Philosophy of M

Philosophy of Mind
A Comprehensive Introduction

William Jaworski

WILEY-BLACKWELL

A John Wiley & Sons, Ltd., Publication

This edition first published 2011
© 2011 William Jaworski

Blackwell Publishing was acquired by John Wiley & Sons in February 2007. Blackwell's publishing program
has been merged with Wiley's global Scientific, Technical, and Medical business to form Wiley-Blackwell.

Registered Office
John Wiley & Sons Ltd, The Atrium, Southern Gate, Chichester, West Sussex, PO19 8SQ, United Kingdom

Editorial Offices
350 Main Street, Malden, MA 02148-5020, USA
9600 Garsington Road, Oxford, OX4 2DQ, UK
The Atrium, Southern Gate, Chichester, West Sussex, PO19 8SQ, UK

For details of our global editorial offices, for customer services, and for information about how to apply for
permission to reuse the copyright material in this book please see our website at www.wiley.com/
wiley-blackwell.

The right of William Jaworski to be identified as the author of work has been asserted in accordance with the
UK Copyright, Designs and Patents Act 1988.

Library of Congress Cataloging-in-Publication Data
Jaworski, William.
    Philosophy of mind : a comprehensive introduction / William Jaworski.
      p. cm.
    ISBN 978-1-4443-3367-1 (hardback : alk. paper) – ISBN 978-1-4443-3368-8 (pbk. : alk. paper)
  1. Philosophy of mind.   2. Mind and body.   3. Materialism.   I. Title.
    BD418.3.J39 2011
    128'.2–dc22

                                                                                2010049303

A catalogue record for this book is available from the British Library.
This book is published in the following electronic formats: ePDFs 9781444397574; ePub 9781444397581

Set in 11/13 pt Dante by Toppan Best-set Premedia Limited

Printed in the UK

Contents

Contents

Contents

Preface

Philosophy of mind is one of the liveliest fields in contemporary philosophy – a hub of activity that intersects with metaphysics, ethics, epistemology, and the philosophies of science and language. The field is usefully divided into five areas of research: (1) mind and body, (2) consciousness, (3) mental representation, (4) the philosophy of psychology and neuroscience, and (5) action theory. This book introduces readers to these topics by focusing on mind–body problems and the range of theories that address them. It is more comprehensive than other available texts. Like other texts, it discusses familiar forms of substance dualism, physicalism, and dual-attribute theory, but it also covers theories off the beaten path such as neutral monism, idealism, and hylomorphism. It covers prominent arguments in the philosophical literature, but also arguments that typically receive short shrift such as Wittgenstein's private language argument, and the embodied mind objection to functionalism. In addition, it discusses how recent developments in neuroscience, psychology, and cognitive science have impacted mind–body debates, a topic that often goes unaddressed.

The book is written in a nontechnical style aimed primarily at upper-division undergraduates, graduate students, and interested professionals, but I have frequently used parts of it to teach first-year students. Each chapter begins with an overview and ends with suggestions for further reading, so the book can easily be used by itself or in conjunction with primary sources. It includes a glossary, and many simple illustrations that are helpful for preparing chalkboards, overheads, and PowerPoint slides. Individual units are organized in a straightforward way that is designed to help readers jump into current debates: the problems, the theories, and the main arguments for and against each.

As a complement to the book, two chapters (12 and 13) are available free online at www.wiley.com/go/jaworski. These chapters cover persons and free will, since many professors like to include units on these topics in their philosophy of mind courses. The addition of these chapters makes the book a flexible teaching tool that is easy to use for introductory courses. Here is an example of what a syllabus for an introductory course based on the book might look like:

	Weeks	Topics	Sections
Philosophy of Mind	1–2	Introduction to mind–body theories, mind–body problems, and basic concepts in philosophy of mind	1.1–1.6 2.1–2.5
	3	Substance dualism	3.1
		The argument for substance dualism	3.2
		The problem of interaction	3.5
	4	Physicalism	4.1–4.4
		The argument for physicalism	4.5
		The knowledge argument and qualia	4.7, 4.8
	5	The identity theory	5.4
		Lewis's argument for the identity theory	5.6
		The multiple-realizability argument	6.1
	6	Functionalism	6.3
		The liberalism objection	6.7
		The Chinese room	6.8
	7	Hylomorphism	10.1–10.6, 10.8, 11.1, 11.2
Philosophy of Persons	8–10	Animalism	12.1
		Constitutionalism	12.2
		Souls	12.3
		Brains	12.4
Free Will and Determinism	11–14	The problem of free will and determinism	13.1–13.2
		Compatibilism	13.3–13.6
		Libertarianism	13.7
		Hard determinism and hard incompatibilism	13.8

The book also makes an original contribution to the philosophical literature. It presents hylomorphism not as a mere historical curiosity, but as a theory whose central ideas dovetail with current work in biology, neuroscience, and philosophy of mind. The hylomorphic theory developed here bears many similarities to classic emergentism and forms of nonreductive physicalism, but it differs from these theories in important respects that insulate it from some of the standard objections to them.

Chapter 1

Mind–Body Theories and Mind–Body Problems

Overview

Mind–body theories and mind–body problems form the core subject-matter of philosophy of mind. Mind–body theories offer different ways of understanding how mental and physical phenomena are related. They are divided into two broad categories: monistic theories and dualistic theories. Monistic theories claim that there is fundamentally one kind of thing. Physical monism or physicalism, as it is usually called, claims that everything is physical; everything can be exhaustively described and explained by physics. Mental monism, which is typically called 'idealism', claims that everything is mental – everything can be exhaustively described and explained using our prescientific psychological concepts. Finally, neutral monism claims that everything is neutral; everything can be exhaustively described and explained using a conceptual framework that is neither mental nor physical but neutral.

Unlike monistic theories, dualistic theories deny that a single conceptual framework is sufficient to describe and explain everything. Rather, a complete description and explanation of everything requires that we use both the mental and the physical conceptual frameworks. There are, then, two fundamentally distinct kinds of properties individuals can have: mental properties, which are expressed by the predicates of the mental framework, and physical properties, which are expressed by the predicates of the physical framework. Among dualistic theories, dual-attribute theories claim that the very same individual can have both mental and physical properties. Substance dualistic theories deny this. The very same individual cannot have both mental properties and physical properties, they claim. According to substance dualists, mental beings such as you and I have no physical properties at all, and physical beings such as human bodies have no mental

Philosophy of Mind: A Comprehensive Introduction, First Edition. William Jaworski.
© 2011 William Jaworski. Published 2011 by Blackwell Publishing Ltd.

properties. This implies that there are not only two fundamentally distinct kinds of properties, but also two fundamentally distinct kinds of individuals as well: those with exclusively mental properties, and those with exclusively physical properties.

In addition to the foregoing theories, there are three others that fall outside the main classification of monistic and dualistic theories. Instrumentalism falls outside the classification because it denies a realist understanding of psychological discourse. Mind–body pessimism falls outside the classification because it denies the possibility of giving a completely satisfactory account of how mental and physical phenomena are related, and hylomorphism falls outside the standard classification because it denies that human behavior can be described accurately in terms of a mental–physical distinction.

Mind–body problems have two features in common: the distinction between mental phenomena and physical phenomena, and premises that make it difficult to understand how mental and physical phenomena are related. The problem of other minds is an example. It makes it difficult to understand how it is possible for us to know what other people are thinking or feeling based on our knowledge of their bodily behavior. The problem of psychophysical emergence, on the other hand, makes it difficult to see how it is possible for mental phenomena to exist at all if the world is fundamentally physical, and the problem of mental causation makes it difficult to see how mental and physical phenomena can interact in the ways they appear to.

1.1   Mind and Brain

The surgeon removed the section of skull and cut through the dura mater revealing the brain beneath. It pulsed gently in sync with the patient's heartbeat. He was 12-year-old R. W. (name concealed for privacy). He'd had a difficult birth but had otherwise developed normally until the seizures began. Three years of failed treatments and months of tortured deliberation had brought him and his parents to this point. Doctors were going to remove part of his brain – in theory, the part responsible for his seizures. The difficulty was identifying exactly what part that was and removing it without damaging the surrounding tissue and with it R. W.'s ability to speak or laugh, to recognize faces or remember facts, to play the piano or smell cookies baking in the oven.

R. W. received a local anesthetic as they cut through his scalp, and was mildly sedated now, but was otherwise awake and alert. The lead surgeon began touching one section of brain tissue after another with two metal probes that carried an electric current. Based on R. W.'s symptoms he guessed this was where the seizures were originating. They always began the same way: an experience of colored triangles – like the afterimages of bright lights only clearer. R. W. would then become confused about his surroundings, and see men moving toward him with guns. Those who saw R. W. during one of these episodes could hear the terror in his voice, and see it on his face as his eyes and head moved from right to left, following, it seemed, the movements of the men across the room.

As the surgeon now touched sections of R. W.'s brain he observed R. W.'s behavior carefully, and asked that R. W. describe any changes he experienced. After stimulating one area in particular R. W. said with astonishment, "Oh, gee, gosh, robbers are coming at me with guns!" A few moments later the stimulation was repeated, "Yes, the robbers, they are coming after me ... Oh gosh! There they are, my brother is there. He is aiming an air rifle at me." R. W.'s eyes moved slowly to the left ...[1]

The foregoing story describes a real operation performed by the neurosurgeon Wilder Penfield (1891–1976). Penfield did pioneering work mapping functional areas of the brain using electrical stimulation in an effort to treat patients like R. W. He kept detailed records of his observations. Another of Penfield's cases involved a 32-year-old woman, A. Bra., who began having seizures a year earlier. Penfield's notes report the effects of stimulating various numbered areas of her right temporal lobe:

15. "I hear singing."
15. Repeated. "Yes, it is White Christmas." When asked if anyone was singing, she said, "Yes, a choir." When asked if she remembered it being sung with a choir, she said she thought so.
16. "That is different, a voice – talking – a man."
17. "Yes, I have heard it before. A man's voice – talking."
18. "There is the sound again – like a radio program – a man talking." She said it was like a play, the same voice as before.
19. "The play again!" Then she began to hum. When asked what she was humming, she said she did not know, it was what she heard.
19. Repeated. Patient began to hum. She continued at the ordinary pace of a song. "I know it but I don't know the name – I have heard it before. I hear it, it is an instrument – just one." She thought it was a violin.
26. Patient said, "It hurts." Stimulation was stopped. She said, "I see a picture." She added, "It was a face which comes from a picture."
27. "The same thing. The play and they are banging on something like a drum."
28. "I see people walking."[2]

The effects Penfield produced are familiar to students of neuroscience. Electrical stimulation of the cortex can cause patients to move their limbs, to sense numbness or tingling on the skin, to experience flashes of light or buzzing sensations, to feel fear, experience déjà vu, or have a sense that they are in a dream.[3] It can also inhibit functioning: in a dramatic demonstration reported on the front page of the *New York Times*, for instance, the neuroscientist Jose Delgado stopped a charging bull in its tracks with the push of a button.[4]

Penfield's observations are interesting for many reasons, not least for the philosophical questions they raise. What, for instance, is the relationship between mental phenomena and physical phenomena? What was the relationship between, say, the activation of cells in R. W.'s temporal lobe and his visual experience of seeing robbers? The cells were tiny components that operated according to simple mechanical principles; they were located inside R. W.'s skull; they had mass, volume, and all the other properties physical things have. R. W.'s experience, on the other hand, did not appear to have these properties. It did not appear to be tiny, and the figures he saw seemed as large as ordinary people. Likewise, the experience did not appear to be a mechanical process located inside his skull, but a qualitative awareness in the surrounding room. Nor is it evident that the experience had mass or volume. How after all could we have weighed or measured it? We know how to weigh and measure the brain cells, and we would know how to weigh and measure the robbers if they had existed, but how could we have weighed or measured the experience itself? The experience and the brain cells seem very different, and yet they were obviously intimately related. But how?

Philosophers, scientists, and others disagree about the answer. Some, for instance, would claim that R. W.'s experience was identical to the activity of his brain cells – that the experience and the brain activity were the very same thing described using two different vocabularies. When using an informed, scientific vocabulary, we would call the event in R. W.'s skull 'temporal lobe activity', but when using an ordinary, prescientific vocabulary, we would call it 'seeing robbers approaching with guns'. Other philosophers would deny that R. W.'s experience was identical to the activity of his brain cells. Experiences are not the same thing as brain activity, they would say; experiences are not physical events at all but nonphysical events caused by brain activity. Yet others would take this type of answer a step further: not only are experiences nonphysical, people are too. You, R. W., and I are nonphysical entities that are intimately connected to human bodies. (Incidentally, this is the kind of answer Penfield himself preferred.) Still other philosophers would claim that the question is ill-posed, that it is a mistake to ask how mental and physical phenomena are related since it is a mistake to describe human experience in dichotomous mental and physical terms to begin with.

These answers represent different mind–body theories. Mind–body theories and the problems they try to solve form the subject-matter of philosophy of mind. We will consider them in detail in the chapters that follow: what they claim, why people believe them, what implications they have for our understanding of human life, and most importantly, what reasons we have for thinking they are true or false. We will begin with a brief overview of the main options and some of the problems they attempt to solve.

1.2   Mind–Body Theories

Mind–body theories offer different ways of understanding how mental and physical phenomena are related. There are two broad categories of mind–body theories: monistic and dualistic. Monistic theories claim there is fundamentally one kind of thing; dualistic theories, that there are fundamentally two kinds of things. The divisions among monistic and dualistic theories of mind are represented in Figures 1.1 and 1.2. The first figure shows the divisions among mind–body theories; the second depicts those differences in an intuitive way.

Monistic mind–body theories are of three broad types. **Physical monism** or **physicalism** claims that everything is physical; everything can be exhaustively described and explained by physics. **Mental monism**, on the other hand, which is commonly called **idealism**, claims that everything is mental; everything can be exhaustively described and explained using mentalistic concepts such as *belief*, *desire*, and *feeling*. Finally, **neutral monism** claims that everything is neutral; everything can be exhaustively described and explained using a conceptual framework that is neither mentalistic nor physicalistic but neutral. All monistic theories, then, are committed to the claim that there is fundamentally one kind of thing; they differ over what that one kind of thing is: mental, physical, or neutral.

Dualistic theories, by contrast, deny that there is only one kind of thing. Fundamentally, there are two kinds of things, they claim: mental and physical. Dualistic theories are further subdivided into two broad categories. All of them claim there are two distinct kinds of **properties** or characteristics things can have, mental properties and physical properties, but they differ over the kinds of individuals that have them. **Dual-attribute theories** claim that the very same individual can have both mental and physical properties – that mental and physical properties can coincide in a single individual. **Substance dualistic theories** deny this. The same individual, they say, cannot have both mental and physical properties. According to substance dualists, then, there are not just two distinct kinds of properties; there are also two distinct kinds of individuals: individuals that have only mental properties, and individuals that have only physical properties.

Most of the mind–body theories depicted in Figures 1.1 and 1.2 start with the same picture of the physical universe – a picture of a vast undifferentiated sea of matter and energy, an ocean of fundamental physical particles or materials governed by laws that are described by or will be described by our best physics. Physicalism claims that this is a complete picture of everything; there is nothing but this vast physical sea. Physics, they say, gives us the exhaustive description and explanation of everything that exists: of all the individuals, all their properties, and all the principles governing their behavior. According to most physicalists, however, we can describe these individuals, their properties, and behavior in many different ways. Instead of describing individual electrons or quarks or other fundamental physical particles, for instance, we can describe collections of those

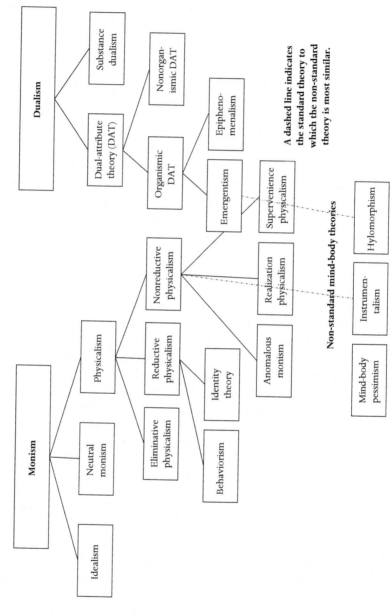

Standard mind–body theories

Monism
- Idealism
- Neutral monism
- Physicalism
  - Eliminative physicalism
  - Reductive physicalism
    - Behaviorism
    - Identity theory
  - Nonreductive physicalism
    - Anomalous monism
    - Realization physicalism
    - Supervenience physicalism
    - Emergentism

Dualism
- Dual-attribute theory (DAT)
  - Organismic DAT
    - Emergentism
    - Epiphenomenalism
  - Nonorganismic DAT
- Substance dualism

A dashed line indicates the standard theory to which the non-standard theory is most similar.

Non-standard mind-body theories

- Mind-body pessimism
- Instrumentalism
- Hylomorphism

Figure 1.1 Standard and non-standard mind-body theories

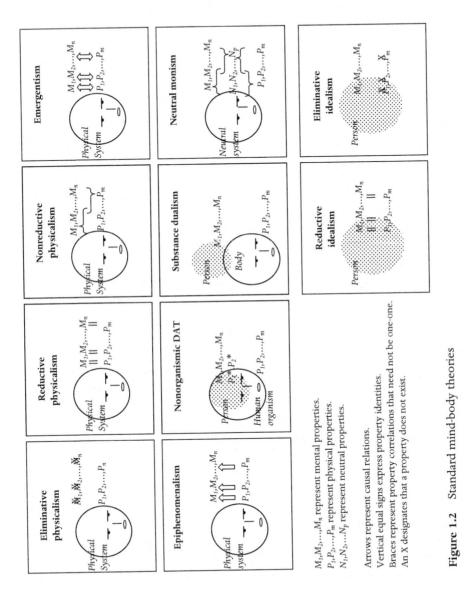

$M_1, M_2, ..., M_n$ represent mental properties.
$P_1, P_2, ..., P_m$ represent physical properties.
$N_1, N_2, ..., N_p$ represent neutral properties.

Arrows represent causal relations.
Vertical equal signs express property identities.
Braces represent property correlations that need not be one-one.
An X designates that a property does not exist.

Figure 1.2 Standard mind-body theories

particles such as tables and chairs or plants and animals. When we use terms such as 'table' or 'human', however, we are not describing entities in addition to those postulated by physics. The table or the human is not an entity in addition to the fundamental physical particles that compose it. Terms such as 'table' and 'human' are terms we use to refer to collections of particles – they are analogous to terms such as 'team'. A team is not an entity in addition to the individual members of the team; the term 'team' is rather a way of referring to the team's individual members; it is a term of collective reference. According to many physicalists, the proper names of humans such as 'Alexander' are analogous to the proper names of teams such as 'The New Jersey Devils': they refer to collections of particles if they refer to anything at all. Moreover, predicates such as 'is alive', 'is in pain', 'believes that there are eight planets in our solar system' do not express properties in addition to those described by physics; they instead express very complex relations among collections of fundamental particles, just as the predicates 'is solid' and 'is liquid' do. Hence, when we speak of Alexander's being alive or experiencing pain or having a belief, we are really expressing a very complex relation among a large collection of fundamental physical particles.

Dual-attribute theories start with the same picture of the physical universe, but they disagree with physicalists about the descriptive and explanatory scope of physics. Physics does not provide an exhaustive description of all individuals and properties, they say, nor is it able to provide an exhaustive explanation of every individual's behavior. Some individuals – people, for instance – have properties in addition to those physics describes and explains. These properties can only be described and explained using different conceptual resources such as those of psychological discourse. Psychological predicates such as 'is in pain' or 'believes that there are eight planets in our solar system' express these properties – nonphysical properties, ones different from those described by physics. To say that Alexander is in pain or has a belief is not to describe a very complex relation among fundamental physical particles, say dual-attribute theorists; it is instead to express Alexander's possession of a unique kind of property distinct from any of those possessed by fundamental physical particles. Dual-attribute theories claim, in other words, that there are two distinct kinds of properties or attributes (hence the name 'dual-attribute theory'), and because there are two distinct kinds of properties or attributes, we need to describe things using both a mental vocabulary and a physical vocabulary.

The most popular dual-attribute theories in recent years have been forms of **epiphenomenalism** and **emergentism**. Both claim that mental properties are produced or caused by physical occurrences. Fundamental physical interactions of the sort described by physics cause or give rise to nonphysical properties – including mental properties such as belief, desire, and pain. Epiphenomenalists and emergentists differ over the causal power of emergent properties – whether those properties are able to exert a causal influence on the physical interactions from which they emerge. Epiphenomenalists say they cannot. According to them, emergent properties, including mental properties, are causally inert; they have no causal power in their own right; they can influence nothing that happens in the universe. They do exist, say epiphenomenalists, and for that reason a complete account of the universe must include a description of them using a vocabulary suited to the task – a mental vocabulary, for instance. But emergent properties are merely causal byproducts of physical processes; they themselves cause or produce nothing. Emergentists disagree with epiphenomenalists about the causal status of mental properties. Mental properties are not causally inert, they say; rather, mental properties have causal powers distinct from those described by physics, and they make a distinctive causal contribution to the flow of physical events.

Dual-attribute theorists and physicalists all claim that any individuals having mental properties also have physical properties. Their views are all compatible, for instance, with the claim that you and I are human organisms – physical beings of a particular sort. But substance dualists disagree. According to them, persons – mental beings – are completely nonphysical. Whereas physicalism implies that physics can describe *all* of my properties, and dual-attribute theory implies that physics can describe *some* of my properties, substance dualism implies that physics can describe *none* of my properties. According to substance dualists, you and I are completely nonphysical entities; we have no physical properties at all. The only properties we have are mental ones: beliefs, desires, hopes, joys, fears, loves, and so forth. According to substance dualists, therefore, you and I are not human organisms. We are not, for instance, the humans we see in the mirror when we shave, or fix our hair, or put on makeup. We are not physical entities of any sort. We might be connected in some way to human organisms, and because of that connection you might take special interest in the appearance or the reproductive destiny of a particular human organism, but you are not that organism. In addition to the universe described by physics, then, substance dualists claim that there is another nonphysical universe described by psychological discourse. We use mental predicates and terms to describe and explain what happens in that nonphysical domain. Nonorganismic dual-attribute theories are similar in spirit to substance dualism. Like substance dualists, nonorganismic dual-attribute theorists deny that we are organisms; they nevertheless claim that we have some physical properties such as spatial location even if we do not have all the physical properties organisms do.

Physicalism, dual-attribute theory, and substance dualism are the most popular mind–body theories, but there are others as well. Idealism is like a reverse image of physicalism: just as physicalism claims that everything is physical, idealism claims that everything is mental. According to most idealists, when we take ourselves to refer to physical entities and properties we are really referring to experiences. When I talk about this table, for instance, I am not really describing an entity that is distinct from my experiences – an entity that could exist in the absence of me or someone else perceiving it. I am instead describing an expanse of color in my visual field, together with a sense of three-dimensional depth, a feeling of solidity, a sensation of texture, and so on. Likewise, when I describe what I take to be a physical property such as solidity or mass, I am not describing a feature that something might possess independent of an experience; I am rather describing one of my experiences using a nonmental vocabulary. When I say that this table is solid, I am really saying that I am having an experience of my hand not passing through it the way it passes through the air. Likewise, when I say the table is heavy, I am saying that I have an experience of anticipating that I would experience effort or exertion if I had the experience of trying to lift it – the experience of trying to lift it, in other words, would be accompanied by an experience of meeting resistance. According to most idealists, then, calling something solid or heavy is really just a way of talking about my experiences, and the same is true of all physical things: our mental and physical vocabularies are just different ways of describing the same phenomena – phenomena that are all mental; there is no mind-independent domain described by physics.

By contrast with the foregoing theories, neutral monism claims that the universe is fundamentally neither mental nor physical. The universe consists, rather, of individuals, properties, and events that can be exhaustively described and explained using a conceptual framework that is neither mental nor physical but neutral. Our mental and physical vocabularies are just ways of expressing properties or events that are neutral.

In addition to the foregoing theories, three require special consideration: **instrumentalism**, **hylomorphism**, and **mind–body pessimism**. These theories are not included among the standard theories depicted in the top portion of Figure 1.1. The reason is that the classification of standard theories is based on three assumptions, and instrumentalism, hylomorphism, and mind–body pessimism each rejects one of them.

First, the standard theories in Figure 1.1 are committed to a **realist** understanding of psychological discourse; they all claim that the predicates of psychological discourse are supposed to express real properties. When we say that Eleanor enjoys the taste of sushi, for instance, realists claim that we are trying to express the possession of a real property by a real individual. Even eliminative physicalists, who deny that mental properties exist, are realists in this sense. They claim that predicates like 'enjoys the taste of sushi' fail to express real properties because there are no such properties. They nevertheless agree that when we use psychological predicates we are at least *trying* to express real properties. Yet this is what instrumentalists deny. Psychological discourse does not aim at expressing real properties, instrumentalists say. Psychological discourse is a mere tool or instrument we use for predicting human behavior. When we describe and explain human behavior using psychological predicates and terms we are concerned not with getting an accurate picture of reality, but simply with making useful predictions of what people will do. Consequently, although there are beliefs, desires, and other mental states, according to instrumentalists, this claim does not carry an ontological commitment as strong as realists suppose. To claim that there are beliefs and desires is simply to claim that it is useful to describe and explain people's behavior using the predicates 'believes' and 'desires'.

Second, the standard theories represented in Figure 1.1 are all committed to the mental–physical distinction. They disagree about whether mental phenomena are identical to physical phenomena: dualists claim that psychological language and physical language express two different kinds of phenomena, and monists deny this. But monists and dualists alike agree that there are two vocabularies or conceptual frameworks for describing and explaining human behavior: a mental vocabulary and a physical one. Hylomorphists reject this claim. Human behavior can only be adequately described and explained, they say, using a unique vocabulary that is neither mental nor physical but that shares features of both. Neutral monists say something similar, but, unlike neutral monists, hylomorphists reject monism. They deny that there is a single conceptual framework – mental, physical, or neutral – that is sufficient to describe and explain everything that exists. The distinctive vocabulary we use to describe and explain human behavior, for instance, can be used to describe the behavior of other living things only by drawing analogies with human behavior. Other living things have their own distinctive structures and patterns of behavior, however, and because of that we have to use descriptive and explanatory resources that are suited to them if we want to give fully accurate descriptions and explanations of their behavior. Because hylomorphists reject the mental–physical distinction, hylomorphism does not fit into the standard classification of mind–body theories.

Finally, exponents of the standard theories in Figure 1.1 are all committed to the idea that it is possible to give a satisfactory account of how mental and physical phenomena are related. Mind–body pessimists reject this assumption. They claim that it is impossible to give a satisfactory account of mind–body relations because there are inbuilt limitations on human cognitive capacities that will prevent us from ever understanding how mental and physical phenomena are related. There may be a coherent account of mental–physical relations; there may even be entities in the universe whose minds are powerful enough to grasp what those relations are, but our minds are not. Our cognitive powers are limited in such a way that we will never be able to solve **mind–body problems**.

Now that we have surveyed some mind–body theories, let us consider some mind–body problems.

1.3 Mind–Body Problems

Mind–body problems arise when we try to understand how thought, feeling, perception, action, and other mental phenomena are related to events in the human nervous system. In our day-to-day dealings we take ourselves to be free beings who act as we do because we have beliefs, desires, hopes, and fears. We describe ourselves as beings who experience joy and sadness, love and hate, pain and pleasure; beings who act to get what we want, who make choices, and who can be held accountable for the choices we make, whose actions, habits, and character traits can be evaluated as good or bad, right or wrong. In our scientific dealings, however, we see the universe as a vast sea of matter and energy that at a fundamental level has none of the features we recognize in our day-to-day lives. At the level of fundamental physics there are no differences among humans, rocks, trees, and other living things. All of them are made of the same basic materials, and at the level of those materials there is nothing that distinguishes you from a rock or a dog. The subatomic particles we find in you are the same as the subatomic particles we find in them, and those particles behave in you and in them in exactly the same ways. From the standpoint of fundamental physics, then, the familiar objects of ordinary experience are just so many collections of the same kinds of microscopic particles – particles that have none of the features we take to distinguish people from other things. Electrons and quarks do not have beliefs or desires, hopes or fears; they do not want things or deliberate about how to get them. They are not free; they do not choose to act. Their behavior is not subject to moral praise or blame, nor do they develop personalities, form character traits or habits, or experience love or hate, sadness or joy.

We thus confront two images of human life: the everyday, prescientific image of ourselves as free, rational beings with mental and moral lives, and the scientific image of ourselves as complex biochemical systems. Understanding how there can be free, mental, moral beings in a universe that at a fundamental physical level has none of these features is one of the principal issues that philosophers, scientists, theologians, and others have struggled with for the past 350 years. It has been the basis of some of the major problems of modern philosophy including the **problem of free will and determinism**, the problems generated by the fact–value dichotomy, and mind–body problems. All of these problems originate in the disparity between the way we describe the world scientifically and the way we describe it in our everyday dealings. The astronomer and physicist Sir Arthur Eddington (1882–1944) once illustrated the disparity in a memorable way:

> I have settled down to the task of writing these lectures and have drawn up my chairs to my two tables. Two tables! Yes ... One of them has been familiar to me from earliest years. It is a commonplace object of that environment which I call the world ... It has extension; it is comparatively permanent; it is colored ... Table No. 2 is my scientific table ... [T]here is a vast difference between [it] ... and the table of everyday conception ... It does not belong to the world previously mentioned – that world which spontaneously appears around me when I open my eyes ... My scientific table is mostly emptiness. Sparsely scattered in that emptiness are numerous electric charges rushing about with great speed ... [M]odern physics has by delicate test and remorseless logic assured me that my second scientific table is

the only one which is really there … On the other hand … modern physics will never succeed in exorcising that first table … which lies visible to my eyes and tangible to my grasp.[5]

Eddington describes a tension between two descriptions of the world: a scientific description, and a commonsense, prescientific one. Only one, it seems, can lay claim to describing the real table. There is, in other words, a single descriptive role to be filled, the role labeled 'real', and only one description can occupy it. Consequently, if we accept the description offered by science, we must reject the description offered by common sense, and if we accept the description offered by common sense, we must reject the description offered by science. The problem is that we do not want to reject either description, and we have good reason to think both are true. As a result, we have difficulty understanding how the scientific description is related to the prescientific one.

Mind–body problems have a similar structure. We have two frameworks for describing and explaining human behavior: a scientific framework and a commonsense, prescientific one. Each has conceptual resources that seem fully adequate for describing and explaining human thought, feeling, and action. Consider an example: an action such as raising your arm over your head. Go ahead and try it. Notice that we can explain your action in two different ways. We can explain it scientifically by appeal to the contractions of muscles in your shoulder and the activity of neurons in a particular region of your brain. Yet we can also explain your action mentally by appeal to your desires and beliefs – a desire, for instance, to understand mind–body problems and a belief that raising your arm might help. What is true of action is also true of perception. We can describe your current visual experience in terms of its qualitative features – a series of small black shapes on a white background, say. But we can also describe it in terms of the states of the neurons in your eyes and brain, and the atomic structure of the paper and ink that reflect light to them. Science and common sense each provide resources that seem fully adequate for describing and explaining our actions and experiences; each purports to satisfy our requests for information; each purports to reveal the reasons why people act and perceive as they do. But if there can be only one such reason – the *real* reason, as we might refer to it – then science and common sense look like rivals competing to occupy a single explanatory role, and we face the vexing task of judging between them; we face a mind–body problem. Consider another example: the **problem of psychophysical emergence**.

1.4 The Problem of Psychophysical Emergence

Life and mind did not always exist in the universe. Early in the universe's history there were not even atoms since energy levels were too high to allow protons and electrons to form stable pairs. Life and consciousness are thus relative newcomers on the cosmic scene. To many people, this suggests that the physical conditions that existed before their emergence had to be responsible in some way for bringing them about. Scientists are becoming increasingly clear about the physical conditions that were responsible for the emergence of life, but consciousness is a different story.

We are conscious beings: we have experiences. Yet we are composed entirely of nonconscious parts: molecules, atoms, and other microscopic entities described by physics. These microscopic entities are not conscious the way we are. How, then, do our conscious experiences emerge out of these nonconscious physical interactions? It is difficult to see how they could. Consider the difference between the rich, colorful, quality-laden features of conscious experiences and basic properties of matter – the difference, for instance, between R. W.'s visual experiences and the cells in his brain, or between your current visual, auditory, and other experiences, and the mass of an electron. How could collisions among a number of nonconscious subatomic particles combine to produce something as rich and varied as your current awareness of the various colors, sounds, smells, and textures that surround you? If the movements of some number N of fundamental physical particles do not constitute a conscious experience, it is implausible to suppose $N+1$ particles could. What difference, after all, could one particle make to whether or not something is conscious? Surely an individual particle does not have the power magically to produce consciousness. Consequently, if N particles are insufficient to produce consciousness, it looks like $N+1$ particles will be insufficient as well, and, in that case, it looks like no number of subatomic collisions will be sufficient to produce conscious experiences. Why? Well, we can agree that the movement of just one subatomic particle is insufficient to produce consciousness; after all, if the movement of just one subatomic particle were sufficient to produce consciousness, then consciousness would probably not have emerged as late in the universe's history as it did, for subatomic particles existed almost from the beginning. We also just agreed, however, that if the movement of one subatomic particle is insufficient to produce consciousness, then the movements of two subatomic particles will be insufficient as well: if N particles are insufficient, then $N+1$ particles are insufficient too. So if one particle is insufficient, so are two. The same is true, moreover, of two subatomic particles: if their movements are insufficient to produce consciousness, then so are the movements of three, and if the movements of three particles are insufficient, then so are the movements of four, and also the movements of five, and of six, and seven, and so on for any number N. It appears, then, that no number of subatomic collisions will be sufficient to produce consciousness. How, then, did consciousness manage to emerge in the course of the universe's history? And how, for that matter, does consciousness manage to emerge in you and me right now? This is the problem of psychophysical emergence.

Notice that I have formulated the problem by advancing some considerations that lead to a puzzling question. Another way of formulating the problem is to present a set of jointly inconsistent claims such as the following:

1 We are conscious beings.
2 We are composed entirely of nonconscious parts.
3 No number of nonconscious parts could combine to produce a conscious whole.
4 The properties of a whole are determined by the properties of its parts.

Claim (1) says that I am conscious, and claim (4) implies that my consciousness should be determined by my parts. My mass, for instance, is determined by the masses of the microscopic particles composing me; it thus seems plausible that if I am conscious, my consciousness is determined by the properties of my parts just as my mass is. But now we face a problem: According to claim (2), none of my parts is conscious, and according to (3) these parts cannot produce consciousness either. So claims (1) and (4) imply that my consciousness must be produced by my parts, but claims (2) and (3) imply that it cannot. Given reasonable assumptions, then, claims (1)–(4) are inconsistent with one another; they cannot all be true, and yet it is not clear which is false since there are good reasons for endorsing each.

One benefit of formulating philosophical problems this way is that the formulation makes it clear what any solution must accomplish: A solution must show either that one of the claims is false, or else that, despite appearances, the claims are not really inconsistent. A solution to the problem of psychophysical emergence, for instance, must either show that (1), or (2), or (3), or (4) is false, or else show that despite appearances these claims are not really inconsistent.

Another benefit of formulating philosophical problems this way is that it helps us evaluate solutions various philosophers have to offer (Figure 1.3). Consider some proposed solutions to the problem of psychophysical emergence. Eliminative physicalists reject claim (1). They deny there is any such thing as consciousness, and hence deny that we are conscious beings. Some dual-attribute theorists – panpsychists and panprotopsychists in particular – reject claim (2). They claim that the entities that compose us, including fundamental physical particles, have conscious or protoconscious states. Substance dualists, idealists, and nonorganismic dual-attribute theorists also reject (2) but for different reasons. They deny that we are composed of physical materials at all. Many emergentists and epiphenomenalists, by contrast, reject claim (3); they claim that consciousness emerges from nonconscious materials by virtue of brute psychophysical laws. Reductive physicalists (whose position we will discuss in detail in Chapter 5) also reject (3). They look to identify conscious states with complex relations among physical particles. Consequently, if enough physical particles stand in the right relations, there are

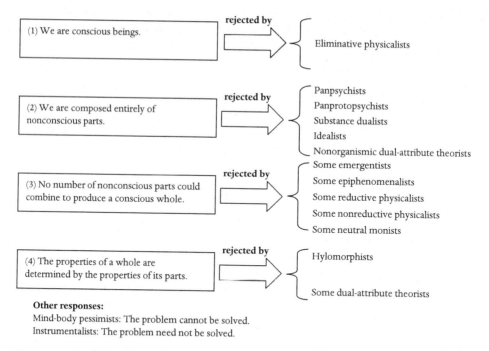

Figure 1.3　Solutions to the problem of psychophysical emergence

conscious states. Neutral monists and nonreductive physicalists (whose position we will discuss in Chapter 6) say something similar. The relations between conscious states and physical particles are not as straightforward as reductive physicalists suppose, they say, but whenever we talk about conscious states we are still talking about complex relations among physical or neutral particles. Hylomorphists, on the other hand, reject claim (4). Living wholes, they say, are structured in ways that confer on them capacities not had by their parts – including the ability to be conscious. Something's structure, however, is not produced or determined by the materials it configures; structure is instead a basic ontological and explanatory principle in addition to those that govern materials in their own right. Finally, some mind–body pessimists claim that the problem is insoluble, that there are absolute limits on our ability to know and understand the world, and these limits manifest themselves in philosophical problems that cannot be solved like this one. Instrumentalists, on the other hand, do not insist that the problem cannot be solved but emphasize that it need not be solved. Psychological discourse is a useful tool, they say, and we need not solve mind–body problems to continue using it.

　　Knowing how different theories solve a given mind–body problem is not the end of a philosopher's task, however, but only the beginning, for in order to evaluate the proposed solutions, a philosopher must evaluate the theories themselves, and this is a complicated task. Proponents of each theory advance reasons for thinking their theory is true, and opponents of each theory advance reasons for thinking it is false. Evaluating the arguments for and against mind–body theories will be our primary concern in the chapters that follow. But first let us consider some more mind–body problems.

1.5   The Problem of Other Minds

The problem of other minds arises from a tension between our objective, third-person knowledge of human behavior, and our apparently subjective, first-person knowledge of our own conscious states. One of our basic starting points for understanding who and what we are is the idea that we are social beings. We know, for instance, that there are other people in the world, and that we often know through our ordinary interactions with them what they think and how they feel. Yet it is difficult to see how this kind of knowledge is possible. Mental states seem to be private, subjective phenomena. You do not have direct access to my mental states, nor do I have direct access to yours. You can hide your thoughts and feelings from me, and I can hide my thoughts and feelings from you. Thoughts and feelings seem to belong to a private, inner domain of subjective experiences – a domain distinct from the public, outer domain of bodily behavior. But if thoughts and feelings are private, if I alone have access to my mental states, then other people cannot know what my mental states are; in fact, they cannot even know whether I have any mental states since a human body seems capable of operating in just the way it does without having any conscious states at all. Even if I had no conscious experiences, it would still be possible for my nervous system to produce the kinds of bodily movements we associate with intelligent action. Conversely, because I cannot access other people's mental states, I cannot really know what their mental states are, or even whether they have any mental states. For all I know, the public, objectively observable human bodies I see around me might be completely devoid of consciousness – they might simply be automata that act in every way as if they have conscious experiences like mine, while yet having no inner mental life at all. How, then, is it possible to have the knowledge of people we ordinarily take ourselves to have?

We can formulate the problem of other minds in terms of the following jointly inconsistent claims:

1   We often know what other people think and how they feel.
2   What other people think and how they feel belong to a private, subjective domain.
3   If what other people think and how they feel belong to a private, subjective domain, then we cannot know what other people think and how they feel as often as we suppose.

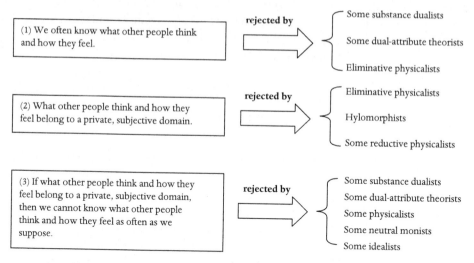

Figure 1.4   Solutions to the problem of other minds

There are several ways of solving the problem. Consider some examples (Figure 1.4). Some substance dualists and dual-attribute theorists reject claim (1). Our reasons for believing that mental states are subjective occurrences are stronger, they say, than our reasons for believing we know other people's mental states. Eliminative physicalists reject (1) as well and also (2): if there are no thoughts or feelings, then there are no thoughts or feelings that belong to a subjective domain. Moreover, say eliminativists, since we cannot know about something that doesn't exist, we cannot know about other people's mental states. Hylomorphists and some physicalists also reject claim (2) but for different reasons. Thoughts and feelings are not private subjective occurrences, they say, but patterns of social and environmental interaction that are just as objectively observable as patterns on a chessboard. Finally, many philosophers reject claim (3). Dual-attribute theorists, some substance dualists, as well as many physicalists and neutral monists claim that we are able to know other people's mental states by making inferences from the objectively observable behavior of human bodies. In addition, some substance dualists and idealists claim that we can know other people's thoughts and feelings directly through a special mind-reading faculty that we possess.

1.6   The Problem of Mental Causation

Consider one more mind–body problem: the **problem of mental causation**. It arises from a tension between our commonsense understanding of people's reasons for performing actions and our scientific understanding of the physical mechanisms involved in their performance. We take it for granted that our beliefs, desires, and other mental states are able to influence the physical universe. When I order dinner at a restaurant, I take it for granted that my body's speech mechanisms are triggered by my desire to order or my intention to speak. Likewise, when I step into an automobile, I assume that it is my beliefs and desires about where to go and how to get there that will govern how my body steers the wheel, presses the accelerator, or applies the brakes. In general, I assume that my mental states are responsible for producing my actions. In fact, the very existence of actions seems to presuppose that mental states can influence physical behavior. Actions, at least the sort involving bodily movements, appear to be physical events with mental causes. If I accidentally trip on the rug we do not call it an action: if, however, I am clowning around and *intend* to trip on the rug, we do call it an action. Why does the one case count as an action while the other does not? The difference is not a physical one. Both cases might involve exactly the same physical occurrences: my foot catching the rug, my frame catapulting forward, my hands striking the floor, and so on. The difference, it seems, is mental. The second case qualifies as an action because it has a mental cause: my intention to trip on the rug. One of our basic assumptions about the world, then, seems to be that beliefs, desires, and other mental states can cause changes in the physical universe – an assumption as basic as our belief that there are such things as actions.

Physical events, however, can be triggered by other physical events. If we stimulate your nervous system in the right way, we can trigger exactly the same bodily movements that are involved in your actions. The neuroscientist Jose Delgado was a pioneer of the technique of neural manipulation. He once implanted electrodes in a bull's midbrain that were activated by remote control – a device he called a 'stimoceiver'. Using the device, he was able to make the bull halt in mid-charge with the push of a button – a dramatic demonstration of neural manipulation reported on the front page of the *New York Times*. Delgado performed experiments on other animals as well – cats, monkeys, chimpanzees, and also humans. He altered the behavior of over 20 human subjects – their feelings, moods, and movements – by electrically stimulating regions of their brains. The human body is after all a vast collection of fundamental physical particles governed by fundamental physical laws. We can manipulate its movements and states in the same ways we can manipulate the movements and states of any other physical system. Usually, however, we leave it to our nervous systems to manage their own affairs. The physical movements involved in your actions are typically caused by other physical events in your nervous system not by external devices, but the principles involved in producing those movements are the same in both cases; they are the kinds of principles described by physics.

With these points in mind, consider a simple action – reaching for an object near at hand, say. This action cannot occur without the contraction of muscles in your arm and shoulder. These contractions are caused by events in your nervous system, the firings of neurons. These neuronal firings are caused in turn by other neuronal firings, and those by yet other physical events such as the impact on your nervous system by light, sound, pressure, airborne chemicals, and other environmental influences. Recall, however, that in order for your reaching to count as an action it must have a mental cause as well – a desire to grasp an object, for instance. But now we face a problem: your action has a physical cause, an event or series of events in your nervous system, and it also has a mental cause, your desire to reach. How are the mental cause of your action and its physical cause related? We can formulate this problem in terms of the following jointly inconsistent claims:

1   Actions have mental causes.
2   Actions have physical causes.
3   Mental causes and physical causes are distinct.
4   An action does not have more than one cause.

Claims (1) and (2) imply that any given action has a mental cause and also a physical cause. According to claim (3), an action's mental cause and its physical cause are distinct. The action must therefore have at least two causes, yet (4) rules this out. It says that an action does not have more than one cause. Consequently, claims (1)–(4) are inconsistent. Claims (1)–(3) imply that actions have multiple causes while claim (4) implies that they do not.

There are several ways of solving the problem of mental causation. Here are some examples (Figure 1.5). Eliminativists reject claim (1): since there are

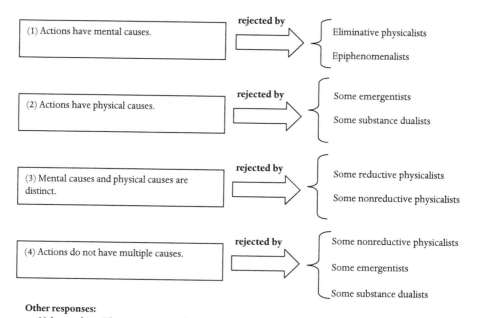

Other responses:
    Hylomorphists: The inconsistency of (1)-(4) is merely apparent since there is an equivocation on the term 'cause'. There are many different kinds of causes.

Figure 1.5   Solutions to the problem of mental causation

no mental events, there are no mental events that cause actions. Epiphenomenalists also reject claim (1) but for different reasons: there are mental events, they say, but those events do not causally contribute to anything. Some emergentists and substance dualists reject (2). They claim that physical laws are periodically violated. Whenever we perform an action such as your act of reaching, the action's physical antecedents cease to be causally efficacious – the events in your nervous system, for instance, no longer have the effects they normally would. Your reaching has only a mental cause, your desire; events in your nervous system are not responsible for bringing about your bodily movements whenever you act. Some reductive physicalists – in particular identity theorists (whose position we discuss in Chapter 5) – and some nonreductive physicalists reject (3). Your reaching has only one cause, they say; the neural firings just *are* your desire. The word 'desire', in other words, is just another way of referring to certain events in your nervous system, the way 'water' is just another way of referring to H_2O molecules. Some dual-attribute theories and substance dualists reject (4). Your reaching has two independent causes: The desire and the neuronal firings both bring about the action, the way you and a friend might both pull a single lever even though each of you is capable of doing it on your own. Your action is thus *overdetermined*, it has more than one independent, fully sufficient cause. Hylomorphists, on the other hand, argue that claims (1)–(4) are not really inconsistent. They claim that there is an equivocation on the term 'cause'. By analogy, there is an equivocation on the term 'law' in the following sentences:

The Supreme Court can overturn any law.
The Supreme Court cannot overturn the law of gravity.

Because the term 'law' is used in different ways in these two sentences, neither implies the falsity of the other. Something analogous is true, say hylomorphists, of the term 'cause' in (1)–(4). Because that term is used in different ways in the four claims, they are not really inconsistent.

We now have a preliminary understanding of mind–body theories and mind–body problems. It is time to consider them in greater detail. We begin in the next chapter by considering the distinctive characteristics of mental and physical phenomena – what philosophers take themselves to mean when they use the words 'mental' and 'physical'.

Further Reading

For more on cortical mapping and the effects of stimulating the brain electrically see Kolb and Whishaw (2003). Jose Delgado's work in neural stimulation is discussed by John Horgan (2005). Substance dualism is discussed in detail in Chapter 3. The general physicalist worldview is discussed in Chapter 4. Reductive and nonreductive physicalism are discussed in chapters 5 and 6, respectively. Eliminativism, instrumentalism, and anomalous monism are discussed in Chapter 7. Dual-attribute theories are the subject of Chapter 8. Neutral monism, idealism, and mind–body pessimism are discussed in Chapter 9, and hylomorphism is discussed in Chapters 10 and 11.

Notes

1 Wilder Penfield and Phanor Perot, 1963, "The Brain's Record of Auditory and Visual Experience: A Final Summary and Discussion," *Brain* 86: 595–696, 615–17.
2 Penfield and Perot, 618.
3 Bryan Kolb and Ian Q. Whishaw, 2003, *Fundamentals of Human Neuropsychology*, 5th edn, New York: Worth Publishers, Chapter 11.
4 John A. Osmundsen, 1965, "'Matador' with a Radio Stops Wired Bull," *New York Times*, May 17.
5 Arthur Stanley Eddington, 1928, *The Nature of the Physical World*, New York: Macmillan Company, ix–xii.

Chapter 2

The Mental–Physical Distinction

Overview

Mind–body problems have two features in common: a distinction between mental and physical phenomena, and premises that make it difficult to understand how the two are related. The seventeenth-century philosopher René Descartes was chiefly responsible for introducing the mental–physical distinction as we currently understand it. By doing so he was effectively rejecting an Aristotelian view of nature that had many more gradations.

The physical domain is defined by the natural sciences, paradigmatically physics. It is the domain that physics is in principle capable of describing and explaining. The mental domain is defined by our prescientific ways of describing and explaining human behavior using categories such as belief, desire, hope, joy, fear, love, choice, responsibility, character, and personality.

There are two broad ways of characterizing mental phenomena: private and public. A private conception of mental phenomena focuses on the notions of first-person authority, subjectivity, phenomenal consciousness, and qualia. A public conception of mental phenomena focuses on the notions of intentionality, mental representation, propositional content, and rationality.

2.1 Mental versus Physical

Few things seem as obvious to us now as the distinction between mental phenomena and physical phenomena. It is commonplace in our culture to distinguish

Philosophy of Mind: A Comprehensive Introduction, First Edition. William Jaworski.
© 2011 William Jaworski. Published 2011 by Blackwell Publishing Ltd.

mental health from physical health, or the mental aspects of athletic performance from its physical aspects. But this division of reality into distinct physical and mental components was due largely to the seventeenth-century philosopher René Descartes (1596–1650).

Before Descartes many philosophers did not approach the universe with a mental–physical dichotomy in mind. In particular, they had a much narrower picture of the mental domain, and a broader, more differentiated picture of the rest of the universe. Mental capacities were associated with what they called *intellect*: the ability to understand universal principles and make judgments of the sort we express in language. Descartes expanded the definition of the mental domain to include things that philosophers had previously not considered mental at all such as the experience of pain. The Greek philosopher Aristotle (384–322 BCE) and his medieval followers, for instance, took pain, perception, action, and related phenomena to be neither mental nor physical in Descartes' sense, and they did not take the physical universe to be a vast, undifferentiated sea of physical material. The universe instead consisted of physical materials that were structured or organized in various ways, and although living things were made out of the same materials as everything else, those materials were structured or organized in ways that conferred on them capacities not had by inanimate objects. These included capacities that could be described and explained using a mental vocabulary, but also capacities that could be described and explained using a nonmental biological vocabulary – not the vocabulary of fundamental physics, but a vocabulary that occupied a position between fundamental physics and psychological discourse.

Twentieth-century philosophers of mind reintroduced a multilevel picture of reality, and biologists and philosophers of biology have recently reintroduced the idea that different levels of reality correspond to different kinds of structure or organization (topics we will consider in connection with physicalism, dual-attribute theory, and hylomorphism), but post-Cartesian categories continue to dominate the way philosophers approach what we are, what capacities we have, and what place we occupy in the broader world. For that reason we begin our discussion of mind–body theories with the division between mental and physical phenomena.

2.2   Physical Phenomena

People are often confused about what philosophers of mind mean when they call something 'mental' or 'physical'. One of the most common confusions – one frequently committed even by professional philosophers – is to suppose that **mental** and **physical** are mutually exclusive categories, that calling something 'mental' implies that it is not physical or conversely that calling something 'physical' implies that it is not mental. We saw in Chapter 1, however, that some physicalist theories claim that mental phenomena are physical, while some idealist theories claim that physical phenomena are mental. Mental and physical phenomena are not defined by mutual exclusion, then. Calling something mental does not imply by definition that it is not physical, nor does calling something physical imply by definition that it is not mental; 'mental' and 'physical' are defined on independent grounds.

We use the term 'physical' in a broad range of ways in our everyday dealings. To avoid unnecessary confusion, however, it is important that in philosophy we use the term 'physical' in a more precise way than is typical in our everyday dealings. 'Physical', in this context, is defined by the descriptive and explanatory resources of modern physics.

The methods and principles of modern physics began crystallizing in the sixteenth and seventeenth centuries in what we now call the **Scientific Revolution**. The changes brought by the Revolution included an increased effort to describe natural phenomena in mathematical terms. People became increasingly confident that we could gain knowledge of the natural world that was as universal and precise as our knowledge of geometrical figures. For over a thousand years, the axioms of Euclidean geometry were held up as a model of universal knowledge. If people wanted to know and explain why any given triangle, circle, or other figure had the properties it had, Euclid's axioms enabled them to do it. They enabled people to describe and explain the features of all abstract figures and solids. When Newton developed his laws of motion, they offered a natural analogue of Euclid's axioms. Just as the axioms enabled us to describe and explain the features of abstract figures and solids, people were confident that laws like Newton's would enable us to describe and explain the features of all concrete bodies. The science of physics continued to develop through the eighteenth and nineteenth centuries so that eventually people were able to give mathematically precise descriptions not just of solid bodies, but of the complex behaviors of fluids, electricity, magnetism, and light. Modern physics seemed on the way, then, to realizing a form of knowledge that was universal and precise. It thus became the paradigmatic natural science, and in more ways than one its methods and principles have come to define what it means to do science.

When we speak of physical phenomena or the physical domain, then, we are speaking of the phenomena or the domain described by physics. There have been different attempts to give a more informative definition of the physical domain. Descartes tried to define it in terms of extension, for instance, the property of taking up space. That definition was eventually abandoned, however, since some things – electrons, for instance – do not take up space, but are still physical entities, things described by physics. People also tried to define the physical domain as the domain of things composed of matter. By the nineteenth century, however, it was clear to physicists that energy not matter was the fundamental category which unified the subject-matter of physics.

The alternative to defining the physical domain in these ways is to stick with the more open-ended definition in terms of physics itself: the physical domain is the domain described and explained by physics. It contains whatever physics says it does, and has whatever features physics says it has.

2.3   First-Person Authority and Subjectivity

Mental phenomena are defined by the descriptive and explanatory resources of psychological discourse. They are the kinds of things we describe and explain using predicates and terms such as 'believes', 'desires', 'hopes', 'wants', 'wishes', 'loves', 'hates', 'pain', 'anger', 'joy', 'sadness', 'embarrassment', 'surprise', 'excitement', 'fear', and so on.

Philosophers tend to work with two different conceptions of mental phenomena: a private conception and a public one. The private conception of mental phenomena focuses on notions like **first-person authority**, **subjectivity**, and **consciousness**. It takes mental phenomena to be inner, subjective occurrences to which only the individual person experiencing them has direct access. The public conception of mental phenomena focuses on notions like intentionality, mental representation, and rationality. It takes mental phenomena to consist in the various ways we comport ourselves toward engagement with the world – ways that can be described and evaluated in rational terms. We will consider these conceptions of mental phenomena in order.

The private conception of mental phenomena derives in part from something philosophers call *first-person authority*. First-person authority is the idea that the knowledge each of us has of his or her own mental states is in some sense privileged. You can be wrong about what I believe, or desire, or feel in a way that you cannot be wrong about what you yourself believe, or desire, or feel. First-person authority is not the same as first-person *infallibility*, the idea that it is impossible for someone to be wrong about what he or she believes, or desires, or feels. Nor is first-person authority the same as first-person *incorrigibility*, the idea that it is impossible for other people to correct us about what we think, feel, or want. First-person authority does not imply that my beliefs about my own mental states are impervious to correction, that others cannot correct my ideas about what I think, feel, or want. The idea of first-person authority implies something much more modest: roughly, if I am convinced that I believe or want or feel something, and I am in error, then the burden of proof is on others to establish this. If, for instance, I assert sincerely, "I believe the Sun orbits the earth," there is a presumption in favor of what I say; we accept that I really do believe this unless someone provides evidence to the contrary. In what might such evidence consist? In this case, evidence to the contrary might include something I said or did in another context that contradicts this – you produce an article I wrote, for instance, in which I assert sincerely that the Sun does not orbit the earth, or you bring testimony that I once wagered a large sum of money that the Sun did not orbit the earth. In other cases, evidence to the contrary would be different. If, for instance, you assert sincerely that you are in pain, evidence to the contrary might consist in certain physiological or behavioral cues: that your tone of voice is relaxed, your pupils are not dilated, your heart rate has not increased, your nervous system is not displaying any of the activity that is normally present when humans experience pain, and so on.

The private conception of mental phenomena also derives from some mundane observations about thoughts, feelings, and actions. Examples include the following:

1   We can keep our thoughts to ourselves: if you ask me what I think of the hot pink color you've chosen to paint your otherwise austere living room I might not verbalize everything that crosses my mind.

2   We cannot feel each other's pains, itches, and other sensations: you can see me jerk my arm away from you when you try to touch it, see the grimace on my face, perhaps even measure the activity of my sensory neurons, but you do not have sensory access to the burning sensation I feel in my elbow the way you have sensory access to these other things – at the very least, it is difficult to see how you could.

3   We can misinterpret others' actions and intentions: I might have come to the carnival booth with the intention of harming my rival, who operates one of the booths. When you witness me approach the booth, hurl a baseball, and hit the target, you might suppose mistakenly that I was trying to hit the target when I was in fact trying to hit my rival. You can be mistaken about my intentions and therefore about the nature of my action in a way you cannot be mistaken about my bodily movements – that I picked up a ball and hurled it.

Philosophers have sometimes taken observations like these to indicate that mental phenomena belong to an inner domain of private experiences to which only the person experiencing them has direct access. The idea that mental phenomena are private in this way is closely related to the notion of subjectivity.

The idea that mental states or experiences are subjective is roughly the idea that they are accessible in principle to only one person – the person whose mental states or experiences they are. The idea that something is **objective**, by contrast, is the idea that it is accessible in principle to more than one person. When Galileo first spotted moons orbiting Jupiter through his telescope, for instance, he was the only person to observe the moons in fact; it was nevertheless possible in principle for other people to observe those moons as well. The existence and behavior of Jupiter's moons is something objective.

In philosophy of mind the subjective–objective distinction is closely related to the *internal–external* or *inner–outer* distinction. The idea is roughly that your mental states comprise an inner, subjective domain to which you and you alone have direct access while your physical states belong to the outer, objective domain of bodily behavior that is accessible in principle to other people. On this understanding of mental phenomena, the access you have to your bodily movements is in no way privileged or distinct from the kind of access that I or some third party has. Any properly situated observer could witness your bodily behavior at least as well as you yourself can. According to most exponents of a subjective conception of mental phenomena, however, your mental states are not like this. We cannot witness each others' conscious states the way we can witness each others' limb movements and facial expressions. According to exponents of a subjective conception of mental phenomena, your knowledge of my mental condition is thus indirect in a way that your knowledge of my bodily behavior is not. You can directly witness my limb movements, facial gestures, and other bodily states, and you also have direct access your own mental states. When it comes to my mental states, however, you can only infer that I have a particular belief, desire, or feeling. Exponents of a subjective conception of mental phenomena thus claim that your access to my mental states is *indirect and inferential*, whereas your access to your own mental states is *direct and noninferential*.

2.4   Qualia and Phenomenal Consciousness

A subjective conception of mental phenomena is also closely associated with several other ideas – the idea of second- or third-person *inaccessibility*, for instance. On the basis of my objective bodily behavior, you might be able to infer that I am having certain subjective experiences. If you witness me wincing and writhing, for instance, you might infer that I am experiencing pain. But witnessing my behavior does not guarantee that I am really experiencing pain. According to the subjective conception of mental phenomena, my bodily behavior need not give you accurate information about what I am experiencing; in fact, according to the subjective conception, it need not give you any information about my experiences at all, for on that conception it is possible that my entire body might be anesthetized while I yet continue to have conscious experiences. Even more surprisingly, it is possible that the human bodies I see around me might be behaving exactly as if they are having conscious experiences and yet lack them entirely – they might be what philosophers call **qualia zombies**, beings that do not have any subjective experiences despite behaving in every objective way as if they do.

The Latin term 'qualia' means literally *qualities* (the corresponding singular term is 'quale'). Many philosophers use the term to refer to the qualitative or phenomenal aspects of experience. Paradigmatic examples of **qualia** include the qualitative aspects of pain, taste, smell, and other sensory experiences. Each has a certain characteristic feel or quale. To use an expression that has become popular in philosophical circles, there is "something it is like" to live through them. There is, for instance, something it is like to eat crème brûlée: a peculiar texture, odor, and flavor – a qualitative dimension to the experience that is impossible to express verbally, but that someone has to live through in order to understand fully. If someone asks, "What is it like to eat crème brûlée?" we can attempt to describe the experience: "It is sweet and creamy, similar in texture to custard or gelato, yet with a crunchy addition due to the caramelized sugar on the surface – that's roughly what it's like to eat crème brûlée." Of course, the verbal description falls short of the actual experience. The reason is that the experience has something – a qualitative or phenomenal dimension – that the description lacks, and that it is impossible to communicate verbally. Likewise, imagine two scenarios in which you go to the dentist to have your tooth drilled. In the first scenario, your tooth is drilled with anesthetic; you don't feel a thing. In the second scenario, however, your tooth is drilled without anesthetic; you feel excruciating pain. In the second scenario, the drilling of your tooth is accompanied by the qualitative experience – the quale – of pain; it has a certain *phenomenal character* that is absent in the first scenario. That qualitative difference, the difference between actually eating crème brûlée and merely thinking about it or describing it is what many philosophers use the term 'consciousness' to refer to.

This notion of consciousness needs to be contrasted with another notion that refers to publicly observable aspects of something's behavior. When emergency medical technicians are trained to assess someone's state of consciousness, for instance, they are trained to determine whether the person can talk, whether he or she is responsive to verbal commands, or responds to painful stimuli. To distinguish consciousness in this behavioral sense from consciousness in the foregoing qualitative sense, many philosophers refer to the qualitative notion as **phenomenal consciousness**. There are several notions of phenomenal consciousness. According to one standard notion, phenomenal consciousness is *nonrelational* and *unanalyzable* (or *intrinsic* and *simple*, as it is sometimes stated). It is possible to analyze the brain mechanisms involved in, for instance, seeing a ripe tomato. They involve complex relations to other brain mechanisms and states of the environment. According to exponents of this view of phenomenal consciousness, however, the qualitative dimension of seeing a ripe tomato cannot be analyzed into the activities of and relations among discrete mechanical components. Likewise, to borrow an example from the American philosopher Wilfrid Sellars (1912–1989), when we look at a pink ice cube we experience a simple, continuous, homogenous quality. This quality can be contrasted with the physical structure of the ice cube which is not simple, continuous, and homogeneous, but rather involves complex relations among heterogeneous pockets of discrete atoms and molecules.

2.5   Intentionality, Mental Representation, and Propositional Attitudes

By contrast with the concepts that are central to a private conception of mental phenomena, the concepts that are central to a public conception of mental phenomena are those of **intentionality** and **rationality**. Intentionality is the feature some mental states have of being *directed at* something – of being *about* or *of* or *for* something. This is a harder notion to understand than the notion of consciousness. Suppose, for instance, that you believe there are exactly eight planets in our solar system. Your belief is a belief *about* the planets; it is a mental state that is directed to the number of planets as its subject-matter. Likewise, in order to be afraid your fear has to be *about* something – there must be something *of* which you are afraid. Similarly in order to have or to entertain a hope or desire you have to want or hope *for* something. To say that these mental states are *about* or *of* or *for* something is to say that they have intentionality.

The word 'intentionality' derives from the Latin word *intensio*, which was used to describe an archer with his bow drawn – having the bow *in tension*, aimed at a target. In an analogous way mental states such as belief and desire seem to be aimed at the world. A more suitable English word for 'intentionality' might be 'directedness' or 'aboutness': the feature certain mental states have of being aimed at or being about something.

Somewhat confusingly, intentionality does not have anything directly to do with intending – with, for instance, forming an intention to do this or that. Intending to do something is merely one example of a kind of mental state that has intentionality. When I intend to write a letter, the intention I form is about letter-writing. But intending is not the only kind of mental state that has intentionality.

One important feature of mental states with intentionality is that they can fail to "hit" the world the way an archer can fail to hit the target. To say that I believe that there are exactly eight planets in our solar system is not automatically to say that there really are exactly eight planets in our solar system. Beliefs can be false. Although they are aimed at the world, they can miss the mark. Similarly, to say that I want a pay raise is not automatically to say that I will receive a pay raise. Desires can remain unfulfilled. Like beliefs, they are aimed at the world but can miss the mark. It is thus an important feature of intentionality that what a mental state is about or of or for need not exist. I can believe that the present King of France is bald even if there is no present King of France. Likewise, I might be afraid that there is a monster under my bed, but my having that fear does not imply that there really is a monster under my bed.

Sometimes philosophers speak of intentionality in terms of **mental representation**. To say that I believe there are exactly eight planets in the solar system is to say that I have a certain representation of the solar system. I represent the solar system to myself as having exactly eight planets, but this representation need not correspond to reality. Philosophers also refer to intentional mental states as states with intentional or representational *contents*. The content of my belief, for instance, is expressed by the sentence 'There are exactly eight planets in our solar system'.

Philosophers also speak of the mental states such as beliefs and desires as **propositional attitudes**. This terminology derives from the idea that intentional states are attitudes that we take toward certain statements or propositions – a feature of intentional states that is reflected in English in our use of the word 'that' in indirect discourse. Consider, for instance, the following statement:

1   Gabriel believes that the glass is filled with water.

The dependent clause that follows the word 'that' expresses a proposition, namely *The glass is filled with water*. When we utter Statement (1), we seem to be saying that Gabriel has a certain attitude toward that proposition; that he is taking a certain stance toward it: he believes that it is true. He could have taken a different attitude toward it such as the attitude described by the following statement:

2   Gabriel doubts that the glass is filled with water.

Like Statement (1), Statement (2) describes Gabriel's attitude toward the proposition *The glass is filled with water*, but the attitude it describes Gabriel having is different: doubt versus belief. The claims that Gabriel believes that the glass is filled with water, doubts that the glass is filled with water, hopes that the glass is filled with water, sees that the glass is filled with water, guesses that the glass is filled with water, and so on, all express intentional states or attitudes that Gabriel can have toward the proposition *The glass is filled with water*.

2.6   Rationality

The notion of intentionality is closely related to the notion of rationality. To describe people's behavior in terms of their beliefs, desires, and other intentional mental states is to classify that behavior as something that is explainable by appeal to reasons. Compare the following cases:

1   Johnson opened the front door, and stepped halfway through, but saw the look of the sky, and reached back in for his umbrella. He locked the door behind him, and proceeded down the path.
2   A few minutes after taking the new medication, Johnson began convulsing uncontrollably.

In Case 1, Johnson's behavior – his decision to take an umbrella – clearly counts as something done for a reason, whereas in Case 2 it clearly does not. In Case 1, we explain Johnson's behavior by appeal to what he believes about the weather;

in Case 2, we explain his behavior not by appeal to his beliefs, but by appeal to certain chemical or physiological conditions: the interaction of the new medication with his nervous system. When we describe someone's behavior in terms of beliefs, desires, and other intentional states, we implicitly locate that behavior within a broader pattern of rational relations: we are committed to viewing that behavior as something that was done for a reason, something describable in terms of concepts such as deliberation and choice. Spasms or convulsions of the sort mentioned in Case 2 are not behaviors of this sort. To describe Johnson's behavior as 'convulsive' in this context implies that it is not something he chose to do in light of certain beliefs, desires, or other attitudes. It is not the type of behavior that qualifies as rational – it is *nonrational*.

Calling Johnson's behavior in this case nonrational is different from calling his behavior *irrational*. To call someone's behavior irrational is to say that it is subject to rational evaluation, but has failed to satisfy a particular criterion for rational evaluation. For example, if Gabriel is trying to light the grill, and he knows this bottle is filled with water, and he knows dousing the coals with water will prevent him from lighting the grill, then it would be irrational for Gabriel to empty the contents of the bottle onto the coals. This is different from a case in which we are trying to describe the behavior of, say, a rock. Unlike Gabriel, a rock's behavior is not even a candidate for rational evaluation. Because the rock is incapable of deliberation and choice in light of reasons, its behavior is not subject to rational evaluation at all. It is completely nonrational, and for that reason it cannot be accused of acting irrationally. In Case 2, Johnson's behavior is like the behavior of the rock. It is not subject to rational evaluation. It does not fit into a broader pattern of reasons; it is nonrational, and for that reason it cannot qualify as irrational.

The private and public conceptions of mental phenomena have both played important roles in philosophy of mind; although at different times philosophers have taken to emphasizing the problems and issues associated with one conception over the other. During the 1950s and 60s, for instance, American philosophers such as Wilfrid Sellars, Roderick Chisholm (1916–1999), and Donald Davidson (1917–2003) focused on the public conception. Meanwhile, Australian philosophers such as J. J. C. Smart focused on the private conception. Later we will see that each conception of mental phenomena is associated with its own family of mind–body problems and that each has its own distinctive implications for mind–body theories. We will also see that there have been attempts to bridge the gap between the two notions. There are theories of consciousness, for instance, that claim that conscious states are species of intentional or representational states – that the private conception of mental phenomena can be assimilated by the public conception.

Further Reading

Descartes' *Meditations on First Philosophy* is the *locus classicus* for the mental–physical distinction (in Descartes 1984). Aristotle's views of human psychological capacities are developed in a number of his works (in Aristotle 1984). These are often referred to by their Latin titles which are included here alongside the English titles: books II and III of *On the Soul* (*De Anima*), chapters 1–5 of *On Sense* (*De Sensu*), chapters 7–10 of *On the Movement of Animals* (*De Motu*). Well-known philosophers who have mistakenly supposed that *mental* and *physical* are mutually exclusive categories include the seventeenth-century philosopher Thomas Hobbes in the Third Set of Objections to Descartes' *Meditations* (in Descartes 1984), and more recently John Searle (1992: Chapter 1; 2004: Introduction).

There are many excellent books on the Scientific Revolution and its implications for modern philosophy. Butterfield (1997) provides a good introduction, and Shapin (1998) provides a readable overview of some of the developments that made the Scientific Revolution revolutionary. Richard S. Westfall (1977) and A. Rupert Hall (1981) discuss the development of modern physics from Johannes Kepler and Galileo Galilei to Isaac Newton. P. M. Harman (1982) discusses the nineteenth-century shift from matter to energy as the unifying subject-matter of physics.

Definitions of the physical domain that appeal to physics include Herbert Feigl's (1958) definition of 'physical$_2$', J. J. C. Smart's (1959) definition, and more recently the definitions of Jeffrey Poland (1994) and Andrew Melnyk (2003). Definitions that attempt to provide an independent characterization of the domain described by physics include Descartes' characterization in Meditation II of his *Meditations on First Philosophy*; Meehl and Sellars's (1956) definition of 'physical$_1$' which they characterize as the spatiotemporal domain; Feigl's (1958) definition of the term 'physical$_1$,' which he uses to refer to the domain of space, time, and causality; and Meehl and Sellars's (1956) term 'physical$_2$,' which they use to refer to the domain of inorganic phenomena.

A private conception of mental phenomena was introduced by Descartes in Meditation II, and was also endorsed by John Locke (1959 [1690]). The expression 'something it is like' to describe consciousness was introduced by Thomas Nagel (1974). Nagel (1989) also discusses the distinction between subjectivity and objectivity, and David Chalmers (1996: Chapter 1; 2002) provides a helpful discussion of phenomenal consciousness, qualia, and the notion of qualia zombies.

The modern notion of intentionality was introduced by the nineteenth-century Austrian philosopher Franz Brentano (1973). The notion was developed by Brentano's student Edmund Husserl (1970 [1900–1]: Volume 2, 533ff.) and by the American philosopher Roderick Chisholm (1957). Searle (1983) and Sokolowski (2000) offer two helpful introductory discussions of intentionality, and Donald Davidson (2001a; 2001c; 2001e; 2001g) discusses the notion of rationality, although his papers are often very difficult.

Chapter 3

Substance Dualism

Overview

Substance dualism claims that persons and bodies are distinct. Persons, such as you and I, are purely mental beings; we have no physical properties. Bodies, on the other hand, including human organisms, are purely physical beings; they have no mental properties. Consequently, according to substance dualists, you and I are not humans. Although each of us might be connected in some way to a human organism, you and I are not human organisms ourselves.

The argument for substance dualism runs as follows: (1) If we can exist without bodies, then we cannot be bodies; (2) we can exist without bodies; therefore, we cannot be bodies. Persons and bodies, in other words, are distinct. Premise (1) follows from the axioms of identity: a thing cannot exist without itself, so if I am a body, I cannot exist without a body. If, on the other hand, I can exist without a body, it follows that I cannot be a body. Premise (2) is more controversial. There are at least two arguments for it. The first argument runs as follows: (i) If it is conceivable that I can exist without a body, then I can exist without a body. Moreover, (ii) it is in fact conceivable that I can exist without a body. Therefore, I can exist without a body. Conceivability-possibility principles like Premise (i) play an important role in philosophy of mind, but they are controversial and subject to restrictions. Substance dualists typically defend Premise (ii) by appeal to examples – situations in which we appear to be able to conceive of ourselves existing without any bodies existing. Critics argue, however, that in these situations we are not really conceiving of ourselves existing without a body. The second argument for Premise (2) sidesteps some of these issues. It claims that having thought or experience is my only essential property – the only property I need in order to exist. If thought or experience is all I need to exist, then I do not need physical

Philosophy of Mind: A Comprehensive Introduction, First Edition. William Jaworski.
© 2011 William Jaworski. Published 2011 by Blackwell Publishing Ltd.

properties to exist, and if I do not need physical properties to exist, then I do not need a body to exist, for a body is simply a thing with physical properties. Consequently, says the argument, I can exist without a body. One liability of the second argument for Premise (2) is that it is implicitly committed to conceptual essentialism, a controversial view of how we come to know something's essential properties. In addition, it faces several objections including the claim that it commits the fallacy of begging the question – that it implicitly assumes I am not a body instead of proving it.

There are many arguments against substance dualism. Critics argue that substance dualism generates a serious problem of other minds; that it has difficulty explaining mental–physical interaction, and that it is empirically inadequate. These arguments fall short of refuting substance dualism since there are ways substance dualists can respond to them. The theoretical costs of doing so, however, are potentially very high. Substance dualists must therefore weigh the costs against the potential benefits very carefully, and consider whether any other mind–body theories can give them what they are looking for without the added expense.

3.1 Substance Dualism: Its Claims and Motivations

Substance dualism has a venerable history. It was endorsed in the ancient world by the Greek philosopher Plato (427–347 BCE) and his followers, and by Neoplatonists during the middle ages. From the seventeenth century until the twentieth, moreover, it was probably the most popular mind–body theory. Some version of it was endorsed by philosophers such as René Descartes, Gottfried Wilhelm von Leibniz (1646–1716), and Nicholas Malebranche (1638–1715). Even in the twentieth century, it was favored by distinguished brain scientists such as Charles Sherrington (1857–1952), John Eccles (1903–1997), and Wilder Penfield, and it has maintained a following among well-known philosophers such as Alvin Plantinga and Richard Swinburne.

Substance dualism claims that there are fundamentally two distinct kinds of individuals in the world: persons and bodies. According to substance dualists, persons are purely mental beings; they have only mental properties. Bodies, on the other hand, are purely physical beings; they have only physical properties. Not only, then, are there two distinct kinds of properties, mental and physical, but there are also two distinct kinds of individuals: individuals that have only mental properties, and individuals that have only physical properties. This is what gives substance dualism its name, for 'substance' is the traditional philosophical term for what we have been calling an individual.

Substance dualists start with the same picture of the physical universe as physicalists. They claim that bodies of all sorts operate according to the principles described by physics. The difference between an electron and a human body is a difference in degree not in kind. Human bodies may be constituted by vast numbers of fundamental physical particles, but they operate according to exactly the same principles as those particles. It is thus possible to give an exhaustive description and explanation of human behavior in purely physical terms in just the way it is possible to give an exhaustive description and explanation of electron behavior in purely physical terms. **Persons,** however, are different. According to substance dualists, persons, such as you and I, are not organisms. We are instead completely nonphysical beings – beings with no properties that can be physically described.

In ordinary English we tend to use the term 'person' synonymously with the term 'human'. When we hear a reporter say that 40 people were killed yesterday in Baghdad, we take it for granted that the reporter means 40 humans were killed. But there is another use of 'person' that applies to roughly any being with psychological capacities similar to those possessed by normal humans. If we were to discover an intelligent race of aliens, we might feel justified in claiming that it was wrong to torture them for the very same reasons it is wrong to torture humans – intelligent aliens are people too: they deserve the same kind of respect and solicitude we extend to humans.

This use of the term 'person' is important for our discussion of substance dualism because according to substance dualists humans are not persons, nor are persons such as you and I humans. This is one of substance dualism's most striking implications. We can sum it up by considering the following two claims:

1   I have beliefs, desires, hopes, joys, fears, loves, and other mental properties.
2   I am an organism such as a human being.

When we utter statements (1) and (2), most of us take ourselves to be saying something true in both cases: most of us, in other words, are convinced that we have mental properties, and yet that we are also living beings, organisms – humans in particular. If substance dualism is true, however, most of us are wrong, for substance dualism implies that one of these statements must be false. According to substance dualism, the same individual cannot have both mental and physical properties. Consequently, if I have mental properties as statement (1) says, then I cannot have any physical properties. But human organisms are physical beings with physical properties. Pick up virtually any biology textbook, and you will find descriptions of many of the physical properties human organisms possess. But if human organisms have physical properties, and I have none, then according to substance dualism, I cannot be a human organism. So according to substance dualism, if statement (1) is true, statement (2) must be false.

This is a striking result. It implies among other things that I am not the organism I see in the mirror when I shave, or fix my hair, or put on my makeup. I am not the organism whose appearance and activities or whose reproductive destiny I take considerable interest in, or whose safety concerns me when it crosses busy streets. Substance dualists are free to claim that I am "attached" in some way to a human organism, but I am certainly not identical to one, and I do not have the kinds of properties human organisms have. I have no hair, for instance, no face, no hands, fingers, or limbs. I have no heart, no brain – no organs at all. I am not capable of being hit by a bus, or being burned in a fire. These are all physical attributes, and if substance dualism is true, I have no physical attributes – not even spatial location: if substance dualism is true I am literally located nowhere.

Similarly, if substance dualism is true, the human organisms you see around you are not persons. Those organisms might be attached to persons, but they are not persons themselves. Organisms are bodies, physical beings, and according to substance dualism persons and bodies are distinct: the former are purely mental beings, the latter purely physical ones. Consequently, if substance dualism is true, it is impossible for you to strike, for instance, or embrace another person. Striking after all involves one body impacting another, and embracing involves one body wrapping itself or part of itself around another, but if substance dualism is true, you have no body, and neither has any other person. You are thus incapable of striking something, and incapable of being struck. Likewise, because you have no arms or other bodily parts, you are incapable of embracing anything and are incapable of being embraced.

Substance dualists can argue that these implications are not as striking as they might at first seem. Because persons are attached to bodies, they can claim, we can easily makes sense of descriptions that suggest we are bodies. When we say, "Eleanor struck Gabriel," for instance, what we are really saying is that Eleanor caused her body – the body to which she is attached – to strike Gabriel's body, a situation depicted in Figure 3.1. Here Eleanor and Gabriel are nonphysical entities depicted by the cloudy patches above their bodies. The arrows represent causal relations. In the figure, Eleanor causes the limbs of her body (the human organism

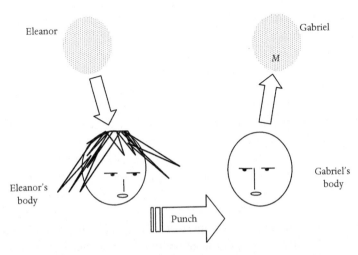

Figure 3.1   Substance dualism on person-body interaction

depicted on the left) to strike Gabriel's body (the human organism depicted on the right); as a result of being struck, Gabriel's body in turn causes a mental state in Gabriel such as pain, anger, or surprise. According to substance dualists, then, their view is not as counterintuitive as it might initially seem. We are intimately connected to our bodies – so intimately connected, in fact, that we often speak of the behavior of our bodies as if it were our own.

Despite this, many people find the substance dualistic view of human nature bizarre. Why would someone be inclined to endorse it? To answer this question it's helpful to consider two things: the motivations for substance dualism, and the arguments for it. People's motivations for endorsing a theory needn't be reasons for believing the theory to be true. By 'motivations' here, we mean something like reasons people might be inclined to think or to want the theory to be true. Sometimes reasons and motivations amount to the same thing, but sometimes they do not. Sometimes people are motivated to believe something in the absence of good reasons for believing that it is true.

Let us start by considering some of the motivations for substance dualism and then consider the arguments for it. The motivations for substance dualism are various, but they share a commitment to placing persons outside of the physical domain. The motivation for doing so might be something as simple as not wanting to believe that persons are vulnerable to the thousand natural shocks that flesh is heir to. But the motivations could be quite sophisticated as well – the desire, for instance, to avoid the problem of free will and determinism. One version of that problem suggests that if we are part of the physical universe, we must be completely governed by fundamental physical laws, and hence cannot really be free: our choices cannot make a difference to how things happen. One way of trying to avoid this problem is to claim that we are not part of the physical universe, but are instead completely nonphysical beings.

Motivations for substance dualism often stem from religious beliefs as well. The doctrine of reincarnation in some Eastern religions, for instance, presupposes that we are nonphysical beings who are capable of being attached to different kinds of organisms. In one lifetime, for instance, I might be attached to a cow. When that cow dies, I survive and am reincarnated – reattached – to an organism of a different kind such as a human. In Western religions, moreover, substance dualism has often presented itself as a way of understanding the claim that we are or have immortal spirits or souls. The ancient Greek philosopher Plato, for instance, was one of the first to argue for a substance dualistic understanding of the soul. Under the influence of his philosophy, some Neoplatonists of late antiquity and the early middle ages came to interpret the teachings of Christianity in a substance dualistic way as well.

These are some of the motivations for substance dualism, but whatever their motivations, substance dualists have advanced real arguments in favor of their position – real reasons for thinking that substance dualism is true. Let us consider one of them.

3.2   The Argument For Substance Dualism

The best-known philosophical argument for substance dualism runs as follows:

1   If we can exist without bodies, then we cannot be bodies.
2   We can exist without bodies.

Therefore, we cannot be bodies.

Persons and bodies, in other words, are distinct. This is often called the **modal argument for substance dualism** since it appeals to the **possibility** of persons existing without bodies (the notion of possibility is a *modal* notion). The argument's conclusion follows validly from its premises: if (1) and (2) are true, then the conclusion must be true as well. And, say substance dualists, there is good reason to think (1) and (2) are both true.

Premise (1) follows directly from the axioms of **identity**. In ordinary English, we often use the term 'identity' to speak of someone's personal characteristics – features such as distinctive personality or character traits that we use to distinguish him or her from other people. In philosophy, however, the term is used differently. 'Identity' is synonymous with 'sameness' – in the strictest sense of that term. To say that x is identical to y is to say that x and y are the very same object, or property, or event; that is, 'x' and 'y' are just two different labels for the very same thing. Samuel Clemens, for instance, was identical to Mark Twain – 'Samuel Clemens' and 'Mark Twain' were two different names for the very same individual. Likewise, the predicate 'has a mass of 1 kg' and the predicate 'has a mass of 2.2 pounds' are two different ways of expressing the very same property.

Now clearly, if x is identical to y – if x and y are the very same thing – then x cannot exist without y. The reason is very simple: it is impossible for a thing to exist without itself; x cannot exist without x; Mark Twain cannot exist without Mark Twain. Suppose, then, that x is the very same individual as y. In that case, x cannot exist without y any more than x can exist without x, for in that case y is x. If Samuel Clemens is the very same individual as Mark Twain, then clearly Mark Twain cannot exist without Samuel Clemens any more than Mark Twain can exist without Mark Twain, for in that case he *is* Samuel Clemens. In general, then, if x and y are identical, then x cannot exist without y. Consequently, if we were to discover that x *can* exist without y, we would succeed in showing x is *not* identical to y. If we discovered that Mark Twain had died, for instance, but that Samuel Clemens was still alive and well, we would know that Samuel Clemens and Mark Twain must be different individuals.

Consider the implications of all this for the argument: If I am identical to a body – my body, the human body I see before me – then I cannot exist without that body. A thing cannot exist without itself, so if that body and I are the very same thing, if we are like Sam Clemens and Mark Twain, then it is impossible for one of us to exist without the other. Suppose, however, that it were possible for one of us to exist without the other; suppose we could prove that it was possible for me to exist without my body; that I do not need that body to exist. In that case, we would prove that I was not in fact that body; we would prove that my body and I must be different individuals – that persons and bodies are distinct. And, say substance dualists, we can prove that it is possible for me to exist without my body or any other body. Why should we suppose that is the case?

There are at least two arguments in favor of Premise (2), the claim that I can exist without a body. Let us call the first of these arguments the **conceivability argument**. It appeals directly to a **conceivability-possibility principle**. Conceivability-possibility principles (CPs) claim that conceivability is a reliable guide to possibility: roughly, if we are able to conceive of something, then it must be possible. If, for instance, I want to know whether it is possible to maneuver this table through the doorway without disassembling it, I can try to determine this by imagining or conceiving a way of moving the table through the doorway. Likewise, if I am planning my schedule for next semester and want to know whether it is possible to take both a course in metaphysics and a course in calculus, I do not travel into the future to see if that schedule has worked out. I instead try to conceive whether it is possible by looking up the days and times those courses are offered, and seeing whether there is a conflict. This procedure of putting together a schedule seems to assume that conceivability is a reliable guide to possibility – that if I can conceive of the schedule working out, it can work out in fact. Conversely, CPs imply that what is impossible is also inconceivable. On this view, the reason we are unable to conceive of the existence of a married bachelor or a four-sided triangle is that the existence of such entities is impossible: there could not be a four-sided object with exactly three sides, or a married unmarried man. So if we can conceive of something, say exponents of CPs, it must really be possible. Consequently, says the argument for Premise (2), if it is conceivable that I can exist without a body, then I must really be able to exist without one. And, says the argument, it is conceivable that a person – a mental being like myself – can exist without a body. Consider some examples:

Example 1   Many people claim that they are able to conceive of themselves existing despite having their bodies cease to exist. People who believe in life after death, for instance, are tacitly committed to conceiving of themselves existing despite their bodies ceasing to exist. So this is one example of a case in which people appear to be able to conceive of themselves existing without a body. You do not have to believe in life after death to be able to conceive of it. By analogy, you do not have to believe that there exists a mountain made of solid gold to be able to conceive of one. All that matters is that you be able to form a conception of yourself existing despite the death of your body. But conceiving of life after death is not the only way of conceiving of yourself existing without your body.

Example 2   Imagine that you are watching your body from a third-person vantage point – the sort of vantage point you occupy when, for instance, you see your body through the security camera at the local convenience store. Imagine, for instance, that you are watching your body reading this text right now from a third-person point of view, and that your body is suddenly annihilated: it vanishes from sight, and you are left staring at an empty chair where your body was previously seated. In that case, you seem to be conceiving of yourself existing in the absence of your body. You are conceiving of yourself having a visual experience – the experience of seeing the empty chair – despite your body ceasing to exist. In other words, you seem to be able to conceive of a situation in which you can exist even though your body does not.

Example 3   Descartes' *Meditations on First Philosophy* suggests another way that you can conceive of yourself existing without any bodies existing: you can conceive of yourself having experiences that are all inaccurate. Consider what you are experiencing right now: you probably take yourself to be in a physical environment surrounded by physical objects: a table perhaps, a chair, a book, and so on. Imagine, however, that what you are experiencing right now is a massive hallucination; that none of your experiences correspond to anything in reality. Imagine that although you seem to be seeing, hearing, and touching bodies around you, in fact none of these things exist; in reality there are no bodies of the sort you take yourself to perceive. Imagine, in other words, that the situation is similar to a dream. While dreaming you can be having an experience as if you are wide awake on some exotic beach when in fact your body is really asleep in bed. Likewise, in this case, you are conceiving of yourself having an experience as if you are situated in a physical environment surrounded by various bodies though none of these bodies exist – including your own. If this kind of situation is conceivable – if you can imagine that you might be subject to a massive hallucination of this sort – then you can conceive of a situation in which you exist and yet no bodies exist, a situation in which you are having experiences (and hence you exist) and yet because those experiences are illusory, because they correspond to nothing in reality, there are no bodies in fact.

According to exponents of the conceivability argument, examples like this illustrate that it is conceivable that a person can exist without a body. But if cases like this are conceivable, and conceivability is a reliable guide to possibility, then it follows that it is possible for a person to exist without a body.

A second argument in support of the claim that persons can exist without bodies appeals to the notion of an essential property. Let us call it the **essential property argument**. It was originally advanced by Descartes in Meditation II of his *Meditations on First Philosophy*. An *essential* property is a property that is necessary for something to exist. Being three-sided, for instance, is an essential property of a triangle – it is impossible for a triangle to exist without being three-sided. Likewise, being a mammal is essential to dogs; it is impossible for a dog to exist without being a mammal. An *accidental* property, by contrast, is a property that is not necessary for something to exist. The property of being Eleanor's favorite shape, for instance, is an accidental property of a triangle. It is possible for a triangle to exist without being Eleanor's favorite shape – before Eleanor was born, for instance, no triangle had that property. Similarly, being a pet is an accidental property of dogs; it is possible for a dog to exist without being a pet.

Consider now persons such as you and I. What essential properties do we have? According to the essential property argument each of us has only one essential property, the property of having experiences, or *thinking*, as Descartes put it. Under the heading of 'thinking' Descartes included everything that we have been discussing under the heading of 'mental phenomena': not just beliefs and desires, but feelings, sensations, and other mental states. According to the essential property argument, thought or experience is the only property you and I need to exist.[1] But if thought is the only property we need to exist, then we do not need any other properties to exist; we do not, for instance, need physical properties to exist. If we do not need physical properties to exist, however, then clearly you and I can exist without a body, for a body is simply a thing with physical properties, and we do not need any physical properties to exist. Hence, the argument concludes, we can exist without bodies.

The central premise of this argument is that thinking is a person's only essential property. But why should we accept this claim? The way substance dualists answer this question derives from the way many of them answer a more general question: How do we discern the essential properties of anything? There are at least two approaches to our knowledge of essential properties. **Conceptual essentialists** claim that we can know the essential properties of things purely *a priori* – purely by consulting definitions or by undertaking some other purely conceptual procedure. **Empirical essentialists**, by contrast, claim that we can know the essential properties of things only *a posteriori* – only by studying them empirically. Like many substance dualists, Descartes was a conceptual essentialist; he claimed we could discern something's essential properties by following an imaginative or conceptual procedure.

According to Descartes, if we want to discern the essential properties of some object, *a*, we start by compiling a list of all the properties we take *a* to possess. Suppose, for instance, that $P_1, P_2, P_3, \ldots, P_n$ is a list of those properties. We next take each property on the list, and consider whether it is possible for *a* to exist without it. We try to imagine or conceive of *a* existing without P_1, of *a* existing without P_2, and so on. If we can conceive of *a* existing without P_1, then we can conclude that *a* can exist without P_1; we can conclude, in other words, that P_1 is not an essential property of *a*, that it is not a property *a* needs in order to exist.

If, by contrast, we cannot conceive of *a* existing without P_1, then we can conclude that P_1 is an essential property of *a*, that *a* needs P_1 to exist. By following this procedure for every property on the list, Descartes thinks, we arrive at a list of *a*'s essential properties.

Consider now how this procedure applies to the essential properties of persons, such as you and I. We start by compiling a list of all the properties we take ourselves to have. We might take ourselves to be bodily beings, for instance, who are capable of seeing, feeling, moving about, eating, thinking, and so on. Next, we take each property on this list, and consider whether it is possible for us to exist without it. We try to imagine or conceive of ourselves existing without eating or moving about, or having limbs, or other bodily parts. In the case of every one of these properties, says Descartes, it is possible to form a conception of oneself existing without it. We can form a conception of ourselves continuing to have experiences even though we lack a stomach, or limbs, or other bodily parts and the capacities for eating or moving associated with them. The only exception, he says, is thought or experience. Unlike the other properties on the list, we cannot form a conception of ourselves not having experiences. Although we can remove bodily parts and capacities from ourselves in imagination, we cannot remove experiences from ourselves in imagination. Once you eliminate from your imagination the having of experiences, you eliminate any conception you have of yourself existing at all. You cannot conceive of yourself without experiences. What this indicates, says Descartes, is that thought or experience is one of your essential properties. In fact, it is your only essential property; it is the only property without which you can form no conception of yourself. The essence of a person thus consists in thinking or having experience; it is something a person needs to exist, and the only thing a person needs to exist.[2] But if having experience is the only thing a person needs to exist, then persons do not need bodies to exist. If their existence depends on having experience alone, then their existence does not depend on having a body. It is thus possible for persons, such as you and I, to exist without bodies.

3.3 Objections to the Argument for Substance Dualism

There are several ways of challenging the substance dualist's argument. It should be clear, however, that Premise (1) is a not a viable target. That premise follows directly from the axioms of identity. If I can exist without a body, then I cannot be the same thing as a body. The only viable way of challenging the argument targets Premise (2), the claim that persons can exist without bodies.

We have considered two arguments for Premise (2): the conceivability argument, and the essential property argument. There are serious objections to both. Critics of the conceivability argument object to it in at least two ways. Some of them argue that examples like 1–3 do not really establish that it is conceivable for us to exist without bodies. Others argue that conceivability is not a reliable guide to possibility. We will consider these objections in order.

To appreciate the first objection, consider an example from the philosopher Michael Tye:

> Suppose … you just imagined the number π's having seven consecutive sevens in its decimal expansion … [W]hat exactly did you imagine? Suppose you report the following: you mentally visualized yourself sitting down with a pen and paper and doing some arithmetic, and you visualized further seven consecutive sevens showing up when you divided twenty-two by seven … [In that case] you did not really imagine the number *itself* having seven consecutive sevens in its expansion.[3]

Tye's example suggests that it is possible for us to be mistaken about what we conceive. It would be a mistake, for instance, for someone to put together visual experiences of the sort Tye describes and claim to have formed a conception of the number π itself having seven consecutive sevens in its decimal expansion. But if we can be mistaken about what we conceive in cases like this, then it seems we can be mistaken about what we conceive in examples 1–3. In Example 2, for instance, you are conceiving of yourself having certain visual experiences – an experience of, say, seeing your body seated in a chair, followed by an experience of seeing that chair empty. By forming these images have you really managed to conceive of yourself existing without a body? Critics of the conceivability argument can argue that you have not, that this is instead a case like the one involving the number π: by putting together these visual images, you have not succeeded in imaging *yourself* any more than you have succeeded in imagining the number π in Tye's example. What you have succeeded in imagining is instead someone who looks just like you vanishing from the chair. Moreover, critics can urge, it is doubtful that having a visual experience is conceivable apart from having visual organs – physical structures that receive light from the environment. Consequently, what you are really imagining in Example 2 is not yourself lacking a body, but yourself – an ordinary human – with ordinary human visual capacities and ordinary human visual organs, watching in an ordinary human way another human who looks just like you vanishing from a chair. And something analogous is true of Examples 1 and 3, and any other examples that are alleged to demonstrate the conceivability of persons existing without bodies. In all such examples, say critics, substance dualists misdescribe what we are conceiving. Substance dualists thus fail to establish that we are really able to conceive of persons existing without bodies.

A second criticism of the conceivability argument challenges the claim that conceivability is a reliable guide to possibility. There are many different kinds of CPs, and clearly not all of them are true, say critics. People once conceived of humans flying with birdlike wings, and yet human flight with birdlike wings is physically impossible. Similarly, prior to the twentieth century people might have conceived that it was possible for there to be a solid sphere of pure uranium with a mass of 1,000 kg. This is another physical impossibility since the critical mass of uranium is approximately 50 kg. Other counterexamples concern the notion of conceivability. It is unclear, for instance, whether the conceptions people form of things while drunk or drugged can serve as reliable guides to possibility at all.

In response to examples of this sort, exponents of conceivability arguments typically do not endorse *unrestricted CPs*, CPs that place no qualifications on the notion of conceivability or limits on the notion of possibility. Instead exponents of conceivability arguments endorse CPs that are restricted in one of three ways: they are restricted to a particular type of conceivability, restricted to a particular type of possibility, or restricted to a particular subject-matter. In his own argument for substance dualism, for instance, Descartes endorsed a CP that was restricted to *clear and distinct* conceivability; he made no claims about drunk and drugged conceivability, or warm and fuzzy conceivability, or any other kind of conceivability. Moreover, Descartes took clear and distinct conceivability to be a reliable guide not to any kind of possibility, but only to *metaphysical* possibility – or as he put it, to the kinds of circumstances God could have brought about. To understand this second restriction, consider these definitions:

It is *technologically possible* that p if and only if p is consistent with current technological constraints.

It is *physically possible* that p if and only if p is consistent with the laws of physics.

It is *metaphysically possible* that p if and only if p is consistent with itself.

Each of these definitions expresses a different notion of possibility. We can see this by considering some examples. It is technologically impossible to construct a robotic system that behaves in every way exactly like a human. Constructing such a system exceeds our current technological constraints; we currently lack the technology to do it. This does not imply, however, that it is physically impossible to construct such a system. Many things that are technologically impossible are still physically possible, and with time, some of these physical possibilities might become technological possibilities as well. Two hundred years ago, long-distance communication with satellite and radio was technologically impossible. It was still physically possible, however, and with time it became technologically possible too. Similarly, a uranium sphere with a mass of 1,000 kg and human birdlike flight are physically impossible; they are incompatible with the laws of physics. This does not imply, however, that they are metaphysically impossible. Many things that are physically impossible are still metaphysically possible. Suppose, for instance, that the laws of physics did not obtain; that the universe obeyed different physical laws.

Under those conditions, a uranium sphere with a mass of 1,000 kg and human birdlike flight might be possible after all.

The differences among these notions of possibility are important for exponents of the conceivability argument because the argument's success does not depend on every kind of possibility. In fact, for the argument to succeed, substance dualists need only establish the metaphysical possibility of persons existing without bodies. If it is possible for persons to exist without bodies under *any* circumstances, then persons cannot be bodies. This gives substance dualists a clear response to critics: the examples of the uranium sphere and human birdlike flight are not examples of metaphysical impossibilities. Examples of metaphysical impossibilities would include the likes of married bachelors and four-sided triangles. A uranium sphere with a mass of 1,000 kg or human flight with birdlike wings are physically impossible, but they are not metaphysically impossible the way married bachelors and four-sided triangles are. A uranium sphere with a mass of 1,000 kg would be possible if the laws of physics were different. A married bachelor or four-sided triangle would not be possible under any circumstances. They are not just physically impossible; they are metaphysically impossible as well. As a result, the examples of the uranium sphere and human birdlike flight do not falsify restricted CPs like the following:

CP*   If it is clearly and distinctly conceivable that *x* can exist without *y*, then it is metaphysically possible that *x* can exist without *y*.

And restricted CPs like this are all that substance dualists need for their argument to succeed.

There is nevertheless a second way critics can attack the conceivability argument. They can argue not that conceivability is never a reliable guide to possibility, but that it is a reliable guide only if we have information that substance dualists fail to provide. Consider again the examples of the uranium sphere and human birdlike flight. These examples may not succeed in falsifying restricted CPs, critics can say, but they do succeed in doing something else: they highlight the dependence of those CPs on scientific knowledge; they show that sometimes our conceptions of what is possible or impossible are only as reliable as our best scientific knowledge.

Consider technological possibility. Knowing whether or not something is technologically possible requires knowing what technological constraints there currently are. But we can know what technological constraints there currently are only empirically – only by studying the world. Likewise physical possibility involves consistency with the laws of physics. But knowing whether or not something is consistent with those laws requires knowing what those laws are, and that is something we can discover only empirically, by studying the world. Our conceptions of what is technologically or physically possible are only as accurate, therefore, as our knowledge of the corresponding laws and constraints. If we do not know what those laws or constraints are, then our conceptions about what is or is not technologically or physically possible are bound to be inaccurate. That is why people once believed inaccurately that it was physically possible for humans to fly with birdlike wings: they were ignorant of the laws of aerodynamics and bird physiology. Because their knowledge of these laws was limited, their ability to conceptualize accurately what was physically possible was similarly limited. Someone who knew the relevant laws might find the idea of human flight with birdlike wings inconceivable: a human body is too heavy and its muscles too feeble to enable a person to flap a pair of wings with enough force to hold itself aloft.

Our knowledge of physical and technological possibility thus depends on having accurate scientific knowledge. Consider now metaphysical possibility: How do we know what is or is not metaphysically possible? Sometimes we can know metaphysical possibilities and impossibilities on purely logical grounds. We can know on purely logical grounds, for instance, that someone cannot be both married and unmarried at the same time and in the same way because we know in general that necessarily any statement with the form 'q & $\sim q$' is false. We know, for instance, that the statement 'Someone is married and also unmarried' must be false: it is inconsistent with itself, or *self-referentially* inconsistent.

Sometimes, however, logic does not suffice to tell us what is metaphysically possible or impossible. On purely logical grounds, for instance, we cannot know that it is impossible for a bachelor to be married. To know that, we need to know something in addition to basic logical principles. We need to know something about the definition of 'bachelor': something is a bachelor only if it is unmarried. Statements whose truth or falsity can be known on purely logical grounds are called *logical* truths and falsehoods. Statements whose truth or falsity can be known on the basis of logic in conjunction with definitions of key terms are often called *analytic* truths and falsehoods. We know the truth values of logical and analytical truths and falsehoods purely *a priori*, by consulting logic and definitions; no study of the world is needed.

Yet not all metaphysical possibilities and impossibilities are knowable *a priori*. Sometimes we can know what is metaphysically possible or impossible only *a posteriori* in the way we come to know a physical possibility, namely by studying the world. Water, for instance, is H_2O. It is thus metaphysically impossible for water to exist without H_2O molecules. But there is nothing in the definition of the term 'water' that would have told us this. Originally, people might have defined water as the substance we drink, that we bathe with, that falls from the sky as rain, that turns to ice in winter, and that fills rivers, lakes, and oceans. Nothing in such a definition tells us that water is H_2O molecules. The identity of water with H_2O had to be discovered empirically – by studying the world, not simply by consulting logic and definitions.

Consider now persons and bodies. How do we know whether it is metaphysically possible for persons to exist without bodies? If the case of persons and bodies is similar to the case of water and H_2O, then we can know this only *a posteriori*, only by studying the world and acquiring information about what properties persons and bodies essentially have. And this, critics claim, is a problem for exponents of the conceivability argument. Exponents of the conceivability argument assume that we are able to determine the truth of the claim that persons can exist without bodies purely conceptually, without undertaking any empirical investigation into the nature of persons and bodies. But what justifies this assumption? Exponents of the conceivability argument appear to say nothing in its favor. They appear to take it for granted that our conceptions are a reliable guide to metaphysical possibility however uninformed by empirical considerations those conceptions may be. This objection to the conceivability argument is related to objections to the essential property argument as well.

There are at least three objections to the essential property argument. The first concerns its commitment to conceptual essentialism. According to Descartes, we determine whether or not a thing can exist without a property by trying to conceive of its existence without that property. Our ability to conceive of *a*'s existence clearly and distinctly apart from a property is supposed to be sufficient to determine whether it is possible for *a* to exist without that property, and hence whether *a* has that property essentially. But empirical essentialists deny the sufficiency of a conceptual procedure of this sort for determining whether or not an object can exist without a property. According to empirical essentialists, discerning something's essential properties is not a task that can be accomplished from an armchair, so to speak, through the manipulation or analysis of concepts. Discerning something's essential properties requires actual scientific investigation since the conceptions we initially form of things may not correspond to their essential properties. Consider an example.

We may have learned to identify water by a certain characteristic look or smell or taste, but if we brought a bottle of water to a distant planet with a strange atmosphere that affected our senses in unusual ways, the contents of the bottle might no longer look, smell, or taste to us the same way. Would this mean that the substance in the bottle was no longer water? Of course not, say empirical essentialists. It would still be the same substance; it would simply be affecting our senses differently on account of the planet's strange atmosphere. It would still be water, in other words, despite lacking the characteristics we originally conceived water to have. The essential properties of water would remain the same even if its accidental properties underwent a change. According to empirical essentialists, the essential properties of something, the properties that make it what it is, and that enable us to say with confidence that the bottle is filled with the same substance on the distant planet that it was on Earth, are properties it is up to science to discern – properties that might nevertheless not correspond to our prescientific conception of water. We discovered the essential properties of water not by trying to imagine water's existence apart from the various properties we initially took it to have; we discovered them scientifically, by means of chemical analysis. But if determining something's essence is an empirical undertaking of this sort, if it requires serious scientific investigation, then I could not discover the essential properties of persons – not even my own – simply by trying to conceive of their existence apart from bodies. Discovering the essential properties of persons would require serious scientific investigation.

Closely related to this objection is a second. It claims that the essential property argument commits the fallacy of begging the question: it implicitly assumes the very thing it is supposed to prove. The objection is based on the plausible premise that the essential properties of physical beings can only be discovered empirically. Even most substance dualists are willing to grant that when it comes to our knowledge of physical beings, science is the ultimate authority. If bodies are governed by the laws of physics, then it makes sense to suppose that physics gives us the final word on them and their properties – including their essential properties. Suppose, then, that this assumption is true, and the essential properties of physical beings can only be discovered empirically. The essential property argument is based on the assumption that we can discover the essential properties of persons conceptually. But if the essential properties of physical beings can only be discovered empirically, and the essential property argument assumes that we can discover the essential properties of persons conceptually, then it looks like the argument assumes from the outset that persons are not physical beings, for if persons were physical beings, we could discover their essential properties only empirically – just as we can discover the essential properties of water only empirically. If I were a physical being, for instance, it would be possible to discover my essential properties only through scientific investigation. To assume, then, as exponents of the essential property argument do, that we can discover my essential properties conceptually, apart from any scientific investigation, is to assume from the outset that I am not a physical being. According to the objection, then, the essential property argument does not prove that persons are not physical; it instead assumes it.

The final objection to the essential property argument was noted by Descartes' contemporary Antoine Arnauld (1612–1694). It concerns the list of properties we initially take an object to possess. Let us assume for the moment that clear and distinct conceivability can be taken as a reliable guide to metaphysical possibility, and that Descartes' procedure does enable us discern whether or not a property is essential to something. Even in this case, says the objection, Descartes' procedure is still liable to error, for an object will often have properties we do not initially recognize. Consider electromagnetic properties. Before the development of electromagnetic theory, people were largely unaware of the broad spectrum of electromagnetic properties most objects possess. If these people had compiled a list of the properties various objects possessed, their list would have been inaccurate since it would have omitted these properties. Having an impoverished initial conception of an object exposes us to the possibility of error. Here is why: imagine a case in which an object, a, has exactly three properties: P_1, P_2, and P_3, and that two of these properties, P_2 and P_3, are essential to it. It turns out, however, that our initial conception of a includes only the properties P_1 and P_2. We do not know, in other words, that *a* also has property P_3. We then follow Descartes' procedure for discerning essential properties and find that we can conceive of *a* existing without P_1, but we cannot conceive of it existing without P_2. We thus conclude – wrongly – that P_2 is *a*'s only essential property. Consider the implications of this for the essential property argument: if the initial conception we have of persons is in any way impoverished, we could be led by Descartes' procedure to draw the wrong conclusion about what essential properties persons have.

3.4   Substance Dualism and the Problem of Other Minds

The foregoing objections challenge the argument that substance dualism is true. In addition, there are arguments that purport to show that substance dualism is false. First, substance dualism faces a serious version of the **problem of other minds**.

One of our basic starting points for understanding who and what we are is the idea that we are social beings. We know, for instance, that there are other people in the world, and that we often know through our interactions with them what they think and how they feel. Yet if substance dualism is true, it is difficult to see how this kind of knowledge is possible. The problem can be stated as follows:

1   If substance dualism is true, then we cannot know what mental states other people have or that other people exist.
2   We can know what mental states other people have and that other people exist.

Therefore, substance dualism is false.

Let us consider the argument in detail starting with reasons behind Premise (1). According to the argument, we can know what mental states other people have only if we either directly perceive those mental states or else infer what those mental states are on the basis of overt bodily behavior. If substance dualism is true, however, it looks like we can know about other people's mental states in neither of these ways. We cannot directly perceive other people's mental states, for if substance dualism is true, mental states are subjective phenomena that are accessible in principle only to the person whose mental states they are. If only the person experiencing a mental state has access to it, then it is impossible for me to know other people's mental states directly. Bodily behavior, both the behavior of human bodies and of other bodies, is objectively observable, and for that reason, it might provide a basis for inferring what mental states other people have. If, for instance, a human body utters the words, "There are eight planets in our solar system," with a sincere look on its face, this might provide a basis for inferring that the person believes there are eight planets in our solar system. If substance dualism is true, however, we cannot know what mental states other people have on this basis either, for if substance dualism is true, the behavior of bodies tells me almost nothing about other people's mental states: what mental states they have, and whether or not other people even exist. Why is that the case? If substance dualism is true, the human bodies I see around me could be acting exactly as they are even if none of them are attached to persons. Bodies are purely physical entities, according to substance dualism; their behavior can be exhaustively described and explained by physics without any reference to persons and their mental states. Consequently, the behavior of a body attached to a person could be completely indistinguishable from the behavior of a body not attached to a person. To illustrate this point consider the scenarios depicted in Figure 3.2.

In each scenario, we witness the behavior of a human body alongside the behavior of a table. The human body moves about, talks, gestures, and so on, while the table just sits there as tables are wont to do. In our ordinary dealings we take it for granted that the human body behaves as it does on account of beliefs, desires, pains, and other mental states, and that the table does not behave as it does on account of such states. In a substance dualistic framework we would understand this situation in the way depicted in Figure 3.2(A). Here the human body is connected to a person and the table is not. If substance dualism is true, however, persons and bodies do not have to be related to each other in this way. Our ordinary sense of what bodily behaviors are due to mental causes could be

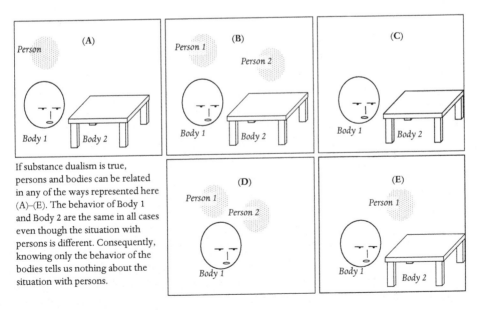

If substance dualism is true, persons and bodies can be related in any of the ways represented here (A)–(E). The behavior of Body 1 and Body 2 are the same in all cases even though the situation with persons is different. Consequently, knowing only the behavior of the bodies tells us nothing about the situation with persons.

Figure 3.2   The problem of other minds

completely wrong. It could be the case, for instance, that every body is connected to a person – the human body as well as the table, as depicted in Figure 3.2(B). If the table fails to move, talk, or gesture, this does not indicate that it isn't connected to a person, but only that it lacks the physical mechanisms necessary to engage in these activities. If persons and bodies are distinct, however, there is nothing that requires that persons be connected to bodies of one sort as opposed to another. Tables, chairs, and other inanimate bodies could all be connected to persons without their behavior reflecting this connection in any way. Similarly, it could be the case that no bodies are connected to persons – neither the human body nor the table, as in Figure 3.2(C). If the human body moves, talks, and gestures, that does not indicate that it is connected to a person. Its speech mechanisms and motor mechanisms could be triggered by states of its nerves and by environmental impacts on its auditory and visual systems in just the way the mechanisms of any complex machine could be triggered. Consequently, if this human body were displaying the kinds of behavior we normally associate with intelligence, we could still not conclude with certainty that it was connected to an intelligent being. If bodies are purely physical entities, their behavior can be exhaustively described and explained by physics irrespective of whether or not they are connected to persons. Since the behavior of both the human and the table can be exhaustively described and explained this way, it is possible for their behavior to be exactly the same in scenarios (A), (B), and (C) even though their relations to persons are different in each case.

If substance dualism is true, therefore, the behavior of bodies can be correlated with persons in any number of different ways. Imagine, then, that we observe a human body carrying on a conversation while the table at which it sits remains silent and immobile. Intuitively, we want to say that we know on the basis of their behavior that the human body is connected to a person and the table is not, that the human body would not be behaving the way it is unless it were connected to a person, and that the table would not be behaving the way it is unless it were not connected to a person. But if substance dualism is true, we can say neither of these things, for the bodies we see around us could be behaving exactly as they are even though the situation with persons is radically different from what we intuitively suspect. Based just on the behavior of the human body and the table, substance dualism gives us no way of knowing whether or not either is connected to a person. Perhaps every body is connected to a person: the human body, the table, this oxygen atom, this piece of hair, these finger tips, and so on. Perhaps no body is connected to a person. Perhaps individual bodies are connected to multiple persons, as in Figure 3.2(D), or an individual person is connected to multiple bodies, as in Figure 3.2(E), or different persons are attached to different bodies at different times – any of these could be the case if substance dualism is true, and yet the behavior of bodies could be exactly the same in each case. Consequently, if substance dualism is true, the behavior of bodies tells us nothing about other people – not even that they exist.

If substance dualism is true, therefore, we cannot know what mental states other people have by directly perceiving them, nor can we know what mental states other people have by making inferences from bodily behavior. Nor can we know that other people exist. If persons and bodies are distinct, then we cannot perceive them the way we perceive bodies, and the behavior of those bodies does not tell us for certain whether other people exist. Consequently, if substance dualism is true, we cannot know what mental states other people have or that other people exist.

But that is absurd, says the argument. Surely we have more knowledge of other people than substance dualism allows; surely we often can and do know that other people exist, and often can and do know what they think or how they feel. Since substance dualism is incompatible with this knowledge, the argument concludes, substance dualism must be false.

Substance dualists can respond by denying one of the argument's premises. In response to Premise (2), for instance, substance dualists can challenge critics to support the claim that we have more knowledge of other people than substance dualism allows. The premise is little more than an appeal to intuition, substance dualists can argue, but intuitions are largely byproducts of cultural conditioning. If we have been enculturated in ways that are opposed to substance dualism, then of course we are going to think that we have more knowledge of other people than substance dualism allows. But that doesn't make it so. Perhaps our intuitions are just plain wrong.

Critics of substance dualism might reply as follows: We expect theories to explain certain facts or phenomena. Among the facts we expect mind–body theories to explain are facts concerning our knowledge of other people, including our knowledge that they exist, and that they have certain thoughts and feelings. These are some of the basic starting points for constructing mind–body theories – points that enable us to construct mind–body theories in the first place. If a mind–body theory is unable to accommodate these basic facts, if it asks us to revise our pre-philosophical understanding of the world so fundamentally, chances are there is something seriously wrong with it. By analogy, if we asked some physicists to construct a theory explaining the behavior of light, and they came back to us with a theory that implied there was no such thing as light, this would mark a serious flaw in their theory.

Of course, sometimes we do endorse theories that require radical revisions of our pre-theoretical starting points. But when we decide to endorse these theories, it is because there are very strong arguments in their favor. Based on the earlier assessment of the argument for substance dualism, however, it is not clear that there are very strong reasons to endorse it. At the very least, it seems that our reasons for thinking substance dualism is true are no stronger and probably much weaker than our reasons for thinking we know other people exist and have certain thoughts and feeling. If it is a toss-up, therefore, between rejecting substance dualism and rejecting the idea that we know other people exist and have mental states, there can be no question, say critics, that it is substance dualism that must go.

Substance dualists can respond to the argument, however, by denying Premise (1), the claim that substance dualism is incompatible with knowing that other people exist and have certain mental states. There are at least two ways that substance dualists can challenge this claim. First, they can argue that if substance dualism is true, we can in fact have direct knowledge of other people's mental states. Substance dualists can claim that each of us possesses a capacity like extra-sensory perception (ESP) that enables us to experience directly the thoughts and feelings of others.

Critics will argue that there are at least two problems with this response. First, there is little evidence to suggest we possess a capacity of this sort. Experiments aimed at measuring whether there is such a thing as ESP have almost always shown there is no reason to believe it exists. Second, and more importantly, even if some people did possess a capacity like ESP, it seems clear that not everyone does. It is fairly clear to me, for instance, that I have no such capacity, and yet I still take myself to know that there are other people and to know at times what they are thinking and how they are feeling. Even if there were such a thing as ESP, therefore, substance dualism would still imply that we have much less knowledge of other people than we appear to have in fact.

The second way substance dualists can challenge Premise (1) is to deny that the behavior of bodies can tell us nothing about persons. One strategy for doing this is called the *argument from analogy*. It claims that I can know that other people are related to bodies by knowing that I am related to a body and that other people and their bodies are similar to me and mine. According to substance dualists, then, we can make an inductive generalization about other people based on the knowledge each of us has of himself or herself.

Inductive generalization is a form of argument that starts out with an initial sample of things of a certain kind and then makes a generalization about all things of that kind based on the initial sample. We often use inductive generalization in the sciences. If all pieces of copper observed so far conduct electricity, we conclude that all copper conducts electricity. In a similar way substance dualists can argue as follows: We can be confident that the human bodies we see around us are connected to people and the tables we see around us are not, and we can be confident that the human bodies are acting the way they are because of the mental states of the people they are connected to. Why can we be confident of these things? Each of us knows that he or she is connected to a human body, and that the operations of that body are due to his or her mental states. I know, for instance, that this human body – my own – is attached to a person, and that my beliefs, desires, pains, and other mental states are responsible for much of this body's behavior. Based on my knowledge that I am related to my body in this way, I can infer that similar behavior in other human bodies most likely has similar causes, that other people's mental states are responsible for much of the behavior of their bodies, just as my mental states are responsible for the behavior of mine. Substance dualists can thus claim that their theory is compatible with each of us knowing that there are other people, and that those people have mental states similar to our own.

The problem with this argument, say critics, is that the initial sample is not large enough to support the generalization it makes. The strength of an inductive generalization depends to a large extent on the size of the initial sample. If I have studied only one piece of copper and make a generalization concerning all pieces of copper, that generalization will be much weaker than if I have studied numerous pieces of copper. Substance dualists, however, make a generalization about the way all human bodies (or a least a great number of them) are related to persons on the basis of only one case: how my body is related to me. Given that there are so many human bodies in the world, and that the initial sample represents less than one billionth of the total group size, this generalization is extremely weak. The observation of my own case – my relation to my body – provides very little evidence that all bodies are related to persons in the same way.

Consequently, say critics, if substance dualism is true, we end up having very little information about other people – so little, in fact, that we cannot even be confident other people exist. Our knowledge of other people, however, is a fundamental starting point for understanding who and what we are. To reject this basic pre-philosophical conviction in favor of a mind–body theory that denies it would require very powerful arguments. But substance dualists offer no arguments to rival our pre-philosophical conviction that we know about other people and their mental states. Because substance dualism is incompatible with this conviction, say critics, substance dualism must be false.

3.5   The Problem of Interaction

The problem of interaction was formulated independently by several of Descartes' contemporaries including Pierre Gassendi (1592–1655) and the Princess Elisabeth of Bohemia (1618–1680), who was Descartes' pupil. It was also among the criticisms the Greek philosopher Aristotle made of the dualists in Plato's academy. The problem concerns whether it is possible for persons, who according to substance dualism are completely nonphysical entities, to interact causally with bodies, which are physical entities.

Intuitively, we want to say that our beliefs, desires, pains, and other mental occurrences causally influence physical events in the world. Many kinds of actions, for instance, would appear to be physical events that have mental causes. If I accidentally trip and fall, my behavior does not count as an action, but if a clown *intends* to trip and fall, it does count as an action. The difference between these cases is not a physical one. We can easily imagine that the physical events in each case are the same: an experienced clown can feign tripping and falling in a manner indistinguishable from a genuine, accidental trip and fall. What is it, then, that distinguishes the real trip and fall from the feigned one? Why does one count as an action while the other does not? The answer seems clear: in the one case the physical events in question have a mental cause, the intention to trip, while in the other case they do not. What distinguishes actions from physical events of other sorts, then, would appear to be the way they are caused: actions are physical events that have mental causes. But if actions are physical events with mental causes, and there are actions, then it follows that persons, the only entities capable of under-going mental events, must be able to interact causally with bodies, the only entities capable of undergoing physical events. The problem with substance dualism is that it appears to be incompatible with this type of causation: if it is true, it seems to imply that persons cannot interact causally with bodies – at least it is difficult to see how they could.

If substance dualism is true, then persons are completely nonphysical entities, and it seems impossible that nonphysical entities could have a causal impact on physical ones. The reason is that physical events occur in space and involve forces or changes in energy. But if you and I are entirely nonphysical, then we have no spatial location; and it is not clear how something without spatial location could influence something in space, or in general how something could manipulate forces or energy states without being in some way physical. An example will help illustrate this point.

In order to drive an automobile forward something has to liberate the energy stored in the chemical bonds of the gasoline. In most vehicles this happens through combustion initiated by the engine's spark plugs. The firing of the plugs is in turn caused by a high-voltage pulse generated by the coil and fed to the plugs by the distributor. When the gasoline undergoes combustion, the liberated energy drives the pistons. They in turn drive the crankshaft, the crankshaft drives the axle, and the axle drives the wheels. An automobile is driven, then, by a series of physical events that occur at particular locations and that involve changes in energy. In order for something to intervene in that series of events, it would have to influence one of the steps in the series: it would either have to turn the crankshaft, or drive the pistons, or ignite the gasoline, or bring about some other event in the series. Bringing about any of the events in that series, however, requires a transfer of energy or the manipulation of forces.

A human body operates in a similar way. The movements of the limbs are produced by muscular contractions. Those in turn are triggered by ions which are released by neuronal firings. Those neuronal firings are triggered in turn by the depolarization of the neuronal membranes, something that typically results either from the presence of ions released by other neurons, or from some type of envi-ronmental stimulus such as light, heat, or pressure. Like the movements of the automobile, the movements of the human body are driven by a series of physical events. In order for something to intervene in that series of events, it would have to bring about one of the steps in the series. But bringing about any of these steps requires a transfer of energy. As a result, it is difficult to see how substance dualism is compatible with persons influencing the behavior of bodies, for according to substance dualism persons are completely nonphysical entities, and it is difficult to see how nonphysical entities could influence bodily behavior for at least two reasons.

First, the energy transformations involved in all of the aforementioned physical processes occur at specific spatial locations – in the combustion chamber, at the point where the crankshaft meets the axle, on the muscle fiber, at the cell membrane, and so on. Because these events occur in space, it seems plausible to suppose that they could only be brought about by something in space. At the very least, it is unclear how something without any location at all could manage to bring them about – how it could manage to depolarize the membrane at this location, for instance, or break the chemical bonds at that location, or exert a force here or there. To have a nonphysical entity causally impact a physical event would be analogous to having a train on one track impact a train on a completely separate track.

Second, as the examples of the automobile and the human body illustrate, normally something can bring about a change in a physical system only if it has energy. It is only because the gasoline stores energy in its chemical bonds that it is capable of driving the piston, and it is only because the ions released by neurons have electromagnetic energy that they are able to bring about muscular contractions, and it is only because the neuronal membrane has an electrical potential that it is able to release ions. But energy is something physical. In fact, since the nineteenth century, physicists have taken energy to unify the subject-matter of physics. It seems, then, that a system capable of manipulating states of energy would have to be a physical system, the sort that is capable of being described by physics. It is thus difficult to see how persons, their beliefs, desires, and other mental states could have energy without being physical. The idea that a nonphysical system might be capable of influencing a physical one thus borders on incoherence.

In short, the problem of interaction can be stated as follows:

1   If substance dualism is true, persons cannot causally influence bodies.
2   Persons can causally influence bodies.

Therefore, substance dualism is false.

As we have seen, critics of substance dualism support Premise (2) by appeal to the existence of actions: actions exist, they argue, only if persons can causally influence bodies. In support of Premise (1), critics argue that it is impossible for nonphysical entities to causally influence physical ones. If substance dualism is true, however, then persons are nonphysical entities; consequently, if substance dualism is true, persons cannot causally influence bodies. Why is it impossible for non-physical entities to causally influence physical ones? Critics argue that something can causally influence a body only if it has features that nonphysical entities lack – features such as spatial location or states of energy.

Substance dualists can respond to the problem of interaction in several ways. One is to reject Premise (1): substance dualists can argue that their theory is in fact compatible with person–body interaction. Persons may be nonphysical enti-ties, substance dualists can say, but that does not prevent them from interacting with bodies. How is it possible for nonphysical entities to causally influence physical ones? Substance dualists who reject Premise (1) can insist that this ques-tion is misguided, that there is no explanation for how there can be causal interac-tions between physical and nonphysical entities; rather, the existence of such causal interactions must be accepted as a brute matter of fact in just the way most of us accept the existence of causal interactions between physical entities and other physical entities as a brute matter of fact. Most of us do not demand an explanation of how it is possible for there to be causal interactions between physi-cal entities and other physical ones. Why, then, should we demand an explanation of how it is possible for there to be causal interactions between physical entities and nonphysical ones? There seems to be no good reason, substance dualists can argue. Consequently, there is no good reason substance dualists cannot simply posit brute causal connections between nonphysical entities and physical ones. A response along these lines is what Descartes suggested in response to the Princess Elisabeth.[4]

One problem with this response is that it seems to require a violation of con-servation laws. Conservation of energy is a basic principle of physics. It says that the total amount of energy in a system is fixed: energy is neither created nor destroyed but merely transformed. The automobile and its surrounding environ-ment and the human body and its environment are *energetically closed systems*. The total amount of energy in those systems neither increases nor decreases; it simply changes from one form to another. The energy stored in the chemical bonds of the gasoline, for instance, is transformed into mechanical energy as the expanding gas in the combustion chamber moves the piston, and the mechanical energy of the wheels and axle is transformed into heat when the brakes are applied. Likewise, the chemical energy stored in the molecules that drive the metabolic processes of human cells is converted into mechanical energy and heat when the body moves. Throughout all of these occurrences, energy is neither gained nor lost but merely transformed. The same is true of the entire physical universe. It is an energetically closed system with a fixed amount of energy. The total amount of energy in the universe neither increases nor decreases; it merely changes from one form to another.

Because there is a fixed amount of energy involved in the movements of the automobile, and the human body, and any other physical system, it seems that a nonphysical entity could causally influence a physical one only if it violated the principle of conservation of energy. The reason is that the nonphysical entity would be bringing about physical changes not through the energy in the physical system, but through energy of a different sort, not included in the physical domain. In that case, however, the physical universe would not be an energetically closed system; it would be a system that was open to the addition of nonphysical energy. Consequently, even if substance dualists can manage to give a coherent account of how there can be nonphysical energy, the influence of that energy on the physical universe seems to require a violation of conservation laws.

The foregoing considerations suggest that substance dualists can countenance causal relations between the mental and physical domains only if they reject the laws of physics. But if it is a toss-up between rejecting substance dualism and rejecting our best science, say critics, there can be no question that substance dualism has to go. After all, our reasons for accepting physical laws are much stronger than any reasons we have for accepting substance dualism. The existence of mental–physical causal relations together with the conservation of energy thus suggests that substance dualism is false.

3.6 Noninteractionist Views: Parallelism and Occasionalism

But perhaps persons do not causally influence bodies after all. At least two kinds of substance dualists target not Premise (1) of the **problem of interaction**, but Premise (2): they deny that persons and bodies causally interact. Exponents of this noninteractionist approach include **parallelists** and **occasionalists**.

Parallelists claim that persons and bodies do not causally influence one another, but merely seem to do so because they are running in parallel. Consider an analogy: We wind two grandfather clocks so that they are running synchronously. We then remove the chimes from Clock A and the hands from Clock B (Figure 3.3). Because they are running in sync, the clocks continue to tell exactly the same time despite the absence of chimes in Clock A and the absence of hands on Clock B. Consider how the clocks might appear to a casual observer who is unaware that they have been wound in sync. If the observer hears Clock B chiming whenever Clock A reaches the hour, the observer might conclude that the clocks are causally connected, that Clock A is causing Clock B to chime. We know, however, that the casual observer would be wrong. There are no causal connections between Clock A and Clock B. The reason Clock B chimes whenever the hands of Clock A reach the hour is not that A causes the chiming of B; it is that the clocks have been wound in sync. This synchrony is what explains the appearance of a causal connection between the clocks even though no real causal connection exists.

According to parallelists, something analogous is true of persons and bodies. The mental states of persons and the physical states of bodies appear to causally

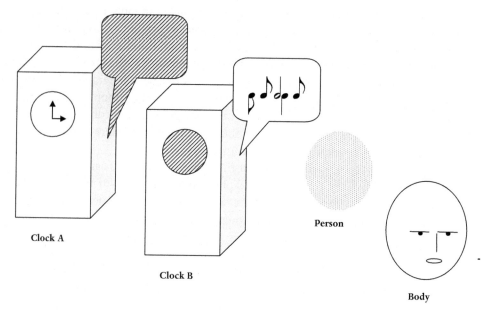

Clock A

Clock B

Person

Body

Figure 3.3   Parallelism

interact. In reality, however, there is no causal interaction; there only appears to be because, like the clocks, persons and bodies are running in sync. Whenever my body stubs its toe, it turns out that at that time I am experiencing pain – not because the stubbing causes me to feel pain, but simply because my body and I are operating in parallel.

Critics might complain that parallelism has the absurd consequence that actions do not exist, for it implies that there are no physical events that have mental causes. In response, however, parallelists can argue that actions are not physical events that have mental causes, that they are rather physical events that *seem* to have mental causes. The clown's feigned tripping *seems* to be caused by his intention, whereas a genuinely accidental trip does not even seem to have a mental cause. The difference between actions and nonactions, then, is not a difference in their causes but in their appearances: actions appear to have mental causes, nonactions do not.

One potential problem for parallelism is that in the clock example there is a clear explanation for why the clocks are running in sync; namely, we have wound them that way. But what explains the synchronous operation of persons and bodies? Parallelists can answer this question in different ways. Leibniz, for instance, claimed that the parallel operation of persons and bodies was due to God. The doctrine of *pre-established harmony* claims that God set up the world in such a way that persons and bodies are running in sync in just the way Clocks A and B are.

But parallelists are also free to claim that the synchronous operation of persons and bodies must simply be accepted as a brute matter of fact.

The second noninteractionist form of substance dualism is occasionalism. It was endorsed by Nicolas Malebranche. Like parallelists, occasionalists deny that there is any causal connection between persons and bodies, but, according to them, this does not imply that there is no causal agency at all. Occasionalists claim that God acts as a causal middleman who, so to speak, brokers the transaction between persons and bodies. Although I cannot directly affect my body, and my body cannot directly affect me, God can directly affect both. God observes my mental states and produces changes in my body that correspond to those states, and likewise, God observes the states of my body and produces the appropriate mental states in me.

There are at least two worries about occasionalism. One is that it implies God is the only real agent that exists. This has been taken to have unacceptable moral and theological implications. Suppose, for instance, that my body shoots and kills another body – your body, say. I cannot be held accountable for the death of your body, at least not directly, for I was not the agent who caused my body to pull the trigger. It was instead God. According to occasionalists, you and I are not causally responsible for anything that happens in the physical universe; the only individual who is causally responsible for what happens in the universe is God. This has awkward implications both for people who do not want to ascribe morally blame-worthy behavior to God, and for people who want to ascribe morally blamewor-thy behavior to people like you and me.

A second problem with occasionalism is that the appeal to God seems ad hoc. 'Ad hoc' is a Latin expression that means literally 'to this'. It is used to refer to a claim that is adopted not on any principled basis, but simply in order to respond *to this* or that unanticipated objection. Consider an example. Suppose I make a sweeping generalization such as "All cows are white," and you then proceed to falsify it by producing a brown cow. Instead of admitting that my generalization is false, however, I respond by saying, "This brown cow does not falsify my original claim, for when I said 'All cows are white' I meant all cows are white *except that one!*" My response in this case is ad hoc. There is no principled basis for me to exclude this particular cow from my generalization; I have decided to do so simply to respond to this one counterexample. According to critics, the occasionalist's invocation of God to explain the appearance of mental–physical interaction is similarly ad hoc.

Why are claims that are adopted ad hoc problematic? The reason is that they can significantly weaken a theory. Theories are meant to unify our knowledge of a particular domain. A theory that adopts ad hoc principles amounts to a collection of claims with little overall unity, and hence little ability to unify our understanding of things. Consider by analogy the strength of the following generalizations:

1 All cows are white.
2 All cows are white except the one you just showed me, and the two over in the neighbor's barn, and those six cows out in the field, and the ones in that photograph, and ...

Statement (2) is a much weaker generalization than statement (1). What makes it weaker is that it includes so many exceptions. The addition of all these exceptions empties (2) of any informative content; it amounts to saying all cows are white except the ones that aren't. Claims that are adopted ad hoc weaken a theory in much the same way these exceptions weaken generalization (2). The worry about appealing to God in the way occasionalists do is that it can potentially yield unlimited ad hoc claims. Any philosophical problem that arises for occasionalists can potentially be solved by invoking the will of an omnipotent being. This threatens to empty occasionalism of any genuine philosophical content.

Regardless of the success or failure of these objections to parallelism and occasionalism, both theories imply that our beliefs, desires, and other mental states are powerless to affect the physical universe. Because of this, many people consider parallelism and occasionalism to be very extreme views. They are nevertheless viable options for substance dualists who want to avoid the problem of interaction.

3.7   The Problem of Explanatory Impotence

The Greek philosopher Aristotle was the first to fault substance dualism for being explanatorily impotent. He criticized the dualists in Plato's academy for offering no explanation of why persons would have the bodies they do. If in fact persons are not humans but nonphysical souls that are merely attached to human bodies, then why are human bodies equipped to engage in precisely the kinds of activities that people naturally want to engage in? The Platonists, he said, gave no satisfactory answer.

The version of the explanatory impotence problem we will consider takes the form of an *inference from a worse explanation*. To understand it we first need to understand an *inference to the best explanation*. Inference to the best explanation is an inductive form of argument often used in the sciences. It starts with a body of facts or phenomena together with a set of theories that purport to explain them. In the process of evaluating the theories, we come to reject some in favor of other, better ones until we arrive at the best explanation among them – the theory that best explains the data. Consider an example.

For many years it was unclear exactly how the Moon was formed. Several competing theories were advanced to explain the Moon's formation. According to one theory, the Moon was a wandering planetoid from outside our solar system which was captured by Earth's gravity. According to a second theory, Earth and the Moon formed side-by-side from the original cloud of cosmic dust out of which the rest of the solar system was formed. A third theory claimed that the Moon formed as a result of a massive cosmic collision: a small planet crashed into the early Earth, and ejected debris into space which eventually coalesced to form the Moon. The first theory was rejected because it was highly improbable that the Moon would have ended up with its current orbit if it had been captured by Earth's gravity. The second theory was rejected because it was not able to explain the absence in the Moon of an iron core: if Earth and the Moon had been formed from the same cloud of cosmic dust, scientists reasoned, then most likely the Moon would have ended up with an iron core just like Earth's. After examining the available evidence, then, scientists concluded that the best explanation of the Moon's formation was the third: the Moon formed as a result of a massive collision between a small planet and the Earth.

This example illustrates both an inference to the best explanation and inference from a worse one. In the process of moving toward the best explanation for the Moon's formation, scientists moved away from competing explanations that did not fit the data as well. In the process of making an inference to the best explanation, they were simultaneously making an inference away from worse ones. An inference to the best explanation, then, always involves a movement from away from worse explanations. The problem of explanatory impotence claims that substance dualism provides an explanation of certain facts that is worse than the explanations provided by other theories. Consequently, as we move closer to the best explanation of those facts – the best mind–body theory – we will simultaneously move away from substance dualism. Our reasons for believing other theories are true, in other words, are also reasons for believing substance dualism is false.

Consider now some facts about the relations between mental and physical phenomena that appear to give substance dualists difficulty. Most of us take it for granted that mental phenomena are not related to just any kind of body – not just any body has or is associated with mental states. Large-brained mammals such as humans are associated with them, for instance, but not tables, pencils, and rocks. Why are mental states associated with some physical systems but not with others? Exponents of different mind–body theories explain this fact in different ways. According to psychophysical identity theorists, for instance, the reason is that mental states are brain states (see Section 5.4). Because large-brained mammals have brains, but tables, pencils, and rocks do not, it is easy to see why humans would have mental states but rocks, tables, and pencils would lack them. Likewise, according to dual-attribute theorists, such as emergentists and epiphenomenalists, mental states are generated by brain states (see sections 8.3 and 8.10). Because tables, pencils, and rocks do not have brains, they cannot generate mental states; large-brained mammals, on the other hand, can. How, by contrast, do substance dualists explain the correlation between mental states and large-brained mammals? The answer: They don't! If substance dualism is true, mental phenomena are not essentially related to physical phenomena – mental states need not be correlated with any physical systems at all. As a result, if mental phenomena are correlated with specific kinds of physical systems such as large-brained mammals, substance dualists can offer no principled way of explaining those correlations; their existence must be accepted as a brute matter of fact.

Consider another example. Not only are mental phenomena correlated with large-brained mammals as opposed to rocks and tables, but they are correlated only with specific parts of those large-brained mammals: their nervous systems. Why are mental states correlated only with states of the nervous system and not with, say, states of fingernails or hair? Again, different mind–body theories offer different explanations. According to psychophysical identity theorists, the reason is that mental states *are* states of the nervous system, and so mental states will be correlated only with those. Likewise, according to emergentists and epiphenomenalists, mental states are caused by states of the nervous system, not by states of the fingernails or hair. How, by contrast, do substance dualists explain the correlation between mental states and states of the nervous system? The answer, again, is that they do not. Because they claim that mental phenomena are not essentially tied to physical phenomena, substance dualists must take mental–physical correlations as brute matters of fact.

What do these examples show? According to critics, they show that substance dualism is explanatorily inferior to other theories, and this gives us good reason to think substance dualism is false. Theories are formulated to explain phenomena in a given domain. One of the jobs of a mind–body theory is to explain mental–physical correlations. When it comes to explaining these correlations, however, other theories such as the psychophysical identity theory, emergentism, and epiphenomenalism do a better job. In fact, say critics, substance dualism does the worst job possible: it offers no explanation of mental–physical correlations at all. Because it does not explain the empirical facts as well as other theories – because there are theories that better explain those facts, we have good reason to think that substance dualism is false. We might not know yet which among the range of alternative theories is true – we might not know which provides the best explanation for the facts about mental–physical correlations, but we do not need to know which of these other theories is the best to know that each is better than substance dualism. And if these theories are better than substance dualism, we know that in the process of moving toward the best explanation among them – the theory that is true – we will be moving away from substance dualism, a theory that is false.

In response to this argument, substance dualists can argue that it is merely inductive. Even if other theories do a better job of explaining mental–physical correlations, they can say, this still does not prove that substance dualism is false. Moreover, substance dualists could argue that failure to explain mental–physical correlations is not really a demerit at all, that there is no good reason to consider a theory that explains mental–physical correlations to be superior to a theory that accepts those correlations as brute unexplainable facts. In this case, then, as in the others we have considered, substance dualists have a way of responding to the criticism.

3.8 Substance Dualism in Perspective

We have considered some arguments against substance dualism, and indicated the ways substance dualists can respond to them. One point that should be clear is that substance dualism is a very resilient theory. If substance dualists are willing to reject conservation laws or the existence of mental–physical causal relations; if they are willing to deny that we know that other people exist, or are willing to reject the demand that a theory of mind explain mental–physical correlations, there is very little critics can say. And yet the price of endorsing substance dualism in the face of the objections seems very high. Rejecting conservation laws or the idea that we know other people exist seems a very high price to pay for a theory that is supported by an argument that is indecisive at best. Consequently, the interesting question for prospective substance dualists is not so much *Can substance dualists respond to these objections?* for as we have seen, they can; the interesting question is rather *Why would someone want to respond to these objections in the first place? Why would someone want to endorse substance dualism given the high price of doing so?* In answering these questions, it is important for prospective substance dualists to consider carefully why they are motivated to endorse substance dualism, and whether there are any mind–body theories that can give them what they are looking for without forcing them to pay the corresponding costs. Examples might include nonorganismic dual-attribute theory (Section 8.2), and the view that we are humans with nonphysical parts (Section 12.3). Many exponents of these views were originally substance dualists, but considered the alternatives and decided that another theory could give them what they wanted without paying the high price the objections to substance dualism exact.

Further Reading

The *locus classicus* for modern substance dualism is Descartes' *Meditations on First Philosophy*. He presents the main argument for substance dualism in Meditation VI, and defends the claim that he is essentially only a thinking thing in Meditation II. Several distinguished scholars responded to the *Meditations* including Thomas Hobbes, Antoine Arnauld, and Pierre Gassendi who wrote the Third, Fourth, and Fifth Sets of Objections to the Meditations, respectively (in Descartes 1984: Volume 2). Descartes' *Principles of Philosophy* is the mature exposition of his views (in Descartes 1984: Volume 1), and his correspondence, including his letters to the

Princess Elisabeth, often contain helpful discussions as well (Descartes 1984: Volume 3).

Substance dualism has been defended more recently by Alvin Plantinga (1974), Richard Swinburne (1997), and W. D. Hart (1988); although Hart's view is more accurately described as a nonorganismic dual-attribute theory (see Section 8.2). Plato argued for substance dualism in the *Phaedo* (in Plato 1997). The influence of Platonic philosophy on religious ideas about immortality is perhaps most evident in Gnostic sects of Christianity. Gnostic Christians saw the physical universe as evil or corrupt and saw us as prisoners within a fleshy prison from which we would be liberated at death to achieve a new state of enlightenment or knowledge (*gnosis* in Greek) of God. Substance dualism nevertheless sits uncomfortably with Western religious traditions that emphasize resurrection of the dead. The Catholic Church, for instance, condemned the substance dualism of the medieval philosopher Peter John Olivi in the document *Fidei catholicae fundamento* at the Council of Vienne in 1312 (Tanner 1990: Volume 1). Likewise, although the thirteenth-century philosopher and theologian Thomas Aquinas claimed that the human soul was immortal, he denied that you and I were immortal in "Commentary on Paul's First Epistle to the Corinthians," (in Aquinas 1995: see especially sections 924–5 on Chapter 15 verses 12–19).

The legitimacy of conceivability-possibility principles remains a source of controversy. The essays in Gendler and Hawthorne (2002) are helpful, although some are probably too technical for introductory purposes. Conceptual essentialism was en vogue for a long time in modern philosophy, but empirical essentialism experienced a revival in the late twentieth century due to the work of philosophers such as Saul Kripke (1980) and Hilary Putnam (1975c). Modern empirical essentialism can be understood as a way of developing the kind of essentialism found in Book II, chapters 1 and 2, of Aristotle's *Physics* (see Aristotle 1984).

Gilbert Ryle (1949: Chapter 1) has a helpful discussion of the problem of other minds. Pierre Gassendi's formulation of the problem of interaction appears in The Fifth Set of Objections to Descartes' Meditations. Daniel Garber (1982) provides a helpful discussion of the problem of interaction. It includes quotes from the Princess Elisabeth along with Descartes' replies, and an alternative reply crafted along Cartesian lines. P.M. Harman (1982) discusses the development of energy physics in the nineteenth century. Leibniz (1989) discusses the idea of parallelism and the doctrine of pre-established harmony in Section 33 of his *Discourse on Metaphysics*, and in sections 78–82 of the *Monadology*. Malebranche (1997a [1688]; 1997b [1674–5]) argues for occasionalism in both his *Dialogues on Metaphysics and on Religion* and his *The Search after Truth*. Aristotle's formulation of the problem of explanatory impotence can be found in Book I, Chapter 3 (lines 407b14–25) of *On the Soul*, a work frequently referred to by its Latin name, *De Anima* (see Aristotle 1984). He mentions the problem of interaction in the same passage. The argument from explanatory impotence has been advanced more recently by Paul Churchland (1984: Chapter 2).

Notes

1   In his later work, *The Principles of Philosophy*, Descartes stated this point by saying that every individual has a single principal attribute which defines its essence. According to Descartes, my principal attribute is thinking, whereas the principal attribute of bodies is extension. If thinking is my principal attribute – the only attribute I need to exist – then I do not need extension or any other physical attribute.

2   After applying the procedure to persons in Meditation II, Descartes went on to apply it to bodies, a piece of wax in particular. He said that he could conceive of the wax existing without the odor, texture, temperature, and all other properties it appeared to possess with one exception: extension. He could form no conception of the wax existing unextended – of the wax not taking up space. Since he could form no conception of the wax being unextended, he concluded that extension was essential to the wax – the only essential property of the wax and of any other body.

3   Michael Tye, 1995, *Ten Problems of Consciousness*, Cambridge, MA: MIT Press, 187.

4   Descartes wrote to Elisabeth (May 21, 1643) that in addition to our notion of physical causation – the type of causation involving extension, shape, and movement – we also have another notion of causation that pertains to the union of mind and body. This notion, he insists, is as irreducible and unanalyzable (primitive, he says) as the notion of physical causation.

Chapter 4

The Physicalist Worldview

Overview

Physicalism claims that everything is physical; everything can be exhaustively described and explained by physics. There are three broad types of physicalism: eliminative, reductive, and nonreductive. They differ over the descriptive and explanatory legitimacy of conceptual frameworks other than physics – conceptual frameworks such as ordinary psychological discourse. According to eliminative physicalists, ordinary psychological discourse has no descriptive or explanatory legitimacy. When scientists finally develop the true physical account of human behavior, we will see that psychological descriptions and explanations correspond to nothing in that account, just as talk of the god Zeus corresponds to nothing in the true physical account of the weather. Reductive and nonreductive physicalists disagree with this assessment. When scientists develop the true physical account of human behavior, we will see that psychological descriptions and explanations do correspond to something in that account. In just the way talk of water corresponds to talk of H_2O molecules, so too we will discover that talk of beliefs and desires corresponds to talk of brain states or talk of internal states of some sort that are responsible for behavior.

Physicalism is motivated by confidence in the descriptive and explanatory power of science, and the argument for physicalism derives from past scientific success. In the past, argue physicalists, whenever people have tried to explain phenomena by appeal to nonphysical entities, their explanations have failed and have been replaced by physical explanations that succeeded. Since this has always happened in the past, we have every reason to think that it will continue to happen in the future – that nonphysical explanations will always fail and will be replaced by physical explanations that succeed. We have every reason to think, in other

Philosophy of Mind: A Comprehensive Introduction, First Edition. William Jaworski.
© 2011 William Jaworski. Published 2011 by Blackwell Publishing Ltd.

words, that everything will be explainable physically and nothing will be explainable nonphysically. In that case, however, we have good reason to think that everything is physical. The principal liability of this argument is that it is merely inductive. It is possible for the premises of inductive arguments to be true and yet for the conclusions to be false. It is possible, in other words, that physicalists might be right about the history of science and yet wrong that everything is physical.

One argument against physicalism is Hempel's dilemma. It claims that physicalism is either false or else lacking in content: either it is false to say that everything is physical, or else we do not know clearly enough what it means to say that everything is physical to be able to evaluate that claim. Physicalists have several ways of responding to this argument.

Other arguments against physicalism appeal to a private conception of mental phenomena. Physicalism, they say, has trouble accommodating phenomenal consciousness or subjectivity. The knowledge argument claims, for instance, that it is possible to know all the physical facts without knowing all the facts. If physicalism is true, then all facts are physical facts. But if someone can know all the physical facts without knowing all the facts (without knowing facts about phenomenal consciousness, say), then not all facts are physical facts, and physicalism must be false. Other objections of this sort claim that it is possible for two people to be physically identical and yet mentally distinct. Person A and Person B might be physically indistinguishable and stand in exactly the same physical relationships to a ripe tomato which they both see, and yet have different qualitative experiences of the tomato. But if that is the case, says the argument, physicalism must be false, for if it were true, systems that were indistinguishable physically would have to be indistinguishable in every respect.

Physicalists have several ways of responding to these arguments. Some responses appeal to theories of consciousness that are compatible with physicalism. These include representational, higher-order, and sensorimotor theories of consciousness. These theories remain highly controversial, as do the objections to physicalism. Physicalism nevertheless remains the most popular mind–body theory today.

4.1 What Physicalism Claims

Physicalism claims that everything is physical – everything can be exhaustively described and explained by physics. Physicalism is far and away the most popular form of monism. Since the middle of the twentieth century, moreover, it has also been the most popular mind–body theory in general, and has generated an extensive literature. Because it occupies such an important place in contemporary philosophy of mind four chapters will be devoted to it. The goal of this chapter is to describe the general physicalist worldview. Subsequent chapters will focus on different varieties of physicalism: reductive, nonreductive, and eliminative physicalism, as well as instrumentalism – a variety of physicalism that stands outside the standard mind–body theories outlined in Chapter 1.

The claim that everything is physical is ambiguous. Some people might interpret it in the following way for instance:

1 Every individual has some features or engages in some behaviors that can be exhaustively described and explained by physics.

This, however, is not the way physicalists interpret it. They take the claim that everything is physical to be much stronger:

2 Every feature of every individual and everything every individual does can be exhaustively described and explained by physics.

Claim (2) says not merely that *some* features of an individual thing can be physically described, or that *some* of its behavior can be physically explained; it says that *all* of an individual's features and *all* of its behavior can be physically described and explained. Moreover, these physical descriptions and explanations are *exhaustive*; that is, they leave out nothing, but provide the complete truth about the individual, its features and behavior. This is physicalism.

Physicalism implies that it is possible to describe and explain every feature of, say, a human being and every type of behavior a human engages in using only the conceptual resources of physics. Once we give a physical account of what humans are and what humans do, there is nothing more to be said; we have exhausted the truth about human beings and human behavior. We are of course free to describe humans and their behavior using other vocabularies or conceptual frameworks, but we need not do so. According to physicalists a purely physical account of human behavior, one that never mentioned beliefs, desires, reasons, motives, pains, and joys, would be missing nothing. Physics is fully sufficient to give us the complete account of what humans are, how they behave, and why they behave as they do.

To illustrate the implications of a physicalist worldview, imagine a godlike being that possesses complete physical knowledge of the universe. Call this being the *Super Physicist*. The Super Physicist knows all the fundamental physical individuals in the universe, as well as their properties and relations, and all the laws governing their behavior. Imagine, however, that the Super Physicist does not have a mental conceptual framework or even a biological conceptual framework. It does not have the perceptual or conceptual tools to distinguish living things from nonliving ones or mental beings from nonmental ones. As a result, when it describes the universe, its description is framed solely in terms of the positions, properties, and relations of all the fundamental physical particles that exist, and nothing else. Because it does not have the concepts to distinguish living things from nonliving ones or mental beings from nonmental ones, its description of the universe makes no mention of plants, animals, or people, nor does it mention any distinctive biological or psychological activities such as growth, reproduction, perception, belief, and desire.

Some of us might be inclined to think the Super Physicist's description would be missing something very important: the distinction between life and non-life, for instance, or between intelligence and non-intelligence. But if physicalism is true, the Super Physicist's description misses nothing important – indeed, it misses nothing at all. Its description of the universe is complete as is. The fact that you and I describe the universe in a way that recognizes the distinctions between living things and nonliving ones or mental beings and nonmental beings is a comment not about what the universe contains but about how we go about describing it. Fundamentally everything is physical, and at the level of fundamental physics, there is no difference between a mental being and a nonmental one, or between a living being and a corpse. All of them are collections of the same kinds of fundamental physical particles or materials that have the same kinds of properties and are governed by the same set of fundamental physical laws. The distinctions between life and non-life or intelligence and non-intelligence are distinctions that we introduce because we have the peculiar descriptive and explanatory interests we have. But these interests need not correspond to anything deep in reality. In reality, physicalists claim, everything is physical – everything can be given an exhaustive description and explanation in purely physical terms. This is why the Super Physicist's description is missing nothing. The Super Physicist does not describe the universe in the way that we do, but according to physicalists, this does not represent a deficiency in its conceptual outlook. It is not as though the Super Physicist is out of touch with what the universe really contains; it is simply that it describes what the universe contains in a language that does not make the distinctions our language does. The idea that the conceptual resources of physics are sufficient to describe and explain everything that exists is perhaps the most striking implication of any physicalist theory.

4.2 Varieties of Physicalism: Eliminative, Reductive, and Nonreductive

There are three broad varieties of physicalism: eliminative physicalism, reductive physicalism, and nonreductive physicalism. They differ over the descriptive and explanatory legitimacy of conceptual frameworks other than physics. These frameworks are often called **special sciences.** They include chemistry, biology, scientific psychology, and economics, as well as forms of discourse that are not strictly speaking scientific, such as ordinary psychological discourse.

By itself, physicalism does not say anything about the accuracy or inaccuracy of special scientific discourse. It does not say anything, for instance, about whether or not there are beliefs, desires, or other mental phenomena. All it says is that everything is physical. This implies that there are no nonphysical phenomena, but this does not mean there are no beliefs or desires since it could turn out that beliefs and desires are really physical states such as states of the brain. It's true that there are physicalists who claim that there are no mental phenomena. They are **elimina-tive physicalists**. Eliminativists deny that the mental conceptual framework has any descriptive or explanatory legitimacy. Psychological descriptions correspond to nothing in reality, they say; in reality, there are no beliefs, desires, hopes, joys, or pains. According to eliminativists, trying to describe and explain human behavior by appeal to mental states is like trying to describe and explain the weather by appeal to the Greek gods: it is the byproduct of a defective conceptual framework that may have been useful at one time, but that will be eliminated as soon as a complete scientific understanding of the phenomenon is achieved (hence the label 'eliminative').

Most physicalists, however, are not eliminativists. They claim that psychological discourse has some descriptive and explanatory legitimacy; some phenomena can be accurately described and explained in mental terms, and when we finally achieve a complete physical account of human behavior, we will see that it vindicates at least some aspects of ordinary psychological discourse. What we had originally called 'pain' and 'belief', for instance, are really just physical states such as states of the brain. According to most physicalists, in other words, we will eventually discover that our psychological ways of describing human behavior correspond to physical ways of describing it, that the mental and physical conceptual frameworks are just two different frameworks for describing the same things. By analogy, the statements 'The pen in my hand is 4 inches long' and 'The pen in my hand is 10.16 cm long' do not describe different pens or different lengths; they describe the very same length of a single pen using two different frameworks for measurement. English and metric systems of measurement do not describe different lengths, weights, and volumes; they describe the same lengths, weights, and volumes using different systems. Most physicalists claim that something analogous is true about the mental and physical conceptual frameworks: they are two different frameworks for describing and explaining the same set of physical phenomena.

Early on, physicalists of this sort expected that psychological categories would correspond to physical categories in some straightforward way. They thought, for instance, that for every mental category such as *belief* or *desire* there would be a corresponding physical category such as *temporal lobe activity* or *c-fiber firing*. Because they envisioned neat correspondence relations of this sort, they were confident that psychological discourse and all the special sciences would eventually be reduced to physics. This view is called **reductive physicalism**.

The term 'reduction' is used in a variety of ways in philosophy and the sciences, and it has been used in a variety of ways just within philosophy of mind. We discuss the notion of reduction in detail in Chapter 5, but for the time being we can understand it simply as the ability of one theory or conceptual framework to take over the descriptive and explanatory jobs of another. We can view theories and conceptual frameworks generally as tools we use to describe and explain things. All physicalists agree that we will eventually be able to use theories in physics to describe and explain everything. Reductive physicalists think that we will also be able to use those theories to perform all the descriptive and explanatory jobs we currently use theories in the special sciences to perform. They believe that the neat correspondence relations between the categories of the special sciences and the categories of physics will eventually allow us to identify mental properties and other special scientific properties with physical properties. We will be able to say that belief, for instance, just *is* a state of the brain. The identification of special scientific properties with physical properties will then allow us to use the descriptions and explanations of physics in place of the descriptions and explanations of the special sciences. Physics will thus be able to take over the descriptive and explanatory roles played by every special science; everything will be reducible to physics.

Reductivism was the dominant physicalist position for many years, but by the early 1970s, developments discussed in detail in Chapter 6 persuaded many physicalists that the categories of the special sciences and the categories of physics were correlated in ways that were much messier than reductivists had supposed. This idea formed the basis of **nonreductive physicalism**, the physicalist outlook that has dominated philosophy of mind for almost 40 years.

Like all physicalist theories, nonreductivism claims that everything can be exhaustively described and explained by physics. What distinguishes it is the idea that we have many different ways of describing the world, and these different ways of describing the world satisfy many different descriptive and explanatory interests – including interests different from those satisfied by physics. When we describe things using the language of physics we do so because we are interested in describing and explaining the behavior of things by appeal to laws that hold universally and without exception – the laws of physics. But we are not always interested in describing things in this way. We often have other descriptive and explanatory interests that physics cannot satisfy. To satisfy these we use the special sciences. But if physics cannot satisfy the interests satisfied by the special sciences, then physics is incapable of taking over the descriptive and explanatory roles the special sciences play. The special sciences are thus irreducible to physics – irreducible not because there are nonphysical individuals, properties, or events, but because we have special interests that the conceptual resources of physics cannot satisfy.

In short, then, all varieties of physicalism claim that physics is sufficient to provide an exhaustive description and explanation of everything – every individual, property, and event. By itself, however, this claim implies nothing about whether psychological discourse or any other special science manages to describe or explain anything in reality. Eliminativists deny that psychological discourse does. Science, they say, will not vindicate ordinary psychological modes of description and explanation; it will instead provide a basis for eliminating them in favor of scientific alternatives. Reductivists and nonreductivists disagree; they claim that the sciences will eventually vindicate psychological descriptions, that psychological discourse does successfully manage to describe and explain something in reality. What distinguish reductivists and nonreductivists are their respective understandings of how exactly science will manage to do this.

4.3   Implications of Physicalist Theories

Any physicalist theory implies the possibility of providing an exhaustive description and explanation of all human behavior in purely physical terms. But particular varieties of physicalism have further implications besides. Eliminativism, for instance, has the striking implication that we are not in any way mental beings. It implies that you and I have no beliefs or desires, no fears or hopes; that we do not experience pain or anger, sadness or joy, expectation or longing. According to eliminativists there are no such things as beliefs or desires or pains. The mental framework has no descriptive or explanatory legitimacy; it is instead a radically defective way of trying to describe and explain human behavior – a way so radically defective it corresponds to nothing in reality. According to eliminativists, for instance, when a married person says, "I love my spouse," what he or she says is always false – not in the sense that he or she married for money or for convenience or for something other than love, but in the sense that there is no such condition as love in which anyone can be or fail to be. Likewise, there are no such states as hate or indifference in which people can be. When we try to explain human behavior by appeal to beliefs, desires, and other mental states, what we say is always false because beliefs, desires, and other mental states do not exist.

Of course, in our practical dealings, we are often willing to treat false claims as if they are true. Consider, for instance, the statement 'The Sun just moved behind the Time-Warner building' uttered on a sunny afternoon in Manhattan. This statement is literally false. The Sun did not really move. What really happened was rather that we were situated on the surface of the Earth in such a way that the Earth's rotation resulted in the interposition of the Time-Warner building between us and the Sun. In our practical dealings, however, that is a mouthful, and in part because of that we are willing to treat the statement 'The Sun just moved behind the Time-Warner building' as if it is true. In the same way, it might be very difficult in any given situation to articulate the true scientific story of human behavior, and so for practical purposes we might always be willing to treat psychological statements such as 'I love my spouse' or 'I prefer espresso to coffee' as if they are true even if they are literally false. Eliminativism has the striking implication, then, that all of our mentalistic statements are literally false; that we merely treat them as if they are true out of custom or convenience.

Reductive physicalism has some striking implications as well. It implies, for instance, that mental states have physical features. Suppose I am currently entertaining the belief that there are exactly eight planets in our solar system. According to reductivists, this belief is something physical – a state of the brain, say, such as the firing of a certain group of cells. What physical state it corresponds to is something it is up to scientists to determine, say reductivists, but the important point for our purposes is that according to reductivists, that belief corresponds to something physical, and this has implications many people find counterintuitive. Consider: in our everyday dealings we are used to describing mental states such as beliefs as true or false, well-warranted or unsupported, reasonable or crazy. But it would certainly be unusual to say that a belief was pinkish-grey in color, that it was located four centimeters into my skull, that it had a vein running through it, and so forth. Yet, if my belief is a physical state, then it will have all the features that a physical state has. If my skull were opened up during surgery, you would be able to touch my belief that there are eight planets in our solar system with your fingers; you might even be able to remove it – not in the sense that you might persuade me of its falsity, but literally by removing the relevant bits of brain tissue.

4.4   Motivations For Physicalism

The striking implications of physicalist theories might lead someone to wonder why anyone would want to endorse physicalism. How has physicalism managed to become the most popular mind–body framework if physicalist theories have such counterintuitive implications?

The principal motivation for physicalism is the success of scientific endeavor over the past 400 years. For most of human history – tens of thousands of years – humans failed to understand correctly how the universe operated. Their understanding was distorted by inaccuracy and superstition, but the Scientific Revolution of the sixteenth and seventeenth centuries changed all that. It instituted new methods for studying the natural world that enabled us to describe and explain accurately how and why things happen as they do – methods that enabled us to improve human life in ways that were unthinkable in centuries past. Physicalism is based on confidence that scientific progress will continue, and that eventually science will be able to answer all the questions we have about the universe (or at least all the questions that can be answered at all). A more modest way of stating the point is to say that physicalists are convinced that among various ways of coming to understand the world, science is the most reliable. It may not be perfect; it may not be able to answer all our questions (there may be questions that simply do not have answers we are capable of discovering), but to the extent that our questions can be answered at all, science is the most reliable way of discovering the answers; it is the most reliable way of studying the natural world there is.

All physicalists, then, are guided by a sense that the natural sciences are the key to understanding the world if anything is. The motivations for endorsing specific forms of physicalism (reductive, nonreductive, and eliminative) are based on episodes in the history of science. Reductivists appeal to success stories, cases in which our prescientific descriptions and explanations have been vindicated by scientific ones. Consider the case of water. We initially described water using an ordinary prescientific vocabulary. When we developed atomic and molecular theory, we did not conclude that there was no such thing as water; we concluded instead that water was really just H_2O molecules. Something similar happened in the case of light. When we developed electromagnetic theory, and were able to show that light could be understood in terms of electromagnetic principles, we did not conclude there was no such thing as light; we concluded that light was really electromagnetic radiation. In these cases, and in many others in the history of science, there was something we initially described in ordinary prescientific terms, and the accurate scientific account of it vindicated our prescientific descriptions. The categories we used to describe and explain phenomena in our prescientific dealings ended up corresponding to the categories scientists eventually developed for giving a complete account of those phenomena. According to reductivists, this is what will most likely happen with psychological discourse. When we finally develop an accurate scientific account of human behavior, we will discover that our ordinary, prescientific modes of psychological description correspond to something in that account. Nonreductivists agree; although they think that the correspondence between scientific and prescientific modes of description will be messier than the cases of water and light indicate.

Eliminativists are motivated by different kinds of examples – cases of descriptive and explanatory failure. At one time, for instance, people tried to explain the phenomenon of combustion by appeal to a substance they called *phlogiston*. Phlogiston, they said, was a subtle fluid that permeated all combustible bodies. When we ignite something – when, for instance, we put a match to a piece of paper – the phlogiston is liberated and flows into the surrounding air, and the resulting ash is de-phlogistonated paper. When scientists finally formulated the oxidative theory of combustion they did not declare that phlogiston was really oxygen molecules; they instead declared that there was no phlogiston. Phlogiston represented a defective attempt to describe and explain the phenomenon of combustion. There are other examples in the history of science of this sort as well. Consider heat transfer: you have a hot cup of coffee, you put it down on the table, and a few minutes later the coffee is no longer hot, but room temperature. At one time people tried to explain this phenomenon by claiming there was a subtle fluid, *caloric*, that permeated all thermal bodies. The caloric, they said, leaked out of the coffee into the surrounding air, and this leakage explained the phenomenon of heat transfer. When scientists formulated the kinetic theory of heat – when they theorized that heat was really just the average kinetic energy of molecules – they did not try to salvage the caloric theory; they did not say that caloric was really mean molecular kinetic energy; they said instead that there was no caloric, that caloric represented a misguided attempt to explain the phenomenon of heat transfer.

Eliminativists claim that what happened to the caloric theory of heat and the phlogiston theory of combustion is going to happen to psychological descriptions and explanations of human behavior. When we finally have a complete scientific account of human behavior, they say, we will see that those descriptions and explanations correspond to nothing in that account. We will see, in other words, that psychological categories such as belief, desire, and pain are on a par with phlogiston and caloric; they represent misguided attempts to explain phenomena which can be given more accurate descriptions and explanations in purely scientific terms. What motivates eliminativists, then, is the sense that psychological categories do not and will not correspond to the kinds of categories scientists will eventually use to give a complete and accurate description and explanation of human behavior.

4.5 The Argument For Physicalism: Past Scientific Success

The main argument for physicalism, like the motivation for it, derives from the success of scientific endeavor. In the past, say physicalists, whenever people tried to explain phenomena by appeal to nonphysical entities, their attempted explanations always failed, and, by contrast, when they attempted to explain those phenomena by appeal to physical entities alone, their explanations succeeded (or they were at least stepping-stones to the development of physical explanations that succeeded). If that is the case, however; if nonphysical explanations have always failed and been replaced by physical explanations that succeeded, then we have good reason to think that nonphysical explanations will always fail, and physical explanations will always succeed. But if nonphysical explanations always fail and physical explanations always succeed, we have good reason to think that nothing is nonphysical and that on the contrary everything is physical – that everything can be physically described and explained. We have good reason, in other words, to think physicalism is true.

The main premise of the physicalist argument claims that in the past nonphysical explanations have always failed and been replaced by physical explanations that succeeded. In support of this premise physicalists can cite many examples, including the following:

Nonphysical explanations of magnetism At one time, people tried to explain the phenomenon of magnetism by appeal to the presence of nonphysical spirits which they claimed inhabited magnetized rocks or pieces of metal. This explanation turned out to be false, and was replaced by a physical explanation in terms of electromagnetic force.

Nonphysical explanations of planetary motion   People once tried to explain the movements of the planets by appeal to nonphysical intelligences that were responsible for producing the orbital movements of the planets. This explanation turned out to be false, and was replaced by a physical explanation in terms of the curvature of spacetime: the planets move in orbit because spacetime is warped by massive objects such as the Sun.

Nonphysical explanations of life   People once tried to explain the difference between living things and nonliving ones (the difference between, say, a living human and a corpse) by appeal to the presence in living things of nonphysical vital spirits. This explanation turned out to be false, and was replaced by a physical explanation in terms of metabolic processes at a cellular level.

Nonphysical explanations of mental illness   People once tried to explain abnormal human behavior by appeal to the presence of nonphysical demons which they claimed had taken possession of afflicted individuals. This explanation turned out to be false, and was replaced by a physical explanation in terms of brain abnormalities.

In each of the foregoing cases, people tried to explain something by appeal to nonphysical entities, but in each of these cases the nonphysical explanations were falsified and replaced by physical ones. The history of science is replete with cases of just this sort, physicalists argue – cases in which nonphysical explanations have failed and been replaced by physical explanations that succeeded. Since these cases have always been the norm in the past, they say, we have every reason to expect they will remain the norm in the future. We have every reason to expect, in other words, that every attempt to explain phenomena by appeal to nonphysical entities will fail, and every attempt to explain those same phenomena by appeal to physical entities will succeed. Consequently, we have good reason to expect that nothing will be explainable nonphysically, and on the contrary everything will be explainable physically. We thus have good reason to think that the physical sciences are capable in principle of explaining everything. But to say that the physical sciences can explain everything is to say that everything is physical. According to physicalists, then, the history of science gives us good reason to think that physicalism is true.

The principal liability of the physicalist's argument is that it is merely inductive. Its premises give us some reason to think that physicalism is true – all inductive arguments provide *some* reason to think their conclusions are true – but those reasons are not decisive. If the premises of an inductive argument are true, the conclusion could still be false. At one time, for instance, Europeans argued inductively as follows: All swans observed so far are white; therefore, all swans are white. This is an example of an inductive argument with a true premise but a false conclusion. Although the observation of so many white swans provided some reason to think all swans were white, these reasons were not decisive, and the discovery of black swans in Australia showed that the conclusion was false. Likewise, all the cases in the history of science in which nonphysical explanations failed and physical explanations succeeded provide some reason – perhaps very strong reason – to think all future cases will follow the same pattern, but these reasons are not decisive.

Consider, for instance, how a substance dualist could respond to the argument: "In each of the examples you physicalists cite, people were trying to provide nonphysical explanations for purely physical phenomena such as magnetism and planetary motion. We agree entirely that physical phenomena can only be explained physically, and that it is a mistake to try to explain them nonphysically. It is thus no surprise that attempts to explain these phenomena nonphysically failed. But that does not show that nonphysical explanations will always fail or that there are no nonphysical phenomena of the sort we substance dualists endorse. It merely shows that when dealing with a fairly limited domain, the domain of physical phenomena, we have good reason to think nonphysical explanations will always fail. But this is perfectly compatible with nonphysicalist theories such as our own. Hence, the argument does not provide strong support for physicalism over and against the nonphysicalist alternatives." Exponents of other mind–body theories such as dual-attribute theorists and hylomorphists can construct analogous objections based on the principles of their own theories. Their general strategy is to accept the physicalist's premise, the premise that in the past nonphysical explanations have failed and been replaced by physical explanations that succeeded, while yet rejecting the physicalist's conclusion.

4.6   Hempel's Dilemma

There are several arguments against physicalism. One is called **Hempel's dilemma** after the philosopher of science, Carl Hempel (1905–1997), who first articulated it. Physicalism claims that everything is physical, that everything can be exhaustively described and explained by physics. But, says the argument, this reliance on physics presents physicalists with a problem: (1) Physicalists must define physics either relative to a preliminary stage of its development or relative to the final, ideal stage of its development. But (2) if physicalists define physics relative to a preliminary stage of its development, then physicalism ends up being false. On the other hand, (3) if they define physics relative to the final, ideal stage of its development, then physicalism ends up lacking content. Physicalism is, therefore, either false or else lacking in content.

Hempel's dilemma originates in the observation that science is a progressive endeavor. We advance theories to explain various phenomena, and then test those

theories through experimentation. Theories we initially advance to explain something are typically falsified by experiments, and replaced by other, incrementally
better theories – ones that are able to accommodate the newly discovered experimental results. Science is thus a process of theorizing, experimenting, falsifying,
and re-theorizing with the goal of achieving a theory that is not subject to further
falsification – an accurate theory that stands in need of no further revision.
Because science is a progressive endeavor of this sort, the theories that are advanced
in particular branches of science are constantly subject to change. That includes
theories in physics. One physical theory is replaced by another, which is replaced
in turn by another, and that by another, and so on. Because physical theories are
subject to constant revision and replacement in this way, the field of physics is
always changing. As a result, it does not make sense to speak of physics in general
but only of physics as it is understood at a particular time or stage in its development. Consequently, when physicalists say that everything can be exhaustively
described and explained by physics, they must specify which stage in the development of physics they have in mind – seventeenth-century physics, for instance, or
nineteenth-century physics, or current physics. But whatever stage they have in
mind, says the argument, it will belong to one of two categories: either it will be
a preliminary stage at which physical theories are subject to falsification and revision, or it will be the final, ideal stage of physics at which physical theories are no
longer subject to falsification and revision. Whichever stage it is, says the argument, physicalists face a problem (Figure 4.1).

Suppose that physicalists define physics relative to a preliminary stage of its
development. In that case, physicalism ends up being false. Why? Because theories
advanced at a preliminary stage of science are false. Suppose, for instance, that
physicalists define physics as nineteenth-century physics. Physicalism would
then be the claim that everything can be exhaustively described and explained
by nineteenth-century physics; it would say that everything is exactly the way
nineteenth-century physics says it is. The problem is that this claim is false: not
everything is the way nineteenth-century physics says it is. Nineteenth-century
physical theories were falsified and replaced by twentieth-century physical
theories. Physicalism thus ends up being false if physicalists define physics as
nineteenth-century physics. The same is true if physicalists define physics as twentieth-
century physics. Twentieth-century physical theories were falsified and replaced
by our current physical theories. Consequently, not everything is the way twentieth-
century physics says it is. Physicalism thus ends up being false if physicalists
define physics as twentieth-century physics. The same is true, moreover, if physicalists define physics relative to our best current physical theories. In that
case, physicalism ends up being the claim that everything can be exhaustively
described and explained by current physics – that everything is exactly the way
current physics says it is. We can be confident that this claim too is false, that not
everything is the way current physics says it is. The reason is once again that
physics is progressive: we know that our current understanding of the physical

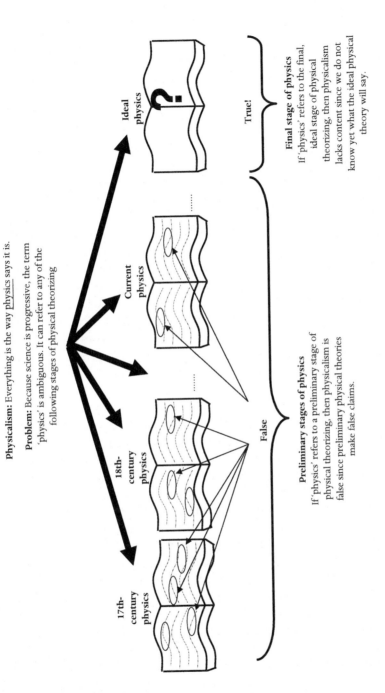

Physicalism: Everything is the way <u>physics</u> says it is.

Problem: Because science is progressive, the term 'physics' is ambiguous. It can refer to any of the following stages of physical theorizing

17th-century physics

18th-century physics

Current physics

Ideal physics

True!

False

Preliminary stages of physics
If 'physics' refers to a preliminary stage of physical theorizing, then physicalism is false since preliminary physical theories make false claims.

Final stage of physics
If 'physics' refers to the final, ideal stage of physical theorizing, then physicalism lacks content since we do not know yet what the ideal physical theory will say.

Figure 4.1 Hempel's dilemma

universe will most likely be replaced by a more adequate understanding in the foreseeable future; we know, in other words, that our current physical theories are most likely false. Because we have not yet reached the ideal stage of physical theorizing, then – the stage at which physical theory is no longer subject to falsification and revision – the physicalist's attempt to define physics relative to current physics or any other preliminary stage of physics yields the conclusion that physicalism is false.

Suppose, then, that physicalists do not define physics relative to a preliminary stage of its development; suppose that they define it instead relative to the final, ideal stage. In that case, physicalism ends up being the claim that everything can be exhaustively described and explained by the final, ideal physical theory – that everything is exactly the way the final, ideal physical theory says it is. If physicalists define physics this way, says the argument, they face a different problem: their theory ends up lacking content: we literally have no idea what it is saying. Why is that the case? Because at this point in history we have no idea what the fully accurate, unrevisable physical theory says. At this point in history, that theory is a mere ideal, something we are striving toward, not something we have actually achieved. Consequently, we have no idea what it says. But if we have no idea what the ideal, unrevisable physical theory says, then we have no idea what it means to say that everything is the way the ideal, unrevisable physical theory says it is. Consequently, says the argument, if physicalists define physics relative to the final, ideal stage of its development, then we can no longer understand what physicalism is saying. But if we can no longer understand what physicalism is saying, then physicalism is no longer a theory we can take seriously.

Physicalists can respond to Hempel's dilemma in several ways. The most obvious is to challenge the argument's premises, but this has not been the most popular response. Most physicalists have not objected to the argument's premises, nor have they disagreed with its conclusion. They have instead argued that the conclusion is not as bad as critics of physicalism insist. Hempel's dilemma has two horns. The first claims that physicalism is false; the second claims that it lacks content. Physicalists who grasp the first horn of the dilemma argue that the falsity of their theory is not as serious a worry as critics suppose. Consider, they say, an analogy with physics. If physics is a progressive science of the sort just described, then physicists must carry out their research agendas despite the falsity of their best theories. They nevertheless remain undaunted in their efforts; they seem to recognize that advancing false theories is just part of the cost of doing physics – an occupational hazard, as it were. Physicalists who grasp the first horn of Hempel's dilemma take a cue from physicists. If physicists can continue to forge ahead despite the likelihood that their best theories will be falsified and replaced by better ones in the foreseeable future, they say, then it is plausible to suppose physicalists can do the same. Like physicists, physicalists can remain confident in their ability to arrive incrementally at better accounts of reality, and hopefully in the end a fully accurate account, despite the falsity of their best current formulations of physicalism. Consequently, say many physicalists, the falsity of physicalism is not as bad as critics insist.

Physicalists who grasp the second horn of Hempel's dilemma look to define physicalism relative to ideal physics. They concede that this definition lacks content, but deny that this poses a serious threat to their view. It would pose a serious threat if it showed that physicalism was *completely* lacking in content, they say, but the argument does not show that. We may not know exactly what the ideal physical theory will claim, but we know enough to give physicalism some content. The reason is that past physical theories give us some insight into future ones, so if we know something about physical theories of the past and present, we gain some insight into the physical theories of the future including the ideal, unrevisable theory at which physicists hope eventually to arrive. We may not know exactly what kinds of fundamental physical individuals or events the ideal physics will postulate or what kinds of properties it will attribute to them, but on the basis of past and present physical theories we can be fairly confident that it will not claim that persons are among the basic physical entities that exist, and that properties like consciousness or intentionality are among the basic physical properties they possess. Physical theories past and present tell us enough about the ideal physics to know that it will not claim that fundamental physical entities are of this sort. If physicalism is defined relative to ideal physics, therefore, physicalism does end up lacking content, but, say physicalists, that does not mean physicalism ends up being completely lacking in content, and, for that reason, the conclusion of Hempel's dilemma is not as bad critics insist. There are, then, several strategies physicalists can adopt in order to deal with Hempel's dilemma.

4.7   The Knowledge Argument

Other arguments against physicalism claim that physicalism is incapable of coun-tenancing a private conception of mental phenomena – a conception that claims mental phenomena such as consciousness are private or subjective. Perhaps the most famous of these is called the **knowledge argument**. It was originally advanced by the philosopher Frank Jackson. Physicalism claims that everything can be exhaustively described and explained by physics. Another way of stating this idea is to say that all facts can be described and explained by physics; all facts, in other words, are physical facts. Roughly, a fact is what gets expressed by a true statement. The statement 'Two and two equal four', for instance, expresses the fact that two and two equal four. Physical facts are facts that are expressed by true statements formulated in the vocabulary of physics. If physicalism is true, then physics can give us an exhaustive description of everything: every fact can be expressed by statements formulated in the language of physics; every fact is a physical fact. But according to the knowledge argument there is good reason to think that not every fact is a physical fact.

Consider the case of Mary. Mary is a unique person in two respects. First, she has complete physical knowledge: like the Super Physicist described earlier, Mary knows all the physical facts there are to know. She has access to a completed physics, a completed chemistry, a completed biology, a completed neuroscience, and so on. Second, Mary has never before experienced colors such as red, yellow, and green. She has been raised and educated in a completely black and white environment. One day, however, Mary leaves that environment and for the first time in her life experiences the color red: she sees a ripe tomato. It seems clear that Mary learns something new about the world when she sees the tomato. She learns what it is like to experience the color red. Of course, prior to seeing the tomato, she always knew that people experienced red; she always knew that experiencing red involved objects with a certain reflectance spectrum, that the light reflected from those objects would strike the retinas of the experiencer, and that the retinal cells would fire and cause the firing of other neurons in the experiencer's nervous system. She knew all about the physical aspects of seeing red: all about the electromagnetic radiation, and the patterns of neuronal activity associated with it. What she never knew about before, however, were the qualitative aspects of seeing red: the qualia associated with those physical occurrences. She never knew what it was like to see red.

Upon seeing the ripe tomato, then, Mary learned that certain events in her nervous system were accompanied by a very particular qualitative experience. Since she learned this fact only upon seeing the ripe tomato, it is not a fact that Mary could have known before since it is not possible to learn something that you already know. Since Mary learned a new fact upon seeing the ripe tomato, then, she could not have known that fact prior to seeing it. Yet prior to seeing it, she knew all the physical facts. Hence, the fact that she learned could not have been a physical fact. Since she knew all the physical facts, and yet did not know all the facts, it follows that not all facts are physical facts. But if not all facts are physical facts, then physicalism must be false.

The knowledge argument is based on the following premises:

1   If physicalism is true, then all facts are physical facts.
2   If it is possible for someone to know all the physical facts without knowing all the facts, then not all facts are physical facts.
3   If it is conceivable that someone can know all the physical facts without knowing all the facts, then it is possible for someone to know all the physical facts without knowing all the facts.
4   It is conceivable that someone can know all the physical facts without knowing all the facts.

I have already discussed the reasons behind Premise (1): if physicalism is true, then all facts can be expressed in a physical vocabulary. Consider the reasons behind

Premise (2): Imagine that I know all the physical facts but not all the facts. Since I do not know all the facts, there must be a fact, q, which I do not know. Now, if q were a physical fact, then I would know it since I know all the physical facts. Since I do not know q, therefore, it follows that q cannot be a physical fact. Consequently, if it is possible to know all the physical facts without knowing all the facts, then not all facts are physical facts.

The really crucial premises here are (3) and (4). Premise (3) is a conceivability-possibility principle of the sort discussed in connection with the argument for substance dualism (Section 3.2): it claims that the conceivability of Mary's case is a reliable guide to its possibility. We have already discussed some of the concerns surrounding conceivability-possibility principles in the discussion of substance dualism (Section 3.3). In what follows, then, we will focus on Premise (4).

Support for (4) derives from the example of Mary. According to the argument, the following are jointly conceivable: (i) Mary knows all the physical facts, but (ii) she has never experienced color, and yet (iii) she learns a new fact upon experiencing color for the first time. Because (iv) no one can learn something that he or she already knows, claims (i)–(iii) seem to imply (4).

Critics of (4) can respond by arguing that either (i), (ii), or (iii) is not conceivable on its own, or that (i), (ii), and (iii) are not conceivable taken in conjunction – that at least one of them implies the falsity of one of the others. Against the conceivability of (i), for instance, someone might argue that it is unthinkable for someone to have complete physical knowledge of the sort Mary is purported to have, that the possession of such knowledge is inconceivable. Think again about Hempel's dilemma: it suggests that science works in incremental steps which culminate in a complete and accurate knowledge of the world. Imagine, however, that this ideal is not really achievable, that scientific progress is asymptotic: just as an asymptotic curve in mathematics gets infinitesimally closer to a limit without ever reaching it, so too scientific progress gets closer and closer to providing better and better descriptions of reality without ever achieving a completely accurate description of reality. This picture of scientific progress represents one type of *scientific fallibilism*. If fallibilism of this sort is true, then the very idea of having complete physical knowledge is incoherent; the case of Mary is thus inconceivable.

Similarly, against the conjunction of (i) and (ii), critics could argue that it is inconceivable for someone to gain complete physical knowledge without having had color experiences. They could argue, in other words, that some physical facts are knowable only if one has had the corresponding experiences, and thus that Mary could not have learned all the physical facts while yet having been deprived of color experiences.

Another, very popular way of attacking (4) is to attack the conjunction of (i) and (iii). One way of doing this is to deny that Mary learns something when she sees the ripe tomato. What happens instead, some critics say, is that she comes to see the same physical facts under a different kind of description – a first-person, subjective description as opposed to a third-person, objective one. This point is often expressed by saying that Mary knows the same *old facts under new representations*. Another response that attacks the conjunction of (i) and (iii) claims that the physical facts logically entail facts about conscious experience. Someone who knew all the physical facts the way Mary does would be able to deduce all the facts about phenomenal consciousness. Knowing, for instance, that seeing red triggers events in the eye and brain would enable Mary to deduce what it was like to see red without ever actually seeing it.

A third strategy for attacking the conjunction of (i) and (iii) is sometimes called the **ability hypothesis**. The ability hypothesis does not deny that Mary learns something when she sees the ripe tomato; it denies instead that what she learns is a new fact. According to this argument, what Mary learns is a new *skill* or *ability*. The ability hypothesis trades on the distinction between knowing-how and knowing-that. I can know *that* Go is a board game without knowing *how* to play it. Conversely, a nineteenth-century physician might have known *how* to treat a particular illness without knowing *that* the treatment worked by influencing the patient's immune response. In general, knowledge-that concerns facts, whereas knowledge-how concerns skills or abilities. This objection to the conjunction of (i) and (iii) claims that when Mary sees the ripe tomato, she learns how to do something she was not able to do before; she gains a new ability; she does not gain knowledge of a new fact.

The knowledge argument and physicalist responses to it remain highly controversial.

4.8   Absent and Inverted Qualia

The knowledge argument is not the only objection to physicalism that appeals to a private conception of mental phenomena. Another appeals to the notion of absent or inverted qualia. It runs as follows:

1   If absent or inverted qualia are possible, then physicalism is false.
2   Absent or inverted qualia are possible.

Therefore, physicalism is false.

What are absent and inverted qualia? Recall that according to a private conception of consciousness, the qualitative aspects of experience needn't be correlated with any publicly observable manifestations in someone's movements or gestures (Section 2.4). It is possible, for instance, that the human bodies I see around me might be behaving exactly as if they have phenomenal states like my own while yet having very different phenomenal states or lacking phenomenal states altogether. The qualitative experience that accompanies the eating of crème brûlée in me might be different from the qualitative experience that accompanies eating crème brûlée in you. Likewise, the quality you experience when the light reflected from a ripe tomato strikes your retinas might be different from the quality I experience when the light reflected from a ripe tomato strikes mine. The idea that it is possible for different types of qualia to accompany the same type of publicly observable behavior is sometimes called the possibility of *qualia inversion* (Figure 4.2(A)). (In the case of color experiences, it is sometimes called the possibility of *inverted spectra*.) Likewise, say exponents of the argument, it is possible for there to be **absent qualia** (Figure 4.2(B)); it is possible, in other words, that, in me, eating crème brûlée is not accompanied by any qualitative experiences of the sort that accompany eating crème brûlée in you. In fact, it is possible that none of my behavior might be accompanied by any qualitative experiences of the sort you have: I might be a qualia zombie, a being who acts in every objective way exactly as if it has conscious states, but who altogether lacks them.

Why should we suppose that the premises of the inverted/absent qualia argument are true? In defense of Premise (2) exponents of the argument typically appeal to a conceivability argument like the one endorsed by exponents of the

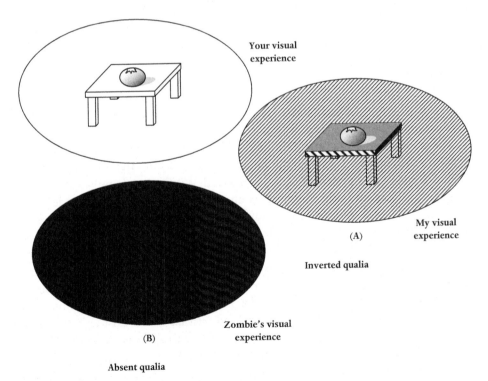

Figure 4.2 Absent and inverted qualia

88 *The Physicalist Worldview*

knowledge argument. If something is conceivable, they argue, then it is metaphysically possible; and, they say, it is conceivable that there could be absent or inverted qualia, that there could be beings who behave in every way exactly as if they have phenomenal states like mine while yet having different phenomenal states or lacking phenomenal states altogether.

The argument for Premise (1) is more complicated. If physicalism is true, says the argument, then either (i) qualia must not exist, or else (ii) qualia must be physical states of some sort. If physicalism is true, after all, everything is physical, so either qualia must be physical, or else they must not exist. But qualia do exist, say exponents of the argument, so if physicalism is true, qualia must be physical states. But if it is possible for there to be absent or inverted qualia, then qualia cannot be physical states. The reason is that identity implies necessary coextension. If, for instance, having a mass of 1 kg is identical to having a mass of 2.2 pounds, then it is impossible for something to have a mass of 1 kg without having a mass of 2.2 pounds. Similarly, if a certain phenomenal experience – the quale associated with eating crème brûlée, say – is identical to a physical state such as brain state B, then it is impossible for something to have that phenomenal experience without having brain state B. If inverted or absent qualia are possible, however, then it is possible for something to have brain state B without having that phenomenal experience, for in cases of absent and inverted qualia two things are exactly alike physically while yet differing from each other phenomenally. Gabriel and Xavier might be molecule-for-molecule twins having all the same physical states and yet having completely different phenomenal states. But if two things can be exactly alike physically and yet differ phenomenally, then phenomenal states cannot be identical to physical states, for the identity of phenomenal states with physical states would imply that physical twins had to be phenomenal twins. Consequently, says the argument, if absent or inverted qualia are possible, physicalism must be false.

Physicalists can respond to this argument in several ways. First, they can deny that qualia exist. There are several arguments to this effect including Daniel Dennett's argument against qualia and Wittgenstein's private language argument. These and other arguments against qualia are discussed in detail in Chapter 8. Second, physicalists can argue that even though qualia exist, it is impossible for two systems to be physically identical yet phenomenally distinct. The burden for physicalists who take this approach is either to argue that conceivability is a not a reliable guide to possibility, or to argue that cases of absent and inverted qualia are not genuinely conceivable. We discussed conceivability-possibility principles in Sections 3.2 and 3.3 in connection with the argument for substance dualism. Finally, physicalists can admit that qualia exist and that cases of absent and inverted qualia are possible, but argue that this is nevertheless compatible with physicalism. Resources for this strategy are provided by representational, higher-order, and sensorimotor theories of consciousness, the subject-matter of the next section.

4.9 Representational, Higher-Order, and Sensorimotor Theories of Consciousness

Qualia-based objections to physicalism rely on a conception of phenomenal consciousness that is difficult for physicalists to accommodate. That conception takes qualia to be properties or events that are nonrelational, unanalyzable, and accessible only to the person experiencing them. There are nevertheless alternative conceptions of phenomenal consciousness that physicalists can accommodate more easily. These include representational theories of consciousness, higher-order theories of consciousness, and sensorimotor theories of consciousness.

Representational theories of consciousness claim that conscious states are really internal representational states – states that represent properties of the objects we experience. Qualia, on these accounts, are properties of those objects themselves. The sweetness we experience when eating crème brûlée, for instance, is just a chemical property of the crème brûlée, a property we represent internally using our taste organs. Likewise, the redness we experience when seeing a ripe tomato is a property of the tomato's surface which we represent using our visual organs. Exponents of representational theories claim that their view reflects a commonsense understanding of sensory experience. In our pedestrian dealings, we take our experiences to be experiences of the objects around us and their properties, they say. We take the sweetness to be a feature of the crème brûlée itself, the redness a feature of the tomato itself, and so on. Consequently, say exponents of representational theories, the qualitative aspects of experience – qualia – are best understood as properties of the objects we see, smell, taste, and experience in other ways. There is, then, no internal domain of nonrelational, unanalyzable, subjective impressions, but only the external domain of familiar objects, properties, and events. Facts about the qualitative aspects of experience are all facts about these objects, properties, and events, and the ways our nervous systems have of representing them.

Physicalists who endorse representational theories of consciousness are committed to a further claim: mental representations and the properties they represent are all physical; they can all be given an exhaustive physical description and explanation. Consider the implications of this view: if facts about qualia are really facts about mental representation, and facts about mental representation are really facts about physical objects, properties, and relations, then the facts about qualia are really facts about physical objects, properties, and relations as well. Consequently, say physicalists who endorse representational theories, qualia do not present their view with any special difficulties.

To appreciate this approach to qualia, we need to consider two things. First, we need to consider what mental representation consists in, what representationalists mean when they say that we have internal states that represent features of the environment. Second, we need to consider how physicalists who endorse representational theories of consciousness look to accommodate the possibility of absent and inverted qualia.

There are many different accounts of mental representation. The simplest claim that mental representation consists in some type of *causal covariation*. States of our nervous systems, they say, undergo changes that correspond to or covary with states in the environment in a lawlike way, and because of these causal covariation relations, the states of our nervous systems represent the states of the environment. Consider an example. Suppose that my nervous system has a component, c, that is capable of being in two states, ON and OFF, and that these states covary with the presence and absence of sugar: c is ON when it comes into contact with sugar, and it is OFF otherwise. Because c's states covary with the presence of sugar, those states indicate the presence of sugar in something analogous to the way smoke indicates the presence of fire. Fire reliably causes smoke, and hence the presence of smoke typically conveys the information that there is fire. In the same way, sugar reliably causes c to be ON, and hence c's being ON typically conveys the information that there is sugar in the environment. According to simple covariation theories, causal covariation relations of this sort are all that mental representation consists in. To have an internal representation of sugar is to have an internal component that is activated if and only if something in the environment has sugar; to have an internal representation of redness is to have an internal component that is activated if and only if something in the environment is red; to have an internal representation of a bear is to have an internal component that is activated if and only if something in the environment is a bear, and so on.

Simple covariation theories of mental representation nevertheless face serious difficulties. For the most part, those difficulties concern what is called the *content* of the mental representations – what the representations are *of* or *about*. Simple covariation theories have a difficult time explaining how a representation's content gets determined – explaining what it is that makes a representation about this object, property, or event as opposed to that one. According to simple covariation theories, a representation's content should be determined entirely by causal covariation relations. My belief that something in the environment is a bear, for instance, should get the content *That is a bear* (as opposed to, say, *That is a dog* or *That is a cat*) because its occurrence is reliably caused by bears and not by dogs or cats. The problem is that a belief that something is a bear can also be reliably caused by things that are not bears – by koalas, for instance. What is it, then, that makes my belief a belief about bears instead of a belief about bears-or-koalas? Simple covariation theories do not provide a satisfactory answer to this question, and because of that they do not provide a satisfactory account of mental representation. Problems like this have led most exponents of representational theories to abandon simple covariation accounts of mental representation in favor of sophisticated ones.

Sophisticated covariation theories agree that mental representation involves causal covariation between the internal states of a system and features of its environment, but they claim that mental representation involves more besides. An example is the theory of mental representation developed by the philosopher Fred Dretske. It claims that mental representation consists not simply in what something indicates, but in what it has the job or function of indicating within a broader system.

On Dretske's view, the components of a system perform various jobs or functions within it: the function of the spark plugs in an automobile engine is to ignite the fuel; the function of the heart in the human body is to pump the blood, and so on. In the case of artifacts, the functions performed by various components are determined by a designer – by someone who wants to construct a system to perform a task, and designs the system with parts that contribute to that task. In the case of natural systems such as human organisms, the functions performed by various components are determined by natural selection. It plays a role in the development of organisms analogous to the role a designer plays in the production of artifacts. Just as the engine designer is responsible for determining the function of the spark plugs in the automobile engine, natural selection is responsible for determining the function of the heart and other biological components in the organism. These components include various sensory organs or subsystems. Their functions are to supply the organism with information about the environment, and according to theories like Dretske's, they supply that information by having internal states that covary with features of the environment.

A sophisticated account of mental representation like Dretske's is what many exponents of representational theories of consciousness endorse. Physicalists argue, moreover, that this type of theory is compatible with physicalism. The causal relations connecting states of the nervous system to features of the environment, they say, as well as the natural selective mechanisms that determine something's function, can all be given exhaustive physical descriptions and explanations. If they are right, then mental representation is a phenomenon that can be exhaustively described and explained by appeal to physics, and the same is true of qualia if qualia can be exhaustively described and explained by appeal to mental representation.

Consider now how exponents of representational theories of consciousness try to handle the problem of absent and inverted qualia. Exponents of sophisticated representational theories like Dretske's argue that it is possible for two systems to be physically indistinguishable and yet have different phenomenally conscious states. The reason, they say, is that phenomenally conscious states are representational states, and it is possible for two physically indistinguishable systems to have different representational states. How is that possible? Recall that on a view like Dretske's, mental representation involves components that have the function of indicating features of the environment. If a system does not have any components whose functions are to indicate features of the environment, then that system cannot have any representational states. So if phenomenally conscious states are representational states, that system cannot have any phenomenally conscious states either. Suppose, then, that there are two systems that are physically indistinguishable. Is it possible for them to have components with different functions? On a view like Dretske's it is, for on that type of view something's function depends on more than its physical constitution; it also depends on the system's history since a component's function within a system is determined either by a designer or by natural selection. If a system is a product neither of design nor of natural selection, then it cannot have any components that perform a function – including the function of indicating features of the environment. Imagine, then, two physically indistinguishable systems with different histories. The first is Gabriel, a normal human whose components have had their functions determined by natural selection. The second is Xavier, a physical duplicate of Gabriel that is nevertheless not a product of natural selection descended from human parents, nor a product of design. Xavier is instead the product of a chance event: a lightning bolt struck a swamp and assembled bits of swamp sludge into a physical duplicate of Gabriel. Because Xavier was produced this way, he is a product neither of design nor of natural selection; his components have thus not been assigned any functions. In that case, though, he has no components with the function of indicating features of the environment, and that means he has no internal states that represent features of the environment. He thus has no experiences, no phenomenally conscious states. It is therefore possible, say exponents of views like Dretske's, that two systems could be physical duplicates and yet have different phenomenally conscious states. When Gabriel encounters objects in the environment, he has experiences; there is something it is like for him to live through those encounters. When Xavier encounters objects in the environment, by contrast, he has no experiences, for on a representational view like Dretske's, having experiences amounts to having representational states, and Xavier has no representational states. Physicalists who endorse views like Dretske's thus claim to be able to accommodate the idea of absent qualia, the idea that it is possible for two systems to be the same physically while yet differing from each other phenomenally.

Physicalist exponents of representational theories of consciousness look to accommodate the possibility of inverted qualia in an analogous way. It is possible, they say, for physically indistinguishable systems to have qualitatively different phenomenal experiences. Qualitative similarities and differences, they say, correspond to similarities and differences in something's discriminatory power – its ability to discriminate things of one kind from things of another kind. And it is possible for physically indistinguishable systems to differ in their discriminatory powers. The reason is that a system's discriminatory powers depend on what its sensory components have the function of indicating, and as we have already seen, exponents of theories like Dretske's claim that it is possible for physical duplicates to have components that perform different functions. Consider an analogy.

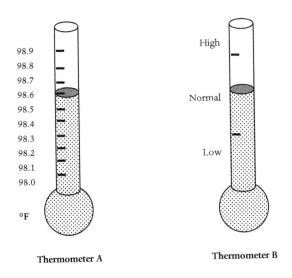

Thermometers A and B are exactly alike physically, yet the level of mercury represents different things in each. In A, it represents a temperature of 98.6°F, while in B it represents a normal temperature. These are the temperatures A and B have the functions of indicating, and because they have different indicator functions, A and B represent different things. It is thus possible for two systems to be the same physically while yet differing representationally.

Figure 4.3   Physically indistinguishable systems that represent different things

Imagine two physically indistinguishable thermometers, A and B (Figure 4.3). The mercury has risen to the same level in each, but that level of mercury does not represent the same thing in each. In Thermometer A it represents a temperature of 98.6 degrees Fahrenheit, while in Thermometer B it represents a normal temperature. These are the respective temperatures A and B have the functions of indicating, the respective temperatures A and B represent. If we were to describe A and B in experiential terms, we would say that A and B experience the temperature in different ways: the temperature seems to be 98.6 degrees Fahrenheit to Thermometer A while it seems to be normal to Thermometer B. If qualitatively different experiences involve differences in the way things phenomenally seem to the experiencing subject, then we can say that A and B have qualitatively different experiences of the temperature, for the temperatures A and B experience seem different to them, and this is the case even though A and B are physical duplicates.

According to exponents of representational views, we can imagine cases in which something analogous is true of systems with components whose functions are to indicate colors, textures, sounds, smells, and other sensory qualities. We can imagine two systems that operate physically in exactly the same way, but that nevertheless have phenomenally different experiences, for just as the designers of thermometers A and B have assigned different functions to the level of mercury in those two physically indistinguishable thermometers, natural selection can assign different functions to the sensory components of two physically indistinguishable organisms. Physicalists who endorse views like Dretske's thus claim to be able to accommodate the idea of inverted qualia, the idea that physically indistinguishable systems might nevertheless have phenomenally different experiences.

Physicalists who appeal to representational theories of consciousness to deal with qualia-related objections have been challenged in several different ways. Recall that the physicalist position relies on two claims:

1   Phenomenal consciousness can be given an exhaustive account in terms of mental representation.
2   Mental representation can be exhaustively described and explained by appeal to physics.

Critics of physicalist appeals to representational theories can target either claim. Critics of Claim (1) have argued against it in several ways. Some have argued that representational theories of consciousness must be false because there are clear examples of phenomenal states that are not representational. We often have mental states such as undirected feelings of anxiety, they say – feelings that are not due to or directed toward anything. Since these mental states are not directed toward anything, they do not represent anything, and yet they still have a distinctive qualitative feel. Consequently, say critics, phenomenal consciousness cannot be given an exhaustive account in terms of representational states; representational theories of consciousness must be false.

Other critics of Claim (1) argue against specific representational theories. Critics of Dretske's theory, for instance, have argued that it has absurd consequences. Consider again the example of Xavier. On Dretske's view, Xavier does not have any experiences despite having eyes, ears, a nose, mouth, and other parts that are affected by the environment in the same way Gabriel's eyes, ears, nose, mouth, and other sensory organs are. But this is absurd, say critics; if Xavier and Gabriel are constituted physically in exactly the same way, then surely Xavier must have experiences if Gabriel does. Since Dretske's theory implies otherwise, Dretske's theory must be false.

Yet other critics of Claim (1) deny the existence of phenomenal consciousness. If phenomenal consciousness does not exist, then clearly it is false to say that its existence can be given an exhaustive account in terms of mental representation – if phenomenal consciousness does not exist, then its existence cannot be given an account in terms of anything. Finally, some critics of Claim (1) deny the existence of mental representations; they deny that our experiences consist in having internal representations of an external world. Exponents of sensorimotor theories of consciousness have sometimes criticized representational theories in this way by appeal to experiments in cognitive science (see Section 11.4).

Other critics of the physicalist appeal to mental representation target Claim (2). Critics of (2) are free to admit that phenomenal consciousness can be understood in terms of mental representation, they simply deny that the appeal to mental representation can provide physicalists with a response to qualia-based objections. The reason, they say, is that mental representation is not a physical phenomenon; it cannot be exhaustively described and explained by appeal to physics. Why might this be the case? Consider again a theory of mental representation like Dretske's. It relies on the notion of natural selection. Suppose, however, that natural selection cannot be given an exhaustive description and explanation in terms of physics, that it is a specifically biological phenomenon that cannot be given an account without appeal to the special descriptive and explanatory resources of biology. If natural selection cannot be given an exhaustive physical description and explanation, and mental representation depends on the notion of natural selection, then mental representation cannot be given an exhaustive description and explanation in terms of physics either. This is one example of how critics might target Claim (2).

Consider now **higher-order theories of consciousness**. Higher-order theories are closely related to representational theories. They claim that conscious states are internal states that are represented or monitored by other internal states. When I consciously experience crème brûlée, say exponents of higher-order theories, the chemical properties of the dessert affect my sensory apparatus in a certain way; my sensory organs register the presence of the dessert's chemical properties in roughly the way representational theories of consciousness claim. This sensory state is nevertheless accompanied by another internal state, one that registers the occurrence of the sensory state itself. Suppose, for instance, that in addition to component c there is another component, d, that is capable of being in two states, S1 and S2. Component d is in state S1 except when component c is ON. When that happens, d enters state S2. d is thus a representational component of my nervous system like c; what it represents, however, is not a state of the environment, but the state of another internal component: it represents c's being ON. According to higher-order theories of consciousness, internal states are conscious when they are monitored in this way by other internal states of the system. c's being ON is a conscious state, for instance, when another internal state, such as d's being in S2, indicates that c is ON.

Exponents of higher-order theories disagree on the nature of the internal monitoring states. Exponents of **higher-order perception theories** claim that the monitoring states are like internal perceptual states; we have inner senses that perceive conscious states in something analogous to the way our outer senses perceive environmental states. The philosopher David Armstrong states the idea in the following terms:

[C]onsciousness is no more than awareness (perception) of inner mental states by the person whose states they are ... [It] is simply a further mental state ... 'directed'

towards the original inner states ... [I]f this further mental state ... can be ... identified with a state of the brain, it will be a process in which one part of the brain
scans another part of the brain. In perception the brain scans the environment. In
awareness of the perception another process in the brain scans that scanning.[1]

Exponents of **higher-order thought theories**, on the other hand, claim that the
internal monitoring states are not like perceptions of sensory states; they are
instead like thoughts about those states. To be conscious of something's sweetness
is not like perceiving c's being ON; it is instead like thinking or believing that
c is ON.

Higher-order theories of consciousness have been challenged in a number of
ways. Some critics argue, for instance, that internal monitoring is not sufficient to
make an internal state conscious. There are many examples, they say, of states
that are monitored internally and yet are not conscious. We remain unaware of
the many processes in the brain that are involved in the production of speech and
movement, for instance, yet those processes are monitored by other brain states.
Clearly, then, there must be more to a state being conscious than being monitored
by another internal state. In addition, say some critics, it is not clear how internal
monitoring could yield conscious states at all. It is not in general the case that
having a mental state directed toward something makes that thing conscious.
Imagine an inanimate, unconscious object such as a table or a rock. Suppose now
that you perceive that object or have a thought about it. Does your perceiving the
object or having a thought about the object suddenly make it conscious? Of course
not, say critics. But if perceiving or thinking about a nonconscious being cannot
make that being conscious, then there is no reason to believe that perceiving or
thinking about an internal state can make that internal state conscious either.
There is thus no reason to think that phenomenal consciousness can be given an
account in terms of internal monitoring.

Representational and higher-order theories of consciousness depend on the
idea that phenomenal experience consists in having internal states that represent the external world. **Sensorimotor theories of consciousness** deny this.
Phenomenal experience, they say, consists instead in patterns of interaction involving the environment and experiencing subjects – in externally directed activities,
the ways organisms go about exploring their environments, not in the occurrence
of internal representational states.

Sensorimotor theories of consciousness derive their name from the idea that
exploring the environment is a sensorimotor process, one that involves the activity
not just of an organism's sensory components, but also of the components that
enable it to move around in search of information. Representational and higher-
order theories sometimes give the impression that perceptual awareness is a
passive process in which an organism registers features of the environment in the
passive way that, say, a camera registers light. But real perception is not like this,
say exponents of sensorimotor theories. Real perception is an exploratory activity

in which an organism strives to position and reposition itself to acquire information about the environment. Consider a simple example: people who are looking
at something interesting while in the midst of a crowd tilt their heads, crane their
necks, stand on their tiptoes, pull themselves forward, and twist their torsos to fit
between other people. This is how real perception works, say sensorimotor exponents; it is a matter of exercising both sensory and motor capacities to explore
and interact with features of the environment. Feeling the texture of a surface is
not simply a matter of placing my hand on it; it is matter of moving my hand
across it. Similarly, tasting crème brûlée is not merely a matter of placing it in
my mouth; it is also a matter of manipulating it with my tongue in an effort
to sense more effectively the properties it has. According to exponents of sensorimotor theories, phenomenal consciousness can be understood in terms of sensorimotor interactions with the environment of this sort.

Each sensory modality is characterized by distinctive patterns of sensorimotor
interaction, they say. Movements, sensations, and features of the environment all
change in response to each other in lawlike ways. Consider, for instance, our
experience of the cubical object depicted in Figure 4.4. We know that if we were
looking at the object from the angle depicted in Figure 4.4(A) and moved ourselves
around the object to the right, we would be presented with a visual profile like
the one depicted in Figure 4.4(B). We know, in other words, that our visual experience of the object would change in a particular way relative to our movements.
The same is true of other sense modalities. We know, for instance, that the taste
of crème brûlée after a sip of espresso would be different from its taste after a sip
of orange juice, and that the color of a tomato would look different under different colored lights.

According to exponents of sensorimotor theories, the qualitative looks, tastes,
and feels of things consist in the various sensory profiles they present to us as we

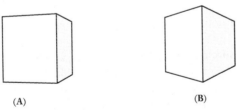

(A)   (B)

Moving around the object shown in (A) toward its right-
hand side will bring into view the profile shown in (B).
Our knowledge of how our perspective on the object's
shape will vary with certain movements we make is an
example of a sensorimotor contingency. According to
sensorimotor theorists, our experiences of objects –
their characteristic looks and feels – are constituted by
our mastery of sensorimotor contingencies.

Figure 4.4   Visual profiles of a cubical object

interact with them using our sensory and motor subsystems – both the sensory profiles they present to us in fact and our implicit knowledge of which sensory profiles they would present to us under a range of different conditions. The qualitative experience of the cube's shape, for instance, consists in the visual profile it presents to me as I look at it right now together with my implicit knowledge that it would present other visual profiles under different conditions – if I were to move around it to the right or the left, say. Likewise, the taste of the crème brûlée consists in the flavor profiles it presents to me as I place it in my mouth and manipulate it with my tongue, together with my implicit knowledge that it would present other flavor profiles if, say, I were to taste it after sipping espresso or finishing a glass of red wine. According to sensorimotor theorists, then, the lawlike interdependence of movement, sensation, and the environment is something each of us implicitly understands, and our knowledge of these lawlike interdependence relations (what are sometimes called *sensorimotor contingencies*), and our exploitation of them as we interact with the environment, constitutes the qualitative character of our experience.

What do sensorimotor theorists have to say about qualia? In one sense, they say, there are no qualia – at least not in the sense we have been discussing them. The qualitative character of our experience does not consist in there being subjective, nonrelational, unanalyzable properties or events, they say; it consists instead in patterns of interaction involving organisms and their environments. Consider an analogy due to the philosopher Alva Noë and the cognitive scientist J. Kevin O'Regan: What is it like to drive a Porsche? In what do the distinctive qualitative aspects of the experience consist? They do not consist in the possession of nonrelational, unanalyzable occurrences in an inner, subjective domain, say Noë and O'Regan; they consist instead in sensorimotor interactions between the driver and the vehicle – the way the driver presses the gas pedal, the way the car accelerates in response, how the driver turns the steering wheel, the way the car handles around a corner, and so on. Sensorimotor interactions like this collectively constitute what it is like to drive a Porsche, and something analogous is true of what it is like to taste crème brûlée or to see the color red:

> [S]eeing ... is constituted by ... the various things one does when one sees ... Suppose you stand before a red wall ... What is it like for you to see this red wall? Try to describe the experience. How do you fulfill this instruction? One thing you might do is direct your attention to one aspect or another of the wall's redness ... its hue, or its brightness ... In what does your focusing on the red hue of the wall consist? It consists in the (implicit) knowledge associated with seeing redness: the knowledge that if you were to move your eyes, there would be changes in the incoming information that are typical of sampling with the eye or typical of the nonhomogeneous way the retina samples color; knowledge that if you were to move your head around, there might be changes in the incoming information typical of what happens when illumination is uneven, and so forth ... [T]here is not *one* thing in which the focusing of your attention on the hue (say) consists ... no simple,

unanalyzable core of the experience. There are just the different things you do when you interact with the redness of the wall.[2]

The taste of the crème brûlée, the look of a red wall, the feel of grass versus artificial turf – these consist not of properties or events in some occult inner domain; they consist instead of patterns of sensorimotor interaction with things in the environment.

Because exponents of sensorimotor theories take the qualitative features of experience to consist in patterns of sensorimotor interaction, they deny that there are qualia in the sense that exponents of qualia-based objections assume. Noë and O'Regan, for instance, state their position as follows:

> Qualia are meant to be properties of experiential states or events. But experiences … are not states. They are ways of acting … things we do … Hence, there are, in this sense at least, no (visual) qualia … [W]e are not denying that experience has qualitative character … [T]he qualitative character of experience … is constituted by the character of the sensorimotor contingencies at play when we perceive. Our claim, rather, is that it is confused to think of the qualitative character of experience in terms of the occurrence of something (whether in the mind or brain). Experience is something one does, and its qualitative features are aspects of this activity.[3]

According to sensorimotor theorists, then, there is no internal domain of non-relational, unanalyzable, subjective impressions, but only the external domain of familiar objects, properties, and events. Facts about the qualitative aspects of experience are all facts about these objects, properties, and events, and our sensorimotor ways of interacting with them. Physicalists who endorse sensorimotor theories of consciousness are committed to a further claim: sensorimotor patterns of interaction with the environment are all physical; they can all be given an exhaustive physical description and explanation. Physicalists who appeal to sensorimotor theories to handle qualia-based objections are thus committed to the following two claims:

1 Phenomenal consciousness can be given an exhaustive account in terms of sensorimotor interaction with the environment.
2 Sensorimotor interaction with the environment can be exhaustively described and explained by appeal to physics.

Critics of physicalist appeals to sensorimotor theories can target either claim. Critics who target Claim (1) can argue, for instance, that there is more to phenomenal consciousness than sensorimotor interaction. They can agree that perception involves patterns of sensorimotor interaction, but deny that these patterns provide an exhaustive account of what perception is. In addition to the patterns, they can insist, there are also qualia – nonrelational, unanalyzable occurrences in a subjective domain.

Critics who target Claim (2), on the other hand, can agree that phenomenal consciousness can be exhaustively understood in terms of sensorimotor interaction; they can simply deny that the appeal to sensorimotor interaction can provide physicalists with a way of handling qualia-based objections, for sensorimotor interaction cannot be exhaustively described and explained by appeal to physics. The reason, critics of (2) might insist, is that patterns of sensorimotor interaction cannot be described and explained without appeal to the special descriptive and explanatory resources of biology, and these are resources physics by itself is unable to supply or replace. This, in any event, is one example of how critics of (2) might argue.

Qualia-based arguments against physicalism as well as physicalist responses to them remain extremely controversial. Now that we have considered them and the other arguments for and against the general physicalist worldview, it is time to consider specific forms of physicalism: reductive physicalism, nonreductive physicalism, and eliminative physicalism, as well as instrumentalism and anomalous monism.

Further Reading

An early Greek version of physicalism was endorsed by Democritus. Aristotle (1984) discusses several similar theories in Book I of *On the Soul* (often referred to by its Latin name, *De Anima*). An early modern physicalist account of human nature is advanced by Thomas Hobbes (1991 [1642]; 1996 [1651]), and an important eighteenth-century formulation is offered by Julien Offray de la Mettrie (1996 [1747]). Since the middle of the twentieth century, a commitment to physicalism has operated as a background assumption for most debates in philosophy of mind – a point discussed by Jaegwon Kim (1998: Chapter 1). The French mathematician Pierre-Simon Laplace (1951) introduced the idea of an imaginary Super Physicist (what is often referred to as 'Laplace's demon') albeit to illustrate the concept of determinism not physicalism: physicalists need not be determinists, nor is it necessary for determinists to be physicalists.

For more on the examples of phlogiston and caloric see Hankins (1985) and Harman (1982). The inductive generalization from past scientific success is articulated in very compressed ways by J. J. C. Smart (1959) and David Lewis (1966). A more sophisticated inductive argument is advanced by Andrew Melnyk (2003).

Hempel's dilemma was originally articulated by Carl Hempel (1969). It has been articulated more forcefully by others including Tim Crane and D.H. Mellor (1990). Andrew Melnyk (2003: Chapter 1) grasps the first horn of Hempel's dilemma, and Jeffrey Poland (1994: Chapter 2) grasps the second horn.

The knowledge argument was originally advanced by Frank Jackson (1982), but his later article "What Mary Didn't Know" (1986) is briefer and more accessible, and covers some of the objections to the knowledge argument discussed here. A version of the argument was also suggested by Thomas Nagel (1974). The old-facts-under-new-representations objection is advanced by Terence Horgan (1984) and Brian Loar (1990). Michael Tye (2000) argues that facts about consciousness can be deduced from physical facts. The ability hypothesis was introduced by David Lewis (1983) and Laurence Nemirow (1990). Other versions of the ability hypothesis have been advanced by Earl Conee (1994) and by John Bigelow and Robert Pargetter (1990). Jackson (1998; 2003) himself now appears to reject the knowledge argument in favor of a version of the ability hypothesis.

Exponents of representational theories of consciousness include Fred Dretske (1995) and Michael Tye (1995). Tye challenges the claim that absent or inverted qualia are possible in Chapter 7 of the same book. Dretske (1995: chapters 3 and 5) develops a different approach to inverted and absent qualia. For more on the problems facing simple covariation theories of mental representation see Fodor (1987: Chapter 4); Dretske (1988: Chapter 3); and Sterelny (1990: Chapter 6). More sophisticated theories of representation are developed in those same books.

The seventeenth-century British philosopher John Locke (1959: Book II, Chapter 1, Section 4) suggested a higher-order perception theory. More recently higher-order perception theories have been defended by David M. Armstrong (1993: especially Chapter 6, sections IX and X), and by William G. Lycan (1996). Exponents of higher-order thought theories include David M. Rosenthal (2005) and Peter Carruthers (2003). Alvin Goldman (1993: 366) criticizes higher-order theories in the ways described earlier. Alva Noë and J. Kevin O'Regan (2002) defend a sensorimotor theory of consciousness. See also O'Regan (2009), and Noë (2004: Chapter 4). The sensorimotor account builds on the ecological theory of perception originally defended by the psychologist J. J. Gibson (1986).

Notes

1 David M. Armstrong, 1993, *A Materialist Theory of the Mind*, 2nd edn, New York: Routledge, 94.
2 Alva Noë and J. Kevin O'Regan, 2002, "On the Brain-Basis of Visual Consciousness: A Sensorimotor Account." In *Vision and Mind: Selected Readings in the Philosophy of Perception*, edited by Alva Noë and Evan Thompson. Cambridge: MIT Press, 567, 571–2.
3 Noë and O'Regan, "On the Brain-Basis of Visual Consciousness: A Sensorimotor Account," 579–80.

Chapter 5

Reductive Physicalism

Overview

Reductive physicalism claims that ordinary psychological discourse will be retained when we develop a complete scientific account of human behavior, and that its categories will correspond in some straightforward way to the categories of physical theory. Logical behaviorism was the first serious reductivist theory. Behaviorists sought to establish mental–physical correlations *a priori* through analyses of psychological language. Problems with behaviorism quickly led to its abandonment. The psychophysical identity theory was developed to circumvent these problems. Identity theorists sought to establish mental–physical correlations *a posteriori* through scientific investigation. The identity theory continues to be the mainstay of reductivist thinking.

There are two arguments for the identity theory which appeal to two different models of *a posteriori* identification. The first claims that given a choice between the identity theory and property dualism, we should choose the identity theory because it has a simpler ontology; that is, it posits fewer basic properties. According to the identity theory, all properties including mental properties are physical. According to property dualism, by contrast, mental properties form a distinct class of properties in addition to physical ones; property dualism is thus committed to twice as many basic types of properties as the identity theory. The second argument claims that endorsing the identity theory is not a matter of choice, but is instead an implication of scientific investigation. Mental states are defined by their typical causes and effects. Pain, for instance, is the state that is typically caused by pinpricks, burns, and abrasions, and that typically causes winces, groans, and similar behavior. The only kinds of states that are capable of having these typical causes and effects are physical states. The job of scientific investigation is then to reveal what those physical states are. Critics of the identity theory dismiss the first argument because it is merely inductive. Critics of the second argument fall into two categories. Some deny that mental states are defined by their causes and

Philosophy of Mind: A Comprehensive Introduction, First Edition. William Jaworski.
© 2011 William Jaworski. Published 2011 by Blackwell Publishing Ltd.

effects. They argue, for instance, that qualia, the qualitative aspects of conscious experience, do not admit of causal analyses, or that psychological discourse is not like a theory that postulates states that can be identified with physical states. Other critics of the argument deny that physical states are the only ones capable of having the physical causes and effects that define mental states.

Both behaviorism and the identity theory have been closely associated with psychophysical reductivism, the idea that physical theory is capable of taking over the descriptive and explanatory roles played by psychological discourse. Reductivism formed the basis of the original physicalist multilevel worldview. According to that view, the physical universe can be divided into different levels corresponding to different sciences. The lowest level corresponds to fundamental physics, followed by atomic physics, chemistry, cell biology, organismic biology, and finally the social sciences. Individuals at each level constitute individuals at each higher level, and theories at each higher level are reducible to theories at each lower level. Because reduction is a transitive relation (if A is reducible to B, and B is reducible to C, then A is reducible to C), all theories on the reductivist view are ultimately reducible to fundamental physics. According to reductivists, this is what it means to say that everything is physical.

Confidence in the reductivist program remained strong until the late 1960s when it began to seem increasingly unlikely that psychological categories corresponded neatly to physical categories. Some arguments suggested instead that mental and physical correlations were not neat one–one correlations, but messy one–many correlations, that instances of a given mental property did not correspond to instances of a single physical property, but to multiple distinct types of physical properties. This idea was the basis of **nonreductive physicalism**, the subject of Chapter 6.

5.1 Behaviorism

The basic physicalist idea has been around since the time of Greek natural philosophers such as Democritus (b. 460 BCE). Early modern formulations of it were advanced by Thomas Hobbes (1588–1679) in the seventeenth century and by Julien Offray de La Mettrie (1709–1751) in the eighteenth century. But unlike substance dualism which was in full flower by then, physicalism did not blossom into a serious theory of mind until the twentieth century. By the 1950s, moreover, physicalism had become the dominant position in philosophy of mind, and it continues to dominate philosophy of mind today.

In this chapter and the next, we will trace the development of mainline physicalist thinking in the twentieth century – the development of reductive and nonreductive physicalism. Both claim that psychological discourse is to some extent accurate, that the entities it postulates (beliefs, desires, and other mental states) will correspond to something in a complete scientific account of human behavior. The burden for exponents of these theories is to explain the nature of this correspondence. There are at least two ways of doing so. Reductivists claim that the predicates and terms of psychological discourse correspond neatly to those of physical theory. In the most straightforward case, a mental property or state corresponds to exactly one physical property or state. The first serious reductivist theory was logical behaviorism.

The term 'behaviorism' is used in different ways in philosophy and in psychology. In psychology, the term is used as a label for two different claims. The first is that psychology should concern itself only with observable phenomena. This claim is often called **methodological behaviorism**. The second claim represents a restrictive interpretation of this methodological claim: psychology should concern itself only with observable phenomena in the strict sense that psychologists should not even postulate inner causal mechanisms to explain overt behavior. This claim is often called *radical behaviorism*.

Methodological behaviorism was pioneered by the psychologist J. B. Watson (1878–1958). Watson was chagrined that psychology had made so little progress since the seventeenth century by comparison with physics. By the beginning of the twentieth century, physics had managed to revolutionize our entire understanding of the universe, and it was clear that this progress was going to continue. Psychology, by contrast, seemed not to have gotten beyond the understanding developed by the Greeks over 2,000 years earlier. What was worse, the methods psychologists employed seemed to offer not even a chance of greater success. At the time, introspection was the dominant method in psychology. Psychologists tried to study mental phenomena using something like Descartes' method of examining the contents and qualitative characteristics of conscious states. Scandalized by the lack of progress, Watson suggested a new methodological imperative for psychological science: psychologists should concern themselves only with observable behavior. If psychology was ever to become a rigorous science like physics, it had to imitate the methods of physics as much as possible. That meant that psychologists had to concern themselves with measurable, objective phenomena – phenomena that were open to study and evaluation by more than one person. Since the contents of consciousness were supposedly private or subjective, phenomena to which only one person had access in principle, they were not a suitable subject-matter for psychological study. Instead, said Watson, psychologists should study the correlations between sensory stimuli and behavioral responses to them.

By the 1930s, methodological behaviorism had become the dominant methodology in psychology, and it remains the dominant methodology today. But there are different ways of interpreting the injunction that psychology should study only objective, measurable phenomena. Some psychologists thought that in order for psychology to be truly scientific, psychologists had to avoid even the practice of postulating unobservable mechanisms to explain observed stimulus–response correlations. These were radical behaviorists such as B. F. Skinner (1904–1990). To most psychologists working today radical behaviorism seems like an excessively restrictive methodological program. After all, even physicists postulate unobservable entities to explain the behavior of observable ones. This postulation is in fact one of the principal means whereby physics progresses. Consider, for instance, the observable behavior of water – its freezing at 0°C, its boiling at 100°C, its expansion when frozen, and so forth. Physicalists explain these observable phenomena by postulating entities they cannot observe: atoms and molecules. Water expands when it freezes, for instance, because water molecules align themselves into crystals as the temperature drops, and these crystals have more volume than water molecules in a liquid state. Although radical behaviorism dominated psychology during the 1940s and 1950s, the 1960s ushered in a more relaxed understanding of psychological method. That relaxed understanding has come to be called *cognitive psychology*. Unlike radical behaviorists, cognitive psychologists postulate internal correlational mechanisms to explain observed human behaviors – mechanisms that are candidates for identification with components of the nervous system.

By contrast with its use in psychology, the term 'behaviorism' is used in philosophy to refer to a different type of claim altogether – a claim not about what psychological science should study, but about the meaning of psychological expressions. *Analytic* or **logical behaviorism**, as it is often called, is the claim that psychological descriptions are abbreviations for physical descriptions of actual and potential behavior. According to logical behaviorists, a statement such as 'I am in pain' is really an abbreviation for a much longer description of what I am actually doing, or what I would do under various counterfactual circumstances. It might mean, for instance, 'I am perspiring; my pupils are dilated; I am wincing; I am trying to escape from a potentially harmful stimulus; I am saying "Ow! Ow!"; if asked, "Are you in pain?" I would answer, "Yes!",' and so on.

One way of understanding the behaviorist thesis is to do the following: Take a psychological statement such as

A   WJ believes that behaviorism is false.

Next, consider the kinds of occurrences that would lead you to suspect that Statement (A) is true. A preliminary list might include the following:

B   WJ has said explicitly that he believes behaviorism is false, and whenever asked whether he really believes that it is false, he says, "Most assuredly!"; and when discussing behaviorism in class WJ always presents the view with a particularly incisive contempt, and he articulates objections to it with an enjoyment bordering on mania; and WJ has anti-behaviorist bumper stickers; and he donates money to anti-behaviorist organizations such as PBFW (Partnership for a Behaviorist-Free World), and AUAB (Americans United Against Behaviorism), and in his more radical moments even VAB (Violence Against Behaviorists); and when at a bar, WJ challenges all the behaviorists present to a debate or to a fistfight; and ...

Again, the idea here is to construct a description of WJ's actual and potential behavior (what WJ is doing, has done, and would do under various counterfactual circumstances) that would lead you to suspect that Statement (A) is true. The idea, in other words is to describe your evidence in favor of Statement (A). Now, according to behaviorists such a description provides not merely evidence for Statement (A), but the actual *meaning* of Statement (A): Statement (A) is really just an abbreviation of Statement (B). According to behaviorists, then, psychological statements are really just disguised statements about actual and potential behavior.

Someone might ask what exactly behaviorists mean by 'behavior' – what exactly is behavior supposed to consist in? Importantly, what behaviorists count as behavior must satisfy two conditions. First, it must be something that can be exhaustively described and explained by physics. My wincing, my escape-directed behavior, my utterances, the particular look I have on my face, and so on, can all be given exhaustive physical descriptions, it seems. Second, these occurrences must be observable by ordinary people in what we might call "pedestrian" circumstances: people with ordinary perceptual capacities can witness them without the use of any special equipment such as electroencephalograms, x-rays, or magnetic resonance images. The reason for this second condition is that psychological predicates and terms are supposed to express behavioral conditions. Since people are able to use psychological predicates and terms in pedestrian circumstances, the behavioral conditions that psychological expressions are supposed to abbreviate must be observable in pedestrian circumstances as well. Behaviorists were not always careful about satisfying this pedestrian constraint on behavioral conditions. The philosopher Carl Hempel, for instance, one of the originators of logical behaviorism, once claimed that the range of relevant behavioral data included facts about people's heart rates, skin conductivity, and hormone levels. Since these are not features people would ordinarily be able to observe, it is unlikely that psychological expressions could be abbreviations for these kinds of conditions.

5.2   Arguments For and Against Behaviorism

Behaviorism was popular during the 1930s and 1940s, but by the 1960s it was generally considered dead. The reasons for its demise are complex. First, general support for the theory waned because philosophers lost confidence in the broader philosophical program of which it was a part: **logical positivism**. Logical positivists aimed to show that philosophical problems were all based on linguistic or conceptual mistakes. Once we clarified the logical structure of our language through the process of linguistic or conceptual analysis, the apparent problems would disappear. The British philosopher Bertrand Russell (1872–1970) had achieved some early success solving problems in metaphysics using the method of conceptual analysis, and positivists were confident that this success could be replicated in other domains. When positivists such as Rudolph Carnap (1891–1970), Herbert Feigl (1902–1988), and Carl Hempel sought to use the method of conceptual analysis to solve mind–body problems, the result was logical behaviorism. By the early 1950s, however, it was clear that positivists had been overly optimistic, and had overestimated the ability of conceptual analysis to solve philosophical problems. This was revealed in part by the problems surrounding their theory of meaning.

Logical positivists argued that the meaning of a statement was its verification conditions – roughly, conditions sufficient for knowing that the statement was true. The identification of meaning with verification conditions was known as the **verifiability theory of meaning** (VTM). Based on the VTM, behaviorists argued that since the truth of psychological statements was known by observing people's behavior, the meaning of psychological statements must consist in behavioral conditions. Whenever we describe people's beliefs, desires, or other mental states, they argued, we are really describing their actual and potential behavior: what they are doing or what they would do in various counterfactual circumstances. The argument for behaviorism thus hinged on two premises: the VTM, and the claim that we know the truth of psychological statements on the basis of actual and potential behavior.

There were serious problems with the behaviorist argument, however. Foremost was that the VTM was shown to be incoherent. Because the VTM claims that a statement's meaning consists in its verification conditions, it implies that a statement that is unverifiable must be meaningless. Positivists generally agreed, moreover, that statements were verifiable in only two ways: *analytically*, on the basis of the definitions of their constitutive terms, and *empirically*, on the basis of some type of experiment or observation. The VTM thus implied that every meaningful statement was verifiable either analytically or empirically. But consider the VTM itself. It does not seem to be verifiable in either of these ways: there is nothing in the definition of 'meaning' that implies that a statement's meaning must consist in its verification conditions, and there does not appear to be any experiment or observation that would be sufficient to prove the VTM true. But if the VTM is neither analytically nor empirically verifiable, then it fails to satisfy its own criterion of meaningfulness; it implies that it itself is meaningless. (For this reason many positivists stopped referring to the VTM as a claim or proposition, and began referring to it instead as a *methodological principle*.)

Behaviorism also faced problems on account of the *holism* of psychological discourse. Psychological predicates and terms form a tight network of interconnections. Consider a description of someone's reasons for performing an action:

1   Johnson took an umbrella when he left home because he believed it was going to rain and thought that bringing an umbrella would be the best means of staying dry.

(1) marks the attempt to describe Johnson's reason for acting by appeal to his beliefs alone. But Johnson's beliefs can explain his action only in conjunction with some type of want or desire. If, for instance, Johnson wants to get wet, his belief that it will rain, and his judgment that umbrellas are the best means of staying dry will no longer explain why he took the umbrella. It is only against the background of assumptions about Johnson's desires, his desire to stay dry, for instance, that (1) is able to explain his behavior. The same would be true if we attempted to explain Johnson's behavior by appeal to a want or desire alone:

> 2   Johnson took an umbrella when he left home because he didn't want to get wet.

A desire not to get wet can explain Johnson's action only on the assumption that he believes he will not get wet if he brings an umbrella.

These examples illustrate that beliefs, desires, and actions are logically interconnected: beliefs and desires can explain actions only in conjunction with one another. Moreover, the connections between Johnson's belief that it will rain, his desire not to get wet, and his act of taking an umbrella are mediated by a range of yet other mental conditions: knowing that exposure to rain can result in wetness, believing that there is a fairly good chance he may be exposed to rain if it should come, supposing that the rain will fall at an angle he can catch with an umbrella, knowing that umbrellas are typically not constructed of materials that disintegrate in water, and so on.

The holism of psychological discourse posed two problems for behaviorism. First, behaviorists argued that behavioral conditions were sufficient for knowing someone's mental states. But the holism of psychological discourse suggested that behavioral conditions could not be sufficient for knowing someone's mental states. Imagine, for instance, that we observe the following episode:

> Johnson opened the front door, and stepped halfway through, but saw the look of the sky, and reached back in for his umbrella. He locked the door behind him, and proceeded down the path.

We might take Johnson's behavior to indicate that he believes it will rain. But Johnson's behavior can be taken as sufficient grounds for this only if we assume that he has a number of other beliefs and desires as well, such as a desire to stay dry and a belief that taking an umbrella will help him do so. Only against the background of these assumptions does Johnson's umbrella-taking count as evidence that he believes it will rain. Consequently, the verification conditions of a psychological statement are not purely behavioral; they invariably make reference to other mental states.

Second, the holism of psychological discourse posed a challenge not just to the argument for behaviorism, but to behaviorism itself. If behaviorism is true, then psychological statements are just abbreviated statements about actual and potential behavior. Behaviorism thus implies that it is possible in principle to translate a psychological statement into a statement about actual and potential behavior without any loss of meaning – just as I might be able to translate the abbreviated expression 'S♥J' without loss of meaning into the English expression 'Sally loves John'. The holism of psychological discourse suggested, however, that the relevant translations could never be performed because the translation of one psychological expression would always require the translation of countless others. Consider an example.

Behaviorism implies that Statement (A) ('WJ believes that behaviorism is false') can be translated into a statement about WJ's behavior such as Statement (B), and it implies that the behavioral conditions cited in that translation are sufficient for knowing that (A) is true. But the conditions cited in (B) are sufficient for knowing that (A) is true only if we make countless further assumptions about WJ's mental states. For example, the behavioral conditions cited in (B) are sufficient to know that WJ believes behaviorism is false only if we assume that WJ is not suffering from some large-scale psychological repression – only if we assume, for instance, that he is not a closet behaviorist who is so ashamed of his condition that he is driven to attempt to convince others and himself that he really believes behaviorism is false. So in order for (B) to provide an accurate translation of (A), we would have to add Condition (C): 'WJ is not a repressed behaviorist: he does not secretly harbor behaviorist sympathies of which he is ashamed, and does not intend to deceive other people or himself about his actual beliefs'. Notice, however, that (C) introduces a number of other psychological concepts: the concept of secretly believing or wanting to believe behaviorism, the concept of feeling ashamed of one's sympathies, and the concept of intending to deceive. If we are to translate (A) into a purely behavioral statement like (B), these additional concepts will have to be given behavioral analyses of their own. But in the process of giving them purely behavioral analyses, we encounter the same problem we encountered with (A): doing so introduces additional psychological concepts, and analyzing these additional psychological concepts requires the addition of yet further ones, and analyzing those requires the addition of further ones yet again, and so on. In practice, then, it would appear to be impossible for us to translate even a single psychological expression into a statement purely about actual and potential behavior.

In addition to these problems, behaviorism faced others. It implied an implausible account of first-person authority, for instance (Chapter 2). If my beliefs, desires, and pains are just different types of behavior, then it seems that I can know what my beliefs, desires, and pains are only by observing my own behavior in the way I observe the behavior of others. I can know that I am in pain, for instance, only if I am capable of observing that my pupils are dilated, that I am sweating, wincing, and so on. But that seems implausible; surely I know that I am in pain by directly feeling it.

This worry about first-person knowledge was closely related to worries about subjectivity. Part of the motivation for behaviorism derived from its ability to avoid the problem of other minds (Section 1.5). Recall that that problem derives from the idea that beliefs, desires, pains, and other mental states are subjective phenomena that are accessible only to the person experiencing them. If mental phenomena are subjective, then it is impossible for any of us to know what mental states other people have. But if mental phenomena are not subjective occurrences but objective ones such as bodily movements, then there is no problem knowing what mental states other people have since bodily movements are as publicly observable as anything can be. Many philosophers of mind, however, are convinced that mental phenomena are subjective, or at least have a subjective component (Section 2.3). If that is the case, critics of behaviorism argue, then behaviorism must be false since behaviorism implies that mental phenomena are not subjective.

In addition, there seemed to be counterexamples to behavioral analyses of psychological concepts. The philosopher Hilary Putnam argued, for instance, that it was possible for there to be *super actors*, people who could replicate all the behavior associated with pain yet without actually being in pain. He also argued that it was possible for there to be *super Spartans*, people who could be experiencing pain without any of the behavior associated with it – without even having dispositions to pain behavior. If behaviorism were true, then cases like these would be impossible, for the claim that some person, S, is in pain would be equivalent to a description of S's actual and potential behavior. Yet a description of the super actor's actual and potential behavior is the same as a description of someone who is in pain even though the super actor is not in pain. Likewise, description of the super Spartan's actual and potential behavior is the same as a description of someone who is not in pain even though the super Spartan is in pain. These examples appear to show that there is more to pain than actual and potential behavior; the claim that S is in pain cannot, therefore, be analyzed in the way behaviorists suppose.

Putnam's examples were closely associated with another worry about behaviorism, the worry that psychological language did not describe overt behavior but the *causes* of overt behavior. It seemed plausible to suppose that pain was not the wincing, groaning, and escape-directed movements, but that it was instead the cause of the wincing, groaning, and escape-directed movements.

Despite these difficulties, it is unclear that behaviorism was ever really refuted. It would perhaps be more accurate to say that by the mid-1950s many philosophers had become disaffected with positivism and saw behaviorism's shortcomings as symptomatic of the more general failure of the positivist program. They were no longer confident that conceptual analysis could solve all philosophical problems, and were ready to explore new approaches in philosophy of mind. As a result, the real *coup de grace* for behaviorism came not in the form of a devastating objection, but in the form of what seemed to many a more plausible alternative, one based on the idea that psychological discourse is theoretical discourse, that it is a scientific or protoscientific theory.

5.3   The Theory Model of Psychological Discourse

At the time of behaviorism's demise a widely endorsed view of scientific method saw science as a leapfrogging process involving theory and observation. The scientific process began with scientists making observations, and formulating theories to explain them. Those theories were then tested against further experimental observations which either verified or falsified the theories. In line with this view of scientific method, positivists had distinguished two kinds of language used in science: theoretical language and observational language. The idea was roughly that our initial observations about the world were formulated in a pre-theoretical, observation vocabulary that differed from the vocabulary used to formulate theories – a difference that was evident from the new predicates and terms theories often introduced. Behaviorists had taken psychological discourse to be like an observation language, a vocabulary used to express pre-theoretical observations of human behavior. To say that Alexander was in pain was to report an observation about how Alexander was behaving or how he would behave under various conditions. The problems with behaviorism inspired philosophers to look for a different understanding of psychological language. In light of the theory/observation distinction, the most obvious suggestion was that psychological language was a theoretical language. Let us call this the **theory model of psychological discourse**, the claim that psychological discourse is or is relevantly like a theory.

The term 'theory' is used in many different ways in philosophy and other disciplines. The distinctive mark of theories in the sense relevant here is that they explain observations by postulating unobservable, hypothetical entities. Consider, for instance, the theory we use to explain our observations of water freezing. That theory postulates the existence of unobservable entities – water molecules – which are related to each other in ways described by chemistry and physics. The relations of these entities to one another are supposed to explain why water freezes in the way we observe: when the water drops below 4°C, there is not enough thermal energy to overcome the hydrogen bonds between water molecules, and, as a result, the molecules end up being less tightly packed than they would be at a higher temperature.

According to the theory model of psychological discourse, psychological explanation is a species of theoretical explanation. Psychological discourse is a prescientific or protoscientific theory – what is often called a 'folk theory'. We use it in our pedestrian dealings to explain observable human behavior. Suppose, for instance, that we explain why Caesar crossed the Rubicon by saying he *wanted* to secure political power and *believed* marching on Rome the best means of securing it. According to the theory model, when we explain Caesar's behavior in this way, we are appealing to a theory that postulates hypothetical entities – beliefs and desires – that are related to each other in ways that enable us to explain why Caesar acted as he did. For example, beliefs and desires might be related to each other in the way expressed by the following generalization:

> When x wants y, and believes doing z the best means of attaining y, then if nothing inhibits x's pursuit of y, x will generally do z.

If beliefs and desires are related to each other in this way, then Caesar's beliefs and desires would explain why he crossed the Rubicon.

  With the exception of behaviorism, the theory model remains a basic tenet of almost every physicalist theory of mind. Its initial popularity, moreover, was due in part to its ability to explain behaviorism's failures. The predicates and terms introduced by a theory are defined largely by their relations to one another. They thus form an interlocking network of concepts. Consequently, if psychological discourse is like a theory, this would explain its holistic character – the very holistic character that contributed to behaviorism's demise. Likewise, the theory model was able to accommodate the intuition that beliefs, desires, and other mental states were the causes of overt behavior, for according to the theory model, when we explain Caesar's behavior by appeal to his mental states, we are postulating hypothetical causes of that behavior: his desire for political power and his belief that marching on Rome was the best means of achieving it. The belief and the desire are the states that together caused Caesar to cross the Rubicon. Finally, the theory model introduced an important ontological idea: the idea that the hypothetical entities postulated by psychological predicates and terms were candidates for identification with states of the nervous system. This idea was the basis of the **psychophysical identity theory**.

5.4   The Psychophysical Identity Theory

Behaviorists had proposed to identify mental states with physical states *a priori*, on the basis of conceptual analysis. By contrast, identity theorists proposed to identify mental states with physical states *a posteriori*, on the basis of scientific investigation into the workings of the nervous system. The history of science provided numerous examples of this type of *a posteriori* identification. Water had been identified with H_2O not by undertaking an analysis of the term 'water', but by studying experimentally what water was. Heat had been identified with mean molecular kinetic energy, and light with electromagnetic radiation in the same way. In each case, people had developed descriptive and explanatory frameworks with different vocabularies and later discovered that those frameworks referred to or expressed the very same phenomena. The terms 'light' and 'electromagnetic radiation with wavelengths of 380–750 nm', for instance, originally belonged to different conceptual frameworks: one to electromagnetic theory, the other to a prescientific vocabulary. Those terms were nevertheless discovered to refer to the very same phenomenon. Identifications of this sort are often called **theoretical identifications**. According to identity theorists, neuroscience would eventually lead to the theoretical identification of beliefs, desires, and other mental states with states of the human nervous system.

The theoretical identification of X with Y is supposed to be marked by two features. First, the identity is supposed to be discovered empirically. By analogy, members of a certain linguistic community might use the name 'Hesperus' to refer to a star that appears in the West in the early evening, and they might use the name 'Phosphorus' to refer to a star that appears in the East in the early morning, and yet they might not know but discover only later that those names refer to the same star. Importantly, the identity of Hesperus and Phosphorus is not something that can be discovered through conceptual analysis. The expressions 'star that appears in the West in the early evening' and 'star that appears in the East in the early morning' clearly have different meanings. Analyzing those meanings will not reveal that those expressions refer to the same individual. The identity of Hesperus with Phosphorus can only be discovered empirically. Second, however, unlike the Hesperus–Phosphorus case, in the case of theoretical identifications, at least one of the predicates or terms, 'X' or 'Y', is supposed to belong to a theory.

Identity theorists endorsed two different models of theoretical identification. Originally, they thought that theoretical identification was a matter of choice. Scientists would discover correlations between certain types of mental states and certain types of physical states. They would discover, for instance, that pain occurred if and only if brain state B occurred. They would then *choose* to identify pain with brain state B on grounds of parsimony; that is, because it yielded a more simple or elegant theory – a theory that postulated a single entity with two different names ('pain' and 'brain state B'), as opposed to two distinct entities corresponding to each name. In addition, this identification would avoid the potentially embarrassing task of having to explain how and why pain and brain state B managed to be correlated if they were in fact distinct. This model of theoretical identification was originally championed by the philosopher J. J. C. Smart.

It was soon criticized, however, by the philosopher David Lewis. Lewis advanced an alternative model of theoretical identification that was also advanced independently by David Armstrong. According to the Lewis-Armstrong alternative, theoretical identifications were not chosen on grounds of parsimony, but were actually *implied* by the logic of scientific investigation. In our ordinary, prescientific dealings we often introduce terms to refer to things that we are able to identify initially only on the basis of their causes and effects. For example, crime-scene investigators might introduce the name 'Mack the Knife' to refer to the person who killed

Miller. Initially, we have no way of identifying Mack the Knife other than by his causal role in Miller's death. Importantly, though, that causal role provides clues about who Mack the Knife is. Forensic investigation might reveal that the person who killed Miller is Jones. In that case, forensic investigation would reveal that Jones is Mack the Knife. In other words, in this case, Mack the Knife was initially defined as Miller's killer. Scientific investigation then revealed that Jones was the individual who killed Miller. Scientific investigation thus reveals that Jones is Mack the knife. According to Lewis and Armstrong, theoretical identification works the same way. We initially define something by reference to narrow profile of its features. We define water, for instance, as the stuff in this bottle. Scientific investigation then reveals that the stuff in this bottle is H_2O. Scientific investigation thus reveals that water is H_2O.

The advantage of the Lewis-Armstrong model of theoretical identification over the appeal to parsimony is that on this model the identifications follow validly by the transitivity of identity. The transitivity of identity is the logical principle represented in Figure 5.1. It says that if $x = y$, and $y = z$, then $x = z$. Recall that if x is identical to y (that is, $x = y$), then 'x' and 'y' are just two different terms for the same entity. Likewise, if y is identical to z (that is, $y = z$), then 'y' and 'z' refer to

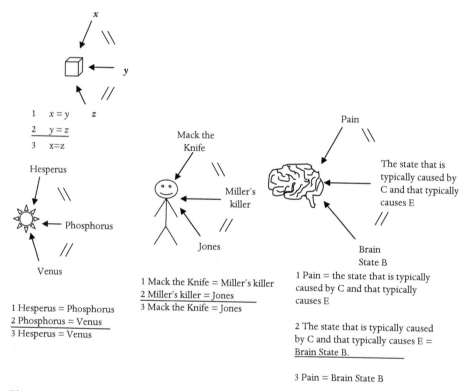

Figure 5.1   Transitivity of identity

the same entity. So if '*x*' and '*y*' refer to the same entity, and '*y*' and '*z*' refer to the same entity, then clearly '*x*' and '*z*' must refer to the same entity (that is, $x = z$). According to Lewis and Armstrong, this is exactly the form theoretical identifications take. Theoretical identification is not a matter of choice; scientists did not choose to identify water with H_2O; they were *forced* to identify water with H_2O by the transitivity of identity and the scientific evidence.

Consider now the application of this model to our mental states. According to Lewis and Armstrong, in our prescientific dealings we define mental states by their typical environmental causes and typical behavioral effects. We initially define pain, for instance, as the state (whatever it turns out to be) that is typically caused by pinpricks, burns, and abrasions, and that typically causes winces, groans, and similar behavior. That state then becomes a target for further scientific investigation which aims to discover what pain is in fact. Pain is thus identified by definition with the state that has such-and-such typical causes and effects, and that state is then identified by scientific investigation with brain state B. Pain is thus identified with brain state B by the transitivity of identity:

1	Pain = the state that is typically caused by pinpricks, burns, and abrasions, and that typically causes winces, groans, and similar behavior.	Established by definition
2	The state that is typically caused by pinpricks, burns, and abrasions, and that typically causes winces, groans, and similar behavior = brain state B.	Established by scientific investigation
3	Pain = brain state B	Follows from (1) and (2) by the transitivity of identity

There are at least three arguments for the identity theory. One is based on a criticism of dual-attribute theories: those theories cannot solve the problem of mental causation, identity theorists argue, and this failure gives us good reason to think the identity theory is true. We consider this argument in detail in Chapter 8. The two arguments we consider in Chapter 5 are based on the aforementioned models of theoretical identification. The first is advanced by J. J. C. Smart; the second by David Lewis.

5.5   Smart's Argument For the Identity Theory: Ockham's Razor

J. J. C. Smart's argument for the identity theory is an appeal to **Ockham's razor**. Ockham's razor is a methodological principle named after William of Ockham (1287–1347), the fourteenth-century philosopher credited with having originally formulated it. The traditional formulation of Ockham's razor says that entities should not be multiplied beyond necessity. The gist of the principle is that we should try to explain phenomena using the simplest theoretical apparatus possible. Ockham's razor is similar to a principle many of us use in our everyday dealings: money should not be spent beyond necessity. Imagine, for instance, that you need to buy medication to fill a prescription. The pharmacist gives you a choice: you can buy a generic version of the drug, or you can buy the name-brand drug for twice as much. You learn that the generic and the name-brand drug have exactly the same active ingredients, and are alike in all the respects that concern you except that one of them is costlier. If you are like most of us, then under the circumstances you would opt for the less expensive drug. Ockham's razor says something analogous about theories: if you have a choice between two theories, TA and TB, which are alike in all relevant respects, but TA has a simpler ontology – that is, TA postulates fewer basic entities than TB – then you should choose TA since it is the ontologically "cheaper" theory.

Smart's argument for the identity theory appeals to Ockham's razor. The identity theory and property dualism are alike in all relevant respects. We assume, for instance, that both are coherent; that neither, for instance, has any internal inconsistencies. We also assume that both are compatible with all the scientific data about how mental phenomena and physical phenomena are related, and we assume that they are explanatorily equivalent, that the identity theory is able to explain everything that property dualism can, and property dualism can explain everything that the identity theory can. There is nevertheless a significant difference between the identity theory and property dualism: the identity theory has a simpler ontology; it postulates fewer basic entities. Identity theorists identify mental states such as pain with physical states such as brain state B. Property dualists, by contrast, distinguish them. As a result, property dualists end up being committed to the existence of at least twice as many entities. Identity theorists claim, for instance, that there is only one entity expressed by the terms 'pain' and 'brain state B', whereas property dualists claim that there are at least two, one expressed by each term. Because the identity theory and property dualism are alike empirically and explanatorily, and the only significant difference is in the sizes of their ontologies, we should choose the identity theory because its ontology is smaller and simpler.

There are at least two ways critics can respond to Smart's argument. The first rejects one of the argument's premises. Critics argue either that the identity theory is incoherent, or that it is incompatible with the scientific data, or else that it is explanatorily weaker than property dualism. If any of these is the case, then the appeal to Ockham's razor is moot, for if TA is incoherent, inconsistent with the empirical data, or explanatorily weaker than TB, then TA is not preferable to TB however much simpler TA's ontology may be.

The second response to Smart's argument accepts the argument's premises but rejects its conclusion. Although it is generally good theoretical practice to choose a theory with a simpler ontology, critics argue, ontological simplicity does not guarantee that a theory with a simpler ontology is true. If the premises of Smart's argument are true, they provide some reason to think that the identity theory is true – all inductive arguments provide *some* reason to think their conclusions are true, but those reasons are not decisive.

5.6 Lewis's Argument For the Identity Theory

By contrast with Smart's argument, Lewis's argument for the identity theory is not inductive but deductive.

1 Mental states are defined by their typical environmental causes and typical behavioral effects.
2 The only states capable of having those typical causes and effects are physical states.

Therefore, mental states must be physical states.

Lewis supports Premise (1) by appeal to examples such as the example of pain described earlier. It seems plausible to suppose that we introduce the term 'pain' to refer to the state that is typically caused by pinpricks, burns, and abrasions, and that typically causes winces, groans, and similar behavior. Consider likewise belief – the belief, for instance, that there are exactly eight planets in our solar system. We might define this as the state that is typically caused by having attended a lecture or read an article on the number of planets, and that typically causes someone to respond, "Eight," to the question "How many planets are in our solar system?" or to respond, "Yes," to the question, "Are there exactly eight planets in our solar system?" Examples like these suggest that mental states are defined by their typical causes and effects.

Premise (2) is sometimes called the *causal* or *explanatory completeness of physics*. It says that physics is capable in principle of providing an exhaustive description and explanation of all causes. What reasons are there to accept this premise? There are at least three arguments supporting it. Lewis's own argument for (2) runs as follows. If physicalism is true, then everything is physical. Consequently, if physicalism is true, any states that exist, including any states with typical causes and effects, are physical states. And physicalism is in fact true, says Lewis. So if there are in fact states with typical causes and effects, then they must be physical states. The claim that physicalism is true is the most controversial premise. Lewis defends it by appeal to an argument like the inductive generalization from past scientific success discussed in Section 4.5: in the past, scientists have always been successful in discovering the causes of the phenomena they were seeking to explain, and that success gives us good reason to suppose that their success is going to continue. We have every reason to suppose that the natural sciences are capable of discovering all the causes that can be discovered at all.

In addition, exponents of Premise (2) could take a cue from opponents of substance dualism: if Premise (2) is false, they could argue, then either (i) there are no states that are capable of having the causes and effects that define mental states, or else (ii) there are nonphysical states capable of having those causes and effects. But implication (i) seems absurd for reasons discussed in Section 3.5. It seems to imply, for instance, that there is no such thing as human action. What distinguishes actions from other physical events is that they have mental causes. If there are no mental causes, then there are no actions. Suppose, moreover, that there are no states that have causes and effects, and that Premise (1) of Lewis's argument is true: mental states are defined by their typical causes and effects. From these claims it would seem to follow that there are no mental states either. For these reasons, implication (i) seems unacceptable. And yet, exponents of Premise (2) could argue, implication (ii) is unacceptable as well for reasons also discussed in Section 3.5: the existence of nonphysical causes for physical events would end up violating the conservation laws of physics. Neither implication (i) nor implication (ii) is acceptable, therefore, and yet these would appear to be the implications of denying Premise (2). Since the implications of rejecting the premise are unacceptable, we have good reasons for accepting it.

Finally, exponents of (2) could argue that something like the causal completeness of physics is a basic methodological assumption of the sciences: if scientists were not confident that they could discover the causes of things using scientific techniques, the sort used to study the physical universe, then they would not spend the time or effort trying to discover those causes. It is only because they are confident that scientific techniques are capable of discovering causes that scientists employ them. Notice what this means, though: scientists tacitly assume that the causes they are trying to discover are physical – that they are the kinds of causes that can be revealed using scientific techniques. The very practice of science, then, seems to assume a principle like the causal completeness of physics.

Consider now some challenges to Lewis's argument. One challenge to Premise (1) derives from concerns over qualia. According to (1), mental states such as pain can be analyzed in terms of their relations to other things – their typical causes and effects, for instance. Some critics of (1) argue, however, that some mental states – qualia in particular – cannot be causally analyzed in this way. Qualia, these critics say, are nonrelational and unanalyzable, and it is possible that a single kind of qualitative experience might be correlated with multiple different kinds of causal processes. This is a version of the absent/inverted qualia argument discussed in Section 4.8.

Recall that according to that argument, it is possible that the human organisms I see around me might be behaving exactly as if they have phenomenal states like my own while yet having very different phenomenal states or lacking phenomenal states altogether. The qualitative experiences that accompany my behavior might be different from the qualitative experiences that accompany your behavior (Figure 4.2(A)). In fact, it is possible that none of my behavior might be accompanied by any qualitative experiences of the sort you have: I might be a qualia zombie, a being who acts in every objective way exactly as if it has conscious states, but who altogether lacks them (Figure 4.2(B)). Critics of (1) argue in a similar way that the qualitative experience that accompanies pinpricks, burns, and abrasions in me might be different from the qualitative experience that accompanies pinpricks, burns, and abrasions in you. Likewise, it is possible that in me pinpricks, burns, and abrasions are not accompanied by any qualitative experiences at all of the sort that accompany pinpricks, burns, and abrasions in you. If qualia inversion and absent qualia are possible, then this suggests qualia cannot be given analyses in terms of their typical causes and effects since any given qualitative experience could accompany or fail to accompany any given causal process.

There are several ways identity theorists can respond to this argument. We considered some of them in Section 4.9: representational, higher-order, and sensorimotor theories of consciousness can provide identity theorists with resources for accommodating the possibility of absent and inverted qualia. Alternatively, identity theorists could deny that absent and inverted qualia are possible, or deny that qualia exist. We consider arguments for these claims in Section 8.5.

A second way of challenging Premise (1) derives from criticisms of the theory model of psychological discourse. If psychological discourse is not a theory, then mental states are not hypothetical entities postulated by a theory. In that case, however, mental states can be neither hypothetical effects that are defined initially by appeal to their typical environmental causes, nor hypothetical causes that are defined initially by appeal to typical behavioral effects. But if they are neither of these, then it is difficult to see how mental states could be defined by their typical environmental causes and typical behavioral effects at all. Consequently, if the theory model of psychological discourse is false, it is difficult to see how Premise (1) of Lewis's argument could be true. Is there any reason to believe that the theory model of psychological discourse is false? In Section 11.7 we consider an alternative to it, namely the **pattern expression theory** of psychological discourse. If the pattern expression theory turns out to be superior to the theory model in various respects, then there is good reason to think the theory model is false, and, in that case, there is good reason to think Premise (1) is false as well.

Consider now challenges to Premise (2). They derive from several sources and target the arguments in support of Premise (2). The first argument for Premise (2), for instance, depends on the premise that physicalism is true. Opponents of the argument can nevertheless challenge this claim in the ways discussed in Chapter 4.

In response to the second argument for (2), moreover, opponents could argue either that the denial of Premise (2) does not have implications (i) or (ii), or else that these implications are not really absurd. We will see in Chapter 8, for instance, that epiphenomenalists deny that implication (i) is absurd: if mental states are causally inert, they argue, this does not have the absurd implication that there are no actions. Moreover, in Chapter 11 we will see that hylomorphists deny that implication (ii) is absurd as well: The existence of causes other than those described by physics, they argue, does not imply that physical laws must be violated, nor does it have other absurd consequences such as the overdetermination of actions. In addition, some philosophers will embrace the violation of physical laws or the overdetermination of actions, and deny that these implications are absurd. Substance dualists, for instance, and those sympathetic to a dualistic outlook will likely be undaunted by a violation of physical laws.

Finally, critics of the third argument for Premise (2) can argue that methodological considerations support a conclusion only inductively, and hence it is possible to accept the premises of the argument while yet denying Premise (2). In addition, they can argue that exponents of the third argument derive the wrong conclusion from their premises. Those premises support the conclusion that scientific techniques are capable of discovering causes, but they do not support the conclusion that those causes must be exhaustively describable by physics. The premises of the argument are compatible with the existence of scientific techniques that reveal causes that can only be described by biology or psychology or some branch of social science. Lewis's argument for the identity theory and the responses to it remain controversial.

5.7   Reductivism

The identity theory has been closely associated with psychophysical reductivism: the idea that the descriptive and explanatory resources of psychological discourse can be taken over by those of physical theory.

The term 'reduction' is used in a confusing variety of ways in philosophy and in the sciences. Here the term refers to a particular kind of ontological and epistemological situation (Figure 5.2). Imagine that Domain A is included within Domain B, but because of the way humans come to know the world, they come to know and describe A-entities in a way that is different from the way they come to know and describe other B-entities. As a result, they describe and explain the behavior of A-entities using a theoretical framework, TA, that is different from the framework they have used to describe and explain the behavior of other B-entities, the framework TB. The result is that they do not initially recognize the inclusion of Domain A in Domain B. People later discover, however, that Domain A is really part of Domain B, that A-entities really just *are* B-entities of a certain sort, and hence the behavior of A-entities can be exhaustively described and explained using TB. This situation is reflected in a certain relationship between

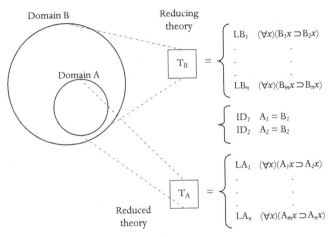

A-entities are B-entities, but since we do not initially recognize this we develop two different theoretical frameworks, T_A and T_B, to describe and explain the behavior of As and the behavior of the other Bs, respectively. Because As are Bs, As are governed by the same laws that govern Bs. Consequently, when we finally discover that As are Bs, we are able to describe and explain the behavior of As using the conceptual resources of T_B. T_B is thus able to assume the descriptive and explanatory roles formerly played by T_A. In this case, T_A is said to have been reduced to T_B. The Nagel model of reduction claims that theories are sets of law statements and that explanation consists in deduction from law statements. According to the Nagel model, then, the reduction of T_A to T_B consists in the deduction of the law statements of T_A (LA_1, …, LA_n) from the law statements of T_B(LB_1, … ,LB_n). Because the laws of T_A and the laws of T_B have different predicates, the deduction requires bridge principles. ID_1 and ID_2, for instance, allow for the deduction of LA_1 from LB_1.

Figure 5.2   Reduction of T_A to T_B

TA and TB. The principles governing the behavior of A-entities, the principles expressed by the law statements of TA, are just special applications of the principles governing the behavior of B-entities in general – the principles expressed by the law statements of TB. The laws of TA, people say, *are reducible to* the laws of TB; and they say that we can provide *a reductive description and explanation* of A-behavior using the conceptual resources of TB. A-statements can be derived from B-statements given certain assumptions about the conditions that distinguish A-entities from B-entities of other sorts – so-called *boundary conditions*. The descriptive and explanatory roles played by the law statements of TA, the *reduced theory*, are thus taken over by the law statements of the more inclusive *reducing theory*, TB. Because it is a relation between theories, reduction in this sense is typically called *intertheoretic reduction*.

Consider an example. Kepler's laws are thought to have been reduced to Newton's laws. Newton's laws imply that massive bodies will behave in very specific ways given the application of certain forces. If those laws are applied to planetary bodies in particular – if, in other words, people examine the implications of those laws within the boundaries of our planetary system – the laws predict that those bodies will behave in roughly the way Kepler's laws describe. Kepler's laws, the laws of a reduced theory, are thus shown to be special applications of Newton's laws, the laws of a reducing theory. To the extent that they are accurate, Kepler's laws really express the application of Newton's laws to planetary bodies. One upshot of this circumstance is that people can appeal to Newton's laws to explain why Kepler's laws obtain: Kepler's laws obtain because Newtonian laws imply that a system operating within the parameters of our planetary system will behave in roughly the way Kepler's laws describe.

There have been many attempts to give a precise account of intertheoretic reduction. Those attempts depend on assumptions about the nature of theories and the nature of explanation. One of the earliest and most influential attempts to formulate the notion of intertheoretic reduction was that of Ernest Nagel (1901–1985). Nagel endorsed a *syntactic* model of theories and a *covering-law* model of explanation. Roughly, the syntactic model of theories claimed that theories were sets of law statements, and the covering-law model of explanation claimed that explanation was deduction from law statements. According to Nagel's model of reduction, to say that TA was reducible to TB was to say that the law statements of TA were deducible from the law statements of TB in conjunction with statements describing various boundary conditions and **bridge principles** if necessary. Bridge principles are empirically supported premises that connect the vocabularies of theories that do not share the same stock of predicates and terms. On the Nagel model of reduction, bridge principles are necessary for intertheoretic reduction if the reduced theory's vocabulary has predicates and terms that the vocabulary of the reducing theory lacks. Suppose, for instance, that LA is a law statement of TA that is slated for deduction from LB, a law statement of TB:

LA   For any x, if x is A_1, then x is A_2.
LB   For any x, if x is B_1, then x is B_2.

Since the vocabulary of TB does not include the predicates A_1 or A_2, additional premises such as the following are required for the deduction:

ID_1 $A_1 = B_1$
ID_2 $A_2 = B_2$

Given ID_1 and ID_2, LA can be derived from LB by the substitution of equivalent expressions.

The reduction of thermodynamics to statistical mechanics is often cited as an example of reduction via bridge principles. The term 'heat', which occurs in the law statements of thermodynamics, is not included in the vocabulary of statistical mechanics. As a result, the deduction of thermodynamic law statements from mechanical ones requires the use of additional premises connecting the theories' respective vocabularies. An example might be the following:

Heat = mean molecular kinetic energy.

As mentioned earlier, identity statements of this sort are called 'theoretical identifications'. In the Nagel model of reduction, theoretical identifications operate as bridge principles linking the vocabularies of reduced theories with vocabularies of reducing theories. Theoretical identifications thus underwrite the possibility of intertheoretic reductions.

The Nagel model of reduction has been extensively criticized, and alternative models of reduction have been based on different assumptions about the nature of theories and explanation. But the idea that reduction involves the inclusion of one domain in another implies that the entities postulated by the reduced theory are identical to entities postulated by the reducing theory. In claiming to have reduced Kepler's laws to Newton's, for instance, the assumption is that planets *are* massive bodies, not merely objects whose behaviors are correlated with the behaviors of massive bodies.

To illustrate the necessity of identity for reduction, imagine that domains A and B comprise completely distinct entities whose behaviors are nevertheless correlated with each other. It turns out, for instance, that the principles governing A-entities and those governing B-entities mirror each other in the following sense: for every A-law there is a corresponding B-law and vice versa, and instances of A-properties are correlated one–one with instances of B-properties. Because A-principles and A-properties mirror B-principles and B-properties, biconditional sentences such as the following end up being true:

BC$_1$ Necessarily, for any x, x is A_1 if and only if x is B_1.
BC$_2$ Necessarily, for any x, x is A_2 if and only if x is B_2.

Such biconditionals could underwrite the deduction of law statements such as LA from law statements such as LB: if BC$_1$ and BC$_2$ are both true, for instance, it is possible to derive LA from LB. What these biconditionals could *not* underwrite, however, is the claim that TA is reducible to TB. The reason is that A and B are completely distinct domains which merely *happen* to be correlated. This is not a case in which one domain is discovered to be part of another, more inclusive domain, and hence it is not a case in which the laws of one domain can be explained by appeal to the laws of another. Without identity statements such as ID$_1$ and ID$_2$, there is no inclusion of one domain in another, and without that sort of inclusion, there is no explanation of the reduced theory's laws in terms of the reducing theory's laws.

Several philosophers have argued that the bridge principles needed for reduction must be identity statements such as ID$_1$ and ID$_2$. The philosopher of science Lawrence Sklar, for instance, argued for this using the example of the Wiedemann-Franz law. The Wiedemann-Franz law expresses a correlation between thermal conductivity and electrical conductivity in metals. It allows for the deduction of law statements about the latter from law statements about the former. This deducibility, however, has never been understood to warrant the claim that the theory of electrical conductivity is reducible to the theory of heat conductivity, or vice versa. Rather, it points in the direction of a different reduction, the reduction of the macroscopic theory of matter to the microscopic theory of matter: the electrical conductivity of metals and the thermal conductivity of metals are both explainable by appeal to the properties of atoms and subatomic particles.

When applied to psychological discourse, the foregoing account of reduction implies that psychophysical reduction requires mental–physical property identities. The reduction of psychological discourse to some branch of natural science would require that mental entities be identified with entities postulated by the relevant branch of natural science. It could not involve two distinct yet coordinate domains. This is clear if we imagine a case involving psychophysical parallelism (Section 3.6).

Imagine two completely distinct ontological domains, one comprising bodies, the other nonphysical Cartesian egos. Imagine, moreover, that these domains happen to mirror each other in the sense just described: the laws governing the behavior of bodies parallel the laws governing the behavior of the Cartesian egos, and the states of the Cartesian egos are distinct from but nevertheless correlated one–one with the states of bodies. In that case, it would be possible to make deductions about the behavior of Cartesian egos on the basis of the behavior of bodies. This deducibility, however, would not warrant the claim that the behavior of Cartesian egos was reducible to the behavior of bodies. Perhaps the behavior of bodies would provide a helpful model or heuristic for understanding or predicting the behavior of Cartesian egos, but it would not provide a reducing theory which explained why the laws governing Cartesian egos obtained. The same point would follow if some type of neutral monism were true – if, say, mental and physical phenomena were correlated with each other, but were both reducible to some third conceptual framework which was neither mental nor physical but neutral. Mere correlations between instances of mental properties and instances of physical properties – even correlations that are lawlike – are not sufficient to underwrite psychophysical reduction. Psychophysical reduction requires that mental states be identical to physical states.

5.8   The Multilevel Worldview

The idea that psychological discourse is reducible to physical theory has often been combined with a multilayered or **multilevel worldview**. A multilevel worldview takes the world to consist of levels or layers that correspond to different scientific disciplines. These disciplines differ from each other in many respects: each, for instance, has its own distinctive research methods and protocols, its own distinctive vocabulary of predicates and terms, and its own distinctive principles for describing the behavior of the entities in its domain. The vocabulary biology uses to describe and explain metabolic processes is different from the vocabulary

physics uses to describe and explain the behavior of fundamental physical particles, and the vocabulary economics uses to describe and explain the behavior of
free markets is different from the vocabulary psychology uses to describe and
explain the behavior of individual human organisms.

A multilevel worldview takes these vocabularies to correspond to different
domains in reality which are related hierarchically in the manner depicted in
Figure 5.3. What determines the hierarchy is principally the relation of composition: the entities postulated by lower-level frameworks compose the entities postulated by higher-level ones. Fundamental physical entities such as quarks,
electrons, and gluons, for instance, compose protons and neutrons; protons and
neutrons compose atoms; atoms compose molecules; molecules compose tissues;

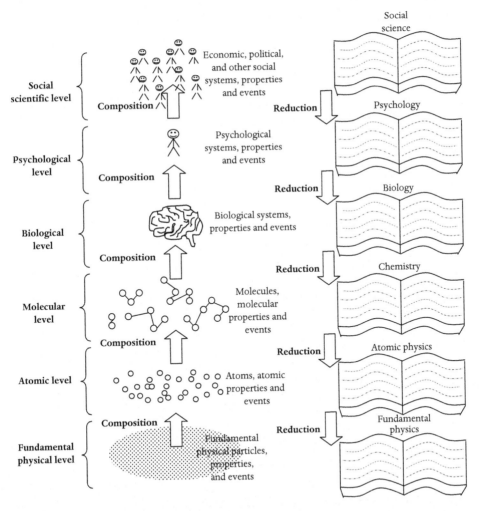

Figure 5.3   The reductivist multilevel worldview

tissues compose organs; organs compose organisms; and organisms compose economic, political, and other social systems.

In addition, exponents of multilevel worldviews typically take composition relations among entities to mirror relations among scientific theories. Reductive physicalists, for instance, take these relations to be reductive: higher-level theories, they say, are reducible to lower-level ones in the sense described earlier. The principles of, say, social science, are reducible to those of psychology: political, economic, and other social scientific regularities are to be explained by appeal to psychological regularities. Psychological discourse is thus capable in principle of taking over all the descriptive and explanatory roles played by the social sciences. Similarly, the principles of psychology are reducible to those of biology. We can explain why a psychological principle is true by the appeal to the principles of biology. We can explain, for instance, why people will typically perform action A when they want x, and believe that performing A will secure x by appeal to neural or other biological principles. Biological principles can be explained in turn by appeal to chemical principles, and those in turn by appeal to the principles governing atomic or subatomic interactions.

On the reductivist view, then, each higher-level theoretical framework is taken to be reducible in principle to a lower-level one. Moreover, this relationship of reducibility is taken to be transitive: if TA is reducible to TB, and TB is reducible to TC, then TA is also reducible to TC. Consequently, every conceptual framework is taken to be reducible ultimately to fundamental physics. Fundamental physics is thus capable of taking over the descriptive and explanatory roles played by every scientific framework there is. On the reductivist view, this is what it means for everything to be describable and explainable by appeal to physics. The categories of conceptual frameworks other than physics – the special sciences, as they are customarily called – line up neatly with the categories of the most general science, fundamental physics. There is thus one set of fundamental physical individuals, one set of fundamental physical properties, one set of fundamental physical principles governing them, and one set of categories in terms of which everything can be described and explained – the categories of fundamental physics. The categories of every special science correspond to these categories, and the correspondence relations underwrite theoretical identifications which in turn enable fundamental physics to take over the descriptive and explanatory roles of every branch of science. On the reductivists' view, then, the various sciences all describe a single fundamentally physical world – the world as described by fundamental physics.

Further Reading

Logical behaviorism was defended by Carl Hempel (1980) and also Rudolf Carnap (1959). Gilbert Ryle (1949) and Ludwig Wittgenstein (2001) are often characterized as behaviorists, but this is a contested claim, and there are good reasons to think they merely endorsed a pattern expression theory of psychological language (Section 11.7). A. J. Ayer (1952) provides an accessible definition and defense of the verifiability theory of meaning. Helpful but more technical discussions of it include Hempel (1950) and Quine (1964) . The collapse of logical positivism was also due to work in the history of science by philosophers such as Thomas Kuhn (1996). They argued that the positivist conception of scientific progress was flawed: actual science did not conform to the positivist idea of science.

Both Peter Geach (1967: Chapter 1) and Roderick Chisholm (1957: Chapter 11) argued against behaviorism by appeal to the holism of psychological discourse. For more on the history of psychology in the twentieth century see Flanagan (1991) and Gardner (1985).

The theory model of psychological discourse was suggested independently by several authors including Hilary Putnam (1975a), Wilfrid Sellars (1956), Herbert Feigl (1958), and Jerry Fodor (1968). The principal defenders of the theory model, however, have been eliminative physicalists (Section 7.1). Paul Churchland (1981) is an example. Importantly, the theory model of psychological discourse is not the same as what psychologists and cognitive scientists call 'theory of mind'. The latter term refers to the ability to understand other people's beliefs, desires, and other mental states. The theory model of psychological discourse and scientific research on theory of mind have a complex history together, and many psychologists who work on theory of mind implicitly endorse the theory model of psychological discourse. But the theory model and theory of mind are not the same thing. The ability to understand each other's mental states is compatible with rejecting the theory model.

Critics of the theory model of psychological discourse include Kathleen V. Wilkes (1991), Robert A. Sharpe (1987), John Haldane (1988), and M. R. Bennett and P. M. S. Hacker (2003: Section 13.2). The papers by Wilkes, Sharpe, and Haldane, along with several others discussing the pros and cons of the theory model can be found in Christiansen and Turner (1993). An alternative account of psychological language is endorsed by exponents of a hylomorphic theory of mind (Section 11.7).

The identity theory was suggested by the psychologist U. T. Place (1956), but its clearest initial formulation was given by J. J. C. Smart (1959). Herbert Feigl (1958), a former positivist, also articulated an identity theory. Around the same time, Wilfrid Sellars (1956; 1963) insightfully anticipated many of the issues, arguments, and counterarguments that would occupy philosophers of mind for the next several decades.

David Lewis (1966; 1972) and David Armstrong (1981; 1993) defended versions of the identity theory that were very similar to each other. David Chalmers (1996: Chapter 3) argues against the causal analysis of consciousness by appeal to inverted spectra and absent qualia. See the discussion of epiphenomenalism in Chapter 8 for more on this point. The idea of inverted qualia was first suggested by the seventeenth-century philosopher John Locke (1959[1690]: Book II, Chapter 32, Section 15).

The seminal formulation of the reductivist multilevel worldview was given by Oppenheim and Putnam (1958). Ernest Nagel's seminal account of intertheoretic reduction appears in Chapter 11 of his *The Structure of Science* (1979). The syntactic model of theories and the covering-law model of explanation on which Nagel's account is based were articulated by Carl Hempel (1965). Important critical discussions of Nagel's account of reduction include Lawrence Sklar (1967), Kenneth Schaffner (1967), Robert Causey (1977: Chapter 4), Clifford Hooker (1981), and Patricia Churchland (1986: Chapter 7). More recently, John Bickle (1998; 2003) has defended reductivism. These discussions are rather technical. Among them Churchland's is probably the most accessible.

Importantly (and confusingly), many biologists and some philosophers have used the term 'reduction' to refer to a method of scientific investigation – the method of functional analysis (Section 10.3). Examples of philosophers who sometimes use the term 'reduction' in this way include William Bechtel (2007). This notion of reduction is completely different from the notion of reduction discussed in this chapter. It is bound up with a notion of composition and mechanistic explanation (Section 10.7) – topics we discuss in detail in Chapter 10 on hylomorphism.

Chapter 6

Nonreductive Physicalism

Overview

The reductivist worldview dominated philosophy of mind for many years, but arguments against the identity theory changed that. Foremost among them was the multiple-realizability argument. Together with functionalism, a theory of mind based on a computational model of psychological discourse, the multiple-realizability argument inspired a new type of mind–body theory: nonreductive physicalism. Nonreductive physicalism soon became the new orthodoxy in philosophy of mind, and although it has been subjected to criticism, it remains the most popular type of physicalism today.

Like physicalism of any sort, nonreductive physicalism claims that everything can be exhaustively described and explained by physics. It also claims, however, that there are many different ways of describing physical reality. The categories of special sciences such as psychology, economics, and biology, are more abstract than those of fundamental physics, and because they are more abstract, they are capable of satisfying descriptive and explanatory interests that fundamental physics cannot. As a result, fundamental physics cannot take over the descriptive and explanatory roles the special sciences play. The special sciences are not reducible to physics, therefore, not because there are nonphysical individuals, properties, or events, but because we have special descriptive and explanatory interests that cannot be satisfied using the conceptual resources of physics.

The burden for nonreductive physicalists is to explain how the categories of the special sciences manage to describe reality: If everything is described and explained by physics, and the categories of the special sciences are different from the categories of physics, how do those categories manage to correspond to reality? For the most part, nonreductivists answer this question in one of two

Philosophy of Mind: A Comprehensive Introduction, First Edition. William Jaworski.
© 2011 William Jaworski. Published 2011 by Blackwell Publishing Ltd.

ways. Realization physicalists claim that mental phenomena are realized by physical phenomena, and supervenience physicalists claim that mental phenomena supervene on physical phenomena.

Realization physicalism is based on functionalism, a theory that takes psychological discourse to be a species of abstract, computational discourse. Because it is based on functionalism, realization physicalism inherits the worries associated with functionalism. The liberalism objection, for instance, claims that functionalism leads us to attribute mental states to systems that do not have them. If mental states are abstract states as functionalists claim, then almost anything can have mental states, but that seems false: surely mental states are not distributed as widely as functionalism allows. In response to the liberalism objection, some functionalists have adopted a teleological understanding of functions which places limits on the kinds of systems that are capable of realizing psychological descriptions. In addition, the Chinese room argument suggests that functionalism cannot adequately accommodate a public conception of mental phenomena, and qualia-based arguments suggest it cannot adequately accommodate a private conception of mental phenomena either. Moreover, the embodied mind objection, which derives from work in cognitive science, argues that psychological discourse is not abstract in the way functionalists claim. Other objections to nonreductive physicalism do not target functionalism, but the conjunction of functionalism with physicalism. Kim's trilemma, for instance, argues that realization physicalism is an unstable theory that ends up collapsing either into a form of reductivism, a form of eliminativism, or a form of dualism. In addition, Kim's exclusion argument claims that nonreductive physicalists must deny the causal efficacy of mental properties the way epiphenomenalists do.

Supervenience physicalism confronts other problems. The formulation problem is the problem of specifying the right kind of supervenience relation. There are many different kinds of supervenience relations, and it is not clear which of them if any provides an adequate basis for a physicalist theory that is nonreductive. The asymmetry problem, on the other hand, is based on the observation that supervenience is not an asymmetrical relation: the supervenience of special-scientific properties on physical properties is compatible with the supervenience of physical properties on special-scientific ones. Physicalists nevertheless need special-scientific properties to be asymmetrically dependent on physical properties. Consequently, it seems supervenience is not sufficient to give physicalists what they need. The explanation problem arrives at a similar conclusion. Supervenience is compatible with a broad range of very different theories: physicalism, dual-attribute theory, neutral monism, hylomorphism. This suggests that supervenience is not by itself sufficient to characterize a physicalist theory.

When these arguments are combined with criticisms of the multiple-realizability argument, they pose a serious challenge to the nonreductivist consensus in philosophy of mind.

6.1   The Multiple-Realizability Argument

The multiple-realizability argument posed a serious challenge to the identity theory and played a pivotal role in bringing about the nonreductivist consensus that has dominated philosophy of mind since the 1970s. According to the argument, mental states are multiply realizable and because they are multiply realizable they cannot be identical to physical states. Consider an example.

Imagine we discover that Alexander's pains are intimately correlated in a way we label 'realization' with a certain type of physical occurrence, brain state B. We also discover that Madeleine's pains are correlated in the same way with a different type of physical occurrence – not brain state B but brain state C. Since brain state B does not in any way involve brain state C, and brain state C does not in any way involve brain state B, we conclude that pain can occur without brain state B, and that it can also occur without brain state C. We conclude, in other words, that neither brain state B nor brain state C is by itself necessary for the occurrence of pain. In that case, however, it seems that pain cannot be identical to either type of physical occurrence. The reason is that property identity requires necessary coextension: if, for instance, having a mass of 1 kg is identical to having a mass of 2.2 pounds, then something can have a mass of 1 kg if and only if it has a mass of 2.2 pounds. Consequently, if pain is identical to brain state B, then something can have pain if and only if it has brain state B, and, likewise, if pain is identical to brain state C, then something can have pain if and only if it has brain state C. But Madeleine experiences pain without brain state B, and Alexander experiences pain without brain state C. Therefore, pain is not correlated with a single type of physical state, and that means pain cannot be identical to a single type of physical state. Moreover, because the identity of pain with a given type of physical state P would imply that *necessarily* every instance of pain was an instance of P, we need not actually discover the correlation of pain with different types of physical states; the bare *possibility* of such correlations is sufficient for the argument to succeed: if the case of Alexander and Madeleine is even possible, it would follow that pain is not a type of physical state; and, says the argument, it seems that this type of situation is possible not only for pain, but for *all* types of mental states. Hence, the argument concludes, the identity theory must be false. In addition, because psychophysical reductivism requires psychophysical identities, it follows that psychophysical reductivism must be false as well.

The foregoing line of reasoning has been extremely influential since the late 1960s when it was originally formulated. It is largely responsible for what has been and continues to be a widespread, decades-long consensus that the identity theory and psychophysical reductivism are false. The multiple-realizability argument relies on the following premises:

1   Mental states are multiply realizable.
2   If mental states are multiply realizable, then they are not identical to physical states.
3   If mental states are not identical to physical states, then psychological discourse is not reducible to physical theory.

Among these claims, the most controversial has been Premise (1), the multiple-realizability thesis (MRT). Exponents of the argument have supported it both *a priori* by appeal to conceivability-possibility principles, and *a posteriori* by appeal to findings in biology, neuroscience, and artificial intelligence research.

Conceivability arguments for the MRT claim that conceivability is a reliable guide to possibility. If that is the case, and it is conceivable that instances of a given type of mental state might be correlated with instances of different types of physical states, then it is possible that this might be the case. And, say exponents of the argument, psychophysical correlations of this sort are surely conceivable. Science fiction writers routinely conceive of scenarios in which robots and extraterrestrials with physiological features very different from ours are capable of experiencing pain, belief, desire, and other mental states without the benefit of cerebral hemispheres or any of the other physical components that are correlated with mental states in humans. If these scenarios are conceivable and conceivability is a reliable guide to possibility, then these scenarios must really be possible.

Conceivability-possibility principles have been a staple in philosophy of mind since at least the time of Descartes. They are nevertheless liable to the restrictions and worries discussed in sections 3.2–3.3. Exponents of empirical arguments for the MRT look to avoid these worries. They argue that various scientific disciplines provide inductive grounds that support the possibility that a given type of mental state might be realized by different types of physical states. Those disciplines include biology, neuroscience, and artificial intelligence research.

The appeal to biology claims that our knowledge of evolution provides good reason to endorse the MRT. Having psychological capacities like ours is selectively advantageous. The ability to experience pain, for instance, increases an organism's chances of survival. If I am in danger of being burned alive, the pain I experience contributes to behavior aimed at removing the threat. Likewise, if I am in danger of being eaten by a large carnivore, my chances of survival are enhanced if I am able to feel fear and respond to the threat appropriately. Similarly, in many circumstances my chances of surviving and successfully reproducing are improved by having more or less accurate beliefs about the environment – knowing or believing that fires and large carnivores are dangerous, for instance. There are, in short, many reasons to think that having mental states like ours is selectively advantageous. In that case, however, there is good reason to think that there are beings elsewhere in the universe that have evolved psychological capacities like ours, and hence are similar to us mentally. On the other hand, there is good reason to think that these beings are dissimilar to us physically. The last 40 years of biological research have shown that life can evolve in a broad range of very different physical environments. Environments once thought incapable of supporting life such as deep sea volcanic vents have been discovered to support rich and diverse ecosystems. It seems very likely, then, that living things will be capable of evolving in a broad range of physical environments very different from those on Earth, and, in that case, it seems unlikely that any mentally endowed creatures evolving in those environments will be physically similar to humans. Our current state of biological knowledge suggests, then, that there are beings in the universe who are like us mentally but who are unlike us physically. Research in biology thus gives us good reason to suppose the MRT is true.

A second kind of empirical argument appeals to neuroscience. Consider the phenomenon of brain plasticity, the ability of different parts of the brain or nervous system to realize different cognitive or motor abilities. If, for instance, cells in the motor cortex that control thumb movement are damaged, cells in the adjacent sections of cortex are able to take over the functions previously performed by the damaged cells. This suggests that different neural components are capable of realizing the same cognitive operation, and, say exponents of the argument, this gives us good reason to suspect it is possible for a mental state to be realized by more than one type of physical state.

A third type of empirical argument appeals to work in artificial intelligence (AI). Some AI researchers are in the business of constructing computer-based models of cognitive functioning. They look to construct computational systems that mimic various forms of human cognition such as linguistic understanding. Successfully constructing such systems would lend further support to the idea that mental states could be realized by different types of physical states since the cognitive capacities of these systems would be realized not just by human brains but by silicon circuitry.

Critics of the MRT point out that these empirical arguments are merely inductive: even if their premises are true, the MRT could still be false. In addition, some critics of the MRT have claimed that the appeal to biology fails. Careful examination of the biological data, they say, does not support the MRT. Other critics target the appeal to neuroscience. The argument does not accurately reflect the types of physical states postulated by neuroscience, they say; when we look at the kinds of states neuroscientists really postulate, we see that these states do not support the idea that a given mental state might be correlated with different types of physical states. Finally, critics argue that the appeal to AI is flawed because AI researchers have not yet succeeded in producing systems with cognitive capacities like a human's. Until more progress has been made, the appeal to AI is no different from a conceptual argument for the MRT: it claims merely that progress in AI is conceivable and hence possible. In addition, arguments such as Searle's Chinese room purport to show that silicon-based minds are impossible (Section 6.8).

The foregoing considerations mark some of the ways critics have responded to arguments for the MRT. In addition, they have argued directly that the MRT is false.

6.2   Reductivist Responses to the Multiple-Realizability Argument

The most popular criticism of the MRT claims that it depends on a dubious assumption, namely, the assumption that our understanding of mental and physical phenomena will not change with time. *Typology-based responses* to the MRT argue that this assumption is false. Although the categories of our current scientific and psychological theories suggest that a given type of mental state can be correlated with many different types of physical states, future scientific investigation will yield different theories with different categories or typologies: the types of mental and physical states they postulate will be different from the types of mental and physical states our current theories postulate. Once we have these new categories in view, say exponents of typology-based responses, we will see that the MRT is false, that mental and physical states correspond to each other one–one just as reductivists have always insisted.

There are three kinds of typology-based responses to the MRT (Figure 6.1). Our current mental and physical typologies suggest a picture like Column A: a type of mental state, M, is correlated with multiple different types of physical states $P_1, P_2, \ldots, P_n$. Exponents of the multiple-realizability argument conclude from this that M is not a physical property, for, if it were, its instances would be correlated one–one with instances of a single type of physical property. Reductivists who postulate *narrow* or *species-specific mental types*, however, break up M into several narrower types of mental states $M_1, M_2, \ldots, M_n$ each of which corresponds to a single type of physical state as in Column B. Suppose, for instance, that we discover human pains are correlated with brain state B, and Martian pains are correlated with a different type of physical state Z. According to exponents of narrow mental types, future scientific investigation will yield a different mental typology that no longer includes simply *pain*, but multiple different types of pains such as *pain-in-humans* and *pain-in-Martians*. Our current term 'pain', they say, does not refer to

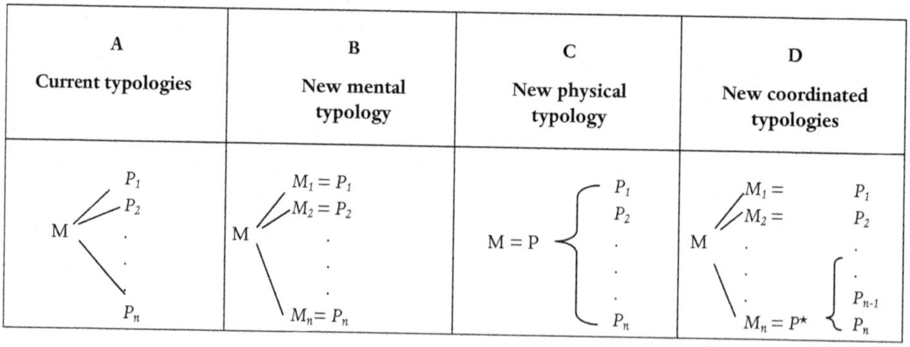

A Current typologies	B New mental typology	C New physical typology	D New coordinated typologies
$M \overset{P_1}{\underset{P_n}{\diagup P_2}}$	$M \overset{M_1=P_1}{\underset{M_n=P_n}{\diagup M_2=P_2}}$	$M=P \left\{ \begin{matrix} P_1 \\ P_2 \\ \vdots \\ P_n \end{matrix} \right.$	$M \overset{M_1=\ \ P_1}{\underset{M_n=P^*}{\diagup M_2=\ \ P_2}} \left\{ \begin{matrix} P_{n-1} \\ P_n \end{matrix} \right.$

Figure 6.1   Typology-based responses to the MRT

a single type of mental state; it is instead a term that refers indiscriminately to many different types of mental states. By analogy, the term 'jade' was originally taken to refer to a single type of mineral; scientific investigation later revealed, however, that what we called jade actually comprised two distinct types of minerals: jadeite and nephrite. Exponents of narrow mental types claim that something similar will happen with our current mental predicates and terms. Our current term 'pain', then, does not refer a single type of mental state found in humans and in Martians; it is instead an imprecise term that refers to many different species-specific types of mental states including pain-in-humans and pain-in-Martians. As a result, they say, the multiple-realizability argument misses the mark: physical states are not correlated one–one with mental states as we currently understand them, but our current understanding will be superseded by a more adequate understanding that does not postulate broad mental states like pain, but narrower, species-specific mental states like pain-in-humans and pain-in-Martians.

Critics of the MRT can also respond by postulating *broad physical types*. They look to bring together different types of physical states under a single overarching physical type, *P*, which corresponds one–one to a single type of mental state *M* as in Column C. Exponents of broad physical types argue that future scientific investigation will yield a different physical typology that no longer distinguishes human brain state B from Martian physical state Z, for instance. We will discover rather that B and Z have something important in common– that they are in fact instances of a broader type of physical state whose instances are correlated one–one with instances of pain. Our current terms 'brain state B' and 'physical state Z' do not in fact refer to different types of physical states; they are instead analogous to the terms 'electricity' and 'magnetism'. These terms were originally taken to refer to different physical phenomena; scientific investigation later revealed, however, that electricity and magnetism belonged to a single overarching type of phenomenon – a discovery still reflected in the name 'electromagnetism'. Exponents of broad physical types claim that something similar will happen with our current physical predicates and terms. 'Brain state B' and 'physical state Z' do not refer to different types of physical states found in humans and in Martians, respectively; rather, human physiology and Martian physiology have important commonalities that we have yet to discover. Once we do discover those commonalities, we will see that the MRT is false, that pain, for instance, is correlated with a broad type of physical state, BZ, found in both humans and Martians.

Finally, critics of the MRT can combine the two aforementioned strategies into a single *coordinated typology strategy*; they can argue that mental and physical typologies will *both* be altered in ways that yield one–one mental–physical correlations as in Column D. Future scientific investigation will result in a revision of both our mental typology and our physical typology. Mental and physical typologies are to some extent interdependent, and as a result they will eventually converge in a way that yields one–one correlations between mental types and physical types.

Because our mental and physical typologies are likely to change in one of these ways, say critics, the multiple-realizability argument does not succeed in showing that mental states are not identical to physical states.

6.3   Functionalism

Despite the aforementioned criticisms, the multiple-realizability argument has been enormously influential. Philosophers have responded to it in several ways. As we have seen, some have responded by rejecting the argument. Others have responded by rejecting physicalism. The most popular response, however, has been to reject neither the argument nor physicalism, but instead the assumption that physicalism must be committed to reductivism. Philosophers who respond this way endorse a nonreductivist understanding of physicalism. That understanding has been inspired largely by **functionalism**, a theory originally formulated by Hilary Putnam as an alternative to the identity theory.

Functionalism claims that psychological states are postulates of abstract descriptions that use categories like those used in computer science. Functionalists agree with identity theorists that psychological discourse constitutes a theory, but they disagree about what kind of theory it is. Psychological discourse is not like a natural scientific theory, functionalists claim, but an *abstract* one. The mental states it postulates are analogous to the angles, lines, and figures postulated by Euclidean geometry. We arrive at Euclidean principles by abstraction, a process in which we focus on a narrow range of properties and then construct idealized descriptions of them. We focus, for instance, on the spatial properties of the objects around us; we ignore their physical details – what they are made of, what colors they have, how much they weigh – and focus simply on their dimensions. We then idealize our descriptions of them: slightly crooked lines we describe as straight, deviant curves we describe as normal, and so on. According to functionalists, something analogous is true of psychological discourse. It provides abstract descriptions of real-world systems, descriptions that ignore the physical details of those systems, the sort described by the natural sciences, and focus simply on a narrow profile of their features. Originally Putnam suggested that those features were analogous to the features postulated by **Turing machines**.

Somewhat confusingly, a Turing machine is not an actual machine like an internal combustion engine or a dishwasher. In fact, it is not a concrete entity at all. A Turing machine is instead an abstract description, one that postulates a set of states that are related to each other and to various inputs and outputs in determinate ways that are stated on what is called its *machine table*. A machine table might say, for instance, that states, $S_1, S_2, \ldots, S_n$, inputs, $I_1, \ldots, I_m$, and outputs $O_1, \ldots, O_p$ are related in the following ways:

If the system is in state S_{13} and receives input I_7, then the system will produce output O_{32}, and enter state S_3.

If the system is in state S_{37} and receives inputs I_5 and I_{23} then the system will produce output O_{15}, and enter states S_{31} and S_{42}.

If the system is in state S_6 and receives input I_{51}, then the system will produce outputs O_{33} and O_{34} and enter state S_{12}.

These statements provide a list of instructions or procedures – a program – that can be carried out or realized by a concrete system. According to Putnam's original theory, which has sometimes been called *machine functionalism* or *computational functionalism* or the **computational theory of mind**, psychological descriptions are like Turing machine descriptions. They are abstract descriptions that postulate inputs, outputs, and internal states that correlate the two. In particular, the beliefs, desires, and other mental states they postulate are internal states that correlate sensory inputs with behavioral outputs.

The name 'Turing machine' derives from the British mathematician Alan Turing (1912–1954) who is generally considered the father of computer science and who pioneered the field of artificial intelligence. Turing suggested a procedure for testing whether an artificially constructed system could qualify as an intelligent being – the **Turing test** (Figure 6.2). Many philosophers and scientists have followed Turing's lead and taken the test to define what it means to be an intelligent being. In the Turing test, a human judge carries on a conversation with two interlocutors. One interlocutor is human, the other an artificially constructed machine. Because the conversation is conducted using a text-only apparatus such as a teletype or internet chat room, the judge is initially unable to tell which interlocutor is a human and which is a machine. If by the end of the conversation the judge still cannot tell which is human and which machine, then the machine will have passed the test: it will qualify as an intelligent being.

The tacit assumption behind the Turing test is that intelligence is a matter of correlating inputs to a system with outputs from it in appropriate ways – the ways that distinguish human verbal interaction, for instance, from the behavior of a thermostat, or a calculator, or a personal computer. To qualify as an intelligent being, in other words, it would be sufficient for a system to be able to correlate inputs to it with outputs from it in the way humans correlate verbal inputs and outputs in conversation. The assumption that having a mind is a matter of correlating inputs with outputs in the right way is the basis of functionalism, and the reason why there has been a lasting association between functionalism and cognitive science – artificial intelligence research especially. The only significant difference between Turing machine descriptions and psychological descriptions, Putnam suggested, was that psychological inputs, outputs, and internal states were related to each other probabilistically not deterministically. If, for instance, Eleanor

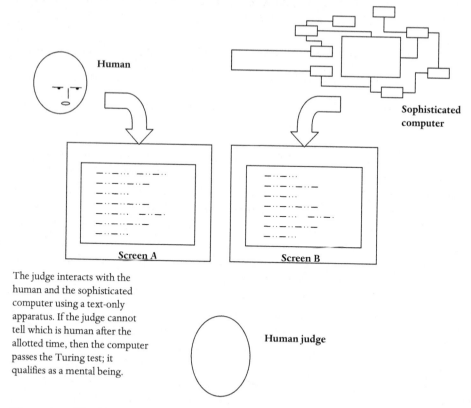

Human

Sophisticated computer

Screen A

Screen B

The judge interacts with the human and the sophisticated computer using a text-only apparatus. If the judge cannot tell which is human after the allotted time, then the computer passes the Turing test; it qualifies as a mental being.

Human judge

Figure 6.2   The Turing test

believes there are exactly eight planets in our solar system, and she receives the auditory input, "Do you believe there are exactly eight planets in our solar system," then she will produce the verbal output, "Yes," not with a deterministic probability of 1, but with a probability between 1 and 0. According to functionalism, then, beliefs, desires, pains, and other mental states are postulates of a theory whose relations to each other and to sensory inputs and behavioral outputs are reflected in generalizations such as 'If someone, S, wants x, and S believes that doing A is the best means of securing x, then probably S will do A'.

Functionalists need not endorse a Turing machine model of psychological discourse; they could instead understand psychological discourse by appeal to models in cognitive psychology or some other discipline. In general, however, functionalists make two claims. First, psychological discourse is abstract discourse that postulates an inventory of objects, properties, states or other entities that are related to each other in ways expressed by the theory's principles. Second, the behavior of concrete systems corresponds to the objects, properties, or states that psychological discourse postulates.

We have so far been using terms such as 'realize' and 'multiple realizability' to refer in a generic way to the relation between mental states and physical states. But, properly speaking, the notion of realization was introduced in connection with functionalism. It concerns this correspondence between abstract descriptions and concrete systems. Let T be a theory describing various relations among its postulates, S_1, S_2, ... , S_n. The relations among the concrete states of a certain concrete system might match the relations among S_1, S_2, ... , S_n. If T says that state S_1 results in state S_2 with a probability of .73 given input I_{15}, it might turn out, for instance, Alexander's brain state B_5 results in brain state B_{67} with a probability of .73 given neural stimulus B_4. It might turn out, in other words, that states B_5, B_{67}, and B_4 in Alexander's brain provide a model of the relations among S_1, S_2, and S_{15} in T (Figure 6.3). If this were true for all of Alexander's brain states, functionalists would say that T described a certain type of *functional organization*, an organization that was *realized* by Alexander's brain, and they would call Alexander's brain a *realization* of T. The states of Alexander's brain are related to each other in ways that match the ways in which S_1, S_2, ... , S_n are related according to T. In fact, concrete systems in general might be said to realize the states

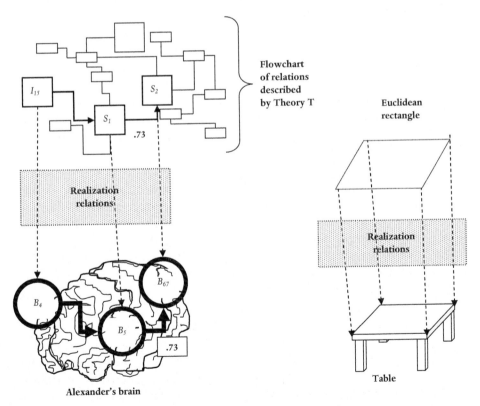

Figure 6.3   Realization relations

postulated by abstract descriptions. The wooden table realizes a Euclidean rectangle: each point on the perimeter of the table can be taken to correspond to a point on the Euclidean rectangle. Similarly, the movements of electrons through the silicon circuitry of a pocket calculator realize an algorithm: they correspond to steps in the algorithm.

6.4   Higher-Order Properties

Realization, then, is a relation between abstract descriptions and concrete systems whose states match or correspond to the states postulated by those descriptions. Philosophers of mind have offered several different accounts of this relation. Perhaps the most influential was suggested by Hilary Putnam. Realization, he said, can be understood as a relation between higher-order and lower-order properties.

Calling a property higher-*order* is not the same as calling it higher-*level*. Higher-order properties are logical constructions out of other properties; their definitions involve the use of logical operators such as conjunction, disjunction, negation, and quantification. Consider an example. Imagine that P_1 and P_2 are properties, and that it would be convenient to have a label for things with either P_1 or P_2. In that case, we might define a new property, Q: Something has Q, we say, if and only if it has either P_1 or P_2. The property Q is thus a logical construction. It is constructed out of the properties P_1 and P_2 using the logical operation of disjunction. Similarly, suppose that juniors are university students in their third year and seniors are university students in their fourth year, and that it would be convenient to have a single term to refer to students who are either juniors or seniors. In that case, we might define an *upperclass student* as a student who is either a junior or a senior. The term 'upperclass student' would then be a logical construction out of the properties of being a junior and being a senior.

Higher-order properties are logical constructions as well; they involve the operation of quantification. A higher-order property is a property whose definition quantifies over other properties. Imagine, for instance, that $P_1, P_2, \ldots, P_n$, are properties, and that we define a new property, R, using the quantifier 'some': the property R, we say, is the property of having *some* P-property or other. Something has R, in other words, if and only if it has P_1, or P_2, or P_3, or $\ldots$, or P_n. The definition of R thus quantifies over P-properties. In that case, R is a higher-order property; its definition quantifies over P-properties.

The order a property belongs to depends on the properties its definition quantifies over. The definitions of first-order properties do not quantify over any properties; the definitions of second-order properties quantify over first-order properties; the definitions of third-order properties quantify over second-order properties, the definitions of fourth-order properties quantify over third-order ones, and so on. So if $P_1, P_2, \ldots, P_n$ are first-order properties, R is a second-order property. A third-order property would be one whose definition quantified over second-order properties. Imagine, for instance, that R and R' are both second-order properties, and we define $R*$ as the property of having some second-order property, R or R'. In that case, $R*$ would be a third-order property.

Importantly, the definitions of higher-order properties are usually not as simple as these examples suggest since those definitions usually specify a condition on the lower-order properties they quantify over. Imagine, for instance, that we define R not just as the property of having some P-property, but as the property of having some P-property *that is typically caused by loud noises*. The definition of R would then place a condition on the P-properties that qualify something as R. Likewise, we might define being a doorstop as being something that stops a door from closing, where the quantifier 'something' ranges over various pieces of wood, metal, and rubber. On this definition, a piece of wood, metal, or rubber qualifies as a doorstop exactly if it satisfies the following condition: it stops a door from closing.

Putnam suggested that mental properties were higher-order properties of this condition-specifying sort: being in a mental state amounted to having some set of first-order internal states that were related to each other in ways that satisfied a functional description. Being in pain, for instance, might be defined as being in some concrete first-order state that correlates pinpricks, burns, and abrasions, with winces and groans, and internal states such as irritation or chagrin. To say that Alexander's brain is currently realizing a state of pain, then, is to say that his brain is currently in a concrete first-order state that is related to other first-order states in the way that satisfies the condition associated with pain.

If mental properties are higher-order properties that specify conditions that lower-order properties must satisfy, then two questions naturally arise. First, what determines what lower-order properties there are? Second, what determines what conditions those lower-order properties must satisfy to qualify as mental properties? Most functionalists take the first question to be an empirical one. It is the job of science, they say, to determine what lower-order properties there are. Some functionalists also take the second question to be an empirical one: science, they say, is ultimately responsible for telling us what conditions define mental states. Other functionalists disagree. They claim that those conditions are implicit in our ordinary prescientific descriptions of human behavior. We do not need science to tell us that pain is typically correlated with pinpricks, burns, and abrasions, they say; this is something we know in advance of any scientific investigation simply by being competent speakers of English.

6.5 Functionalism versus the Identity Theory

Like many terms in philosophy of mind, 'functionalism' has been used in several different ways. It has been used to refer to the theory just described, but it has also been used to refer to the type of identity theory endorsed by David Lewis and David Armstrong (Sections 5.4 and 5.6). These different uses of the term have often been a source of confusion, and for that reason it is important to take a few moments to clarify things.

Functionalism and the Lewis-Armstrong way of articulating the identity theory are similar in the following respect: both claim that mental states can be defined in terms of input–output correlations. In the case of the identity theory, these correlations are taken to be causal: mental states are defined by their typical causes and effects. Functionalism, by contrast, does not specify the nature of the correlations. Causation is an ontological category, and functionalism's official account of mental states and their realizers is ontologically neutral. It characterizes the correlations among a system's inputs, outputs, and internal states in purely abstract, probabilistic terms. It does not specify the nature of those correlations – whether they are causal correlations, for instance, or correlations of some other sort. Perhaps Alexander's brain state B_5 *causes* brain state B_{67} with a probability of .73 given neural stimulus B_4, but perhaps the relation between B_5, B_{67}, and B_4 is not a causal relation at all. Functionalism is compatible with this possibility, with the possibility of noncausal input–output correlations of the sort that, say, parallelists would endorse.

Functionalism's ontological neutrality extends to the nature of mental states, inputs, and outputs as well. Functionalism says that the mental states of a system are internal states that correlate inputs to it with outputs from it in ways that correspond to a functional description of that system – in particular, the kind of functional description that distinguishes human behavior from, say, the behavior of thermostats and pocket calculators. But functionalism does not specify further what the natures of those internal correlational states are, or what kinds of concrete states must realize them. Functional descriptions could be realized by physical states such as those of a human brain or a Martian gamma organ, but they could also be realized by nonphysical states such as those of a Cartesian ego. Unlike the identity theory, then, functionalism is not committed to physicalism. It is *compatible* with physicalism, and in fact most functionalists are also physicalists, but functionalism does not *imply* physicalism. A functionalist could be a substance dualist, a dual-attribute theorist, or even an idealist.

Functionalism's ontological neutrality is often expressed in a slogan: *Matter doesn't matter!* According to functionalists, when it comes to a system having mental states, all that matters is that the system correlates inputs with outputs in the right sorts of ways; it does not matter what does the correlating (Figure 6.4). As a result, functionalism is compatible with the MRT. In you and me, sensory inputs might be correlated with motor outputs through the activity of a human brain, but in a Martian, a sophisticated robotic system, or a Cartesian ego, inputs might be correlated with outputs through the activity of something else – a Martian gamma organ, complex silicon circuitry, or nonphysical ectoplasm. Each of these systems might correlate inputs with outputs in accordance with the same

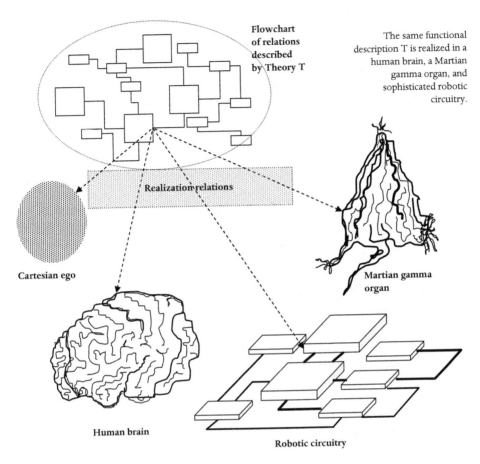

Figure 6.4   Functionalism and the MRT

functional description, and because of that, each would qualify as a mental being. These systems would differ from each other in their ontological makeup, but that difference would have no bearing on their status as mental beings, for again, according to functionalism matter doesn't matter. When it comes to having mental states, it does not matter what kind of matter a system is made of, or even whether it is made of matter at all; all that matters is that the system correlates inputs with outputs in the right sorts of ways.

This difference between the ontological commitments of functionalism and the ontological commitments of the identity theory is also reflected in those theories' accounts of psychological language. Functionalism takes mental states to be *abstract* states, ones postulated by abstract descriptions. The Lewis-Armstrong identity theory takes mental states to be *concrete* physical states that have been described using an abstract vocabulary. To help illustrate the difference consider a very rough analogy with a Platonic versus an Aristotelian understanding of geometrical objects. The Platonist claims that a geometrical term such as 'rectangle' refers to an abstract object postulated by Euclidean geometry. The Aristotelian, by contrast, claims that 'rectangle' is a way of referring to concrete objects such as this table in terms of their dimensions. There is a roughly analogous sense in which the functionalist claims that 'pain' expresses a type of abstract state whereas the Lewis-Armstrong identity theorist claims that 'pain' expresses a concrete physical state such as brain state B. According to the identity theorist, 'pain' refers to a physical state by appeal to a narrow profile of that state's properties such as its typical causes and effects. What a psychological language provides, then, is not an inventory of abstract states, but an apparatus for referring to concrete physical ones.

Because identity theorists and functionalists have different understandings of what mental states are, they also have different understandings of how mental states are related to physical states. According to identity theorists, the relation is identity: mental states *are* physical states. According to functionalists, the relation is not identity but realization: mental states are realized by physical states; they are not identical to them. Because of this difference identity theory and functionalism have different implications when it comes to psychophysical reduction.

6.6   Functionalism and the Nonreductivist Consensus: Realization Physicalism

Functionalism is compatible with the MRT. Having mental states, it says, amounts to having internal states of some sort that correlate inputs with outputs in the right sorts of ways. It does not specify what those states are, and hence it is compatible with those states being realized by the states of many different kinds of things: human brains, Martian gamma organs, even the nonphysical states of Cartesian egos. Functionalism's compatibility with the MRT has had three important implications for philosophy of mind. First, because many philosophers endorse the MRT, functionalism's compatibility with it has often been taken to show that functionalism is superior to the identity theory. Second, because many philosophers take the MRT to rule out psychophysical reduction, many of them have taken functionalism to rule out psychophysical reduction as well. Third, because many of the philosophers who reject psychophysical reduction remain sympathetic to physicalism, many of them have taken functionalism to provide the basis for a new nonreductivist understanding of physicalism.

Because functionalism is ontologically neutral, it is not committed to affirming physicalism nor is it committed to denying it. It does not claim that everything is physical, but it does not deny that everything is physical either. Functionalism is thus compatible with the claim that everything is physical, and that mental states are all realized by physical states in fact even if it is possible for them to be realized by states of other sorts. Functionalism is compatible, in other words, with physicalism being true and also with the MRT being true. By the mid-1970s, functionalism's compatibility with both physicalism and the MRT formed the basis of a growing consensus that some nonreductivist variety of physicalism must be correct.

Nonreductive physicalist theories are committed to the basic physicalist idea that everything can be exhaustively described and explained in the vocabulary of fundamental physics. They claim, however, that there are many different ways of describing the physical universe. Psychological discourse and other special sciences describe the universe using categories that do not correspond to those of fundamental physics. We use these categories because they enable us to satisfy descriptive and explanatory interests that the categories of fundamental physics cannot. The vocabulary of fundamental physics enables us to describe the ontologically basic, first-order properties that exist, but we are not always interested in describing things in this way. We often have descriptive purposes that can only be served by employing a different vocabulary. Imagine, for instance, that fundamental physics distinguishes between systems having P_1 and systems having P_2, and that P_1 and P_2 are the only physical properties that satisfy the condition associated with pain – the only properties associated with the correlation of pinpricks, burns, and abrasions with winces and groans. It thus turns out that every system having pain has either P_1 or P_2. We might nevertheless not be interested in making the distinction between P_1 and P_2 at all. If, for instance, we are interested simply in distinguishing systems that have pain from systems that lack it, it is irrelevant that all systems having pain have either P_1 or P_2. We are not interested in distinguishing the pain-feeling individuals that have P_1 from the pain-feeling individuals that have P_2; we are not interested in the distinction between P_1 and P_2 at all; we are only interested in distinguishing individuals that have pain from individuals that lack it, and, in this regard, the vocabulary of fundamental physics does not help us: 'pain' is not included in its inventory of basic predicates and terms. Dividing the world into individuals that have pain versus individuals that lack it requires a different vocabulary – a special scientific one.

The special sciences thus enable us to describe the world in ways that satisfy special descriptive and explanatory interests. We postulate special scientific objects, properties, and events to satisfy descriptive and explanatory interests we are incapable of satisfying using only the postulates of fundamental physics. To say that fundamental physics cannot satisfy the interests the special sciences do, however, is to say that fundamental physics cannot take over the descriptive and explanatory roles the special sciences play. The special sciences are thus *autonomous* – each is irreducible to the others, and all are irreducible to fundamental physics.

This nonreductivist understanding of the special sciences yields a multilevel worldview (Figure 6.5) different from the reductivist worldview described earlier. Lower-level entities are still taken to compose higher-level ones, and each level of

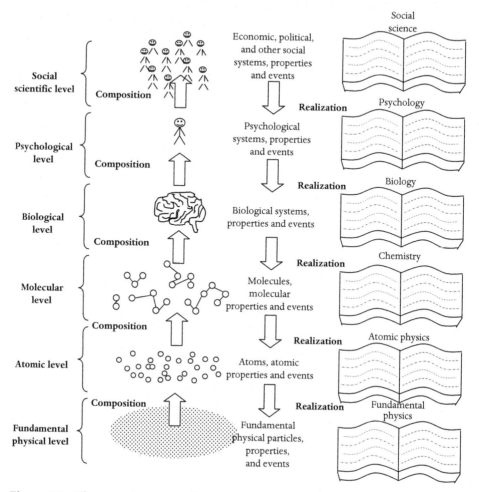

Figure 6.5   The nonreductivist multilevel worldview

composition is still taken to correspond to a distinctive science or conceptual framework with its own unique principles, predicates, and terms for describing and explaining the behavior of the entities at its level. But on the nonreductivist multilevel view, higher-level conceptual frameworks are no longer taken to be reducible to lower-level ones. The principles of social science, for instance, are no longer taken to be reducible to those of psychology. Political, economic, and other social scientific regularities cannot be expressed in lower-level psychological terms, and thus psychological discourse is incapable of taking over the descriptive and explanatory roles the social sciences play. The same is true of psychological principles and their relation to the principles of biology, and biological principles and their relation to the principles of chemistry, and so on. On the nonreductivist view, to say that everything can be described and explained by appeal to physics is to say that the descriptive and explanatory categories of physics correspond to the most basic entities, properties, and laws that exist. This does not mean, however, that the categories of every special science map directly or indirectly onto the categories of physics, or that physics could even in principle take over the descriptive and explanatory roles the special sciences play. The categories of fundamental physics enable us to describe and explain the behavior of the compositionally most basic entities there are, and to formulate the most general laws, but we are not always interested in describing and explaining the most basic entities and formulating the most general laws. Sometimes we have other interests in mind, and according to nonreductive physicalists the categories of the special sciences enable us to satisfy them.

Because they have a different understanding of the special sciences, nonreductivists have to carry a theoretical burden different from that of reductivists. The burden for reductivists is to show that the categories of the special sciences correspond directly to the categories of fundamental physics. The burden for nonreductivists is instead to explain how the special sciences still enable us to describe and explain physical reality if their categories do not correspond to those of physics. If the world is fundamentally physical, and we describe it using categories that correspond directly to those of physics, then it is easy to see how our descriptions manage to correspond to reality. But if the world is fundamentally physical, and we describe it using categories that do not correspond to those of physics, what guarantee is there that our descriptions correspond to reality at all? Nonreductivists have answered this question by placing limits on the extent to which special scientific descriptions can vary relative to those supplied by fundamental physics. Special scientific descriptions may not correspond in a straightforward way to fundamental physical descriptions, say nonreductivists, but they do correspond in *some* way. How exactly? Nonreductivists have tended to answer this question in two ways. **Realization physicalists** claim that special scientific phenomena are realized by lower-level phenomena. **Supervenience physicalists** claim that special scientific phenomena supervene on lower-level phenomena.

Realization physicalism takes the realization relation to hold not just for mathematical postulates, computational procedures, and mental states, but for any form of discourse other than fundamental physics: economics, biology, and even lower-level special sciences such as chemistry. It says that each of these disciplines comprises a vocabulary of abstract predicates and terms that gloss over fine-grained differences marked by the predicates and terms of lower-level disciplines; each postulates higher-order properties that quantify over lower-order properties. Descriptions framed in economic terms, for instance, such as 'inflation', 'interest rates', and 'consumer confidence' can be understood as abstract ways of describing the mental states of individual people – what they desire or think, what they are willing to spend, and so on. Descriptions framed in mental terms can be understood in turn as abstract ways of describing human brain states. Descriptions of these brain states can be taken yet again as abstract ways of describing various chemical reactions, and so on, until we reach the level of fundamental physical description, a level that is no longer abstract. According to realization physicalism, then, psychological discourse, and the special sciences generally, can be taken to describe fundamental physical processes abstractly. The categories of the special sciences abstract from fine-grained differences marked by the categories of fundamental physics.

Because special scientific categories are abstract on this view, the states they postulate are not at odds with physicalism. To appreciate this, suppose that physicalism is true, and that P_1, P_2, ... , P_n are all the physical properties that exist. Suppose, moreover, that we define a higher-order property, pain, as follows:

Something has pain if and only if it has a physical property that satisfies the following condition: it results in the system wincing or groaning with a probability of $.N$ if the system receives pinpricks, burns, or abrasions.

By defining pain in this way, we do not add to the inventory of basic physical properties that exist. We cannot bring about the existence of new fundamental physical properties by sheer fiat – the way we can imagine God, say, bringing about the existence of a new fundamental physical property to add to P_1, P_2, ... , P_n. Defining a higher-order property does not add to the basic physical features of the world; it merely introduces a new way of talking about them: having pain amounts to having some physical property or other that satisfies the aforementioned condition. Saying that something has pain, therefore, is just another way of describing its possession of physical properties – a way that abstracts from the kinds of distinctions made by the vocabulary of fundamental physics.

The distinctions introduced by the predicates and terms of the special sciences are not distinctions written in the book of nature as it comes off the press, but instead notes we jot in the margins – our commentary on a text that is written in the language of physics. When we describe things in special scientific terms, then, we are not describing anything over and above fundamental physical processes; we are describing fundamental physical processes using categories that satisfy interests we cannot satisfy using the categories of fundamental physics. We use the categories of fundamental physics when we are interested in describing the basic first-order properties that exist and the exceptionless laws that govern them. But we are not always interested in describing the world this way. When we have other interests in mind, we use the categories of the special sciences. These categories are different from those of fundamental physics but not completely unrelated to them: higher-level properties are realized by lower-level properties – ultimately the kinds of properties postulated by fundamental physics. Because higher-level properties are all physically realized in this way, the special sciences manage to describe physical reality.

By the 1980s realization physicalism had become the new orthodoxy in philosophy of mind, and it continues to be taken by many as the default position on mind–body issues. It has nevertheless faced some serious criticisms. Because realization physicalism combines physicalism with functionalism, these criticisms have been of at least three sorts: some criticisms have targeted physicalism in general; others have targeted functionalism, and yet others have targeted the combination of the two. Criticisms of physicalism were covered in Chapter 4. Criticisms of functionalism and its combination with physicalism are covered next.

6.7   Troubles with Functionalism: Liberalism and Qualia

Many criticisms of functionalism have been catalogued by the philosopher Ned Block in a paper entitled "Troubles with Functionalism." We will consider two of them: the criticism that functionalism is too liberal with mentality, and the criticism that functionalism cannot countenance qualia.

The multiple-realizability argument suggests that the identity theory is too conservative in attributing mental states to things. If mental states are identical to human brain states, then it is impossible for nonhumans to have mental states. The identity theory thus rules out the possibility of nonhumans such as Martians or sophisticated robotic systems having mental states. Identity theorists are committed to saying, for instance, that a Martian who fell into flames and was displaying all the behavior associated with pain in humans – wincing, screaming, crying, pleading – would nevertheless not be experiencing pain because it would lack a human brain. This strikes many people as absurd. Surely, we could be confident that a Martian in these circumstances would be experiencing pain. The identity theory fails to attribute mental states to systems that have them, critics say.

One apparent advantage of functionalism over the identity theory is that it allows us to attribute mental states to a broader range of systems. Since matter does not matter, according to functionalists, a system like the Martian could have mental states just like a human's. So long as the Martian had internal components of some sort that correlated inputs with outputs in the right sorts of ways, then the Martian would have mental states. Functionalism is thus able to countenance the possibility of nonhumans having mental states. It distributes mental states more liberally than the identity theory, and for that reason it is superior.

According to the liberalism objection, however, this alleged asset is really a liability. If the identity theory is too conservative with mentality, it says, then functionalism is too liberal. The identity theory might fail to attribute mental states to systems that have them, but functionalism goes to the opposite extreme: it attributes mental states to systems that do not have them. Consider an example.

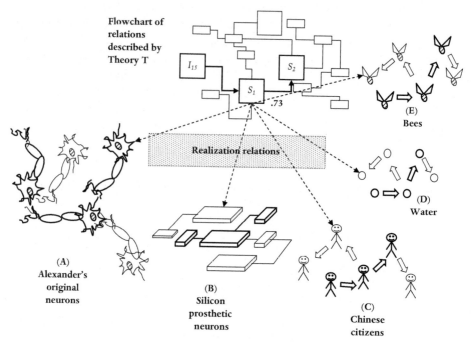

Figure 6.6   The liberalism objection

Let T be a functional description of the relations among states S_1, S_2, ... , S_n – a description realized by the states of Alexander's brain. According to T, for instance, state S_1 results in state S_2 with a probability of .73 given input I_{15}; and states B_5, B_{67}, and B_4 in Alexander's brain provide a model of those relations: Alexander's brain state B_5 results in brain state B_{67} with a probability of .73 given neural stimulus B_4 (Figure 6.6). The same is true of all the states postulated by T; all of them are realized by states of Alexander's brain. Imagine, however, that Alexander has been diagnosed with a degenerative neurological disease that is destroying his brain at a rapid rate. The doctors give him approximately six months to live. Given the grim prognosis, Alexander volunteers for a radical experimental treatment: doctors replace his neurons with silicon prostheses. Each silicon prosthesis operates in exactly the way one of Alexander's neurons does; each interacts with other silicon prostheses and with other bodily tissues in just the way Alexander's neurons do. As a result, Alexander's brain is replaced by a system of sophisticated silicon circuits. After the surgery, it is no longer Alexander's brain states that realize T, but the states of his silicon circuits (Figure 6.6(B)). If functionalism is true, then this situation is possible: it is possible that sophisticated silicon circuitry might realize the same functional description as a human brain. Since Alexander's silicon circuitry realizes T after the surgery in just the way his brain did before, Alexander retains the same mental states after the surgery that he had before it.

Imagine now another scenario. The government of China, very impressed with the results of Alexander's treatment, approaches him with a proposal. In an effort to build solidarity within their country and to secure China's place as a leader in functionalist research, government officials want to replace Alexander's silicon prostheses with something else: people, the citizens of China. Each able-bodied person in China will be outfitted with a radio transmitter and a radio receiver that will enable him or her to interact with other people in China in exactly the way Alexander's silicon prostheses currently interact with each other. In just the way Alexander's silicon circuitry came to realize the functional organization originally realized by his brain, so too the citizens of China will realize the functional organization currently realized by Alexander's silicon circuitry. Of course, because the citizens of China are larger and more spread out than Alexander's circuits, the system will have to be adapted. A radio transmitter will be installed in Alexander's skull. Sensory impulses from his body will be transmitted to a satellite that will relay signals to the citizens of China. The citizens will then interact with each other in just the way Alexander's neurons did originally, and will transmit their outputs to a radio receiver also in Alexander's skull which will in turn trigger the appropriate motor outputs.

If functionalism is true, and the new system consisting of the citizens of China operates exactly the way Alexander's silicon circuitry and Alexander's brain operated (Figure 6.6(C)), then Alexander will not have undergone a mental change at all, for if functionalism is true, matter doesn't matter: it doesn't matter whether Alexander's functional organization is realized by a human brain, by sophisticated silicon circuitry, or by the people of China. All that matters is that the system correlate inputs to it with outputs from it in the way specified by the functional description T. According to the liberalism objection, however, this is absurd. It is absurd to suppose that Alexander's mental states could be realized by a system of this sort. And the same is true of many other systems. Imagine, for instance, that one sunny afternoon the movements of the water molecules in a pond suddenly match relations postulated by T (Figure 6.6(D)): the heat of the sun induces the water molecules to move relative to one another in ways that just happen to correspond to those states. Because the movements of the water molecules in the pond correspond to those states, it seems that the pond must realize that functional description; so if functionalism is true, the pond must realize mental states. We can imagine analogous examples involving all sorts of different systems – the bees in a swarm, for instance, could come to be related to each other momentarily in a way that realizes T (Figure 6.6(E)). If functionalism is true, then it seems that the swarm must momentarily realize mental states. But again, this seems absurd. These examples suggest that functionalism attributes mental states to systems too easily – too liberally. It attributes mental states to systems that do not have them. Intuitively it seems absurd to suppose that the pond, or the swarm, or the people of China could realize a mind. Consequently, the argument concludes, we have good reason to think functionalism is false.

The liberalism objection is based on the following premises:

1   If functionalism is true, then systems like the Chinese nation, the pond, and the swarm of bees can have mental states.
2   Systems like the Chinese nation, the pond, and the swarm of bees cannot have mental states.

Functionalists can respond by rejecting either premise. Against Premise (1), they can argue that functionalism is not really committed to systems like the Chinese nation, the pond, or the swarm having mental states. One way to argue for this is to impose restrictions on the kinds of systems that can realize mental states. There are at least two ways functionalists can do this.

First, functionalists can argue that systems like the pond or the swarm cannot realize mental states because they cannot receive the right kinds of inputs or produce the right kinds of outputs. They cannot receive pinpricks, burns, or abrasions, for instance, or produce winces, groans, knee-jerks, and other escape-directed movements. Call this the *knee-jerk response* to the liberalism objection.

The problem with the knee-jerk response is that it overlooks the scope of the MRT. It is not just mental states that are multiply realizable, according to functionalists; inputs and outputs are multiply realizable as well. We can easily conceive of alien species who are not pained by pinpricks and burns the way humans are, or who respond to pain not with winces and groans, but with some other type of behavior. Moreover, because inputs, outputs, and mental states are all postulates of the same abstract descriptions, what is true of mental states on a functionalist account should also be true of inputs and outputs. In both cases, matter shouldn't matter; it shouldn't matter what realizes an input or an output any more than it matters what realizes an internal correlational state. On a functionalist account, all that should matter is that inputs, outputs, and internal states are all related to each other in the right kind of way, in accordance with the right kind of functional description. Finally, consider the implications of denying the multiple realizability of inputs and outputs: if functionalists claim that, say, any pain-capable system must correlate pinpricks, burns, and abrasions with winces, groans, and escape-directed movements, then functionalism ends up implying that the only systems with mental states are systems with input–output apparatuses like a human's. And if that is the case, functionalism ends up being no more liberal about mentality than the identity theory. It rules out the possibility of intelligent aliens or robotic systems with sensory organs or behavioral systems different from those of a human. For these reasons, it looks like inputs and outputs must be multiply realizable, and if that is the case, the inputs and outputs that define pain need not be realized by pinpricks, burns, winces, and knee-jerks – the kinds of states that realize the inputs and outputs in humans. In the pond, for instance, the inputs that define pain could be realized by a subtle disturbance in the wind, and the outputs that define pain could be realized by a small convection current produced by a subtle rise in temperature.

The knee-jerk response illustrates an important tension in functionalist thinking: if functional descriptions are defined in highly abstract ways, then functionalism is in danger of becoming too liberal; it is in danger of allowing systems like the pond and the swarm to have mental states. If, on the other hand, functional descriptions are defined less abstractly, then functionalism is in danger of becoming too conservative; it is in danger of denying mental states to systems whose input–output apparatuses differ significantly from those of humans.

A better response to the liberalism objection's major premise is given by **teleological functionalists**. Instead of restricting the realization of mental states the way the knee-jerk response does, they restrict the realization of mental states to systems that are teleologically organized. The word 'teleology' derives from the Greek word *telos* which means *end* or *goal*. To say that something is teleological is to say that something serves a purpose or engages in goal-directed behavior. Human intentional action is a species of teleological behavior; it is goal-directed behavior that results from deliberation and choice. Gabriel studies in order to do well on the exam, and studying is something he chooses to do in light of reasons about which he has deliberated. But not all goal-directed behavior involves deliberation and choice. The kinds of teleological behavior described in biology, for instance, typically do not involve deliberation and choice. Phototropism in plants is an example. Plants grow toward sources of light in order to get the energy they need for photosynthesis, the biochemical process that drives their metabolism. But saying that plants grow toward light in order to get energy, that this is the purpose of phototropism, does not imply that plants deliberate about various means to getting energy and finally choose one course of action over another.

According to teleological functionalists, the components of many complex systems operate in order to achieve goals or purposes within that system. Consider a complex artifact such as an internal combustion engine. Its components contribute teleologically to the engine's overall activity. The purpose of the fuel injector, for instance, is to introduce fuel to the combustion chamber to allow for combustion. The fuel injector's behavior is thus directed toward achieving the end of combustion; it makes a contribution to the engine's overall activity. According to teleological functionalists, something analogous is true of natural systems such as organisms. Their components contribute teleologically to their overall behavior. The purpose of the heart, for instance, is to pump blood; its activity is directed toward the goal of maintaining the health of the body's tissues. Likewise, the purpose of the eyelids is to protect the eyes, the purpose of the epiglottis is to prevent us from choking when we swallow, the purpose of the lungs is to oxygenate the blood, and so on. The only significant difference between natural systems and artifacts is the way their teleology is determined. The teleology of an artifact is due to its designer – someone who had a goal in mind, who wanted to construct a system to achieve that goal, who deliberated about how best to construct that system, and finally chose a design that included parts that contributed to that goal in various ways. Natural systems like organisms are not designed in this way however – at least not literally. Their teleology is due instead to natural selection. The role natural selection plays in the development of organisms is analogous to the role a designer plays in the production of artifacts. Just as the engine designer is responsible for the goal-directedness of the fuel injector in the automobile engine, natural selection is responsible for the goal-directedness of the heart, eyelids, epiglottis, and lungs in the organism.

Teleological functionalists restrict the realization of mental states to teleologically organized systems. If a system has not been designed or naturally selected so that its parts contribute teleologically to its overall activity, they say, then that system cannot realize mental states. Consider again the pond and the swarm. They have not been designed or selected to operate teleologically. As a result, say teleological functionalists, they are not candidates for realizing mental states. Because teleological functionalism introduces this restriction on the systems capable of realizing mental states, it is able to rule out many of the cases that have the potential to embarrass functionalists.

Critics of functionalism might nevertheless respond that the appeal to teleology does not give functionalists as much help as they need for at least two reasons. First, the teleology of natural systems is a controversial topic among biologists and philosophers of biology. Although many have come to embrace teleology as a distinctive and irreducible feature of biological description, there are also long-standing efforts to deny the legitimacy of teleological descriptions and explanations in biology. To the extent that a commitment to natural teleology remains controversial, teleological functionalism remains controversial as well.

Second, say critics, even if functionalists manage to develop an empirically adequate account of natural teleology, its helpfulness is limited. Restricting realization to teleologically organized systems helps rule out cases like the pond or the swarm of bees, but it does not help with cases like the nation of China, for the Chinese-nation system was designed to contribute to Alexander's overall activity in just the way his silicon prostheses were. Teleological functionalists cannot rule out the possibility that the citizens of China might realize mental states any more than they can rule out the possibility that silicon circuitry might realize mental states. If they rule out one, then they must also rule out the other, and if they rule out both, then functionalism once again becomes too conservative, for it then implies that the range of systems capable of having mental states is far narrower than the multiple-realizability thesis suggests.

Functionalists can also respond to the liberalism objection by rejecting Premise (2), the claim that systems like the pond, the swarm, or the Chinese nation do not have mental states. Functionalists can argue against (2) in at least two ways: They can argue either that the counterintuitive nature of these examples is not really a problem, or else that these examples are not as counterintuitive as they initially seem. Functionalists who endorse the first response can argue that functionalism is a revolutionary theory, and that revolutionary theories often have counterintuitive implications. General relativity theory and quantum theory, for instance, both have implications that are stunningly counterintuitive. That does not mean they are false, but only that our intuitions have not been trained to appreciate the truth about the physical universe. Likewise, if functionalism's implications seem counterintuitive, say functionalists, that does not show that functionalism is false; it only shows that our intuitions have not been trained to appreciate the truth about mental states. Second, functionalists can urge that examples such as the Chinese nation system are not really as counterintuitive as they at first seem. If, for instance, we were to meet Alexander in pedestrian circumstances, and were able to interact with him, we would notice no difference between his behavior before the operation and his behavior after. The silicon circuitry and the Chinese citizens would coordinate his behavior in exactly the way his brain had done originally. What basis could there possibly be, then, for claiming that he had mental states in the one case but not in the other? There seems to be none.

In addition to the liberalism objection, however, there is another objection that claims there would be a difference in Alexander after his operation. It is a version of the absent/inverted qualia argument discussed in Chapter 4. When Alexander had a brain, it argues, we could be fairly confident that he had conscious experiences with a qualitative dimension. But once his brain is replaced by silicon circuits or the citizens of China, we can no longer be so sure. Unlike the input–output correlations associated with mental states, qualia cannot be given an analysis in terms of inputs and outputs since qualia are nonrelational and unanalyzable. As a result, if two systems are the same functionally, they could still differ mentally: one could have conscious experiences that differ from the other's conscious experiences, or one could have conscious experiences that the other completely lacks. This worry about the possibility of absent and inverted qualia marks a further similarity between functionalism and the identity theory: neither sits comfortably with a private conception of mental phenomena.

The most obvious line of functionalist response to this objection is to deny that qualia are nonrelational and unanalyzable. Like the theories of mental representation discussed in Section 4.9, functionalists can argue that qualia admit of functional analyses. It is plausible, for instance, to suppose that the qualitative awfulness of pain plays a role in the description and explanation of behavior, that the qualitative dimension of pain is in part the reason why pinpricks, burns, and abrasions are correlated with winces, groans, and similar behavior. If so, then it is plausible to suppose that the qualitative dimension of pain admits of an input–output analysis after all. This line of functionalist response, and the worries about liberalism and qualia it is meant to address remain controversial. The same is true of another objection to functionalism: Searle's **Chinese room argument**.

6.8   The Chinese Room

Functionalism claims that mental states are identical to functional states – states postulated by an abstract description of inputs, outputs, and states that correlate the two. If functionalism is true, then it is impossible for two systems to be functionally identical (that is, to correlate inputs with outputs in the same ways), and yet mentally distinct. According to John Searle's Chinese room argument, however, there is good reason to think that it is possible for two systems to be functional identical and mentally distinct.

Imagine the following situation (Figure 6.7): Xavier, a person who knows no Chinese, is placed in a room that is outfitted with an input slot, an output slot, and an elaborate chart. The chart instructs him how to correlate strings of Chinese characters with other strings of Chinese characters. People outside the room write Chinese characters on cards and then pass the cards through the input slot. Xavier receives a card and then follows the instructions on the chart. They tell him how to correlate the Chinese characters printed on the input card with other Chinese characters. Xavier writes those other characters on a second, output card, and then slips that card through the output slot. Because Xavier does not understand Chinese, he does not know that the strings of input characters and the strings of output characters are actually Chinese sentences. A card

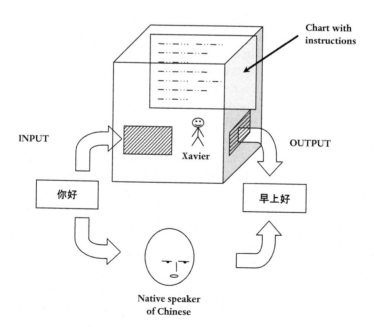

Xavier uses the chart to correlate inputs with outputs in the same way the native speaker does. He and the native speaker are thus functionally identical; they correlate Chinese inputs with Chinese outputs in the same way. Yet Xavier and the native speaker are mentally distinct. Xavier does not understand Chinese, but the native speaker does.

Figure 6.7   The Chinese room

passed to Xavier through the input slot might say in Chinese, "Hello, how are you today?" and by following the instructions on the chart Xavier might pass a card through the output slot on which he has written, "I'm very well today, thank you," and yet never know for an instant the meaning of what he has written or the meaning of the characters on the input card. Despite his ignorance, however, if Xavier becomes adept at using the chart, his input–output correlations might be indistinguishable from those of a native speaker of Chinese. Both he and the native speaker might correlate Chinese inputs with Chinese outputs in exactly the same ways – they might be functionally identical. And yet, says Searle, there would be a difference – a mental difference, for, unlike the native speaker, Xavier would not understand Chinese! Although Xavier and the native speaker would be functionally identical, they would be mentally distinct. If functionalism were true, and mental states such as understanding were functional states, then it would be impossible for two individuals to be functionally identical and yet mentally distinct in the way Xavier and the native speaker are. Hence, says the argument, functionalism must be false.

The Chinese room argument depends on the following premises:

1 If functionalism is true, then it is impossible for two systems to be functionally identical yet mentally distinct.
2 It is possible for two systems to be functionally identical yet mentally distinct.

Therefore, the argument concludes, functionalism is false. Functionalists can respond to this argument in several ways, but it should be clear that Premise (1) is not a viable target. If functionalism is true, then mental states are identical to functional states. Consequently, if two systems have all the same functional states, they must have all the same mental states since a system's mental states are just a subset of its functional states. The controversial premise is (2). It is supported in turn by the following claims:

(i)   If it is conceivable for two systems to be functionally identical yet mentally distinct, then it is possible for two systems to be functionally identical yet mentally distinct.
(ii) It is conceivable for two systems to be functionally identical yet mentally distinct.

Premise (i) is a conceivability-possibility principle like those used to support the argument for substance dualism (Section 3.2) and the knowledge argument against physicalism (Section 4.7). The argument thus inherits the worries and restrictions that attend any appeal to conceivability-possibility principles, and functionalists are free to challenge the premise in the ways discussed in Chapter 3. But most of the discussion about the Chinese room argument has focused on Premise (ii).

Premise (ii) is supported by the example of the Chinese room. In response, functionalists have argued that the Chinese room scenario is not really conceivable. Perhaps the strongest reply along these lines is what Searle dubs the 'Robot Reply'. The Robot Reply trades on two considerations. First, it claims that Xavier's failure to understand Chinese is irrelevant to the argument. The argument purports to show that it is possible for there to be two systems that are functionally identical yet mentally distinct, but Xavier is not the entire Chinese room system; he is only one part of it, the part responsible for correlating inputs with outputs in accordance with the chart. Xavier is analogous to the nervous system of the native speaker. It is not the native speaker's nervous system that understands Chinese, but the native speaker himself – the whole system. Because Xavier is analogous to the native speaker's nervous system, we cannot expect that Xavier himself will understand Chinese. To be effective, the Chinese room argument has to show that the Chinese room *as a whole* does not understand Chinese despite being functionally identical to a native speaker. But, says the Robot Reply, the argument does not show this. The reason is that the Chinese room as a whole is clearly *not* functionally identical to the native speaker.

The Chinese room and the native speaker clearly do not correlate inputs with outputs in the same way. The native speaker's linguistic abilities, for instance, are bound up with perceptual, motivational, and motor subsystems in ways that the Chinese room's linguistic abilities are not. In order for the Chinese room to be functionally identical to a native speaker, it would have to be connected to a sophisticated robotic body; it would have to receive inputs from perceptual and motivational subsystems, produce motor outputs, and so on. Unlike the original Chinese room, a sophisticated robotic system of this sort would be functionally identical to the native speaker; it would be capable of interacting with the environment and other people in the complex ways the native speaker does. But in that case, it is no longer clear what basis there could be for claiming the systems are mentally distinct. Because the systems behave in exactly the same ways, there would be no basis for claiming that one understands Chinese while the other does not. At the very least, if one denies that the robot understands Chinese, it would also make sense to deny that the native speaker does as well since both of them engage in exactly the same kinds of social and environmental interactions. In order for the Chinese room argument to work, then, it must provide an example of a system that satisfies two conditions: (a) the system must be functionally identical to the native speaker, and yet (b) it and the native speaker must be mentally distinct. According to the Robot Reply, the original Chinese room fails to satisfy condition (a), and once we get a system capable of satisfying (a), we no longer have any reason to think it is capable of satisfying (b). Hence, says the Robot Reply, the Chinese room argument fails. The Chinese room and the Robot Reply remain highly controversial.

6.9   The Embodied Mind Objection to Functionalism

Another objection to functionalism claims that the theory misrepresents psychological phenomena and the nature of psychological discourse. Psychological discourse is not abstract discourse as functionalists claim, says the objection; beliefs, desires, and other mental states cannot be defined apart from the specific physiological structures that characterize organisms of this or that specific kind. Let us call this the **embodied mind objection** to functionalism since contemporary versions of it derive from the embodied mind movement in cognitive science. The idea behind the objection nevertheless goes back to Aristotle.

Aristotle once criticized a philosopher named 'Socrates the Younger'. Socrates the Younger appears to have claimed that human activities could be defined abstractly in something analogous to the way we define circles and rectangles. The definitions of these things make no reference to any realizing materials. When we define a circle as an infinite number of points equidistant from a single point, for instance, that definition makes no mention of metal, wood, plastic, air, or any other material. As a result, a circle could be realized in almost anything. According to Socrates the Younger, definitions of human activities and capacities were like the definition of the circle; they made no reference to the particular bodily parts or physiological structures humans possess. Against this view, Aristotle argued that human activities and capacities were tied essentially to particular bodily parts disposed in particular ways, and could not be defined without reference to them. Consider an activity such as punching a heavy bag. Punching isn't just any old striking. Striking with a foot, head, or elbow, for instance, doesn't count as punching, but only striking with a hand. Not just any old striking with a hand counts, moreover: striking with an open hand or with the finger tips does not count as a punch, but only striking *with a fist*, and doing so in a particular way – with the knuckles. An activity like punching, then, cannot be defined apart from specific bodily structures disposed in very specific ways, and the same seems true of many other human activities.[1] Aristotle thus concluded,

> Socrates the Younger was wrong in always comparing an animal with the circle and bronze ... [I]t supposes that a man can exist without his parts, as a circle can exist without the bronze. But in fact, the two cases are not similar, for an animal ... cannot be defined without reference to parts in the right condition.[2]

Aristotle's criticism of Socrates the Younger is relevant because functionalists endorse a view of human psychological capacities similar to the view of Socrates the Younger. Beliefs, desires, pains, and other mental states, they say, are like mathematical postulates; they can be defined abstractly, without reference to any specific realizing structures or materials. This feature of functionalism, recall, is what enables the theory to accommodate the multiple-realizability thesis: if mental states are postulates of abstract descriptions, they can be realized in almost anything – human brains, Martian gamma organs, silicon circuitry, and so on. Against functionalists, contemporary exponents of embodied mind objections argue that human psychological capacities cannot be described or explained in the abstract way functionalists suppose. Descriptions and explanations of those capacities must instead incorporate descriptions and explanations of the physiological systems and subsystems humans possess. Human psychological capacities, in other words, are essentially embodied.

Most of the work in cognitive science that supports the embodied mind objection is very technical. It is nevertheless worth mentioning at least one example even if we do not have the time to consider its technical details. Standard accounts of vision in cognitive science draw their inspiration from the work of David Marr (1945–1980). Marr sought to describe and explain human vision in the way functionalists suggest: in terms of a set of abstract computational processes that are realized in some type of physical material. A growing body of research suggests, however, that vision cannot be described and explained in this way. In particular, it cannot be defined abstractly; it is instead essentially embodied in particular physiological structures. The cognitive scientist Dana Ballard, for instance, argues that vision can only be understood when we take embodiment into account and describe vision not just in terms of abstract operations in conjunction with realizing materials, but in terms of a distinctive embodiment level of description and explanation:

> The functionalist view depends critically on levels of abstraction ... [E]arly work in the field [of human intelligence] has been dominated by the tenets of artificial intelligence. One of the most important of these is that intelligence can be described in purely computational terms without recourse to any particular embodiment ... [T]he special features of the human body and its particular ways of interacting in the world have been seen as secondary to the fundamental problems of intelligence ... [O]ur central thesis is that intelligence has to relate to interactions with the physical world, and that means that the particular form of the human body is an important constraint in delimiting the aspects of intelligent behavior ... [E]mbodiment is crucial and illuminating and, we argue, best handled by positing a distinct ... embodiment level [which] specifies how the constraints of the physical system interact with cognition. One example is the movements of the eyes during the co-ordination of the hand in problem-solving tasks.[3]

According to Ballard, the explanations of hand–eye coordination provided by an embodiment theory are superior to the explanations provided by standard functionalist-oriented theories. The embodiment explanations, he argues, are both simpler and a better fit for the biological data.

The embodied mind objection accuses functionalism of empirical inadequacy. Functionalism, it claims, does not accurately reflect the scientific facts. Because of its empirical character, the success or failure of the argument depends on what science ends up discovering about human psychological capacities. The initial results are promising, say exponents of the objection, and yet even they admit that the results are not all in yet.

6.10   Kim's Trilemma

Another objection to realization physicalism targets not functionalism by itself, but the combination of functionalism and physicalism. Roughly, the argument claims that realization physicalism robs psychological discourse of its causal or explanatory import. According to functionalism, psychological discourse is abstract discourse; it provides an abstract way of describing whatever causal properties and relations there are. If physicalism is true, however, all causal properties and relations can be exhaustively described by physics including those involved in human behavior. If the real, causal story about why humans act as they do is told by physics, however, then it appears that psychological discourse has no causal or explanatory content in its own right.

One influential version of this argument was originally formulated by the philosopher Jaegwon Kim. Let us call it **Kim's trilemma**. Kim's trilemma poses realization physicalists with three uncomfortable options. Realization physicalism is committed to the following three claims:

Physicalism: Everything is physical; everything can be exhaustively described and explained by physics.

Anti-eliminativism: Psychological discourse is to some extent accurate; some mental predicates express genuine properties, and some individuals have the properties those predicates express.

Anti-reductivism: The properties expressed by mental predicates are not the same as those expressed by the predicates of physics.

Kim argues that these three claims are at odds with one another, and as a result realization physicalists face an uncomfortable choice: either (1) they must reject anti-reductivism, or (2) they must reject anti-eliminativism, or (3) they must reject physicalism. In case (1), prospective realization physicalists are forced to endorse reductivism; in case (2), they are forced to endorse eliminativism, and in case (3) they are forced to endorse dualism. In no case, then, are they able to maintain the nonreductive physicalist position they desire.

Kim's argument depends on two assumptions. First, he assumes that genuine properties are ones that make a causal difference to the individuals having them. Philosophers use the term 'property' in at least two different senses. Properties in the broad sense are just the ontological correlates of predicates: Any predicate expresses a property in the broad sense. Properties in a narrow, causal sense are properties in the broad sense that make a causal difference to the entities having them. Hence, *weighing 1 kg* and *weighing 2.2 pounds* are different properties in the broad sense since they correspond to different predicates, but they are not different properties in the causal sense because they have the same causal influence on the things that have them. In fact, Kim says it might be a good idea to speak of properties only in the causal sense, to say there is one (causal) property here that is expressed by different predicates – there is a single (causal) property, in other words, that is expressed by the two different predicates 'weighs 1 kg' and 'weighs 2.2 pounds'.[4]

Second, Kim assumes that if physicalism is true, the only genuine properties – that is, the only causal properties – are physical properties. This would seem to be a direct implication of physicalism: if physics is capable of providing an exhaustive description and explanation of everything, and causal relations are explanatory ones, then physics is capable of giving an exhaustive account of all the causal relations there are. To deny this, says Kim, is tantamount to denying physicalism; it would be to accept the existence of nonphysical causes – causes that cannot be expressed in the language of physics.

Given these assumptions, Kim poses the following difficulty for nonreductive physicalists. Anti-reductivism implies that mental properties are not physical properties. Physicalism implies, however, that all genuine properties – all causal properties – are physical properties. Consequently, if mental properties are not physical properties as anti-reductivism claims, then it looks like mental properties cannot be genuine properties, contrary to anti-eliminativism. Suppose, however, that we accept anti-eliminativism: mental properties, we insist, are genuine properties. Physicalism implies that all genuine properties are physical. Consequently, if mental properties are genuine properties as anti-eliminativism claims, then it looks like mental properties must be physical properties, contrary to anti-reductivism. Suppose, finally, that we accept anti-reductivism and also anti-eliminativism. The properties postulated by psychological discourse are not the same as those postulated by physics, we say, but they are genuine properties nonetheless. In that case, it looks like not all genuine properties are physical, contrary to physicalism. It is thus impossible to endorse physicalism, anti-eliminativism, and anti-reductivism as realization physicalists want.

In response, realization physicalists are likely to argue as follows:

Critics have failed to grasp what is so innovative about realization physicalism. According to realization physicalism, having a mental property amounts to having a physical property that satisfies a certain condition. Being in pain, for instance, might amount to having a physical property whose instances are typically correlated with inputs such as pinpricks, burns, and abrasions, and outputs such as winces, groans, and similar behavior. The benefit of this view of mental properties is that it allows us to endorse anti-eliminativism and anti-reductivism without compromising our commitment to physicalism. Because mental properties are second-order properties their definitions are different from the definitions of physical properties. Consequently, we can claim that mental properties are not the same as physical properties. Yet postulating these properties does not add to the basic inventory of physical properties that exist; it does not posit any new physical properties; it simply introduces a different way of describing whatever physical properties there are – a way that uses an abstract input–output vocabulary. In what sense can we say that mental properties are genuine causal properties? In this sense: mental properties qualify as genuine causal properties because the physical properties that realize them are genuine causal properties. If, for instance, pains in Alexander are realized by brain state B, and pains in Madeleine are realized by brain state C, then 'pain' expresses state B of Alexander's brain when we apply the predicate to him, and it expresses state C of Madeleine's brain when we apply the predicate to her. As a result, Alexander's pain has exactly the causal power that his brain state B has, and Madeleine's pain has exactly the causal power that her brain state C has. In both cases, the predicate 'pain' expresses a genuine property. Consequently, our theory is compatible with anti-eliminativism, anti-reductivism, and physicalism, contrary to what Kim's argument suggests.

But Kim has a counter-response to this realization physicalist argument. It is based on a principle he calls the 'Causal Inheritance Principle', roughly:

If a higher-order property M is realized by a lower-order property P, then the causal powers of this instance of M are identical to the causal powers of P.[5]

Realization physicalism appears to imply the Causal Inheritance Principle. If 'pain' expresses brain state B in Alexander, and brain state C in Madeleine, and whatever physical property realizes pain in this or that individual, then instances of pain are just instances of various physical properties. Consequently, if Alexander's pain is realized by brain state B – if that is what the predicate 'is in pain' expresses in his case – then, in his case, pain is the property of having brain state B. In that case, the causal powers Alexander's pain has are the causal powers of brain state B. Realization physicalism appears to be committed, therefore, to the Causal Inheritance Principle. Why is that a problem for realization physicalists? It is a problem because the Causal Inheritance Principle seems to imply that there is no distinctive property of pain.

If the Causal Inheritance Principle is true, 'pain' does not designate a causal property in its own right; it instead expresses many different physical properties – whichever physical properties happen to realize the input–output correlations that define pain. In that case, however, realization physicalism seems to imply that there is strictly speaking no such thing as pain, for to speak of pain is just to speak of a range of different physical properties that satisfy a certain condition. Kim's argument suggests, therefore, that realization physicalists are committed to denying that 'believes', 'desires', 'hopes', and other mental predicates express genuine properties.

Can realization physicalists claim that these predicates express properties that make a causal difference beyond the difference made by the physical properties that realize them? They cannot since that claim implies property dualism; it requires them to abandon physicalism. Can realization physicalists claim that mental predicates express physical properties, but that they express different properties in different individuals – 'pain', for instance, expresses one type of physical property in Alexander and a different type of physical property in Madeleine? This is a version of the narrow-mental-type strategy discussed earlier (Section 6.2). (Incidentally, this is the option Kim seems to favor.) According to exponents of narrow mental types, the mental properties postulated by our current psychological vocabulary – properties like pain – do not correspond to the physical properties postulated by our current scientific theories. Nevertheless, they say, scientific progress will eventually force us to revise our psychological vocabulary, and bring our inventory of mental properties in line with our inventory of physical properties. There might be no such property as pain *simpliciter*, say exponents of narrow mental types, but there are properties such as pain-in-humans, pain-in-Martians, and pain-in-robots. The problem with this response is that it implies a commitment to reductivism. The only genuine mental properties on this view are narrow mental properties that correspond one–one to physical properties. One way or another, then, it looks like realization physicalists are forced to abandon their position; they are forced to abandon either physicalism, or anti-eliminativism, or anti-reductivism.

The burden for nonreductivists, recall, is to explain how psychological discourse manages to describe and explain physical reality even though its categories do not correspond to those of fundamental physics. Kim's trilemma suggests that realization physicalists fail to carry this burden. The argument remains controversial.

6.11   Supervenience Physicalism

The type of nonreductive physicalism just considered is based on the notion of realization. Another kind of nonreductive physicalism is based on the notion of supervenience. Supervenience is a kind of dependence relation: to say that characteristics of one sort supervene on characteristics of another sort is to say that things cannot differ in characteristics of the first sort without also differing in characteristics of the second sort. Some aesthetic properties, for instance, supervene on physical properties: two individuals cannot differ from each other aesthetically without differing from each other physically. If Painting A is physically indistinguishable from Painting B, if they have exactly the same physical features, then it is impossible for one to be beautiful and the other ugly, or for one to be well proportioned and the other poorly proportioned. If aesthetic properties supervene on physical properties, then physical twins must be aesthetic twins: any aesthetic differences between Painting A and Painting B would be traceable to physical differences between them.

Supervenience physicalism is a type of nonreductive physicalism that claims mental properties supervene on physical properties. It says that two systems cannot differ from each other mentally without differing from each other physically. If, for instance, we were to construct an exact physical replica of you – a physical twin that did not differ from you even at the level of atoms and fundamental physical particles – then you and your twin could not differ from each other mentally either. If you believed that there were exactly eight planets in our solar system, your twin would believe that as well, and if your twin liked coffee ice cream, then you would like coffee ice cream too. Any mental difference between you and your twin would have to be reflected in some type of physical difference between you. If one of you liked coffee ice cream, and the other did not, that mental difference would be traceable to a physical difference such as a difference in your brains. But if there were no differences between you and your twin, if you were exactly the same particle for particle, then, according to supervenience physicalism, it would be impossible for you and your twin to differ from each other mentally. Hence, according to supervenience physicalists, psychological discourse and other special sciences manage to describe physical reality because the properties they postulate supervene on physical properties.

The claim that mental properties supervene on physical properties is not unique to supervenience physicalism. Emergentism, epiphenomenalism, hylomorphism, and other theories are compatible with supervenience, and other physicalist theories such as realization physicalism, eliminativism, and the identity theory actually imply it.[6] What sets supervenience physicalism apart is the idea that supervenience is sufficient to provide a nonreductive physicalist account of how mental properties are related to physical properties.

Supervenience physicalism confronts at least three difficulties. The first is the *formulation problem.* It concerns the attempt to formulate the right kind of supervenience relation, the kind nonreductive physicalists need. There are several kinds of supervenience relations. They differ from each other based on how strongly they take mental properties to depend on physical properties. The goal is to find a supervenience relation that is strong enough to preserve physicalist intuitions, but not so strong that it ends up implying a commitment to reductivism. Finding a relation of this sort has proven difficult, and hence it has proven difficult to formulate an acceptable version of supervenience physicalism. Consider some examples.

The claim that mental properties *weakly supervene* on physical properties is the claim that for any possible world, w, and any individuals x and y in w, if x and *y* are physical twins, they are also mental twins. Since the time of the seventeenth-century philosopher Gottfried Wilhelm von Leibniz, philosophers have often spoken of possibility in terms of *possible worlds*. Possible worlds are ways the world could have been. The world is a certain way in fact. In fact, for instance, you are reading this sentence. But the world did not have to turn out this way. It could have turned out other ways. It could have turned out, for instance, that you had decided never to read this chapter; in fact, it could have turned out that you had never learned to read, or even that you had never been born at all. The world did not turn out in any of these ways, but it could have. The way things are in fact, then, is only one of many ways they could have been – the actual world, in other words, is only one among many possible worlds. To say that it was possible for you not to have read this book, or that was possible for your parents never to have met, or that it was possible for human life on Earth never to have evolved is to say that there is a possible world in which you do not read this book, a possible world in which your parents never meet, and a possible world in which human life on Earth never evolves. Likewise, to say that it is impossible for there to be a married bachelor is to say that there is no possible world in which a married bachelor exists. And to say that it is necessary that $2 + 2 = 4$ is to say that $2 + 2 = 4$ in every possible world.

Weak supervenience says that mental properties in one particular world depend on physical properties in that one world. For any individuals *x* and *y* in world *w*, if *x* and *y* are physical twins in *w*, they must also be mental twins in *w*. Weak supervenience physicalism claims that mental properties weakly supervene on physical properties, that this kind of dependence relation is all physicalists need for a workable nonreductivist theory. The problem with weak supervenience physicalism is that it only specifies a mental–physical dependence relation within a single world. In any *one* world, physical indiscernibility guarantees mental indiscernibility. But knowing mental and physical properties are correlated in this one world tells us nothing about whether and/or how they are correlated in others. As a result, weak supervenience physicalism is compatible with the possibility that a physical replica of me could have radically different mental properties, or perhaps no mental properties at all. Could a molecule-for-molecule replica of me in another world differ from me significantly in his beliefs, desires, and other mental properties? If mental properties supervene on physical properties in only this weak sense, then yes, he could. That result, however, seems inconsistent with physicalist intuitions; in particular, it seems inconsistent with the idea that physical properties *fix* or *determine* all the properties there are. Physicalism requires something stronger.

Global supervenience is a stronger dependence relation than weak supervenience. It is not just the mental and physical properties of individuals in a world that matter, but the distribution of mental and physical properties over *all* individuals in that world. To say that mental properties globally supervene on physical properties is to say that any worlds with indistinguishable distributions of physical properties over individuals would also have indistinguishable distributions of mental properties over individuals. *Global supervenience physicalism* claims that mental properties globally supervene on physical properties, that this kind of dependence relation is all physicalists need for a workable nonreductivist theory.

The problem with global supervenience physicalism is similar to the problem with weak supervenience physicalism. Global supervenience allows for the possibility that a world might differ from the actual world in some minor physical way, and yet differ from it mentally in a major way. Suppose, for instance, that world *w* is physically indistinguishable from the actual world with one exception: the position of a lone hydrogen atom in deep space is slightly different from what its position is in fact. Intuitively, we would expect this to make little or no mental difference to world *w*: why should the position of a single atom in deep space affect the mental properties of persons on Earth, say? Yet global supervenience physicalism is compatible with those persons having radically different mental properties given only this minor physical difference between *w* and the actual world. Again, this seems incompatible with the sort of psychophysical determination demanded by physicalism.

Finally, **strong supervenience** says that for any individuals in any worlds at all – individual *x* in world$_1$ and individual *y* in world$_2$, for instance – physical indiscernibility guarantees mental indiscernibility. It is impossible, in other words, for physical twins to fail to be mental twins even if they are in different worlds. Strong supervenience physicalism claims that mental properties strongly supervene on physical properties, that this kind of dependence relation can give nonreductive physicalists what they want. The problem with strong supervenience physicalism is that it seems to imply some type of reductivism, for, if it is true, something's mental properties end up corresponding one–one to its physical properties. But if that is the case, then strong supervenience physicalism no longer qualifies as a form of physicalism that is nonreductive. In short, then, the formulation problem is the problem of specifying a supervenience relation that is strong enough to satisfy physicalist intuitions but no so strong that it ends up implying reductivism.

The second problem facing supervenience physicalists is the *asymmetry problem*. It concerns whether supervenience is sufficient to capture the kind of dependence or determination relation that physicalists want. That relation is an asymmetrical one: mental phenomena are supposed to depend on physical phenomena in a way that physical phenomena do not depend on mental phenomena. Physicalists want to say, for instance, that the existence of pain or belief depends on the existence of lower-level physical states, but that the existence of lower-level physical states does not depend in turn on the existence of pain or belief. The problem is that supervenience is not an asymmetrical relation: if *A* supervenes on *B*, it is still possible for *B* to supervene on *A*. Consider cases of identity. Property identity implies supervenience: Metric weights, for instance, supervene on English weights: *x* and *y* cannot differ in respect of, say, weighing 1 kg unless they differ also in respect of weighing 2.2 pounds. And yet English weights also supervene on metric weights:

x and y cannot differ in respect of weighing 2.2 pounds unless they also differ in respect of weighing 1 kg. The supervenience of A-properties on B-properties, then, does not rule out the supervenience of B-properties on A-properties. Consequently, supervenience is not sufficient by itself to ground a physicalist theory of mind. Something else is required in addition to secure the asymmetry of psychophysical dependence.

Third, supervenience appears insufficient to ground a physicalist theory of mind for another reason. We can call it the *explanation problem*. Supervenience relations must be explained by something. If mental properties supervene on physical properties, something needs to explain why they supervene on physical properties. The need to explain supervenience relations derives from an observation mentioned earlier: supervenience is compatible with a broad range of very different mind–body theories. Consider two such theories: the identity theory and epiphenomenalism. As we have seen, the identity theory claims that mental properties are identical to physical properties. Pain, for instance, is identical to brain state B. Epiphenomenalism, on the other hand, denies that mental properties are identical to physical properties; it claims rather that mental properties are caused or produced by physical properties. Identity theory and epiphenomenalism differ from each other in a fundamental way: one endorses mental–physical identities, the other denies them. Yet despite this fundamental difference, both theories are compatible with psychophysical supervenience. If mental properties are identical to physical properties, then clearly mental properties supervene on physical properties: if pain is identical to brain state B, then it is impossible for something to be in pain without having brain state B. If, on the other hand, mental properties are caused by physical properties as epiphenomenalists claim, then once again mental properties can supervene on physical properties. Suppose, for instance, that each mental property is caused by a single type of physical property, and the instantiation of that type of physical property always produces an instance of just that type of mental property. Suppose pain, for instance, can only be caused by brain state B, and whenever brain state B occurs, it always causes pain. In that case, x and y can differ from each other mentally only if they differ from each other physically. If x and y differ from each other in some mental respect – if, say, x experiences pain at t and y does not – then that difference will have to correspond to a physical difference. Since pain can only be caused by brain state B, and x is experiencing pain, x must have brain state B. On the other hand, since brain state B always causes pain, and y is not in pain, y cannot have brain state B. Every mental difference requires a physical difference. Hence, physical twins will turn out to be mental twins. On this epiphenomenalist view, then, mental properties supervene on physical properties.

The identity theory and this version of epiphenomenalism are very different mind–body theories, yet both are committed to mental properties supervening on physical properties. If supervenience relations can be grounded in theories that are this different, then whenever we hear that mental properties supervene on physical properties, we always have to ask why they do so. A mind–body theory must provide answers to basic ontological questions. Are, for instance, mental properties identical to physical properties?' Because supervenience is compatible with theories that endorse mental–physical property identities and also with theories that reject them, knowing simply that mental properties supervene on physical properties does not provide us with an answer to this very basic question. Consequently, if we are told that mental properties supervene on physical properties, we must always ask: What explains this supervenience? This is the case even when we limit the discussion to physicalist theories. As we have just seen with the example of the identity theory, reductivists are committed to mental–physical supervenience relations, and provide an explanation for them: mental properties supervene on physical properties because they *are* physical properties. This kind of explanation is not available to nonreductivists, and in the absence of some more basic fact about, say, mental and physical property identity, it seems that supervenience physicalists must postulate mental–physical supervenience relations as brute, unexplainable facts. Why does the belief that 2 + 2 = 4 supervene on frontal lobe activity? In the absence of a more basic fact about mental phenomena, the answer it seems is that it just *does*, and this answer is bound to make physicalists very uncomfortable. The reason is that physicalists share a sense that whatever psychophysical correlations there are, those correlations must be explainable in physical terms. Physics is supposed to be not just ontologically authoritative, but explanatorily authoritative as well. Consequently, the brute obtaining of supervenience relations is insufficient to capture physicalist intuitions. As a result, supervenience by itself seems insufficient to ground a physicalist theory of mind. Just as would-be supervenience physicalists must provide something that secures the asymmetry of mental–physical supervenience relations, so likewise they must provide something that explains mental–physical supervenience relations.

The formulation problem, the asymmetry problem, and the explanation problem do not show that mental properties fail to supervene on physical properties. Indeed, many philosophers – physicalists and nonphysicalists alike – endorse some type of mental–physical supervenience. The problems show, rather, that the attempt to base a physicalist theory of mind on supervenience alone may be misguided; that supervenience by itself is not up to the task; more is required for a workable physicalist theory of mind. The adequacy of supervenience as a basis for nonreductive physicalism remains a source of controversy.

6.12   The Exclusion Argument

Kim's trilemma is closely related to another argument: the **exclusion argument**, sometimes called the *exclusion problem* or the *problem of causal/explanatory exclusion*

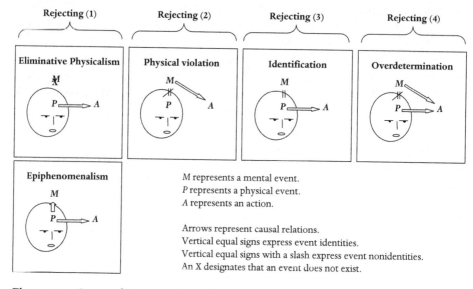

Figure 6.8   Some solutions to the problem of mental causation

(Kim sometimes calls it the *supervenience argument*). It is a version of the problem of mental causation described in Section 1.6.

Imagine you reach for an object near at hand. This action cannot occur without the contraction of muscles in your arm. These contractions are caused by events in your nervous system: the firings of neurons. Recall, however, that in order for your reaching to count as an action it must have a mental cause – it must be caused, for instance, by your desire to grasp an object. But now nonreductivists must answer a question: How are the mental cause of your action and the physical cause of your action related? There are only a handful of possible answers (Figure 6.8).

To understand them let us formulate the problem in terms of the following jointly inconsistent claims:

1   Actions have mental causes.
2   Actions have physical causes.
3   Mental causes and physical causes are distinct.
4   An action does not have more than one cause.

Claims (1) and (2) imply that any given action has a mental cause and also a physical cause. According to Claim (3), an action's mental cause and its physical cause are distinct. The action must therefore have at least two causes, yet (4) rules this out; it says that an action does not have more than one cause. Consequently, claims (1)–(4) are inconsistent. Claims (1)–(3) imply that actions have multiple causes while Claim (4) implies that they do not. The task for nonreductivist physicalists is to resolve the inconsistency by rejecting one of the claims. But, says the argument, there is no satisfactory way for them to do so; rejecting any one of the claims lands them in difficulty. Consider each option.

There are two ways of rejecting Claim (1). The first denies that there are mental events. It is endorsed by eliminativists. The second admits that there are mental events, but denies that they can causally influence anything. This is the option endorsed by epiphenomenalists. The first approach is not available to nonreductive physicalists since they are committed to anti-eliminativism, and the second approach has very awkward consequences (Section 8.8). It implies, for instance, that our mental states have no causal influence on our behavior, that our thoughts and feelings do not in any way influence or explain what we do. If actions are physical events with mental causes, moreover, then it also implies that there are no such things as actions since it implies that there are no such things as mental causes. These are highly counterintuitive results.

Consider likewise Claim (2): rejecting it seems at odds with nonreductivists' commitment to physicalism. Rejecting (2) requires rejecting the principle we called the *causal completeness of physics* (Section 5.6), what is sometimes called the *causal closure of the physical domain*. The principle says that the natural sciences, paradigmatically physics, are capable in principle of providing an exhaustive account of all causes. We can state the idea as follows:

Physical Closure: If a physical event has a cause at time t, then it has a physical cause at t.

Physical closure implies that in searching for the causes of physical events, we need never search outside the physical domain. Any physical event that has a cause at all will have a physical cause. Physical closure is an important physicalist commitment. Its rejection implies that some physical events have nonphysical causes, and this is incompatible with physicalism.

Rejecting Claim (3), on the other hand, appears to be at odds with nonreductivists' commitment to anti-reductivism. It implies that an action's physical cause and its mental cause are identical, that the neural events responsible for your reaching are identical to your desire to reach. This is the approach endorsed by identity theorists. The word 'desire', they say, is just another way of referring to the events in your nervous system, the way 'water' is just another way of referring to H_2O. This does not seem to be an option for nonreductivists. Their anti-reductivism commits them to denying that mental states are identical to physical states.

That leaves Claim (4). Rejecting (4) implies that actions are overdetermined, that they have multiple independent fully sufficient causes. The overdetermination of actions has several awkward implications which we consider in detail in Section 8.11. But Kim argues that nonreductive physicalists cannot endorse the overdetermination of actions in any event. Genuine cases of overdetermination involve two

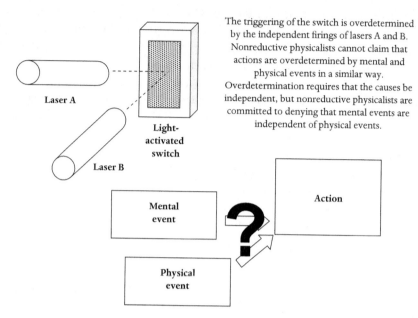

The triggering of the switch is overdetermined by the independent firings of lasers A and B. Nonreductive physicalists cannot claim that actions are overdetermined by mental and physical events in a similar way. Overdetermination requires that the causes be independent, but nonreductive physicalists are committed to denying that mental events are independent of physical events.

Figure 6.9   Nonreductive physicalism and overdetermination

separate and independent causal chains. Consider the two lasers in Figure 6.9. They simultaneously trigger a light-sensitive switch. The lasers operate independently of each other (one can be activated without the other), and either can trigger the switch by itself: if Laser A were fired without Laser B, it would be sufficient by itself to trigger the switch, and, likewise, if Laser B were fired without Laser A, it would be sufficient by itself to trigger the switch. Because either laser can trigger the switch by itself, yet both trigger the switch in fact, the triggering of the switch is overdetermined; it has multiple, independent, fully sufficient causes.

Can nonreductive physicalists claim that actions are overdetermined by mental and physical causes in an analogous way? No, says Kim, for, if nonreductive physicalism is true, mental events are not independent of physical events. Either mental events are realized by physical events, or else mental events supervene on physical events, but either way mental events depend on physical events for their existence. Consequently, mental events and physical events cannot supply independent fully sufficient causes for actions. Actions cannot be overdetermined by mental and physical events.

Nonreductive physicalists might object to this last point as follows:

Kim has argued that if nonreductive physicalism is true, mental events and physical events cannot be independent causes of actions. But nonreductivists do not need to claim that mental and physical events are independent causes of actions to reject Claim (4). They only have to claim that an action has more than one cause; they do not have to claim in addition that these causes are independent. They can say that an action has more than one cause and that one of these causes, the mental cause, depends on the other, the physical cause.

Call this the *dependent cause response* to the exclusion problem.

The problem with the dependent cause response, Kim argues, is that it threatens to rob the mental event of any real causal role in the production of action. Nonreductive physicalists, after all, are committed to Physical Closure. On their view, any physical event that has a cause must have a physical cause. If your action has a mental cause, therefore, it must have a physical cause. According to nonreductive physicalists, the mental cause and physical cause must be distinct as Claim (3) says. Yet according to exponents of the dependent cause response, the mental event is not an independent cause of the action. In what way, then, can the mental cause contribute to an explanation of the effect? It seems that it cannot contribute at all, for, if it did, it would make a causal contribution beyond the contribution made by the physical cause, and, in that case, exponents of the dependent cause response would be abandoning physicalism in favor of some type of property dualism. Exponents of the dependent cause response seem committed, therefore, to denying that mental events have any causal influence on our behavior. If nonreductive physicalism is true, the occurrence of a physical cause excludes the occurrence of a mental one – hence the label 'exclusion argument'.

Nonreductive physicalists seem left without options, therefore. They cannot reject (1) or (4) without rejecting the causal efficacy of mental events; they cannot reject (2) without rejecting their commitment to physicalism, and they cannot reject (3) without rejecting their commitment to anti-reductivism.

The exclusion argument is controversial, and nonreductive physicalists have responded to it in several ways. Let us consider one of them. Some nonreductive physicalists argue that the exclusion argument fails to make an important distinction between properties and events. Claim (3) concerns causes, they say, and causes are events not properties. Anti-reductivism might commit them to claiming that mental properties are distinct from physical properties, but it does not commit them to claiming that mental events are distinct from physical events. Mental and physical events can be identical even if mental and physical properties are distinct. Consequently, say nonreductivists, they are free to reject Claim (3). They can identify mental events with physical events without taking the further step of identifying mental properties with physical properties the way identity theorists do. Let us call this the *token physicalist response* to the exclusion problem.

'Token physicalism' is a label that is frequently used to describe nonreductive physicalism. It is based on the **type–token distinction** originally drawn by the American philosopher Charles Sanders Peirce (1839–1914). A type is a general category and tokens are its individual members or instances. The following characters, for instance, are five tokens of a single type:

A   A   A   A   A

Tokens, in other words, are particular existing things, such as particular instances of the letter A, whereas types are the general categories to which tokens belong. Nonreductive physicalism is often called *token physicalism* because according to nonreductivists every token is a physical token even if not every type is a physical type. The types postulated by the special sciences, for instance, are not physical types; they are not physical categories such as the categories of fundamental physics since they do not correspond to the categories of fundamental physics. Reductive physicalism, on the other hand, is often called *type physicalism*. Reductive physicalists claim that the categories of the special sciences correspond directly to those of physics, so not only is every token a physical token, every type is a physical type as well.

The success of the token physicalist response to the exclusion problem depends on an account of tokens and types. The type–token distinction can be applied to a broad range of ontological categories, so claims about types and tokens tell us very little unless we know what the types and tokens are. When it comes to the exclusion problem, nonreductivists take the types to be properties and tokens events. There are several prominent theories of events in philosophy. One is based on a *substance–attribute ontology*. An ontology is an inventory of the entities that exist, and a substance–attribute ontology claims that substances and attributes – that is, individuals and properties – are the most basic entities in any such inventory, that any other entities depend on individuals and properties for their existence. Consider, for instance, *property instances* such as *this table's greenness*, or *that building's height*, or *Eleanor's enjoyment of sushi*, or *William and Cecilia's being married*. Each property instance consists of an individual or individuals having a property or standing in a relation. This table, that building, Eleanor, and William and Cecilia are all individuals; greenness, height, and enjoyment of sushi are all properties, and being married is a relation. A *property instantiation* or *property exemplification* theory of events claims that events are property instances. Each consists of an individual or individuals having a property or standing in a relation at a time. A baseball game, for instance, is an event that consists of a number of individuals performing various activities with each other for nine innings – in other words, it consists of those individuals standing in a very complex relation for a certain amount of time.

Kim's original formulation of the exclusion problem takes events to be property exemplifications in this sense. Because events on this view consist of individuals having properties at times, Event$_A$ and Event$_B$ are identical only if they consist of the same individual having the same property at the same time: a's having property F at time t is identical to b's having property G at time t' only if a is identical to b, F is identical to G, and t is identical to t'. Consequently, on a property exem-

plification theory of events, event identity requires property identity. Mental
events cannot be identical to physical events unless mental properties are identical
to physical properties. You having a desire at time *t* can be identical to you having
neural firings at time *t* only if having a desire – that property – is identical to
having neural firings. If events are property-exemplifications, therefore, nonreductive physicalists cannot reject Claim (3), for their commitment to rejecting mental–
physical property identities would commit them to rejecting mental–physical
event identities as well. Nonreductive physicalists who want to reject Claim (3)
must endorse a different theory of events, one that does not require property
identity for event identity. The philosopher Donald Davidson's account of events
is an example.

On Davidson's account, events are not distinguished by their constituent individuals, properties, and times, but by their causes and effects (Figure 6.10). What
distinguishes $Event_1$ from $Event_2$ is that $Event_1$ is caused by $Event_0$ and causes
$Event_2$, whereas $Event_2$ is caused by $Event_1$ and causes $Event_3$. On Davidson's own
view, an event qualifies as mental if it is describable using a mental vocabulary,
and it qualifies as physical if it is describable using a physical vocabulary. Moreover,
a given event might be describable using both vocabularies. Hence, the very same

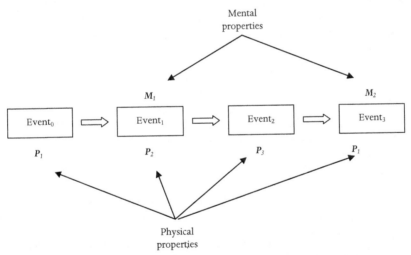

On a Davidsonian account, events are individuated by their causes and effects. Here the arrows
represent causal relations. What distinguishes events in the causal chain is that each has a
different cause and a different effect. Some philosophers add to this an account of properties:
events have properties, they say, and an event qualifies as mental if it has mental properties, and
it qualifies as physical if it has physical properties. Hence, all the events depicted here are physical
events since they all have physical properties. In addition, $Event_1$ and $Event_3$ are mental events
since they have mental properties. The very same event, then, can have both mental and physical
properties. Mental and physical events can be identical even if mental and physical properties are
distinct.

Figure 6.10   A Davidsonian theory of events plus properties

event can be both a mental event and a physical event. Some nonreductive physicalists, however, endorse an account of events like Davidson's, but instead of speaking of descriptions, as Davidson does, they speak of properties. On their view, an event qualifies as mental if it has a mental property, and it qualifies as physical if it has a physical property. According to these nonreductivists, the same event can have both mental and physical properties, so the very same event can be both mental and physical. In Figure 6.10, for instance, the event with mental property M_1 is identical to the event with physical property P_2. Importantly, on this view the M_1-event can be identical to the P_2-event even if property M_1 is not identical to property P_2. Nonreductivists who endorse a theory of events along these lines are thus free to claim that mental and physical events are identical even though mental and physical properties are distinct. But, in that case, they argue, they are free to reject (3) without compromising their commitment to anti-reductivism.

The token physicalist response to the exclusion problem is controversial. One worry is that it might rob mental properties of any causal role in the explanation of behavior. If physicalism is true, then everything can be explained by physics, and if that is the case, then the only properties that can make a causal difference to what happens are physical properties. Consequently, if mental properties are not physical properties, as the token physicalist response claims, then it looks as though mental properties cannot make any causal difference to what happens in the world. (Incidentally, Davidson's own nonreductivist theory, **anomalous monism**, has a similar problem with mental causation (Section 7.7).)

The burden for nonreductive physicalists, recall, is to explain how special scientific descriptions and explanations manage to correspond to reality if special scientific categories do not correspond to physical ones. Kim's exclusion argument suggests that this is a burden nonreductive physicalists have failed to carry, that they have no good account of how psychological and other special scientific explanations manage to express the real reasons things happen as they do.

6.13   Nonreductive Physicalism in Perspective

In recent years 'nonreductive physicalism' has become a popular label for any view that combines the claim that we are physical beings with the claim that psychological discourse is not reducible to physical theory. But the label is often misapplied. Nonreductive physicalism is not the only mind–body theory that is compatible with these claims, and people often use the label to refer to theories such as emergentism that are not forms of physicalism at all. Another common mistake is to suppose that nonreductive physicalism's commitment to anti-reductionism implies that physics cannot give an exhaustive description and explanation of everything, that there are, for instance, certain aspects of human behavior that elude physical description. But nonreductive physicalism implies exactly the opposite: because it is a form of physicalism, it implies that physics can exhaustively describe and explain everything – including human behavior. Like any form of physicalism, it implies that if a being like the Super Physicist described in Chapter 4 were to give an account of all fundamental physical interactions, its description of the universe would miss nothing, and our feeling that the Super Physicist's description would miss something – the distinction between, say, living and nonliving or mental and nonmental – simply reflects a different set of descriptive and explanatory interests – interests that according to nonreductive physicalists do not correspond to anything deep in reality. Philosophers who are attracted to nonreductive physicalism, then, but who want a deeper metaphysical anchor for their anti-reductionism should consider dual-attribute theory (Chapter 8) or hylomorphism (Chapters 10 and 11).

Philosophers who are comfortable with physicalism, on the other hand, face a more complicated set of choices. The problems with supervenience physicalism suggest that supervenience relations are by themselves inadequate to ground a physicalist theory of mind. Importantly, realization physicalists have argued that their theory implies a commitment to supervenience relations as well. Moreover, they have argued, their theory is able to provide a basis both for explaining supervenience relations and for securing the asymmetry of mental–physical dependence. If that is the case, would-be nonreductive physicalists are advised to explore some version of realization physicalism. If they are persuaded that the problems with realization physicalism are insurmountable, however, they should consider anomalous monism (Sections 7.5–7.7). If they are not satisfied with anomalous monism, then they are advised to reconsider their commitment to anti-reductionism, and look to a version of reductivism that can handle the multiple-realizability argument. These include reductivist theories that postulate narrow mental types, those that postulate broad physical types, and those that endorse some type of coordinated typology strategy. The downside of postulating broad physical types or holding out for coordinated mental and physical typologies is that both strategies rely heavily on future scientific investigation. They thus require reductivists to issue fairly hefty promissory notes. Perhaps for this reason the postulation of narrow mental types has tended to be the strategy of choice among reductivists.

Prospective physicalists who are still dissatisfied should consider two, more radical alternatives: instrumentalism and eliminativism. These theories together with anomalous monism are the subject of the next chapter.

Further Reading

The characterization of nonreductive physicalism and the nonreductivist worldview presented in this chapter follows Jerry Fodor's (1974) influential characterization, which was reprinted as Chapter 1 of Fodor (1975). This characterization is controversial in some respects. In particular, it differs from approaches that characterize nonreductive physicalism in terms of a commitment to some type of property dualism. For an introductory example of the property-dualistic approach see Horgan (1994). Property-dualistic definitions of nonreductive physicalism have been a source of confusion in philosophy of mind. The difference between nonreductive physicalism and property dualism is discussed in detail in Chapter 8.

The multiple-realizability argument was originally advanced by Hilary Putnam (1975f). Putnam defended the MRT *a posteriori* by appeal to evolutionary biology. Ned Block and Jerry Fodor (1972) followed suit and bolstered the case for the MRT by appeal to neuroscience and artificial intelligence research. See Brian Kolb and Ian Whishaw (2003: 621–41) for a description of brain plasticity and research related to it. Jaegwon Kim (1972) was the first to appreciate the range of possible reductivist responses to the MRT. David Lewis articulates his response to the multiple-realizability argument in Lewis (1980). In addition, an increasing number of philosophers have looked to criticize the MRT on scientific grounds; Shapiro (2004) provides an example. For an introductory discussion of these responses and a survey of the literature on the multiple-realizability argument see William Jaworski's article "Mind and Multiple Realizability" in the Internet Encyclopedia of Philosophy (http://www.iep.utm.edu/).

Functionalism was inspired by Alan Turing (1950), but it was Hilary Putnam (1975b; 1975e; 1975f) who first articulated the view in a series of papers first published in the 1960s. See Putnam (1970) for his discussion of higher-order properties. Putnam (1980) expressed misgivings about functionalism, and later advanced several arguments against it in Putnam (1988). More recently Putnam expressed sympathy for hylomorphism (Nussbaum and Putnam 1992), a theory we consider in chapters 10 and 11. Among Putnam's arguments is an appeal to Gödel's theorem to disprove that mental states are computational states. The physicist Roger Penrose (1990; 1994) has also appealed to Gödel's theorem in an effort to refute the computational theory of mind.

Andrew Melnyk (2003) offers a recent formulation of realization physicalism. See Block (1980) for more on the liberalism objection to functionalism. William G. Lycan (1987: Chapter 4) defends teleological functionalism (he calls his version of the view 'homuncular functionalism' or 'homunctionalism'). The introduction to Lycan (1990) is also a helpful source of information about the troubles confronting functionalism and attempts to solve them. Searle (1980) presents the Chinese room argument and several objections to it including the Robot Reply. Raymond Gibbs (2006) is an accessible introduction to the embodied mind movement in cognitive science. Some of the central articles defending embodiment are collected in Noë and Thompson (2002). Many contemporary exponents of embodiment have been inspired by the ideas of the French phenomenologist Maurice Merleau-Ponty (1962). For a discussion of Aristotle's views on embodiment, including his criticism of Socrates the Younger, see Nussbaum and Putnam (1992).

Jaegwon Kim (1989; 1992b; 1993b: Chapter 4) has been the most forceful critic of nonreductive physicalism in recent years. His papers on the trilemma, the exclusion problem, and the worries about supervenience physicalism are collected in Kim (1993b). He develops the arguments further, discusses some objections to them, and offers replies in Kim (1998: Chapters 1 and 4), and Kim (2005: Chapters 1 and 2).

Notes

1   Aristotle's favorite way of arguing for this point was by drawing an analogy with *the snub*. Snubness, he said, could not be defined simply as concavity; it was, he said, concavity *in a nose*. A better example would be something like a smile. A smile cannot be defined simply as a curvature; it is a curvature *of the mouth*. According to Aristotle, the definitions of human activities and capacities were analogous to the definitions of snubness and a smile.

2   *Metaphysics* Book VII, Chapter 11 1037a22–31. See also *De Anima* Book I, Chapter 1, 403a3–b15, and *Physics* Book II, Chapter 2, 194a1–27.

3   Dana Ballard, "On the Function of Visual Representation." Reprinted in *Vision and Mind: Selected Readings in the Philosophy of Perception*, edited by Alva Noë and Evan Thompson, 466–8.

4   Jaegwon Kim, 1998, *Mind in a Physical World: An Essay on the Mind–Body Problem and Mental Causation*, Cambridge, MA: MIT Press, Chapter 4.

5   See, for instance, p. 326 of Kim's "Multiple Realizability and the Metaphysics of Reduction." Reprinted in his *Supervenience and Mind*, New York: Cambridge University Press

6   It might seem surprising that eliminativism implies supervenience. But eliminativists deny that there are mental properties, and consequently they deny that two things could differ from each other mentally. If X and Y are physical twins, they must also be mental twins since they are bound to have exactly the same mental properties, namely none.

Chapter 7

Eliminative Physicalism, Instrumentalism, and Anomalous Monism

Overview

Eliminative physicalism claims that mental entities do not exist. Psychological categories are not the categories in terms of which an accurate scientific account of human behavior is to be framed, and, as a result, psychological discourse will eventually be eliminated in favor of a scientific account of human behavior instead of being retained as part of it. The argument for eliminativism begins with a premise shared with identity theorists: psychological discourse is like a scientific theory. Scientific theories are open to revision or outright rejection in light of accumulating evidence. According to eliminativists, psychological discourse has all the features of a failed theory: it is explanatorily impotent, it is not fruitful, and it does not fit in with the rest of what we know. In all likelihood, then, psychological discourse will be completely rejected in the process of developing a scientific account of human behavior. Critics of the eliminativist argument say either that psychological discourse is not like a scientific theory, or else that psychological discourse is not defective in the ways eliminativists claim. Moreover, if eliminativism is true, critics argue, then there is no explanation for how psychological discourse manages to be as successful for describing and explaining human behavior as it appears to be.

Unlike eliminativism, instrumentalism and anomalous monism are both committed to mental realism, to the claim that beliefs, desires, and other mental states exist. Both, however, provide an interpretation of this claim that is weaker than the interpretations provided by other forms of physicalism. These interpretations

Philosophy of Mind: A Comprehensive Introduction, First Edition. William Jaworski.
© 2011 William Jaworski. Published 2011 by Blackwell Publishing Ltd.

are based on the rejection of assumptions other physicalist theories make. Instrumentalism rejects the assumption that psychological discourse aims at expressing real properties. Psychological discourse is instead a mere tool or instrument for predicting human behavior – a tool whose use carries with it no significant ontological implications.

The argument for instrumentalism claims that the goal of theorizing is not truth but empirical adequacy: having a theory that fits the facts. Claiming in addition that there are unobservable entities that correspond to the theory's postulates is both unnecessary and undesirable. The argument against instrumentalism is analogous to the argument against eliminativism: it seems incapable of explaining how psychological discourse manages to be a useful tool for describing and explaining human behavior if its predicates do not correspond to real properties.

Anomalous monism weakens the implications of mental realism by rejecting an ontology of individuals and properties in favor of an ontology of events, and by understanding psychological discourse as a framework for rationally interpreting someone's behavior. The argument for anomalous monism is based on three premises: (1) mental events cause physical events; (2) causal relations require strict laws connecting causes to their effects, and (3) there are no strict laws that can be formulated in a psychological vocabulary; psychological discourse, in other words, is anomalous. From these premises it follows that the laws connecting mental causes to their physical effects cannot be formulated in a psychological vocabulary; they can only be formulated in a physical vocabulary. If that is the case, however, then mental causes must be describable in a physical vocabulary, and from this it follows that those causes must be physical events. Hence, mental events are physical events – this is the 'monism' in anomalous monism; all events are physical events. Critics of anomalous monism claim that premises (2) and (3) are not adequately supported, and that the theory has problems accommodating (1).

7.1 The Argument For Eliminativism

Eliminativism seems to many people an extreme and even bizarre view, but many distinguished philosophers have flirted with it including Willard van Orman Quine, Richard Rorty (1931–2007), and Paul Feyerabend (1924–1994). Moreover, eliminativists have argued forcefully in its favor. The philosopher who has done the most to articulate and defend the view is Paul M. Churchland. Other eliminativists have tended to follow his lead, so it is his version of eliminativism and the argument for it that we will focus on.

Churchland's argument for eliminativism runs as follows: Any highly defective scientific theory is a candidate for complete rejection in favor of a better theory. But ordinary psychological discourse – often called 'folk psychology' – is a highly

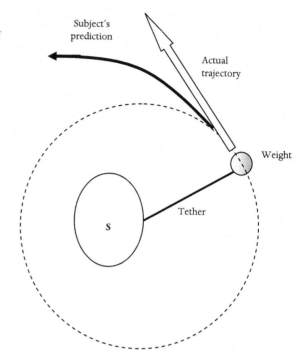

Test subjects are asked to predict the trajectory of a weight tethered to a rope that S swings in a circular path. The actual trajectory dictated by physical laws is tangential to the circular path, but many subjects inaccurately predict a curved path instead. Some researchers conclude that most people operate with an intuitive and largely inaccurate prescientific theory about the physical universe – a folk theory.

Subject's prediction

Actual trajectory

Weight

Tether

S

Figure 7.1   Folk physics

defective scientific theory. Consequently, folk psychology is a candidate for complete rejection in favor of a better scientific theory.

'Folk psychology' is a derogatory label for ordinary psychological discourse. It was coined by analogy with 'folk physics'. In the 1970s and 80s psychologists began studying people's intuitive ideas about how the physical universe operated. They discovered that many people – even most – had inaccurate ideas about how physical systems behave. For example, they would present test subjects with the scenario depicted in Figure 7.1. Here an individual, S, is swinging a weight by a tether along the circular path. The researchers asked test subjects to describe what trajectory the weight would take if S let go of the tether. The correct answer is that the weight will follow a rectilinear path at a tangent to the circular path it was following initially. But most subjects failed to answer correctly. In fact, most subjects failed to answer a large number of such questions correctly. Researchers concluded that most people operate with an intuitive and largely inaccurate prescientific theory about the physical universe – a folk theory – to which they appeal when trying to describe and explain the behavior of the physical systems around them. This theory was dubbed 'folk physics'. Eliminativists claim that ordinary psychological discourse is a folk theory analogous to folk physics. It is an intuitive but largely inaccurate prescientific theory about human behavior – a theory so inaccurate that it will ultimately be rejected entirely in favor of a superior one.

Scientific theorizing is always a gamble. Any theory we advance is open to the possibility of falsification in light of accumulating evidence. When a theory is falsified we can do one of two things with it. If its flaws are relatively minor, we can revise the theory in relatively minor ways to bring it in line with the data. If, for instance, our theory of gravitation postulates a gravitational constant of $6.673 \times 10^{-11} \, \mathrm{m^3/kg(s^2)}$, and experimental evidence shows that this is false, that the gravitational constant is $6.674 \times 10^{-11} \, \mathrm{m^3/kg(s^2)}$ instead, then we will most likely revise our theory by adopting a different value for the gravitational constant instead of rejecting the entire theoretical framework. On the other hand, there are times when a theory is so inaccurate, that we do reject it entirely. As we saw in Section 4.4, these are the episodes in the history of science that motivate eliminativists – episodes in which a theory has been so radically mistaken that no minor tweaking could bring it in line with the facts. In these cases a theory is not revised, but simply rejected in favor of a better theory.

When a theory is completely rejected in this way, its ontology is rejected as well. A theory's ontology is the inventory of entities that it claims exist. Atomic theory, for instance, claims that atoms exist; atoms are thus included in its ontology. Similarly, phlogiston was included in the ontology of the phlogiston theory of combustion. The phlogiston theory claimed that all combustible bodies were permeated by subtle fluid called 'phlogiston' which was released when those bodies were ignited. This theory was ultimately rejected, and replaced by a better one: the oxidative theory of combustion which claimed that bodies combusted on account of their atoms combining with oxygen in the atmosphere. When the phlogiston theory was rejected, scientists did not continue to believe in the existence of phlogiston. The idea that there was such a substance, they concluded, was a mistake: there was no phlogiston; combustion was really due to oxygen. When the phlogiston theory was replaced by the oxidative theory, its ontology was replaced by the ontology of the new theory as well.

What happened in the case of phlogiston has happened many other times in the history of science. The same thing happened with the caloric theory of heat and the aether theory of light. Both postulated the existence of fluid-like substances to explain thermal phenomena and optic phenomena, respectively; and each was replaced by a better theory: the kinetic theory of heat in the former case, and the electromagnetic theory of light in the latter. In both cases, the ontology of the rejected theory was replaced by the ontology of the superior theory: we now know that there is no such material as caloric; thermal phenomena are due to the kinetic energy of molecules. Likewise, we know that there is no such material as luminiferous aether; light is instead a form of electromagnetic radiation. According to eliminativists, something analogous will be true of our folk psychological theory of human behavior.

Folk psychology, say eliminativists, is a crude theory that most of us use in our pedestrian dealings to describe and explain human behavior. Suppose, for instance, that we explain why Caesar crossed the Rubicon by saying he *wanted* to secure political power and *believed* marching on Rome the best means of securing it. Eliminativists and others who endorse the theory model of psychological discourse (Section 5.3), such as identity theorists and functionalists, claim that in saying this we are appealing to a theory that includes beliefs and desires in its ontology, and that according to this theory, beliefs and desires are related to each other in ways that explain why Caesar acted as he did. For example, beliefs and desires might be related to each other in the way expressed by the following generalization:

When x wants y, and believes doing z the best means of attaining y, then if nothing inhibits x's pursuit of y, x will generally do z.

According to the theory model, beliefs and desires are entities postulated by a theory that aims at explaining human behavior. Whether or not that theory is true is for the natural sciences to determine. According to most physicalists, the sciences will prove that the theory is true, that there really are beliefs, desires, and other mental states. But according to eliminativists, the sciences will prove that the theory is false, that there really are no such things as beliefs, desires, or other mental states. The real explanation for human behavior has nothing to do with such entities, say eliminativists. Once we get the accurate scientific theory of human behavior, we will discover that the entities in its ontology do not correspond in any way to the entities in the ontology of folk psychology; we will discover that the physical categories in terms of which human behavior is accurately explained will not correspond in any way to beliefs, desires, or other mental states. In short, folk psychology will not be revised in light of accumulating evidence about human behavior; it will be completely rejected in favor of the superior theory.

But why should we suppose that the science is going to turn out this way? Even if we accept that ordinary psychological discourse is a theory, why should we suppose that it is radically defective – so radically defective that a complete scientific account of human behavior will result not in its revision but in its complete rejection? There are at least three arguments to this effect.

First, worthy scientific theories, ones that are likely to be revised not rejected, are explanatorily powerful. At the very least, a worthy scientific theory is able to explain the behavior of the entities in its ontology. But, says the argument, folk psychology is explanatorily impotent. The ontology of folk psychology includes phenomena such as sleep, dreaming, and vision; and yet folk psychology is not able to explain why we sleep, why we dream, or how we are able to construct a three-dimensional visual experience from a pair of two-dimensional retinal images.

If folk psychology were a worthy scientific theory, it would be able to explain these phenomena, but it cannot.

Second, worthy scientific theories are *fertile*: they make novel predictions, suggest avenues for further research, and develop over time. Einstein's general theory of relativity, for instance, made a novel prediction about the effects of gravity on light. It predicted that a massive body such as a star would warp space-time in a way that acted like a lens. This suggested an avenue for new research and experimentation, and, in 1919, the astrophysicist Arthur Eddington confirmed the lensing effect of the sun's gravity: during a solar eclipse, he observed that the light from stars passing near the sun was slightly bent. Similarly, quantum theory began with only a handful of particles in its ontology, but over time the research avenues it opened led to the discovery of an entire particle zoo. By contrast with these theories, folk psychology does not make novel predictions, and it has not developed over time. The folk psychology that we have today is more or less exactly the same as the folk psychology of our ancient human ancestors.

Third, worthy scientific theories fit in with the rest of what we know. Part of what we know about human beings is that we are products of natural selection whose development is governed by DNA, protein synthesis, and other physiological processes. When we begin describing these processes it becomes increasingly unclear how folk psychology is supposed to fit into the broader scientific picture of human nature we have been developing over the past 100 years. Folk psychology's lack of fit with the rest of what science tells us about human nature gives us good reason to suppose that folk psychology is a radically defective theory, one that will be rejected not revised as science advances.

Critics of eliminativism have attacked both the argument for it and the theory itself. Criticisms of the argument have tended to focus on the second premise, the claim that folk psychology is a highly defective theory. This premise is really a conjunction of two claims: (1) folk psychology is a theory, and (2) it is highly defective. Critics of Claim (1) argue on various grounds that psychological discourse is not a theory. Their arguments motivate alternative accounts of psychological discourse such as the account endorsed by hylomorphists (Section 11.7). According to hylomorphists, psychological predicates and terms do not postulate unobservable hypothetical entities; they instead refer to or express directly observable patterns of social and environmental interaction. If hylomorphists are right, then Claim (1) is false.

Most critics of eliminativism, however, accept Claim (1) and instead target Claim (2). Eliminativist arguments for this claim are flawed, they say. Consider first the appeal to explanatory impotence. It is flawed because theories are typically designed to play a limited set of explanatory roles, and we do not consider a theory defective if it fails to play a role it wasn't designed to play. Consider an example.

Gresham's Law is a principle in economics often expressed by the generalization 'Bad money drives out good'. Imagine, for instance, that the US mint began producing pennies made of solid gold. The value of these pennies as currency would be 1 cent. Their value as gold bullion, however, would (by current market value) be approximately $200.[1] According to Gresham's Law, the gold pennies would eventually go out of circulation as people began keeping them to resell as bullion in contrast to using them as 1 cent pieces. As a result, the cheap copper-alloy pennies – the "bad" pennies – would be the only ones left in circulation; they would have driven out the "good" gold pennies: bad money drives out good. Imagine now that somebody argued as follows:

> Gresham's Law is radically defective. It cannot explain the behavior of the objects in its domain. It says that there is such a thing as money. Pennies are money, so Gresham's Law should be able to explain why pennies behave as they do. But it can't. It can't explain, for instance, why copper pennies but not gold pennies turn green when they corrode!

It should be clear what is wrong with this argument: Gresham's Law is a law of economics, and economics is not in the business of trying to explain every kind of behavior but only economic behavior. As a result, it is not a strike against Gresham's Law that it cannot explain metallic corrosion; that is not the kind of behavior economic laws are supposed to explain; it is not the kind of behavior they are in the business of explaining.

An analogous point seems to apply to the argument against folk psychology. Different sciences are in different lines of work. If folk psychology cannot explain why we sleep or why we dream, or how we are able to construct a three-dimensional visual experience from a pair of two-dimensional retinal images, perhaps the reason is not that folk psychology is defective, but that folk psychology is in a different line of work. Perhaps, for instance, it is merely in the business of explaining people's choices, feelings, personality, and character traits and not the physiological processes that make these things possible.

Consider likewise the eliminativist's second argument, the appeal to theoretical infertility. The problem with this argument, say critics, is that a theory may be infertile for at least two different reasons: it could be highly defective, or it could be *complete*. Imagine, for instance, that somebody ran the following argument:

> Basic arithmetic is a radically defective theory that will eventually be eliminated. Successful theories are fertile; they grow; they make novel predictions; they suggest avenues for further research. But basic arithmetic has not grown, or made novel predictions, or suggested avenues for further research throughout all of recorded history.

The problem with this argument is that if arithmetic has failed to develop it is not because it is defective, but because its basic axioms or principles have grown as far as it is possible for them to grow: they are complete. Something analogous might be true of folk psychology: perhaps its basic principles have failed to grow because it too is complete.

Finally, say critics, it is not clear that folk psychology fails to fit in with the rest of what we know about humans and their place in the natural world. The field of evolutionary psychology, which has been developing over the past 25 years, might be able to locate folk psychology within a broader evolutionary picture of human life. Consider, for instance, what is often called the *Machiavellian intelligence hypothesis* or the *social brain hypothesis*. It claims that psychological discourse evolved principally as a tool for social interaction and manipulation. Individual animals who possessed that tool had a selective advantage over those who did not: they ended up being able to manipulate social situations more effectively and thus gained for themselves a competitive edge in social hierarchies, in mate selection, and in other aspects of social life that had a bearing on reproductive success. If some version of the Machiavellian intelligence hypothesis turns out to be correct, then it will be clear how folk psychology fits into the broader scientific story of human nature – mastery of folk psychology was selectively advantageous for animals like us.

In addition to targeting the arguments for Claim (2), critics of eliminativism have also argued directly that the claim is false. Psychological discourse, they say, is not highly defective. It is instead a highly effective framework for describing and explaining human behavior, one that we use all the time in our pedestrian dealings precisely because it is so effective. We will return to this idea momentarily since it is the basis of the main argument against eliminativism.

7.2   The Argument Against Eliminativism

The foregoing considerations target the argument for eliminativism, but critics have also argued against eliminativism itself. One common if misguided objection to eliminativism claims that the theory is self-refuting. Eliminativists claim that there are no beliefs, says the objection, and yet they themselves must believe their own theory. Their view is thus incoherent: it implies both that there are beliefs and that there are not beliefs. The obvious flaw in this argument is that it assumes wrongly that eliminativists must believe their own theory. In response, eliminativists can argue as follows:

> We do not believe our theory, nor do we disbelieve it. In point of fact, there are no such things as beliefs or disbeliefs to have; there are no propositional attitudes at all. To assume, as the objection does, that we must believe our theory is therefore implicitly to beg the question against us, for it assumes that there are such things as beliefs, yet this is precisely what we eliminativists deny.

A stronger argument against eliminativism is based on the descriptive and explanatory success of psychological discourse. We use folk psychology in our pedestrian dealings with great effectiveness. In fact, there is no better way of making sense of human behavior – of describing, predicting, or explaining it – than by the use of psychological predicates and terms. If I want to predict what you will do under certain circumstances, the most effective means I have at my disposal is my knowledge of what you tend to believe or desire, or how you tend to feel about this or that. Likewise, if I want to explain your behavior, the best means I have of doing so is to appeal to what I know about your beliefs, your desires, your feelings, and other mental states. For the most part, in our pedestrian dealings these appeals are very effective.

Moreover, when we fail to predict accurately what someone will do, or when we fail to explain accurately why someone acted as he or she did, we do not take it as an indication that the entire system of psychological predicates and terms is flawed, or that we have reached the limits of its effective range; we take it as an indication, rather, that we need to learn more about that person's beliefs, desires, and other mental states. If your behavior surprises me, I conclude that I have not altogether understood who you are, what you think, or how you feel; I do not conclude that you have no beliefs, desires, or feelings.

Psychological discourse is thus very effective for describing and explaining human behavior. This effectiveness requires some type of explanation, however, and the most obvious explanation is that there really are beliefs, desires, and other mental states. Conversely, if there are no beliefs, desires, or other mental states, then it becomes unclear how the effectiveness of psychological discourse can be explained at all. The biggest challenge facing eliminativists, then, and what many are likely to see as its biggest flaw, is that it seems incapable of explaining how psychological discourse manages to be as effective as it is if there are in fact no properties of the sort it postulates.

Because eliminativism is so counterintuitive and also seems incapable of explaining the apparent success of psychological discourse, it has always been a marginal theory in philosophy of mind. In practice it operates more as a constraint on theorizing than a serious theory in its own right: if a theory of mind implies eliminativism, this is typically considered a strike against the theory. Most physicalists, then, are reductivists or nonreductivists not eliminativists.

7.3   Instrumentalism

Instrumentalism differs from other forms of physicalism because it rejects a *realist* understanding of psychological discourse. The physicalist theories considered so far, forms of reductivism, nonreductivism, and eliminativism, all assume that when we use psychological discourse we are at least trying to express real

properties, that the purpose of psychological discourse is to describe real properties that things possess. Instrumentalists reject this assumption. They claim
instead that psychological discourse is merely a tool or instrument that we use
for the purpose of predicting human behavior. Instrumentalism in philosophy
of mind is an application of a more general understanding of theoretical discourse. With the exception of behaviorism, the physicalist theories considered
so far all agree that psychological discourse is theoretical discourse, that our
ordinary psychological ways of describing human behavior constitute a theory.
Instrumentalists agree that psychological discourse is a theory, but they disagree
about the nature of theoretical discourse. The views considered so far claim
that theoretical predicates and terms aim to describe real objects and properties.
When we use theoretical terms such as 'electron' we actually aim to refer to
mind-independent objects in the world. Instrumentalists reject this understanding
of theoretical talk. According to them, theoretical terms such as 'electron' are
simply tools we use in an effort to predict the behavior of things around
us. Speaking of electrons, for instance, helps us to predict how an electronic
device will work, or how some experimental equipment set up by physicists
will operate. But in using the term 'electron' we are not thereby committed to
the real existence of such entities. Consider an analogy with the depiction of
the solar system in Figure 7.2(A) and the depiction of a plane dropping a bomb
in Figure 7.2(B).

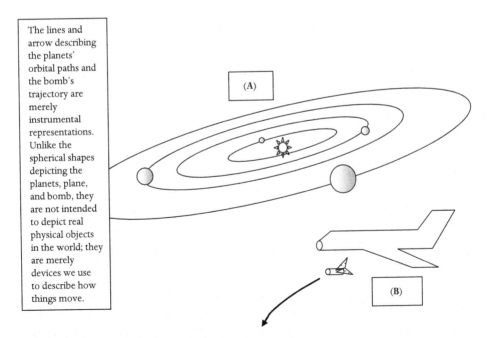

The lines and arrow describing the planets' orbital paths and the bomb's trajectory are merely instrumental representations. Unlike the spherical shapes depicting the planets, plane, and bomb, they are not intended to depict real physical objects in the world; they are merely devices we use to describe how things move.

(A)

(B)

Figure 7.2   Real versus instrumental representations

The depiction of the solar system consists of representations drawn on paper. These representations are of at least two different types that operate in two different ways. The circular image of the Sun at the center, and the circular images of the planets farther out are all meant to represent actual objects that a suitably situated observer might be able to see. By contrast, the lines depicting the orbital paths of the planets around the Sun are not meant to depict real objects at all. They are meant to depict the ways in which the planets move, not entities that a suitably situated observer would be able to see. The same is true of Figure 7.2(B): the representations of the airplane and the bomb are meant to depict real objects; the arrow, by contrast, is not meant to depict a real object, but the bomb's trajectory. There are thus two different kinds of representations in Figures 7.2(A) and 7.2(B): representations whose purpose is to depict real objects in the world, and representations whose purpose is to depict not real objects in the world, but the way real objects behave; they are tools we use to describe how real objects move.

The distinction between the two types of representations in Figures 7.2(A) and 7.2(B) is analogous to the distinction instrumentalists draw between theoretical and non-theoretical ways of describing the world. Non-theoretical discourse aims at describing real objects and properties, but theoretical discourse is not like this. Theoretical descriptions are mere tools we use to achieve certain predictive goals. In our efforts to predict the behavior of the objects around us, we end up coining theoretical predicates and terms.

7.4   Arguments For and Against Instrumentalism

The argument for instrumentalism claims that a realist interpretation of theoretical discourse is burdened with unnecessary ontological baggage. Theories, say instrumentalists, are instruments that enable us to make predications. If a theory is *empirically adequate* – if it fits the empirical facts of the matter and enables us to make accurate predications – then that theory does its job. We need not expect more of a theory than empirical adequacy. Realists suppose that the entities a theory postulates must really exist in the way the objects of pedestrian acquaintance really exist. They suppose, in other words, that theories must be true in the sense that they correspond to the world. But, say instrumentalists, this supposition trades on a mistaken understanding of theoretical discourse. The goal of theoretical discourse is not truth, but empirical adequacy – the ability accurately to control and predict the behavior of the systems we encounter. From a theoretical standpoint, say instrumentalists, the demand that we have theories that are true adds nothing worthwhile. Consider, for instance, the reasons we would want a theory to be true. They seem to be precisely the reasons we want a theory to be empirically adequate: a true theory would enable us to predict and control the systems we encounter just as an empirically adequate theory does. What, then, would the demand for a true theory supply in addition to empirical adequacy? All it could really supply, say instrumentalists, is a further burden: a demand not only that the theory allow for accurate prediction and control, but that the theory actually correspond to things that exist. One problem with this demand, according to instrumentalists, is that it might be impossible for us ever to satisfy it. The best evidence for a theory's truth is its empirical adequacy. What in addition to the empirical facts of the matter could prove that a theory was true? Not only does the goal of achieving truth place an additional, unnecessary burden on us, say instrumentalists, it might place a burden on us that is ultimately impossible to carry.

The argument against instrumentalism is similar to the argument against eliminativism. According to instrumentalists, psychological discourse is empirically adequate. We can use it successfully to describe, explain, predict, and manipulate human behavior. But if psychological discourse is useful for all these purposes, critics ask, what explains that usefulness? The most obvious answer is a realist one: psychological discourse is useful because it is accurate – because its predicates and terms correspond to real objects and properties. Instrumentalists are likely to respond that requesting an explanation for the success of psychological discourse is misguided and question-begging – misguided because the goal of theorizing is to construct empirically adequate theories, not to explain why those theories manage to be empirically adequate; and question-begging because the demand that we explain why theories manage to be empirically adequate already presupposes that there is more to the task of theorizing than achieving empirical adequacy; it already presupposes, in other words, that instrumentalism must be false. Instrumentalism nevertheless remains a marginal view in philosophy of mind.

7.5   Anomalous Monism

The 'monism' in 'anomalous monism' refers to physicalism. Like the physicalist theories considered so far, anomalous monism is committed to the claim that everything is physical. But anomalous monism is different from the other physicalist theories we've considered because of two factors: its ontology and its account of psychological language.

Our discussion of mind–body theories has so far been based on a *substance–attribute ontology*. An ontology is an inventory of the kinds of entities that exist. A substance–attribute ontology takes substances and attributes – that is individuals and properties – to be the basic entities, and it understands other entities in terms of these. Exponents of substance–attribute ontologies often take events, for instance, to consist in individuals having properties at times. This is often called a *property-instantiation* or *property-exemplification* theory of events. The event *Madeleine's playing chess this morning*, for instance, consists in an individual, *Madeleine*, having a property, *playing chess*, at a time, *this morning*. Anomalous

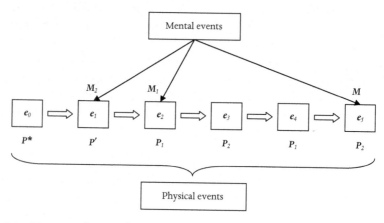

Figure 7.3   Events and anomalous monism

monism is based on a different understanding of events. On a substance–attribute theory of events, events are distinguished from each other by the individual, properties, and times they comprise. If $Event_1$ and $Event_2$ involve different individuals or different properties or occur at different times, then they are different events. What distinguishes Eleanor's playing the flute at time t from Gabriel's playing the flute at time t, for instance, is that these events involve different individuals: Eleanor versus Gabriel. Similarly what distinguishes Eleanor's playing the flute at time t from Eleanor's being 5 feet tall at time t is that these events involve different properties: playing the flute versus being 5 feet tall. Finally, what distinguishes Eleanor's playing the flute yesterday from Eleanor's playing the flute today is that these events occur at different times. On Davidson's view, however, events are not distinguished by their constituent individuals, properties, and times, but by their causes and effects. Figure 7.3 illustrates this idea. It depicts a series of events. Each event in the series is caused by an antecedent event and causes a subsequent event. What distinguishes each event in the chain from every other event in the chain is its cause and its effect. What distinguishes e_1 from e_2, for instance, is that e_1 is caused by e_0 and causes e_2, whereas e_2 is caused by e_1 and causes e_3.

The Ms and the Ps in the diagram represent mental and physical descriptions, respectively. According to Davidson, events can be described using different vocabularies. In the figure, an event accompanied by an 'M' is describable using a mental vocabulary, and an event accompanied by a 'P' is describable using a physical vocabulary. On Davidson's view, an event qualifies as mental if it is describable using a mental vocabulary, and it qualifies as physical if it is describable using a physical vocabulary. Moreover, a given event might be describable using both vocabularies. In this way, anomalous monism is similar to the psychophysical identity theory discussed earlier. The identity theory claims that the same property can be expressed by two different predicates, a mental predicate and a physical predicate. In the same way, anomalous monism claims that the same event can be described by two different sentences, a sentence framed in psychological terms such as 'Xavier wants to vacation in Italy' and a sentence framed in physical terms such as 'Xavier's brain has temporal lobe activity'.

According to anomalous monism, all events are physical events; all events are describable in physical terms – hence every event depicted in Figure 7.3 is accompanied by a '*P*'. Some of the events in that series can also be described mentally – hence, some of them are also accompanied by an '*M*'. Because all events are physical, according to anomalous monism, it follows that those mental events are also physical events – they are events which are describable in both a mental vocabulary and a physical vocabulary. Like all anti-eliminative forms of physicalism, then, anomalous monism claims that mental events are physical events.

The other feature that distinguishes anomalous monism from the other physicalist theories considered so far is its account of psychological language. This feature is expressed by the 'anomalous' in 'anomalous monism'. The word 'anomalous' derives from the Greek *nomos*, which means *law*. The prefix 'a-' is like the Latin prefix 'non-': it means 'not' or 'without'. To call something anomalous, then, is to say that it does not operate in a lawlike way; that it operates without law, in the absence of law, in a way that fails to conform to lawlike principles.

According to anomalous monism, psychological discourse is anomalous. There are no strict laws that can be formulated in a psychological vocabulary – no laws that do not admit of exceptions. This implies two things. First, there are no strict laws that can be formulated in purely psychological terms such as the following:

1   If an individual, S, is afraid, then S will experience anxiety.

Second, there are no strict laws that can be formulated in mixed mental and physical terms such as the following:

2   If an individual, S, is afraid, then the cells in S's amygdala will be active.
3   If the cells in the amygdala of an individual, S, are active, then S will be afraid.

Because there are no strict laws connecting mental descriptions with physical descriptions as in (2) and (3), a given type of mental description need not correspond to a single type of physical description. It need not always be the case, for instance, that being afraid corresponds to activity in the amygdala. In one situation the activity of cells in the amygdala might be correlated with fear, and in another not. The reason mental and physical descriptions are not necessarily correlated one–one is that they satisfy different interests. We use physical descriptions when we are interested in describing events in terms of the strict laws that explain causal connections among them. We use mental descriptions when we are interested in describing events in terms of their rational relations to other events, their positions within a broader network of reasons. Psychological discourse is *interpretive*, according to anomalous monists; we use it to construct interpretations of someone's behavior that renders that behavior rational. Because mental and physical descriptions satisfy different interests, physical theory cannot take over the descriptive and explanatory roles played by psychological discourse. As a result, psychological discourse is not reducible to physical theory. Anomalous monism is thus a form of nonreductive physicalism. It claims that everything is physical, and yet it denies that physics is capable of taking over the descriptive and explanatory roles played by psychological discourse.

7.6   The Argument For Anomalous Monism

Davidson's argument for anomalous monism runs as follows:

1 Mental events cause physical events.
2 Mental events cause physical events only if there are strict laws connecting mental events with physical events.
3 No strict laws can be formulated using a psychological vocabulary.

From these premises, Davidson concludes that mental events must be identical to physical events. To see how he arrives at this conclusion, let us consider the premises one at a time.

We appeal to mental events all the time to explain actions. We explain why Caesar crossed the Rubicon, for instance, by appeal to his desire for political power and his belief that marching on Rome was the best means of achieving it. Davidson argues that we would not be able to explain human behavior in this way unless mental events caused physical events. When we describe an event as an action, says Davidson, we locate it within a broader pattern of reasons – the reasons the agent chose to act as he or she did. For any given action, however, there might be many reasons why someone in those circumstances would choose to act the way the agent did. There might be many reasons, for instance, why someone in Alexander's circumstances might choose to kill his rich uncle: revenge, greed, anger, and so on. Among these reasons, what is it that distinguishes the reason Alexander acted as he did from the many other reasons someone in his circumstances might act that way? According to Davidson, the answer is that the agent's reason causes the action. Although someone might kill a rich uncle for revenge, greed, or anger, it was Alexander's greed that caused him to put the cyanide in his uncle's cocktail – that was the reason Alexander acted as he did. Psychological explanation involves identifying the reasons why people act as they do. So, according to Davidson, we can manage to explain human behavior psychologically only if reasons can be causes – only if beliefs, desires, and other mental events manage to cause human behavior. These are the reasons behind Premise (1).

According to Davidson, however, causal relations require strict laws. The universe is an orderly place. Causation does not happen at random, but always in an orderly or predictable way. If A-events cause B-events, they do so according to a rule. There is always a principle, a law, according to which As operate as causes of Bs. It is because there are regularities of this sort that scientists are inspired to look for causes. If we notice that a particular type of detritus always appears on a beach in Northern California after a storm in some far away part of the Pacific, we can be confident that there is a chain of events that connects the storm with the detritus – a chain in which each link is governed by a lawlike regularity. Many lawlike regularities admit of exceptions: there are exceptions to the laws of economics, the laws of psychology, of biology, and even chemistry. But the laws of fundamental physics are different. They are strict; they have no exceptions. According to Davidson, these are the laws that are ultimately responsible for connecting all events in the universe. These are the reasons behind Premise (2).

On Davidson's view, then, causal relations are always underwritten by strict laws. Consequently, since mental events cause physical events, those causal relations must be underwritten by strict laws as well. There must be a strict law, for instance, which connects Alexander's greed with his act of putting cyanide in his uncle's cocktail. And yet, says Davidson, there are no strict psychological laws; there are no laws that can be formulated using a psychological vocabulary. There is, for instance, no law (thankfully) that says, "Every time someone, S, is greedy for an uncle's wealth, S will murder the uncle to secure that wealth." But if there is no strict law of this sort, and if there are no psychological laws in general, then the laws connecting mental events to physical events cannot be psychological laws. They must instead be physical laws since physics is the science that formulates strict laws. But if the laws connecting mental events with physical events are physical laws, then it appears that mental events must be physical events – they must be events that are describable in a physical vocabulary. Consider an example based on Figure 7.3.

Event e_2 causes e_3 – an M_1-event causes a P_2-event. According to Premise (2), there must be a strict law that connects e_2 to e_3, but according to Premise (3), this law cannot be formulated in psychological terms. There can be no law, for instance, that says, "Every M_1-event causes a P_2-event." In that case, however, there must be a physical law that explains the connection between e_2 and e_3. Imagine that P_1-events always cause P_2-events, and that P_1-events are the only events that cause P_2-events. We know that e_3 was caused by e_2, which is a mental event, but since e_3 is a P_2-event, we know that it must have been caused by a P_1-event. We thus conclude that e_2 must be a P_1-event; we conclude, in other words, that the mental event e_2 must be a physical event. There must be a strict physical law that connects Alexander's greed with his act of murder. This law cannot be a psychological law; it must instead be a physical law. Hence, there must be a way of describing Alexander's greed and a way of describing his action in physical terms – a way that corresponds to a strict law connecting physical events. But if Alexander's greed and Alexander's action can be described physically, then his greed and his action must be physical events. Hence, mental events must be physical events.

The crucial premise in this argument, the one we have not yet discussed, is Premise (3). Why should we believe that there are no strict psychological laws? Davidson argues that if there were such laws, they would have to be either (a) laws formulated using a psychological vocabulary by itself, or (b) laws formulated using a psychological vocabulary and a physical vocabulary in conjunction. According to Davidson, however, there are laws of neither sort. Davidson's arguments for these claims are notoriously difficult, and any interpretation of them is bound to be controversial, but their gist is as follows.

In support of (a), the claim that there are there are no strict laws that can be formulated using a psychological vocabulary by itself, Davidson argues that mental occurrences are subject to too many nonmental influences for there to be purely psychological laws. Consider, for instance, our moods and emotions. These are often affected by factors such as the weather, medication, and alcohol. Whether or not fear results in anxiety, for example, depends on a range of physiological factors. But if that is the case, there can be no strict laws that are expressible using only a psychological vocabulary since the truth of any psychological generalization will always depend to some extent on physiological conditions.

In support of (b), the claim that there are no laws that can be formulated using a psychological vocabulary in conjunction with a physical vocabulary, Davidson appeals to two premises: (i) psychological discourse and physical discourse are governed by different principles, and (ii) if two forms of discourse are governed by different principles, their predicates and terms cannot co-occur in law statements. From these premises it follows that psychological and physical predicates and terms cannot co-occur in law statements; that is, there can be no laws that are formulated using a psychological vocabulary and a physical vocabulary in conjunction. The defense of (b) is the most complicated part of Davidson's argument.

According to Davidson, psychological discourse is rational discourse. When we describe events psychologically, we describe them in terms of reasons. Psychological predicates and terms are governed by a principle of rationality, as Davidson puts it. Scientific discourse, by contrast, is not governed by a principle of rationality. When we describe events scientifically, according to Davidson, we describe them not in terms of reasons, but purely in terms of causes. The difference between psychological discourse and natural scientific discourse comes out clearly if we contrast the way we revise psychological descriptions and the way we revise physical ones.

Psychological and physical descriptions are both revisable in light of countervailing evidence, but they are not revisable in the same way. In particular, physical descriptions are not revisable in light of a principle of rationality. We do not alter a scientific theory because it would render the behavior of systems operating by its principles more rational. Revisions to the fabric of natural science are performed independently of considerations of rationality. But this is not the case with psychological descriptions. Suppose we describe Gabriel psychologically as wanting to light the grill, and as believing the use of lighter fluid the best means. If we see him begin dousing the coals with water, we revise our description by saying he believed mistakenly that the water bottle was filled with lighter fluid. If this description is challenged; if, for instance, he says, "Why yes, I did know it was filled with water," we revise our description yet again in a way that renders his behavior rational: we describe him as, say, feeling too embarrassed to admit his mistake, or as really not having wanted to light the grill, but as having wanted only to seem to be doing so. We revise our description of his behavior, in other words, to accommodate the general idea that he is a rational being. Contrast this with a case in which we revise a physical description. Imagine that we observe a number of falling bodies, and formulate a hypothesis implying that terrestrial bodies fall at a rate of $7\,\mathrm{m/s^2}$. If repeated experiments indicate a rate of $9.8\,\mathrm{m/s^2}$ instead, we could revise our description of the situation in a number of ways: by discarding our hypothesis, by discarding the experimental results as somehow flawed, even by discarding the gravitational constant of the universe. But whatever we choose to do, however we choose to alter our description of the situation, our choice does not depend on considerations of rationality; we do not alter our overall set of scientific assumptions with an eye to rendering the behavior of falling bodies more rational. The same is true of any branch of natural science. Natural scientific descriptions are not revisable in the same way as psychological ones; rationality is not a consideration with the former as it is with the latter.

Because psychological discourse and scientific discourse differ in this way, says Davidson; because rationality is a consideration with one but not the other, it is not possible to put psychological predicates and terms together in a single law statement with physical predicates and terms. On this point Davidson draws an analogy with so-called "gruesome" predicates and terms. Consider the following statement:

H1   All emeralds are grue.

Something is grue exactly if it is either observed before, say, December 31, 2017, and is green, or is not observed before that time and is blue. Although (H1) has the look of a genuine law statement, it is not. We can tell, because it is not confirmed by its positive instances the way law statements are. If we discover that this particular piece of copper conducts electricity, that gives us some reason, however slight, to suppose that *all* copper conducts electricity. Likewise, every observation of a green emerald lends credibility however slightly to the following generalization:

H2   All emeralds are green.

But every positive instance of (H2) is also a positive instance of (H1); every emerald observed to be green is also observed to be grue. So if our emerald observations confirm (H2), they should also confirm (H1), but they *don't*, for (H1) predicts falsely that unobserved emeralds are blue! Since law statements are confirmed by their positive instances, and (H1) is not, it follows that (H1) is not a genuine law statement.

Davidson uses this example to show that some predicates are simply not "made for each other," as he puts it. Contrast this with another example:

H3   All emerires are grue.

Something is an emerire just in case it is observed before December 31, 2017, and is an emerald, or is not observed before that time and is a sapphire. This statement does not result in the false prediction that unobserved emeralds are blue; it predicts – truly – that unobserved sapphires are blue. This shows that the problem with statement (H1) is not a function of the predicate 'is grue' all by itself, but of that predicate in combination with the predicate 'is an emerald'. In combination with other "gruesome" predicates such as 'is an emerire', it does not generate the problems associated with (H1). According to Davidson, the predicate 'is grue' is not made for predicates like 'is an emerald', but it *is* made for predicates like 'is an emerire'.

Davidson suggests that attempting to combine psychological predicates and physical predicates would be analogous to attempting to combine 'is grue' and 'is an emerald'. Psychological and physical predicates are not made for each other, and, consequently, any attempt to juxtapose them in a psychophysical law statement would result in a bastardized non-lawlike generalization such as 'All emeralds are grue'. Moreover, says Davidson, whether or not predicates are made for each other in this way is something we can know *a priori*. The claim that all emeralds are green may turn out false, but it at least has a shot at confirmation: it is an empirically respectable hypothesis that can be subject to real testing. The claim that all emeralds are grue, on the other hand, is not even a candidate for lawlike status. The same is true, says Davidson, of psychological predicates and physical predicates: they are not even candidates for co-inclusion in law statements; the rules constituting their respective forms of discourse rule this out.

According to Davidson, then, there are no strict laws that can be formulated using only a psychological vocabulary, and there are no strict laws that can be formulated using a psychological vocabulary in conjunction with a physical vocabulary. But this implies that there can be no strict laws that are formulated using a psychological vocabulary at all. But if there are no strict psychological laws, and yet mental events cause physical events, then the strict laws that govern those

mental–physical causal connections must be physical laws. If those laws are physical, however, and mental events are governed by them, then mental events must
be describable in physical terms, and hence they must be physical events. According
to Davidson, then, the anomalous character of psychological discourse together
with the causal character of psychological discourse shows that physicalism is true.

7.7   Arguments Against Anomalous Monism

Some critics of anomalous monism have argued that causal relations do not
require strict laws connecting causes to their effects. Others have argued against
the claim that there are no strict laws that can be formulated in a psychological
vocabulary. Perhaps the best-known argument against anomalous monism,
however, claims that the theory robs beliefs, desires, and other mental states of
any role in the explanation of behavior. Critics who take this line have sometimes
mistakenly attacked a token physicalist view of the sort described in Section 6.12.
Davidson's own view is similar to that token physicalist view but because it is not
exactly the same, the objection has no purchase. There have nevertheless been
other attempts to formulate the objection so that it targets Davidson's own theory
instead of a superficially similar one.

Suppose that Madeleine takes a drink of water because she is thirsty. We would
ordinarily say that her thirst was what caused her to act. According to Davidson,
however, wherever there are causal relations, there must be strict laws that underwrite them. There must therefore be a strict law that connects Madeleine's thirst
to her act of drinking. Ordinarily we might try to express this law in something
like the following way:

L1   If someone is thirsty, and has water available, then that person will take
a drink provided nothing interferes.

A generalization like this seems to express what we would ordinarily take to be
someone's reasons for drinking water: people drink when they are thirsty, water
is available, and there are no overriding conditions that would prevent them from
drinking. The problem with (L1) is that it is formulated using psychological predicates: The predicate 'is thirsty' expresses a mental state, and the predicate 'take a
drink' expresses an action. According to Davidson, however, strict laws – the sort
needed to express causal relations – cannot be formulated using psychological
predicates. (L1), therefore, cannot express the causal relation that explains
Madeleine's action. We instead need a law statement formulated in a purely physical vocabulary such as the following:

L1*   If someone is in physical state P1 and has some water available, then that person will enter into physical state P2 provided nothing interferes.

It is a strict physical law of this sort that enables us to explain Madeleine's behavior. It expresses the real reason Madeleine acted as she did, and the same is true of all Madeleine's actions, and not just hers, but everyone else's too. According to anomalous monism, causal relations must be underwritten by strict laws, and no strict laws can be formulated using a psychological vocabulary. Generalizations like (L1) must therefore be replaced by generalizations like (L1*) if we want to get at the real reasons why things happen as they do. Notice what this implies: In order to get at the real reasons why people act, we need to purge our explanations of any psychological expressions. Consequently, the real reasons why people act as they do – the real causal story behind their actions – is never a psychological one; it is always a purely physical one. Psychological discourse thus lacks any real causal or explanatory import. Anomalous monism strips it of the causal or explanatory status we ordinarily take it to have. The argument against anomalous monism remains controversial.

Further Reading

W. V. O. Quine (1966) nodded toward eliminativism, but he later endorsed anomalous monism (1985). Unlike Churchland's (1981) eliminativist view, however, Quine's is not committed to the theory model of psychological discourse. Richard Rorty (1965) flirted with eliminativism, as did Paul Feyerabend (1963). Patricia S. Churchland (1986) and Stephen Stich (1983) defend eliminativism as well.

For an introductory discussion of research on folk theories see McCloskey (1983). Criticisms of eliminativism and the argument for it can be found in many of the essays in Christiansen and Turner (1993); see also Fodor (1987: Chapter 1). For more on the Machiavellian intelligence hypothesis see Dunbar (1996) and the essays in Byrne and Whiten (1988) and Whiten and Byrne (1997).

Daniel Dennett's Intensional Systems Theory is a form of instrumentalism. The essays in Dennett (1987) are an accessible introduction to Dennett's views. See especially "True Believers: The Intentional Strategy and Why It Works" (1987: Chapter 2). More recently, Dennett (1991b) has tried to distance himself from the earlier instrumentalist characterization of his views. His more considered position is best understood as a form of nonreductive physicalism with a pragmatic twist: we employ psychological discourse because it affords us certain practical benefits that fundamental physics does not. In particular, it enables us to satisfy our desire for ease and efficiency: we can formulate predictions about human behavior much more quickly and easily using psychological discourse than we can using the conceptual resources of fundamental physics. Devitt and Sterelny (1999: Section 15.2) offer a brief and accessible discussion of the tensions generated by the different strands of Dennett's thought.

Davidson's seminal formulation of anomalous monism occurs in two papers (2001c; 2001d), although regrettably both are difficult. The claim that anomalous monism collapses into epiphenomenalism has been advanced by several people including Jaegwon Kim (1989), Ernest Sosa (1984), and Ted Honderich (1982). Davidson (1993) has replied to the charge in a volume that also includes counter-responses by Kim and Sosa (Heil and Mele 1993).

A good introductory discussion of the concept of substance and related concepts in metaphysics can be found in Loux (2002). The idea that events are property instances is endorsed by Jaegwon Kim (1993a), by Alvin Goldman (1970), and by Jonathan Bennett (1988). Davidson (2001b; 2001c; 2001f) defends an alternative view of events.

Note

1   At the time I am writing this, gold is approximately $1,000 per troy ounce, and I estimate that a penny made of solid gold would weigh about 0.2 troy ounces.

Chapter 8

Dual-Attribute Theory

Overview

Dual-attribute theories (DATs) steer a middle course between substance dualism and physicalism. Like substance dualists, dual-attribute theorists claim there are two distinct kinds of properties. Some individuals, they say, have properties that cannot be expressed using the vocabulary of physics. Unlike substance dualists, however, dual-attribute theorists deny that persons are completely nonphysical entities. Like some physicalists, on the other hand, DATs claim that some individuals have both mental and physical properties. In addition, DATs are similar to forms of nonreductive physicalism, since both theories deny that the special sciences are reducible to fundamental physics. Their reasons for denying this are nevertheless different. According to dual-attribute theorists, the reason is that some things have nonphysical properties. According to nonreductive physicalists, the reason is not that there are nonphysical properties, but that fundamental physics cannot satisfy all of our descriptive and explanatory interests.

There are several different kinds of DATs. They differ on account of two factors: (1) what kinds of individuals have both mental and physical properties, and (2) how those mental and physical properties are related. Regarding factor (1), organismic DATs claim that we are organisms. Nonorganismic DATs reject this claim. One argument in their favor appeals to mereological essentialism, the claim that a composite has all of its parts and only those parts essentially. Mereological essentialism is based on a controversial understanding of parts and wholes that draws its inspiration from the axioms of set theory. Critics argue that this account of parthood is implausible.

Philosophy of Mind: A Comprehensive Introduction, First Edition. William Jaworski.
© 2011 William Jaworski. Published 2011 by Blackwell Publishing Ltd.

Regarding factor (2), the most popular DATs are epiphenomenalism and emergentism. Both claim that mental phenomena are caused by or emerge from physical phenomena, but they differ about whether mental phenomena can have a causal influence on physical phenomena in turn: emergentists claim they can; epiphenomenalists claim they cannot.

The argument for epiphenomenalism claims that human behavior can be explained in purely physical terms, but that qualia, the qualitative aspects of experience, cannot. Hence, qualia are epiphenomenal; they exist, but they are not part of the network of causal relations that explains human behavior; they make no causal contribution to it. Critics of epiphenomenalism claim that the premises of this argument are false, and that the theory is absurd since it implies that, for instance, the unpleasant feelings associated with pain or disgust have no influence on our behavior. Emergentist theories do not have this implication. They nevertheless face problems with mental causation of a different sort. In addition, classic emergentist theories appear to have been falsified on purely empirical grounds: they take emergent properties to be emergent forces, but scientific investigation has shown that all forces are physical. Finally, both epiphenomenalism and emergentism face the problem of psychophysical emergence: both have trouble explaining how higher-level properties emerge from lower-level properties. Theses such as panpsychism and panprotopsychism have been advanced to deal with this problem, but these theses face serious problems of their own.

8.1 Dual-Attribute Theory versus Physicalism and Substance Dualism

Dual-attribute theories (DATs) steer a middle course between substance dualism and physicalism. Like forms of substance dualism and unlike forms of physicalism, they are committed to property dualism. They claim that some individuals have properties that cannot be expressed using the vocabulary of physics. Like forms of physicalism and unlike forms of substance dualism, however, DATs deny that persons are completely nonphysical entities. DATs endorse what we called earlier *psychophysical property coincidence*, the claim that some individuals have both mental and physical properties.

Consider again the following claims discussed in Chapter 4:

1   Every individual has some features or engages in some behaviors that can be exhaustively described and explained by physics.
2   Every feature of every individual and everything every individual does can be exhaustively described and explained by physics.

Recall that physicalism endorses (2). It says not merely that *some* features of an individual thing can be physically described, or that *some* of its behavior can be physically explained, but that *all* the features of *every* individual and *all* of its behavior can be physically described and explained. DATs reject this claim. They deny that every feature of every individual admits of an exhaustive physical description and explanation. According to DATs, some individuals have properties that cannot be expressed in physical terms. Physics is not fully sufficient to describe everything there is; some things can only be described and explained using other conceptual frameworks such as psychological discourse.

   DATs are similar in one respect to forms of nonreductive physicalism: they both deny that the special sciences are reducible to fundamental physics. They nevertheless deny this for different reasons. Recall that reduction involves one theory or conceptual framework taking over the descriptive and explanatory roles played by another. According to dual-attribute theorists, the reason fundamental physics cannot take over the descriptive and explanatory roles played by the special sciences is that there are nonphysical properties – some individuals have properties that cannot be expressed in the vocabulary of physics. Nonreductive physicalists, by contrast, deny the existence of nonphysical properties. Like all physicalists, they claim that the only properties that exist are physical ones. Unlike dual-attribute theorists, then, nonreductivists deny the reducibility of the special sciences for reasons that have nothing to do with ontology. According to them, the reason physics cannot take over the descriptive and explanatory roles of the special sciences has to do with our peculiar descriptive and explanatory interests. Sometimes we have interests that can be satisfied only if we use a vocabulary different from that of fundamental physics, they say, but the inability of fundamental physics to satisfy all our interests has no ontological implications. Consider again the Super Physicist described in Chapter 4. It knows all the fundamental physical individuals in the universe, their properties, their relations, and all the laws governing their behavior. But it does not have any mental or biological concepts that would enable it to distinguish living things from nonliving ones or mental beings from nonmental ones. Like physicalists of any sort, nonreductive physicalists are committed to claiming that the Super Physicist's description of the world would miss nothing. If we find the Super Physicist's description unappealing – if it feels to us as though it is missing something – that can only be because it fails to satisfy some peculiar descriptive interests we have. Dual-attribute theorists, by contrast, claim that the Super Physicist's description really is missing something, namely all of the nonphysical properties some individuals have. Nonreductive physicalists deny the reducibility of the special sciences, then, not for ontological reasons as dual-attribute theorists do, but for reasons that concern our descriptive and explanatory interests.

   The difference between DATs and nonreductive physicalism can be characterized even more clearly if we consider realization physicalism. Realization physicalism, recall, is the nonreductivist theory that claims mental properties and other special scientific properties are higher-order properties, logical constructions whose definitions quantify over lower-order physical properties (Section 6.4). According to realization physicalism, having pain, for instance, amounts to having some lower-order physical property that satisfies a condition such as having instances that typically correlate pinpricks, burns, and abrasions, with winces, groans, and similar behavior. Because realization physicalism postulates higher-order properties in addition to first-order physical properties, it is sometimes called a form of property dualism. But this label is misleading. The postulation of higher-order and lower-order properties is not the kind of property dualism that distinguishes monistic theories from dualistic ones. The monistic–dualistic distinction concerns first-order properties alone. All dualistic theories – DATs and substance dualistic theories alike – claim that there are *first-order* nonphysical properties. DATs deny that mental properties are higher-order properties in the realization physicalist's sense; they deny that mental properties are logical constructions of any sort. Mental properties, they claim, are first-order properties that are distinct from first-order physical properties. It is this strong ontological thesis that distinguishes DATs from physicalist theories of all sorts including nonreductivist ones.

DATs differ from substance dualistic theories as well. Substance dualists are committed to rejecting (1), the claim that every individual has some features and behaviors that can be described and explained by physics. According to substance dualists, some individuals have no features that can be physically described and explained. DATs, on the other hand, are compatible with (1). They claim that some individuals have some features that can be described in a physical vocabulary, and that these individuals engage in some behaviors that can be explained in a physical vocabulary. In fact, dual-attribute theorists are free to claim that *all* individuals have some features and engage in behaviors that can be described and explained in a physical vocabulary. Dual-attribute theories thus split the difference between substance dualism and physicalism. Physicalists accept both (1) and (2). Substance dualists reject both (1) and (2). Dual-attribute theorists can accept (1), but they reject (2).

DATs are sometimes referred to as forms of **property dualism**, in contrast to forms of substance dualism. The label 'property dualism' can be misleading, however, because as we have seen, substance dualistic theories are also committed to property dualism. The label 'dual-aspect' has also been used instead of 'dual-attribute', but this can be misleading as well since 'aspect' suggests that according to DATs the mental–physical distinction is merely a matter of how things appear to us – that we can see the same thing in different aspects depending on the conceptual framework we use to describe them. The term 'attribute' captures the ontological nature of the mental–physical distinction less ambiguously.

Finally, DATs should not be confused with neutral monism (Chapter 9). Like dual-attribute theorists, neutral monists claim that some individuals have both mental and physical properties, and that these mental and physical properties are distinct (at least in the sense that they have different definitions). Neutral monists nevertheless add that these individuals and all individuals can be exhaustively described and explained using a neutral conceptual framework, one that is neither mentalistic nor physicalistic. Dual-attribute theorists reject this additional claim. They deny that there is an essential core of neutral properties that characterize everything, that the mental and physical conceptual frameworks are just different frameworks for describing things that are in themselves neither mental nor physical.

8.2   Nonorganismic Dual-Attribute Theories

There are several different kinds of dual-attribute theories. They are distinguished on the basis of two factors: (1) what kinds of individuals have both mental and physical properties, and (2) how those mental and physical properties are related. Let us consider these factors in order.

Organismic DATs claim that we are organisms. The claim that we are organisms is closely associated with **animalism**, the claim that we are animals. The term 'organism', however, is broader than 'animal'. A complex robotic system is not an animal, but it might count as an organism – an artificially constructed organism in particular. Organismic DATs claim that we are complex beings of this sort, either animals or something similar. **Nonorganismic DATs** deny this.

Nonorganismic DATs are similar in many respects to forms of substance dualism. Consider, for instance, the view that each of us is a ghost or spirit inhabiting a human body. This is a type of nonorganismic DAT. It claims that we have mental properties and also physical properties such as spatial location and extension (the ghost is *in* the body, and is extended throughout it). We thus have both mental properties and physical properties, on this view, yet we are not organisms. We might be intimately related to organisms; we might be constituted by organisms, for instance, or be generated by them, but we are certainly not organisms ourselves. Moreover, although we might have physical properties such as spatial location, we do not have the full range of physical characteristics organisms have since we have no organic parts – no internal organs or other physical components. Because nonorganismic DATs deny we are organisms, moreover, they are like forms of substance dualism in another respect: They imply that one of the following claims is false:

1   I have beliefs, desires, hopes, joys, fears, loves, and other mental properties.
2   I am an organism such as a human being.

Because of their similarities to substance dualistic theories, nonorganismic DATs are often called forms of *non-Cartesian dualism*, and many of their exponents are really disaffected substance dualists: they really wanted to be substance dualists, but they were convinced the problems with substance dualism were insurmountable, and thus opted for the next best thing – nonorganismic DAT. Because nonorganismic DAT is similar in its outlook and implications to substance dualism, it can give disaffected substance dualists the kind of theory they are looking for – a theory that rejects our identity with organisms. Yet because it attributes to us some physical properties, even if only an attenuated list of them, it avoids many of the problems substance dualism faces. Consider, for instance, the problem of interaction (Section 3.5). If you and I are physical beings – ghostly beings who inhabit bodies, for instance, or point particles like electrons only with mental properties – then mental–physical causal interactions become less problematic. Because you and I are physical beings, we can belong to the same network of physical causal relations as the human bodies we interact with. The problem of interaction is thus held in check.

But why should we suppose nonorganismic DAT is true? An argument for it would have to establish both the truth of property dualism and the falsity of the claim that we are organisms. We will consider arguments for property dualism momentarily. In addition, we considered one argument that we are not organisms already, namely the argument for substance dualism (Section 3.2). Consider now a different argument for that claim, one advanced by the philosopher Roderick Chisholm.

If I am identical to an organism, Chisholm argued, then I must have the same properties as an organism. This follows directly from Leibniz's law: if x is identical to y, then x and y must have all the same properties since x and y are the very same thing. But, says the argument, I do not have the same properties as an organism. In particular, you and I exist far longer than any organism does.

Organisms are composites – entities with proper parts.[1] The organism seated in this room, for instance, has hands, arms, a torso, legs, a head, and eyes, among other parts. According to Chisholm, however, every composite has exactly the parts it has essentially: it cannot exist without having exactly those parts. If, for instance, S is composed of the parts A, B, and C, then S cannot exist without A, B, and C. If S were to lose one of those parts, S would cease to exist. Moreover, if S were to gain any additional parts, it would also cease to exist. The claim that a composite has all of its parts and only those parts essentially is called **mereological essentialism**.

A mereology is a theory of parts and wholes – from *meros*, the Greek word for part. Mereological essentialism reflects a mereology modeled on set theory. It understands the relation between a whole and its parts on the model of the relation between a set and its members. A set is defined by its members. The set {A, B, C}, for instance, consists of exactly the members A, B, and C. It is distinct from the set {A, B} and from the set {A, B, C, D} because these sets do not have exactly the same members as {A, B, C}. The set {A, B, C} has a member that the set {A, B} lacks, and it lacks a member that the set {A, B, C, D} has. Mereological essentialists take composite entities to be like sets. A composite, they say, is defined by its parts just as a set is defined by its members. If S is composed of exactly the parts A, B, and C, then it is distinct from S′, the object composed of exactly the parts A and B, and it is also distinct from S″, the object composed of exactly the parts A, B, C, and D.

If the relationship between wholes and their parts is analogous to the relationship between sets and their members, then a composite entity cannot exist without having exactly the parts it has. If S is composed of A, B, and C, and it loses a part – the part C, for instance – it will cease to exist. In its place there will be instead S′, the composite defined by the parts A and B. Conversely, if S gains a part – the part D, say – it will once again cease to exist. In its place will be S″, the composite defined by the parts A, B, C, and D.

Mereological essentialism has important implications for an understanding of organisms. An organism, such as my body, is composed of numerous fundamental physical parts. According to mereological essentialism, my body has exactly these fundamental physical parts essentially. Organisms, however, are constantly gaining and losing fundamental physical parts. The constant exchange of materials with the environment is one of the defining characteristics of organisms. Every time an organism takes a breath, for instance, it takes in materials from the environment – oxygen molecules – which then become parts of it. Likewise, every time an organism exhales, it casts off materials into the environment – carbon dioxide molecules – which used to be parts of it. If mereological essentialism is true, then every time an organism inhales or exhales it ceases to exist, for every time it inhales or exhales it gains or loses parts, and according to mereological essentialism, an organism has all of its parts essentially; it cannot exist without having exactly the parts it has. The moment my body gains or loses a part, it will cease to exist. It will be replaced by another body – one that will most likely be very similar to it because it will have many of the parts my body has now – just as S′ will have most of the parts S has now. In reality, then, the entity I am used to calling 'my body' is not a single entity at all, but a plurality of entities which have come into and gone out of existence in a sequence. At time t_1, the organism I call 'my body' consists of the particles $a_1, a_2, a_3, \ldots, a_n$, but at time t_2, that organism has ceased to exist, and has been replaced by another organism – one I nevertheless still call 'my body'. At time t_3, that organism will be replaced by yet another organism consisting of yet another, different, set of particles – an organism which I will once again call 'my body'. If mereological essentialism is true, therefore, each of these organisms is different from each of the others. So in reality, the term 'my body' refers to a sequence of organisms, not a single organism. If mereological essentialism is true, moreover, each organism in the sequence exists for only a very brief instant. Therefore, the mereological essentialist concludes, organisms exist for only very brief instants of time.

Consider now whether you could be one of these organisms. Unless your body is in a state of suspended animation, any of the organisms in the sequence composing it will have ceased to exist by the time you finish reading this sentence. But consider yourself. Did you cease to exist just now when you finished reading that sentence? You are probably confident that you still exist, and for good reason: you understood that sentence, and it is plausible to suppose that you could not have understood it unless you had read and understood both its beginning and its ending, and yet, it seems that you could not have understood both its beginning and its ending unless you existed at both its beginning and its ending. If you understood that sentence, therefore, there is good reason to think that you existed for as long as it took you to read and understand it. And yet, says the argument, no organism can exist that long. In the amount of time it took you to read that sentence, the organism composing your body and most likely every other organism in the universe ceased to exist and was replaced by a different organism with different parts. Consequently, people like you and I exist far longer than any organisms do. But if you and I exist longer than organisms do, then you and I cannot be organisms. Hence, the argument concludes, we are not organisms.

Chisholm's argument depends on the following premises:

1   Any organism that exists at time t_1 gains or loses physical parts at time t_2 by exchanging materials with its environment.
2   If an organism that exists at time t_1 gains or loses physical parts at time t_2 by exchanging materials with its environment, then that organism ceases to exist at t_2.
3   You and I exist longer than the duration between t_1 and t_2.

Premises (1) and (2) imply that no organism exists longer than the duration between t_1 and t_2. From this conclusion and Premise (3) it follows by Leibniz's law that you and I are not organisms. What is the duration between t_1 and t_2? That is an empirical matter, exponents of the argument say. It is up to biologists to fill in the exact details, but we know enough about the biological data to know that the time it takes for an organism to exchange materials with its environment is far shorter than, say, the time it takes for you to read a sentence.

Few critics of the argument are likely to target Premise (1). Nor are they likely to target Premise (3). The most likely target is Premise (2), the claim that when an organism exchanges materials with its environment, it ceases to exist. This is the premise based on mereological essentialism. If mereological essentialism is true, then composites have their parts essentially. Since organisms are composites, it follows that organisms must have their parts essentially. Consequently, if an organism loses a part at time t_2, it ceases to exist at t_2. Again, critics are unlikely to deny that organisms are composites. The really controversial premise is mereological essentialism. To challenge it, critics can offer an alternative mereology, one that is not based on set theory.

Hylomorphists, for instance, endorse an alternative mereology (Section 10.3). It claims that an organism is more than the sum of its fundamental physical parts. In addition to the fundamental physical parts that compose it, there is also the way those parts are organized or structured. That organization has a bearing on whether or not the organism is able to exist through time. If the organism retains the same organization or structure, then it can continue to exist despite undergoing a constant exchange of materials with the environment. When it breathes, for instance, the oxygen atoms it inhales come to be organized in a particular way – they are integrated into its metabolic activities, and thereby become parts of it. Conversely, the carbon atoms it exhales cease to be part of it; they cease to contribute to its metabolic activities, and thus cease to be integrated into its overall structure. A structural notion of composition along these lines is reflected even in the way we treat inanimate objects. We suppose that tables and chairs can continue to exist so long as the pieces of wood that compose them retain their organization. If this table loses some of its fundamental physical parts as a result of being scratched, say, we do not conclude that the table has ceased to exist, but that it continues to exist minus some of its fundamental physical parts. If composition involves structure or organization, as hylomorphists claim, then Chisholm's argument fails. We will consider this notion of organization in greater detail in Chapter 10.

Moreover, in Chapter 12 we will consider arguments in support of animalism. If animalism is true, then we are organisms, and nonorganismic DATs must be false. Nonorganismic DATs face other problems as well. Although they have an easier time handling the problem of interaction than substance dualists, it is not clear that they avoid the problem of other minds or the problem of explanatory impotence (Sections 3.4 and 3.7). Versions of both problems can be reformulated as objections to nonorganismic DAT. In addition, like all DATs, nonorganismic DATs face a problem with mental causation. We discuss this problem in Section 8.11 in connection with emergentism.

8.3   Epiphenomenalism

Organismic DATs are the paradigmatic dual-attribute theories. They claim that we are organisms who nevertheless possess two irreducibly distinct kinds of properties. To many people organismic DAT seems like the most obvious way of understanding human nature; it seems obvious to them that we are organisms, that some aspects of our behavior can be described and explained in physical terms, but that other aspects cannot. If I bungee jump from a height, you can describe and explain the trajectory I take and why I took that trajectory in purely physical terms. If you want to know my reasons for bungee jumping, however, physics is no help. My reasons can only be expressed in a mental vocabulary, and hence a complete description and explanation of my behavior will require using both the mental and physical conceptual frameworks.

Different organismic DATs are distinguished from each other on the basis of how they understand the relationship between mental and physical properties. The most popular organismic DATs are epiphenomenalism and emergentism. Both epiphenomenalism and emergentism claim that an organism's physical properties are responsible for generating its mental properties. Fundamental physical interactions of the sort described by physics cause or give rise to nonphysical properties – including mental properties such as belief, desire, and pain. What distinguish epiphenomenalism and emergentism from each other are their respective views on whether mental properties can exert a causal influence on the physical interactions from which they emerge. Epiphenomenalists claim that emergent mental phenomena are causally inert; they have no causal powers in their own right, and can influence nothing that happens in the physical universe. Mental phenomena exist, and because they exist a complete account of the universe must include a description of them using a vocabulary that is appropriate to the task – a mental vocabulary. But according to epiphenomenalists, emergent mental properties are merely causal byproducts of certain physical processes; they themselves produce or give rise to nothing. Emergentists disagree with epiphenomenalists about the causal status of emergent mental properties. They deny that those properties are causally inert. Emergent mental properties have causal powers distinct from those described by fundamental physics, and they make a causal difference to the flow of physical events.

Emergentism and epiphenomenalism have both experienced a renaissance in recent years. In the case of epiphenomenalism this has been due to increased sympathy for a private conception of mental phenomena (Section 2.4). Epiphenomenalists are generally satisfied with a physicalist worldview – a physicalist view of human behavior in particular. They are nevertheless convinced that mental states cannot be given an analysis in terms of inputs and outputs or typical environmental causes and behavioral effects. For that reason they tend to view mental phenomena as causal byproducts of the operation of the brain. Brain states are triggered by environmental causes, and they in turn trigger behavioral effects, but, in the process, they also produce mental states as a sort of phenomenal residue – a residue that is causally inert. Consider an analogy: An automobile engine is responsible for producing the automobile's behavior, its movements. In the process of producing these movements, however, it also produces heat, a causal byproduct of its movement-generating operations. If we imagine that the heat produced by the engine is dissipated into the surrounding environment in a way that does not affect the automobile, then we have a rough analogy with the epiphenomenalist view of mental phenomena. According to epiphenomenalists, emergent mental states are related to brain states in something analogous to the way heat in the example is related to the internal operations of the engine. Emergent mental states are produced by brain states in accordance with brute psychophysical laws such as a law that brain state B always produces pain. But pain and other emergent mental states do not affect the states of the brain or any other physical states.

There are different types of epiphenomenalist theories. One type is unrestricted in its scope. It claims that all mental properties are epiphenomenal. This type of epiphenomenalism is not especially popular. A second type of epiphenomenalism is more modest. It claims that only some mental properties are epiphenomenal. This type of epiphenomenalism has become increasingly popular in recent years. It focuses on qualia, and was championed by Frank Jackson in the 1980s and by David Chalmers in the 1990s. This is the type of epiphenomenalism that will concern us most in what follows. To understand it, we can start by recalling the kind of identity theory endorsed by David Lewis and David Armstrong (Sections 5.4 and 5.6) since the epiphenomenalist's view of human behavior is similar to the identity theorist's.

Recall that according to the Lewis-Armstrong version of the identity theory mental states are defined by their typical environmental causes and behavioral effects. We use the term 'pain', for instance, to refer to a type of occurrence that is typically caused by, say, pinpricks, burns, abrasions, and other stimuli, and that typically causes winces, groans, and similar behavior. That type of occurrence then becomes a target for scientific investigation that aims to discover what pain is in fact – what internal physical state has those typical environmental causes and behavioral effects. Pain is thus identified by definition with the type of occurrence that has certain typical causes and effects, and that type of occurrence is then identified by scientific investigation with some type of physical state, *P*. Epiphenomenalists like Chalmers think that Lewis and Armstrong give a correct account of beliefs, desires, and other mental states that conform to a public conception of mental phenomena (Sections 2.5–2.6). These mental states, they think, can be defined by appeal to their typical causes and effects, and can therefore be identified with physical states. Importantly, these are the mental states responsible for producing behavior. We explain people's behavior by appeal to their beliefs, desires, and other intentional states. Since these states are identical to physical states on the epiphenomenalist view, it follows that human behavior – the way people correlate environmental causes with behavioral effects – can be given an exhaustive physical description and explanation. Epiphenomenalists thus agree with identity theorists about mental states that admit of causal analyses. But they disagree that all mental states are like this. Qualia, they say, do not admit of causal analyses. Qualia are nonrelational, unanalyzable, and epiphenomenal. Qualia are not part of the causal network that produces human behavior. Because qualia are real, epiphenomenalists say, a complete account of human nature must include them, but qualia do not play any role in the production of behavior; they are not in any way responsible for what we say or do.

8.4   The Argument For Epiphenomenalism

The argument for epiphenomenalism has two parts. The first part tries to show that beliefs, desires, and other mental states of the public variety are identical to physical states. This argument was discussed in Section 5.6. The second part of the epiphenomenalist's argument tries to show that no such account is possible for qualia, that private mental states are not among the states responsible for causing or explaining behavior. This argument has two premises:

1   There are qualia.
2   Qualia cannot be physically described or explained.

If qualia cannot be physically described or explained, then they are not part of the network of physical causal relations that are responsible for human behavior. If qualia are not part of that causal network, however, then they make no causal contribution to human behavior; they are epiphenomenal.

   Premise (2) of the epiphenomenalist argument has generated more controversy in the recent literature than Premise (1). Discussions of Premise (2) have often been countenanced under the heading of the **explanatory gap**. The term 'explanatory gap' is used to express the idea that there is an unbridgeable distinction between the descriptive and explanatory resources of physics and the descriptive and explanatory resources of psychological discourse – at least those used to describe and explain qualia. Several arguments support the existence of the explanatory gap. Some we have discussed already. Consider again the problem of psychophysical emergence discussed in Section 1.4. It claims that it is impossible for any number of nonconscious fundamental physical interactions to combine to produce conscious experience. If that is true, then no matter how detailed our knowledge of fundamental physical interactions gets, none of that knowledge will tell us anything about conscious experiences. There is a gap between our knowledge of physical things and our knowledge of consciousness.

   Consider likewise, the absent/inverted qualia argument discussed in Section 4.8 and again in Section 6.7: if absent or inverted qualia are possible – if, for instance, it is possible for there to be beings who behave in every way exactly as if they have conscious experiences even though they do not, then it is possible for two systems, A and B, to be physically indistinguishable yet phenomenally distinct. If that is possible, however, then there seems to be a gap between physical descriptions and explanations and phenomenal ones. Suppose, for instance, that A and B are physically indistinguishable, and that A has phenomenally conscious states, but B does not. In that case, the physical description of A and the physical description of B will be indistinguishable from each other, and the physical explanation of A's behavior will be indistinguishable from the physical description of B's. On the basis of these descriptions, then, how can we know that A is phenomenally conscious and B is not? We cannot know, says the argument. Because the physical description is the same in both cases, there is nothing in that description that would enable us to know that A was conscious and B was not. Hence, there is an unbridgeable gap between our physical descriptions and explanations and our phenomenal ones.

Another argument, advanced by the philosopher Thomas Nagel, is based on the subjective/objective distinction. Descriptions of conscious states are always made from a particular point of view, a particular first-person perspective, says Nagel. Physical descriptions, however, are not tied to particular points of view. On the contrary, says Nagel, because they are framed in the vocabulary of science, physical descriptions exclude the subjectivity that is characteristic of conscious experience. Science looks to describe and explain what happens in the world not from any one subjective perspective, but objectively – that is, apart from any particular point of view. It strives to achieve *a view from nowhere*, as Nagel puts it. As a result, we will never be able to give a physical description or explanation of consciousness since science tries to eliminate from view the very subjectivity that makes phenomenal experience what it is.

There are also several challenges to Premise (2). Some of them we discussed earlier. Physicalists who endorse representational theories of consciousness, higher-order theories of consciousness, and sensorimotor theories of consciousness all argue that it is possible to give a physical account of qualia (Section 4.9). According to representational theories, for instance, the facts about phenomenal experiences are not facts about unanalyzable, nonrelational, subjective occurrences; they are instead facts about familiar physical objects, properties, and events, and the ways my sensory organs represent them. According to physicalists, these facts are all physical facts; they can all be exhaustively described and explained by physics. But if facts about qualia are really facts about mental representation, and facts about mental representation are really facts about physical objects, properties, and relations, then the facts about qualia are really facts about physical objects, properties, and relations as well. Physicalists who endorse higher-order theories of consciousness and sensorimotor theories of consciousness challenge Premise (2) for similar reasons. If they are right, then qualia can be described and explained physically.

A second challenge to Premise (2) comes from mind–body pessimists like Colin McGinn (Section 9.6). Mind–body pessimists agree with other critics of (2) that qualia can be given straightforward physical descriptions and explanations. But, they say, we will never be able to articulate those descriptions and explanations. The reason is that there are inbuilt limitations on human cognitive capacities that will forever prevent us from understanding how physical states and phenomenal states are related. Conscious experiences are in fact caused by the activity of the brain in a way that is entirely unmysterious – a way that could be physically described and explained by, for instance, beings who weren't hindered by the kinds of cognitive limitations we ourselves have. Consequently, Premise (2) is false:

qualia can be physically described and explained. Yet those descriptions and explanations are cognitively inaccessible to us the way colors are cognitively inaccessible to a blind person. As a result, it will always seem to us that there is an unbridgeable gap between our physical descriptions and explanations and our phenomenal ones. That gap, however, does not reflect the existence of two kinds of properties in reality, but the limitations on our way of coming to know reality. Premise (2) and the arguments for and against it remain highly controversial.

8.5   Do Qualia Exist?

Consider now Premise (1) of the epiphenomenalist argument, the claim that qualia exist. This claim has played a central role in many of the arguments we have discussed, not just the epiphenomenalist argument, but also the knowledge argument (Section 4.7), and the absent/inverted qualia argument (Sections 4.8 and 6.7). It might come as a surprise, then, that philosophers have advanced very few arguments in its favor. Those who believe in qualia share a sense that the existence of qualia is too obvious to require argument. Arguments proceed from premises that are better known to us than their conclusions, but what could be better known than the existence of conscious, phenomenal states? Because they take the obviousness of qualia for granted, exponents of qualia take the burden of proof to lie with their opponents. David Chalmers, for instance, has this to say about what he calls *type-A materialism* – his label for any view that denies the existence of qualia:

> The obvious problem with type-A materialism is that it appears to deny the manifest
> … [W]e have the various functional capacities of access, control, report, and the like
> … But in addition … we are conscious, and this phenomenon seems to pose a
> further explanandum. It is this explanandum that raises the interesting problems of
> consciousness. To flatly deny … without argument that there is [consciousness] …
> would be to make a highly counterintuitive claim that begs the important questions.
> This is not to say that highly counterintuitive claims are always false, but they need
> to be supported by extremely strong arguments. So the crucial question is: are there
> any compelling *arguments* for the claim[?][2]

According to Chalmers, the natural science of human behavior is able to account for the ways we interact with each other and the environment, but it is incapable of explaining the existence of phenomenal consciousness. Denying that there is such a thing, he says, is highly counterintuitive and must be supported by strong arguments. Many philosophers agree. Few things could seem more counterintuitive than denying we are conscious! And yet, it is not obvious that the existence of qualia is as obvious as exponents of qualia suppose.

People are often mistaken about what qualia skeptics deny. Qualia skeptics do not deny first-person authority, for instance (Section 2.3). They do not deny that the knowledge each of us has of his or her own mental states is often in some sense privileged – that you can be wrong about my pains and sensations, for instance, in a way that you cannot be wrong about your own. Nor do qualia skeptics deny mundane truisms about thoughts, feelings, and actions: that we often have thoughts and feelings that go unexpressed in our overt behavior, that we cannot feel each other's pains, itches, and other sensations, that we often mis-interpret other people's actions, intentions, and so on. Qualia skeptics can endorse all of these claims. What they deny is that first-person authority and mundane observations like these provide any support for the idea that there are private, subjective, inaccessible occurrences that constitute our mental lives. We can accept all of these truisms about human experience, they say, and yet reject the claim that qualia exist.

Skepticism about the existence of qualia derives from several sources. One source is historical. Prior to the seventeenth century, people did not endorse a private conception of mental phenomena. Most philosophers claimed that psy-chological discourse was expressive of the ways animals like us interact with each other and the environment. So entrenched was this idea in the philosophical culture of the time that Descartes felt compelled to argue for a different, private conception of mental phenomena. Descartes' audience did not believe the exist-ence of qualia was too obvious to require argument, and neither did Descartes. He came to endorse a private conception of mental phenomena not because of its alleged obviousness, but because it played a central role in his broader project. He was concerned with establishing an indubitable foundation for the natural sciences. As a first step, he sought to establish that the contents of his mind were better known than anything else, and argued on behalf of that claim. Historical considerations of this sort raise questions about whether the existence of qualia is really too obvious to require any argument.

Another source of qualia skepticism derives from a competing explanation for the alleged obviousness of qualia. It claims that the existence of qualia only *seems* obvious to exponents of qualia because they have been indoctrinated in post-Cartesian ways of thinking – they have been trained to see mental phenomena through the lens of a post-Cartesian theory. On this skeptical view, our intuitions are *theory-laden*: what seems obvious to us is shaped in part by the kinds of theories we endorse. If intuitions are theory-laden, this suggests that qualia are not pre-theoretical data that a theory of mind must try to explain; they instead represent a particular kind of theoretical commitment; they are entities postulated by a private conception of mental phenomena. But if the existence of qualia seems obvious to people who endorse a private conception of mental phenomena, this does not automatically imply that a private conception of mental phenomena is true. It seems true to people who endorse it, but it does not seem true to people who reject it – it would not have seemed true to philosophers prior to the seventeenth century, for instance, or to Descartes' contemporaries. In that case, however, it will not do for exponents of qualia to claim that their ideas are too obvious to require argument. If qualia represent a particular kind of theoretical commitment, then exponents of qualia must argue for their theory, and that means they have to argue that qualia exist.

A third source of skepticism about qualia derives from our use of psychological language. If words such as 'pain' referred to private, subjective experiences, as exponents of qualia claim, then we would expect psychological language to have certain characteristics that it in fact lacks. Consider, for instance, language learning. If 'pain' referred to a subjective state, then we would expect children to learn how to use the word 'pain' only by a process of introspection – only by teaching them to focus on inner, private states, and attaching names to those states. In point of fact, this does not seem to be the way children learn to use words like 'pain'. The philosopher P. M. S. Hacker and the neuroscientist M. R. Bennett describe the learning process in the following way:

> The child learns to substitute pain-utterances for its natural groans and cries. He learns to scream "Ow" ... later to say, first, "Hurts" and then "It hurts!" ... and later still to say "I have a pain." The *primitive* or *elementary* pain-utterance is learnt as an extension of natural *expressive behavior* ... Something similar holds in the case of "Want" ... the child displays conative behaviour – he *tries* to get things, reaches for a toy that is outside the cot or for some appealing food beyond his reach, and cries or screams in frustration. He learns that this is an efficacious means of getting its parent to give him the object. The parent picks up the object, saying, for example, "Does Tommy want Teddy? Here it is." And, in due course, the child learns to say "Want," and later "I want Teddy," and so forth. The child's *primitive* or *elementary* use of "I want" is *as an extension of its natural conative behaviour* ... the child is learning a new form of conative behaviour – learning to give verbal expression to its wants.[3]

According to Bennett and Hacker, children learn to use words like 'pain' not by reflecting on private experiences, but by learning how to substitute linguistic behavior such as saying, "That hurts," for nonlinguistic behavior such as screaming or crying. There is nothing private or subjective about the process of language learning. Observations about how we learn and use language thus provide a further source of skeptical worries about the alleged obviousness of qualia.

A fourth source of qualia skepticism derives from the failure of a private conception of mental phenomena to cohere with a naturalistic picture of human mental life. This argument stands the epiphenomenalist argument on its head: if Premise (2) of the argument is true, say qualia skeptics, if it is true that qualia cannot be explained in physical terms, then there must be something wrong with the very idea of qualia. Nor are physicalists the only ones inclined to argue this way. Emergentists, hylomorphists, and anyone else who demands a naturalistic or scientifically respectable account of human psychological capacities might be skeptical of qualia for the same reason: the alleged disconnect between qualia and physical explanation.

A fifth source of skepticism derives from the philosophical problems qualia generate, especially the problem of other minds (Section 1.5). That problem affects not just substance dualism but any theory committed to a private conception of mental phenomena. If mental states really are subjective, as exponents of qualia claim, then we have no way of knowing whether other people are really experiencing the world in the way we are. The human organisms we see around us could be qualia zombies – they could be behaving exactly as they are and yet not have any of the qualitative experiences we take them to have. But surely, say qualia skeptics, this type of worry is absurd; it is absurd to suppose that the people we see around us might be qualia zombies. Could anyone seriously question, for instance, that a person who has fallen into flames and is writhing and shrieking is experiencing pain? Philosophers who answer affirmatively should take more care to preach what they practice, say qualia skeptics. It might be possible to question such things in the detached coolness of philosophical speculation, but in the heated currents of real human life it is not, and the way we think, feel, and act in real life tells us something important about the true nature of human psychological capacities.

Finally, there are at least four arguments that directly attack the existence of qualia. The first is the argument for eliminativism discussed in Section 7.2: qualia are postulates of a defective scientific theory, the argument claims – a folk theory that will be eliminated once we achieve a complete physical account of human behavior.

Another similar argument claims that we have good reasons for thinking qualia do not exist since appeals to qualia are scientifically useless. The argument appeals to *ontological naturalism*, the claim when it comes to determining what things exist, the sciences play a starring role. Science is our best guide to what exists, say naturalists. It may not be the only guide, but it is certainly the most reliable, and its results should enjoy a privileged status when it comes to determining what exists and what doesn't. In particular, if our best scientific explanations postulate entities of kind K, then we have good reason to think Ks exist. If, however, our best scientific explanations do not postulate entities of kind K, we have little or no reason to think Ks exist. Consider now our best explanations of human behavior. Epiphenomenalists claim that qualia play no role in those explanations. They openly assert that qualia contribute nothing to our behavior, that everything we do can be exhaustively explained without making any appeal to phenomenal states. In that case, however, there is little reason to think qualia really exist. They are not included in our best scientific account of human behavior, and science is our best guide to knowing what exists.

Two more arguments against qualia are advanced by the philosophers Daniel Dennett and Ludwig Wittgenstein, respectively. Both argue that the very idea of qualia is incoherent. Wittgenstein argues that if mental phenomena were subjective as qualia exponents claim, it would be impossible for us to use psychological predicates and terms in the way we do in fact. This is often called the **private language argument** since it purports to show that expressions in our language could not refer to private, subjective phenomena of the sort endorsed by exponents of qualia. Dennett, on the other hand, argues that the concept of qualia is problematic because it is impossible for something to have all the features qualia are typically defined as having. We will consider both arguments in the sections that follow.

8.6 Dennett's Argument Against Qualia

Exponents of qualia typically define qualia as properties that are both nonrelational and directly knowable. Qualia are nonrelational in the sense that they cannot be given causal analyses of the sort that would enable us to identify them with physical properties, and they are directly knowable in the sense that people are directly acquainted with the qualia they experience, and do not need to infer that those qualia exist on the basis of, say, bodily behavior. Dennett argues, however, that qualia cannot be both nonrelational and directly knowable. One way of interpreting his argument goes as follows: (1) Exponents of qualia must claim either that qualia influence behavior in conjunction with our beliefs, desires, and other propositional attitudes, or that qualia influence behavior directly, completely independent of our propositional attitudes. However, (2) if qualia affect behavior independent of any contribution from our propositional attitudes, then qualia cannot be nonrelational. On the other hand, (3) if qualia influence behavior in conjunction with our propositional attitudes, then qualia cannot be directly knowable. Hence, qualia cannot be both nonrelational and directly knowable. But since qualia are supposed to be nonrelational and directly knowable – since these features are supposed to define what qualia essentially are – Dennett concludes that qualia must not exist.

Dennett's argument assumes that the existence of qualia must be reflected somehow in people's behavior – that the possession of one type of qualitative experience in contrast to another must make a difference to how someone behaves. If there are color qualia, for instance, their possession must be taken to have some bearing on, say, our ability to match colors or our ability to describe our experiences – my disposition to say, "I see a red ball," for instance, in contrast to, "I see a blue ball." If verbal reports such as, "I see a red ball," are to have any link to private qualitative experiences, then those experiences must contribute to an explanation of why I say, "I see a red ball," instead of "I see a blue ball." But if qualia have an influence on behavior, then that influence, it seems, must either be direct or else it must involve other mental states such as beliefs and desires. If my experience of a red quale were to have any influence on my verbal behavior, it would either have to contribute directly to my uttering "I see a red ball" in contrast to "I see a blue ball" or else it would have to contribute to my utterance indirectly via my beliefs and desires about that quale – my uttering "I see a red ball" in contrast to "I see a blue ball" would be due not to the red quale itself, but to my *belief*, say, that I have a red quale.

Now, according to Dennett, if my red quale were directly responsible for my utterance, then having a red quale would not be a nonrelational property. On the contrary, it would be defined by a particular causal relation: it would be the state that was responsible for my uttering "I see a red ball" instead of "I see a blue ball." On the other hand, says Dennett, if my red quale influenced my behavior indirectly – because I had certain beliefs about it, say – then my red quale would not be directly knowable by me. For if my behavior resulted not just from my quale but from my quale in conjunction with my beliefs, then I would have to know about both my quale and my beliefs. But if that were the case, qualia would not be directly knowable, for people, including myself, would have to know a great deal about my circumstances to know about my qualia. Why would that be the case? Here Dennett asks us to consider some thought experiments. Consider first a case in which a mad neuroscientist has manipulated my brain in my sleep. Upon awakening I declare that my sensory experiences are qualitatively different from the way they were before – that color qualia seem different to me. Someone might be inclined to say that the mad neuroscientist has succeeded in altering my qualia, but this is not necessarily the case. The mad neuroscientist could have produced the same result – my declaration that my sensory experiences are qualitatively different – by having altered my memories of how things used to appear. Since either alteration of my brain would have resulted in me reporting a change in my experience, how could I know which was the case? According to Dennett, there would be no way of knowing directly. I would have to know more about my circumstances; I would have to know, for instance, which parts of my brain the neuroscientist manipulated. In that case, however, knowledge about my qualia – whether they have stayed the same or changed over time – would not be direct; it would require knowledge of other things. In the mad neuroscientist scenario, for instance, it would require knowledge of my memories and brain states.

The same is true of another case, says Dennett: Chase and Sanborn are tasters for Maxwell House coffee who after several years on the job report that their experience of tasting the coffee has undergone a change: both claim that they no longer enjoy the flavor of Maxwell House. They nevertheless describe the change in different ways. Chase claims that his qualia have remained the same as always, but that his attitudes toward those qualia have changed – he no longer likes that taste, the quale associated with Maxwell House. Sanborn, on the other hand, claims that his attitudes toward the taste of Maxwell House have not changed, but that his qualia have – he still thinks the taste of Maxwell House can't be beat, he just no longer experiences that quale when he drinks the coffee.

Chase and Sanborn's verbal behavior can be explained in one of three ways: Either (i) Chase has the right idea: the qualia associated with Maxwell House have stayed the same, but the attitudes toward those qualia have changed, or (ii) Sanborn has the right idea: the attitudes toward Maxwell House qualia have stayed the same, but the qualia themselves have changed, or (iii) the attitudes and the qualia have both changed. How can anyone know which of these explanations, (i), (ii), or (iii), is correct? According to Dennett, there is no direct way of knowing; we must instead know more about Chase and Sanborn's circumstances. If, for instance, Chase were able to distinguish the taste of Maxwell House from the taste of other coffees just as effectively as he always had, then we would have reason to suppose that (i) was correct. If, on the other hand, he failed to distinguish the taste of Maxwell House from the taste of other coffees as he had before, then we would have good reason to suppose that (i) was incorrect. As in the case of the mad neuroscientist, knowing about people's qualia requires knowing about their circumstances, and that suggests that qualia are not directly knowable in the way qualia exponents claim.

So if qualia affect behavior directly without any contribution from beliefs, desires, and other propositional attitudes, then qualia are not nonrelational properties; they are instead defined by causal relations. If, on the other hand, qualia affect behavior only in conjunction with beliefs, desires, and other propositional attitudes, then qualia are not directly knowable, for knowing about someone's qualitative states – even my own – requires knowing about that person's circumstances. Hence, qualia cannot be both nonrelational and directly knowable. Since being nonrelational and being directly knowable are supposed to be essential, defining features of qualia, it follows that qualia must not exist.

Dennett goes on to argue that a public conception of mental phenomena can accommodate all the facts that have inspired people to suppose that qualia exist. Many properties that initially seem nonrelational, for instance, are really not. He cites an example from the philosopher Jonathan Bennett: the chemical phenol-thio-urea tastes very bitter to most people, but to some people it is as tasteless as water. The bitter flavor of phenol-thio-urea might seem like an intrinsic property, but it is clearly relational: it depends on the taste buds of the people sampling it. When we talk about the qualitative dimension of our experiences, we are really talking about the impact of the environment on the states of our sensory organs – organs whose jobs are to detect the properties that objects have. In speaking of how things taste, or look, or smell to us, we are talking about complex relations between objects with certain physically describable properties and the states of our sensory organs. We met this idea earlier in discussing representational theories of consciousness (Section 4.9). The upshot, says Dennett, is that a public conception of mental phenomena can accommodate all the alleged facts about allegedly private experiences.

One criticism of Dennett's argument is that it trades on the assumption that qualia must be reflected somehow in behavior – that qualia would have an impact on behavior either directly or in conjunction with propositional attitudes. His argument assumes that exponents of qualia are not thoroughgoing epiphenomenalists, but are instead committed to the idea that people's qualia are reflected in their behavior in some way or other. Epiphenomenalists are free to reject this assumption. Defenders of the assumption can respond that if qualia are denied to have any influence on behavior, then epiphenomenalism is an extremely implausible theory – more on this response when we consider the arguments against epiphenomenalism.

8.7   Wittgenstein's Private Language Argument

Wittgenstein's private language argument has been an inspiration to many opponents of qualia. Wittgenstein used the term 'private language' to refer to a language in which predicates and terms are supposed to refer to or express private, subjective experiences. Because exponents of qualia claim that some of our mental vocabulary refers to or expresses subjective phenomenal states, exponents of qualia are committed to psychological discourse being a private language in Wittgenstein's sense. Wittgenstein nevertheless argues that the idea of a private language is incoherent; that it would be impossible for the words in a language to be useful for interpersonal communication if they referred to subjective experiences. Since psychological discourse is in fact useful for interpersonal communication, it follows that psychological discourse must not be a private language; its predicates and terms must not refer to or express subjective experiences.

Wittgenstein's private language argument is notoriously difficult and obscure. Any presentation of it is bound to be controversial. According to one interpretation, the argument is based on the following premises:

1   A word can have a meaning in a language only if it is possible for speakers of that language to determine that the word is being used in accordance with established usage.
2   If words in a language referred to subjective phenomena, then it would be impossible for speakers of that language to determine that the word was being used in accordance with established usage.

Therefore, if words in a language referred to subjective phenomena, they could not be meaningful; we could not use them for interpersonal communication. There could be no language in which words referred to subjective phenomena – to use Wittgenstein's term, there could be no private language. Now,

3   Words in our language such as 'pain', 'itch', and 'tickle' are meaningful.

These words are useful for interpersonal communication. Hence, these words must not belong to a private language; they must not refer to subjective phenomena. Let us consider the argument in detail.

Symbols in a language must be assigned meanings. The reason is that the relationship between a symbol and its meaning is a contingent one. Symbols need not have the meanings they have in fact. In English, for example, the expression 'dog' refers to a mammal not a mollusk, but it could have been otherwise. Things could have worked out so that speakers of English used the symbol 'dog' to refer to what we actually call a squid, or it could have been used in a way that was completely non-referential – the way the expression 'Hello' is used. Because a symbol has the meaning it has only contingently, there must be a process whereby symbols in a language are assigned their meanings – whereby speakers of the language either learn or establish rules for using them. We catch a glimpse of how symbols are assigned meanings when learning a language. We typically learn a language by practicing the sounds that fluent speakers utter and producing the symbols fluent speakers produce in the same kinds of contexts in which fluent speakers utter or produce them. Many of us have gone through this process in learning a foreign language, and all of us have gone through it in learning our native tongue. According to Wittgenstein, however, if words in a language referred to subjective episodes, as exponents of qualia claim, then this type of language-learning process would be impossible. It would be impossible for anyone to learn the meaning of a word because it would be impossible to assign a meaning to that word at all. Consequently, if exponents of qualia were right, words like 'pain' would be meaningless; we would not be able to use them to communicate. Since we do use words like 'pain' to communicate, it follows that those words must not refer to private episodes. Exponents of qualia must be wrong.

Why would it be impossible to assign meanings to symbols if those symbols referred to subjective experiences – if, in other words, those symbols belonged to a private language? Here is one line of argument among several Wittgenstein suggests. In order to assign a meaning to a symbol at least two conditions must be met. First, the symbol must be used in a consistent manner. Second, it must be possible for speakers of the language to check that it is being used in a consistent manner. Let us consider these conditions one at a time.

Imagine that I want to introduce a term – 'gzink' – to refer to a certain kind of plant I have just discovered. In order for that meaning to stick, in order for it to be assigned to that word, other speakers and I must use the term in a manner consistent with that usage. We are free to use the term in other ways – to refer to red wagons, for instance, or as an expression of surprise – but however we decide to use the term, there must be consistency in its usage. An analogy with games is helpful here. Without consistent rules, there can be no game. To illustrate this, try to imagine a game in which the rules could be changed at will by any player without warning. Imagine something like a card game, for instance, in which each player could determine on the spot what constituted a high hand, and could change that at any point. Or try to imagine a game like chess in which Player A suddenly moved several of his pieces at once – and several of Player B's pieces as well – into a checkmate of Player B's king, and then declared this a legal move on account of a newly instituted rule. If any player could change the rules of the game in these ways at will there would be no game of cards, there would be no game of chess, there would be no game at all. According to Wittgenstein, language works the same way. Using words in a language is analogous to making moves in a game. There must be consistency in their usage just as there must be rules to a game. Just as the rules of a game establish criteria for correct and incorrect performance, the established use of a term does the same. Speakers cannot use a term in any way they please and still make sense. Meaning depends on consistent usage. The symbol 'gzink' can refer to the plant I discovered only if other speakers and I continue to use the symbol in that way. When I say, "This is a gzink," therefore, I mean to establish a consistent use for the word 'gzink'. That use establishes a criterion for correct usage. Someone who says of a cat, "That is a gzink," has not used the term correctly – has not used it in accordance with established usage.

But meaning requires more than consistent usage; it also requires that speakers be able to check that someone's usage is consistent. Think again about the process of learning a language. Part of what makes that process possible is that there are criteria for correctly applying words in the language, and speakers of the language are able to check whether a word is being used correctly. In our day-to-day lives, this checking happens so naturally we scarcely notice it. If, for instance, someone says of a cat, "That is a gzink," and we know better, we simply say, "No, that is not a gzink. Gzinks are plants." In this way, the speaker's use of the term gets corrected by other speakers. This correction doesn't always happen explicitly; it can happen implicitly as well: a speaker who requests a gzink at a store and is disappointed to have the salesperson return with a plant instead of an animal receives an implicit reprimand for misusing the word. All meaningful expressions have in common the possibility of some type of correction along these lines. This type of correction is possible not only because there are correct and incorrect ways of using a term, but also because speakers of the language are able to determine whether that term is being used correctly or incorrectly. If speakers were incapable of knowing whether an expression was being used correctly, the effect would be no different from there being no correct usage at all. Think again about the analogy with games: in order for there to be a game, not only must there be rules; it must also be possible for players to know what those rules are. If there were no way of checking whether Player A's move was legal, there would be no way of ruling A's move illegal, and hence there would be no way of preventing A from making that move. It would be precisely as if there were no rule outlawing A's move. Without some way of knowing what the rules are or of determining whether the rules are being followed, the net effect is the same as having no rules at all. Likewise, unless there is some way for speakers to know how the words of a language are used, and some way to determine whether someone is using words in a manner consistent with their established usage, the net effect is the same as having no established uses for those words at all. There can be no meaning, no language, unless speakers can determine whether someone is using words in accordance with established usage.

According to the first premise of the private language argument, then, a word can have a meaning in a language only if it is possible for speakers of that language to determine that the word is being used in accordance with established usage. The examples involving 'gzink' illustrate ordinary cases in which speakers exercise their ability to determine whether a word is being used in accordance with established usage, but these examples involve a word in a public language – a language in which the criteria for correctly applying the word can be assessed by people other than the speaker. Wittgenstein argues that checking for consistent usage would be impossible in a private language. If a word such as 'pain' were used to refer to a subjective episode, it would be impossible for anyone to check whether it was being used consistently. Wittgenstein's argument for this claim proceeds in two steps. First, he argues that if 'pain' referred to a subjective episode it would be impossible for the speaker to determine whether the word was being used consistently. Second, he argues that if 'pain' referred to a subjective episode it would be impossible for anyone else to determine whether the word was being used consistently. He thus concludes that if 'pain' referred to a subjective episode, no one – neither the speaker nor anyone else – would be able to determine whether the word was being used consistently. Let us consider the premises of this argument in reverse order.

Imagine that 'pain' really did refer to a subjective episode. Imagine that I underwent a subjective experience at time t_1, and introduced the term 'pain' to refer to that type of experience. I concentrate my attention on that experience, I utter, "This is pain," and I look thereby to establish a consistent usage for the term 'pain'. Just as I introduced the term 'gzink' to refer to a certain type of plant, I now introduce the term 'pain' to refer to a certain type of subjective experience, the type I am having at t_1. In order for 'pain' to refer to this type of experience, however, future uses of the term must be consistent with the usage I am introducing now. I have to use the term to refer just to the type of experience I had at t_1. Moreover, I have to be able to determine that I am actually using the term in this way. Imagine, then, that I utter, "I am in pain," at time t_2. If the experience I am calling 'pain' is subjective, only I can have access to it. Only I can have access to my inner, subjective states. Consequently, no one other than myself could determine whether I was using the term 'pain' at t_2 in a manner consistent with the usage I introduced at t_1. Checking the consistency of my usage would require someone to have access not just to the utterance 'pain' but also to what that utterance referred to. In the case of a private language, that utterance would refer to a subjective state, one to which only I could have access. Consequently, if pain were a subjective state, then no one other than I could determine whether I was using the word 'pain' at t_2 to refer to the same type of subjective state I called 'pain' at t_1. I would thus be the only person who had any chance of determining whether I was using the word 'pain' consistently. But, Wittgenstein argues, even I would not be able to determine whether I was using the word 'pain' consistently.

Determining whether a speaker is using a term correctly, in accordance with established usage, requires some type of corroboration. Imagine how this corroboration might work in the case of 'gzink'. Since I am the world authority on gzinks, people look to me to correct their usage of the term 'gzink'. They thus rely on me to use the term consistently. To avoid mistakes, I take steps to insure that this is the case. I take a photograph of the original plant I dubbed a gzink at time t_1. Consequently, if I come across another plant at time t_2 and say "This is a gzink," I can consult the photograph just to be sure. Comparing the plant in the photograph with the plant I see before me corroborates my belief that this is the same type of plant I earlier dubbed a gzink. The photograph thus provides an independent source of information that corroborates my belief that I am using the term 'gzink' correctly.

Consider now the case of 'pain'. It is tempting to suppose that it should work exactly the way 'gzink' does. I take a mental photograph, as it were, of my experience at t_1, and then consult that mental photograph at time t_2 to ensure that I am using 'pain' consistently. According to Wittgenstein, however, this cannot be the case. Mental photographs are not real photographs. To say that I am consulting a mental image is simply to say that I am remembering what I saw at some earlier time. But, says Wittgenstein, memory cannot corroborate my belief that I am using the term 'pain' correctly in the way a photograph can corroborate my belief that I am using the term 'gzink' correctly. The reason is that corroborating evidence must be independent of what it corroborates. If I were a murder suspect, for instance, I could not say, "My claim that I was in Mexico at the time of the murder is corroborated by my earlier statement that I was in Mexico at the time of the murder." To use Wittgenstein's analogy, that would be like buying multiple copies of the same newspaper to check that what the paper said was accurate. Corroborating evidence must come from a source independent of the person making the claim. Thus, I cannot provide corroborating evidence that my own statements are accurate, and in a similar way, Wittgenstein suggests, I cannot provide corroborating evidence that my own mental states are accurate. I cannot corroborate my belief that I am using the term 'pain' to refer to the same experience I had at t_1 by appeal to my memory of what happened at t_1. Saying, "I remember that at t_1 I referred to this type of experience as 'pain'," is tantamount to saying, "I believe that I am using the term 'pain' right now to refer to the same type of experience I had at t_1." Appealing to my memory to corroborate my belief that I am using the term 'pain' to refer to the same type of experience I had at t_1 is tantamount to appealing to my belief that I am using the term 'pain' to refer to the same experience I had at t_1 to corroborate my belief that I am using the term 'pain' to refer to the same experience I had at t_1. It is tantamount, in other words, to appealing to the belief to corroborate itself. Since corroboration must come from an independent source, we cannot speak of corroboration here at all. But if there can be no corroboration that I am using the term 'pain' in accordance with the usage I introduced at t_1, then there is no way for me determine whether I am really using the word 'pain' consistently. Consequently, I can really have no idea what 'pain' refers to.

But if I can have no idea what 'pain' refers to, then nobody can have any idea what 'pain' refers to. Not only am I incapable of determining whether I am using 'pain' consistently, if 'pain' refers to a subjective experience, nobody else is capable of determining whether I am using 'pain' consistently either. But if speakers of a language cannot determine whether a word is used consistently, then that word cannot have a meaning in the language since meaning requires that speakers be able to determine whether a word is being used in accordance with established usage. Judging whether I was using words consistently in a private language would be analogous to trying to play a game in which neither I nor any other player had a rulebook. In such a case, there would be no way of knowing whether anyone was playing in accordance with the rules. If there were a private language, there would be no way of knowing whether words in the language were being used consistently; there would be no way of knowing what the words in the language meant. Thus, 'pain' could not have a meaning if it referred to a subjective experience.

The implication of the foregoing considerations is this: if mental expressions refer to subjective episodes as exponents of qualia claim, then there is no way of knowing what those expressions mean because there is no way of checking whether those expressions are being used consistently. Since meaning requires not just that an expression be used consistently, but that it be possible to check that it is being used consistently, words in a private language could not be meaningful; they could not be assigned meanings of the sort that characterize real language. Consequently, 'pain' could not have a meaning if it referred to a subjective experience.

And yet, says the argument, surely 'pain' does have a meaning; surely we use that word and similar words such as 'itch' and 'tickle' for interpersonal communication all the time. In that case, however, these words cannot refer to subjective episodes. They cannot be words in a private language. They can only be words in a public one. So if the private conception of mental phenomena were true, mental expressions such as 'pain' would be meaningless; we would be incapable of using them for interpersonal communication. But mental expressions are not meaningless; we can and do use them for interpersonal communication. Hence, the private conception of mental phenomena must be false.

The upshot of Wittgenstein's private language argument for the epiphenomenalist argument, and any other appeal to qualia such as the knowledge argument, seems to be this: there may in fact be qualia, but if there are, none of our mental expressions refer to them. Words like 'pain', 'tickle', 'itch', and the terms we use to describe the qualitative aspects of what we experience do not refer to subjective episodes; they do not refer to qualia. As a result, we would not be able to name examples of qualia, and in that case we would not even be able to say that they exist. According to exponents of the epiphenomenalist argument, the knowledge argument, and other arguments that appeal to qualia, the claim that there are qualia is supported by appeal to examples: *a* exists, they argue, and *a* is a quale; therefore, qualia exist. But what examples of qualia are there? The private language argument suggests there cannot be any – at least none of the examples qualia exponents typically cite can count. Terms such as 'pain', 'itch', 'tickle', and so on cannot refer to subjective episodes – none of the words in our language can. Given that this is the case, however, it is difficult to see by what means anyone could support the claim that there are qualia, or what real reason people could have for thinking that qualia exist.

According to exponents of qualia, qualia skeptics deny what is obvious, namely that qualia exist. But the foregoing considerations – the eliminativist argument, the ontological naturalist argument, Dennett's argument, the private language argument, the historical and other considerations discussed earlier – all suggest that the existence of qualia is not obvious at all, that qualia exponents must endeavor to argue on behalf of their controversial claim.

8.8   Arguments Against Epiphenomenalism

There are at least four arguments against epiphenomenalism. First, critics argue that epiphenomenalism has highly counterintuitive implications. In particular, it implies that our conscious states have no causal influence on our behavior. According to epiphenomenalists, our feelings of anger, pain, or sadness do not in any way influence or explain what we do. Human behavior can be given an exhaustive physical explanation since the mental states that have a bearing on that behavior are really physical states. The idea that qualia make no causal contribution to human behavior strikes many people as a very odd view. Moreover, an unrestricted version of epiphenomenalism, one that claims not only that qualia are epiphenomenal but that *all* mental states are epiphenomenal, has an additional problem: it implies that there are no actions. If actions are physical events with mental causes, and there are no mental causes, then it follows that there are no actions. Again, this strikes many people as a highly counterintuitive view.

A second objection claims that epiphenomenalism, like substance dualism, generates a resilient strain of the problem of other minds. If there is an explanatory gap between physical states and mental ones – if it is indeed possible that there could be qualia zombies, for instance, who behave in every way exactly as if they have consciousness even though they really don't – then the behavior of human organisms and other bodies tells us next to nothing about other people's mental states. Unlike the substance dualistic case, we at least know that other people exist since most epiphenomenalists claim that people are organisms. Moreover, on a restricted version of epiphenomenalism people's behavior can tell us something about their beliefs, desires, and other intentional mental states since these are just physical states on the restricted epiphenomenalist view. But our knowledge of human physical states still cannot tell us whether these people have conscious, phenomenal states like ours, or whether they are really just zombies. Consequently, if epiphenomenalism is true, we end up having less information about other people than we ordinarily take ourselves to have.

A third objection claims that epiphenomenalists have no good response to the problem of psychophysical emergence. How it is possible for consciousness to emerge out of fundamental physical processes? If there is a gap between our physical descriptions and explanations and our phenomenal ones, then how is it possible for physical processes, however complex, to give rise to conscious states? According to critics, epiphenomenalists have no good answer.

This objection is closely related to a fourth: epiphenomenalism does not fit comfortably with a naturalistic worldview, say critics, a worldview based on the natural sciences. This objection effectively stands the epiphenomenalist's argument on its head. Epiphenomenalists appeal to the existence of an explanatory gap between physical descriptions and mental ones to support their position, but, critics say, the existence of an explanatory gap is a liability not an asset. Because it is difficult to see how lower-level physical processes could give rise to qualia, epiphenomenalism seems like a gerrymandered theory that pastes together two distinct pictures of ourselves: a physicalist picture which is true of the mental states responsible for human behavior, and a substance dualistic picture which is true of qualia. As a result, epiphenomenalism looks less like a solution to the mind–body problem and more like a restatement of it.

8.9   Explaining Emergence: Panpsychism, Panprotopsychism, Psychophysical Laws and Structure

Epiphenomenalists have responded to the last two objections in several ways.

Some have argued that there are psychophysical laws that are every bit as basic as the laws governing purely physical interactions. Just as certain physical events are guaranteed to result from antecedent physical events, likewise certain mental events are guaranteed to result from physical events. If that is the case, however, then contrary to the fourth objection, epiphenomenalism does fit with a naturalistic picture of the world: the world just is a place in which physical events produce mental events in accordance with basic psychophysical laws – laws that the sciences are capable of discovering.

In addition, the postulation of brute psychophysical laws goes some of the way toward addressing the problem of psychophysical emergence, say epiphenomenalists. If there is a gap between our physical descriptions and explanations and our phenomenal ones, how is it possible for physical processes to give rise to conscious states? The answer, according to some epiphenomenalists, is that there are psychophysical laws that bridge the gap. Knowing only that Alexander has brain state B might tell me nothing about his phenomenal states. But knowing that Alexander has brain state B, and also that occurrences of brain state B reliably cause pain would tell me something about his phenomenal states. A psychophysical law linking brain state B to pain would go some of the way toward explaining how mental states emerge from physical states.

Critics of this response nevertheless argue that psychophysical laws do not really address the problem. Knowing that there is a psychophysical law linking pain to brain state B might explain why this or that instance of pain is correlated with this or that instance of B, but it does not explain why there is a correlation between pain and B in the first place. Exponents of psychophysical laws accept the existence of these correlations as brute, unexplainable matters of fact: the universe, they say, just is the sort of place that includes psychophysical laws – end of story. Some critics insist that some further account must be given, that the existence of psychophysical laws requires some type of explanation.

Related to this is another worry: that the existence of psychophysical laws does not address the problem of psychophysical emergence so much as attach a label to it. Saying that there are psychophysical laws does not explain how the rapid vibrations of countless tiny physical particles could generate the stable, homogeneous experience of seeing a pink ice cube. It simply says that the generating happens as a regular, lawlike matter of fact. If we want to know how there could be such a law, what explains the connection between physical events and phenomenal consciousness, there is no answer. Psychophysical laws, then, are every bit as mysterious as the psychophysical connections they are supposed to explain, and because of that, say critics, they do not offer a solution to the problem of psychophysical emergence.

Finally, some critics doubt that there are psychophysical laws. Epiphenomenalists claim that psychophysical laws can be discovered empirically, and that is why their view qualifies as naturalistic: science is capable of discovering what psychophysical laws there are. But have the sciences really discovered any such laws? It is not clear that they have. This does not imply that psychophysical laws do not exist, but it also does nothing to support the claim that they do exist. It also illustrates that epiphenomenalists are making an empirical gamble whose results needn't turn out in their favor.

Another way epiphenomenalists can address the problem of psychophysical emergence is to deny that fundamental physical particles lack conscious states. The problem of psychophysical emergence is based on the assumption that conscious states must emerge from nonconscious processes. The reason it seems impossible for consciousness to arise out of fundamental physical processes, epi-phenomenalists argue, is that the properties of fundamental physical particles seem to be very different from the qualitative properties of conscious experiences. There is, for instance, an enormous difference between the rapid vibrations of countless tiny particles and the steady, homogeneous color we experience when looking at a pink ice cube. Because the properties of the particles and the proper-ties of our experience are so different, we feel as though it is impossible for the former to give rise to the latter. Suppose, however, that we are wrong about the properties that fundamental physical particles possess. Suppose that fundamental physical particles have conscious states just like our own. In that case, there is no longer a problem explaining how composites of fundamental physical particles could have conscious states. We do not need to explain how consciousness arises from nonconscious processes because on this view there are no nonconscious processes. Consciousness is present at every level of reality, even the fundamental physical one. This is what **panpsychism** claims. According to panpsychists, every-thing has mental states.

Panpsychism strikes many people as highly counterintuitive. It seems highly counterintuitive that quarks, electrons, and other fundamental physical particles should have conscious states like our own. Can we really believe than an electron has a rich qualitative experience of the world the way you and I do? Some epiphe-nomenalists have looked to soften the counterintuitive implications of panpsy-chism by claiming that the conscious experiences of fundamental physical particles are not as qualitatively rich as our own. This is what **panprotopsychists** claim. According to panprotopsychists, fundamental physical particles do not have con-scious states of the sort we experience; they instead have *protoconscious* states. These states are simpler precursors of our qualitatively rich conscious states in something analogous perhaps to the way atoms are simpler precursors of mole-cules. When fundamental physical particles interact with each other, they give rise to protoconscious states that are more sophisticated. The protoconscious states of atoms and molecules, for instance, are more sophisticated than the protocon-scious states of fundamental physical particles. Likewise, when atoms and mole-cules interact with each other, when for instance they constitute neural tissues, or different parts of the brain, those tissues and brain components end up having protoconscious states that are more sophisticated than those of their constitutive atoms and molecules. Finally, when different parts of our brains interact with each other, they constitute the qualitatively rich conscious states we are familiar with in our everyday dealings.

Critics of the panprotopsychist response argue that it does not really solve the problem of psychophysical emergence so much as replace it with a different problem. First, it is not clear what protoconscious or protomental states are sup-posed to be. We know what beliefs or desires are, but what are protobeliefs and protodesires? I believe that $2 + 2 = 4$, for instance, but what would it mean to have a protobelief that $2 + 2 = 4$? Or are protobeliefs not supposed to have

Not a good retort since only at an appropriate This would "emerge" amount of complexity

propositional contents – contents that can be expressed by statements such as '2 + 2 = 4'? If so, then in what sense can they qualify as protobeliefs? Second, even if we could get clear about the nature of protomental states, it would still be unclear how protomental states could collectively form regular mental states. Panprotopsychism assumes that protomental properties are what the philosopher of biology William Wimsatt has called aggregative properties such as mass. If x has a mass of 1 kg and y has a mass of 1 kg, then x and y have a collective mass of 2 kg.[4] But it is unclear how mental properties – or protomental properties – could manage to be aggregative in this way. It thus remains unclear whether panprotopsychism really offers a solution to the problem of psychophysical emergence.

A third response to the problem of psychophysical emergence appeals to the notion of structure or organization. Exponents of this response agree that the reason it seems impossible for consciousness to arise out of fundamental physical processes is that the properties of fundamental physical particles are very different from the qualitative properties of conscious experiences. There is no way to account for how the rapid vibrations of countless tiny particles could produce by themselves the steady, homogeneous pinkness of the ice cube. But there is more to psychophysical emergence than the particles themselves; there is also the way they are structured or organized. Not just any arrangement of fundamental physical particles can generate conscious states. A tree trunk and a human brain, for instance, are composed of the same kinds of fundamental physical particles. Why is it, then, that the brain gives rise to conscious states but the tree trunk does not? The answer, say exponents of structure, is that the brain but not the tree trunk has those particles organized in the right sort of way – a way that is capable of producing consciousness.

Exponents of structure argue that their approach avoids the counterintuitive implications of panpsychism and panprotopsychism. In addition, they say, their view has an advantage over a view that postulates psychophysical laws by themselves; namely, it can explain any psychophysical laws that exist. The reason why pain is correlated with brain state B, for instance, as opposed to some other type of physical state is that brain state B has the right kind of structure or organization, one that is apt for producing experiences of pain. Exponents of structure can thus endorse the existence of psychophysical laws, but they can also explain why those laws obtain, and this, they say, gives their view an advantage over views that postulate psychophysical laws without also postulating structures.

Critics might nevertheless argue that the appeal to structure fails to solve the problem of psychophysical emergence. A view that posits psychophysical laws together with structures does little better than a view that posits psychophysical laws alone. The existence of structures might explain the existence of laws, but how are structures supposed to explain the emergence of conscious states? It is unclear that they can. Suppose a certain number of fundamental physical particles do not generate any conscious states (Figure 8.1(A)). We then rearrange the particles by imposing on them a certain organization or structure (Figure 8.1(B)).

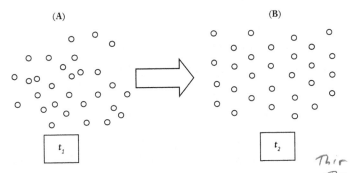

Figure 8.1 Structure and emergence

This is ridiculous. The structure has to functionally structured.

How is this repositioning supposed to explain the emergence of conscious states? *structured.*
If the particles in Figure 8.1(A) do not give rise to consciousness, how could chang-
ing their spatial relations make any difference? It does not seem as though it could. ← *So bad,*
According to critics, then, a response that appeals to psychophysical laws plus
structure does no better than a response that appeals to psychophysical laws alone.
Both responses attach a label to a mystery without doing anything to resolve it.
It is a mystery how a number of fundamental physical interactions could produce
consciousness, but it is equally mysterious how they could do so in a lawlike way,
say critics, and how reorganizing them could make any difference at all.

8.10 Emergentism

Emergentism is similar to epiphenomenalism: both are DATs, and both claim that
physical occurrences produce or give rise to mental ones. But there are at least
three differences between the theories. First, emergentists have tended to emphasize the role of structure or organization more than epiphenomenalists have.
Perhaps the most common emergentist account of psychophysical emergence
combines psychophysical laws with structure in the manner described in Section
8.9: when lower-level conditions achieve the right kind of organization, emergentists say, higher-level properties emerge in reliable lawlike ways. Second, emergentists
have tended not to limit the scope of emergence to qualia the way epiphenomenalists have, and many have not endorsed a private conception of mental phenomena
at all. Qualia do not occupy a privileged place in emergentist theories, therefore,
the way they do in popular versions of epiphenomenalism. Third, and most
important, emergentists claim that emergent properties make a causal difference *yes*
to the individuals having them.
　Emergentists endorse a multilevel worldview similar to the nonreductive physicalist worldview (Figure 8.2). According to emergentists, however, the relation

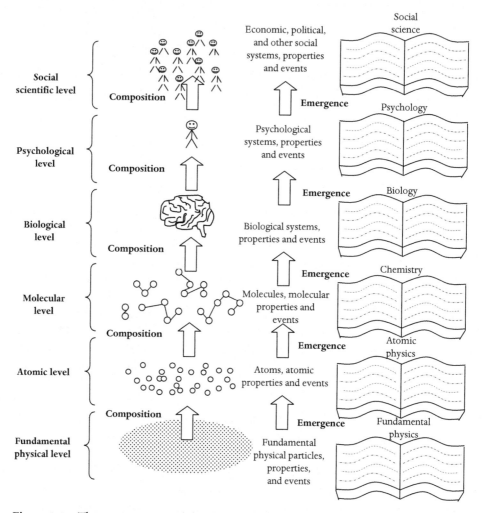

Figure 8.2   The emergentist multilevel worldview

between levels is not realization but emergence, and higher levels do not correspond to abstract ways of describing lower-level processes, but to distinctive classes
of properties that result from the organization of lower-level components.

Emergentists might disagree about exactly what characteristics emergent properties have, but most would agree that they have the following four:

1   Emergent properties are possessed by a system on account of the organization
    of its components.

2   Emergent properties are not possessed by any of a system's components
    individually since the organization responsible for their emergence is not a

feature of any one component considered in isolation, but of all of them together.

3 Emergent properties are not epiphenomenal. They are not causally or explanatorily inert, but make a distinctive causal or explanatory contribution to a system's behavior. At least some of that behavior is due to the system's emergent properties.

4 Emergent properties are not logical constructions out of lower-level properties; they do not represent abstract ways of describing lower-level occurrences or processes.

Characteristic (1) is what distinguishes emergentism from panprotopsychism. It implies that emergent properties are not what the philosopher of biology William Wimsatt calls *aggregative properties* such as mass. A system's mass is equal to the sum of the masses of its constituent parts irrespective of how those parts are organized. Eleanor has a mass of 50 kg for the same reason a 50 kg rock does: their fundamental physical constituents have masses that when taken together equal 50 kg. Characteristic (1) implies that emergent properties are not aggregative properties of this sort – the sort panprotopsychists take them to be.

Characteristic (2) distinguishes emergentism from panpsychism. According to panpsychists, lower-level entities have the same kinds of properties as the higher-level systems they compose. Characteristic (2) implies that emergent properties are not properties of this sort.

Characteristic (3) distinguishes emergentism from epiphenomenalism, and Characteristic (4) distinguishes emergentism from nonreductive physicalism. Recall that according to some nonreductive physicalists (realization physicalists), being in pain amounts to being in some lower-level state that satisfies a condition such as having certain typical causes and effects (Section 6.4). One implication of this view is that higher-level properties do not have any causal powers beyond those of their lower-level realizers (Section 6.10). According to emergentists, higher-level properties are not logical constructions out of lower-level properties. When we describe the contributions that beliefs, desires, and pains make to someone's behavior we are not describing fundamental physical processes using an abstract vocabulary; we are rather describing a distinctive class of first-order properties and relations that emerge as a result of the complex organization of lower-level components. These higher-level emergent properties make a causal difference to the individuals having them beyond the difference made by the lower-level properties of their components. According to emergentists, moreover, higher-level properties are able to exert a causal influence on lower-level components different from the influence of lower-level causal factors – an idea that is often called 'downward causation'.

Classic emergentist theories such as that of C. D. Broad (1887–1971) understand downward causation and the causal powers of emergent properties on the model of forces in physics. Emergent properties are *force-generating properties,* they say, like the properties postulated by physics. The only difference is that emergent properties are tied to higher levels of organization.[5] The neuroscientist Roger Sperry (1913–1994), another exponent of classic emergentism, describes the idea as follows:

> [T]he molecules of higher living things are moved around mostly by the living, vital powers of the particular species in which they're embedded. They're flown through the air, galloped across the plains, swung through the jungle, propelled through the water, not by molecular forces of quantum mechanics but by the specific holistic vital and also mental properties ... possessed by the organisms in question.[6]

On Sperry's view, which is representative of classic emergentist thinking, the properties postulated by lower-level sciences such as physics and chemistry and the properties postulated by higher-level sciences such as biology, psychology, and economics are all species of forces; they are all causal factors that operate on the world in just the way the causal factors postulated by physics do. Emergent forces are able to influence lower-level materials in the same way fundamental physical forces do, and for that reason they are able to override or nullify the influence of those lower-level forces. Were it not for those forces, the molecules that compose me would behave no differently in me from the way they behave in a corpse. The difference is due to the emergence of biological and psychological forces. Those forces are responsible for the metabolic and other biological processes in which those molecules are engaged, as well as the thoughts, feelings, and actions that distinguish my behavior from a corpse's.

8.11   Arguments For and Against Emergentism

The traditional argument for emergentism is an inference to the best explanation. According to emergentists, their theory provides the best explanation for the scientific facts – in particular, facts about the differences between composites and the things composing them. Consider, for instance, the difference between table salt and the sodium and chlorine atoms that compose it. Taken by themselves sodium and chlorine are poisonous to humans. In combination, however, they are necessary for human life. The same atoms have properties in isolation that are different from their properties in combination. Why? What explains the difference? According to emergentists, the best explanation is that new properties emerge when sodium and chlorine are combined, and these emergent properties override or nullify the effects of the sodium and chlorine when taken in isolation. Consider an analogy. A soccer ball left to its own devices remains stationary. The forces acting on it do not produce any movements of the sort produced by the activity of the soccer players. They exert forces on the ball that override the forces that would otherwise keep the ball stationary. According to emergentists, emergent forces operate on lower-level entities in something analogous to the way the soccer players operate on the ball. They are able to override or nullify the behavior that would be produced by lower-level forces operating on their own. Emergentists claim that something analogous is true of the differences between humans and the organs that compose them. Taken by themselves those organs cannot think, or feel, or act. In combination, however, they constitute a human that can think, feel, and act. What explains the difference between a human and the parts that compose it? According to emergentists, the best explanation is that new properties emerge when these parts are combined, and these emergent properties override or nullify the nonthinking, nonfeeling, nonacting characteristics of the parts taken in isolation.

Critics of the emergentist argument claim that as a matter of empirical fact emergentism is not the best explanation for the differences between composites and the things that compose them. Emergentism was very popular in the first quarter of the twentieth century prior to groundbreaking discoveries in chemistry and biology. As a result, many emergentists formulated their claims as empirical conjectures that ended up being false. Scientists now know, for instance, that the difference between the nontoxicity of table salt, on the one hand, and the toxicity of sodium and chlorine, on the other, can be explained by features of the atoms themselves and the ways they interact with human tissue. The real explanation makes no appeal to emergent forces. The same is true of the metabolic and other biological processes in which living things engage, critics say. These processes can be explained in terms of the interactions of various atoms and molecules without appeal to any forces beyond those postulated by physics. The actual empirical data thus support an explanation of these phenomena different from the emergentist's.

Some critics, moreover, take this empirical idea a step further. They use it to advance an objection not just to the argument for emergentism but to the theory itself. According to emergentists there are emergent forces, but, critics say, there is good empirical reason to think there are no emergent forces. As a matter of empirical fact, it seems that all the forces that exist can be described and explained by physics. The philosopher Brian McLaughlin has stated the point as follows:

British Emergentism ... went wrong for deep empirical reasons ... That there are [configurational] forces is, on the evidence, enormously implausible. The lattice forces that hold together organismic molecules are electro-magnetic in origin. And there are no vital or psychological forces. The doctrine of emergent determination due to configurational vital, psychological, or social forces is ... simply false. As truly remarkable as it is, it seems to be a fact about our world that the fundamental forces which influence acceleration (the electro-magnetic-weak force and the strong force) are all exerted at the subatomic level.[7]

'Configurational' is McLaughlin's term for emergent forces. He suggests that classic emergentism (what he calls 'British Emergentism') failed not for strictly philosophical reasons, but for empirical ones: science has shown that the emergent forces postulated by classic emergentist theories do not actually exist.

Emergentists can argue in response that the scientific facts might require them to modify their claims about the chemical and biological levels of nature, but the data do not require them to reject their entire view. Even if emergent forces are not necessary to explain chemical and biological phenomena, emergentists can argue, they are still necessary to explain psychological and social phenomena; the empirical data have not shown that these phenomena can be explained without appeal to emergent forces. On this modified emergentist view, therefore, novel forces emerge at the mental and social levels even if they do not emerge at the chemical and biological levels.

This response might save the emergentist theory from empirical refutation, critics can retort, but it will not save the emergentist argument. That argument claims that emergentism provides the best explanation for the empirical data, but the claim that emergentism is the best explanation is based largely on phenomena at the chemical and biological levels. Emergentists claim there is good reason to think that differences at each level in nature are best explained by appeal to emergent forces. Why do they claim this? Because, they say, there is good reason to think the differences between biological and chemical phenomena, on the one hand, and physical phenomena, on the other, are best explained by appeal to emergent forces. But, say critics, if differences at these levels are not explained by appeal to emergent forces, then there is no longer any reason to think differences at other levels are explained this way. Consequently, say critics, even if the empirical data do not succeed in refuting the emergentist theory, they at least succeed in refuting the emergentist argument.

In addition to the foregoing worry about empirical inadequacy, there are at least two more objections to emergentism. First, emergentism, like epiphenomenalism, claims that mental properties emerge from lower-level physical interactions. Consequently, emergentists face the same problem with psychophysical emergence that epiphenomenalists do (Section 8.9). Second, although emergentists avoid the sorts of problems epiphenomenalists face with mental causation, they face problems with mental causation of a different sort. The first problem, as we have seen, is empirical: emergentists have tended to understand the causal influence of higher-level properties on the model of forces in physics. But if higher-level properties are understood in this way, the existence of emergent properties implies the existence of emergent forces. According to critics, however, there is good empirical reason to think there are no emergent forces.

A second problem with mental causation is a species of the problem of mental causation discussed in Chapter 1. It runs as follows:

(i)   If emergentism is true, then either actions are overdetermined by mental and physical causes, or else physical laws are periodically violated.

(ii) Actions are not overdetermined by mental and physical causes, and physical laws are not periodically violated.

Therefore, the argument concludes, emergentism is false. Why should we suppose the premises of the argument are true? Recall the discussion of mental causation in Section 1.6. Suppose that you reach for an object near at hand. This action cannot occur without the contraction of muscles in your arm. These contractions are caused by events in your nervous system: the firings of neurons. These neuronal firings are caused by other neuronal firings in turn, and those by yet other physical events such as the impact on your nervous system of light, sound, pressure, airborne chemicals, and other environmental factors. Recall, however, that in order for your reaching to count as an action it must have a mental cause – it must be caused, for instance, by your desire to grasp an object. But now emergentists must answer a question: How are the mental cause of your action and the physical cause of your action related? There are only a handful of possible answers (Figure 8.3).

To understand them let us formulate the problem in terms of the following jointly inconsistent claims:

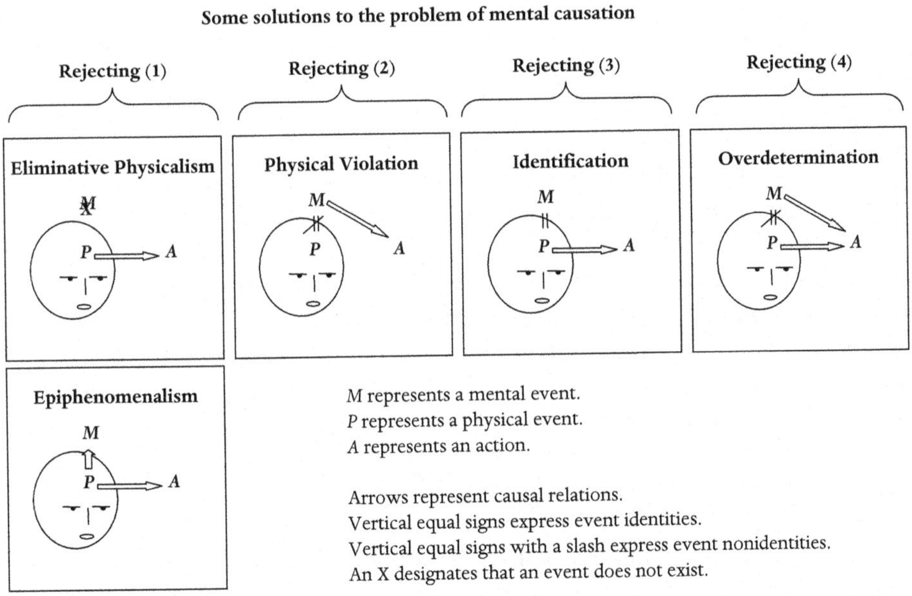

Figure 8.3   Some solutions to the problem of mental causation

1   Actions have mental causes.
2   Actions have physical causes.
3   Mental causes and physical causes are distinct.
4   An action does not have more than one cause.

Claims (1) and (2) imply that any given action has a mental cause and also a physical cause. According to Claim (3), an action's mental cause and its physical cause are distinct. The action must therefore have at least two causes, yet (4) rules this out. It says that an action does not have more than one cause. Consequently, claims (1)–(4) are inconsistent. Claims (1)–(3) imply that actions have multiple causes while Claim (4) implies that they do not. The problem for emergentists is to resolve the apparent inconsistency.

Eliminativists reject Claim (1): Since there are no mental events, they say, there are no mental events that cause actions. Epiphenomenalists also reject Claim (1) but for different reasons: there are mental events, say epiphenomenalists, but those events do not causally contribute to anything. Rejecting (1) is not an option for emergentists, however, for unlike eliminativists they claim that there are mental events, and unlike epiphenomenalists they claim that mental events can have a causal influence on physical ones. Identity theorists reject Claim (3): your reaching has only one cause, they say; the neural firings are identical to your desire. The word 'desire', in other words, is just another way of referring to the events in your nervous system, the way 'water' is just another way of referring to H$_2$O. But rejecting Claim (3) is not an option for emergentists either. Emergentists are property dualists; they are committed to denying that the term 'desire' refers to the same property as, say, 'brain state B'. Consequently, they are committed to denying that your desire could be identical to the events in your nervous systems.[8] That leaves emergentists with two options: rejecting (2) or rejecting (4). But both of these options are implausible, say critics. Let us consider them in reverse order.

Rejecting (4) commits emergentists to the **overdetermination** of actions. To say that something is overdetermined is to say that it has two or more independent, fully sufficient causes. Consider an example of overdetermination: the light-sensitive switch depicted in Figure 8.4 is simultaneously triggered by two independent beams of light emitted by Laser A and Laser B. Either beam is capable of triggering the switch by itself independently of the other. If Laser A were fired without Laser B, it would be sufficient by itself to trigger the switch, and likewise, if Laser B were fired without Laser A, it would be sufficient by itself to trigger the switch. Because either laser is sufficient to trigger the switch by itself, yet both trigger the switch in fact, the triggering of the switch is overdetermined; it has more than one fully sufficient cause.

According to critics, emergentists who reject (4) are committed to saying something similar about your action: it is overdetermined. In Chapter 1 we saw that events in your nervous system are by themselves fully sufficient to bring about the movements of your limbs; by themselves, they are sufficient to make your

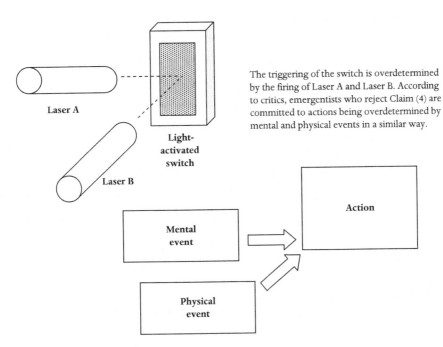

The triggering of the switch is overdetermined by the firing of Laser A and Laser B. According to critics, emergentists who reject Claim (4) are committed to actions being overdetermined by mental and physical events in a similar way.

Figure 8.4 Overdetermination

arm reach, your foot stomp, and so on. But, say critics, emergentists are also committed to mental states being fully sufficient to bring about your actions. In that case, however, the events in your nervous system and your mental events are both fully sufficient to bring about your actions. But because the events in your nervous system and your mental events are distinct, your action is overdetermined: it has more than one fully sufficient cause.

Why is the overdetermination of actions a problem? It is a problem, say critics, because it has absurd consequences. Consider what overdetermination implies: If the triggering of the switch is overdetermined by Laser A and Laser B, that implies that the switch could have been triggered by A alone without B, or by B alone without A. Similarly, if your action is overdetermined by your mental states and the events in your nervous system, that implies that your action could have been caused by the events in your nervous system alone without your mental states, or that it could have been caused by your mental states alone without the events in your nervous system. But both of these results seem absurd. It seems absurd to suppose that your action could have occurred without your beliefs or desires: simply to qualify as an action an event needs a mental cause. Conversely, it seems absurd to suppose that your action could have occurred without the events in your nervous system – the events that were responsible for triggering the muscular contractions in your limbs. Both of these results seem absurd, and yet both are implied by the overdetermination of actions.

The only remaining alternative is for emergentists to reject (2). But the problem with this option, say critics, is that it seems false as a scientific matter of fact. When you reach, your limbs cannot move unless something triggers the appropriate muscular contractions. Normally what triggers those contractions are events in your nervous system – physical events that we can actually witness if we use the right equipment. Neuroscientists have devices that can measure the activity of individual neurons. Using these devices, we can actually observe the triggering of muscular contractions in your limbs by events in your nervous system. Emergentists claim that mental properties make a causal difference to the individuals having them distinct from the causal difference made by lower-level physical properties. Moreover, if emergentists want to avoid the overdetermination of actions, it seems as if the only thing they can say is that when we perform actions, the causal influence of mental properties somehow manages to override or nullify the causal influence of physical occurrences like the events in your nervous system. In that case, though, it looks like physical laws will be violated every time someone performs an action. At the very least, this type of view implies a rejection of what we earlier called the *causal* or *explanatory completeness of physics*, sometimes called the *causal closure of the physical domain*.

The causal completeness of physics says that the natural sciences, paradigmatically physics, are capable in principle of providing an exhaustive account of all causes. This premise is typically supported by appeal to an inductive generalization from past scientific success similar to the argument for physicalism discussed in Section 4.5: in the past, scientists have always been successful in discovering the causes of the phenomena they were seeking to explain, and that success gives us good reason to suppose that their success is going to continue. We have every reason to suppose that the natural sciences are capable of discovering all the causes that can be discovered at all. In addition, one might argue that the postulation of nonphysical causes ends up violating the conservation laws of physics (Section 3.5). Finally, one could argue that something like the causal completeness of physics is a basic methodological assumption of scientific endeavor: if scientists were not confident that they could discover the causes of things using scientific techniques – techniques that investigate the physical universe – then they would not spend time or effort trying to discover the causes of things. It is only because they are confident that those techniques are capable of discovering causes that they employ them. This means that scientists tacitly assume that the causes they are trying to discover are physical. The very practice of science, then, seems to assume a principle like the causal completeness of physics. Emergentists who reject (2) are thus committed to rejecting an assumption that is empirically well-supported. In addition, say critics, they face the awkward task of having to explain how the natural sciences have managed to discover the causes of so many phenomena if not all causal occurrences are physical – if in fact actions do not have physical causes.

According to critics, the foregoing considerations should be enough to convince us that rejecting (2) is not a viable option for emergentists. But if rejecting (2) is not a viable option and neither is rejecting (4), then, say critics, it looks like emergentism must be false, for these are the only options emergentists are free to endorse.

8.12   Dual-Attribute Theory in Perspective

Both emergentism and epiphenomenalism face serious problems with mental causation – emergentism because it claims mental properties have a causal influence on the physical domain, epiphenomenalism because it denies this. Physicalists and hylomorphists view these problems as opportunities to argue for their own theories.

Identity theorists argue that their theory avoids the problems besetting both kinds of DAT. When it comes to solving the problem of mental causation, they say, rejecting Claim (iii) provides the most elegant solution. Unlike epiphenomenalist theories, identity theory is able to accommodate mental causation, but unlike emergentist theories, it is able to do so without endorsing overdetermination or rejecting the causal completeness of physics.

Hylomorphists argue in a similar way. Their strategy for solving the problem of mental causation, however, is not to reject one of the claims (i)–(iv), but to argue that the apparent inconsistency is due to a fallacy of equivocation. Once we clarify what each of these claims means, say hylomorphists, we see that (i)–(iv) are not really inconsistent. We will consider the hylomorphic approach to the problem of mental causation in Section 11.11.

Many philosophers are attracted to DAT because they want a deep metaphysical anchor for their anti-reductionism and nonreductive physicalism cannot provide it. Given the problems DATs face, however, these philosophers have a three-way choice: either (1) they can defend DATs against the objections, or (2) they can abandon their aspiration for a metaphysically grounded form of anti-reductionism and accept some form of nonreductive physicalism (Chapter 6), or (c) they can consider a nonstandard mind–body theory like hylomorphism which provides a different kind of metaphysical grounding for anti-reductionism (Chapters 10–11).

Further Reading

Roderick Chisholm (1989) argued that we are not organisms, and also entertained the view that we are tiny beings, like point particles, that inhabit the brains of human organisms. Eric Olson (1996) defends animalism, and Peter van Inwagen (1990) defends an approach to mereology similar to the hylomorphic approach. P. F. Strawson (1959) defends an organic dual-attribute theory.

T. H. Huxley (1874) was a nineteenth-century exponent of epiphenomenalism; David Chalmers (1996; 2002) advances the argument for epiphenomenalism. Joseph Levine (1983) was responsible for introducing the expression 'explanatory gap'. William Lycan (1996) suggests a way of closing the explanatory gap.

Anthony Kenny (1968) discusses the public conception of mental phenomena that held sway before Descartes. Alva Noë and Kevin O'Regan (2002) argue that intuitions are theory-laden. Dennett (1991a; 1993) criticizes qualia. Wittgenstein's private language argument appears in Part I of the Philosophical Investigations (2001 [1953]) starting at Section 243 and continuing into the mid-300s. Good intro-ductory discussions of the argument can be found in Bennett and Hacker (2003: Section 3.9) and Kenny (1973: Chapter 10). McGinn (1997: Chapter 4) defends a version of the argument different from the version outlined here. Bennett and Hacker (2003) use Wittgensteinian techniques to criticize appeals to a private conception of mental phenomena by neuroscientists and philosophers in Part III of their book. Other Wittgenstein-inspired critics of qualia include Kenny (1989), Malcolm (1956), and more recently Hilary Putnam (1999: Part II). Gilbert Ryle (1949) and P. F. Strawson (1959) are also sources of arguments against a private conception of mental phenomena.

For many years epiphenomenalism's place in philosophy of mind was analo-gous to eliminativism's: if your theory implied that mental states were epiphe-nomenal, people assumed there must be something wrong with your theory. Recently, however, epiphenomenalism has won some surprising converts includ-ing Jaegwon Kim (2005), a former defender of physicalism.

Classic emergentism was originally formulated by John Stuart Mill (1965 [1843]: Book III, Chapter 6), and was subsequently endorsed by Samuel Alexander (1966) and C. Lloyd Morgan (1923). But the theory reached maturity in C. D. Broad (1925). It has been endorsed more recently by the neuroscientist Roger Sperry (1975), and Timothy O'Connor (2000: Chapter 6). The philoso-pher John Searle (1992) is sometimes classified as an emergentist, but on exami-nation his theory turns out to be a confused amalgam of ideas taken from emergentists and nonreductive physicalists. He claims, for instance, that mental states are both caused by the brain and realized in it. The causal claim sug-gests an emergentist or epiphenomenalist view, but the realization claim suggests a nonreductive physicalist view. The history of classic emergentism is traced by Brian McLaughlin (1992). In that article McLaughlin also discusses classic emergentism's problem with empirical inadequacy. Jaegwon Kim (1993c; 1999; 2006) has done the most to articulate emergentist problems with mental causation.

Notes

1   In the formal theory of parts and wholes, every object is a part of itself – just as every set is a subset of itself. The set S is a proper subset of the set S′ exactly if S is a subset of S′, and S ≠ S′. Likewise, x is a proper part of y exactly if x is a part of y, and $x ≠ y$. In ordinary English we typically use the term 'part' to refer to proper parts.

2   Chalmers, 2002, "Consciousness and Its Place in Nature." In *Philosophy of Mind: Classical and Contemporary Readings*, edited by David John Chalmers, 247–72, New York: Oxford University Press, 251–2.

3   M. R. Bennett and P. M. S. Hacker, 2003, *Philosophical Foundations of Neuroscience*, Malden: Blackwell Publishers, pp. 101–2.

4   William C. Wimsatt, 1985, "Forms of Aggregativity." In *Human Nature and Natural Knowledge*, edited by Marjorie Grene, Alan Donagan, Anthony N. Perovich, and Michael V. Wedin. Dordrecht: Reidel.

5   In "The Rise and Fall of British Emergentism" (*Emergence or Reduction?: Essays on the Prospects of Nonreductive Physicalism*, 1992, edited by Ansgar Beckermann, H. Flohr, and Jaegwon Kim, 49–93, Berlin: W. de Gruyter), Brian McLaughlin explains the emergentist position as follows: "Wholes can possess force-generating properties of a sort not possessed by any of their parts ... Such properties will endow the whole with the power to exert a fundamental force not exerted by any less complex wholes" (79).

6   *The Omni Interviews*, 1984, edited by Pamela Weintraub, New York: Ticknor & Fields, 201. This passage is quoted by Jaegwon Kim in "'Downward Causation' in Emergentism and Nonreductive Physicalism" (*Emergence or Reduction?: Essays on the Prospects of Nonreductive Physicalism*, 1992, edited by Ansgar Beckermann, H. Flohr, and Jaegwon Kim, 119–38, Berlin: W. de Gruyter, 120).

7   McLaughlin, "The Rise and Fall of British Emergentism," 91.

8   This inference is based on the assumption that event identity requires property identity, that the event *my desiring x at time t*, for instance, is identical to the event *my having firing neurons at time t* only if desiring x is identical to having firing neurons. For more on a view of events like this see: Jaegwon Kim, "Events as Property Exemplifications," in his *Supervenience and Mind*, 1993, 33–52, New York: Cambridge University Press; Alvin Goldman, *A Theory of Human Action*, 1970, Englewood Cliffs: Prentice-Hall; or Jonathan Bennett, *Events and Their Names*, 1988, Indianapolis: Hackett Publishing Co.

Chapter 9

Idealism, Neutral Monism, and Mind–Body Pessimism

Overview

The term 'idealism' has been used in many different ways. It is important to distinguish ontological idealism, the claim that everything is mental, from conceptual idealism, the claim that our experience of the world depends in part on concepts or structures supplied by our minds. Berkeley's idealism is an example of ontological idealism; Kant's transcendental idealism is an example of conceptual idealism. We are concerned here only with ontological idealism. Ontological idealism is like an inverse image of physicalism. It implies that everything can in principle be given an exhaustive description and explanation in psychological terms. The most common version of ontological idealism claims that what we ordinarily take to be mind-independent objects (tables, chairs, humans, trees) are really just collections of experiences. This chair, for instance, is really just a collection of color, texture, and solidity experiences. One argument for ontological idealism relies on two premises: (1) ordinary objects such as chairs, tables, humans, and trees consist entirely of qualities or characteristics we perceive by the senses, but (2) the only things we perceive by the senses are our own ideas or experiences. Hence, ordinary objects consist simply of our own ideas or experiences; they are just collections of them. There are serious challenges to both premises, but the second poses the greatest liability. It relies on assumptions that were common in the seventeenth and eighteenth centuries, but that most philosophers now reject. In addition, idealism is highly counterintuitive: it rejects the commonsense assumption that we inhabit a world of mind-independent objects, and has difficulty accommodating the commonsense distinction between reality and appearance. Given its counterintuitive implications, critics argue that idealists must carry the burden of proof

Philosophy of Mind: A Comprehensive Introduction, First Edition. William Jaworski.
© 2011 William Jaworski. Published 2011 by Blackwell Publishing Ltd.

– they must prove that common sense is wrong. But, say critics, this is something idealists have failed to do.

Neutral monism claims that everything is neutral; everything can be exhaustively described and explained in terms of a conceptual framework that is neither mental nor physical but neutral. Physical events are neutral events that satisfy one type of condition, and mental events are neutral events that satisfy another type of condition. The argument for neutral monism proceeds in two steps. The first argues for the superiority of monism to dualism by appeal to ontological parsimony or Ockham's razor. The second argues that among monistic theories, neutral monism is superior to physicalism and idealism because it solves mind–body problems more effectively than the other two. Perhaps the strongest criticism of neutral monism claims that neutral monists have failed to provide an informative account of what neutral entities are. As a result, neutral monism remains merely an abstract possibility, not a theory whose merits and demerits can be evaluated alongside the other theories we have considered.

Mind–body pessimism claims that it is impossible for us to solve mind–body problems because there are inbuilt limitations on our cognitive powers. Just as small children have cognitive limitations that prevent them from understanding quantum physics, so too we have cognitive limitations that prevent us from understanding how, say, states of consciousness emerge from states of the brain. Critics of mind–body pessimism argue against it in several ways. Some argue that there is good reason to think we will eventually be able to solve mind–body problems. Others argue that there are more plausible explanations for the existence of mind–body problems than the explanation pessimists give.

9.1 Varieties of Idealism

This chapter covers three theories that occupy marginal positions in contemporary philosophy of mind. Perhaps their marginalization is justified and perhaps not, but they are worth considering in any event because they raise interesting issues, and pose significant challenges to the mainstream. The first two theories we will consider are forms of monism. We will begin with idealism.

The label 'idealism' has been used in a variety of ways in philosophy. It is helpful to distinguish forms of *conceptual idealism* from forms of *ontological idealism*. Forms of conceptual idealism claim that our experience of the world is unavoidably shaped by our concepts. The transcendental idealism endorsed by the eighteenth-century philosopher Immanuel Kant (1724–1804) is an example. According to Kant, our mind supplies concepts or categories – the categories of space, time, and causation, for instance – that give structure to the raw, unstructured data of sensation.[1] What appears to us as an experience of a spatiotemporal domain of mind-independent objects – what we typically take our experiences to be experiences *of* – is an amalgam of raw sensory data together with categories and concepts supplied by our minds. What mind-independent objects there are and what those objects are like in themselves apart from our experiences we cannot know, according to Kant, for our knowledge of the world is limited to our experiences, and our experiences do not reveal how things are in themselves, but only how they appear to us when filtered through the categories supplied by our minds. Forms of German idealism such as the philosophies of J. G. Fichte (1762–1814) and G. W. F. Hegel (1770–1831) represented responses to or developments of Kant's idealism that took that idealism in an ontological direction. The forms of idealism endorsed at the end of the nineteenth century by British philosophers such as F. H. Bradley (1846–1924) and J. M. E. McTaggart (1866–1925) represented developments of German idealism in turn. Our principal concern, however, is not with Kantian conceptual idealism, nor the forms of idealism inspired by Kant, but with ontological idealism of another sort.

The ontological idealism that interests us is like an inverse image of physicalism. It claims that everything is mental in something analogous to the way physicalists claim that everything is physical. The claim that everything is mental might remind some readers of panpsychism (Section 8.9). But idealism and panpsychism are very different theories. Idealism is a form of monism; panpsychism is a dual-attribute theory. Panpsychism, in other words, is committed to property dualism; it claims that in addition to mental properties there are distinct physical properties. Everything has mental properties, according to panpsychists, but they still deny that all the properties that exist are mental properties. Idealists, by contrast, claim precisely that all properties are mental; unlike panpsychists, they deny that there is a distinct class of physical properties.

Because idealists claim that all properties are mental, their views on physical properties are analogous to the views of physicalists on mental ones. Idealists of an eliminativist stripe claim that physical properties do not exist – that statements about, say, the mass or solidity of mind-independent objects are false in something analogous to the way statements about the characteristics of the Greek gods or the present king of France are false. But eliminativism has not been the dominant position among idealists. The most famous ontological idealist, George Berkeley (1685–1753), took a reductivist stance toward physical phenomena, and subsequent idealists have tended to follow his lead.

According to reductive idealists like Berkeley, what we ordinarily take to be mind-independent physical objects and properties are really just collections of experiences, an idea Berkeley famously expressed with the Latin slogan *esse est percipi* – to be is to be perceived. According to reductive idealists, talk of physical objects is really just talk of experiences. When I say this table is solid or heavy, for instance, I am saying that when I have an experience of trying to push through it or lift it, that experience is accompanied by another experience: meeting resistance. According to reductive idealists, in other words, physical properties like solidity and mass can be identified with particular experiences or collections of experiences.

Forms of reductive idealism are sometimes called forms of **phenomenalism**. Among forms of phenomenalism, moreover, there is a distinction analogous to the distinction between behaviorism and the identity theory, the forms of reductive physicalism discussed in Chapter 5. *Analytic phenomenalism* claims that statements that are apparently about mind-independent physical objects can be analyzed or translated into statements about someone's actual or potential experiences in something analogous to the way analytic behaviorism claims that statements about beliefs, desires, and other mental states can be analyzed or translated into statements about someone's actual or potential behavior. *Nonanalytic phenomenalism*, on the other hand, is not committed to the idea that such analyses are possible; it endorses a type of reductive idealism analogous to the identity theory, which identifies physical properties with mental ones not by linguistic analysis but by other means. Analytic phenomenalism was somewhat popular during the era of logical positivism when it was defended by philosophers such as A. J. Ayer (1910–1989). It was nevertheless forcefully criticized, and subsequent idealists have tended to favor nonanalytic phenomenalism.

9.2 The Motivation and Argument For Ontological Idealism

Ontological idealism has been a marginal position in the history of philosophy. The principal reason is that it goes against the commonsense idea that the objects we experience have a mind-independent status – that the table in front of me, for instance, is an entity that would exist and have size, position, mass, solidity, and other physical properties even if no one were experiencing it. Given its counterintuitive implications, why would anyone want to endorse ontological idealism?

The motivations for ontological idealism have often been similar to those for substance dualism. Exponents of both tend to see the sciences as a threat to our prescientific understanding of things; although idealists take the threat to be more serious. Substance dualists are at least willing to countenance the existence of mind-independent objects and properties of the sort described by physics; idealists are unwilling to allow even that. They take the existence of any mind-independent objects and properties to be incompatible with what they take to be certain core, prescientific beliefs about ourselves and the universe. Berkeley in particular took those beliefs to concern our knowledge of the world and the existence of God.

If our knowledge of the world was limited to our experiences, Berkeley reasoned, and the world consisted of objects that existed independent of those experiences, then there would be room for skeptics to argue that we do not really have knowledge of the world at all (knowledge of what objects and properties really exist) but only knowledge of our experiences – experiences that might give us no information at all about how things are in themselves. Likewise, thought Berkeley, if the world consisted of objects capable of existing independent of anyone experiencing them, then there would be room for atheists to argue that the world could exist independent of God, a conclusion he wished to avoid. Although there are many philosophers who have shared Berkeley's aversion to skepticism and atheism, most consider his idealism a rather extreme response to both, and are convinced there are better ways of responding to each.

Berkeley nevertheless argued in favor of idealism. His original argument relied on two premises:

1   Ordinary objects such as chairs, tables, humans, and trees consist entirely of qualities or characteristics we perceive by the senses.
2   The only things we perceive by the senses are our own ideas or experiences.

Therefore, Berkeley concluded, ordinary objects must consist only of our own ideas or experiences; there are no experience- or mind-independent chairs, tables, humans, or trees; all of them are simply collections of experiences. The table I see before me is simply a collection of colors, shapes, textures, and other experiences, and the same is true of the chair I perceive myself to be sitting on and the humans and trees I see out the window. Each is simply a bundle of sensory or other experiences.

Both premises of Berkeley's argument have been controversial. In defense of (1), Berkeley argued that the very idea of an unperceived object was incoherent:

> the reader need only reflect and try to separate in his own thoughts the being of a sensible thing from its being perceived … But say you, surely there is nothing easier than to imagine trees, for instance, in a park, or books existing in a closet, and nobody by to perceive them … But what is all this … more than framing in your mind certain ideas which you call *books* and *trees* … [D]o not you yourself perceive or think of them all the while? … [I]t is necessary that you conceive them existing unconceived or unthought of, which is a manifest repugnancy.[2]

This is often called Berkeley's 'master argument'. It claims that it is impossible for us to form a conception of an unconceived object on the grounds that conceiving of an object that is unconceived implies a contradiction. According to the argument, if I try to conceive of an unconceived object, I will be trying to conceive of something that is both conceived by someone, namely me, and yet not conceived by anyone. But nothing can be both conceived by someone and not conceived by anyone; that is a manifest contradiction. Hence, the idea of a mind-independent object, one that can exist without being conceived by anyone is incoherent; there can be no such object. Everything that exists depends on the mind: tables, chairs, humans, trees – all of them are simply collections of sensory and other experiences.

One worry about the master argument is that it appears to conflate the distinction between the act of conceiving and what is conceived. To illustrate this, imagine a parallel argument:

> I am immortal: it is impossible for me not to exist. The reason is that it is impossible to form a conception of myself not existing. Such a conception implies a contradiction because for me to form a conception of myself I must exist. Hence, for me to form of a conception of myself not existing, I would have to exist, and that means it would be necessary for me both to exist and not to exist. But that is a manifest contradiction; nothing can both exist and not exist. Hence, it is inconceivable that I should fail to exist. I am thus immortal.

This argument conflates the distinction between my act of conceiving and the situations I am able to conceive. It is true that I cannot engage in the act of conceiving unless I exist, but it does not follow from this that the only situations I am able to conceive are situations in which I exist. I can easily conceive all sorts of situations in which I do not exist – situations that occurred before I was born, for instance, or that would have occurred if I hadn't been born at all. The argument is thus flawed insofar as it moves illicitly from a premise about my act of conceiving (that I can conceive of something only if I exist) to a conclusion about what I am able to conceive (that I can conceive only of situations in which I exist). Berkeley's master argument seems to commit a similar mistake. While it is true that I can conceive of this book only if I am conceiving of it, it does not follow from this that I can conceive only of situations in which the book is being conceived by someone. I can easily conceive of all sorts of situations in which the book is unconceived by anyone – situations, for instance, in which the book exists unperceived in a closet. There is thus good reason to think that Berkeley has failed to make the case for Premise (1).

Consider now Premise (2). A central concept in Berkeley's philosophy of mind and many early modern philosophies of mind was the concept of an idea. For Berkeley and for many early modern philosophers, an idea was supposed to be anything that could be "present before the mind," as they sometimes put it. An idea, in other words, was roughly anything that we are or could be aware of or experience. (Although philosophers like Berkeley used terms like 'perception' or 'conception' instead of 'awareness' or 'experience'). According to Premise (2), ideas are the only things we are ever aware of or experience. Although we would say in our ordinary discourse that I perceive a book in front of me, what I am perceiving, according to Premise (2) is, strictly speaking, not a book but the *idea* of a book.

Premise (2) was an assumption common among Berkeley's contemporaries. Philosophers like René Descartes and John Locke took our experiences to constitute something like an inner theatre of subjective impressions that could fail to reflect things in the external world. Since these philosophers were Berkeley's chief interlocutors, it is likely that Berkeley accepted this understanding of the mind as a basic starting point – the price of admission to the debates in which he wanted to participate. But the popularity of Premise (2) among these philosophers does not make it true, nor does it insulate it from criticism. Opponents of (2) are likely to argue that what we perceive are not mere ideas but actual mind-independent things. I do not perceive the idea of the book, opponents will say, but the book itself – a mind-independent object. Likewise, it is not the idea of sweetness that I perceive when I eat the ice cream but the sweetness of the ice cream itself – a mind-independent property.

There are at least two ways of formulating the claim that we perceive actual objects and properties and not mere ideas of them. The first claims that external objects produce representations of themselves in us, and that we therefore perceive the table and the sweetness indirectly through the mediation of these internal representations. This is the *representationalist* view. The second view denies that there is an inner domain of representations; it claims that we perceive the table and the sweetness directly without the mediation of any inner mental representations. This is the *direct realist* view.

Berkeley does not appear to have been familiar with direct realist views of perception. They pose a serious challenge to his argument, but it is not clear what he would have said in response to them. He nevertheless was familiar with representationalist views, and advanced at least two arguments against them. The first has three premises: (i) If there are inner representations of mind-independent objects, then those representations would have to be ideas, for they would be present to the perceiving mind. But (ii) the relation of representation involves resemblance: inner representations must resemble whatever they represent. Consequently, if I really had an inner representation of the book, that representation would have to resemble the actual book in the world. Likewise, if I had an inner representation of the ice cream's sweetness, it would have to resemble the actual sweetness of the ice cream. But (iii) ideas can only resemble other ideas. Consequently, if I really had inner representations, those representations could only represent other ideas since ideas are the only things that ideas can resemble. Since, however, representationalists insist that inner representations are of mind-independent things, and premises (i)–(iii) show there can be no representations of mind-independent things, it follows that representationalism must be false.

Perhaps the easiest way for representationalists to counter this argument is to attack Premise (ii), the claim that representation requires resemblance. Consider symbolic systems such as languages; they provide numerous examples that seem to challenge this claim. The English word 'red', for instance, represents the color red, but it is not clear in what significant sense the letters 'red' can be said to resemble the color. Likewise, the word 'dog' represents a dog, but it is not clear in what sense the word can be said to resemble a furry animal with teeth. There is room, then, for representationalists to argue that Berkeley's first argument against them fails.

Berkeley's second argument against representationalism is reminiscent of the problem of interaction confronting substance dualists (Section 3.5). Berkeley argues that representationalists give no account of how it is possible for mind-independent entities to produce ideas – of how it is possible, in other words, for nonmental entities to causally influence mental ones – and this gives us good reason to think representationalism is false.

In response, representationalists can argue that an account of causal relations is either unnecessary or else a source of difficulty not just for them but for idealists as well. Every theory, representationalists can argue, is forced to take some assumptions as brute, unexplainable facts. Idealists complain that representationalists do not explain how nonmental entities are able to causally influence mental entities, yet idealists themselves do not explain how mental entities are able to causally influence other mental entities; they do not endeavor to explain how it is possible for one idea to cause another. Idealists choose to take causal relations among ideas as unexplainable givens, whereas representationalists choose to take causal relations between ideas and external things as unexplainable givens. Since idealists provide no grounds for asserting that their basic assumptions are superior to those of representationalists, their objection to representationalism is ineffective, for if it counts as a strike against a theory that it does not account for how certain types of causal relations are possible, then it is a strike not just against representationalism, but against idealism as well.

To summarize, then, the arguments Berkeley advances in favor of (1) and (2) are questionable at best. The argument he advances in favor of (1) appears flawed, and there are reasons to reject (2) based on representationalist and direct realist theories of perception.

9.3   Arguments Against Idealism

In addition to criticisms of the argument for idealism, there are also arguments that purport to show that idealism is false. One objection to idealism claims the theory is false because it has absurd consequences. If tables, trees, mountains, and other objects are just bundles of experiences, then idealism implies that these objects would cease to exist if no one were experiencing them. If I were alone, for instance, and there were no one else around to see this table, idealism implies that the table would cease to exist if I were to leave the room, for in that case, there would no longer be anyone around to experience it. But this is absurd, says the objection, surely the table would continue to exist if I stepped into the hallway.

Idealists can respond to this argument in at least two ways, both of which are found in Berkeley's work. First, idealists can appeal not just to actual experiences to ground the existence of objects but to potential experiences as well – not just what people actually see or hear but what they could see or hear under certain circumstances. Although I might not actually be seeing the table when I leave the room, idealists can say, I *could* see the table if I were to re-enter it; and the mere potential that the table might be seen is sufficient for it to exist. The table's existence, in other words, consists not merely in being actually experienced, but in being potentially experienced as well.

One problem with this response is that it makes it difficult for idealists to draw a distinction between reality and appearance. Consider the kinds of experiences we would ordinarily classify as hallucinations. It seems possible that I could have the experience of seeing a pink elephant – that I could perceive the idea of a pink elephant, as Berkeley might put it. The idea of a pink elephant thus has the potential to be experienced by me. But if something's existence consists not merely in being actually experienced but in being potentially experienced as well, then it seems that idealists are committed to saying that the pink elephant really exists. The original objection claimed that idealism was too ontologically exclusive – that it implied the nonexistence of things that seem to exist. The worry about this response is that it makes idealism too ontologically inclusive; that it implies the existence of things that seem not to exist.

Considerations of this sort are perhaps what led Berkeley to adopt a second strategy for responding to the objection. It posits God or some other being as an eternal, omnipresent perceiver. God, it claims, always has an experience of everything. God, for instance, always perceives the table even when nobody else does. Thus, when I leave the room, the table continues to be perceived by someone, namely God, and it thus continues to exist.

This response seems to allow idealists to countenance the existence of objects we ourselves do not perceive, but it still does not address the worry that idealism cannot draw a distinction between appearance and reality. It seems that there is no way for idealists to distinguish what we would ordinarily consider hallucinations, for instance, from genuine perceptions. If I were having an experience of there being a pink elephant in front of me – if I were perceiving that idea – then it seems the idealist is committed to saying that a pink elephant really exists. Berkeley was familiar with this worry. To handle it, he appealed to the idea that there are laws of nature.

Most philosophers believe that there are laws of nature; they believe that things do not happen at random but in predictable patterns and according to regular principles: bodies in motion conform to the law $F = ma$ (force equals mass times acceleration); a cup of hot coffee will get cooler if left for a few minutes in a cool room; sugar dissolves in water; oil does not, and so on. Some philosophers treat laws of nature as basic entities; others ground them in the powers and capacities of individual things – the power of sugar to dissolve in water, for instance, or the power of silicon crystals to produce electricity when exposed to certain wavelengths of light. Berkeley grounded laws of nature in the power of God to produce ideas in regular ways. God, he said, is the source of all regularity in the universe. It is because God decides to produce ideas in us in regular ways that our experiences of, say, bodies in motion conforms to the law $F = ma$, and that a cup of hot coffee will get cooler not hotter if left in a cool room.

The idea that there are laws of nature grounded in God's will provides idealists like Berkeley with a basis for drawing a distinction between appearance and reality – between experiences that we would consider hallucinations, for instance, and experiences that we would consider veridical such as instances of genuine perception. The behavior of real things conforms to the laws of nature, they can claim, whereas hallucinations and other nonveridical experiences do not. Consequently, if I have an experience that does not conform to the laws of nature, I have good reason to believe that that experience is illusory. If, for instance, the pink elephant were real, I would be able not merely to see it but also to feel, smell, and hear it. Consequently, if I attempt to reach out and touch the elephant and discover that it is intangible – that my hand goes right through it, say – then I have grounds to conclude that I am suffering from some type of visual hallucination. Similarly, because God produces ideas in all of us in regular ways, the experiences of other people could also provide evidence for or against the reality of the elephant. If I were the only person in the room who was having a visual experience of a pink elephant, if other people denied that they could see a pink elephant, then I would once again have good reason to believe that my experience was illusory.

By appealing to laws of the nature, then, idealists are able to bring their view closer to the dictates of common sense. Yet their effort to do so forms the basis of another, more general objection to idealism. If the goal of these idealist maneuvers (the appeal to potential experiences, to God's omni-perception, and to laws of nature) is to allow idealists to accommodate a commonsense view of things, why endorse idealism at all? Why not just endorse a commonsense view straightaway and be done with it? If there were compelling reasons to reject a commonsense view of things – if, for instance, a commonsense view generated the kinds of contradictions Berkeley claimed it did, then we might reasonably be expected to abandon it in favor some alternative such as idealism. But as we have seen, Berkeley's argument fails to establish the incoherence of the commonsense view, and, in the absence of such an argument, the commonsense view of things operates as our default view of reality.

Here is another way of stating the point: our pre-philosophical intuitions give us some reason to think that a commonsense view of the world is true – that the world consists of mind-independent entities. If our pre-philosophical intuitions have any evidential value at all, then the burden is on idealists to show that the commonsense view is false. Yet it seems that this is a burden idealists have failed to carry. Common sense may not be a decisive or infallible source of information, but if someone asks us to reject the deliverances of common sense, it is fair of us to demand good reasons why. Consequently, if idealists ask us to reject our commonsense commitment to the mind-independence of physical entities, it is fair of us to demand a compelling argument against that commitment, and this is something idealists have so far failed to provide.

9.4   Neutral Monism

Neutral monism claims that everything is neutral. The basic entities that exist are in themselves neither mental nor physical; they can be accurately described as mental or physical if they satisfy certain extrinsic conditions, but they needn't be described in these ways since they can all be exhaustively described and explained in terms of a neutral conceptual framework, one that is neither mentalistic nor physicalistic. According to neutral monists, in other words, what we call 'mental events' are really neutral events that satisfy one type of condition, and what we call 'physical events' are really neutral events that satisfy another type of condition. These conditions ground the distinction between the mental and physical conceptual frameworks, but the phenomena we are ultimately describing in terms of these conceptual frameworks are in themselves neither mental nor physical; they only qualify as mental or physical insofar as they satisfy certain extrinsic conditions. Perhaps the easiest way to understand neutral monism is to draw an analogy with functionalism (Sections 6.3–6.4).

Recall that according to functionalists, being in a mental state amounts to being in some state that satisfies a certain condition. Being in pain, for instance, might amount to being in some state that correlates pinpricks, burns, and abrasions with winces, groans, and escape-directed movements. Moreover, according to functionalists who are also physicalists (we called them 'realization physicalists' in Chapter 6) the only states that correlate pinpricks, burns, and abrasions with winces, groans, and escape-directed movements are physical states. According to realization physicalists, then, being in pain amounts to being in some *physical* state that correlates pinpricks, burns, and abrasions with winces, groans, and escape-directed movements. Neutral monists say something similar except that for them the basic states that correlate inputs to a system with outputs from it are not physical but neutral. Being in pain, for instance, amounts to being in some neutral state that correlates pinpricks, burns, and abrasions with winces, groans, and escape-directed movements. Moreover, according to neutral monists it is not just mental phenomena that are defined in this way; physical phenomena are defined in this way as well. Being in a physical state such as having a certain mass amounts to being in some neutral state that conforms to the laws of physics – that, say, satisfies the variable 'm' in the formula $F = ma$.

According to neutral monists, then, there are conditions that qualify neutral events as mental and other conditions that qualify neutral events as physical. It is possible, moreover, for the same neutral event to satisfy conditions of both sorts – just as one man can satisfy the conditions that qualify him both as a brother and as a father. A neutral event that satisfies conditions of both sorts qualifies as both a mental event and a physical event. Hence, a particular neutral state might qualify both as a pain and as a brain state because it both (1) correlates pinpricks, burns, and abrasions with winces, groans, and escape-directed movements, and (2) stands in causal relations that conform to the laws of physics. Neutral monism thus allows the very same event to be both mental and physical without having to provide an account of how mental events are nothing but physical events, or how physical events are nothing but mental ones. Neutral monism thus promises to secure monism without having to provide the kind of reductivist account endorsed by reductive physicalists and reductive idealists. The promise of such an account is in part what motivates neutral monists.

9.5   The Arguments For and Against Neutral Monism

Neutral monists often look to resolve mind–body problems by characterizing mental and physical phenomena as species of phenomena that belong to a more general type. Consider an analogy involving some imaginary mathematicians. The imaginary mathematicians, let us suppose, are concerned with giving a unified account of what triangles and rectangles are. One group of them tries to define rectangles as a species of triangle. A second group tries to define triangles as a species of rectangle. Despite their efforts, both groups fail; try as they might, their proposed definitions always run into contradictions: three-sided figures, it seems, cannot be defined as a species of four-sided figure, nor can four-sided figures be defined as a species of three-sided figure. Given the problems confronting the first two groups, a third group of mathematicians suggests an alternative strategy: instead of defining rectangles as a species of triangle or triangles as a species of rectangle, they look to define both triangles and rectangles as species of *polygons* – species, in other words, of a more general type of mathematical entity. Since triangles and rectangles both count as polygons, on their account, it has the advantage of being able to explain the features rectangles and triangles have in common. Yet because there are always features that distinguish one species of a general type of object from another species, it is also able to explain the features that distinguish rectangles and triangles. In addition, say exponents of this third strategy, their account can explain why the first two groups of mathematicians failed in their efforts to provide a unified account: rectangles and triangles cannot be defined in terms of each other since neither is a variety of the other; both are instead varieties of a third, more general, type of entity.

Many neutral monists see in the history of mind–body problems something analogous to the case of the imaginary mathematicians. Philosophers have been looking to construct a unified, monistic account of mental and physical phenomena. One group, physicalists, have attempted to account for mental phenomena in terms of physical phenomena. A second group, idealists, have attempted to account for physical phenomena in terms of mental ones. Despite their best efforts, however, neither physicalists nor idealists have been successful. Try as they might, both encounter mind–body problems. Given the problems confronting physicalists and idealists, neutral monists suggest an alternative strategy for constructing a monistic theory of mind. Mental phenomena should not be understood as a species of physical phenomena, nor should physical phenomena be understood as a species of mental phenomena; rather, phenomena of both sorts should be understood as species of a more general type of phenomenon: both should be understood as species of neutral phenomena. Such an account would enable us to explain what mental and physical phenomena have in common – their ability, for instance, to enter into causal relations with one another. If all events are of the same general type, then there is no problem explaining how those events can causally interact. On the other hand, such an account would also enable us to explain why mental and physical phenomena differ: different species within a general category are always associated with different conditions; there are thus different conditions associated with being mental and being physical. Finally, such an account would enable us to explain why philosophers have been struggling so long with mind–body problems. The reason physicalists and idealists have failed to construct a workable theory of mind is like the reason the first two groups of imaginary mathematicians failed to construct a unified account of rectangles and triangles: mental entities are not species of physical entities, nor are physical entities species of mental ones; both, rather, are species of neutral entities, and because philosophers have failed to recognize this, they have become entangled in mind–body problems.

The foregoing considerations describe one of the motivations for neutral monism. But what are the actual arguments in favor of it? What are the reasons for thinking neutral monism is true? Disappointingly, neutral monists have typically not argued very much in support of their theory. Even neutral monism's most prominent defender, Bertrand Russell, said that the theory, though "simple and unifying" was nevertheless "not demonstrable."[3] The foregoing considerations nevertheless suggest an argumentative strategy. It proceeds in two steps: the first argues for the superiority of monism to dualism; the second, for the superiority of neutral monism to physicalism and idealism.

Neutral monists can argue that monism is superior to dualism in the way physicalists like J. J. C. Smart do, namely by appeal to ontological parsimony or Ockham's razor (Section 5.5). All things being equal, neutral monists can say, a coherent monistic theory is preferable to a coherent dualistic one. The reason is that a monistic theory posits fewer kinds of entities than a dualistic one, and ontological frugality is preferable to ontological profligacy. In general, theoretical entities should not be multiplied beyond necessity, so a theory that does an explanatory job with fewer entities is preferable to a theory that does that same explanatory job with more. Monistic theories promise to do the same explanatory job as dualistic theories using fewer basic entities. Dualists, after all, posit twice as many basic types of entities as monists; they say that there are fundamentally two distinct types of properties, whereas monists are committed to there being fundamentally only one. Provided, then, that monistic theories can do the same explanatory work as dualistic ones, monistic theories are preferable. Second, when it comes to competing monistic theories, neutral monists can argue that their theory is superior on the grounds that it does a better job of solving mind–body problems: (1) physicalism and idealism cannot solve mind–body problems in a satisfactory way, neutral monists can urge, yet (2) neutral monism can solve those problems, and (3) neutral monism does not have any problems that are as serious as or more serious than those facing physicalism and idealism. The ability of a theory to solve problems its competitors can't is something that weighs in its favor. So if neutral monism can solve problems that physicalism and idealism can't, and there are no problems with neutral monism that offset this benefit, then there is good reason to consider neutral monism superior to other monistic theories.

Critics of neutral monism will respond to this argument in several ways. Dualists will challenge the appeal to ontological parsimony. If two theories, T_A and T_B, are equally matched in every other respect – if both are coherent, both are consistent with the available scientific data, both can explain the same range of phenomena – then ontological parsimony becomes a relevant factor in choosing between T_A and T_B. But if one theory is incoherent, or is falsified by the scientific data, or cannot explain phenomena that the other can, then these factors trump any appeal to ontological parsimony. And, dualists can argue, monistic theories have problems with coherence, problems explaining the scientific data, or problems achieving adequate explanatory power. The simplicity of their ontologies is thus insufficient for rejecting dualism.

In addition, many monists will challenge premises (1)–(3). Physicalists and idealists can argue against Premise (1), for instance, that their own theories provide satisfactory solutions to mind–body problems. They can also argue that neutral monists have failed to articulate a proposal detailed enough to support premises (2) and (3). In particular, they can urge that at least two features of neutral monism require further clarification: first, neutral monists need to state clearly exactly what neutral entities or occurrences are, and second, they need to specify exactly what kinds of conditions qualify neutral entities or occurrences as mental and what kinds of conditions qualify neutral entities or occurrences as physical. Let us consider these points in reverse order.

Neutral monists have had different things to say about the conditions that qualify neutral occurrences as mental or physical. One type of account follows Bertrand Russell in describing these conditions in terms of laws. A neutral occurrence qualifies as a mental event, on this view, exactly if it is related to other neutral occurrences in a way described by a psychological law. A neutral occurrence qualifies as a physical event, on the other hand, exactly if it is related to other neutral occurrences in a way described by a physical law. Consider an example. Imagine that the following statement expresses a psychological law:

L1   If someone, S, wants x, and believes that doing A will secure x, then typically S's beliefs and wants will cause S to do A.

On this account, neutral occurrences N_1, N_2, and N_3 might qualify as instances of wanting, believing, and doing A, respectively, exactly if they are related to each other in the way L1 describes. Likewise, imagine that the following statement expresses a physical law:

> L2   Brain state B is always caused by sensory stimulus S, and always causes motor response M.

On this account, neutral occurrences N_1, N_2, and N_3 might qualify as instances of brain state B, sensory stimulus S, and motor response M, respectively, exactly if they are related to each other in the way L2 describes. If it turns out, moreover, that the very same neutral occurrence is related to other neutral occurrences in a way described by both laws, then that neutral occurrence qualifies both as a mental event and as a physical event. N_1, for instance, might qualify both as an instance of wanting and as an instance of brain state B. The appeal to psychological and physical laws thus provides neutral monists with a basis for developing a fuller account of what conditions qualify neutral events as mental or as physical. (Exactly what physical and psychological laws there are is an empirical matter, something neutral monists leave to the relevant branches of science to determine.) It thus appears that neutral monists have something to say about the conditions that qualify neutral entities as mental or physical.

Perhaps the biggest challenge facing neutral monists, however, is providing a clear account of what neutral entities are. We have a fairly clear conception of what physical entities are: they are paradigmatically the entities described and explained by physics. Likewise, we have fairly clear examples of what mental entities are: they include beliefs, desires, feelings, pains, and so on. But what are neutral entities?

According to neutral monists, neutral entities are supposed to be entities that are in themselves neither mental nor physical but that qualify as mental or physical if they satisfy certain conditions. Some neutral monists have been tempted to say little more than this. They define neutral entities in terms of their alleged relations to mental and physical ones. They say, for instance, that neutral entities are the ones that can factor into both physical and psychological laws, or that neutral entities are the entities that are capable of satisfying the conditions associated both with being mental and with being physical. The problem with these definitions is that they fail to provide us with adequate means of identifying which entities in the world the neutral entities are, or of determining whether neutral entities even exist. Consider an analogy.

Imagine that we arrive together at a meeting of an organization, and you want to know from me which person in the room is the organization's president. I respond: "Well obviously the president is the person in the room who sets the meeting's agenda, who organizes the annual fundraiser, who was elected by the membership last January, who … ," and I continue to describe the relations that define the role the president occupies within the organization – relations to the meeting, the fundraiser, the electorate that are had by anyone who occupies the presidential role. You are doubtless disappointed by my response. The reason is that for all the information it supplies, it does not supply information that enables you to pick out which person in the room actually occupies the presidential role. Yet that is precisely what you want: information that tells you which person in the room is president. Attempts to define neutral entities simply in terms of their relations to mental and physical entities are analogous to my response, and seem to have an analogous shortcoming: They describe the role neutral entities are supposed to occupy within neutral monistic theory – relations to mental and physical entities that would be had by anything that qualified as a neutral entity. But they do not supply any information that would enable us to pick out which entities in the world, if any, actually occupy that role. If neutral monists cannot supply a definition that enables us to do this, then neutral monism remains merely an abstract possibility in logical space – merely a suggestion, not a genuine theory whose merits and demerits can be evaluated alongside the other theories we have considered.

Not all neutral monists have rested content with purely relational definitions of the foregoing sort, but attempts to give more informative definitions have faced other problems. For instance, informative definitions of neutral entities have often had a mentalistic cast, and this has generated suspicions that neutral monists' so-called neutral entities are not really neutral but mental, and that would-be neutral monists are really closet idealists. William James, for instance, claimed that neutral phenomena were *pure experiences* – a category that sounded suspiciously mentalistic. Bertrand Russell criticized mentalistic characterizations like James's, yet at one time Russell himself characterized the basic entities in his ontology in a similar way. The basic entities, he said, were *sensibilia*, a category of entities he introduced by expanding the mentalistic notion of sense data. According to Russell, sense data were the basic units of experience – a color patch here, a flavor there, and so on. Our overall experience of reality was constructed out of these bits of sensory data, and sensibilia were the more general category to which these sense data belonged. In other words, there are in addition to the sense data we experience other entities of the very same type that go unexperienced by anyone, and these unexperienced entities together with sense data constitute the class of all sensibilia. These sensibilia, Russell said at the time, are the basic entities that exist.

At other times, however, Russell characterized the basic entities in other terms. Later in his career, for instance, he characterized fundamental reality as an underlying *material* or *stuff* that was in itself neither mental nor physical. Although this characterization avoided the worry that neutral monism is really a form of idealism, it gave rise to the equal and opposite worry that neutral monism was really a form of physicalism since the categories of material and stuff suggest something physical. Russell later abandoned this vocabulary as well. In the end, he seems to have favored describing the neutral entities simply as events.

The category of events seems neutral enough: there is nothing built into the concept of an event that implies that events be mental, nor is there anything that implies that events be physical. Neutral monists like Russell might thus hope to avoid the charge that their theory is a disguised form of idealism or physicalism by appealing to an ontology of events. The problem with this characterization of neutral entities is that it borders on being uninformative in the way the relational characterizations of neutral entities discussed a moment ago were uninformative. What, after all, qualifies an event as neutral on this account? Granted, there is nothing built into the concept of an event that implies that events must be mental or physical, but by the same token there is nothing built into the concept of an event that implies that they must be neutral – that implies, in other words, that they must be in themselves neither mental nor physical but something else. Characterizing the basic entities simply as events falls short of specifying what qualifies any events that exist as neutral entities.

Neutral monists might respond that the events that exist qualify as neutral because they can factor into both mental and physical laws. In that case, however, neutral monists would be settling for a relational definition of neutral entities of the sort discussed earlier – a definition that describes the role neutral entities are supposed to play in neutral monistic theory, but that fails to supply any information that would enable us to pick out which entities in the world, if any, actually occupy that role. To the extent that neutral monists settle for a definition of this sort, they endorse what amounts to a mere abstract possibility – a suggestion, not a genuine theory that can be evaluated alongside its competitors.

The foregoing considerations present neutral monists with a problem, for opponents of the theory can turn those considerations into an argument that the theory is false. Neutral monists endorse the existence of neutral entities, they can say, and yet neutral monists are incapable of describing these entities in neutral terms: their descriptions end up being either mentalistic, or physicalistic, or uninformative. The repeated failures of neutral monists to provide informative descriptions of neutral entities give us some reason to doubt that neutral entities really exist. There are good reasons to believe that mental and physical entities exist; there are, after all, mental and physical conceptual frameworks, and these frameworks appear to have some purchase on reality since we routinely use them successfully for description and explanation. By contrast, there does not appear to be a neutral conceptual framework to stand alongside these others. Why not? The best explanation, opponents of neutral monism can urge, is that there are no neutral entities. The basic entities that exist are either mental or physical, not neutral, as neutral monists claim.

The demand for an informative characterization of neutral phenomena thus poses a serious challenge both to the argument for neutral monism and to the theory itself. It is not clear that neutral monists have yet found the resources needed to provide an adequate response.

9.6   Mind–Body Pessimism

The mind–body theories we have considered so far are all based on the assumption that mind–body problems can be solved in a satisfactory way. Mind–body pessimists reject this assumption. Unlike other mind–body theorists, mind–body pessimists claim that mind–body problems cannot be solved. The reason, they say, is that human cognitive capacities are limited in ways that will forever prevent us from discovering solutions.

The idea that philosophical problems are due not to the way things are in reality but rather to inbuilt limitations on our cognitive powers is not new. The eighteenth-century philosopher Immanuel Kant claimed that philosophical problems concerning topics such as the existence of God, or the possibility of human freedom in a deterministic universe, were the result of people trying to exceed the limits of their cognitive capacities. These problems reflected not some deep paradox at the heart of reality, but rather the limits on our ability to understand reality.

Mind–body pessimists have a similar view of mind–body problems. Mind–body problems are insoluble, they say, not because there is anything paradoxical about the relation between mental and physical phenomena, but simply because our ability to understand the world has limits, and those limits make it impossible for us to understand fully how mental phenomena are related to physical phenomena. There are, by analogy, limitations on a child's ability to understand the physical universe – limitations that prevent the child from, say, understanding quantum mechanics or general relativity theory. If, therefore, certain aspects of the physical universe seem puzzling, paradoxical, or magical to the child, the implication is not that the physical universe really is puzzling, paradoxical, or magical, but rather that the child's ability to understand the physical universe is limited. The puzzles and paradoxes reflect limitations in his or her cognitive powers, not the way things are in reality. Mind–body pessimists insist that something analogous is true of human cognitive powers in general: there are inbuilt limitations on our ability to understand the world – limitations that prevent us from understanding fully how mental and physical phenomena are related. As a result, the mental–physical relation can seem puzzling, paradoxical, even magical to us. This does not imply that the mental–physical relation really is puzzling, paradoxical, or magical in reality, but rather that our ability to understand the world is limited, and this cognitive limitation prevents us from understanding fully how, say, mental phenomena can emerge from physical phenomena, or how mental events can cause physical events, or how we are able to know anything about each others' mental states.

The foremost mind–body pessimist in recent years has been Colin McGinn. According to McGinn, our cognitive limitations will forever prevent us from solving the problem of psychophysical emergence – the problem of explaining how states of the brain can produce consciousness in particular (Sections 1.4,

8.8–8.9). Even though the brain produces consciousness in a straightforward way, says McGinn, we will never be able to understand what that way is. By analogy, a blind person may never be able to understand exactly what the color red is: the causal connection between brain states and conscious states is cognitively inaccessible to us in the way colors are cognitively inaccessible to a blind person. As a result, psychophysical emergence will forever seem mysterious to us even though in reality conscious experience is caused by the activity of the brain in a way that is entirely unmysterious – a way that could be described scientifically, for instance, by beings who weren't hindered by the kinds of cognitive limitations we ourselves have.

In favor of mind–body pessimism, McGinn argues as follows: (1) The emergence of consciousness can be explained straightforwardly by a property of the brain; nevertheless, (2) that property is cognitively inaccessible to us; we can never know what it is. Hence, the causal connection between consciousness and the brain will always seem problematic and mysterious even though in reality it is not.

In support of Premise (1), McGinn draws an analogy with the emergence of life. We know that life emerged from nonliving materials without any sort of supernatural intervention. As a result, we can infer that there must have been some type of natural mechanism that was responsible for producing living things even if we do not yet know what that mechanism was. The same is true of consciousness. It too is a biological phenomenon, and so we infer that there must be some type of natural mechanism that is responsible for producing conscious states; we simply do not know what that mechanism is. The only significant difference between the emergence of life and the emergence of consciousness, on McGinn's view, is the possibility of discovering the causal mechanism responsible for each. We can be optimistic that we will one day discover the mechanism responsible for the emergence of life, according to McGinn, but we will never be able to discover the mechanism responsible for the emergence of consciousness. That mechanism is cognitively inaccessible to us.

But why should we suppose that the causal mechanism responsible for consciousness is cognitively inaccessible? In support of Premise (2), McGinn advances at least two arguments. First, he argues that the mechanism responsible for producing consciousness is not something we could ever discover. That mechanism could be discovered, he argues, only by appeal either to introspection or to brain science. Yet neither of these is capable of supplying the information we need. To reveal the brain mechanism responsible for consciousness, these methods would have to reveal both sides of the mind–brain connection. The problem is that introspection and brain science each reveal only one side of that connection. Introspection reveals only the mental side; it reveals nothing about how our mental states are related to states of the brain. Simply reflecting on my current state of consciousness does not reveal anything to me about how that state is produced, by what brain states, or even whether it is produced by brain states at all. Brain science, on the other hand, reveals only the physical side of the mind–

brain connection; it reveals nothing about how brain states are related to states of consciousness. When we study the brain of a conscious subject we don't have any access to the conscious states of that subject. I might see that certain cells in your visual cortex are active, but I don't thereby come to have your visual experiences; I don't thereby come to see what you are seeing. Moreover, says McGinn, it's difficult even to conceive of an observed property of the brain that might disclose something's conscious states – like trying to imagine a property of a rock that would reveal to us that it was conscious. Since introspection and brain science are the only two ways we could discover the causal mechanism linking consciousness to the brain, and neither is able to reveal that mechanism, the exact nature of the mind–brain connection will remain forever inaccessible to us.

Second, McGinn argues that it is impossible for us ever to construct a theory that explains how states of consciousness are related to states of the brain. To see this, imagine that there were a theory, T, that stated how physical states produced states of consciousness. T would say, for instance, that a property of a bat's brain, B, was responsible for producing a certain state of consciousness, C, in the bat. To be able to grasp what T said, we would have to be able to understand both what B was and also what C was. Yet most exponents of consciousness agree that it is impossible for us to understand what the experiences of other kinds of beings are like. It is impossible, for instance, for us to understand what it is like to be a bat. That would require us to have conscious experiences like a bat has, but according to most exponents of consciousness we cannot have such experiences; we cannot know what it is like to be a bat. If we can never know what it is like to be a bat, however, then we could never understand what T was saying since we could never understand what one of its terms, namely 'C', was referring to. It is impossible, then, for us ever to construct a theory that would explain how physical states could produce states of consciousness, and without such a theory, the link between consciousness and the brain is bound to remain forever inaccessible to us.

According to McGinn, then, there is a natural and straightforward explanation of how consciousness emerges from the brain; we can simply never know what that explanation is. Consequently, there is no real problem of consciousness – no real mystery about how consciousness is produced by the brain; there is only the appearance of a mystery – an appearance due to the limitations of our cognitive powers.

There are several ways of responding to McGinn's argument. Critics of Premise (1), for instance, can argue that the considerations McGinn advances do not support the conclusion that we have inbuilt cognitive limitations that prevent us from discovering the mechanism that produces consciousness; rather, McGinn's considerations support the conclusion that consciousness is not produced by the brain at all. If we cannot discover the causal mechanisms responsible for consciousness, says the objection, it is plausible to conclude that there are no such mechanisms. At the very least, it seems more plausible to draw this conclusion than the conclusion that there are limitations on our cognitive powers that blind us to certain features of the world.

A second type of response takes issue with Premise (2). Critics of (2) can argue that the analogy McGinn draws between the emergence of consciousness and the emergence of life supports a conclusion different from McGinn's. Just as we have good reason to think that we will eventually be able to bridge the gap in our understanding of how life emerges from inorganic processes, so too, critics can argue, we have good reason to think that we will eventually be able to bridge the gap in our understanding of how consciousness emerges from the brain. Just as we can be optimistic that we will eventually discover causal laws linking inorganic processes to the emergence of life, so too we can be optimistic that we will eventually discover causal laws linking brain states to the emergence of consciousness.

In addition, critics can argue that at best McGinn's second argument for Premise (2) rules out a global theory of consciousness, one with laws linking physical states to conscious states in any conscious being whatsoever. But, critics can urge, the argument does not rule out the possibility of a local, species-specific theory of consciousness with laws linking physical states to conscious states in humans specifically. McGinn's tacit assumption seems to be that giving an account of consciousness for one kind of conscious being would involve giving an account of consciousness for every kind of conscious being. An assumption like this is plausible in the case of natural kinds. A theory that enabled you to explain the essential features of this quantity of copper, for instance, would be the same as a theory that enabled you to explain the essential features of any quantity of copper. The reason is that copper is the same kind of material wherever it exists – if you can account for one sample of copper you can account for them all. If consciousness is a single kind of thing wherever it exists, if it is a natural kind like copper, then McGinn's assumption is plausible. But why should we assume that consciousness is a natural kind? McGinn offers no argument. He seems to take it as a basic assumption, and that assumption, critics can argue, is dubious at best.

Another objection to McGinn's argument looks to deny the existence of consciousness as McGinn understands it – roughly, a private domain of subjective impressions. Those who take a cue from Wittgenstein's or Dennett's arguments against qualia (Chapter 8), for instance, are likely to deny McGinn's claims about the inscrutability of a bat's conscious states, and the same is true of those who endorse representational or higher-order theories of consciousness (Section 4.9).

Finally, critics of mind–body pessimism in general are likely to argue either that mind–body problems can be solved in satisfactory way, or else that the insolubility of those problems is due to something other than inbuilt cognitive limitations. Someone might argue in line with critics of Premise (2), for instance, that the emergence of consciousness seems mysterious to us right now because we have only been studying consciousness scientifically for a few decades. As science progresses we can expect breakthroughs that will bridge the explanatory gap.

Alternatively, someone might agree that mind–body problems are insoluble, but argue that the reason for their insolubility has nothing to do with the inbuilt cognitive limitations pessimists postulate. Consider, for instance, the kind of historical explanation that the qualia skeptics described in sections 8.5–8.7 might advance: the reason mind–body problems are insoluble, skeptics might argue, is that those problems are based on false assumptions about the nature of mind – assumptions that were adopted in the wake of the Scientific Revolution, and whose falsity is revealed precisely by the insolubility of the problems they generate. If mind–body problems are insoluble, then, the explanation might have nothing to do with any deep metaphysical or epistemological story about inbuilt cognitive limitations; it might have simply to do with mundane historical facts about the adoption of misguided assumptions by Western philosophers at a certain point in their history. Although McGinn defends his view against several alternative explanations for the insolubility of mind–body problems, this is one he does not address.

Further Reading

Berkeley (1998a [1710]; 1998b [1713]) argues for ontological idealism in the opening sections of *A Treatise Concerning the Principles of Human Knowledge*, and through the character of Philonous in *Three Dialogues between Hylas and Philonous*. John Foster (1982; 1991) is perhaps the sole contemporary defender of ontological idealism. He advances an argument for idealism different from Berkeley's. "The Succinct Case for Idealism" (Foster 1993) is a helpful introduction to his views. Foster defends nonanalytic phenomenalism, unlike A. J. Ayer (1952) who defended analytic phenomenalism. Analytic phenomenalism was criticized by Roderick Chisholm (1948).

Kant's (1998 [1781]) *Critique of Pure Reason* is the *locus classicus* for his transcendental idealism. His discussion of insoluble philosophical problems is contained in the same work. Nicholas Rescher (1998) defends a contemporary version of conceptual idealism.

The representationalists of Berkeley's day included John Locke, the target of many of Berkeley's arguments. For a more recent defense of representationalism see Fodor (1987). Direct realism was the default position in the philosophy of perception prior to the seventeenth century. Aristotle, for instance, appears to have been a direct realist. In addition, the eighteenth-century Scottish philosopher Thomas Reid (2002 [1785]) defended direct realism. More recent defenders of direct realism include the philosophers John McDowell (1994) and Hilary Putnam (1999), and the psychologist J. J. Gibson (1986).

The ideas that inspired neutral monism were first articulated in the nineteenth century by the philosopher and physicist Ernst Mach (1959). A version of the theory was endorsed by William James (1984a [1904]; 1984b [1904]) who called it 'radical empiricism'. Several American philosophers in the first quarter of the twentieth century followed James's lead, including R. B. Perry (1968) and E. B. Holt (1973). The theory was nevertheless articulated most clearly by the British philosopher Bertrand Russell who coined the term 'neutral monism'. Russell was critical of the neutral monistic theories of his predecessors, but he later came to defend his own version of the theory (Russell 1956; 2005 [1921]). Information theory, a branch of mathematics, might provide neutral monists with their best chance to date of providing a satisfactory characterization of neutral phenomena. An information-theoretic version of neutral monism has been defended by Kenneth Sayre (1976).

Colin McGinn (1989) argues for mind–body pessimism. The private conception of consciousness he appeals to was originally expressed by Thomas Nagel (1974). McGinn's idea that the emergence of consciousness will inevitably seem mysterious to us has sometimes earned his view the label 'mysterianism'.

Notes

1 Kant himself did not use the terms 'concept' and 'category' to refer to space and time. He called them instead 'forms of intuition'. Kant used 'concept' and 'category' in technical senses.
2 Berkeley, *A Treatise Concerning the Principles of Human Knowledge*, sections 7 and 23.
3 Russell, 1956, "Mind and Matter," in *Portraits from Memory and Other Essays*, New York: Simon and Schuster, 158.

Chapter 10

The Hylomorphic Worldview

Overview

Hylomorphism claims that individuals consist of materials that are structured or organized in various ways. You and I are not mere collections of physical particles; we are collections of physical particles with a certain organization or structure. That structure is a basic ontological and explanatory principle. It is the reason why you and I are humans as opposed to dogs or rocks, and it is the reason why humans possess the particular developmental, metabolic, reproductive, perceptive, and cognitive capacities they do.

Hylomorphism's view of organization is closely associated with an account of composition: roughly, x is a part of y if x contributes to the activities of y. An electron is a part of me, for instance, if it contributes to my activities – if, say, it depolarizes one of my cellular membranes. This notion of composition dovetails with work in biology, philosophy of biology, and philosophy of neuroscience.

Hylomorphism also implies that there are emergent properties. A strand of DNA has physical properties such as mass irrespective of its surroundings, but it acquires new properties when incorporated into a cell: it makes a contribution to the cell's metabolic and reproductive activities. The strand of DNA thus has two types of properties: properties due to its integration into a structured individual, and properties it possesses independent of any such integration. What is true of an organism's parts are true of it as well. Eleanor has a mass of 50 kg because her fundamental physical constituents have masses that add up to 50 kg irrespective of their organization. Her abilities to speak, or to remember or perceive, by contrast, depend to a large extent on how her fundamental physical constituents are organized. Alter the structure of her nervous system, for instance, and she would lose those capacities.

Philosophy of Mind: A Comprehensive Introduction, First Edition. William Jaworski.
© 2011 William Jaworski. Published 2011 by Blackwell Publishing Ltd.

Hylomorphism differs from physicalism because it postulates structure or organization as a basic ontological and explanatory principle distinct from the principles of fundamental physics. Hylomorphism differs from classic forms of emergentism in several respects. One is that it denies emergent properties are emergent forces. It instead endorses causal pluralism, the claim that there are many different kinds of causes and many different kinds of causal relations. Hylomorphism takes causes to be explanatory factors, and it takes causal relations to mirror explanatory ones. Since there are many different kinds of explanatory factors, hylomorphists argue, and also many different kinds of explanatory relations, there are many different kinds of causes and many different kinds of causal relations. Two kinds of explanations that are important to distinguish are rational explanations, which explain why people behave as they do by appeal to their reasons, and mechanistic explanations, which explain how organisms and other complex systems behave as they do by analyzing their activities into subactivities performed by subsystems – a research strategy called 'functional analysis'.

Different kinds of organisms engage in different kinds of activities. Because each kind of organism has its own distinctive activities, each kind of organism comprises its own hierarchy of levels, subactivities, and subsystems or parts. According to hylomorphism, then, levels in nature are not to be understood in a global, kind-generic way, but in a local, kind-specific way with only the lowest level or levels cutting across kind-specific boundaries.

One argument for hylomorphism is an inference to the best explanation. It proceeds in two steps. First, say hylomorphists, a commitment to organization as a basic ontological and explanatory principle best reflects the distinctive character of the ontological and explanatory principles used in the biological sciences. Second, among the theories that acknowledge structure as a basic ontological and explanatory principle, hylomorphism is the best alternative since it avoids the philosophical and empirical problems competing theories face.

10.1   What Is Hylomorphism?

The term 'hylomorphism' is a compound of the Greek words *hyle* and *morphe*, which are typically translated 'matter' and 'form' respectively. According to hylomorphism, individual organisms consist of both matter and form, both a structure and materials that are structured. Consider again the Super Physicist introduced in Chapter 4. When hylomorphists look at the world, they see the same vast sea of matter and energy the Super Physicist describes. But they see something more besides: the way that matter and energy is structured or organized. According to hylomorphists, structure or organization is a basic ontological and explanatory feature of the world. The hylomorphic notion of structure or organization finds its most ready application in the biological domain. Organisms are not just chunks of matter and energy; they are chunks of matter and energy that are structured or organized in various ways. That structure or organization is what is responsible for organisms having the distinctive capacities they have such as the capacities for growth and development, reproduction, perception, movement, and cognition. It is because organisms have these capacities that they qualify as living things as opposed to nonliving ones, and it is because they possess distinctive types of developmental, reproductive, and other capacities that they qualify as living things of one or another kind: mammal, fish, bird, primate. The capacities that categorize us humans as the kind of living things we are include capacities for engaging in activities described and explained in a vocabulary of psychological predicates and terms: thought, feeling, intentional action, personality, character, and so on.

Hylomorphism was the dominant philosophy of nature prior to the seventeenth century. It bears many similarities to classic emergentism and forms of nonreductive physicalism, but it differs from these theories in important respects. Moreover, it represents a general view of the natural world different from all of the post-Cartesian theories considered so far. For that reason we will devote two chapters to it. This chapter is concerned with presenting the general hylomorphic worldview. The next chapter presents a hylomorphic approach to mind–body problems – a hylomorphic theory of mind.

10.2   The Hylomorphic Worldview

Perhaps the easiest way to understand the hylomorphic worldview is to consider a passage from a popular biology textbook:

> Life is highly organized into a hierarchy of structural levels, with each level building on the levels below ... Biological order exists at all levels ... [A]toms ... are ordered into ... molecules ... [T]he molecules ... are arranged into minute structures called organelles, which are in turn the components of cells. Cells are subunits of organisms ... [A]n animal or plant is not a random collection of individual cells, but a multicellular cooperative ... Similar cells are grouped into tissues ... [A]rrangements of different tissues form organs, and organs are grouped into organ systems ... [Moreover] there are tiers beyond the individual organism. A population is a localized group of organisms belonging to the same species; populations of different species living in the same area make up a biological community; and community interactions that include nonliving features of the environment, such as soil and water, form an ecosystem ... Identifying biological organization at its many levels is fundamental to the study of life ... With each step upward in the hierarchy of biological order, novel properties emerge that were not present at the simpler levels of organization ... A molecule such as a protein has attributes not exhibited by any of its component atoms, and a cell is certainly much more than a bag of molecules. If the intricate organization of the human brain is disrupted by a head injury, that

organ will cease to function properly, even though all its parts may still be present. And an organism is a living whole greater than the sum of its parts ... [W]e cannot fully explain a higher level of order by breaking it down into its parts. A dissected animal no longer functions; a cell reduced to its chemical ingredients is no longer a cell. Disrupting a living system interferes with the meaningful explanation of its processes.[1]

This passage highlights a number of important features of biological systems and biological science – features that are also central to the hylomorphic worldview.

First, living things such as human beings are exhaustively decomposable into fundamental physical particles or materials of the sort described by physics – the very same fundamental physical materials found in nonliving things. At a fundamental physical level, there is no difference between the materials composing a human and the materials composing a dog or a rock. Hylomorphism is thus at odds with views that would try to distinguish living beings from nonliving ones or mental beings from nonmental ones on the basis of something at the fundamental physical level. Greek atomists such as Democritus, for instance, claimed that the differences between living things and nonliving ones could be explained by the possession of a greater number of round atoms. Since those atoms were round, they reasoned, they could slide past one another more easily and were thus capable of producing the movements we associate with living things – the beating of the heart, the movements of the limbs, and so on. More recently, the physicist Roger Penrose has made an analogous suggestion about mental phenomena: the difference between conscious beings and nonconscious ones, he suggests, is something that can be explained by quantum phenomena at a fundamental physical level. Hylomorphism is opposed to views like those of Democritus and Penrose. According to hylomorphism, what distinguishes living things from nonliving ones and mental beings from nonmental ones is not the fundamental physical materials that compose them, but the way those materials are structured or organized.

Hylomorphism takes structure or organization (or order or arrangement) to be a basic ontological and explanatory principle. Structure is a basic ontological principle in the sense that an individual's structure is responsible for its being categorized as a member of this or that kind. A quantity of fundamental physical material arranged one way composes a human while the same quantity arranged another way composes a dog, a tree, or a rock. What categorizes something as a human as opposed to a dog or a rock is not the materials composing it, but the way those materials are structured or arranged. Structure is also a basic explanatory principle in the sense that it explains why members of this or that kind are able to engage in the behaviors they do. It is because humans are organized as they are, for instance, that they are able to speak, to learn, and to engage in the range of activities that distinguish them from other living things and from nonliving ones. Disrupting something's structure compromises its capacities – as in the example of the head injury in the passage quoted above.

Second, because organisms consist of both structures and materials that are structured, hylomorphism implies that a complete account of their behavior must appeal to both. Knowing only about one or the other will be insufficient to provide a complete account of the organism's behavior. Consider an analogy: Imagine that you are in the market for a piano. In order to be able to evaluate various instruments, you need to know both something about the materials that compose them, and something about their workmanship – how those materials are put together or arranged. Knowing only that the manufacturer used high-quality materials is not sufficient for knowing whether the instrument is a good one since good materials can be assembled in a shoddy way. Likewise, knowing only that the best craftsmen were employed to impose the best design on the available materials is not sufficient for knowing whether the instrument is a good one since good design and workmanship cannot overcome the limitations of shoddy materials. A good piano requires both good workmanship and good materials. In a similar way, say hylomorphists, understanding the behavior of a living thing requires knowing something both about its structure and about the materials that are structured in that way. If you are riding a rollercoaster, we will be able to explain some of what you are experiencing purely by appeal to physical principles such as Newton's laws of motion. Other aspects of your behavior, however, will require us to describe specific biological structures and capacities such as your vestibular system and how it enables you to maintain your balance and negotiate your environment, and yet other aspects of your behavior will require us to describe specific psychological structures such as a penchant for thrill-seeking.

Saying that something's structure and its materials both contribute to an explanation of its behavior is tantamount to saying that some individuals have two types of properties: properties due to their materials and properties due to their structures or their integration into individuals with structures. Consider an example. Electrons have physical properties such as mass and charge irrespective of their surroundings. Under the right conditions, however, electrons contribute to the activities of living things. In living cells, for instance, electrons can operate as membrane depolarizers, contributors to the cells' organic processes. Subatomic particles, atoms, molecules, and other entities are all capable of contributing to an individual's activities in this way. Nucleic acids, hormones, and neural transmitters are examples; they are genes, growth factors, metabolic and behavioral regulators, and so on. Each of these things admits of two types of descriptions which are expressive of two types of properties. Each can be described organically, in terms of the contributions it makes to a structured system, but each is also independently describable in nonorganic, non-contribution-oriented terms. Descriptions of the former, organic sort are expressive of the properties characteristic of organisms and their parts. Descriptions of the latter, nonorganic sort are expressive of the properties things possess independently of their integration into organic wholes. A strand of DNA, for instance, might always have various atomic or fundamental physical properties regardless of its environment, but that strand acquires new properties when it is integrated into a cell since it makes a goal-directed contribution to the cell's activities. It becomes a gene, a part of the cell that plays a role in, for instance, protein synthesis.

Hylomorphism implies, then, that there are two distinct kinds of properties: properties due to something's structure and properties things possess independently of a broader structure. According to hylomorphism, properties of both sorts make a causal difference to the things having them. In this sense, hylomorphism's view of properties is similar to the emergentist theories discussed in Section 8.10. Recall the features of emergent properties discussed there:

1   Emergent properties are possessed by a system on account of the organization of its components.
2   Emergent properties are not possessed by any of a system's components individually since the organization responsible for their emergence is not a feature of any one component considered in isolation, but of all of them together.
3   Emergent properties are not epiphenomenal. They are not causally or explanatorily inert, but make a distinctive causal or explanatory contribution to a system's behavior. At least some of that behavior is due to the system's emergent properties.
4   Emergent properties are not logical constructions out of lower-level properties; they do not represent abstract ways of describing lower-level occurrences or processes.

Feature (1) implies that emergent properties are not aggregative properties such as mass. Eleanor has a mass of 50 kg for the same reason a 50 kg rock does: their fundamental physical constituents have masses that when taken together equal 50 kg. Feature (1) implies that emergent properties are not aggregative properties of this sort. Feature (4), moreover, is what distinguishes the hylomorphic view of properties from the view endorsed by nonreductive physicalists. Nonreductive physicalists claim that being in pain amounts to being in some lower-level state that satisfies a condition such as having a range of typical causes and effects. Feature (4) implies that logical constructions of this sort do not count as emergent properties. When we describe the contributions the DNA makes to the cell's overall activity we are not describing fundamental physical processes using an abstract vocabulary; we are rather describing properties and relations that are distinctive of biological organization.

A third feature of the hylomorphic view is that despite the possession of irreducible, emergent properties, the behavior of organized systems never violates any lower-level physical laws. Because they are composed of fundamental physical materials, those systems are still subject to the laws governing those materials such as the laws of gravitation and electromagnetism. In fact, the higher-level behavior of organized systems depends on those laws. It is because lower-level entities behave in stable, characteristic ways that they can be recruited to play in organisms the higher-level roles they do. It is because electrons have a characteristic mass and charge, for instance, that they are able to operate as membrane depolarizers within certain structures. Higher-level behavior thus depends on lower-level regularities. Consequently, we must appeal both to lower-level principles and to higher-level ones in order to explain the behavior of organized systems.

10.3 Organic Composition and Functional Analysis

Hylomorphism's account of organization is closely related to an account of composition or parthood. This notion of parthood was discussed briefly in Section 8.2. It claims that organisms are more than the sums of their parts; in addition to the fundamental physical particles that compose them, there is also the way those particles are organized or structured. According to hylomorphism, lower-level entities such as atoms and electrons are integrated into higher-level entities such as organisms by contributing to the activities of those organisms. An electron is a part of me, for instance, exactly if it contributes to my overall functioning – if, for instance, it contributes to depolarizing one of my cellular membranes or plays a role in the metabolic processes of one of my cells. Consider again the strand of DNA described earlier. When it is integrated into a cell, it makes a goal-directed contribution to the activity of the whole. As a result, it gains the status of an organic part. It and parts like it are literally *organ-ized* in living things: they become organs. On the hylomorphic view of composition, then, parts contribute to the activities of the wholes they compose, and different parts of a whole contribute to its activity in different ways. Genes and messenger molecules are both parts of cells; they both contribute to the cells' activities, and what distinguish them from each other are the different roles they play in protein synthesis: their different jobs within the cell qualify them as different parts of it.

The philosopher Peter van Inwagen has recently defended a similar account of composition. According to van Inwagen, something qualifies as a part if and only if it is "caught up in a life." He explains:

> [T]o say that x is caught up in a life is to say that there are [objects, call them 'the ys'] whose activity constitutes a life and x is one of the ys ... [I]t follows that x is a (proper) part of something if and only if x is caught up in a life ... Alice drinks a cup of tea in which a lump of sugar has been dissolved. A certain carbon atom ... is carried along with the rest of the sugar by Alice's digestive system to the intestine. It passes through the intestinal wall and into the bloodstream, whence it is carried to the biceps muscle of Alice's left arm. There it is oxidized in several indirect stages (yielding in the process energy ... for muscular contraction) and is finally carried by Alice's circulatory system to her lungs and there breathed out as a part of a carbon dioxide molecule ... Here we have a case in which a thing, the carbon atom, was ... caught up in the life of an organism, Alice. It is ... a case in which a thing

became however briefly, a *part* of a larger thing when it was a part of nothing before or after.[2]

Hylomorphism's account of organic composition can be understood as a way of elaborating van Inwagen's basic idea: to be caught up in the life of something is to make a goal-directed contribution to its metabolic activities. The electron that depolarizes one of my neural membranes or that is involved in the production of ATP in one of my cells contributes in a small way to my overall operation. This contribution qualifies it as one of my parts. The electron that makes no such contribution is not a part of me, even if it is located "inside" of me or is in some way "attached" to me.

An account of composition like this has also been articulated by several philosophers of biology including William Bechtel, a philosopher of neuroscience:

> The component parts of a mechanism are the entities that perform the operations which together realize the phenomenon of interest. A structure within the mechanism may be well delineated (it has boundaries, continues to exist over time, is differentiated from the things around it, etc.). However, if it does not perform an operation that contributes to the realization of the phenomenon, it is not a working part of that mechanism. For example, while the gyri and sulci of the brain are well delineated, they are not working parts of the brain but byproducts of the way brains fold to conserve the length of axons.[3]

According to Bechtel, something qualifies as a component part of a whole mechanism only if it performs an operation that contributes to the activity of the mechanism.

Philosophers of biology and neuroscience have been attracted to a view of composition along these lines because this is the type of view suggested by actual work in biology and neuroscience – both the methods of those sciences and the kinds of explanations they employ. Of central importance is a method of scientific investigation philosophers often call **functional analysis**. Biologists, cognitive scientists, engineers, and others often study complex systems by analyzing their activities into subactivities performed by subsystems. Consider a complex artifact such as an internal combustion engine. We can understand how the engine operates by analyzing its activity into a number of subactivities performed by subsystems: the generation of an electrical charge by the coil, the distribution of that charge to the spark plugs by the distributor, the injection of the fuel into the combustion chamber by the fuel injectors, the ignition of the fuel by the spark plugs, the movement of the piston produced by the expanding gas, and so on. Once we have analyzed the engine's activity into subactivities performed by subsystems, we can iterate the process and analyze each of the subactivities into sub-subactivities performed by sub-subsystems. The ignition of the fuel by the plugs, for instance, can be analyzed into the build-up of electrostatic charge on the spark plug head, the overcoming of the air's resistance by that charge, and so on. We can continue to iterate the analytic process until we reach a level at which no further functional analysis is possible – a level at which it no longer makes sense to ask how the system manages to behave as it does.

The activity of biological systems can be studied in the same way as the internal combustion engine. Consider a human activity such as running. Functional analysis reveals that running involves among other things a circulatory subsystem that is responsible for supplying oxygenated blood to the muscles. Functional analysis of that subsystem reveals in turn that it has a component responsible for pumping the blood – a heart. Functional analysis of the heart's pumping activity shows that the heart is composed of muscle tissues that undergo frequent contraction and relaxation. Functional analyses of the activities of the muscle tissue reveal that it is composed of cells. Functional analyses of their activities reveal that these cells are composed of organelles such the cell membrane, the mitochondria, and the nucleus. Functional analyses of these organelles reveal that they are composed in turn of complex molecules. The cell membrane, for instance, is composed of a double layer of phospholipids. An analysis of these phospholipids reveals that each has a hydrophobic end that repels water, and a hydrophilic end that attracts water, and it is because they have both water-repellant and water-attractive ends that the phospholipids are able to form a two-layered membrane that separates the environment outside the cell from the environment inside it. Functional analysis of the water-attractive end of a phospholipid molecule further reveals that it is composed of a phosphate group, an arrangement of atoms with a distribution of electrons capable of attracting water molecules. The electrons are able to perform this role because they are negatively charged. Here functional analysis most likely comes to an end: if electrons have their charges not on account of the activity of some lower-level subsystem, but simply because they are negatively charged particles, then no further functional analysis is possible.

Five remarks are in order about the method of functional analysis: first, a remark about the label 'functional analysis'. Although this is the label that has frequently been used by philosophers, biologists have often called the method of functional analysis 'reduction'. Consider a passage from the same biology textbook quoted earlier:

> [R]educing complex systems to simpler components that are more manageable to study ... is a powerful strategy in biology ... Biology balances the reductionist strategy with the longer-range objective of understanding how the parts of cells, organisms, and higher levels of order, such as ecosystems, are functionally integrated.[4]

It should be clear that this passage represents a notion of reduction different from the one we discussed in connection with mind–body theories (Section 5.7). Reduction in the philosophical sense we have discussed so far concerns the ability of one conceptual framework to take over the descriptive and explanatory roles of another. To say that psychology is reducible to physical theory in this sense is to say that all the descriptive and explanatory roles currently played by psychological discourse could be taken over in principle by physical theory – that the conceptual resources of physical theory are fully sufficient to describe and explain everything we currently use psychological discourse to describe and explain. This is typically not the sense of reduction that biologists have in mind when they speak of reduction. When they speak of reduction, they are typically speaking not of one conceptual framework taking over the descriptive and explanatory roles of another, but of a method for studying the behavior of complex systems – the method we have been referring to as 'functional analysis'. Endorsing this method does not imply a commitment to reduction in the philosophical sense: saying that we can investigate something's activities by analyzing them into subactivities does not imply that a description of lower-level subsystems can take over the descriptive and explanatory roles played by higher-level forms of discourse. To avoid confusion, then, we will continue to refer to the aforementioned method of studying complex systems as 'functional analysis', and will reserve the term 'reduction' for cases in which one conceptual framework is capable of taking over the descriptive and explanatory roles of another.

Second, the notion of function that gives functional analysis its name is different from the notion of function discussed earlier in connection with functionalism (Section 6.3). In the context of functional analysis, the notion has a teleological dimension: subsystems *contribute* to the activities of the wholes to which they belong. The heart contributes to running, for instance, by pumping oxygenated blood to the muscles. Teleological functionalists appeal to a teleological notion of function along these lines as well (Section 6.7). Recall, however, that, like all functionalists, teleological functionalists claim that higher-level properties are higher-order properties; they are not first-order properties in their own right, but logical constructions that quantify over lower-order properties. Hylomorphists reject this understanding of higher-level properties in the same way emergentists do (Section 8.10). So although hylomorphism and teleological functionalism are both committed to the idea that a system's components contribute teleologically to its overall operation, they disagree on how that notion of contribution is to be understood. According to teleological functionalists, higher-level conceptual frameworks represent different ways of describing lower-level occurrences. According to hylomorphists, by contrast, higher-level descriptions correspond to distinctive ontological structures.

Third, according to hylomorphists, the method of functional analysis provides a basis for understanding the notion that parts contribute to the activities of wholes or are caught up in the lives of those wholes. To say that a part, x, contributes to the activities of a whole, y, on this view, is to say the following:

1   y engages in an activity A;
2   There is a functional analysis of A into subactivities; and
3   x performs one of those subactivities.

Gabriel's circulatory system is part of Gabriel, for instance, because there is a functional analysis of Gabriel's running into subactivities, and Gabriel's circulatory system performs one of those subactivities.

Fourth, however, according to hylomorphism, not just any kind of contribution qualifies something as a part. In order for something to qualify as part of an organism, it must be caught up in the organism's life, as van Inwagen puts it. Roughly, it must be part of the organism's living tissue. There are at least two ways this can occur. First, something can be composed of living materials. Imagine for instance that an individual, Gabriel, is engaged in running. Functional analysis of his running reveals that he has a circulatory system, and that the components of that circulatory system include something that pumps blood – a human heart. Functional analysis of the heart's pumping activity reveals that it is composed of muscle tissues which are composed in turn of cells. Cells are living things – the simplest things that display the full range of behaviors that biologists take to be characteristic of life: the acquisition and use of nutrients from the environment, the excretion of waste materials, reproduction, response to environmental stimuli, and so on. Something that is composed of cells is composed of living materials. So because Gabriel's heart is composed of living materials, his heart qualifies as a part of him on the hylomorphic view.

But being composed of cells at some level is not the only way that something can be caught up in the life of an organism. The organelles of single-celled organisms such as amoebas are parts of those organisms; they are caught up in the lives of those organisms, and yet they are not composed of cells. What qualifies them as parts of those organisms is not that they are composed at some level of cells, then, but that they contribute in some way to the activities of cells. A cell membrane, for instance, is caught up in the life of the cell because it contributes to the cell's homeostatic activity: the maintenance of its internal environment. The phospholipids that compose the membrane also qualify as parts of the cell since they contribute to the activity of the cell membrane. Likewise, the electrons at the hydrophilic end of the phospholipid molecule qualify as parts of the cell because they contribute to the molecule's water-attractive activity. In short, then, to be caught up in the life of an organism consists either in composing cells or in being composed of cells. My heart qualifies as a part of me because it is composed of cells, whereas the electrons in my heart qualify as parts of me because they compose cells.

Finally, the hylomorphic view of composition implies that so-called "artificial organs" – artificial hearts, pacemakers, prosthetic limbs, cochlear implants, neural stimulation devices, and so on – are not parts of the organisms in which they are implanted. Consider again Gabriel's running. This time, however, imagine that the blood-pumping component of Gabriel's circulatory system is not a human heart, but a different device. Functional analysis of its activities reveals that it does not have cells as components at any level. It is not composed of living materials but of titanium and plastic. Since the device is neither composed of cells nor

composes cells, it is not caught up in Gabriel's life. Consequently, on the hylomorphic view, it is not a part of him. It is merely an artifact that contributes to Gabriel's
activity in the way a human heart normally would. Artificial devices of this sort
can contribute to our activities in important ways – ways that are every bit as
important as the organs they are meant to replace. But that importance does not
qualify them as parts. They are merely artifacts, albeit organ-like artifacts that
contribute to our activities in the way organic parts normally would.

On the hylomorphic view of composition, then, our status as living things
is manifest on many levels. Organisms are *multistructure complexes*; they comprise
multiple levels of structural or organizational complexity. That organizational
complexity is apparent in the biological structures we have considered so far: the
organization of subcellular materials into cells, of cells into tissues, tissues into
organs, and so on. But on the hylomorphic view, biological organization also
comprises patterns of social and environmental interaction including, as we
shall see, the patterns of social and environmental interaction we describe as
thought, feeling, perception, and action. To understand this idea we need to say
more about the notion of structure or organization at the heart of hylomorphic
thinking.

10.4   The Concept of Organization

Hylomorphism has two central concepts: the concept of structure or organization, and the concept of materials that get structured or organized. Aristotle is
generally credited with having been the first to develop these concepts in a philo-
sophically precise way. He used the word *hyle* – typically translated 'matter' – to
designate anything on which a structure might be imposed. Consider a pile of
timbers, nails, and other materials that lie collectively unstructured in the lumber-
yard at time t_1, and the same timbers, nails, and materials that are collectively
structured in a house built from them at time t_2. Consider likewise various chemical compounds that were collectively unstructured in the soil but that are now
collectively structured in the cells of a tree. Consider also various activities. Pieces
of wood lying inertly in a box come to play a role in our behavior when we begin
a game of chess. Like the bricks and timbers, they come to be structured in a
certain way; we conscript them to play roles in our game (queen, knight, rook) in
the same way we conscript the bricks and timbers to play roles in our house (top
plate, header, wall). Like the house, the activity of game-playing constitutes a
structure into which these pieces of wood are integrated. Moreover, the ability to
play chess could be integrated into yet another, more encompassing, structured
activity. It could be used to further certain educational ends, for instance, such
as the development of analytical skills, and those skills might be integrated into
a further program of social structuring – the effort to develop a citizenry with

critical acumen, say. The timbers, nails, and other building materials are matter for the house; they are capable of being organized house-wise. Likewise, the tissues that composed the tree trunk are matter for the timbers, and chemicals that were in the soil are matter for the tissues. Similarly, physiological components, their states, and certain environmental conditions are matter for the activities or structured interactions with the environment we call 'seeing', 'hearing', and 'tasting'. These forms of interaction are in turn matter for more complex behaviors such as the visual planning and pattern recognition involved in chess, or the auditory pattern recognition involved in music. Likewise, our responses to feelings of anger, desire, fear, and other emotional states are matter for character traits: being mild-mannered or irascible, temperate or overindulgent, courageous or cowardly all represent patterns of choice vis-à-vis various orectic and emotional promptings.

In hylomorphic philosophy, matter is not self-organizing – especially when it comes to the complex arrangements we find in organisms and artifacts. Left to its own devices a heap of materials – a pile of timbers, say – does not spontaneously organize itself into a house. Nor do various quantities of fundamental physical materials spontaneously converge to yield organisms and their parts. The organization that characterizes these things – their form or structure – has to be imposed. Aristotle frequently drew analogies between highly structured natural entities – organisms, their activities and capacities – and artifacts. Just as highly structured artifacts come into being by human agency from relatively unorganized nonbiological raw materials, likewise said Aristotle, organisms come into being by the operation of natural processes from relatively unorganized biological materials, processes, or states. Moreover, the production of artifacts and the production of natural things both involve what is typically a gradual process of construction (or *training*, in the case of skills and character traits) whereby the relevant structures are imposed. And in both the natural and the artifactual cases, once the relevant structures are imposed the results are discrete individuals belonging to natural or artifactual kinds such as *house* or *human*, or stable capacities or character traits, or tokens of certain types of activities such as seeing or chess-playing.

For Aristotle living things were the paradigmatic natural entities. Like many of the Greeks, he used the term *psyche* to refer to what it is that distinguishes living things from nonliving ones. Some of the Greeks, such as Democritus, thought that *psyche* was something that could be described at a fundamental physical level such as a greater number of round atoms. Other Greeks, such as the followers of Plato, endorsed a biological analogue of substance dualism: they thought *psyche* was a nonphysical component added to the fundamental physical materials that composed an organism. By contrast with both views, Aristotle claimed that *psyche* was a living thing's organization or structure. The term *psyche* is typically translated 'soul', but this translation is misleading. Since the seventeenth century and perhaps for much longer, talk of souls has been closely associated with substance dualism or views like it. Consequently, this translation suggests that according to Aristotle soul is something that is capable of existing independent of a body. But this is not the case. According to Aristotle, soul is the organization or structure that distinguishes a living thing from nonliving ones. Peter van Inwagen has more recently used the term 'life' to express the same idea.[5]

On Aristotle's view, living things are distinguished from nonliving ones at the most basic level by the capacity for growth and reproduction: roughly, the capacity to assimilate materials from the environment by imposing their structures on them, and the capacity to replicate those structures in other materials. But the behaviors of some living things are structured in ways that are more complex, and that we describe using terms such as 'perception', 'memory', 'learning', and 'imagination'. The interactions between a young child and the candy hidden in the cupboard are at first almost completely unstructured – or, more precisely, they are structured in ways we can describe and explain merely by appeal to the conceptual resources of physics: the child and candy exert a gravitational influence on each other, for instance. But the interactions between the child and the candy become structured in more complex ways once the cupboard door is opened. We describe these ways by saying the child *wants* the candy, is *trying to get* it, and *remembers* that it is there once its mother has re-closed the cupboard door. The same is true of the child's interactions with its mother and with other people: it is *chagrined* and *frustrated* by her refusal to give the candy, but *knows* that its father is more pliable. Similarly, the father's *pliability* and the mother's *prudence* are also types of complex structured behavior. They represent broad patterns of choice, decision, thought, feeling, and action with long histories and long-term implications for future behavior.

According to hylomorphists, then, organisms are multistructure complexes: each comprises a complex hierarchy of structures and substructures. And when it comes to human behavior in particular, various biological activities and capacities are incorporated into patterns of rational behavior, the sort described in Section 2.6: distinctive patterns of behavior that admit of evaluation in terms of rational, moral, aesthetic, and similar categories. What get structured in these rational ways include states of various organic parts, such as the parts that enable humans to engage with and respond to their social and physical environments. Some of these forms of engagement and response, and the criteria we use to evaluate them are expressed by psychological predicates and terms. What psychological discourse expresses on the hylomorphic view, then, are high-level structured behaviors having various organic states as their substructures or matter (Section 11.7).

Hylomorphists are not the only ones who appeal to a notion of organization or structure along these lines. Many philosophers and scientists speak of organization or structure in ways that resemble the hylomorphic notion even if they do not make the connection to Aristotelian philosophy. William Bechtel is a recent example among philosophers:

[T]he organization of ... components typically integrates them into an entity that has an identity of its own ... Organization itself is not something inherent in the parts ... Accordingly, investigators who already understand in detail how the parts behave are often surprised by what happens when they are organized in particular ways ... In virtue of being organized systems, mechanisms do things beyond what their components do ... Not only can one study the performance of a mechanism without knowing its component parts and their operations, but what the mechanism as a whole does is typically quite different than the operations performed by its parts ... [T]he mechanism as a whole may in fact constitute a component of a larger mechanism that does something still different ... The fact that mechanisms perform different activities than do their parts manifests itself in the fact that the activities of whole mechanisms are typically described in different vocabulary [sic] than are component operations.[6]

The American philosopher John Dewey endorsed a similar view:

The difference between the animate plant and the inanimate iron molecule is not that the former has something in addition to physico-chemical energy; it lies in the *way* in which physico-chemical energies are interconnected and operate ... Iron as a genuine constituent of an organized body acts so as to tend to maintain the type of activity of the organism to which it belongs. If we identify ... the physical as such with the inanimate we need another word to denote the activity of organisms as such. Psycho-physical is an appropriate term ... In the compound word, the prefix 'psycho' denotes that physical activity has acquired additional properties ... Psycho-physical does not denote an abrogation of the physico-chemical; nor a peculiar mixture of something physical and something psychical ... it denotes the possession of certain qualities and efficacies not displayed by the inanimate. Thus conceived there is no problem of the relation of physical *and* psychic. There are specifiable empirical events marked by distinctive qualities and efficacies. There is first of all, *organization* ... Each "part" of an organism is itself organized, and so of the "parts" of the part ... "mind" is an added property assumed by a feeling creature, when it reaches that organized interaction with other living creatures which is language, communication.[7]

Consider also the seventeenth-century philosopher John Locke:

[C]onsider wherein an oak differs from a mass of matter ... [O]ne is only the cohesion of particles of matter any how united, the other such a disposition of them as constitutes the parts of an oak; and such an organization of those parts as is fit to receive and distribute nourishment, so as to continue and frame the wood, bark, and leaves, &c., of an oak, in which consists the vegetable life ... For this organization ... *is* that individual life ... The case is not so much different in *brutes* ... Something we have like this in machines ... [F]or example, what is a watch? ... [N]othing but a fit organization or construction of parts to a certain end ... If we would suppose this machine one continued body, all whose organized parts were repaired, increased, or diminished by a constant addition or separation of insensible parts, with one common life, we should have something very much like the body of an animal ... An animal is a living organized body; and consequently the same animal ... is the same continued life communicated to different particles of matter, as they happened successively to be united to that organized living body ... This also shows wherein the identity of the same man consists; viz. in nothing but a participation of the same continued life, by constantly fleeting particles of matter, in succession vitally united to the same organized body.[8]

Many scientists appeal to a notion of organization along these lines as well. Examples include Gerd Sommerhoff:

The physico-chemical picture of the living organism is only half the truth. The missing half concerns the nature of the organizational relationships that make the behavior of obviously living systems uniquely different from that of obviously non-living systems ... In many ways this is the more important half. For here lie the differences between life and death, and between higher and lower forms of life as they affect us most ... Even if we knew down to the last molecular detail what goes on inside a living organism, we should still be up against the fact that a living system is an organized whole which by virtue of the distinctive nature of its organization shows unique forms of behaviour which must be studied and understood at their own level.[9]

Consider likewise the neurophysiologist Jonathan Miller:

[T]he physical universe tends towards a state of uniform disorder ... In such a world the survival of form depends on ... the intrinsic stability of the materials from which the object is made, or the energetic replenishment and reorganisation of the material which is constantly flowing through it ... The configuration of a fountain ... is intrinsically unstable, and it can retain its shape only by endlessly renewing the material which constitutes it; that is, by organising and imposing structure on the unremitting flow of its own substance ... The persistence of a living organism is an achievement of the same order as that of a fountain ... it can maintain its configuration only by flowing through a system which is capable of reorganising and renewing the configuration from one moment to the next. But the engine which keeps a fountain aloft exists independently of the watery form for which it is responsible, whereas the engine which supports and maintains the form of a living organism is an inherent part of its characteristic structure.[10]

The scientists who have done the most to illustrate the usefulness of the notion of organization for describing and explaining living things have been biologists such as Neil A. Campbell in a passage quoted earlier, as well as G. G. Simpson, J. Z. Young, and Ernst Mayr:

[T]o understand organisms one must explain their organization ... [O]ne must know what is organized and how it is organized, but that does not explain the fact or the nature of the organization itself. Such explanation requires knowledge of how an organism came to be organized and what functions the organization serves ... The aim of biology is to understand the structure, functioning ... and history of organisms.[11]

The essence of a living thing is that it consists of atoms ... caught up into the living system and made part of it for a while. The living activity takes them up and organizes them in its characteristic way. The life of a man consists essentially in the activity he imposes upon that stuff.[12]

All biologists are thorough-going "materialists" in the sense that they recognize no supernatural or immaterial forces, but only such that are physico-chemical ... [T]he modern biologist rejects in any form whatsoever the notion that a "vital force" exists in living organisms which does not obey the laws of physics and chemistry. All processes in organisms, from the interaction of molecules to the complex functions of the brain and other whole organs, strictly obey these physical laws ... But [biologists] do not accept the naïve mechanistic explanation of the seventeenth century and disagree with the statement that animals are "nothing but" machines ... Where organisms differ from inanimate matter is in the organization of their systems. Organismic biologists stress the fact that organisms have many characteristics that are without parallel in the world of inanimate objects. The explanatory equipment of the physical sciences is insufficient to explain complex living systems.[13]

These quotations represent a type of view that has become increasingly popular in biology and the philosophy of biology over the past 25 years. The foregoing philosophers and scientists share a commitment to an empirically grounded notion of organization or structure that acts as a fundamental ontological and explanatory principle. Although most of the authors we have quoted may not know it, this commitment marks a return to a central tenet of Aristotelian natural philosophy. That philosophy was largely abandoned during the Scientific Revolution. Seventeenth-century natural philosophers such as Francis Bacon, Robert Boyle, and Thomas Hobbes ridiculed the Aristotelian notion of form. Now that the sciences have had time to mature, and have turned their attention to the phenomena of life and mind, the notion is experiencing a renaissance. Biologists have become increasingly convinced that explanations of living behavior require conceptual resources beyond those provided by physics. Biological science is not just an abstract way of describing fundamental physical processes; it corresponds to a distinctive kind of natural organization and behavior. Hylomorphism is best seen, therefore, as situating an empirically useful concept within a broader philosophical framework that provides a systematic understanding of the natural world.

10.5 Hylomorphism and the Multilevel Worldview

Hylomorphism is committed to a multilevel worldview similar to those endorsed by physicalists and emergentists. Like those multilevel views, it claims that lower-level entities compose higher-level ones. If the entities $x_1, x_2, \ldots, x_n$ compose y, then $x_1, x_2, \ldots, x_n$ belong to a lower level than y. The hylomorphic view is nevertheless different because of the way it defines levels. The multilevel views discussed so far define levels *globally*: levels are defined relative to branches of science whose categories cut across the features that distinguish one kind of living thing from another. There is, then, a single set of levels for the entire natural world irrespective of the specific kinds of organisms that exist. The biological, chemical, and physical levels we find in dogs, for instance, are the same as the biological, chemical, and physical levels we find in humans, or spiders, or cats. Hylomorphism does not deny that some levels cut across kind-specific boundaries. Fundamental physics, for instance, describes the basic materials that are liable to further structuring in entities of all kinds. According to hylomorphists, however, not all levels are like this; not all can be defined globally. Some levels, it claims, can only be defined *locally*, so that different kinds of living things comprise different hierarchies of levels. The levels we find in dogs, for instance, might be very different from those we find in cats. The reason, according to hylomorphists, is that levels are defined primarily by the relation of parthood or composition, and, on the hylomorphic view, composition consists in the contributions parts make to the activities of the wholes to which they belong. Consequently, if dogs and cats engage in different activities or if their parts contribute to their respective activities in different ways, then dogs and cats will comprise different kinds of parts, and that means they will comprise different hierarchies of levels. Moreover, it seems to be an empirical matter of fact that different kinds of living things engage in different activities and that they have parts that contribute to their respective activities in different ways. Consider an example.

Humans and spiders engage in different kinds of activities. Spiders, but not humans, for instance, spin webs; and conversely humans, but not spiders, speak and sing. These differences in human and spider activity are reflected in differences in human and spider parts. Spiders, but not humans, have spinnerets; and humans, but not spiders, have vocal cords. When describing and explaining the behavior of humans and of spiders, then, we use different predicates and terms to refer to or express their different activities and the different kinds of parts those activities involve. Moreover, even when we use the same predicates and terms to describe the activities of both, there are still significant differences in what these predicates and terms refer to or express. Consider, for instance, eating. We can apply the term 'eating' both to an activity in which humans engage and to an activity in which spiders engage. But while eating in humans and eating in spiders have some features in common, there are significant differences that become apparent as soon as we consider how members of each species eat. Humans eat by biting off morsels of food with their incisors and chewing them with their molars. Human saliva contains enzymes that partially digest the morsels which are eventually swallowed and carried to the stomach by the peristaltic motion of the esophagus where they are further digested by acids and enzymes. Spiders, on the other hand, eat by regurgitating stomach fluids onto their prey while grinding at the prey with their chelicerae (their jaws). The chewing action of the chelicerae in combination with the enzymes in the stomach fluid breaks down the prey's tissues into a soupy mixture which is sucked through the spider's mouth by the pumping action of its stomach while hairs around the mouth filter out any unliquefied pieces. Despite the common label, human eating and spider eating are very different activities that comprise very different subactivities and subsystems. Humans do not have chelicerae, nor do spiders have molars. The human stomach does not engage in pumping as the spider stomach does, nor does the spider bring food to its stomach by peristalsis as the human esophagus does. Humans and spiders, then, are composed of different kinds of parts suited to different kinds of activities.

But if levels are defined by composition, and humans and spiders are composed of different kinds of parts, then humans and spiders will comprise different hierarchies of levels. Each animal will comprise a hierarchy unique to members of its kind. Hylomorphism thus defines levels in a local, kind-specific way. Except for fundamental physics, and perhaps some other lower-level disciplines, the levels comprised by one kind of organism may not be found in organisms of any other kind. As a result, the hylomorphic multilevel worldview countenances a plurality of level hierarchies each of which is tied to a distinctive kind of living thing. What emerges is a picture of organisms as multistructure complexes each of which comprises a kind-specific hierarchy of structural levels (Figure 10.1).

Hylomorphism's local definition of levels converges with some recent work in the philosophy of science. Philosophers of neuroscience such as William Bechtel

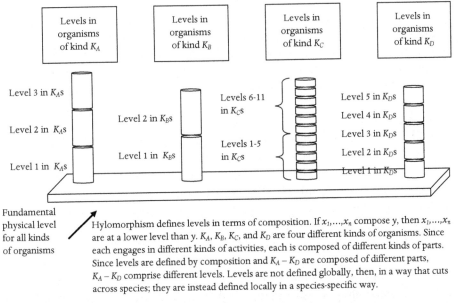

Hylomorphism defines levels in terms of composition. If $x_1,...,x_n$ compose y, then $x_1,...,x_n$ are at a lower level than y. K_A, K_B, K_C, and K_D are four different kinds of organisms. Since each engages in different kinds of activities, each is composed of different kinds of parts. Since levels are defined by composition and $K_A - K_D$ are composed of different parts, $K_A - K_D$ comprise different levels. Levels are not defined globally, then, in a way that cuts across species; they are instead defined locally in a species-specific way.

Figure 10.1   The hylomorphic multilevel worldview: locally-defined levels

and Carl Craver have reached the conclusion that a local definition of levels is the most natural way to make sense of the explanations used in neuroscience. Craver, for instance, says the following:

> [L]evels of mechanisms are not monolithic divisions in the structure of the world ... [They] are far more local than the monolithic image suggests. They are defined only within a given compositional hierarchy. Different levels of mechanisms are found in the spatial memory system, the circulatory system, the osmoregulatory system, and the visual system. How many levels there are, and which levels are included, are questions to be answered on a case-by-case basis by discovering which components at which size scales are explanatorily relevant for a given phenomenon. They cannot be read off a menu of levels in advance.[14]

Once again, then, the claims of hylomorphism appear to dovetail with work in the natural sciences.

10.6 Hylomorphism versus Physicalism and Classic Emergentism

Among the theories considered so far hylomorphism most closely resembles forms of nonreductive physicalism and emergentism. It is thus helpful to consider how hylomorphism is similar to and different from these theories. Consider first the similarities and differences with nonreductive physicalism.

Hylomorphism claims that living things and nonliving ones are ultimately composed of the same fundamental physical materials, and hence nothing can violate fundamental physical laws. According to hylomorphists, then, physicalists are in one sense exactly right: physics is the most general and the most fundamental natural science. But saying everything obeys physical laws is a far cry from saying everything is *determined* by physical laws, or that it is possible to describe and explain everything by appeal to physics. Two chess players might obey all the rules of chess, but those rules do not determine every aspect of how the game is played, and not every aspect of the game can be described and explained purely by appeal to the rules. The description and explanation of various tactics and strategies, for instance, involves the use of a distinctive vocabulary. To use the philosopher Gilbert Ryle's expression: if everything is governed by the rules, it still does not follow that everything is *ordained* by them.[15]

An important feature of the physicalist worldview – reductivist, nonreductivist, or otherwise – is that there is nothing in nature independent of our interests that distinguishes the subject-matters of the special sciences from the subject-matter of fundamental physics. Any differences that are discoverable in nature are either differences that can be exhaustively characterized in physical terms, or else differences that we have postulated to suit our peculiar interests. When we describe and explain things in the vocabulary of physics it is with an eye to expressing basic laws. When we describe and explain things in the vocabulary of chemistry, biology, psychology, economics, or other special sciences, it is with an eye to satisfying other interests. Consequently, if what distinguishes humans from dogs or from rocks is not something that can be described at a fundamental physical level, the distinctions between humans and dogs or humans and rocks are distinctions adopted merely to suit our special descriptive and explanatory interests. So while there is most likely a real difference between, say, positive and negative charges – that is, a difference explicable in the language of physics – there is most likely no real, natural, or interest-independent difference on a physicalist view between living things and nonliving ones, or between psychologically endowed beings and the rest of the physical world, for it is unlikely that there is any difference in the fundamental physical materials that compose living things as opposed to dead ones, or mental beings as opposed to nonmental ones.

Importantly, then, on the physicalist worldview there is no such thing as structure or organization that would operate as a basic ontological and explanatory principle to mark out different kinds of individuals and different subject-matters for the sciences. This is not to say that physicalists cannot speak of something's distinctive structure or organization; it is simply that they cannot admit that such talk amounts to an endorsement of ontological or explanatory principles distinct from those postulated by physics. If there are structural principles in nature, they must be principles that can be exhaustively described and explained by physics. Physicalists are thus committed to denying the type of view suggested by the earlier quote from the scientist Gerd Sommerhoff:

> The physico-chemical picture of the living organism is only half the truth. The missing half concerns the nature of the organizational relationships that make the behavior of obviously living systems uniquely different from that of obviously non-living systems ... In many ways this is the more important half. For here lie the differences between life and death, and between higher and lower forms of life as they affect us most ... Even if we knew down to the last molecular detail what goes on inside a living organism, we should still be up against the fact that a living system is an organized whole which by virtue of the distinctive nature of its organization shows unique forms of behaviour which must be studied and understood at their own level.[16]

What physicalists balk at here is the idea that there are unique, irreducible forms of behavior that are due to something's organization and that account for the distinctions between the living and the nonliving, the mental and the nonmental. And it is not just physicalists who balk at this, but anyone who endorses a similar view of human behavior. Epiphenomenalists, nonorganismic dual-attribute theorists, and even substance dualists, for instance, think that the behavior of human organisms can be given an exhaustive description and explanation in purely physical terms. They all deny that organization or structure operates as a basic ontological and explanatory principle. Together with physicalists they view the human body as a mere collection of fundamental physical materials – a view of human bodies introduced in the wake of the Scientific Revolution. By contrast with this view, hylomorphism denies that human bodies are mere collections of fundamental physical materials; they are instead collections of fundamental physical materials that are *organized* or *structured* in a distinctively human way. That way of being structured is what distinguishes humans from the rest of the physical universe in respect both of what they are and of how they behave.

Consider now hylomorphism's similarities to and differences from the emergentist theories discussed earlier (Section 8.10). Hylomorphists and classic emergentists both deny that physics is capable of providing an exhaustive account of everything. Both agree that the Super Physicist's description of the universe is missing something important. Moreover, like hylomorphists, many classic emergentists appeal to a notion of organization or structure. It is the organization of lower-level entities, they claim, that is responsible for the generation of emergent properties. These are significant similarities between hylomorphism and classic emergentism, but there are at least three significant differences.

First, hylomorphists reject the classic emergentist idea that emergent properties are forces or force-like properties. Second, unlike classic emergentists, hylomorphists do not claim that higher-level properties are produced or generated by lower-level systems on account of their organization. They claim instead that higher-level phenomena represent ways in which lower-level phenomena are organized. Mental phenomena, for instance, are not generated by states of the brain; they are instead ways in which states of the brain can be structured or integrated into higher-level patterns of behavior. This has important implications for their approach to mental causation (Section 11.11). Third, when it comes to psychological phenomena, hylomorphists reject the mental–physical dichotomy (Section 11.10). They deny that it is possible to describe and explain human behavior in dichotomous mental and physical terms. The vocabulary we really use to describe and explain human behavior, they claim, is neither mentalistic nor physicalistic nor a hybrid of mentalistic and physicalistic elements. It is instead a special vocabulary suited to describing and explaining distinctively human patterns of behavior – a vocabulary that cuts across the mental–physical distinction. Let us consider these points further starting with a discussion of hylomorphism's causal pluralism, and moving on to the second and third points in Chapter 11.

10.7   Causal Pluralism

Recall that classic emergentists take emergent properties to be force-generating properties like those postulated by physics. The only difference between emergent properties and physical ones on the classic emergentist view is that emergent properties are tied to higher levels of organization. Recall, moreover, that this view of emergent properties is a serious liability for emergentist theories since the scientific data suggest that there are no nonphysical or emergent forces. As a matter of empirical fact, it seems that the emergent forces classic emergentist theories postulate do not actually exist (Section 8.11). According to hylomorphists, one advantage their theory has over classic emergentism is that it is not liable to this type of empirical objection. Classic emergentists tacitly assume that higher-level properties can make a causal difference to the world only if they influence the world in the same way the forces postulated by physics do. Hylomorphists, on the other hand, endorse **causal pluralism**. They claim that there are causal properties and relations that do not fit the mold set by physics. Because they distinguish among different kinds of causation, hylomorphists argue, their view is compatible with all forces operating at a fundamental physical level, and is therefore immune to the empirical objections raised against emergentism.

Hylomorphists' causal pluralism is committed two claims: first, there are many different kinds of causal factors; second, there are many different kinds of causal relations. To understand these claims it is helpful to appreciate how hylomorphists understand the connection between causation and explanation. According to hylomorphists, causes are explanatory factors. We invariably respond to questions such as *What caused Zidane's ejection from the 2006 World Cup Final?* or *What caused the Arab-Israeli War of 1973?* by attempting to *explain* the events in question. That is why explanatory sentences such as (1) can easily be reformulated as causal sentences such as (2) without any apparent loss of meaning:

1 Socrates died because he drank the hemlock.
2 Socrates' death was caused by his drinking the hemlock.

Many philosophers apply the term 'cause' to a narrow range of explanatory contexts. Classic emergentists, for instance, limit the application of 'cause' to the operation of forces. Hylomorphists, by contrast, do not try to narrow the application of 'cause' to explanatory contexts of one or another sort. They claim instead that different explanatory contexts reveal different types of causal factors and different types of causal relations.

Because causes are explanatory factors, hylomorphists claim that it is often – even typically – unhelpful to speak of *the* cause of something. In any given explanatory context, there are always multiple contributing factors. Imagine, for instance, that we want to explain an automobile accident. A close examination of the case reveals the following contributing factors among others:

(i)   Poor brake design.
(ii)   Grading that is insufficient for a sharp curve in the road.
(iii) Inadequate signage warning drivers of the curve.
(iv)   The driver's high blood-alcohol level.

In a given context, any one of these factors might be cited as a cause or the cause of the crash. Each factor, moreover, contributes to an explanation of the crash in a different way. The way the grading of the roadway contributed to the crash, for instance, is very different from the way the driver's blood-alcohol level did. In the former case, we can describe the contribution purely by appeal to physical factors such as the car's velocity and the tires' coefficients of friction. In the latter case, we need to bring in other factors – biological factors such as the effects of alcohol on perception and reaction time. Not only are there different explanatory factors, then, there are also different explanatory relations – different ways something contributes to an explanation of an effect.

Because causation and explanation are so closely related, hylomorphists argue, we can understand causation by understanding explanation. Explanations are answers to certain kinds of questions – typically why-questions and how-questions. There are many different kinds of why- and how-questions. This is apparent if we consider the many different questions that can be expressed by a single sentence. Consider an example due to the philosopher of science Bas van Fraassen: the sentence 'Why did Adam eat the apple?' could express any of the following:

Q1   Why did Adam eat *the apple* (in contrast to having eaten something else)?

Q2   Why did Adam *eat* the apple (in contrast to having done something else with it)?

Q3   Why did *Adam* eat the apple (in contrast to someone else having eaten it)?

According to van Fraassen, this example shows that explanation is *contrastive*: a why-question always presupposes a *contrast class* of propositions. In the case of Q1, the contrast class consists of the propositions 'Adam ate the apple', 'Adam ate the pear', 'Adam ate the mango', 'Adam ate the banana', 'Adam ate the strawberry', and so on. One of these statements, 'Adam ate the apple', is what van Fraassen calls the question's *topic*. When we ask a why-question we assume that its topic is true, and we assume that the other statements in the contrast class are false.

In addition to having a contrast class every why-question assumes a *relevance relation* to the topic and contrast class. Not just any true statement regarding them can count as an answer. Consider an example: You and I are roommates. One day you come home to discover a hideous and disturbingly erotic sculpture on the coffee table in our living room – a space we often use to entertain guests, including your staid, respectable friends and co-workers. The doubts you have long harbored about my aesthetic sensibilities now come to fore: "Why," you ask, "is that object on our coffee table (in contrast to somewhere else)?" I respond: "It is on our coffee table (in contrast to somewhere else) because its atoms are on our coffee table (in contrast to somewhere else)." It should be obvious that this response does not answer your question. Although it addresses the question's topic and contrast class, it does not do so in a way that is *relevant* to your interests. The causal factors that you are interested in are my reasons for choosing to place the object on our coffee table as opposed to somewhere else. We can nevertheless imagine a context in which my answer would be relevant: You and I are debating the merits and demerits of various theories of material constitution. You want to know what it is on my theory that explains the location of composite objects such as the object on our coffee table. You ask: "Why is that object on our coffee table (in contrast to somewhere else)?" "Because its atoms are there," I respond. In this case, my answer is entirely relevant to your question.

The foregoing examples illustrate that a why-question has three components: a topic, a contrast class, and a relevance relation. Different why-questions are distinguished from each other on the basis of these components.

There are many different kinds of how-questions as well. Consider an example that illustrates this:

SWAT TEAM CAPTAIN   Headquarters, there's a high yield explosive timed to detonate in four minutes! How do we disarm it?

HEADQUARTERS   Very carefully!

The answer strikes us as ridiculous because we assume the captain was requesting a *method* for disarming the bomb – a series of steps, not a directive of *manner*. Likewise:

How did Judith kill Holofernes?
Answer A   With a mixture of revulsion and determination.
Answer B   With a mixture of bile and snake venom.
Answer C   With a mixture of seduction and cunning.

The first answer supplies the manner with which Judith killed Holofernes; the second supplies the method whereby she did so, and the third supplies the means whereby she was able to administer the deadly concoction.

How-questions are of at least three types. How-questions of *manner* ask for a more determinate description of the manner in which something is accomplished. Second, there are how-questions of *cognitive resolution*. These arise when the context implies a set of claims which seem jointly improbable, perhaps inconsistent, and a request is made to remove the appearance of improbability. The familiar how-questions that express philosophical problems are examples, including:

How can we be free and yet live in a deterministic universe?
How can God exist and yet evil exist as well?

Finally, there are *analytic* how-questions. These request a description of steps which contribute to the accomplishment of some activity or procedure. They include questions that ask for *means*, *methods*, and *mechanisms*. In response to the question "How does one dance a swing?" for instance, the answer, "First, get a good teacher; then practice, practice, practice," takes the question to ask for means. The answer, "Backstep, one-two-three, one-two-three," accompanied by a demonstration takes the question to ask for a method. A mechanistic interpretation is harder to imagine, but suppose a student in a neuroscience class complained as follows: "Look, all we've been talking about all semester is how individual neurons perform simple little tasks. What I want to know is how humans manage to perform big complicated tasks. For instance, how does one dance a swing?" The answers, "Usually quite awkwardly," and "First, get a good teacher," and "Backstep, one-two-three, one-two-three" – answers which take the question to ask for manner, means, and method, respectively – are clearly out of place. What the student has in mind is an answer such as, "The primary motor cortex has a group of cells which generate actions potentials; and these generate action potentials in the adjacent cells, and those in turn ..." Such an answer aims at describing the mechanisms at work in dancing a swing.

How-questions of mechanism are often a starting point for scientific investigation: for a type of explanation that is sometimes called *mechanistic explanation*. Mechanistic explanation is the type of explanation yielded by the method of functional analysis. The aim of functional analysis is to explain how a system is able to perform an activity by describing how its subsystems or parts contribute to that activity. This is what a mechanistic explanation of the system's behavior consists in. We provide a mechanistic explanation of how a human heart or an internal combustion engine operates by describing how its components contribute to its activity.

Mechanistic explanations are distinct from other explanations of living behavior. This point was made by Plato in a famous passage from the *Phaedo* in which Socrates describes his experience reading the pre-Socratic philosopher Anaxagoras:

> My wondrous hopes were swept away, my friend, when I proceeded to read, and saw [Anaxagoras] neither appealing to thought, nor citing any of the causes responsible for the ordering of things, but instead citing air, and aether, and water, and many other absurdities as causes. To me it seemed exactly the same as someone saying that Socrates does everything he does with thought, and then in undertaking to state the causes of each thing I do were to say that I am sitting here now because, first, my body is composed of bones and sinews, and the bones are hard and have joints separating them, while the sinews for their part contract and relax, and cover the bones along with the flesh and skin that contains them, and that because the bones move freely in their joints, the contracting and relaxing of the sinews somehow enables me to bend my limbs now, and this is the cause of my sitting here in a bent position ... But to call such things causes is most absurd. If someone were to say that without having bones, and sinews, and such, I would not be able to do what I believe best, that would be true. But to say that I do what I do *because* of these, and therein act with thought, but not on account of choosing what I believe best – *that* would be an extremely careless way of speaking.[17]

According to Socrates, the problem with Anaxagoras' account of human action is not that he misunderstands the physiological mechanisms of human action, but that he assumes those mechanisms are relevant to answering the questions about human behavior Socrates is interested in. Human action, Socrates thinks, can only be explained psychologically by appeal to reasons: thoughts and choices based on beliefs about what is best. Consider another example.

Cecilia is waiting anxiously by the door for Madeleine to come downstairs so they can leave in time for an appointment. Upon being told that Madeleine is reading a book she asks, "Why is Madeleine reading (in contrast to hurrying down the stairs)?" and receives the following response:

A1   Madeleine is reading (in contrast to hurrying down the stairs) because light reflected off the pages of the book is striking Madeleine's retinas, and the muscles in her eyes are moving in such-and-such ways, and such-and-such neurons are firing in her cortex.

A response along these lines is clearly irrelevant to Cecilia's question. What Cecilia wants is a response that locates Madeleine's behavior within a broader pattern of reasons, as the following response does:

A2   Madeleine is reading (in contrast to hurrying down the stairs) because she thinks finishing the chapter is more important than being on time.

Contrast this example with another. Madeleine's seizures have not responded to drug treatment and the only remaining course of action is lobectomy: doctors must remove part of her brain. To prepare for the operation they must first identify the damaged sections of brain tissue. They do so using a new minimally invasive technique: Madeleine wears a cap-like apparatus during her daily activities which collects data about her brain states for later examination in conjunction with a video record of her activities. When doctors examine the data they discover an anomaly: the brain regions that in most people are active as they engage in voluntary leg movements, such as hurrying down stairs, are active in Madeleine when she is reading. "Why is Madeleine reading (in contrast to hurrying down the stairs)?" the doctors ask. In this context, they are probably looking for an explanation such as:

A3   Madeleine is reading (in contrast to hurrying down the stairs) because during her development certain neural structures had to be "re-wired" to avoid the damaged sections of brain tissue.

Whatever the details, they are certainly not looking for a response that reveals Madeleine's reasons for reading; they are not concerned with the rational structure of Madeleine's behavior but with something else: the states of the various physiological substructures that enable Madeleine to engage in the activities she does.

According to hylomorphists, there are as many different kinds of causal relations as there are explanatory relations, and there are as many different kinds of
causes as there are explanatory factors. Because there are many different kinds
of explanatory relations and explanatory factors, there are also many different
kinds of causal relations and causes. Providing a complete account of any given
phenomenon might require describing a broad range of them. In particular,
because living things have both a structure and materials that are structured, a
complete account of their behavior must involve a description of both. Yet a
thing's materials and its structure contribute to its behavior in different ways –
ways reflected in different types of causal or explanatory relations.

Aristotle defended an account of causation and explanation along these lines.
It is often called the *doctrine of the four causes*. According to Aristotle, determining
what living things there are, how those things behave, and why they behave as
they do are all empirical matters. Although actual empirical investigation gives
rise to a varied and complex range of questions and answers, the main questions
concern four factors: (1) the structures or forms of things, (2) the materials that
get structured or formed in those ways – their "matter", (3) what is responsible
for bringing about the structuring of that matter, and, where appropriate, (4) what
that structuring is *for*, what contributions it makes to a yet broader scheme of
organization. Points (1)–(4) each highlight a distinctive type of explanatory factor
or *aitia* – a Greek term typically translated 'cause'. Taken in conjunction these
explanatory factors are supposed to provide a complete account of something's
behavior. Because living things have both a structure and materials that are structured, a complete account of their behavior will include the contributions made
by both. Consequently, while some aspects of living behavior might be explainable
by appeal to the principles governing fundamental physical materials, other aspects
will only be describable and explainable using categories such as *growth, reproduction, perception, desire*, and *thought*.

This kind of causal pluralism marks a key difference between hylomorphism
and classic emergentism. It also provides hylomorphists with resources for solving
the problem of mental causation in a unique way (Section 11.11). But before
considering the implications of hylomorphism for philosophy of mind, it will be
helpful to consider the argument for the general hylomorphic worldview.

10.8   The Argument For Hylomorphism

The main argument for hylomorphism is inductive. It proceeds in two steps. The
first defends structure as a real and irreducible ontological and explanatory principle. The second argues that among theories that recognize the reality and irreducibility of structure, hylomorphism is superior to classic emergentism, its
principal competitor.

The argument that structure is a real and irreducible ontological and explanatory principle is an inference to the best explanation. It claims that the reality and irreducibility of structure is the best explanation for why appeals to structure in, say, biology and biological subdisciplines such as neuroscience manage to be successful for describing and explaining the behavior of living things. Biologists, neuroscientists, and others make free use of concepts such as organization, order, arrangement, and structure, say hylomorphists, and they clearly suggest that something's organization or structure makes a distinctive contribution to what it is and what it does. Hylomorphists take these claims at face value; they take what scientists have to say about the structure or organization of living things as grounds for taking structure to be a real feature of those things. The reason we can successfully explain the behavior of living things by appeal to their structures, hylomophists say, is that living things really do have structures that make a difference to their behavior. This is the simplest, most direct explanation for why appeals to structure in biology, neuroscience, and other biological subdisciplines are successful. If there is a better explanation, say hylomorphists, the burden of proof is on structure's opponents to provide it. According to hylomorphists, then, we should take talk of structure in the sciences at face value in the absence of compelling reasons to do otherwise – reasons it is the job of structure's opponents to provide.

Hylomorphists are not the only ones who claim that structure is a basic ontological and explanatory principle however. Some emergentists do as well. Recall from Chapter 8 that classic emergentists sometimes appeal to structure as a way of addressing the problem of psychophysical emergence. Mental properties emerge from physical systems, they say, on account of the way those systems are structured. The hylomorphic approach to structure differs from the emergentist approach in the ways described in Section 10.6, and hylomorphists argue that their approach is superior on both philosophical and empirical grounds. Classic emergentism has serious philosophical and empirical problems, hylomorphists say – problems their own theory does not have. Since their theory does not have these problems, or any others that are as or more serious, there is good reason to think that hylomorphism is a superior theory, that it provides a superior way of accommodating the reality and irreducibility of structure. But if hylomorphism is the best way of accommodating structure, and there are good empirical reasons to think that structure really exists, then there are good empirical reasons to think hylomorphism is true. Let us consider this argument in greater detail starting with the claim that structure is a *real* ontological and explanatory principle.

Hylomorphists argue that the reality of structure is the most obvious way of explaining the scientific facts – that we should take talk of structure in the sciences at face value in the absence of compelling reasons to do otherwise. What might constitute reasons of this sort? To answer this question let us first consider who the opponents of structure are and what they claim.

Opponents of structure claim that everything can in principle be described and explained without making any appeal to structure. They fall into three categories:

structural eliminativists, *structural reductivists*, and *structural nonreductivists*. Structural eliminativists claim that the structures postulated by biologists, neuroscientists, and others do not really exist, that descriptions and explanations that appeal to structure are all false. Appeals to structure might be useful for certain practical purposes, they say, but they are no more true than descriptions and explanations that appeal to the Greek gods. Structural reductivists, on the other hand, claim that some descriptions and explanations that appeal to structure are true, but that what makes them true is something that can be described and explained without appeal to structure. Talk of structure, in other words, can be reduced to talk of something nonstructural. Finally, structural nonreductivists agree with reductivists that some descriptions and explanations that appeal to structure are true, and they agree that what makes them true is something that can be described and explained without appeal to structure, but they disagree that talk of structure can be reduced to talk of something nonstructural. Reduction requires that the reducing framework take over the descriptive and explanatory jobs of the framework being reduced (Section 5.7), but it is unlikely, say nonreductivists, that nonstructural discourse will be able to take over the descriptive and explanatory jobs that biologists, neuroscientists, and others employ structure to perform. Talk of structure satisfies unique descriptive and explanatory interests that nonstructural discourse cannot satisfy, and that means talk of structure will not be reducible to talk of something nonstructural even if what makes talk of structure true is always something nonstructural in fact.

The divisions among opponents of structure correspond to the divisions among physicalist theories, and physicalists are included among structure's opponents. But physicalists are not the only opponents of structure. Many substance dualists and epiphenomenalists, for instance, are inclined to reject the existence of structure as well. They deny that physics can exhaustively describe and explain the behavior of everything, but they are free to claim that physics can exhaustively describe and explain the behavior of *all bodies*. What physics fails to describe and explain, they say, are nonphysical properties or the behavior of nonphysical individuals, but substance dualists and epiphenomenalists need not deny that physics can exhaustively describe and explain all physical properties and the behavior of all physical individuals. They are thus free to deny that structure is a real and irreducible ontological and explanatory principle as hylomorphists take it to be.

Consider now how hylomorphists respond to opponents of structure who deny structure's reality. There are two challenges here. Structural eliminativists claim that all appeals to structure are false. Structural nonreductivists, on the other hand, claim that although some appeals to structure are true, structure corresponds to nothing deep in reality; we employ the concept of structure simply because it satisfies some of our peculiar descriptive and explanatory interests. Against eliminativists, hylomorphists argue the way most anti-eliminativists do. Recall, for instance, the argument against psychological eliminativism discussed in Section 7.2. Opponents of psychological eliminativism argue that the real existence of mental properties is the best explanation for why psychological discourse manages to be successful for describing and explaining human behavior. Hylomorphists argue in a similar way that the real existence of structure is the best explanation for why appeals to structure in the sciences manage to be successful for describing and explaining biological and other phenomena. We appeal to structure in our scientific dealings very effectively, and this effectiveness requires some type of explanation. The most obvious explanation is that there really is such a thing as structure. If there is not, then it is unclear how the effectiveness of appeals to structure in the sciences can be explained at all. For that reason, say hylomorphists, the burden of proof is on eliminativists: they must either provide an alternative explanation for the apparent success of structural descriptions and explanations or else show that those descriptions and explanations are not really successful after all.

Hylomorphists argue against structural nonreductivists in at least two ways. First, they argue that structural nonreductivism has problems analogous to those of nonreductive physicalism. Recall that the burden for nonreductive physicalists is to explain how special scientific descriptions and explanations manage to correspond to reality if everything is physical and special scientific categories do not correspond to the categories of physics. Structural nonreductivists face an analogous challenge, say hylomorphists. They must explain how descriptions and explanations that appeal to structure manage to correspond to reality if in reality there are no structures of the sort to which biologists, psychologists, and others appeal.

According to structural nonreductivists, there is no such thing as structure or organization in nature other than what we find at a fundamental physical level. We have many different descriptive and explanatory interests, and because of that we tend to describe and explain things in many different ways including ways that involve predicates and terms such as 'structure' and 'organized'. Using these predicates and terms enables us to satisfy descriptive and explanatory interests that we cannot satisfy using only the predicates and terms of fundamental physics, but by using them we are not describing any features of the world that are not described by physics. When biologists use terms such as 'structure' or 'organization', they are not describing anything over and above unstructured processes; they are simply describing unstructured processes in a different way. Structure is not something written in the book of nature as it comes off the press; it represents instead notes we jot in the margins – our commentary on a text written entirely in nonstructural terms. If this is the case, however, then how do appeals to structure manage to correspond to reality if fundamentally everything is not structured, if the structures postulated by the special sciences do not correspond to what exists at a fundamental level? The simple fact that appeals to structure satisfy some of our interests does not guarantee that those appeals will manage to be successful at describing or explaining anything. Accounting for the descriptive and explanatory success of structural discourse requires something in addition to its ability to satisfy our interests. In Chapter 6 we saw that nonreductive physicalists attempt to supply this additional element by appealing to notions of realization and super-venience. We also saw, however, that these attempts face serious challenges. Because the nonreductivist account of structural discourse is analogous to nonre-ductive physicalism, say hylomorphists, it is bound to face analogous challenges, and until those challenges are answered satisfactorily, there are good reasons to reject structural nonreductivism in favor of the more direct hylomorphic alterna-tive which claims that structure exists independent of our descriptive and explana-tory interests.

Second, say hylomorphists, structural nonreductivists face an additional explan-atory challenge. Nonreductivists claim that we use structural predicates and terms because they enable us to satisfy peculiar descriptive and explanatory interests. But what explains the fact that we have these interests? Surely, say hylomorphists, the best explanation is that we are interested in describing and explaining the real behavior of things, and that behavior involves various kinds of structure. So the best explanation for the descriptive and explanatory interests we have, say hylo-morphists, – the very interests nonreductivists appeal to – is that structure really does correspond to something deep in reality.

Consider now the claim that structure is an *irreducible* ontological and explana-tory principle, and how hylomorphists respond to structural reductivists. There is a plurality of scientific disciplines, say hylomorphists. It is an empirical matter of fact that biologists, psychologists, economists, and other practitioners of the special sciences describe and explain human behavior using categories other than those of fundamental physics. Nor does the success of these descriptions and explanations depend on the idea that they are reducible to fundamental physical ones. Given the autonomous status of special scientific descriptions and explana-tions, say hylomorphists, reductivists carry the burden of proof: if it is possible exhaustively to describe and explain human behavior using only the categories of fundamental physics, if we can do without the conceptual resources of the special sciences, as reductivists claim, then the burden is surely on them to establish this. They must show that nonstructural discourse can take over the descriptive and explanatory roles of structural discourse. And, say hylomorphists, they have not shown this.

Structural reductivists might argue that although they have not shown this yet, there are good reasons to think they eventually will. Any textbook in biology or in a biological subdiscipline such as neuroscience has extensive descriptions of the lower-level mechanisms that underwrite higher-level behavior. And this, reductiv-ists might argue, is a promising indication that eventually it will be possible to give an exhaustive description and explanation of all living behavior in purely nonstruc-tural terms.

Hylomorphists can nevertheless respond that the discovery of lower-level mechanisms does not support the reductivist position for at least two reasons. First, the discovery of these mechanisms is perfectly compatible with the irreduc-ibility of structure. In fact, these mechanisms are exactly what one would expect to discover if structure is something irreducible, and organisms comprise many levels of structural complexity. Second, the behavior of lower-level mechanisms is itself something that is often described and explained by appeal to structures. Opiate drugs, for instance, are able to affect the nervous system as they do because they are structurally similar to the endorphins produced by the human body. Chemical structure thus plays a crucial role in explaining the influence of those drugs on human behavior. So the effectiveness of functional analysis as a research method, and the discovery of lower-level mechanisms do not by themselves support the idea that structure can be reduced to something nonstructural, say hylomorphists. The scientific data are perfectly compatible with the claim that structure is an irreducible descriptive and explanatory principle, and in fact, say hylomorphists, many examples suggest that the irreducibility of structure fits the data more comfortably than structural reductivism.

In short, then, hylomorphists argue that there are good empirical reasons to take the autonomy of structural talk in the special sciences at face value. They thus shift the burden of proof onto the shoulders of reductivists: If it really is possible to reduce structural talk to something nonstructural, they say, the burden is on reductivists to establish this.

Consider finally a general argument that opponents of structure might advance. It appeals to Ockham's razor in something analogous to the way J. J. C. Smart argues on behalf of the identity theory (Section 5.5). In general, says the argument, we should not multiply entities beyond necessity. Other things being equal, we should choose the simplest theory we can. Consequently, if the behavior of bodies can be exhaustively described and explained in nonstructural terms, we should not seek to explain the behavior of bodies by appeal to structure as well. Hence, a rejection of structure should be our default position.

Hylomorphists can respond to this argument in at least two ways. First, while it might be true that we should prefer a simpler theory if all other things are equal, other things might not be equal. Recall from Section 5.5 that ontological simplicity only becomes a decisive factor in theory choice when competing theories are all coherent, all consistent with the scientific data, and equal in explanatory power. If theories that reject structure are not coherent, if they have insoluble philosophical problems, if they are not consistent with the scientific data, or lack the explanatory power of theories that endorse structure, then it does not matter how much simpler their ontologies are, these other factors trump that simplicity. We saw a moment ago, moreover, that according to hylomorphists, opponents of structure have yet to establish that their theories are consistent with the scientific data, and have explanatory power to rival that of theories that endorse structure; they have yet to establish that we can describe and explain living behavior without appeal to structure, or that we can reduce appeals to structure to something nonstructural.

Second, hylomorphists can attack the claim that competing theories really are simpler or more economical than their own. There are different ways of reckoning

a theory's simplicity, they can argue. The theories offered by opponents of structure are simpler than hylomorphism in one sense; namely, they do not posit
structure as a basic ontological and explanatory principle in addition to the materials that are structured. But their theories are not simpler in another sense, namely
in the way they explain how talk of structure in the special sciences manages to
be successful. Consider an example.

Hylomorphists offer the simplest, most direct explanation for the success of
descriptions and explanations that appeal to structure: those descriptions and
explanations are successful because structure really exists. Opponents of structure
have to offer different explanations, and those explanations are liable to make their
theories at least as complicated as hylomorphism – if not ontologically, then in
other ways. Structural nonreductivists, for instance, claim that talk of structure is
successful because it satisfies our peculiar descriptive and explanatory interests.
They appeal to interests, in other words, to explain the success of structure talk.
Interests thus play a role in the nonreductivist theory analogous to the role
structure plays in hylomorphism: structures and interests are both introduced to
explain the success of appeals to structure. In this sense, then, the nonreductivist's
theory is no simpler than the hylomorphist's. Moreover, in another sense it would
appear less simple. Hylomorphists offer the most straightforward explanation
for the success of appeals to structure. Any story structural nonreductivists
tell about the success of structure talk is bound to be more complicated because
it will require a more complicated semantics for structure talk – a more complicated account of what talk of structure refers to or expresses. There are thus
multiple ways of reckoning whether one theory is simpler than another, and these
different ways of reckoning simplicity must be weighed against one another when
assessing the relative merits and demerits of competing theories. As a result, say
hylomorphists, it is not clear that the appeal to Ockham's razor really favors
opponents of structure.

That concludes the first part of the argument for hylomorphism, the part that
purports to show that structure is a real and irreducible ontological and explanatory principle. The second part argues that hylomorphism is the best way of
accommodating structure. Hylomorphists are not the only ones who treat structure as a real and irreducible ontological and explanatory principle. Many classic
emergentists do as well. Hylomorphists argue that their theory is superior to
classic emergentism on both empirical and philosophical grounds.

Recall that classic emergentist theories understand emergent properties on
the model of forces. They tacitly assume that the only way a property can make
a causal difference to the individuals having it is if that property operates on the
world in the way forces do. Because they assume this, emergentists postulate
not just emergent properties but also emergent forces. We saw in Section 8.11,
however, that one problem with this claim is that it appears to be false: as an
empirical matter of fact, there do not appear to be any emergent forces. All the
forces that exist in nature can be exhaustively described in physical terms.

As a result, classic emergentism would appear to be false as an empirical matter of fact.

By contrast with classic emergentism, hylomorphism denies that causal properties must influence things in the way forces do. There are many different kinds of causes and many different kinds of causal relations. As a result, hylomorphists are free to claim that physics gives us an exhaustive description and explanation of all forces. What they deny is that an exhaustive account of all forces amounts to an exhaustive account of all behavior. According to hylomorphists, there are properties that make a causal difference to the individuals having them but that do not influence the behavior of those individuals in the way forces do. As a result, hylomorphists argue, their theory is superior to classic emergentism on empirical grounds.

In addition, hylomorphists claim that their theory is superior on philosophical grounds, for unlike classic emergentism, they argue, their theory can solve both the problem of mental causation and the problem of psychophysical emergence. The claim that classic emergentism faces these problems was discussed in Section 8.11. The claim that hylomorphism does not face these problems will be discussed in Chapter 11 in connection with a hylomorphic theory of mind. In short, then, hylomorphists and classic emergentists both accept structure as a basic ontological and explanatory principle. Hylomorphists argue, however, that their way of accommodating structure is superior to classic emergentism on both empirical and philosophical grounds. So if structure is to be accepted as an irreducible descriptive and explanatory principle, hylomorphists argue, their theory is the best way of accommodating it.

Classic emergentists can respond to this argument in at least two ways. First, they can challenge the claim that classic emergentism faces the problems of empirical inadequacy, psychophysical emergence, and mental causation. Second, they can argue that hylomorphism faces problems as well – either the same problems as classic emergentism or other problems that are at least as serious as these. Either of these strategies would weaken the contention that hylomorphism is superior to classic emergentism. We will consider these points later, in connection with a hylomorphic theory of mind.

We have just considered the general argument for hylomorphism, some of the ways opponents might challenge it, and how hylomorphists are likely to respond. Next we will consider hylomorphism's implications for the philosophy of mind. Because a hylomorphic theory of mind claims that you and I are organisms, it represents a specific application of general hylomorphic principles. It effectively extends the biological notion of structure discussed in this chapter into the psychological domain. Psychological phenomena, it claims, represent a level of behavioral organization higher than the kinds of organization we have focused on so far. Thoughts, feelings, and intentional actions represent different ways our interactions with each other and the environment can be organized or structured.

Further Reading

Many of the ideas that are central to hylomorphism are found in the literature on biology and philosophy of biology. Hylomorphists are sympathetic to several trends in that literature. For instance, they endorse the autonomy of biological science defended by Francisco Ayala (1968), G. G. Simpson (1964), and Ernst Mayr (1982; 1988). This view of biology is also reflected in biology textbooks such as Campbell (1996) and Campbell and Reece (2009). Again biologists tend to use the term 'reduction' differently from philosophers. What they call the method of reduction in biology we have been calling the method of functional analysis, and what they call 'reductive explanation' we have been calling 'mechanistic explanation'.

For more on Democritus, see Barnes (2001: Chapter 21). See Penrose (1990; 1994; 1997) for Penrose's views on consciousness.

Aristotle's original articulation of the notion of structure or form appears in Chapters 7–9 of Book I of the *Physics*. In chapters 1 and 2 of Book II, he uses the notion to articulate his philosophy of nature, and in Chapter 3 he articulates his causal pluralism. Aristotle's causal pluralism is often called the doctrine of the four causes, but calling them 'causes' is often misleading since modern philosophers tend to use 'cause' in a very narrow sense, one that corresponds only to what medieval Aristotelians called the 'efficient cause' – the cause responsible for bringing about a change. Aristotle says explicitly that a cause (*aitia* in Greek) answers the question *dia ti*; that is 'Why?' or 'On account of what?' Aristotle applies the hylomorphic framework to animal life in *On the Soul* (*De Anima*) and in the works on biology that are generally called the *Parva Naturalia*. He treats more technical aspects of the account in books VII and VIII of the *Metaphysics*, but these books are notoriously difficult. The application of the hylomorphic framework to character traits can be found in the *Nicomachean Ethics*, especially books I and II. In Chapter 7 of Book I Aristotle presents the so-called *ergon argument*, that we are no different from other living things when it comes to the evaluation of our behavior, and he draws an analogy between the evaluation of artifacts and the evaluation of living things: we can reckon a human being good or bad, he says, in the same way we reckon a tool good or bad: by whether it performs well its distinctive activity – what he calls its *ergon*, a term typically translated 'function'. Aristotle discusses the acquisition of character traits in chapters 1–5 of Book II.

Nancy Cartwright (1999) defends a contemporary form of causal pluralism. See van Fraassen (1980: Chapter 5) for an account of explanation and the logic of why-questions. On the logic of how-questions see Jaworski (2009). On mechanistic explanation and functional analysis see Robert Cummins (1975), William Lycan (1987: Chapter 4), and William Bechtel (2007).

Notes

1   Neil A. Campbell, 1996, *Biology*, 4th edn., Benjamin/Cummings Publishing Company, Inc, 2–4.
2   Peter van Inwagen, 1990, *Material Beings*, Ithaca: Cornell University Press, 94–5.
3   William Bechtel, 2007, "Reducing Psychology While Maintaining Its Autonomy Via Mechanistic Explanation," in *The Matter of the Mind: Philosophical Essays on Psychology, Neuroscience, and Reduction*, edited by Maurice Kenneth Davy Schouten and Huibert Looren de Jong, 172–98, Malden: Blackwell Publishers, 180.
4   Campbell, *Biology*, 4.
5   Van Inwagen, *Material Beings*, 81–97.
6   Bechtel, "Reducing Psychology While Maintaining Its Autonomy Via Mechanistic Explanations," 185–6.
7   John Dewey, 1958, *Experience and Nature*, New York: Dover Publications, 253–8.
8   John Locke, 1959 [1690], *An Essay Concerning Human Understanding*. 2 vols. New York: Dover Publications, Inc., Book II, Chapter 27, Sections 5–9.
9   Gerd Sommerhoff, 1969, "The Abstract Characteristics of Living Systems," in *Systems Thinking: Selected Readings*, edited by F. E. Emery, 147–202. Harmondsworth: Penguin, 147–8.
10 Jonathan Miller, 1982, *The Body in Question*, New York: Vintage Books, 140–1. Miller is quoted by Peter van Inwagen in *Material Beings*, 92–3.
11 George Gaylord Simpson, 1964, *This View of Life: The World of an Evolutionist*, New York: Harcourt, 113.
12 J. Z. Young, 1971, *An Introduction to the Study of Man*, Oxford: Clarendon Press, 86–7. Young has been quoted by both Peter van Inwagen, *Material Beings*, 92, and David Wiggins, *Sameness and Substance*, vii. Both van Inwagen and Wiggins endorse a view similar to the one outlined here.
13 Ernst Mayr, 1982, *The Growth of Biological Thought: Diversity, Evolution, and Inheritance*, Cambridge: Belknap Press, 2, 52; see also Ernst Mayr, 1988, *Toward a New Philosophy of Biology: Observations of an Evolutionist*, Cambridge: Belknap Press.
14 Carl Craver, 2007, *Explaining the Brain: Mechanisms and the Mosaic Unity of Neuroscience*, New York: Oxford University Press, 190–91.
15 Gilbert Ryle, 1949, *The Concept of Mind*, New York: Barnes & Noble, 76.
16 Sommerhoff, "The Abstract Characteristics of Living Systems," 147–8.
17 *Phaedo* 98c–99b.

Chapter 11

A Hylomorphic Theory of Mind

Overview

A hylomorphic theory of mind extends the biological notion of structure discussed in Chapter 10 into the psychological domain. The discussion of structures
in Chapter 10 tended to focus on mechanical structures: spatial arrangements
among a thing's parts that enable those parts to interact in novel ways. According
to hylomorphists, however, mechanical structures are not the only structures that
exist. The characteristic ways that living things interact with each other and their
environments are structured phenomena as well. Plants, animals, and other living
things are not just organized assemblages of parts; they are zones of structured
activity that include patterns of social and environmental interaction. According
to a hylomorphic theory of mind, beliefs, desires, hopes, joys, fears, and pains are
really just ways that animals like us interact with each other and the environment.
At some levels, these forms of interaction include the patterns we describe in
perceptual or sensory terms: seeing, hearing, tasting, feeling, having an itch. At
other levels, they include patterns into which these lower-level activities are integrated, such as believing, wanting, and remembering; and these higher-level patterns are often themselves integrated into behavioral patterns that are more
complex still, such as intellectual habits, or personality or character traits.

A hylomorphic theory of mind differs from most other mind–body theories
because it rejects the inner mind picture of mental phenomena. The inner mind
picture is a loose collection of ideas that depict beliefs, desires, and other mental
states as internal states of some sort. Hylomorphists deny that mental states are
occurrences in some hidden inner chamber; they are instead patterns of social and

environmental interaction. Those patterns might incorporate internal states such as states of the nervous system, but they are not identical to those internal states since they also involve social and environmental factors.

In addition to rejecting the idea that our experiences are inner states, hylomorphists reject the idea that accurate and inaccurate experiences have an inner experiential element in common. They favor disjunctivism instead, the idea that there need not be an inner experiential element that is common to both accurate and inaccurate experiences. Hylomorphists also reject the idea that we can know what mental states other people have only by making inferences from the behavior of bodies. We can know what mental states other people have, they say, by directly perceiving those mental states in something analogous to the way we directly perceive patterns on a chessboard. In line with this, hylomorphists reject the idea that psychological discourse is like a scientific theory that postulates hypothetical inner entities (mental states) whose relations to one another are supposed to explain observable human behavior. Rather, they say, psychological discourse is a form of social behavior that uses symbols to express directly observable patterns of social and environmental interaction in which people participate. Hylomorphists also reject the claim that mental states can be defined abstractly, independently of social, physical, and environmental conditions. Rather, they say, mental states are essentially embodied; they cannot be defined independently of the specific bodily parts humans possess and the environments and communities humans inhabit.

The hylomorphic view of embodiment has important implications for how hylomorphists understand multiple realizability. We can apply our psychological predicates and terms to nonhuman things not because psychological capacities are abstractly defined, they say, but because we are able to draw analogies between the behavior of nonhuman things and our own. The hylomorphic view of embodiment also has implications for how hylomorphists understand the mental–physical dichotomy. Because thoughts, feelings, perceptions, and actions are essentially embodied, they cannot qualify as nonphysical phenomena, say hylomorphists, and conversely because the fundamental physical processes that occur in human organisms contribute to higher-level human behavior (thought, feeling, and action), those processes cannot qualify as non-psychological phenomena. Higher-level human activities, and the substructures and subactivities they comprise all count as social, psychological, biological, and also physical phenomena. Human beings are psychophysical wholes; our ordinary psychological vocabulary comprises predicates and terms that are tailor-made for describing and explaining the capacities humans possess and the activities in which they engage. Biological, psychological, social, chemical, and physical phenomena do not exist in separation from each other in real human behavior; they together constitute a single zone of psychophysical activity. The mental–physical dichotomy is at best a logical construction, one that abstracts from the way psychological, social, physical, and other phenomena are incorporated into real human behavior.

Hylomorphists also offer distinctive solutions to mind–body problems. The problem of other minds arises, for instance, only if we do not have direct knowledge of other people's beliefs, desires, pains, and other mental states. Hylomorphists claim, however, that we do have direct knowledge of other people's mental states. Beliefs, desires, pain, and other mental phenomena are patterns of social and environmental interaction which normal humans have the ability to discern in something analogous to the way chess players have the ability to discern mating or tactical patterns on a chessboard. This approach to mental phenomena can easily be confused with behaviorism. Hylomorphism and behaviorism both reject aspects of the inner mind picture. They nevertheless differ from each other in at least three respects. First, hylomorphists reject physicalism, behaviorists do not. Second, hylomorphists have a broader conception of what counts as behavior than behaviorists do. And third, hylomorphists have a different understanding of psychological language.

The problem of mental causation arises, on the other hand, because our scientific and nonscientific descriptions appear to provide competing explanations for human behavior. Hylomorphists argue, however, that actions are complex phenomena that integrate many different noncompeting causal or explanatory factors. By analogy, there are many factors that contribute to explaining a car crash: insufficient grading, poor brake design, inadequate signage, high blood-alcohol level, and so on. When we ask for an explanation of the crash, we are typically not asking for a list of all the contributing factors, but only a select subset: the civil engineer is interested in the grading of the roadway, the mechanical engineer in the brake design, the judge in the high blood-alcohol level. The same is true when we ask for explanations of human behavior; we select the factors we are interested in and focus on those. In most cases, we are interested in people's reasons for choosing certain courses of action – the rational structure of their behavior, as opposed to the physiological mechanisms that enable that behavior to occur. This does not imply that these mechanisms do not contribute to actions any more than the mechanical engineer's explanation implies that the driver's blood-alcohol level did not contribute to the crash. What it does imply is that explanations that appeal to reasons and explanations that appeal to physiological mechanisms do not in any way compete to occupy a single explanatory role – the role of being the one and only cause of the action, just as the brake mechanism and the alcohol do not compete to be the one and only cause of the crash. There is no need, then, to claim either that mental states do not contribute to actions, or that physical states do not contribute to actions, or that mental and physical states share the same explanatory role and are thus overdetermining causes of actions.

Finally, the problem of psychophysical emergence arises only if lower-level physiological occurrences are taken to generate or produce higher-level behavior. But hylomorphists deny that brains generate beliefs, desires, and other mental states. Brains do not generate mental states, they say, any more than wood and metal generate pianos. Rather, brains are subsystems that enable humans to interact with each other and the environment in the highly structured ways we call 'belief', 'desire', and 'pain'. Mental phenomena are not causal byproducts of lower-level neural processes; they are rather patterns of social and environmental interaction that comprise lower-level phenomena – ways in which lower-level neural processes can be structured or organized. If mental phenomena are patterns of social and environmental interaction, ways in which physiological occurrences can be structured, then the problem of emergence never even arises. It makes no sense to ask for explanation of how physiological occurrences produce mental phenomena if physiological occurrences do not produce mental phenomena in fact.

There are at least two arguments in favor of a hylomorphic theory of mind. The first appeals to the general hylomorphic worldview. Since there is good reason to endorse hylomorphism in general (Section 10.8), says the argument, there is good reason to endorse a hylomorphic approach to mental phenomena specifically. The second argument claims that a hylomorphic theory of mind does a better job solving mind–body problems than competing theories, and since a hylomorphic theory of mind does not have any problems that are as serious as or more serious than those facing its competitors, there is good reason to think a hylomorphic theory of mind is true. Critics of a hylomorphic theory of mind can challenge these arguments and a hylomorphic theory of mind in several ways. The hylomorphic theory described in this chapter is new enough, however, that it is difficult to assess the objections to it and the responses hylomorphists make. Only time will tell if some version of hylomorphism deserves a lasting place among the other theories we have considered.

11.1 Patterns of Social and Environmental Interaction

A hylomorphic theory of mind extends the biological notion of structure discussed in Chapter 10 into the psychological domain. Most of us are familiar with *mechanical structures* – spatial relations among something's parts that enable those parts to interact in ways that confer capacities on the whole that are not had by the parts taken individually. This is the sense in which we can speak of the structure of a complex artifact such as an internal combustion engine or the structure of an organ such as a heart. But according to hylomorphists, mechanical structures are not the only structures that exist. Determining what kinds of structures exist is an empirical matter, something we discover through scientific investigation, they say, and what scientific investigation reveals is that there are many kinds of structures in addition to mechanical ones. The characteristic ways that living things interact with each other and their environments are structured phenomena as well.

Living things do not act at random. Birds build nests not webs, and lay eggs not acorns. Humans grow lungs instead of gills, and skin instead of scales. Dogs grow fur not feathers, and teeth not beaks. Squirrels bury nuts, and are active during the day; raccoons come out at night, and will rummage through our garbage if we do not take precautions. All of these are examples of patterns in living behavior. Just as the parts of living things are not assembled at random but have distinctive structures, so too the behavior of living things is characterized by distinctive patterns of social and environmental interaction. It might be helpful to consider some of the patterns biologists have discovered in their efforts to describe and explain the behavior of living things.

Some of these patterns involve the ways organisms maintain their distinctive structures against entropy, the physical principle according to which matter tends toward a state of uniform disorder. Maintaining those structures requires energy, and biologists have developed a catalog of the ways in which different living things obtain energy from their environments, the metabolic processes and catalysts involved in utilizing that energy, and the ways organisms maintain the temperatures, fluids, and chemical levels needed to carry out those processes. Other patterns of living behavior involve reproduction, development, and growth. Some organisms reproduce sexually, others asexually. Some have shorter or longer reproductive cycles than others, and those cycles have different stages and can be influenced by a variety of different internal and external factors.

Yet other patterns of living behavior involve an organism's ability to respond to and interact with features of its environment. Organisms can sense and respond to internal and external stimuli in a range of different ways involving a range of different physiological mechanisms: phototropism, gravitotropism, thigmotropism, photoreception with eyecups, photoreception with compound eyes, or with single-lens eyes, mechanoreception, auditory reception with an inner ear, auditory reception with a lateral line system, proprioception with statocysts, proprioception (vestibular or kinesthetic) with other mechanisms, airborne chemoreception, waterborne chemoreception, electroreception, and so on. In addition, these sensory mechanisms have various ranges of sensitivity, thresholds of activation, and rates of adaptation to external stimuli.

Other forms of environmental interaction involve movement. Some organisms are sessile, others are capable of locomotion, and the ways organisms have of moving themselves vary widely and involve many different kinds of physiological mechanisms. Examples include flagellation, ciliation, amoeboid motion, swimming by paddling, swimming by propulsion, swimming by caudal movement, swimming by undulation, crawling by peristalsis, crawling by undulation, crawling by accordion motion, multipedalism, quadrupedalism, bipedalism, brachiation, gliding, and flying.

Other patterns of behavior involve states of motivation or arousal: hunger, thirst, fear, anger, disgust. Others involve cognitive abilities. Some living things are capable of forming memories, short-term or long-term. Others are capable of learning by imprinting, by classical conditioning, or operant conditioning. Some are capable of cognitive learning through observation or imitation, and yet others are capable of thinking: of forming mental images or maps, using symbolic representations, reasoning and problem-solving.

Some patterns of living behavior involve features of the specific types of eco-systems organisms inhabit: tundra, tropical forest, temperate forest, grassland, desert, marsh, lake, ocean. They involve variable soil and terrain, flora and fauna, average temperatures, rainfall, average hours of sunlight, as well as seasonal or other periodic environmental changes: flood, drought, volcanic eruption, fire. Other patterns involve interactions with members of other species: competition, predation, parasitism, disease, and mutualistic relations. And yet other patterns involve relations with members of an organism's own species. Organisms can be solitary or social, and in the latter case they can engage in a variety of group behaviors: flocking, schooling, herding, monogyny with polyandry, monogyny without polyandry, polygyny, and fission–fusion grouping, among others.

The foregoing examples illustrate some of the behavioral patterns found in the living world. According to hylomorphists these patterns include mental phenom-ena. Thought, feeling, perception, and action, say hylomorphists, are patterns of social and environmental interaction. Some of these patterns we describe in per-ceptual or sensory terms: seeing, hearing, tasting, feeling, having an itch. Other patterns are more complex and incorporate perceptual or sensory patterns of these sorts. They include believing, wanting, knowing, and remembering. These higher-level patterns, moreover, are often integrated into behavioral patterns that are more complex still such as intellectual habits or personality or character traits. Consider some examples.

Humans have an evolutionary history that has equipped them with the capacity to identify features of the environment that have an important bearing on their well-being, and to respond to those features in automatic ways that do not require thought or reflection. These patterns of identification and automatic response include fear, anger, surprise, enjoyment, disgust, and other emotions. Here is an example from the psychologist Paul Ekman:

[E]motions evolved to prepare us to deal quickly with the most vital events in our lives. Recall a time when you were driving your car and suddenly another car appeared ... seeming as if it were about to hit you ... In an instant, before you had time to think ... danger was sensed and fear began ... Without consciously choosing to do it, you automatically turned the steering wheel to avoid the other motorist ... At the same time an expression of fear flashed across your face – brows raised and drawn together, eyes opened very wide, and lips stretched back toward your ears. Your heart began to pump more rapidly, you began to sweat, and the blood rushed to the large muscles of your legs ... Emotions prepare us to deal with important events without our having to think about what to do.[1]

Ekman's research indicates, moreover, that emotions are not private responses to environmental stimuli; each has an important social dimension as well. Humans have evolved physiological mechanisms that make their emotions evident to others through movements, gestures, and vocal cues. Ekman explains:

> [E]motions are not private ... [O]ver the course of our evolution it has been useful for others to know when we [experience an emotion] ... Most of our emotions have a distinctive signal that tells others how we are feeling ... [including] distinct, universal, facial expression[s] ... The voice is another emotion signal system ... [T]here are also emotional impulses to physical action ... In anger [for example] ... there is an impulse to move closer to the emotion trigger. In fear there is an impulse to freeze if that will avoid detection, or to get out of harm's way if it won't ... Although individuals differ in how expressive they are, emotions are not invisible or silent. Others who look at us and listen to what we say could tell how we are feeling, unless we were to make a concerted effort to squelch our expressions. Even then, some trace of our emotions might leak out and could be detected.[2]

Empirical work like Ekman's suggests that emotions are patterns of social and environmental interaction – patterns that include the activities and states of muscles and nerves among their subactivities and substructures.

Consider another kind of pattern. Imagine that I am helping Gabriel move some items out of his apartment on the second floor of the building in which he lives. Because he lives in a questionable neighborhood, his door is outfitted with a number of locks. It's a short trip down the stairs, and we intend on coming back as soon as we've carried one of the items out to his car, which is parked directly in front of the building. Before proceeding down the stairs, however, he stops, removes a large ring of keys from his pocket, and proceeds to lock the door. I find this behavior puzzling, "Why are you locking the door?" I ask, "We're coming right back up." He responds: "I'm locking the door because I was recently robbed while on a short trip down the stairs just like this one. And ... ," he adds *sotto voce*, "I suspect my neighbor across the hall may have been the culprit." His answer resolves my puzzlement. Why? The reason, say hylomorphists, is that it enables me to discern a pattern in Gabriel's behavior that I could not discern before. I was puzzled because I made a number of assumptions about Gabriel and his circumstances:

1 Gabriel is a rational being, one who acts on account of reasons.
2 Rational beings tend to act rationally. Moreover,
3 Gabriel wants to save time and unnecessary effort, and
4 Locking the door in the present circumstances needlessly wastes time and effort, yet
5 Gabriel is locking the door.

Together claims (1)–(5) generate a tension I do not know how to resolve. If Gabriel is a rational being who wants to save time and effort, and locking the door is a waste of time and effort, then it seems he shouldn't be locking the door. Conversely, if he is locking the door, and doing so is a needless waste of time and effort, it seems that he must not really want to save time and effort, or else he must be acting irrationally. Because claims (1)–(5) all seem to be true, I am at a loss how to make sense of Gabriel's behavior. Gabriel's answer provides the key. It challenges my commitment to Claim (4). It suggests locking the door is not a needless waste of time and effort, that the chances of being robbed in the time it would take us to return are fatter than I initially suspected. I am thus able to discern a rational pattern in Gabriel's behavior that I was unable to discern before. By analogy, I might be completely puzzled by the way a chess master is playing, but one decisive move can suddenly enable me to discern the strategy that has been there all along. In Gabriel's case, we might describe the pattern I'm able to discern in the following way:

Gabriel is locking the door because he's afraid he might get robbed by his neighbor – something he believes likely on the basis of recent events.

We can easily imagine other answers to my question that would have disclosed a different pattern in Gabriel's behavior. Here are some examples:

"I've lately been trying to cultivate an attitude that is heedless of the constraints of time and effort."

"I'm just checking that this key turns in the lock. The outside door of the building is keyed the same way, and this is not the key I usually use."

"I really just enjoy locking doors; I love the feel of the lock snapping into place and the satisfying sound it makes when it does so."

"Actually, before returning we have to go down the block and pick up something from the corner store."

"Physicists have discovered a temporal anomaly in this building: people walking up the stairs take three times longer to cover the same distance as people outside the anomaly."

Any of these answers could have resolved my puzzlement since each would have enabled me to discern a rational pattern in Gabriel's behavior – patterns we could have described in the following ways:

Gabriel is locking the door as part of a spiritual exercise.

Gabriel is not locking the door; he is merely testing the key.

Gabriel is locking the door for the sheer thrill of doing so.

Gabriel is locking the door because he's afraid he might get robbed by his neighbor – something that he believes could happen in the time it will take us to run to the corner store.

Gabriel is locking the door because he's afraid he might get robbed by his neighbor – something he believes likely on the basis of what physicists have recently discovered about his building.

The core idea of a hylomorphic theory of mind is that sensations, feelings, thoughts, perceptions, actions, and other psychological phenomena are complex patterns of social and environmental interaction of this and similar sorts. They are ways animals like us interact with each other and the environment – ways in which our behavior is structured or organized.

Historically speaking, philosophers have developed this basic idea in many different ways. The Greek philosopher Aristotle suggested one way, for instance, and his ancient and medieval followers suggested others. To be relevant to current mind–body debates, however, a hylomorphic theory of mind has to address the issues that arise within those debates. Since this is a book on current mind–body debates, the sections that follow describe a new kind of hylomorphic theory, one that is based on work in psychology and cognitive science, that builds on some recent developments in the mind–body literature, and that addresses some current mind–body problems.

11.2   Rejecting Inner Minds

A hylomorphic approach to mental phenomena differs in a fundamental way from many of the mind–body theories considered so far. Most of those theories are committed in some way to the idea that mental phenomena are inner states, ones that occur "in the head," so to speak, in an interior domain such as a brain or Cartesian mind. We can call this the *inner mind picture* of mental phenomena. According to exponents of the inner mind picture, the inner mental domain is different from the outer domain of objectively observable bodily movements and gestures. Occurrences in the outer domain are equally accessible to me and to other people. The observations I make of my limb movements are no different in kind from observations you or anybody else can make of them. Any properly situated observer can witness my movements and gestures at least as well as I myself can. According to exponents of the inner mind picture, however, the mental domain is not like this; it is not equally observable by everyone. You and I cannot witness each other's mental states the way we can witness each other's limb movements. In general, people's mental states are not directly observable by other people, at least not in ordinary perceptual circumstances. Instead, each of us must infer what mental states other people have based on things that are directly observable such as bodily movements and gestures.

The idea that mental phenomena are internal states is often combined with a theory model of psychological language (Section 5.3). According to the theory model, recall, psychological discourse is like a scientific theory that postulates hypothetical entities – mental states – whose relations to one another are supposed to explain overt bodily behavior. When we explain why Caesar crossed the Rubicon by saying he wanted to secure political power and believed marching on Rome the best means of securing it, exponents of the theory model claim that we are postulating entities, a belief and a desire, that are related to each other in lawlike ways expressed by generalizations such as the following:

L   When x wants y, and believes doing z the best means of attaining y, then if nothing inhibits x's pursuit of y, x will generally do z.

According to exponents of the theory model, this lawlike relation among hypothetical entities is supposed to explain Caesar's observed behavior.

Exponents of the inner mind picture who endorse the theory model identify the hypothetical entities postulated in laws like (L) with inner states of some sort such as states of a brain, or states caused by states of a brain, or states of a nonphysical mind. Exactly what kinds of inner states mental states are is something that exponents of the inner mind picture take to be an open philosophical question. The reason is that they take mental states to be defined by relations such as (L), and these relations do not specify what kinds of inner states beliefs, desires, and other mental states are. We know mental states must be related in the ways expressed by generalizations like (L), say many exponents of inner minds, but we cannot know on the basis of these generalizations exactly what the natures of these states are. Knowing that is something that requires philosophical investigation.

Whatever inner states mental states turn out to be, however, exponents of the inner mind picture claim that our experience of the world is constituted by them. Each of us, they say, has an internal representation of the external world – a representation that under the best of circumstances accurately reflects events in the world. But our inner experiences can also fail to reflect events in the world, as in cases of hallucination or false belief. There might be no experiential difference between, say, perceiving an elephant and having a hallucination as if there is an elephant, according to many exponents of the inner mind picture; my inner experiential states might be exactly the same in both cases. In both I might have an inner visual experience as if there is an elephant; the difference is simply that in the case of perception my visual experience corresponds to something in the world, whereas in the case of hallucination it does not. The cases nevertheless have an element in common, say exponents of inner minds; they both involve the same kind of inner visual state: an experience as if there is an elephant.

The inner mind picture just described comprises a loose collection of ideas. They include the following:

The inner experience thesis   Our experiences are inner states. Sometimes these inner states accurately represent objects, properties, and events in the external world, but they can also fail to represent them.

The common element thesis   Accurate and inaccurate experiences have an inner experiential element in common – perception and hallucination, for instance, have an inner experience in common.

The inferential access thesis   Other people's mental states are not directly observable; we can know what mental states other people have only by making inferences from the behavior of bodies.

The theory model of psychological discourse   Psychological discourse is like a scientific theory that postulates hypothetical entities (mental states) whose relations to one another are supposed to explain observable human behavior.

The neutrality thesis   Beliefs, desires, and other mental states can be defined independently of physical conditions. The definitions of mental states do not imply anything about how or even whether mental states are correlated with certain kinds of physical states.

Internalism   Beliefs, desires, and other mental states can be defined independently of social and environmental conditions. The definitions of mental states do not imply anything about the communities and environments people inhabit.

Not all philosophers endorse the inner mind picture, and even those who do endorse it typically do not endorse every claim associated with it. Some of those claims have in fact been extensively criticized, and are no longer favored by the majority of philosophers. What sets a hylomorphic approach to mental phenomena apart is that it rejects all of the aforementioned claims. Thoughts, feelings, perceptions, and other mental phenomena are not occurrences in some hidden inner chamber, it says; they are instead patterns of social and environmental interaction. These patterns are not hidden from view but are readily discernible by anyone who has the ability to perceive them, and that includes most humans. Accurate and inaccurate experiences, moreover, are not different species of a common kind of inner experience; they are completely different kinds of phenomena. Seeing an elephant, for instance, is a way of interacting with something in the environment, whereas having a hallucination as if there is an elephant is not a way of interacting with something in the environment, but a situation in which the neural subsystems involved in perception misfire – in which those subsystems are activated apart from the social and environmental factors that make genuine perception what it is. Nor do psychological predicates and terms postulate hypothetical inner entities; they instead refer to or express the patterns of social and environmental interaction in which we ordinarily observe people participating. Those patterns, moreover, cannot be defined independently of social and environmental conditions, nor can they be defined independently of physical ones: beliefs, desires, and other mental phenomena are essentially embodied, say hylomorphists, and their essential embodiment is reflected in the predicates and terms we use to describe them. A hylomorphic theory of mind thus rejects the claims that constitute the inner mind picture, and endorses the following claims instead:

The outer experience thesis   Our experiences are not inner events that reflect events in the external world; they are instead patterns of interaction involving individuals, properties, and events in the world.

Disjunctivism   There need not be an inner experiential element that is common to both accurate and inaccurate experiences.

The direct access thesis   Other people's mental states are directly observable; we can know what mental states other people have by directly perceiving them.

The pattern expression theory of psychological discourse   Psychological discourse is not like a scientific theory that postulates hypothetical entities; it is instead a form of social behavior that uses symbols to express patterns of social and environmental interaction in which we participate.

The embodiment thesis   Beliefs, desires, and other mental phenomena cannot be defined independently of physical conditions. Definitions of mental phenomena imply something about how mental states are correlated with certain kinds of physical states.

Externalism   Beliefs, desires, and other mental phenomena cannot be defined independently of social and environmental factors. The definitions of mental states imply something about the communities and environments people inhabit.

The sections that follow discuss these claims in detail. They begin with a consideration of externalism and the outer experience thesis.

11.3   Externalism

To understand hylomorphism's commitment to externalism and the outer experience thesis it is helpful to start by considering actions. Actions are mental phenomena, say hylomorphists; they are among the things we use psychological
language to describe and explain. We can therefore use actions as a model for
understanding other mental phenomena.

The first thing to recognize about actions, say hylomorphists, is that they are
not series of muscular contractions, bodily movements, or other physiological
events. Actions certainly involve muscular contractions, bodily movements, and
other physiological events, but they are not identical to them since actions involve
social and environmental factors in addition to physiological ones. Consider a
simple act such as reaching for a glass of water. In order for me to perform this
act it is necessary that there be a glass of water in my vicinity. If this environmental
condition is not satisfied, if there is no glass, or if the liquid in the glass is not
water but something else, then I am not reaching for a glass of water. If, for
instance, the glass is filled with gin, then what I am doing is reaching for a glass
of gin. Perhaps I intend to reach for a glass of water; perhaps I mistakenly believe
that I am reaching for a glass of water; but regardless of what I intend or believe,
I cannot be reaching for a glass of water unless the glass I am reaching for contains
water. The same is true if we consider an act such as drinking water. If I begin to
ingest the contents of the glass, I cannot be said to be drinking water if what I
am ingesting is in fact gin. Examples like this show that the performance of an
action depends not just on muscular contractions and other physiological events,
but on environmental factors as well. I cannot reach for or drink a glass of water
unless a particular environmental condition is satisfied; namely, there is a glass in
the vicinity that is filled with water. Because the performance of an action depends
on environmental conditions, an action is not merely a collection of physiological
events. An act of reaching for a glass of water and an act of reaching for a glass
of gin might involve the same kinds of muscular contractions, bodily movements,
and neuronal firings; they would nevertheless still differ on account of the contents
of the glass.

Other examples illustrate that actions depend on social conditions in addition
to environmental ones. Imagine, for instance, that a Congressional aide is charged
with the task of delivering a bill to the White House for the president's signature.
Instead of waiting for the president, however, the aide signs the document in his
own name. Does the bill thereby become law? Of course not, and the reason is
that the act of signing a bill into law requires that a very specific social condition
be met; namely, the bill must be signed by the president, by someone who occupies a very specific social role. Something similar is true of activities such as
reading or purchasing. They depend not on social roles but on other social conditions. Reading, for instance, requires a written language, a socially embedded

system of symbols, and purchasing requires money, a socially embedded instrument for economic exchange. Actions, then, depend not just on states of the nervous system, bodily movements, or other states internal to the organism; they depend on social and environmental factors as well.

What hylomorphists claim about actions, they also claim about perceptions. Just as I cannot be reaching for a glass of water without there being a glass of water, likewise I cannot be seeing a glass of water without there being a glass of water – or be tasting, or touching, or smelling water if what I am tasting, touching, or smelling is something other than water. I can be mistaken about what I am tasting, touching, or smelling. If my taste buds are deranged, I might be incapable of distinguishing water from, say, gin based on their flavors alone, but this does not imply that there is no difference between water and gin, and it does not imply that I am tasting water if the liquid in my mouth is gin.

The idea that actions, perceptions, and other mental phenomena depend on social or environmental conditions is sometimes called **externalism** in the philosophy of mind. In addition to being externalists about actions and perceptions, hylomorphists are also externalists about thoughts – propositional attitudes such as beliefs and desires (Section 2.5). Perhaps the best-known argument for the externalism of thoughts has been advanced by the philosopher Hilary Putnam.

Putnam's argument is based on what are typically called **Twin Earth thought experiments**. Twin Earth thought experiments focus on cases in which two individuals (or a single individual considered in two different circumstances) inhabit environments that differ in some respect, and that environmental difference is responsible for a difference in their beliefs, desires, and other propositional attitudes. Consider, for instance, Gabriel and Xavier. In Gabriel's environment people drink H_2O; they bathe with H_2O; H_2O falls from the sky as rain; it flows from drinking fountains, fills lakes, rivers, and oceans, and so on. In Xavier's environment, by contrast, there is no H_2O, but another substance, XYZ, not found in Gabriel's environment. XYZ is indistinguishable from H_2O in all of its macroscopic features: color, odor, texture, taste, viscosity, and so on. In Xavier's environment it is XYZ that people drink, that they bathe with, that falls from the sky as rain, that flows from drinking fountains, that fills lakes, rivers, and oceans. People in Xavier's environment have never encountered H_2O, and conversely people in Gabriel's environment have never encountered XYZ. Despite this difference, ordinary speakers of English in both environments make the same utterances concerning what they call 'water'. In Gabriel's environment people say, "Water is the stuff that we drink, that we bathe with, that falls from the sky as rain, that freezes in the winter, that fills those lakes, rivers, and oceans." In Xavier's environment people say the same things: "Water is the stuff that we drink, that we bathe with, that falls from the sky as rain, that freezes in the winter, that ..." Even though they utter the same sounds concerning the stuff they call 'water', however, there is an important difference between people in Gabriel's environment and people in Xavier's: when they talk about or think about water, they are talking about or thinking about different kinds of stuff.

When people in Gabriel's environment say or think that water is the stuff that fills rivers, lakes, and oceans, their thoughts are about H_2O. When they want to quench their thirst or when they hope there's enough hot water left for a comfortable shower, they thirst for H_2O, and entertain hopes about H_2O. Because they have never encountered XYZ, it is difficult to see how they could thirst for it, or entertain hopes or beliefs about it. When Gabriel asks the bartender for a glass of water, he is asking the bartender to supply him with the same thirst-quenching liquid he has always drunk in the past; he is not asking the bartender to surprise him with a liquid he has never before tasted. What he is asking for is H_2O. Something analogous is true of Xavier and people in his environment. Their beliefs, desires, and hopes concern not H_2O but XYZ. Because they have never encountered H_2O in their environment, they do not thirst for it, look to bathe with it, or entertain hopes or beliefs about it. People in the two environments have different thoughts, then – different beliefs, desires, hopes, and other propositional attitudes. In Gabriel's environment people's thoughts concern H_2O, while in Xavier's they concern XYZ. The reason people in the two environments have different thoughts, moreover, is that they have been interacting in their respective environments with different stuff: H_2O versus XYZ. What the example of Gabriel and Xavier illustrates, then, is that people's beliefs, desires, and other propositional attitudes depend in part on environmental conditions – they depend in part, for instance, on the kind of stuff they typically interact with.

The philosopher Tyler Burge has extended Putnam's point: Thoughts depend not just on environmental conditions, he argues; they depend on social conditions as well. For this reason externalism is also called *anti-individualism*, for it denies that thought is something that can involve only a single individual. One of the examples Burge advances in favor of anti-individualism involves two different linguistic communities that use the term 'arthritis' to express two different concepts. Suppose that in Gabriel's linguistic community, 'arthritis' is used to refer to an inflammation of the joints, while in Xavier's community, it is used to refer to an inflammation of the joints or the muscles. Gabriel and Xavier can be in identical types of physiological states, and yet have different attitudes about their condition on account of belonging to different linguistic communities. Imagine, for instance, that Gabriel and Xavier both experience chronic pains in their right thighs. Both say, "I suspect I have arthritis in my thigh, and fear the doctor will confirm my suspicions." But when Gabriel and Xavier say this, they are saying different things. Each is effectively saying that he has the medical condition that doctors in his community call 'arthritis'. But those medical conditions are different. In Gabriel's community, 'arthritis' refers to a condition of the joints, while in Xavier's community, it refers to a condition of the joints or muscles. As a result, Xavier's suspicion is well-founded, and his fear could be realized – he could turn out to have the condition that doctors in his linguistic community call 'arthritis'.

But this is not the case with Gabriel. He couldn't be suffering from the condition he calls 'arthritis' in his thigh, and the doctor could not accurately diagnose his condition as arthritis, for in his linguistic community the term 'arthritis' refers to a disease of the joints only, not to a disease of the joints or muscles. As a result, it is clear that Gabriel and Xavier have different propositional attitudes – different fears and suspicions. This difference in their attitudes is due, moreover, to a difference in their social circumstances – to the way their respective linguistic communities use the term 'arthritis'.

In line with externalist arguments, then, a hylomorphic theory of mind claims that the phenomena we describe in psychological terms including thoughts, perceptions, and actions, are complex relational phenomena. When we say that someone is performing an action, or perceiving, believing, or wanting something, we are describing ways in which that individual is related to other people and the environment. Beliefs, desires, and pains are not brain states or internal states produced by brain states; they are instead patterns of social and environmental interaction. These patterns require that our brains be in certain states, just as relating to the environment in the ways we call 'reaching for a glass of water' and 'signing a bill into law' require that our muscles and nerves be in certain states, but these brain states are not the only factors involved in having a belief, desire, or pain, just as the states of our muscles and nerves are not the only factors involved in reaching for a glass of water or signing a bill into law. So just as actions depend on social and environmental factors, say hylomorphists, the same is true of thoughts, feelings, and perceptions.

11.4   Inner Experiences versus Sensorimotor Exploration

Hylomorphists' commitment to externalism is closely related to their rejection of the inner experience thesis. Hylomorphists deny that our experiences are things that occur "in our heads" so to speak. Instead, they say, our experiences occur in the world. Consider an example: perception. Exponents of the inner mind picture often suggest that our perceptual experiences consist in having internal representations of the external world, but hylomorphists reject the idea that our experiences are internal states that mirror external things. They claim instead that our experiences are patterns of interaction involving individuals, properties, and events in the real world itself. One way of developing this idea builds on some recent work in cognitive science.

Sensorimotor theories of consciousness (Section 4.9) claim that perceptual experience is an exploratory activity in which an organism continuously samples features of its environment using its perceptual subsystems. Exponents of sensorimotor theories have supported their view by appeal to experiments involving the phenomenon of *change blindness*. Change blindness is a phenomenon in which test subjects are presented with a picture or scene that undergoes some large and fairly obvious change: the pants of a man in the foreground change color from blue to brown, a banana pointing to the right switches to the left, a large tree disappears in the background, or a large building gradually materializes. Despite the obviousness of these changes, a significant percentage of test subjects – between 25 and 75 percent – fail to detect them.

Change blindness studies suggest that perceptual experience does not consist in having a continuous internal representation of the external world, for if it did, critics say, we would have complete perceptual awareness of every aspect of our visual field; our experience would consist of a number of inner conscious elements – awareness of blue pants here, awareness of a tree there, awareness of a banana pointing to the right, and so on. If our experience consisted of a field of inner conscious elements like this, however, then we would expect test subjects to be aware of any changes in their visual fields since those visual fields would consist in nothing but inner conscious experiences. Change blindness studies show, however, that test subjects are often not aware of changes in their visual fields, and this suggests that perceptual experience does not consist in having an internal representation of the external world. In what, then, does it consist?

According to exponents of sensorimotor theories, it consists in a series of exploratory episodes in which an organism continuously samples features of its environment using its perceptual subsystems. The reason test subjects are blind to changes in the visible environment, say exponents of sensorimotor accounts, is that subjects are not continuously aware of all of the environment's features. An organism's awareness of its environment is not a continuous inner state but a series of externally directed samplings of environmental features. Perceptual experience is a process in which the organism moves around attending to different features of its surroundings at different times. Test subjects miss changes because they are not engaged with every feature of their environments at a given time, and hence miss changes in features they are not engaged with at those times. Perceptual experience does not consist in having a detailed, uninterrupted landscape of inner conscious impressions; it consists rather in a stream of episodes in which we use our sensory and motor subsystems to attend first to one feature of the environment, then another, and another, and so on.

But, someone might urge, it certainly appears as though our conscious experience consists in a continuous landscape of detailed inner impressions. Something has to explain this appearance. According to sensorimotor exponents, our experience seems continuous not because there is a landscape of inner impressions but because the world remains continuously accessible to our sensory exploration. Our exploratory access to the surrounding environment is for the most part unimpeded; we are free to engage with one feature of the environment or another, and because we have free access to those features, it seems to us as though the entire field of conscious experience lies within us as if it were a complete uninterrupted landscape. In reality, though, the field of conscious experience is not within us; it is rather in the world, in our patterns of engagement with the world. The philoso-pher Alva Noë states the point as follows:

> We have the impression that the world is represented in full detail in consciousness because, wherever we look, we encounter detail. All the detail is present but it is only present *virtually*, for example, in the way that a web site's content is present on your desktop ... It is *as if* all the content at the remote server is *present* on your local machine even though it isn't really ... To experience detail virtually, you don't *need* to have all the detail in your head. All you need is quick and easy access to the rel-evant detail when you need it. Just as you don't need to download, say, the entire *New York Times* to be able to read it on your desktop, so you don't need to construct a representation of all the detail of the scene in front to you to have a sense of its detailed presence.[3]

Consider likewise the remarks of the cognitive scientists Erik Myin and J. Kevin O'Regan:

> [T]he scene we are confronted with seems to be detailed, not because we see all of the details all of the time but because we find the details whenever we look for them ... [E]lements of the scene that are in peripheral vision or are currently not attended to are seen only in a secondary sense. The retina registers these elements, but we do not see them fully as we see something we attend to. Only when we turn to them and scrutinize them, do we actually see all the detail ... [T]he impression of seeing everything in the visual field in front of us derives not from all the detail actually being continuously represented [internally], but from its immediate acces-sibility at the mere flick of the eye or of attention. If this is true, then large changes in an image should surely go unnoticed when these occur on parts of the image that are not currently part of what the viewer is visually exploring.[4]

According to exponents of sensorimotor theories, then, perceptual experience does not consist in having detailed internal representations of the environment; it consists instead in a series of exploratory samplings of the environment; it is an overall pattern of environmental interaction. As Myin and O'Regan put it, "Seeing and perceiving are not achievements of an isolated head or brain ... The organism moves its eyes, repositions its body to get a better perceptual grip on the objects that surround it ... The locus of perceptual processing includes the world rather than being just confined to the head."[5] This is the kind of approach to perceptual experience hylomorphists can endorse, an approach that sees perceptual experi-ence not as an internal state, but as a pattern of environmental interaction. And it is the kind of approach that exponents of sensorimotor theories argue is the best explanation for phenomena such as change blindness.

Exponents of the inner experience thesis can respond to this argument by offer-ing a competing explanation of change blindness. The reason test subjects fail to notice changes in their visual field, they can say, is that test subjects fail to attend to features of their detailed inner representations of things. We are not always attending to all the features of our inner representation of the external world, exponents of the inner experience thesis can say, and because of that we can fail to notice changes in that representation. Sensorimotor theorists can nevertheless argue that this explanation is inferior. Among other things, they can say, it runs afoul of Ockham's razor.

Ockham's razor, recall, is a methodological principle that says we should try to explain phenomena using the simplest theoretical apparatus possible (Section 5.5). If you have a choice between two theories, TA and TB, and they are alike in all relevant respects, but TA has a simpler ontology, that is, it postulates fewer basic entities than TB, then you should choose TA since it is the ontologically simpler theory. Exponents of sensorimotor theory can argue that their own explanation of change blindness is superior to the explanation offered by exponents of inner experiences because their own explanation is ontologically simpler. According to sensorimotor theorists, test subjects fail to notice changes in their visual field because they are not attending to every feature of the surrounding environment. Exponents of inner experiences say something similar. According to them, test subjects are not attending to every feature of their internal representations of the surrounding environment. Both sensorimotor theorists and exponents of inner experiences posit a surrounding environment, but exponents of inner experiences posit a second domain of entities in addition, namely a domain of inner representations of that environment. Consequently, say sensorimotor theorists, the explanation offered by exponents of inner experiences is unnecessarily complicated. It uses twice as many entities to do the same amount of explanatory work as sensorimotor theory, and, according to Ockham's razor, that makes sensorimotor theory superior.

The account of perceptual experience favored by hylomorphists and other exponents of sensorimotor theories marks a radical break with the inner mind picture. It denies the need to posit internal representations to account for perceptual experiences. Another component of hylomorphists' rejection of inner minds is disjunctivism, the idea that accurate and inaccurate experiences – perceptions and hallucinations, for instance – need not have an inner experiential element in common.

11.5   Disjunctivism

Many exponents of the inner mind picture take accurate and inaccurate experiences to be species of a single kind of inner occurrence. When I see an elephant and when I have a hallucination as if there is an elephant, they say, I am having the same kind of inner experience in both cases – an inner experience that is related to a real elephant in the case of perception, and that is related to nothing in the case of hallucination. Hylomorphists reject this view. Accurate and inaccurate experiences do not or at least need not have an inner experiential element in common. Perception and hallucination are not species of a single kind of inner mental state but are completely disjoint phenomena. This type of view has sometimes been called **disjunctivism** in the philosophy of mind.

The label 'disjunctivism' derives from the idea that when we make statements about our experiences, those statements have an implicit disjunctive form – a form, in other words, that involves the logical operation of disjunction – *either ... or ...* Consider, for instance, the following statement:

1   I am having an experience as if there is an elephant.

According to many exponents of the inner mind picture, a statement like this can be taken to report the occurrence of an inner mental state. According to disjunctivists, however, this statement should be analyzed as follows:

2   Either I am seeing an elephant, or else I am having a hallucination as if there is an elephant.

According to disjunctivists, in other words, there is not a single kind of inner experience that is reported by Statement (1). Statement (1) is instead an abbreviated way of saying that either I am perceiving something in the environment, or else I am in a state of a completely different sort – I am having a hallucination.

Hylomorphists understand hallucination in terms of the *offline operation* of perceptual subsystems. Our perceptual subsystems can be activated without us actually perceiving. Consider, for instance, the cognitive processes involved in conjuring and manipulating mental images. Figure 11.1 depicts three pairs of pictures.[6] Pairs A and B present pictures of the same object rotated in different directions. Pair C, by contrast, presents pictures of different objects. In a well-known experiment, the psychologists Roger Shepard and Jacqueline Metzler showed test subjects pairs of pictures like these, and asked them to determine whether the left-hand picture of each pair was of the same object as or a different object from the object in the right-hand picture of that pair. Shepard and Metzler found that the time it took subjects to complete the task corresponded to the amount of time it would take a test subject to "rotate" one of the pictures – it was as if test subjects were imagining themselves manipulating three-dimensional objects. Subsequent studies by many researchers using positron emission tomography (PET) and functional magnetic resonance imaging (fMRI) revealed that parts of the brain such as the striate cortex, which were active in actual perception, were also active when people performed tasks involving mental imagery. When we try to imagine an object rotated in space, or imagine what a chessboard would look like if we moved various pieces, or try to imagine ourselves or others performing a task, we are activating some of the visual, tactile, and other perceptual

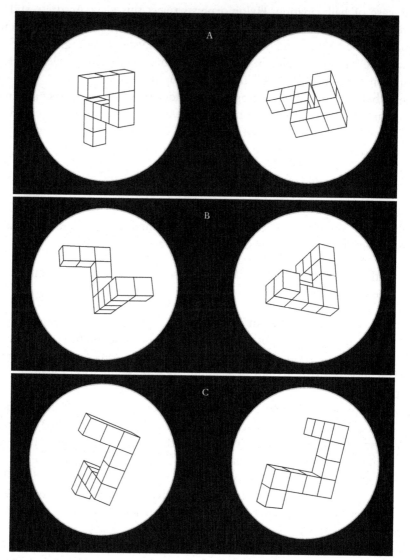

From R.N. Shepard and J. Metzler, 'Mental rotation of three-dimensional objects'. *Science*, 1971.
Reprinted with permission from The American Association for the Advancement of Science.

Figure 11.1   Image rotation experiments

subsystems that are involved in actually seeing, touching, and doing things, yet without actually seeing, touching, or doing them. We are operating those perceptual subsystems offline.

The Greek philosopher Aristotle had a general name for the offline activation of our perceptual subsystems; he called them exercises of *phantasia*. The term *phantasia* has often been translated 'imagination'. This is a misleading label, however, because for Aristotle *phantasia* comprised much more than the activity we call 'imagining'; it comprised a range of activities involving the offline operation of perceptual subsystems. Remembering, imagining, dreaming and many other cognitive processes are all examples of *phantasia* in Aristotle's sense.

Sometimes the offline activation of perceptual subsystems is something in our control. I am responsible for operating my perceptual subsystems offline when I play chess, for instance, or think about how to move a large piece of furniture through a doorway. But sometimes we are not responsible for the offline activation of our perceptual subsystems. Dreaming is one example of this. Hallucination is another. Hallucinations occur when our perceptual subsystems misfire, and lead us to make inaccurate judgments about the environment. They are analogous to misfirings of other sorts: the shortstop accidentally throwing the ball away, the traveler failing to remember how to say 'thief' in Italian, the writer accidentally omitting the article 'the' before a word). In these cases, certain conditions in the nervous system lead to errors in the performance of some higher-level task. Just as certain conditions of the nervous system can result in errors like these, say hylomorphists, so too they can result in errors judging the environment. Hallucinations are examples. It seems to us as if we are perceiving something, but really we are not. If a mad neuroscientist manipulates Madeleine's nervous system, and she declares, "I see a pink elephant!" because it seems to her that she is looking at a pink elephant, hylomorphists respond, "No, that is incorrect; there is no pink elephant here; your visual system is misfiring: it is in a state that makes it seem to you as if you are seeing a pink elephant even though you are not." The cells in Madeleine's nervous system that enable her to see are engaged in various activities – perhaps the same activities in which they would be engaged if there were a pink elephant standing before her. But because they have been caused by the neuroscientist's electrodes, the activities of these cells are not integrated into the pattern of environmental interaction we would call 'seeing a pink elephant'; they are not integrated into a pattern of environmental interaction we would call 'seeing' at all. Seeing requires something seen, say hylomorphists, and in Madeleine's case nothing is being seen. We could give this state of Madeleine's nervous system a name; we could call it 'having a visual experience'; but attaching that label to it wouldn't qualify it as a case of perception. When Madeleine describes her condition as an instance of seeing, her description is strictly speaking incorrect.

Our perceptual subsystems are not the only ones that can be operated offline. The subsystems involved in actions can as well. When, for instance, athletes perform "visualization" exercises in which they imagine themselves performing various tasks without actually performing them, they are operating the subsystems involved in those tasks offline.[7] Moreover, just as there can be misfires of the perceptual subsystem, so too there can be misfires of the subsystems involved in action. Imagine, for instance, that the mad neuroscientist manipulates Eleanor's nervous system and produces neural states and muscular contractions that are indistinguishable from the neural states and muscular contractions of someone playing basketball. Eleanor, however, does not have a ball. Since it is not possible to play basketball without a ball, Eleanor is not playing basketball. Her bodily movements and states might be indistinguishable from those of someone playing basketball – just as the state of Madeleine's visual system might be indistinguishable from the state of someone seeing a pink elephant. Without a ball, however, Eleanor is not playing basketball. Her case is analogous to the case of hallucination. Hallucinations are misfires of the perceptual subsystem, cases in which the activities of our perceptual subsystems are not integrated into the pattern of environmental interaction we call 'perceiving'. In the same way, Eleanor's behavior involves a misfire of the subsystems involved in action; it is a case in which the activities of those subsystems are not integrated into the pattern of environmental interaction we call 'playing basketball'.

One objection to disjunctivism claims that disjunctivists fail to explain how hallucinatory experiences and perceptual experiences can seem qualitatively indistinguishable to the person experiencing them. Imagine, for instance, that Madeleine accurately perceives a ripe tomato. At time t, however, the tomato is instantaneously annihilated and a neural implant is activated that makes it seem to Madeleine as if she is perceiving the same ripe tomato even though she no longer is. The transition happens so seamlessly that Madeleine cannot tell the difference between her experience before t and her experience after t; she cannot tell the difference, in other words, between her perceptual experience of the tomato and her hallucination of it. The perceptual and hallucinatory experiences are qualitatively indistinguishable, say critics of disjunctivism; Madeleine cannot tell the difference between them on the basis of introspection, by reflecting on the qualitative features of her experience. If asked to describe her experience before t and after t, she would say the same thing in both cases: "It seems to me that I am seeing a ripe tomato." Something must explain the qualitative indistinguishability of Madeleine's perceptual and hallucinatory states, critics of disjunctivism insist, and the best explanation is surely that perception and hallucination have an inner experiential element in common, that there is a single kind of inner experience that Madeleine has both before t and after t, namely an inner experience as if there is a ripe tomato, and it is because of this common inner element that Madeleine cannot tell the difference between her perceptual and hallucinatory states. Therefore, say critics, disjunctivism must be false.

Disjunctivists can respond to this objection in several ways. Consider one of them. Disjunctivists can argue that their opponents have described Madeleine's situation in a way that implicitly begs the question against them; that is, their opponents have described Madeleine's situation in a way that assumes rather than proves that disjunctivism is false. Once Madeleine's situation is described in a neutral way, disjunctivists can urge, a way that does not beg the question against disjunctivism, we will see that disjunctivists can explain Madeleine's experiences just as well as their opponents can, and, as a result, the objection fails. Consider, then, what disjunctivists might take to be a neutral description of Madeleine's situation.

Madeleine's environment and nervous system have been altered in ways that bring about a change in her perceptual status. Because of those changes, she was perceiving a ripe tomato before *t*, but is no longer perceiving a ripe tomato after *t*. She nevertheless remains unaware of the change. What if anything needs to be explained here? According to disjunctivists, the only thing that might initially seem puzzling is how Madeleine manages to remain ignorant of the change in her perceptual status, how she remains unaware that a change has taken place. This, in any event, is what opponents of disjunctivism appear to focus on; it is what they take as grounds to posit common inner experiences. Madeleine remains ignorant of the change, they say, because there is an inner experience that remains the same before the change and after it, and because of that common inner experience Madeleine cannot tell the difference between her perceptual status before the change and her perceptual status after it. But do we need to posit an inner experience to explain how Madeleine remains ignorant of the change? We do not, say disjunctivists; all we need is to explain how Madeleine fails to gain information about her perceptual status, and this does not require us to postulate common inner experiences. It only requires us to recognize that perception involves more than we can know through introspection, more than we can know simply by reflecting on our experiences. It involves knowing something about our relation to the environment as well. Consider an analogy.

Alexander has entered a lottery. The winning number is drawn at time *t*, and he in fact wins. He nevertheless remains unaware that he has won. He lacks access to television, internet, or any other sources of information that might inform him that he has won. At time *t*, therefore, Alexander undergoes a change in his status: he was not a winner before *t*, and he is a winner after *t*. He nevertheless remains ignorant of the change that has taken place. Do we need to posit a common inner experience to explain how Alexander remains ignorant of having won? Clearly not. What explains Alexander's ignorance is simply his lack of access to television, internet, and other sources of information about the winning lottery number. He remains ignorant about his changed status because knowing about that change requires knowing about the results of the drawing, and he cannot know the results of the drawing through introspection, simply by reflecting on his experiences.

Something analogous is true of Madeleine's situation, disjunctivists can say. Perception involves standing in certain relations to the environment – relations Madeleine cannot know about through introspection. Through introspection, for instance, Madeleine cannot know that her brain states are being manipulated by a neural implant and that the tomato she previously perceived has been annihilated. Madeleine lacks access to important information about the operation of her nervous system and her relations to the environment, and, as a result, she remains unaware of the change in her perceptual status. Just as we need not posit a common inner experience to explain how Alexander remains ignorant of winning the lottery, we need not posit a common inner experience to explain how Madeleine remains ignorant that she is hallucinating. All we need to explain both cases, disjunctivists can say, is an account of how Alexander and Madeleine lack access to information about their circumstances, and this is something disjunctivists are able to provide. As a result, they can say, the objection to their view fails. Once Madeleine's situation is described in the foregoing way, once it is construed as a case in which we need only explain how Madeleine remains ignorant of a change in her perceptual situation, we see that the disjunctivist explanation is just as good as the alternative.

Opponents of disjunctivism might retort that disjunctivists misconstrue Madeleine's situation. What disjunctivists must explain is not simply how Madeleine remains ignorant of a change in her perceptual status; they must explain how Madeleine's experience before *t* can be qualitatively indistinguishable from her experience after *t*. There is a positive fact about Madeleine's experiences – the fact that some of them cannot be distinguished through introspection – that requires explanation, and it is this, critics can insist, that disjunctivists fail to explain.

It is precisely here, however, that disjunctivists can argue that their opponents commit the fallacy of begging the question, for it seems that their opponents are demanding an explanation of something disjunctivists deny is the case. Opponents of disjunctivism assume that there is something common to Madeleine's experience before *t* and after *t*. In particular, they assume that there are certain experienced qualities – the apparent redness of the apparent tomato, for instance – that are the same before *t* and after *t*. Opponents claim, in other words, that Madeleine's perception and her hallucination share a qualitative element in common, namely, a set of qualitatively indistinguishable features, and it is the sharing of this element that requires explanation. But disjunctivists deny that there is a common element of this sort. They deny that there are experiential elements common to the perception and the hallucination. At the very least, they say, it is not necessary to posit such elements to explain why Madeleine cannot distinguish the perception from the hallucination. If there are good reasons to posit common inner elements, the burden is on opponents of disjunctivism to provide them. But simply to assume that there are such elements, and that disjunctivists must explain them is to beg the question against disjunctivism. It is to assume disjunctivism is false, not to prove it. Consequently, say disjunctivists, either they are able to explain Madeleine's case every bit as well as their opponents, or else their opponents simply beg the question against them. Either way, say disjunctivists, the objection fails.

Disjunctivism is one of several components that belong to hylomorphists' rejection of inner minds. Another important component concerns our knowledge of other people.

11.6 Direct Access, Pattern Recognition, and the Problem of Other Minds

Hylomorphists claim that we can directly perceive other people's thoughts, feelings, perceptions, and actions. They reject the idea that we can know about other people's mental states only by making inferences from bodily behavior, and, because of this, they argue that their theory does not face the problem of other minds that confronts many other mind–body theories (see Sections 1.5, 3.4, and 8.8).

The problem of other minds arises on account of two crucial assumptions. The first is the assumption that we cannot directly perceive other people's mental states, that our knowledge of their mental states depends on making inferences about those states based on bodily behavior. The second is the assumption that the same bodily movements and gestures can be correlated with many different kinds of mental states. Suppose these assumptions are true. According to the first, you can know about my mental states only by making inferences from my bodily behavior. You observe my gestures and movements, and then infer that these gestures and movements could correspond to feelings, desires, and other mental states. According to the second assumption, however, my gestures and movements might be due to a wide range of very different mental states. My grimace might be due to a genuine feeling of pain, for instance, but it might also be due to a desire to deceive you into believing that I am in pain. Because my movements and gestures do not provide decisive evidence that I am in this or that mental state, you have difficulty knowing what mental states I have. In fact, according to some exponents of the inner mind picture, you might have difficulty knowing whether I have any mental states at all. Many exponents of qualia, for instance, insist that qualia zombies are possible – that people could behave in exactly the ways they do while yet lacking phenomenal experiences altogether (Section 4.8). If this is in fact possible, then you cannot infer on the basis of my bodily movements and gestures that I am a conscious being at all.

So if both of the foregoing assumptions are true, if the same bodily behavior can be correlated with many different kinds of mental states, and our only access to other people's mental states is by inference from their bodily behavior, then there is a real problem knowing other people's mental states. If, however, either of the assumptions is false, then the problem disappears. If our knowledge of other people's mental states does not depend on making inferences from bodily behavior, but we are instead able to perceive their beliefs, desires, and pains directly, then the problem of other minds does not arise, and likewise, if the same bodily movements and gestures cannot be correlated with a broad range of different mental states, then the problem also does not arise: someone's movements and gestures provide strong evidence that he or she has a very particular set of

White	Black
1. Q x h8+	K x h8
2. Bf6+	Qg7
3. Re8++	

1. The white queen at b2 takes the rook at h8 – Check! The black king takes the queen.

2. The white bishop at e7 moves to f6 – Check! The black queen moves to g7.

3. The rook at e1 moves to e8 – Checkmate!

The checkmating pattern is not hidden from view; it lies in plain sight. Anyone with the ability to discern mating patterns can see it. According to hylomorphists, mental states are analogous to patterns on a chess board. They are directly observable by anyone who has the ability to discern them, and most normal humans do.

Figure 11.2   Patterns on a chess board

mental states. The falsity of either assumption, then, disposes of the problem, and, according to hylomorphists, both assumptions are false. They reject the first assumption on the grounds that we can directly perceive patterns in each other's behavior, and they reject the second assumption on the grounds that mental phenomena are essentially embodied. We will consider their rejection of the first assumption in this section, and their rejection of the second assumption in Section 11.9.

Hylomorphists claim that beliefs, desires, pains, and other mental phenomena are not occurrences in a hidden inner chamber; they are instead patterns of social and environmental interaction. We are thus able to know and recognize mental phenomena in something analogous to the way we know and recognize patterns on a chessboard or patterns in music. Consider, for instance, the checkmating pattern in Figure 11.2. The pattern is not hidden from view; it lies in plain sight: anyone who has learned to discern checkmating combinations can see it. Likewise, listeners do not infer that a piece of music has a melody; they perceive the melody directly. Chess playing and music appreciation are possible because people have the ability to discern patterns on the chessboard, and patterns in the sounds. According to hylomorphists, something analogous is true of mental phenomena.

Normal humans are equipped with the ability to recognize patterns in each other's behavior including thoughts, feelings, perceptions, and actions. Simple examples of our pattern-discerning abilities include our ability to discern other people's emotional states through facial and vocal expressions. The psychologist Paul Ekman and his colleagues have shown that normal humans have the ability to discern in each other's faces and voices emotional states such as anger, fear, enjoyment, sadness, disgust, and surprise, and that this ability transcends cultural boundaries – facial and vocal recognition of emotional states is a universal human trait.[8]

Another example involves our ability to discern other people's intentions. The psychologist Michael Tomasello and his colleagues have shown, for instance, that humans develop this ability as early as 9–12 months of age. In one experiment, psychologists studied how two different groups of infants went about imitating adult behavior.[9] Infants in the first group witnessed adults performing an activity aimed at achieving a goal and succeeding in achieving that goal. Infants in the second group witnessed adults performing a similar activity but failing to achieve the intended goal. Infants were then given the opportunity to imitate the activities they had observed. The study found that both groups of infants mimicked the goal-directed activities they had observed irrespective of whether or not the original adult performance had been successful. Infants in the second group did not try to replicate the failed performances they had witnessed; they tried instead to achieve the goal that the adults in the second group were trying but failing to achieve. Even though infants in the second group never witnessed the successful achievement of the goal, therefore, they were able to discern what the goal was. They were able to discern not mere bodily movements and gestures, but the intentions of the adults performing them. This type of pattern-recognition is not unique to humans, moreover. Other studies show that great apes such as chimpanzees have the ability to discern intentions as well.[10]

According to hylomorphists, empirical work like this supports the idea that normal humans are equipped to discern emotions, intentions, and other psychological patterns in each other's behavior. And this view, they say, provides resources for avoiding the problem of other minds.

Two further points are noteworthy regarding the hylomorphic approach to other minds. First, the hylomorphic approach implies that we can know that other people have mental states, and can know what mental states they have, but it does not imply that our knowledge of other people's mental states is infallible. The exercise of our psychological pattern-discerning abilities is subject to error in just the way the exercise of a chess player's pattern-discerning abilities is subject to error. A chess player might fail to see mating opportunities in particular cases, and so too, say hylomorphists, we might fail to recognize what people think or feel or do on particular occasions. Second, the hylomorphic approach implies that the knowledge each of us has of his or her own mental states is similarly limited and fallible. Not only can I fail to discern exactly what I believe or desire, but others might be able to discern what I believe or desire more accurately than I do. An analogy with chess is once again helpful: a chess master might be able to discern features of my board position more accurately than I myself can.

11.7   Psychological Language: Pattern Expression versus the Theory Model

The idea that humans have the ability to recognize psychological patterns in each other's behavior is the basis for the hylomorphic view of psychological language. Psychological language, say hylomorphists, is not like a theory; psychological predicates and terms do not postulate hypothetical entities that are supposed to explain directly observable bodily movements and gestures; psychological predicates and terms instead refer to or express directly observable patterns of social and environmental interaction. We see things, feel things, recognize and want them, strive for them, and because we are social animals we have evolved abilities to make our seeings, feelings, recognizings, and wantings known to others. Sometimes we make them known by movements, facial expressions, and vocal cues – "body language" in general. Other times we communicate them by means of symbols in a written or spoken language. According to hylomorphists, psychological language is a form of social behavior of this latter sort, a form that uses symbols to express the psychological patterns of social and environmental interaction in which we participate. We might call this a **pattern expression theory** of psychological language. Several remarks are in order about it.

First, a pattern expression theory of psychological language meshes with *usage-based* accounts of language learning endorsed by some psychologists and linguists. Exponents of usage-based linguistics argue that human children learn to speak a language through a process of interacting with other humans. They discern patterns in those interactions and then learn to use verbal expressions to refer to objects, properties, or events that figure prominently in them. The psychologist Michael Tomasello describes one usage-based account of language learning:

> [Word learning] emerges naturally from situations in which children are engaged in social interactions in which they are attempting to understand and interpret adult communicative intentions as expressed in utterances … [There are] two … aspects of the word learning process: (1) the structured social world into which children are born – full of scripts, routines, social games, and other patterned cultural interactions; and (2) children's … capacities for tuning into and participating in this structured social world – especially [capacities for] joint attention and intention-reading … [H]uman children are born into worlds in which their caregivers have certain activities to perform on a regular basis … Some of these routines are fairly constant across cultures (such as nursing) … Social interactional routines such as feeding … and a host of other activities constitute the formats – joint attentional frames – within which children acquire their earliest linguistic symbols … Learning the communicative significance of an individual word consists in the child first discerning the adult's overall communicative intention … and then identifying the specific functional role this word is playing in the communicative intention as a whole … [T]he shared intentional situation … constrains the interpretation of the speaker's

communicative intention … [C]hildren [thus] acquire linguistic symbols as a kind of by-product of social interaction with adults, in much the same way they learn many other cultural conventions.[11]

According to Tomasello, the interactive activities in which children and their adult caregivers engage provide contexts with items or features to which the children and adults can jointly attend. Because the number of items and features involved in these activities is limited, children are able to discern in the midst of participating in the activity what an adult intends to communicate when using a particular utterance. Children's abilities to participate in an activity with a caregiver and to discern the caregiver's intentions thus provide a basis for discerning what the caregiver's utterances mean. Children then learn to produce the utterances themselves by imitating what their caregivers say and do.

Consider how an account of language learning like Tomasello's might apply to the learning of a psychological expression. A mother and her small child are walking near some shrubbery when a cat unexpectedly jumps out from behind a bush and startles them. They jump back, their eyes widened, brows raised, lips stretched back toward their ears, their hearts race, and the child cries. "Did that scare you?" the mother says, as she picks up the child to comfort her. This episode provides a context in which the child learns to use the expression 'scared'. The child and her mother are both attending to a limited set of social, environmental, and physiological factors: the startling occurrence, the physiological responses to it, and social responses such as the facial expressions, the crying, and the mother's comforting reaction. These factors provide a background against which the child can discern what the mother is trying to communicate when she says 'scared'. Later the child imitates the utterance and the intention behind it, and comes gradually to master the utterance's use. Moreover, because the utterance is just one symbol in an overall system of symbols, it can be used in a broader variety of ways than the original, nonsymbolic expressions of human fear. The child can eventually use it to report fearful episodes ("I was scared"), to issue warnings ("That's scary"), or express anticipated fears ("I'm scared that it will hurt"). On this account of psychological language, then, our use of psychological predicates and terms builds on previously mastered forms of social and environmental interaction. In some cases, our use of a psychological predicate or term gives symbolic expression to a pattern of behavior like crying or grabbing – something in which we are already naturally competent to engage, and in other cases, our usage builds on previously mastered verbal skills in something analogous to the way our ability to solve quadratic equations builds on previously mastered arithmetic skills.

According to hylomorphists, then, psychological language is an extension of our natural emotional, perceptual, cognitive, and conative capacities. It is a form of symbol-using behavior that is grafted onto other forms of expressive behavior, and what we use these symbols to express are patterns of social and environmental interaction. Psychological language is not a theory: when we describe people's beliefs, desires, and other mental states we are not postulating hypothetical entities; we are referring to directly observable patterns in people's behavior. When I say, "Gabriel is locking the door because he's afraid he might get robbed by his neighbor," I am not postulating hypothetical entities to explain my observations of Gabriel's bodily movements and utterances. I am instead describing a directly observable pattern in Gabriel's behavior.

Importantly, hylomorphists claim that the patterns of social and environmental interaction we express with psychological predicates and terms involve more than the social, environmental, and physiological factors we initially use to define them. Emotions, for instance, involve more than just movements, facial expressions, and vocal cues; they also involve the operation of physiological substructures – cells in the limbic system of the brain, for instance. These substructures can only be discerned through scientific investigation; they do not factor into our initial pre-scientific conceptions of anger, fear, and sadness, but they are still included in those patterns of behavior. To understand this idea, consider the view of *natural kind terms* defended by philosophers like Saul Kripke and Hilary Putnam.

Natural kind terms include terms that refer to materials such as 'gold' and 'water', as well as the terms we use to refer to living things such as 'elm' and 'human'. We learn to use natural kind terms by applying them to paradigmatic cases. We learn to use the term 'water', for instance, by applying it to the stuff in this bottle, the stuff that comes out of that showerhead, that fills this lake, that falls in droplets from that cloud, and so on. These interactions *fix the reference* of the term 'water', as Kripke puts it; they determine which stuff in the environment the word 'water' refers to. In addition, some of the features we use to identify water in these interactions might factor into our initial conception of water – our initial understanding of what water is. We might take water, for instance, to be a colorless, odorless, tasteless liquid that we drink, that we bathe with, that fills rivers and lakes, that rains from clouds, and so on. Later on, when we study water scientifically, we might discover other properties it has – that it consists of hydrogen and oxygen atoms, say. Initially, however, what the term 'water' refers to and what our initial conception of water includes are determined by our pedestrian interactions with it.

According to hylomorphists, psychological expressions are defined in an analogous way. We learn what fear is, for instance, by interacting with the environment and the people around us. These interactions fix the references of psychological expressions such as 'fear', 'anger', and 'desire'. Moreover, just as water has properties that we cannot discern in our pedestrian dealings and that do not enter into our initial prescientific conception of 'water', the same is true of psychological patterns of behavior; they involve a broad range of conditions only some of which are apparent to us in our pedestrian dealings – facial expressions, gestures, and vocal cues, together with environmental triggers and social responses.

The analogy with water is also helpful for understanding how, on the hylomorphic view, we can sometimes be in error when describing people's mental states.

We identify water in our pedestrian dealings by appeal to a narrow profile of water's properties, such as the way it looks and tastes to us. As a result, we can mistakenly judge that some other substance is water if it looks and tastes to us like water. Imagine a substance like XYZ in the Twin Earth thought experiment discussed earlier (Section 11.3) – a substance different from water that is nevertheless indistinguishable from it under pedestrian circumstances. Because XYZ looks and tastes like water, because it resembles water in respect of the properties we typically use to identify water, we are liable to misidentifying glasses of XYZ as glasses of water. Something analogous is true of mental states on the hylomorphic view. Because there is more to an emotion, say, than the facial gestures, vocal cues, and other factors we initially use to identify that emotion in our pedestrian dealings, we are liable to misidentifying people's emotional states. Consider likewise patterns of rational behavior such as Gabriel locking the door (Section 11.1). If Gabriel is a pathological individual who delights in deceiving people for its own sake, then his movements and utterances might lead me to mistake his will to deceive for a fear of being robbed.

Finally, the analogy with water is helpful for understanding another point: why on the hylomorphic view we cannot always be wrong about what mental states other people have. Misjudging that something is water depends on being able to identify features typically associated with water. When I judge that the liquid in the glass is water, I am identifying and responding to certain features the liquid has such as its look and taste. If a liquid looks like water, and tastes like water, I judge that it is water. Importantly I identify and respond to the liquid's look and taste both when my judgment is accurate and when it is inaccurate – both when the liquid really is water and when the liquid is something else. In both cases, my judgment is based on a prior ability to identify and respond to the features associated with water. Something analogous is true of mental states on the hylomorphic view. Consider an example.

Paul Ekman and his colleagues have shown that the movements, facial expressions, and vocal cues associated with emotions follow stereotypical patterns that occur involuntarily when people experience those emotions, and that are very difficult to produce voluntarily when they do not experience them. The *orbicularis oculi* muscle surrounding the eye, for instance, contracts involuntarily when people experience enjoyment, and only a small number of people (around 10 percent, according to Ekman) can contract it voluntarily at all. Actors who look convincingly as if they are enjoying themselves might belong to the small group who can contract the muscle voluntarily, but more likely, says Ekman, they are remembering something enjoyable, and the remembered emotion then produces the involuntary muscular contraction.[12] Something analogous is true of other mental states. Gabriel's fear of being robbed by his neighbor might be expressed in a number of different ways – locking the door on short trips, setting up a security camera in his apartment, saying, "I'm afraid my neighbor will rob me," feeling uncomfortable at the prospect of leaving his apartment unlocked. But as in the case of emotion, there are limits on the variability of fear behavior. If Gabriel never locked his door on short trips, never took security precautions of other sorts, denied that he was afraid of being robbed by his neighbor, never felt uncomfortable with the idea of leaving his apartment unlocked, it would be doubtful that he really was afraid of being robbed by his neighbor. It is only because human psychological behavior follows regular patterns like these that there is a possibility of misidentifying what mental states people have.

When I judge that Eleanor is experiencing enjoyment, I am identifying and responding to certain features of her behavior – the contraction of the *orbicularis oculi* muscle, for instance. Eleanor's face looks a certain way, and hence I judge that she is experiencing enjoyment. I identify and respond to that look both when my judgment is accurate and when it is inaccurate – both when Eleanor really is experiencing enjoyment and when she is convincingly feigning it. In both cases, my judgment is based on a prior ability to identify and respond to the features associated with enjoyment. Likewise, when I judge that Gabriel is afraid of being robbed, I am identifying and responding to features of his behavior such as his assertion that he is afraid of being robbed. His behavior looks and sounds a certain way, and on the basis of the way it looks and sounds I judge that he is afraid of being robbed. I identify and respond to these features of Gabriel's behavior both when my judgment is accurate and when it is inaccurate. Making erroneous judgments about what mental states people have depends on the prior ability to identify and respond to the features typically associated with those mental states.

The upshot, say hylomorphists, is that we can be wrong about people's mental states some of the time, but we cannot be wrong about people's mental states all of the time. If that were the case, if there were no social, environmental, or physiological features typically associated with this or that mental state, or if we were not able to identify and respond to those features, then we would not be able to make judgments about other people's mental states at all, rightly or wrongly. The possibility of us being wrong about other people's mental states some of the time depends on us being right about other people's mental states most of the time. According to hylomorphists, this is a further reason to think there can be no real problem of other minds. We must have a reliable source of information about other people's mental states in order to be in error about what mental states other people have.

11.8   Hylomorphism versus Behaviorism

Before discussing other aspects of a hylomorphic theory of mind, it is important to prevent a potential misunderstanding. Several features of a hylomorphic theory of mind are liable to remind readers of behaviorism (Chapter 5). Both theories, for instance, reject aspects of the inner mind picture. Both claim that mental states are in some sense patterns of behavior, both claim that these patterns are directly observable under pedestrian circumstances, and both deny that mental states are hypothetical postulates of a prescientific theory. Despite these similarities, however, hylomorphism and behaviorism are very different theories.

First, hylomorphists reject physicalism, behaviorists do not. A commitment to physicalism is in fact part of what motivates behaviorists to analyze psychological expressions as abbreviated physical descriptions of actual and potential behavior. Hylomorphists, by contrast, reject physicalism as part of their broader commitment to structures in nature (Section 10.6).

Second, hylomorphists do not conceive of behavior as narrowly as behaviorists do. Behaviorists tend to conceive of behavior in terms of bodily movements or utterances – something that can be given an exhaustive description by physics and that is observable under pedestrian circumstances. According to hylomorphists, however, behavior comprises more than this. Thoughts, feelings, perceptions, and actions all involve social and environmental factors in addition to physiological ones. Hylomorphists thus deny the possibility of analyzing psychological predicates and terms into longer descriptions of actual and potential bodily movements and states. Psychological language instead describes distinctive patterns of social and environmental interaction – structures that cannot be analyzed or reduced to unstructured bodily movements, physiological states or dispositions.

Third, the hylomorphic account of psychological language is not the same as the behaviorist account. Behaviorists claim that psychological expressions operate like abbreviations. Hylomorphists, by contrast, claim that psychological expressions operate like natural kind terms.

Hylomorphists are not completely unsympathetic to some of the claims behaviorists make. According to hylomorphists, behaviorists see correctly that psychological expressions imply bodily conditions, and they see correctly that human patterns of social and environmental interaction are complex enough that we can only describe some of them using contrary-to-fact hypotheticals such as, "If the child were to ask the father for the candy, then the father would probably give the candy to the child." But, say hylomorphists, from these observations behaviorists draw the wrong conclusion; they conclude falsely that psychological predicates and terms are abbreviations for more complex physical descriptions of bodily movements and states instead of seeing that psychological predicates and terms express broad patterns of social and environmental interaction into which bodily movements and states are integrated. The bodily movements and states that constitute what behaviorists think of as behavior represent only one of several types of conditions involved in patterns of behavior as hylomorphists conceive of them.

11.9 Embodiment

A hylomorphic theory of mind is also committed to a particular view of **embodiment**. According to hylomorphists, human psychological capacities are essentially embodied; they cannot be defined without reference to the particular bodily parts humans possess. Consider by analogy animals' locomotive capacities: flagellation, ciliation, amoeboid motion, swimming by paddling, bipedalism, brachiation, flying, and so on. We cannot define any of these modes of animal movement without making reference to the bodily parts involved in their occurrence. Moving by ciliation requires cilia. Swimming by caudal movement requires a tail. Walking bipedally requires two feet. Moving by brachiation (swinging by the arms) requires arms. The same is true of reproductive and perceptual activities. Seeing, hearing, tasting, having sexual intercourse – none of these activities can be defined without reference to very specific bodily parts.

According to hylomorphists, our capacities to think and feel are analogous to our capacities to move ourselves, reproduce, and perceive the environment; they cannot be defined apart from specific bodily parts positioned or moved or operated in very specific ways. Consider again the example of emotions. They involve specific kinds of movements, facial expressions, and vocal cues that enable us to discern when someone is experiencing anger, fear, enjoyment, or sadness. As we saw in Section 11.7, hylomorphists claim that these movements, expressions, and cues are among the conditions that enable us to fix the references of emotion words such as 'fear' and 'enjoyment'. Something analogous is true, they say, of more complex patterns of behavior such as those involved in Gabriel fearing his neighbor will rob him: locking the door on short trips, installing security cameras, saying, "I am afraid of being robbed by my neighbor," feeling uncomfortable with leaving the apartment unlocked – these are the kinds of conditions that define the kind of fear Gabriel has, and each involves human bodily parts positioned, moved, or operated in very particular ways.

According to hylomorphists, then, psychological predicates and terms are analogous to the predicates and terms we use to describe the ways organisms move themselves or reproduce or perceive aspects of their environments. Just as something like a smile cannot be defined without reference to a mouth, human psychological capacities cannot be defined without reference to human bodily parts. This view of human psychological capacities has several important implications.

First, it suggests yet another response to the problem of other minds (Section 11.4). Recall that the problem of other minds depends on two assumptions: the assumption that we only infer what mental states other people have on the basis of their bodily movements and gestures, and the assumption that the same bodily movements and gestures can be correlated with many different kinds of mental states. We have already seen that hylomorphists reject the first assumption; they claim that we can directly discern patterns in each other's behavior. They also reject the second: they claim that there are constraints on how human patterns of social and environmental interaction are embodied. Examples of these constraints include the involuntary contraction of the *orbicularis oculi* muscle during enjoyment, or the kinds of actions and utterances involved in being afraid of robbery. If there are constraints on embodiment of this sort, then mental states and physical states cannot vary in relation to each other as much as the problem of other minds assumes.

Second, the hylomorphic view of embodiment implies a rejection of the neutrality thesis. The neutrality thesis, recall, is the claim that the definitions of mental states do not imply anything about what mental states are or whether their occurrence must be correlated with certain physical states. Functionalism is perhaps the clearest expression of this idea (Section 6.3). According to functionalists, the mental states of a system are defined abstractly as the internal states that correlate inputs to it with outputs from it in ways that correspond to a functional description, a description that does not specify what the natures of the inputs, outputs, and internal correlational states are, and that does not imply that they must be realized in materials of any specific type. If hylomorphists are right, and human psychological capacities are essentially embodied, then views like functionalism must be false. And recall that the idea that human psychological capacities are essentially embodied was the basis of the embodied mind objection to functionalism (Section 6.9).

Third, the hylomorphic view of embodiment and psychological language has important implications for how hylomorphists understand multiple realizability (Section 6.1). Multiple realizability, recall, is the idea that a given type of mental state, such as pain, can be correlated with states of many different types – physical states such as those of a human brain, a Martian gamma organ, or complex silicon chip, and perhaps even nonphysical states such as those of a nonphysical Cartesian mind. Functionalists have an easy time accommodating multiple realizability. If mental states are abstractly defined by inputs and outputs, as functionalists claim, then as long as a system correlates inputs with outputs in accordance with the right kind of abstract functional description, that system has mental states. But if mental states are not abstractly defined, if in particular they cannot be defined apart from human bodily parts, as hylomorphists insist, then how can hylomorphists accommodate the idea of multiple realizability?

Hylomorphists agree that we can use psychological predicates and terms to describe and explain the behavior of familiar nonhuman animals such as dogs and cats. They can also admit that we can conceive of using those predicates and terms to describe and explain the behavior of alien species and perhaps even complex robotic systems. According to hylomorphists, however, we can extend the use of our human-defined psychological predicates and terms to nonhuman things not because psychological capacities are abstractly defined, but because we are able to draw analogies between the behavior of nonhuman things and our own. Consider by analogy the way we use the term 'punch' to describe the activity of someone with a prosthetic limb even though punching cannot be performed without a hand oriented and moved in a specific kind of way. We are able to apply our hand-defined term to something other than a hand by drawing an analogy between the prosthetic limb and the real limb it was designed to replace. According to hylomorphists, something analogous is true of the way we apply psychological predicates and terms to nonhuman things.

Familiar nonhuman animals such as dogs and cats, for instance, have body plans and functional parts similar to our own – heads, eyes, noses, mouths. These body plans make it easy for us to discern patterns in their behavior that are similar to the patterns in ours, and these similarities enable us to describe and explain their behavior using predicates and terms such as 'eats', 'sleeps', 'sees', 'believes', and 'wants'.[13] For similar reasons it is conceivable that we might encounter alien species or even complex robotic systems whose behavioral patterns are similar enough to our own that we could apply psychological predicates and terms to them as well. We could even conceive of applying them to alien species that differ from us radically in terms of their overall body plans and functional parts. Consider, for instance, a movie like *The Blob* in which we are invited to describe and explain the behavior of the blob-like creature psychologically. Even though its body plan is very different from ours, the filmmakers include enough scenes displaying how it behaves to enable us to discern human-like patterns of desire or intention. If we were to encounter blob-like creatures in reality, and were able to observe enough of their behavior to discern behavioral patterns similar to those of humans, then we might also be able to apply psychological predicates and terms to them.

There are nevertheless limits on how far we can extend our use of psychological predicates and terms, say hylomorphists. We can describe and explain something's behavior psychologically only if we can discern patterns of social and environmental interaction in that behavior that resemble a human's. A completely nonphysical being, however, would not engage in behaviors in which we could discern any patterns at all. Trying to discern patterns of social and environmental interaction in its behavior would be like trying to discern a chess player's position on a board with invisible pieces. Consequently, say hylomorphists, although it might be conceivable that there could be nonphysical beings, we would never be able to describe and explain their behavior psychologically, for unless a nonphysical being were equipped for the kinds of social and environmental interactions in which humans engage – interactions that require the kinds of bodily parts humans possess – that being could not engage in any behavior in which we would be able to discern a psychological pattern of behavior. Hylomorphists thus deny that we can apply psychological predicates and terms to disembodied beings such as nonphysical Cartesian minds.

One implication of a hylomorphic theory of mind, then, is that substance dualism is not merely false but incoherent; there could not be a disembodied psychological being of the sort substance dualists claim that we are. The only reason substance dualism does not seem incoherent to substance dualists, say hylomorphists, is that they equivocate on psychological predicates and terms; they invent (perhaps unwittingly) abstract definitions for psychological capacities – definitions that ignore the conditions of human embodiment – and use psychological predicates and terms in accordance with these abstract definitions. We are capable of inventing abstract definitions for just about anything. We can, for instance, invent a definition according to which anger is simply a state that correlates inputs with outputs, or a definition of reproduction according to which it is simply a process whereby individuals of a certain kind produce other things of that kind. According to hylomorphists, however, if we define anger and reproduction in these ways, the terms 'anger' and 'reproduction' will lose some of the content they have in our everyday discourse, and, as a result, the invented terms will be of limited usefulness for describing and explaining the behavior of real things. The vocabulary we really use to describe and explain human behavior is tied to the conditions of human embodiment – conditions that a nonphysical being could never satisfy.

In short, then, hylomorphists claim that psychological predicates and terms are of a piece with the predicates and terms we use to describe and explain human movement, perception, and reproduction – all represent patterns of behavior that cannot be defined apart from the specific bodily parts humans possess. Because of this our psychological predicates and terms apply in the first place to concrete human behavior embodied in specifically human bodily structures. If and when we extend our use of these predicates and terms to nonhuman things we do so by drawing analogies between their behavior and ours.

11.10 Hylomorphism and the Mental–Physical Dichotomy

The hylomorphic view of embodiment also has implications for how hylomorphists understand the mental–physical dichotomy. Because thoughts, feelings, perceptions, and actions are essentially embodied, say hylomorphists, they cannot be reckoned nonphysical phenomena. Conversely, say hylomorphists, if fundamental physical occurrences contribute to psychological patterns of behavior – if they are structured psychologically – those fundamental physical events cannot be reckoned nonpsychological. When an electron contributes to depolarizing one of my neural membranes, that event is part of a psychological pattern of behavior; it is also a physical event, one that can be described and explained by physics. According to hylomorphists, physics contributes to a description and explanation of what psychological phenomena are in something analogous to the way it contributes to a description and explanation of what a good piano is. Because a piano has both a structure and materials that are structured, descriptions and explanations of both must be included in an account of what a good piano is. Similarly, because thoughts, feelings, perceptions, and actions have both structures and subactivities that are structured, descriptions and explanations of both must factor into accounts of what they are. Higher-level human activities, and the substructures and subactivities they comprise, all count as social, psychological, biological, and also physical phenomena.

On the hylomorphic view, then, human beings are psychophysical wholes, and our ordinary psychological vocabulary comprises predicates and terms that are tailor-made for describing and explaining the capacities humans possess and the activities in which they engage. When we do draw distinctions among our descriptions and explanations of human behavior, it is on the basis of structures and substructures. By identifying substructures that can exist independently of their incorporation into structured individuals and behaviors, for instance, we can draw distinctions among various branches of biology, psychology, chemistry, and physics. But biological, psychological, chemical, and physical phenomena do not exist in separation in real human behavior. In real human behavior they together constitute a single psychophysical zone of activity. Because real human behavior comprises all of these structural levels, a complete account of human thoughts, feelings, perceptions, and actions would require a description and explanation of all of the levels of organization humans comprise. Usually, however, we are not concerned with giving a complete account of human behavior. Usually, say hylomorphists, we pick out the levels and factors we are interested in and focus on those to the exclusion of others. Consider again the analogy with the car crash: the balding tires, the faulty brake mechanism, the inadequate roadway grading, and the driver's blood-alcohol level all contributed to the crash. A complete account of why the crash occurred would thus have to consider all these factors. In particular contexts, however, we usually select one or two of them: the automotive engineer focuses on the brake mechanism, for instance, the civil engineer on the roadway grading, the prosecutor on the blood-alcohol level, and so on. According to hylomorphists, the same is true of human behavior. A complete account of a simple action such as reaching for a glass of water would have to consider the range of social and environmental factors, and the subactivities and subsystems that contribute to its performance. In most contexts, however, we are not concerned with giving a complete account of that behavior; we instead have a limited set of descriptive and explanatory interests in mind, and focus on a limited set of contributing factors. This picture of explanation has important implications for the way hylomorphists approach the problem of mental causation.

11.11   Hylomorphism and the Problem of Mental Causation

Recall the problem of mental causation facing emergentists (Section 8.11). The following claims seem jointly inconsistent, yet it is difficult to see which claim emergentists should reject:

1   Actions have mental causes.
2   Actions have physical causes.

3   Mental causes and physical causes are distinct.
4   An action does not have more than one cause.

Emergentists cannot reject (1), the claim rejected by eliminative physicalists and epiphenomenalists, nor can they reject (3), the claim rejected by reductive physicalists. Yet Claim (2) appears to commit them to violating physical laws and the causal closure of the physical domain, and rejecting Claim (4) appears to commit them to the overdetermination of actions, an awkward result.

Hylomorphists initially seem to be in the same boat as emergentists. Because they endorse the existence of emergent properties with the features described in Section 10.2, they cannot reject (1) as eliminativists and epiphenomenalists do, nor can they reject (3) as reductivists do. Unlike emergentists, moreover, they cannot reject (2) since they are committed to the idea that higher-level behavior never violates lower-level physical laws. Are they committed, therefore, to rejecting (4), and accepting the overdetermination of actions with all its awkward consequences? No, say hylomorphists, they are not. The reason, they argue, is that claims (1)–(4) are not really inconsistent. They only seem to be inconsistent because there is an equivocation on the term 'cause'. Once that equivocation is recognized, they say, we will see either that all four claims are true but consistent, or else that one of the claims is false but its falsity does not have the awkward consequences it is alleged to have.

The hylomorphic solution to the problem is based on hylomorphism's commitment to causal pluralism (Section 10.7). Hylomorphism claims that there are many different kinds of causes and many different kinds of causal relations. Suppose, then, say hylomorphists, that mental states cause actions in one kind of way – they *rationalize* actions, let us say – and that physical events such as events in the nervous system cause actions in a different kind of way – they *trigger* the muscular subsystems involved in actions. In that case, claims (1), (2), and (3) would have to be rewritten as follows:

1*   Actions are rationalized by beliefs, desires, and other mental states.
2*   Muscular contractions are triggered by events in the nervous system.
3*   Rationalizing causes and triggers are distinct.

Hylomorphists can endorse all three of these claims. What do they make of Claim (4), the claim that rules out an action having multiple causes? Given the distinction between triggering and rationalizing causes, hylomorphists claim that (4) can be rewritten in either of the following ways:

(4*)   An action does not have more than one rationalizing cause.
(4**)   An action does not have more than one trigger.

Hylomorphists are free to endorse both of these claims, and they are also free to reject them. Either way, they argue, they succeed in solving the problem. If they endorse both claims, then they succeed in solving the problem of mental causation since (4*) and (4**) are both consistent with (1*), (2*), and (3*). If, on the other hand, they reject one of the claims, then they still succeed in solving the problem of mental causation since the denial of (4*) and the denial of (4**) are both consistent with (1*)–(3*). So whether they endorse (4*) and (4**) or reject them, say hylomorphists, they solve the problem either way.

This solution to the problem of mental causation nevertheless depends on the distinction between two kinds of causes and causal relations: rationalizing causes versus triggers. Why should we suppose these two kinds of causes and causal relations really exist? According to hylomorphists, their existence is an empirical matter of fact. In fact, they say, we explain things by appeal to causes and causal relations of both sorts. Consider again the example from Section 10.7.

Cecilia is waiting anxiously for Madeleine to come downstairs so they can leave in time for an appointment. When informed that Madeleine is reading a book, Cecilia asks, "Why is Madeleine reading (in contrast to hurrying down the stairs)?" and receives the following response:

A1   Madeleine is reading (in contrast to hurrying down the stairs) because light reflected off the pages of the book is striking Madeleine's retinas, and the muscles in her eyes are moving in such-and-such ways, and such-and-such neurons are firing in her cortex.

A response along these lines is clearly irrelevant to Cecilia's question. What Cecilia wants is a response that rationalizes Madeleine's behavior, that locates it within a broader pattern of reasons, as the following response does:

A2   Madeleine is reading (in contrast to hurrying down the stairs) because she thinks finishing the chapter is more important than being on time.

If, on the other hand, neuroscientists are concerned with the physiological mechanisms that enable Madeleine to read, then they might find a response such as (A1) relevant since they are not interested in the rational structure of Madeleine's behavior in that case, but in the physiological substructures that enable her to engage in the activities she does.

Madeleine's behavior can be given both a rationalizing explanation, then, and a mechanistic explanation. The former appeals to reasons: beliefs, desires, and other mental states; the latter appeals to triggers. These reasons and triggers, moreover, explain their effects in different ways. They answer requests for different kinds of information. Since our actual descriptive and explanatory practices appeal to causes and causal relations of both sorts, say hylomorphists, we have good reason to think there are causes and causal relations of both sorts. At the very least, they argue, if there are not causes and causal relations of both sorts, the burden of proof is on others to show it.

This solution to the problem of mental causation seems very attractive, but it has its critics. Consider two objections to it. First, critics argue that the alleged solution is no solution at all. Hylomorphists distinguish rationalizing causes from triggers, but in that case, say critics, it is possible to reformulate the original problem. Suppose, for instance, that your act of reaching for a bottle of water is rationalized by a desire and is also triggered by an event in your nervous system. In that case, it looks like your action is overdetermined – not by two rationalizing causes or by two triggers, but by the one rationalizing cause together with the one trigger. If hylomorphists want to avoid the awkward implications of overdetermination, therefore, they must either reject the existence of the rationalizing cause, or else reject the existence of the triggering cause. In the former case, however, the hylomorphic solution collapses into a form of epiphenomenalism, and in the latter case it ends up endorsing the violation of physical laws the way some emergentist theories do.

Hylomorphists do nevertheless have a response to this objection. They argue that it is based on two false assumptions. First, they say, it assumes that actions are the sorts of things that could be triggered by physical causes. What (2*) says, however, is not that actions have neural triggers, but that muscular contractions do. Critics, by contrast, endorse the following claim instead:

2?   Actions are triggered by events in the nervous system.

Hylomorphists argue that this claim is false. Actions, they say, have rational structures; triggers, on the other hand, are causes at a lower level of organization; they need not fit into higher-level patterns of reasons. If, for instance, a neuroscientist triggered muscular contractions in your arm using an electrode, and caused your hand to grasp a knife and stab someone, you would not rightly incur moral or legal blame. The reason is that your limb movements would not count as an action, something you chose to perform in light of certain reasons. This understanding of actions and triggers has been borne out in real cases of neural manipulation. Consider the neurosurgeon Wilder Penfield's observations:

> When I have caused a conscious patient to move his hand by applying an electrode to the motor cortex of one hemisphere, I have often asked him about it. Invariably his response was: "I didn't do that. You did." When I caused him to vocalize, he said: "I didn't make that sound. You pulled it out of me." ... The electrode ... can cause him to turn head and eyes, or to move the limbs, or to vocalize and swallow ... But he remains aloof.[14]

The same point comes out in another way, say hylomorphists. Actions involve not only reasons, but social and environmental factors as well. Triggers, however, do not depend on social and environmental factors in the same way. We considered examples that illustrated this point in sections 11.3 and 11.5. The mad neuroscientist can manipulate Eleanor's nervous system to produce neural states and muscular contractions that are indistinguishable from the neural states and muscular contractions of someone playing basketball. Without a ball, however, Eleanor is not playing basketball. Actions might involve bodily movements and other physiological states as subactivities, say hylomorphists, and, because of that, triggers do factor into a complete explanation of human action. But a complete explanation of human action involves more than just the triggers of bodily movement; it involves rational, social, and environmental factors as well, and because of that actions are not the sorts of events that can be triggered the way muscular contractions can.

Second, say hylomorphists, the objection is committed to the idea that mental causes and physical causes compete to occupy a single role – the role of being the one and only cause of the action. An assumption like this has been the basis of many problems and arguments in philosophy of mind including, for instance, Kim's exclusion argument (Section 6.10), and Eddington's problem with the two tables (Section 1.3). Recall that Eddington's problem pitted the scientific description of the table against the commonsense, prescientific one. Only one, he suggested, can lay claim to describing the real table; only one, in other words, can fill the descriptive role labeled 'real'. Consequently, if we accept the description offered by science, we must reject the description offered by common sense, and if we accept the description offered by common sense, we must reject the description offered by science. The problem is that we do not want to reject either description, and we have good reason to think both are true. The objection makes a similar assumption about rationalizing causes and triggers, say hylomorphists. According to critics, rationalizing causes and triggers compete to occupy a single explanatory role, the role of being the one and only cause of an action. Because of this assumption, critics of hylomorphism conclude that hylomorphists are forced either to deny that the rationalizing cause occupies that role, or to deny that the triggering cause occupies that role, or else to accept the absurd idea that the causes occupy that role together.

Hylomorphists argue in response that there is not a single causal role that rationalizing causes and triggers compete to occupy. Actions, they say, are complex multistructure phenomena; each comprises many levels of structural complexity with many different causal factors. Consequently, a complete explanation of an action would require a consideration of a range of social and environmental factors as well as subactivities and substructures at every level with causes at each level contributing to an explanation of the action in different ways. Cecilia, for instance, is interested in the rational structure of Madeleine's behavior, while the neuroscientists are interested in the neural substructures that enable that behavior to occur. Because these causes contribute to Madeleine's behavior in different ways, they do not compete to occupy a single explanatory role; they instead play different noncompeting roles in our explanations of a complex phenomenon. Triggers are causes that operate a level of organization lower than the level at which reasons operate. According to hylomorphists, then, the objection to their solution fails to recognize that there are many different kinds of causal factors and causal relations, and that actions are complex multistructure phenomena that comprise many different kinds of causes and causal relations.

Consider now a second objection to the hylomorphic solution. Like the first objection, it claims that the hylomorphic solution is no solution at all. Hylomorphists are forced to deny that rationalizing causes exercise any real control or influence over human behavior, says the objection. The reason, it says, is that the features something has are determined by the features of its parts. Your features, for instance, including your psychological features are determined by the features of your organic parts such as your brain; the features of your brain, moreover, are determined by the features of the molecules that compose it, and their features are determined by the atoms that compose them, and so on. Ultimately, then, say exponents of the objection, the features of everything are determined by the features of fundamental physical particles since these are the basic constituents of everything. Consider what implications this has for the hylomorphic view. If everything that happens is determined by what happens at a fundamental physical level, then beliefs, desires, and other mental states do not really contribute to an explanation of what people do; the real explanation for human behavior and for everything else is given by fundamental physics. And if that is the case, then beliefs, desires, and other mental states might rationalize actions, as hylomorphists claim, but rationalizations do not have any real causal importance since they do not have any real explanatory importance, and on a hylomorphic view, causes are explanatory factors.

Hylomorphists argue in response that this objection, like the first, is based on two false assumptions. The first assumption is that higher-level and lower-level causes – reasons and triggers, for instance – compete to occupy a single causal role. Exponents of the objection suppose that higher-level and lower-level causes would have to explain their effects in the same ways, and, because of that, they think that higher- and lower-level causes would either have to exclude each other from occupying a single causal role – the role of being the one and only cause of higher-level behavior – or else they would have to share that role and be redundant overdetermining causes of higher-level behavior. We have already seen that hylomorphists reject this understanding of causes and causal relations in favor of causal pluralism, and that they take their causal pluralism to be grounded in our best empirical explanations of why and how things operate as they do. Hylomorphists thus challenge their opponents to show that that the empirical data do not support the hylomorphic view.

The objection's second assumption is that something's properties are determined by the properties of its parts. Let us call this the *lower-level determination thesis*. Determination is a type of necessitation relation. Roughly, if X-things determine Y-things, then the existence of an X-thing results in the existence of a Y-thing, and the existence of that X-thing explains the existence of the Y-thing. According to exponents of the lower-level determination thesis, for instance, if Alexander is composed of certain lower-level components with lower-level properties $F_1, \ldots F_n$, then Alexander is guaranteed to have certain higher-level properties precisely because his lower-level components have properties F_1, ... F_n. Because all of Alexander's properties are explained by lower-level conditions on this view, its exponents think that it undermines the explanatory status of higher-level properties.

Hylomorphists nevertheless argue that the lower-level determination thesis is false. At the very least, they say, the burden of proof is on exponents of lower-level determination to prove that the thesis is true. It might be plausible to endorse something like the lower-level determination thesis when it comes to what we called earlier *aggregative properties* such as mass (Section 10.2). It is plausible to suppose that, for instance, an organism's mass is determined by the masses of its fundamental physical constituents. But not all properties are like this, say hylomorphists. Some properties depend not just on the particles or materials that compose a thing, but on the way those particles or materials are structured or organized, and this is a claim, say hylomorphists, that is based on our best empirical descriptions and explanations of living behavior. Consequently, if critics of hylomorphism want to reject this claim in favor of lower-level determination, the burden of proof is on them to show that it is false. Consider likewise the arguments for externalism discussed in Section 11.3. They suggest that actions, perceptions, and thoughts are not determined by the physical states of an individual organism – by, say, the properties of its parts – since thinking, perceiving, and acting depend on social and environmental conditions in addition to physiological ones. Gabriel and Xavier might be physically indistinguishable from each other – they might have all the same physical properties – and yet differ from each other mentally. Arguments for externalism thus suggest that the lower-level determination thesis described above is false, that exponents of lower-level determination must take into account not only an organism's parts, but the lower-level conditions that constitute its environment as well.

In response, exponents of lower-level determination could say two things. First, they could expand the lower-level determination thesis to include the lower-level conditions that constitute an organism's environment. Second, in defense of lower-level determination, they could appeal to the notion of supervenience (Section 6.11). Supervenience, recall, is a kind of dependence relation. To say that M-properties supervene on P-properties is to say that things cannot differ in their M-properties without also differing in their P-properties, or equivalently, if two things have the same P-properties, they must also have the same M-properties. Many aesthetic properties, for instance, supervene on physical properties. If Painting A is physically indistinguishable from Painting B, then it is impossible for one to be beautiful and the other ugly, or for one to be well proportioned and the other poorly proportioned. If aesthetic properties supervene on physical properties, then physical twins must be aesthetic twins; any aesthetic differences between Painting A and Painting B must be traceable to physical differences between them.

According to many philosophers, not just physicalists, it is plausible to suppose that higher-level properties supervene in some sense on lower-level properties. If two things have the same physical properties they must also have the same mental properties; any mental difference must be traceable to some type of physical difference. But the best explanation for higher-level properties supervening on lower-level properties, say exponents of lower-level determination, is that higher-level properties are determined by lower-level properties. If higher-level conditions are determined by lower-level conditions, then indistinguishable lower-level conditions will yield indistinguishable higher-level ones. Physical twins are guaranteed to be mental twins, for instance. Hence, say exponents of lower-level determination, there is good reason to believe that the lower-level determination thesis is true.

Hylomorphists say two things in response to this argument. First, they argue that hylomorphism is compatible with a broad variety of supervenience relations. Hylomorphists are free to claim, for instance, that mental differences depend on broader social and environmental differences, and that social and environmental differences depend on lower-level physical differences. As a result, hylomorphists are free to claim that mental differences depend on lower-level physical differences – that mental properties supervene on physical properties. Consider an example. Imagine two scenarios: In Scenario A, Alexander believes that there are eight planets in our solar system, and in Scenario B, he believes that there are nine. Hylomorphists are free to claim that this mental difference depends on some social or environmental difference in the two circumstances. It is plausible to suppose, for instance, that differences in beliefs about the planets depend on receiving a certain kind of education, and so Alexander's belief in Scenario A must be due to something in his education (a college lecture on astronomy, say), that is missing from Scenario B. Hylomorphists are also free to claim that this social and environmental difference depends on lower-level physical differences. If the lecture occurs in Scenario A but not in Scenario B, then in one scenario but not the other, the speaker's utterances will vibrate the air molecules that eventually impinge on Alexander's eardrums. Without some sort of lower-level physical differences between the two scenarios, there could not be social and environmental differences, and without these social and environmental differences, there could not be any mental differences. Hylomorphists are free to claim, therefore, that mental differences depend on lower-level physical differences; that mental properties, and higher-level properties in general, supervene on lower-level physical properties. But if that is the case, then a mere commitment to supervenience does not pose a problem for hylomorphists.

Second, because they can accommodate supervenience relations, hylomorphists challenge the claim that lower-level determination provides the best explanation for them. Exponents of lower-level determination provide one kind of explanation for supervenience relations, but hylomorphists provide another. Higher-level conditions are not determined by lower-level conditions, they say, higher-level conditions merely depend on lower-level conditions, and different higher-level conditions depend on different lower-level ones. Having a belief that there are eight planets, for instance, requires lower-level conditions different from having a belief that there are nine. Consequently, Alexander's beliefs about the number of planets cannot differ in Scenarios A and B unless those scenarios differ physically. It is by no means obvious that this is a weaker explanation for supervenience than lower-level determination. At the very least, then, exponents of lower-level determination must show that their explanation is superior in order to support this part of their objection.

11.12   Hylomorphism and the Problem of Psychophysical Emergence

Hylomorphists argue that their view also solves the problem of psychophysical emergence. Beliefs, desires, pains, and other mental phenomena are behavioral structures, they say. Structures, however, do not emerge out of unstructured materials. A piano, for instance, does not emerge out of wood and metal; rather, someone imposes a structure on wood and metal in order to make a piano. According to hylomorphists, brains do not generate thoughts, feelings, and actions any more than wood and metal generate pianos. Mental phenomena are not causal byproducts of lower-level neural processes; they are rather patterns of social and environmental interaction that include lower-level phenomena – ways in which lower-level neural processes can be structured or organized.

If this is what mental phenomena are, if they are patterns of social and environmental interaction – ways in which physiological occurrences can be structured – then the problem of emergence never even arises. It makes no sense to ask for an explanation of how it is possible for physiological occurrences to produce mental phenomena if physiological occurrences do not produce mental phenomena in fact. It is legitimate to request an explanation of how it is possible that p only if it is true that p. Consider an analogy. Imagine someone argued as follows: "Your theory of the weather explains why it rains by appeal to the water cycle: evaporation, condensation, and precipitation. But your theory must be false since it fails to explain how it is possible for Zeus to produce rain." This objection is flawed not because its premise is false. In fact, its premise is true: the water-cycle theory does not explain how it is possible for Zeus to produce rain. The objection is flawed because failing to explain how Zeus produces rain does not count as a strike against the theory. The reason is that we are convinced Zeus does not produce rain. If Zeus does not produce rain, then it is not legitimate to demand an explanation of how he does produce it, and if the request for an explanation is not legitimate, then not providing an explanation does not count as a strike against the theory.

Since hylomorphists deny that structures emerge from unstructured materials, they deny the legitimacy of a request to explain how structures can emerge from unstructured materials. But if it is not legitimate to request an explanation of emergence, it is not a problem if hylomorphists do not answer it.

11.13   Arguments For and Against a Hylomorphic Theory of Mind

There are at least two arguments in favor of a hylomorphic theory of mind. The first appeals to the general hylomorphic worldview. Since there is good reason to endorse hylomorphism in general (Section 10.8), says the argument, there is also good reason to endorse a hylomorphic approach to mental phenomena specifically. The second argument claims that a hylomorphic theory of mind does a better job solving mind–body problems than competing theories. In particular, hylomorphists argue that their theory does a better job solving the problem of other minds, the problem of mental causation, and the problem of psychophysical emergence. Since a hylomorphic theory of mind does not have any problems that are as serious as or more serious than those facing its competitors, say hylomorphists, there is good reason to think a hylomorphic theory of mind is true.

Critics of a hylomorphic theory of mind can challenge these arguments in several ways. First, they can challenge the argument in favor of the general hylomorphic worldview in the ways described in Section 10.8. Second, they can argue that a hylomorphic theory of mind does not do a better job solving mind–body problems than competing theories. Finally, they can argue that hylomorphism has problems of its own that are as serious as or more serious than the problems facing its competitors. What might some of those problems be? Because the hylomorphic theory of mind presented in this chapter is a recent development, it is difficult to find well-rehearsed objections to it in the mind–body literature. There are nevertheless familiar objections to some of its central claims. These include objections to externalism, to disjunctivism, to the hylomorphic account of composition, and to the way hylomorphists approach qualia and inner experiences in general. Consider some examples.

One familiar objection to externalism argues that if externalism is true, beliefs, desires, and other mental states do not play any role in the production or explanation of behavior. If externalism is true, say critics, then mental states are relations between organisms and their environments. The only states that play a role in the production and explanation of an organism's behavior, however, are states internal to the organism such as states of its nervous system. Because these internal states are by themselves fully sufficient to produce the organism's movements and other environmental responses, say critics, the organism's relations to the environment play no role in the production of its behavior. If externalism is true, however, the organism's mental states are included among these relations. Consequently, if externalism is true, an organism's beliefs, desires, and other mental states play no role in the production or explanation of its behavior.

In response, hylomorphists challenge the premise that states of an organism's nervous system are fully sufficient to produce all of its behavior. Consider actions. They involve more than the bodily movements triggered by the organism's nervous system (Sections 11.3, 11.5, and 11.11), say hylomorphists. So if actions are included among an organism's behavior, then clearly the states of an organism's nervous system are not fully sufficient to produce all of its behavior. In addition, because objections to externalism are well-rehearsed, externalist responses to those objections are almost equally well-rehearsed. Hylomorphists can thus appeal to standard externalist responses to defend this aspect of their view.

Something analogous is true of objections to hylomorphism that appeal to qualia. According to exponents of qualia, hylomorphism is akin to physicalism. Views of both sorts have difficulty accommodating private, subjective episodes. Consequently, say critics, it is possible to formulate qualia-based objections to hylomorphism that are analogous to the qualia-based objections advanced against physicalism: the knowledge argument, and the appeal to absent or inverted qualia (Sections 4.7–4.8). Hylomorphists can argue in response that if it is possible to formulate qualia-based objections to hylomorphism that are analogous to the qualia-based objections to physicalism, then it is also possible to formulate hylomorphist replies to those objections that are analogous to the replies made by physicalists. In order to accommodate qualia, for instance, hylomorphists can formulate hylomorphic versions of representational, higher-order, and sensorimotor theories of consciousness. Earlier in fact we considered a sensorimotor account of perceptual experience that hylomorphists are free to endorse (Section 11.4). If critics argue that theories like this do not accommodate everything they have in mind when they talk of phenomenal consciousness, moreover, then hylomorphists, like physicalists, can argue either that the notion of phenomenal consciousness critics have in mind is empirically empty, as exponents of ontological naturalism and Wittgenstein's private language argument claim (Sections 8.5 and 8.7), or else that the notion is incoherent, as exponents of Dennett's argument against qualia claim (Section 8.6).

Other objections to a hylomorphic theory of mind will have less familiar contours. Some critics, for instance, might insist that a hylomorphic theory of mind depends too much on empirical conjectures, that its accounts of psychological knowledge, psychological language, embodiment, and causation, for instance, lie exposed to the threat of empirical falsification. Our best science could end up proving them wrong, critics might say, and this is a serious liability for a mind–body theory.

Hylomorphists can say two things in response. First, they can argue that being empirically falsifiable is an asset in a mind–body theory not a liability. Mind–body theories must fit the empirical facts concerning how mental and physical phenomena are related. We saw in earlier chapters that several mind–body theories encounter problems because critics claim they do not fit the empirical facts. Substance dualism (Section 3.7), functionalism (Section 6.9), and classic emergentism (Section 8.11) are examples. Formulating mind–body theories that fit the empirical facts, however, sometimes involves making conjectures about what the empirical facts are. Making empirical conjectures, then, is an integral part of formulating an empirically adequate mind–body theory. Second, if critics reckon empirical conjecture a liability, then hylomorphism is not alone in having it. Other mind–body theories such as physicalism and classic emergentism rely on empirical conjectures as well. So if being empirically falsifiable is a problem for hylomorphism, it is also a problem for many of its competitors, and in that case this objection does not favor those theories over hylomorphism.

Still, the kind of hylomorphic theory described in this chapter is new enough that it is difficult to assess the arguments for and against it. Only time will tell if some version of it deserves a lasting place among the other theories we have considered.

Further Reading

The classic source for hylomorphic thinking about psychological phenomena is Aristotle's treatise *On the Soul* (*De Anima*). It applies to living behavior the hylomorphic metaphysics that he introduces in books I and II of the *Physics* and that he develops further in books VII and VIII of the *Metaphysics*. He discusses perception in *On the Soul*, Book II, chapters 5–12, and Book III, chapters 1 and 2. He addresses *phantasia* in Chapter 3 of Book III, thought in chapters 4–6, and desire and action in chapters 9–11.

Interpretations of Aristotle's psychology have been controversial. Interpreters who claim Aristotle endorsed some type of dualism or dual-attribute theory include Howard Robinson (1983) and Jonathan Barnes (1971–2). Thomas Slakey (1961), on the other hand, interprets Aristotle as a type of identity theorist, while others interpret him as a type of functionalist, including Marc Cohen (1992), Kathleen Wilkes (1978), and Edwin Hartman (1977). G. R. T. Ross (1973) suggests that Aristotle is a neoparallelist, while Myles Burnyeat (1992) suggests he is committed to a form of panpsychism. Finally, Herbert Granger (1996) claims that Aristotle is committed to a strange view that is ultimately incoherent, and Bernard Williams (1986) claims that Aristotle's view waffles between incoherence and being a form of nonreductive physicalism. The position taken in this chapter is that all of these interpretations are mistaken. A hylomorphic approach to mind–body issues does not fall into any of the standard post-Cartesian categories. While it might be similar to one or another standard mind–body theory in some respect, it differs from each of them in important respects as well. If this is true, it would explain why interpretations of Aristotle's psychology diverge so wildly. We understand others in terms of the categories that are familiar to us, and the categories that are most familiar to contemporary philosophers are so thoroughly informed by post-Cartesian modes of thinking that they can often prevent us from understanding a pre-Cartesian view. As a result, contemporary philosophers have interpreted Aristotle as everything from a substance dualist to an identity theorist.

Contemporary exponents of a hylomorphic approach to mind–body issues are few and far between. Nussbaum and Putnam (1992) endorse a hylomorphic view, as does John Haldane (1989). Many aspects of a hylomorphic approach are apparent also in the works of Neo-Wittgensteinians such as Anthony Kenny (1989) and P. M. S. Hacker (see Bennett and Hacker 2003). Wittgenstein himself has often been classified as a behaviorist, but a careful reading of his *Philosophical Investigations* (2001 [1953]) and other works suggests a theory of psychological language more akin to the view endorsed by hylomorphists. The same is true of Gilbert Ryle (1949).

Externalist accounts of thought are widely endorsed in philosophy of mind due in large part to the influence of Hilary Putnam (1975c) and Tyler Burge (1979). For a more accessible introduction to Burge's views see Burge (1982). Internalist accounts of thought are defended by Jerry Fodor (1987: Chapter 2) and John Searle (1983). Tyler Burge (1989) defends externalism against Fodor. Many of Burge's writings on externalism are collected in Burge (2007). Disjunctivism is discussed in the essays in Byrne and Logue (2009).

See Paul Ekman (2007) for more on the social conditions involved in emotions, and Joseph LeDoux (1996) for more on the neural mechanisms involved in them. Roger Shepard and Jacqueline Metzler present their original experiment with mental imagery in Shepard and Metzler (1971). Stephen Kosslyn (1994) discusses findings about the activity of the visual cortex in both perception and mental imagery; although Stephen Kosslyn (2006) is probably a more accessible introduction to the topic. Alva Noë and J. K. O'Regan (2002) defend a sensorimotor theory of perceptual experience by appeal to change blindness studies. See also O'Regan (2009) and Noë (2004).

A pattern expression theory of psychological language was suggested by Wittgenstein in Part I, Section 244 of the *Philosophical Investigations* (2001 [1953]). Similar views have since been endorsed by Alasdair MacIntyre (1999), by Anthony Kenny (1989), and by M. R. Bennett and P. M. S. Hacker (2003). For more on usage-based linguistics see Michael Tomasello (2003). Saul Kripke (1980) defends an account of natural kind terms, and Hilary Putnam (1975c) defends a similar account.

For more on embodiment and the embodied mind movement in cognitive science see Raymond Gibbs (2006). See also the suggested readings on the embodied mind objection to functionalism at the end of Chapter 6. In addition to work in cognitive science, Wittgenstein (2001 [1953]), Ryle (1949), and Strawson (1959) appear to defend embodiment theses.

Notes

1   Paul Ekman, 2007, *Emotions Revealed: Recognizing Faces and Feelings to Improve Communication and Emotional Life*, 2nd edn., New York: Owl Books, 19–20.

2   Ekman *Emotions Revealed*, 54–5, 58–61.

3   Alva Noë, 2004, *Action in Perception*, Cambridge, MA: MIT Press, 49–50.

4   Erik Myin and J. Kevin O'Regan, 2009, "Situated Perception and Sensation in Vision and Other Modalities: A Sensorimotor Approach," in *The Cambridge Handbook of Situated Cognition*, edited by Philip Robbins and Murat Aydede, 185–200, New York: Cambridge University Press, 187–8.

5   Myin and O'Regan, "Situated Perception and Sensation in Vision and Other Modalities," 185.

6   R. N. Shepard and J. Metzler, 1971, "Mental Rotation of Three-Dimensional Objects," *Science* 171: 701–03.

7   J. Decety, and J. Grezes, 1999, "Neural Mechanisms Subserving the Perception of Human Action," *Trends in Cognitive Science* 3: 172–78; and T. Rossi, F. Tecchio, P. Pasqualetti, et al., 2002, "Somatosensory Processing During Movement Observation in Humans," *Clinical Neurophysiology* 113/1: 16–24.

8   See Ekman, *Emotions Revealed*, for an accessible introduction to this work.

9   A. Meltzoff, 1995, "Understanding the Intentions of Others: Re-enactment of Intended Acts by 18-Month-Old Children," *Developmental Psychology* 31: 838–50. See also Michael Tomasello, 2003, *Constructing a Language: A Usage-Based Theory of Language Acquisition*, Cambridge, MA: Harvard University Press, 26–7.

10 For a summary of some of this research, see Michael Tomasello, 2008, *Origins of Human Communication*, Cambridge, MA: MIT Press, 44–7.

11 Tomasello, *Constructing a Language*, 87–90.

12 Ekman, *Emotions Revealed*, 206.

13 A view of psychological language like this seems to be what the philosopher Ludwig Wittgenstein had in mind when he said, "only of a living human being and what resembles (behaves like) a living human being can one say: it has sensations, it sees; is blind; hears; is deaf; is conscious or unconscious" (*Philosophical Investigations*, Section 281).

14 Wilder Penfield, 1975, *The Mystery of the Mind: A Critical Study of Consciousness and the Human Brain*. Princeton: Princeton University Press, 76–7.

Glossary

Italicized words are references to other glossary entries.

Ability hypothesis   A response to the *knowledge argument*. Exponents of the ability hypothesis deny that Mary learns a new fact when she sees a ripe tomato for the first time; she instead gains a new ability.

Absent qualia   *See* Qualia-based arguments.

Agent-causal indeterminism   *See* Agent-causal theories.

Agent-causal theories   Forms of *libertarianism* that claim that actions are produced not by antecedent events, but directly by agents by means of a special kind of causal relation, agent causation. Critics argue that exponents of agent causation have failed to prove that this type of causal relation really exists.

Animalism   The claim that we are identical to animals.

Anomalous monism   A form of *nonreductive physicalism* originally formulated by *Donald Davidson*. It claims that everything is *physical*, and that psychological discourse is anomalous; that is, there are no laws that can be formulated using a psychological vocabulary. This implies both that there are no laws featuring exclusively *mental* predicates, and that there are no laws featuring mental predicates in combination with physical predicates. Because psychophysical *reduction* requires lawlike connections between mental and physical states, it requires laws featuring mental predicates in combination with physical predicates. Consequently, anomalous monism rejects the possibility of psychophysical reduction. Mental states nevertheless cause physical states, it says, so if causal relations must be underwritten by laws, it follows that there must be laws linking mental states with physical states. Since these laws cannot be formulated in a psychological vocabulary, they must be formulated in a physical vocabulary, and that means that mental states must have physical descriptions; that is, they must be physical states.

Philosophy of Mind: A Comprehensive Introduction, First Edition. William Jaworski.
© 2011 William Jaworski. Published 2011 by Blackwell Publishing Ltd.

Anti-eliminativism   The claim that eliminativism is false. There are mental states; psychological discourse is at least to some extent accurate.

Anti-reductionism   *See* Anti-reductivism.

Anti-reductivism   The claim that mental properties are not identical to physical properties, or that psychological discourse is not reducible to physical theory.

Aquinas, Thomas (1224–1275)   Prominent medieval philosopher who is best known in philosophy of mind as a defender of a medieval Aristotelian theory of the *soul*. The exact nature of his views is a matter of considerable dispute. Some interpreters claim that he endorsed a form of *substance dualism*. Others maintain that he defended a version of *hylomorphism*, and yet others that he defended a version of the *soul view of persons*.

Aristotle (384–322 BCE)   The greatest philosopher of antiquity, best known in philosophy of mind as an early defender of *hylomorphism* who endorsed *causal pluralism* and advanced an early version of the *embodied mind objection* against one of his contemporaries.

Armstrong, David M. (1926–)   Australian philosopher best known in philosophy of mind for defending a version of the *psychophysical identity theory* and a *higher-order theory of consciousness*.

Arnauld, Antoine (1612–1694)   French philosopher best known in philosophy of mind as the author of the Fourth set of objections to Descartes' *Meditations*.

Artificial Intelligence (AI)   A branch of cognitive science that tries to construct artificial systems that either have intelligence or simulate intelligence. The idea that such systems would only simulate intelligence is known as Weak AI; the idea that they would actually have intelligence is known as Strong AI. *John Searle* has argued against Strong AI by appeal to the *Chinese room argument*.

Behaviorism (in philosophy)   *See* Logical behaviorism.

Behaviorism (in psychology)   A term used in psychology to designate the claim that psychologists should concern themselves only with observable phenomena. This is often called 'methodological behaviorism'. It has more and less radical interpretations. Radical behaviorists such as B. F. Skinner claimed that psychologists should not even postulate inner mechanisms to explain overt stimulus–response patterns.

Berkeley, George (1685–1753)   British philosopher best known in philosophy of mind for having defended a reductivist form of ontological *idealism*.

Block, Ned (1942–)   American philosopher best known for his work on *consciousness* and for cataloging the problems with *functionalism* including the *liberalism objection*.

Brentano, Franz (1838–1917)   German philosopher best known in philosophy of mind for reintroducing the notion of *intentionality* into modern philosophy. He was the teacher of *Edmund Husserl*, and influenced the work of *Roderick Chisholm*.

Bridge laws   *See* Bridge principles.

Bridge principles   Empirically supported premises that connect the vocabularies of theories that do not share the same stock of predicates and terms. Bridge principles are necessary for intertheoretic *reduction* if the reduced theory's vocabulary has predicates and terms that the vocabulary of the reducing theory lacks. An example of a bridge principle would be 'heat = mean molecular kinetic energy' which was necessary for the reduction of thermodynamics to statistical mechanics.

Burge, Tyler (1946–)   American philosopher best known for defending *externalism*.

Capacity-based theories of free will and moral responsibility   *Compatibilist* theories that analyze free will in terms of the exercise of certain capacities such as the capacity for rational self-governance. Critics argue that capacity-based theories fail to capture our intuitions about what constitutes moral responsibility.

Causal indeterminism   A form of *libertarianism* that claims that actions are caused indeterministically. Antecedent conditions such as an agent's beliefs and desires make the occurrence of an action more probable, but do not determine it; that is, they do not bring it about with a probability of 1. Critics allege that causal indeterminist theories face a problem with control: if an agent's actions are not determined by the agent's beliefs and desires, then the agent is not completely in control of their occurrence, and in that case the agent cannot be held morally accountable for them.

Causal pluralism   The claim that there are many different kinds of causes and many different kinds of causal relations. *Hylomorphists* appeal to causal pluralism to solve the *problem of mental causation*.

Chinese room argument   An objection to *functionalism* and *Strong AI* originally formulated by the philosopher *John Searle*. If functionalism is true, then it is impossible for two systems to be functionally identical and mentally distinct. Yet it is possible for two systems to be functionally identical and mentally distinct. A person could learn to correlate Chinese language inputs with Chinese language outputs by following instructions on a sophisticated chart, and thereby come to correlate inputs with outputs in the same way a native speaker does. The person and the native speaker would thus be functionally identical, yet they would be mentally distinct since the person, unlike the native speaker, would not understand Chinese. The person operates the same way as a computer, so if the person does not understand Chinese merely by correlating inputs with outputs the way a speaker does, the machine doesn't understand Chinese either.

Chisholm, Roderick (1916–1999)   American philosopher best known in philosophy of mind for defending a *nonorganismic dual-attribute theory* by appeal to *mereological essentialism*, for defending an *agent-causal theory* of free will, and for introducing Anglo-American philosophers to *Franz Brentano's* notion of *intentionality*.

Churchland, Paul M. (1942–) and Patricia S. (1943–)   Canadian-American philosophers best known for defending *eliminative physicalism*.

Compatibilism   A family of solutions to the *problem of free will and determinism* that claim the existence of moral responsibility is compatible with *determinism*. Classic compatibilist theories claim that free will and moral responsibility require the ability to do otherwise, and that this ability is compatible with determinism. Contemporary compatibilist theories deny that moral responsibility requires the ability to do otherwise by appeal to *Frankfurt-type examples*. Contemporary compatibilist theories include *hierarchical theories, capacity-based theories, reactive attitude theories,* and *semicompatibilist theories*.

Computational theory of mind   *See* functionalism.

Conceivability   *See* Conceivability-possibility principles.

Conceivability argument   An argument that supports the substance dualist's claim that persons can exist without bodies. If it is conceivable that persons can exist without bodies, says the argument, then persons can exist without bodies, and it is in fact conceivable that persons can exist without bodies. Therefore, persons can exist without bodies.

Conceivability-possibility principles   Claims with the form 'If it is conceivable that *p*, then it is possible that *p*'. Conceivability-possibility principles are used as premises in many arguments in philosophy of mind and in philosophy generally. Philosophers will often appeal to conceivability-possibility principles without explicitly stating them – a practice that conceals their contentious nature.

Conceptual essentialism   *See* Empirical versus conceptual essentialism.

Consciousness   An ambiguous term used in at least two senses in philosophy of mind. In one sense it refers to certain publicly observable aspects of someone's behavior: whether someone is responsive to verbal commands or painful stimuli, for instance. This is the sense used in ordinary discourse when we say that someone who is asleep or drugged is not conscious. The notion of consciousness that has taken center stage in mind–body debates, however, is often called 'phenomenal consciousness'. It refers to the allegedly private, qualitative aspects of experience – *qualia*. According to one standard account of phenomenal consciousness, qualia are nonrelational and unanalyzable. It is possible to analyze the brain mechanisms involved in, for instance, seeing a ripe tomato, but exponents of this account of consciousness claim that the qualitative dimension of seeing a ripe tomato cannot be analyzed into the activities of and relations among discrete mechanical components. Other accounts of phenomenal consciousness reject the idea that qualia are nonrelational and unanalyzable. These include *representational theories of consciousness*, *higher-order theories of consciousness*, and *sensorimotor theories of consciousness*.

Consequence argument   An argument against *compatibilism*. We are free, says the argument, only if what we do is up to us. If *determinism* is true, however, what we do is not up to us, for if determinism is true, then our actions are necessary consequences of the laws of nature together with events in the past – including events that occurred before we were born. But the laws of nature and events in the past are not up to us. If these things are not up to us, however, then our actions are not up to us since they are the necessary consequences of things that are not up to us. So if determinism is true, what we do is not to us. But if what we do is not up to us, then we are not free. Consequently, if determinism is true, we are not free. Compatibilism must therefore be false. The consequence argument remains controversial.

Constitutionalism   The view that we are constituted by animals. Constitution is supposed to be a relation between two things that share all the same parts but that nevertheless differ in their properties. A statue, for instance, is said to be constituted by a lump of clay. The statue and the lump share all the same parts, but they are different things according to constitutionalists because they have different properties. The lump, for instance, but not the statue can survive being squashed.

Content   *See* Intentionality.

Covariation theories of mental representation   Theories that try to account for mental representation in terms of causal covariation relations between states of the environment and states of experiencing subjects. To have an internal representation of redness, for instance, is to have an internal component that is activated if and only if something in the environment is red. Simple covariation theories claim that causal covariation relations of this sort are all mental representation consists in, but these theories have difficulty explaining what determines the content of mental representations – what the representations are *of* or *about* (*see* Intentionality). Sophisticated covariation theories like *Fred Dretske's* and *Jerry Fodor's* look to address these difficulties.

Davidson, Donald (1917–2003)   American philosopher best known in philosophy of mind for his work on action theory and *anomalous monism*. Davidson argued against followers of *Ludwig Wittgenstein* that psychological explanation was a species of causal explanation. Davidson's argument for anomalous monism develops several ideas of his mentor, the philosopher *W. V. O. Quine*.

Delgado, Jose (1915–)   Neurosurgeon who pioneered techniques of neural manipulation.

Democritus (b. 460 BCE)   Ancient Greek philosopher credited with having been the first to believe in the existence of atoms. Democritus suggests an early version of *reductive physicalism*.

Dennett, Daniel (1942–)   American philosopher known in philosophy of mind for attacking *qualia* and defending *compatibilism* and *instrumentalism*. Dennett's more considered view is not instrumentalist, however, but is best described as a form of *nonreductive physicalism* that emphasizes the practical advantages of psychological explanation: we use psychological discourse because it is more efficient for explaining and predicting human behavior than physics.

Descartes, René (1596–1650)   Prominent French philosopher whose ideas are largely responsible for philosophy of mind as we have understood it since the seventeenth century. Descartes is best known for having defended *substance dualism* by appeal to a *modal argument*, and for his attempt to defend *interactionism*. The exact nature of Descartes' substance dualism is nevertheless a matter of dispute. Some interpreters compare his philosophy of mind to that of *Thomas Aquinas*, but others insist that his philosophy marks a radical break with his medieval predecessors. Descartes' famous works on mind and body include *Meditations on First Philosophy* and *Principles of Philosophy*.

Determinism   The claim that for any given state of the universe at a time, there is exactly one possible resultant state that comes about because of antecedent conditions in conjunction with the laws of nature. *Soft determinism* combines determinism with *compatibilism*, and *hard determinism* combines determinism with *incompatibilism*.

Direct access thesis   The idea that other people's mental states are directly observable; we know what mental states other people have by directly perceiving them not by making inferences from bodily behavior. *Hylomorphists* and *logical behaviorists* both endorse versions of the direct access thesis. It is opposed to the *inferential access thesis*.

Disjunctivism   The view that there need not be an inner experiential element that is common to both accurate and inaccurate experiences. There need not be an inner state

– a visual experience, say – that is common to both perception and hallucination, for instance.

Dretske, Fred (1932–)   American philosopher best known in philosophy of mind for defending a sophisticated *covariation theory of mental representation*. According to Dretske, mental representation consists in what an internal component has the function of indicating within a broader system. The function of a system's sensory organs or subsystems is to supply it with information about the environment, something it does by having internal states that covary with states of the environment.

Dual-aspect theory   *See* Dual-attribute theory.

Dual-attribute theory (DAT)   Dual-attribute theories are committed to the conjunction of *property dualism* and *psychophysical coincidence*; they claim, in other words, that mental and physical *properties* are distinct, and that the same individual can have properties of both sorts. Forms of *substance dualism*, by contrast, endorse property dualism but reject psychophysical coincidence. DATs are sometimes referred to simply as forms of property dualism, but this label is misleading because substance dualism is committed to property dualism as well. DATs are distinguished from each other by two factors: their claims about the things that have both *mental* and *physical* properties, and their claims about how mental and physical properties are related. Organismic DATs claim that the things having both mental and physical properties are organisms. These theories are often committed to *animalism*. Nonorganismic DATs deny that the things having both mental and physical properties are organisms. The most popular forms of DAT are *emergentism* and *epiphenomenalism*. Both claim that mental properties are generated or produced by physical interactions. DATs are sometimes conflated with forms of *nonreductive physicalism*.

Dualism   *See* Monism versus dualism

Eddington, Arthur Stanley (1882–1944)   British astronomer and physicist. Eddington was one of the first scientists to try to confirm Einstein's general relativity theory experimentally. He is known in philosophy for having proposed a philosophical problem concerning two tables: the table described by physics and the table described by common sense.

Eliminative physicalism   A form of physicalism that denies that psychological discourse has any descriptive or explanatory legitimacy. In reality, say eliminativists, there are no beliefs, desires, hopes, joys, or pains. Trying to describe and explain human behavior by appeal to mental states is like trying to describe and explain the weather by appeal to the Greek gods: it is the byproduct of a defective conceptual framework that may have been useful at one time, but that will be eliminated as soon as a complete scientific understanding of human behavior is achieved (hence the label 'eliminative'). By contrast, *reductive* and *nonreductive physicalism* claim that psychological discourse does have descriptive and explanatory legitimacy.

Eliminativism   A term used in this text to refer either to *eliminative physicalism* or to *nihilism*.

Elisabeth of Bohemia (1618–1680)   The Princess Elisabeth is best known as a student of *Descartes* who posed the *problem of interaction*.

Embodied mind objection   An argument against functionalism that claims that human psychological capacities cannot be defined abstractly in the way functionalists suppose.

Mental states are instead essentially embodied in the kinds of substructures or subsystems humans possess. Contemporary exponents of embodied mind objections in cognitive science argue that explanations of cognitive capacities that assume embodiment are superior to functionalist-inspired explanations that do not.

Embodiment thesis A claim endorsed by a *hylomorphic theory of mind*: human psychological capacities are essentially embodied. They cannot be defined without reference to the bodily parts humans possess. Embodiment has implications for how hylomorphists understand *multiple realizability*. We can apply psychological predicates and terms to nonhumans, they say, not because psychological capacities are defined abstractly as, say, *functionalists* claim, but because we are able to draw analogies between the behavior and body plans of nonhuman things and our own.

Emergentism A *dual-attribute theory* that claims, like *epiphenomenalism*, that mental properties are produced by or emerge out of physical interactions. Unlike epiphenomenalists, however, emergentists claim that mental properties exert a causal influence on physical things. Emergentists argue that their theory is the best explanation for certain empirical facts. Critics deny this, and argue that emergentism faces the *problem of psychophysical emergence*, and the *problem of mental causation*.

Empirical essentialism *See* Empirical versus conceptual essentialism.

Empirical versus conceptual essentialism Two competing views of how we discern something's essential properties. Empirical essentialists claim that we discover something's essential properties by studying it empirically. Conceptual essentialists deny that we must study something empirically to discern its essential properties. *Descartes* is an example of a conceptual essentialist, and *Saul Kripke*, *Hilary Putnam*, and *Aristotle* are examples of empirical essentialists.

Epiphenomenalism A dual-attribute theory that claims mental properties are caused by something's physical properties, and that mental properties cannot causally influence anything in turn. Contemporary epiphenomenalist theories claim that *qualia*, and in general mental states that conform to a *private conception of mental phenomena*, are epiphenomenal, but that *propositional attitudes* and mental states that conform to a *public conception of mental phenomena* are not epiphenomenal but are identical to physical states as the *psychophysical identity theory* claims.

Essential property argument An argument advanced by *Descartes* to support the *substance dualistic* claim that persons can exist without bodies. Our only essential property is thinking, says the argument. If that is our only essential property, however, the only property we need to exist, then we do not need physical properties to exist. But if we do not need physical properties to exist, then we do not need bodies to exist. Hence, persons can exist without bodies. The argument is implicitly committed to *conceivability-possibility principles* and *conceptual essentialism*.

Event-causal indeterminism *See* Causal indeterminism.

Events There are at least three theories of events that philosophers of mind appeal to when stating their views. The property-exemplification theory defended by *Jaegwon Kim*, Alvin Goldman, and Jonathan Bennett claims that events are individuals having *properties* or standing in relations at times. *Donald Davidson* defends a different theory of events according to which events are unrepeatable particulars individuated by their causes and effects. Other philosophers endorse bundle theories of events according to which events are bundles of properties.

Exclusion argument A version of the *problem of mental causation* advanced by the philosopher Jaegwon Kim as a criticism of *emergentism* and *nonreductive physicalism*. According to the argument, there is no satisfactory way for emergentists and nonreductive physicalists to solve the problem.

Exclusion problem *See* Exclusion argument.

Explanatory gap A term used to express the idea that there is an unbridgeable gap between the descriptive and explanatory resources of physics and those used to describe and explain qualia.

Externalism The claim that mental states depend in some way on social or environmental conditions external to the individual whose mental states they are. Internalists, by contrast, claim that mental states do not depend on external conditions. Externalism is sometimes called 'anti-individualism'. Although many philosophers of the past have been externalists, interest in contemporary externalism was sparked by *Hilary Putnam's Twin Earth thought experiments*.

First-person authority The idea that the knowledge each of us has of his or her own mental states is in some sense privileged. Each of us can be wrong about what mental states other people have in a way that we cannot be wrong about what mental states ourselves have. First-person authority is not the same as first-person infallibility, the idea that it is impossible for us to be wrong about what we believe, or desire, or feel. Nor is first-person authority the same as first-person incorrigibility, the idea that it is impossible for other people to correct us about what we think, desire, or feel.

Fission problem An argument that purports to show that *psychological-continuity* accounts of personal identity are false. Psychological-continuity accounts claim that personal identity consists in psychological continuity, but it is possible for a person to be psychologically continuous with two different individuals. Since it is not possible for one person to be identical to two, critics argue that psychological-continuity accounts must be false.

Fodor, Jerry (1935–) American philosopher known for defending *functionalism, nonreductive physicalism*, a sophisticated *covariation theory of mental representation*, and the language of thought hypothesis – the idea that mental representations are like symbols in a purely mental language (mentalese) that are combined according to syntactic rules to form sentence-like entities. Fodor has also defended the descriptive and explanatory legitimacy of *folk psychology* against the claims of *eliminativists*, and was at one time a critic of content externalism.

Folk psychology A label (originally derogatory) for ordinary psychological discourse.

Four-dimensionalism *See* Temporal parts theory.

Frankfurt, Harry (1929–) American philosopher best known for presenting *Frankfurt-type examples* against the *Principle of Alternative Possibilities*, and for defending a *hierarchical theory* of free will and moral responsibility.

Frankfurt-type examples   Cases that purport to show that the *Principle of Alternative Possibilities* is false. The cases involve what is sometimes called a 'Frankfurt controller', someone who is capable of controlling an agent's behavior, but who nevertheless does not want to interfere with the agent's behavior unnecessarily. If the agent acts in the way the Frankfurt controller wants, then the controller does not intervene to alter the agent's behavior. Intuitively, we can hold the agent accountable for what he does even though he lacks the ability to do otherwise. Hence, moral responsibility does not require the ability to do otherwise. Frankfurt-type examples remain controversial.

Function   A term used in several different ways in philosophy of mind. Classic functionalist theories conceive of functions as states that correlate inputs to a system with outputs from it. This notion differs from the notion of a teleological function. A teleological function is something's job or purpose within a broader system. The purpose of the heart is to pump blood, that is the job, the function (in the teleological sense) that the heart performs within a human organism. *Teleological functionalists* appeal to a teleological notion of functions to deal with the *liberalism objection* to classic functionalism.

Functional analysis   A method of scientific investigation used by biologists, cognitive scientists, engineers, and others to study how complex systems operate. The method involves analyzing the activities of a system into simpler subactivities performed by simpler subsystems. Confusingly, biologists often refer to functional analysis as 'reduction', but this is different from the philosophical notion of *reduction*. The latter is the notion of one theory taking over the descriptive and explanatory roles of another, but a commitment to functional analysis as a research method does not imply a commitment to reduction in this sense.

Functionalism   A popular theory that claims mental states are functional states that correlate inputs to a system with outputs from it and with other internal states. Although functionalism was originally inspired by the *Turing test* and the ideas of *Alan Turing*, it was first formulated by *Hilary Putnam*. Unlike many other theories in mind–body debates, functionalism does not take a stand on what exists. It does not say, for instance, that everything is physical, or that some things are nonphysical. Functionalism is officially neutral with regard to ontological issues, and simply offers a characterization of psychological language. Psychological discourse, it says, is abstract discourse that ignores the physical or other details of a system and focuses simply on how the system correlates inputs with outputs. Psychological discourse, in other words, is analogous to geometrical discourse which ignores the physical details of something (what it is made of, say) and focuses simply on its spatial properties. According to functionalists, therefore, mental properties are abstract *higher-order properties* that are *realized* by concrete lower-order things. Functionalists argue that their theory provides the most obvious explanation for *multiple realizability*. Critics deny this and argue that functionalism has problems with the *Chinese room argument*, the *embodied mind objection*, and the *liberalism objection*. *Teleological functionalists* attempt to deal with this third problem by placing restrictions on the kinds of systems that can realize mental states. Although functionalism is compatible with *substance dualism, idealism, neutral monism,* and *dual-attribute theory,* it is frequently endorsed in conjunction with *physicalism.* The resulting view is *realization physicalism.*

Gassendi, Pierre (1592–1655)   French philosopher best known in philosophy of mind as the author of the Fifth set of objections to Descartes' *Meditations*, and for posing the *problem of interaction*.

Global supervenience   *See* Supervenience.

Hard determinism   A solution to the *problem of free will and determinism* that denies *compatibilism* and affirms *determinism*. Hard determinists claim that determinism is true and that the truth of determinism is incompatible with the existence of free will. They thus deny the existence of free will.

Hard incompatibilism   A solution to the *problem of free will and determinism* that denies the existence of free will and moral responsibility. Like *hard determinists*, hard incompatibilists deny *compatibilism*, but they do not affirm the truth of *determinism* since they take this to be an empirical matter. They deny the existence of free will and moral responsibility on independent grounds.

Hempel, Carl (1905–1997)   German philosopher of science with influential views on scientific explanation. He is best known in philosophy of mind as an erstwhile *logical positivist* and *logical behaviorist* who later suggested a problem confronting physicalist theories: *Hempel's dilemma*.

Hempel's dilemma   An argument against physicalism suggested by the philosopher of science *Carl Hempel*. Physicalism says that everything is the way physics says it is. But physics must be defined either relative to a preliminary stage of scientific theorizing, or relative to the final, ideal stage of scientific theorizing. If it is defined in the former way, then physicalism is false since preliminary physical theories are false. If it is defined in the latter way, then physics lacks content since we do not yet know what the final, ideal physical theory will say.

Hierarchical theories of free will and moral responsibility   *Compatibilist* theories that analyze free will in terms of the conformity of lower-order desires to *higher-order desires*. Critics argue that hierarchical theories fail to capture our intuitions about what constitutes moral responsibility.

Higher- and lower-level properties   A distinction among properties at different levels in a *multilevel worldview*. The lowest-level properties are those postulated by fundamental physics. Higher-level properties are those postulated by the *special sciences*: chemistry, biology, psychology, economics, and other social sciences. The distinction between higher- and lower-level properties should not be confused with the distinction between *higher- and lower-order properties*. The latter distinction concerns degrees or orders of abstraction, but levels need not be defined in terms of levels of abstraction.

Higher- and lower-order desires   A distinction used in connection with *hierarchical theories of free will and moral responsibility*. Roughly, first-order desires are desires for ordinary things while second-order desires are desires for other desires. If I desire to be a generous person, for instance, I desire to have certain desires such as desires to help other people. Third-order desires are desires for certain second-order desires, and so on. Higher- and lower-order desires should not be confused with *higher- and lower-order properties*.

Higher- and lower-order properties   Higher-order properties are properties whose definitions quantify over other properties. *Realization physicalists* claim that mental properties are higher-order properties. Pain, for instance, is defined as the property of having some physical property that correlates certain inputs with certain outputs. The physical properties are in this case lower-order relative to pain, and particular instances of pain are said to be *realized* by particular instances of physical properties. Higher- and lower-order properties should not be confused with *higher- and lower-level properties* since levels need not correspond to orders of abstraction. They should also not be confused with *higher- and lower-order desires* as these are understood in discussions of *hierarchical theories of free will and moral responsibility*. Finally, higher-order properties should not be confused with the notions of higher-order thought and higher-order perception as they are understood in connection with *higher-order theories of consciousness*.

Higher-order perception   *See* Higher-order theories of consciousness

Higher-order theories of consciousness   Higher-order theories of consciousness claim that conscious states are internal states of a system that are monitored by other internal states of that system. I am conscious of seeing red, for instance, when I have an internal sensory state that registers the presence of redness in the environment, and another internal state that registers the presence of the internal sensory state. There are at least two kinds of higher-order theories of consciousness. Higher-order perception theories claim that the internal monitoring states are like inner perceptions of sensory states; higher-order thought theories claim that the internal monitoring states are like thoughts about sensory states. Higher-order theories of consciousness are very similar to *representational theories of consciousness*. *Physicalists* have looked to both to provide them with resources for responding to *qualia-based arguments* against their view.

Higher-order thought   *See* Higher-order theories of consciousness

Hobbes, Thomas (1588–1679)   British philosopher best known in philosophy of mind for having endorsed an early-modern version of the *psychophysical identity theory*, for having endorsed *compatibilism*, and for having authored the Third set of objections to Descartes' *Meditations*.

Homunctionalism   *See* Teleological functionalism.

Homuncular functionalism   *See* Teleological functionalism.

Husserl, Edmund (1859–1938)   German philosopher, student of *Franz Brentano* and teacher of Martin Heidegger. Husserl is best known as the founder of phenomenology, a philosophical method for studying *intentionality*.

Hylomorphic theory of mind   A theory that applies the principles of *hylomorphism* to *mind–body problems*. While some structures in nature are just spatial arrangements among a thing's parts, say exponents of a hylomorphic theory of mind, the characteristic ways that living things interact with each other and their environments are structured phenomena as well. These patterns of social and environmental interaction include mental states. A hylomorphic theory of mind rejects the idea that mental states are internal states. Mental states might incorporate internal states such as states of the nervous system, but they are not identical to those internal states since they also involve social and environmental factors. A hylomorphic theory of mind is easily confused with *logical behaviorism*.

Both theories reject the idea that mental states are internal states, but they differ in at least three respects: hylomorphists reject *physicalism*, behaviorists do not; hylomorphists have a broader conception of what counts as behavior than behaviorists do; and hylomorphists have a different understanding of psychological language. A hylomorphic theory of mind is committed to *externalism*, to *disjunctivism*, to the *pattern expression theory* of psychological language, to the *direct access thesis*, and to the *embodiment thesis*. Exponents of the theory are also sympathetic to *sensorimotor theories of consciousness*.

Hylomorphism   A theory that claims structure or organization is a real and irreducible ontological and explanatory principle. Things are composed of more than simply fundamental physical materials or particles; they are composed of those materials structured or organized in various ways. Those structures are responsible for distinguishing one kind of thing from another, and for explaining why those things operate as they do. A human and a dog, for instance, are composed of the same kinds of physical materials; what distinguishes them are the ways those materials are structured or organized. Hylomorphism represented the dominant approach to understanding human psychological capacities prior to the *Scientific Revolution*. A *hylomorphic theory of mind* applies the general principles of hylomorphism to *mind–body problems*.

Idealism   The claim that everything is mental. The term 'idealism' is used to refer to either conceptual idealism or ontological idealism. Conceptual idealism claims that our experiences of the world depend in part on concepts or structures supplied by our minds. *Kant's* transcendental idealism is an example of conceptual idealism. Ontological idealism is like an inverse image of physicalism. Its most prominent defender was the British philosopher *George Berkeley*. Ontological idealists have followed Berkeley in being reductivists about physical discourse: our talk of mind-independent objects, they say, can be reduced to talk of our experiences. This type of view is often called 'phenomenalism'.

Identity   The relation every thing bears only to itself. To say x is identical to y is to say that x and y are the very same thing. Identity is defined by several axioms including the *indiscernibility of identicals*, the *necessity of identity*, and the *transitivity of identity*.

Identity conditions   *See* Persistence conditions.

Identity theory   *See* Psychophysical identity theory

Incompatibilism   The denial of *compatibilism*. Incompatibilist theories claim that *determinism* is incompatible with the existence of free will and moral responsibility. *Libertarian* theories are forms of incompatibilism. *Hard determinist* theories are as well.

Indiscernibility of identicals   The principle that if $x = y$, then x and y must have all the same properties. A thing cannot have properties different from the properties it itself has. The indiscernibility of identicals is sometimes called 'Leibniz's law'; although this term is also used for the conjunction of the indiscernibility of identicals with the controversial identity of indiscernibles, the principle that if x and y have all the same properties, then $x = y$. The indiscernibility of identicals is often used as a premise in arguments to show that one thing is not identical to another. If pain is identical to brain state B, for instance, then it is impossible for something to have pain without having brain state B. Consequently, an argument showing that something can have pain without having brain state B or vice versa will show that pain and brain state B are not identical.

Inductive generalization from past scientific success   An argument for physicalism. In the past, whenever people have tried to explain things nonphysically, their attempts have failed, and physical attempts have succeeded. Since this has always been the case in the past, says the argument, we have good reason to think this will always be the case. We have good reason to think, in other words, that nonphysical explanations for phenomena will always fail and that physical explanations for those phenomena will succeed. Hence, we have good reason to think that everything will be explainable physically, and nothing will be explainable nonphysically. Hence, we have good reason to think that everything is physical, that physicalism is true.

Inferential access thesis   The idea that we can know what mental states other people have only by making inferences from bodily behavior. If mental states are *private, subjective* episodes, then we cannot directly witness other people's mental states the way that we can directly witness their objective bodily movements. Consequently, our knowledge of what mental states other people have depends on making inferences from bodily movements and utterances. The inferential access thesis is opposed to the *direct access thesis*.

Instrumentalism   In philosophy of mind, instrumentalism is the view that psychological discourse does not aim at expressing real properties, as realist theories of psychological language claim; rather, psychological discourse is merely a tool or instrument for predicting human behavior whose use carries with it no significant ontological implications.

Intentionality   The feature at least some mental states have of being *about*, or *of*, or *for* something. A fear, for instance, is always fear *of* something, a belief is always a belief *about* something, a desire is always a desire *for* something. The notion of intentionality played an important role in medieval philosophy, but was ignored in the modern period until it was reintroduced in the nineteenth century by the German philosopher *Franz Brentano*, and made its way into Anglo-American philosophy due in part to *Roderick Chisholm*. *John Searle* has done much to clarify the notion. Philosophers also talk about intentionality in terms of mental representation: mental states such as beliefs are said to represent the world. Intentionality is also discussed in terms of propositional attitudes. A belief that $2 + 2 = 4$ is an attitude of acceptance directed toward the proposition '$2 + 2 = 4$'. In addition, that proposition is said to be the content of the intentional state or mental representation. *Physicalists* have often been concerned with giving accounts of intentionality that are compatible with their view. They typically understand intentionality in terms of mental representation, and then try to account for mental representation in terms of relations found throughout the physical universe. *Covariation theories of mental representation*, for instance, try to account for mental representation in terms of causation, something that physicalists claim can be understood exhaustively in terms of physics.

Interactionism versus noninteractionism   Species of substance dualism. Interactionist theories claim that persons and bodies can causally interact. Noninteractionist theories deny this; they include *parallelism* and occasionalism. Although interactionism is the default position for substance dualists, the *problem of interaction* has motivated some substance dualists to endorse noninteractionism. The burden for noninteractionists is to explain why persons and bodies appear to interact if they do not interact in fact. Parallelists such as *Leibniz* claim that persons and bodies operate in parallel: their states are correlated without interacting. Occasionalists such as *Malebranche* claim that God acts a causal middleman who coordinates changes in persons with changes in bodies.

Internalism versus externalism   *See* Externalism.

Inverted qualia   *See* Qualia-based arguments.

Inverted spectrum   *See* Qualia-based arguments.

Jackson, Frank (1943–)   Australian philosopher best known in philosophy of mind for having advanced the *knowledge argument* and for defending *epiphenomenalism*.

James, William (1842–1910)   American philosopher and psychologist best known in philosophy of mind as a defender of *neutral monism*.

Kant, Immanuel (1724–1804)   The greatest philosopher of the eighteenth century. Kant is known for having defended a form of conceptual *idealism* and for defending a *libertarian* solution to the *problem of free will and determinism*. What is distinctive about Kant's libertarianism is that it endorses the existence of libertarian free will while denying the possibility of ever explaining how libertarian free will is possible. We can know that we are free beings, according to Kant, but not how it is possible for us to be free.

Kim, Jaegwon (1934–)   Korean-American philosopher best known in philosophy of mind for his work clarifying the notion of *supervenience* and for his vigorous attacks on *nonreductive physicalism* including *Kim's trilemma* and the *exclusion argument*. Kim was originally sympathetic to the *psychophysical identity theory*. He nevertheless worked on formulations of nonreductive physicalism before endorsing narrow mental types in response to the *multiple-realizability argument*. More recently he has endorsed *epiphenomenalism*.

Kim's trilemma   An argument advanced by *Jaegwon Kim* that purports to show that *realization physicalists* must abandon either their commitment to *physicalism*, their commitment to *anti-eliminativism*, or their commitment to *anti-reductivism*.

Knowledge argument   An anti-physicalist argument advanced by *Frank Jackson*. If physicalism is true, then all facts are physical facts. But not all facts are physical facts, says the argument, since it is possible for someone to know all the physical facts without knowing all the facts. Mary, for instance, has complete physical knowledge. She knows all the physical facts, but she has never before experienced color. When she experiences color for the first time, she learns something new; she gains knowledge of a fact she didn't know before. Since she knew all the physical facts, she must have learned a nonphysical fact. Hence, not all facts are physical facts; physicalism must be false. Criticisms of the argument include the *ability hypothesis*, and the claim that Mary knows the same *old facts under new representations*.

Kripke, Saul (1940–)   American philosopher best known in philosophy of mind for defending *property dualism* and the *necessity of identity*, for developing an influential account of natural kind terms, and for clarifying the distinction between necessity and apriority. Kripke argued that there are necessary truths that are knowable *a posteriori* such as the truth that water is H_2O, and there are contingent truths that are knowable *a priori* such as the truth that the length of a metal bar in Paris is 1 meter. The distinction was a helpful corrective to the claim of *psychophysical identity theorists* that mental states were contingently identical to brain states. If identity is necessary, as Kripke argued, and pain is identical to brain state B, then necessarily pain is brain state B. The correct way for identity theorists to formulate their claim is to say that necessarily pain is identical to brain state B, but this necessary truth is discoverable *a posteriori*. Kripke is well known for having advanced an argument against the identification of mental states with physical states.

Leibniz, Gottfried Wilhelm von (1646–1716)   Prominent German philosopher best known in philosophy of mind as a *substance dualist* who endorsed *parallelism*.

Levels of reality   *See* Multilevel worldview.

Lewis, David K. (1941–2001)   American philosopher best known in philosophy of mind for defending a version of the *psychophysical identity theory*, a model of *theoretical identification* based on the *transitivity of identity*, and for defending *temporal parts theory*.

Liberalism objection to functionalism   If functionalism is true, then almost anything can realize mental states, even systems that are intuitively bizarre such as a giant "brain" that is composed of all the people in China. It is nevertheless absurd to suppose that such systems could really have mental states; therefore, functionalism must be false.

Libertarianism   A family of solutions to the *problem of free will and determinism*. Libertarian theories claim that the existence of free will is compatible with the falsity of determinism. They include *simple indeterminism, causal indeterminism,* and *agent-causal theories*.

Locke, John (1632–1704)   Prominent seventeenth-century British philosopher known in philosophy of mind for having endorsed a higher-order perception theory of consciousness (*see* Higher-order theories of consciousness), and having gestured toward the notion of inverted qualia (*see* Qualia-based arguments). Locke also endorsed a *psychological-continuity* account of personal identity, a structural account of animal identity, and a *compatibilist* account of free will.

Logical behaviorism   An approach to mind–body issues inspired by *logical positivism*. It claims that psychological expressions are abbreviations for longer descriptions of actual and potential behavior, where paradigmatic behavior consists in bodily movements and utterances. Logical behaviorism is motivated by the *reductive physicalist* attempt to show that mental phenomena are physical phenomena. Unlike the *psychophysical identity theory* which tries to show this *a posteriori* through scientific investigation, logical behaviorism tries to show this *a priori* through conceptual analysis. It implies that every psychological expression can be analyzed into an equivalent physical description of actual and potential behavior. Logical behaviorism faced numerous problems, and was largely abandoned with the demise of positivism in the early 1950s.

Logical positivism   A movement in early-twentieth-century philosophy. Positivists in general saw human history as progressing through stages: the religious stage was followed by the philosophical or metaphysical stage, and that stage was followed by the scientific stage. Initiators of each new stage had to struggle to move human understanding past the preceding stage. Logical positivists took themselves to be contributors to the effort to move human understanding beyond the philosophical/metaphysical stage using the logical and linguistic tools developed by the logician and mathematician Gottlob Frege (1848–1925), and the philosophers *Bertrand Russell* and *Ludwig Wittgenstein*. The positivist movement had its heyday in the 1930s and 1940s, but by the early 1950s it was moribund. *Logical behaviorism* was the branch of positivist philosophy that dealt with *mind–body problems*.

Machine functionalism   *See* Functionalism.

Malebranche, Nicholas (1638–1715) French philosopher best known in philosophy of mind for endorsing *substance dualism* and occasionalism (*see* Interactionism versus noninteractionism). Malebranche argued that God was the only agent, the only being capable of causing anything. This claim implies that persons and bodies are incapable of influencing each other causally. To explain the appearance of person–body interaction, Malebranche argued that God causally influenced both.

Materialism *See* Physicalism.

Mental Mental phenomena are defined by psychological discourse. Mental properties and events are those expressed by psychological predicates and descriptions. There are broadly speaking two conceptions of mental phenomena: a *private versus a public conception of mental phenomena*.

Mental content *See* Intentionality.

Mental monism *See* Idealism.

Mental representation *See* Intentionality.

Mereological essentialism The claim that a thing has all of its parts and only those parts essentially. It implies that if a thing gains or loses a part that thing ceases to exist. *Roderick Chisholm* argued against the claim that we are organisms by appeal to mereological essentialism. *Hylomorphism* supplies a competing account of parthood.

Mereological universalism The claim that any objects whatsoever compose a distinct whole. There is, for instance, an object composed of your left hand, the Eiffel Tower, and the president's nose. Mereological universalism is used to support *nihilism*, the claim that people do not exist. *Hylomorphism* supplies a competing account of parthood.

Methodological behaviorism *See* Behaviorism (in psychology).

Mind An ambiguous term that has been used to refer both to mental capacities such as the ability to think or feel, and to the entity that has those capacities. To avoid confusion this text avoids using the term.

Mind–body pessimism A theory that denies the possibility of solving *mind–body problems*.

Mind–body problems Philosophical problems that arise when we try to understand how *mental* phenomena are related to *physical* phenomena. Examples include the *problem of other minds*, the *problem of mental causation*, and the *problem of psychophysical emergence*. Sometimes the expression 'the mind–body problem' with the definite article is used to refer to the range of problems that concern the nature of mental phenomena and their relation to physical phenomena.

Modal argument for substance dualism If I can exist without a body, then I cannot be a body; and I can exist without a body. The second premise is defended by appeal to the *conceivability argument* and the *essential property argument*.

Monism versus dualism In philosophy of mind, the monist–dualist distinction concerns claims about what kinds of things there are. Monists claim there is only one kind of thing. Dualists claim there are two kinds of things. Monist theories include *idealism*, *physicalism*, and *neutral monism*. Dualist theories include *dual-attribute theory* and *substance dualism*.

Multilevel worldview   Also called a 'multilayered worldview': a picture of the universe according to which reality consists of a number of different levels or layers. The levels are often taken to correspond to branches of science, with the lowest level corresponding to the objects, properties, and events postulated by fundamental physics, followed by the objects, properties, and events postulated by atomic physics, chemistry, biology, psychology, and social sciences such as economics. Lower-level objects, properties, and events are taken to compose higher-level objects, properties, and events. Fundamental physical particles are taken to compose atoms, for instance, which compose molecules, which compose organic tissues, which compose organisms, which compose social systems. Different multilevel worldviews understand interlevel relations in different ways: some take higher-level sciences to be *reducible* to lower-level ones; others deny this. Some take higher-level properties to *emerge* from interactions among lower-level systems; others take higher-level properties to be *realized* by lower-level interactions. Yet others take higher-level phenomena to be *embodied* in lower-level subactivities and subsystems. Levels can be defined globally or locally. A global view of levels claims that the same hierarchy of levels exists throughout the natural world. A local view of levels denies that there is a single levels-hierarchy existing throughout the natural world; rather, there are different kinds of levels corresponding to different kinds of things.

Multiple-realizability argument   An argument that was taken to show the falsity of the *psychophysical identity theory* and to support *anti-reductivism*. The argument has three premises. The first is called the multiple-realizability thesis: (1) Mental states are multiply realizable; that is, it is possible for a given type of mental state to be *realized* in more than one type of physical state. Pain, for instance, might be realized by states of a human brain, the states of a Martian gamma organ, or the states of complex robotic circuitry. (2) If mental states are multiply realizable, then they are not identical to physical states. (3) If mental states are not identical to physical states, then psychological discourse is not reducible to physical theory. The multiple-realizability thesis is defended by appeal to *conceivability-possibility principles* and by appeal to work in biology, neuroscience, and *artificial intelligence* research. *Reductive physicalists* can respond to the argument in several ways, so it remains controversial. It has nevertheless been very influential, and together with *functionalism* it inspired *nonreductive physicalism*.

Nagel, Thomas (1937–)   American philosopher best known in philosophy of mind for his views on *subjectivity* and *qualia*.

Necessity of identity   The principle that if $x = y$, then necessarily $x = y$. A thing not only does not exist without itself, it cannot exist without itself.

Neoplatonists   *See* Plato.

Neutral monism   A mind–body theory that claims that fundamentally everything is neither mental nor physical but neutral. Its defenders include the philosophers *William James* and *Bertrand Russell*. Neutral monism has been a marginal view in philosophy of mind largely because its exponents have failed to provide an informative definition of neutral phenomena.

Nihilism (eliminativism about people)   A term used in this text to refer to the claim that people, such as you and I, do not exist. The argument for nihilism appeals to *mereological universalism*. Located exactly where I am there are many different collections of particles all of which constitute wholes that are all candidates for being me. Since there is no principled way of determining which collection the word 'I' refers to, it must refer to none of them. Therefore 'I' has no referent. I do not exist, and the same is true for all people.

Nonorganismic dual-attribute theory   *See* Dual-attribute theory

Nonreductive physicalism   A family of physicalist theories that reject the *reduction of the special sciences* to physics. Unlike *eliminative physicalists* and like *reductive physicalists*, nonreductive physicalists claim that psychological discourse has real descriptive and explanatory legitimacy. Unlike reductive physicalists, however, nonreductivists deny that this legitimacy is due to psychological categories corresponding in a straightforward way to physical categories. It is due instead to psychological categories satisfying special interests we have. We have many different descriptive and explanatory interests. Physics satisfies some of them, but it cannot satisfy all; only the special sciences can. As a result, physics cannot take over the descriptive and explanatory roles the special sciences play. Hence, the special sciences are not reducible to physics. *Dual-attribute theories* deny the reducibility of the special sciences to physics as well, but for different reasons. Unlike nonreductive physicalist theories, they deny that all properties are physical. Because nonreductive physicalism is committed to rejecting reductivism, and because some forms of it distinguish between *higher-order and lower-order properties*, it is sometimes characterized as a form of *property dualism*, but this label is misleading at best. Nonreductive physicalism is committed to *physicalism*, a form of *monism*. It implies that all properties are physical, and is thus incompatible with property dualism. The label 'nonreductive physicalism' has also been used to describe any view that (1) rejects reductivism yet (2) implies that we are composed entirely of physical particles. This too is a misleading label since many nonphysicalist theories endorse (1) and (2) including *hylomorphism* and dual-attribute theories such as *emergentism* and *epiphenomenalism*. Varieties of nonreductive physicalism include *realization physicalism*, *supervenience physicalism*, and *anomalous monism*. Nonreductive physicalism was inspired by arguments against the *psychophysical identity theory* such as the *multiple-realizability argument*.

Nonreductivism   A label used in this text as an abbreviation for *nonreductive physicalism*.

Objective   *See* Subjectivity versus objectivity.

Occasionalism   *See* Interactionism versus noninteractionism

Ockham's razor   A methodological principle named after the fourteenth-century philosopher William of Ockham (1287–1347). It says that when constructing theories entities are not to be multiplied beyond necessity. Given a choice between two theories that are otherwise indistinguishable, Ockham's razor dictates that we should prefer the theory with the simpler ontology, the one that posits fewer basic entities. Ockham's razor is a premise in *J. J. C. Smart's* argument for the *psychophysical identity theory*.

Old facts under new representations   An objection to the *knowledge argument*. It claims that Mary does not learn a new fact when she experiences color for the first time; she instead knows the same old facts but under a new representation.

Ontological naturalism   The claim that when it comes to determining what things exist, the sciences play a starring role. The sciences may not be the only guides to what exists, say ontological naturalists, but they are the most reliable, and their results should enjoy a privileged status when it comes to determining what exists and what doesn't. Appeals to ontological naturalism figure in arguments against *qualia* and against *mereological universalism*.

Overdetermination   An occurrence is overdetermined if it has two or more independent fully sufficient causes.

Panprotopsychism   A dual-attribute theory that tries to solve *the problem of psychophysical emergence* by postulating protoconscious or protomental states. These protomental states are supposed to combine to produce more complex protomental states and ultimately mental states of a familiar sort. Because the theory does not attribute ordinary mental states to fundamental physical particles, panprotopsychism is taken to be more plausible than *panpsychism*.

Panpsychism   A dual-attribute theory that claims that everything has mental states including, for instance, fundamental physical particles. Panpsychism should not be confused with *idealism*, a form of monism that claims everything is mental.

Parallelism   A noninteractionist form of substance dualism. It claims persons and bodies do not interact but merely appear to interact because they operate in parallel: their states are correlated without interacting. *Leibniz* endorsed the doctrine of pre-established harmony to explain the parallel operation of persons and bodies: God created the universe so that persons and bodies would operate in sync. *See also* Interactionism versus noninteractionism.

Pattern expression theory of psychological language   An account of psychological language that was suggested by *Ludwig Wittgenstein*, and that is endorsed by exponents of a *hylomorphic theory of mind*. Psychological language is not like a theory that postulates hypothetical entities, as the *theory model of psychological discourse* claims. Rather, psychological language is a form of social behavior that uses symbols to express directly observable patterns of social and environmental interaction.

Penfield, Wilder (1891–1976)   Canadian neurosurgeon who did pioneering work mapping functional areas of the brain using electrical stimulation. Penfield endorsed a form of *substance dualism*.

Penrose, Roger (1931–)   British physicist best known in philosophy of mind for attacking *functionalism* by appeal to Godel's theorem and for defending the view that future physics will provide resources for explaining the emergence of *consciousness*.

Persistence conditions   Conditions sufficient and necessary for something to exist over time.

Persons   A term used in many different ways in philosophy and ordinary discourse. Some philosophers define persons as mental beings – as things that have mental states or that are capable of having mental states. *See* Psychological-continuity theory of personal identity, Animalism, and Constitutionalism.

Phenomenal consciousness   *See* qualia

Phenomenalism   *See* Idealism.

Physical   Physical phenomena are defined by physics. Physical objects, properties, and events in the strictest sense are those postulated by physics.

Physical closure   The claim that if a physical event has a cause at time *t*, it has a physical cause at time *t*. Closure does not imply that every physical event has a cause; it is compatible with the existence of uncaused physical events. Nor does it imply that physical events cannot have nonphysical causes; it is compatible with a physical event having a physical cause and an *overdetermining* nonphysical cause. Physical closure figures centrally in arguments against *nonreductive physicalism* and *emergentism* that appeal to the *problem of mental causation*. The *exclusion argument* is an example.

Physical monism   *See* Physicalism.

Physicalism   The claim that everything is physical. Physicalism is also called 'materialism'. The latter, older term harkens back to a time when physicists believed that the physical domain was defined by matter. Nineteenth-century energy physics convinced them, however, that matter was not the basic category that unified the subject-matter of physics. Varieties of physicalism include *eliminative physicalism*, *reductive physicalism*, and *nonreductive physicalism*. Physicalism is supported by an *inductive generalization from past scientific success*. Critics argue against it by appeal to *Hempel's dilemma*, the *knowledge argument*, and *qualia-based arguments*.

Plato (427–347 BCE)   Ancient Greek philosopher known in philosophy of mind as an early defender of *substance dualism*. In Plato's dialogue *The Phaedo*, the character of Socrates argues that the *soul* is immortal. Neoplatonists in late antiquity used Plato's ideas to interpret Christian doctrines. Many Neoplatonists, most prominently Gnostic Christians, combined a substance dualistic understanding of the soul with the idea that the physical universe was an evil or corrupt prison from which we would be liberated at death.

Platonists   *See* Plato

Possibility   Arguments about what is possible figure prominently in philosophy of mind and other areas of philosophy. Different notions of possibility have different scopes. Something is technologically possible, for instance, if it is compatible with current technological constraints. Something is physically possible if it is compatible with the laws of physics, and something is metaphysically possible if it is compatible with itself. A married bachelor, for instance, is not merely technologically or physically impossible; it is metaphysically or logically impossible. Metaphysical or broadly logical possibility is possibility simpliciter. Claims about what is possible are often defended by appeal to *conceivability-possibility principles*.

Principle of Alternative Possibilities (PAP)   The claim that moral responsibility requires the ability to do otherwise. PAP is rejected by most contemporary *compatibilists* on the grounds that *Frankfurt-type examples* disprove it.

Private language argument   An argument advanced by *Ludwig Wittgenstein* against a *private conception of mental phenomena*. If psychological expressions such as 'pain' refer to private, *subjective* episodes, then we would not be able to use these expressions for interpersonal communication. Since we do use these expressions for interpersonal communication they must not refer to private, subjective episodes.

Private versus public conceptions of mental phenomena   A private conception of mental phenomena focuses on notions like *first-person authority*, *subjectivity*, and *consciousness*. It takes mental phenomena to be inner, subjective occurrences to which only the individual person experiencing them has direct access. A public conception of mental phenomena, by contrast, focuses on notions like *intentionality*, mental representation, and *rationality*. It takes mental phenomena to consist in the various ways we comport ourselves toward engagement with the world – ways that can be described and evaluated in rational terms.

Privileged access   *See* First-person authority.

Problem of causal/explanatory exclusion   *See* Exclusion argument.

Problem of free will and determinism   A philosophical problem that can be understood in terms of the following claims. (1) Either *determinism* is true, or determinism is false. (2) If determinism is true, then there is no free will. (3) If determinism is false, then there is no free will. (4) There is moral responsibility only if there is free will. (5) There is moral responsibility. Claims (1)–(3) imply that there is no free will, but claims (4) and (5) imply that there is. The claims are thus jointly inconsistent, but it is difficult to know which is false. *Compatibilist* theories try to solve the problem by rejecting Claim (2) or Claim (4). *Libertarian* theories try to solve the problem by rejecting Claim (3), and *hard determinist* and *hard incompatibilist* theories try to solve the problem by rejecting Claim (5).

Problem of interaction   A version of the problem of mental causation that is used as an objection to *substance dualism*. If substance dualism is true, says the argument, then persons and bodies cannot causally interact, but persons and bodies can causally interact; therefore, substance dualism must be false.

Problem of mental causation   Actions have physical causes, events in the nervous system. They also have mental causes – beliefs and desires, for instance. Understanding how the mental causes and the physical causes of actions are related poses a philosophical problem: (1) actions have mental causes; (2) actions have physical causes; (3) mental causes and physical causes are distinct; (4) an action does not have more than one cause. Claims (1)–(3) imply that any given action has more than one cause, but Claim (4) rules this out. *Eliminative physicalists* and *epiphenomenalists* reject Claim (1). *Psychophysical identity theorists* reject Claim (3). *Emergentists*, *nonreductive physicalists*, and *substance dualists* reject either Claim (2) or Claim (4), and *hylomorphists* argue by appeal to *causal pluralism* that the problem equivocates on the term 'cause', and once the equivocation is resolved, claims (1)–(4) are no longer inconsistent. Kim's *exclusion argument* appeals to the problem to disprove *nonreductive physicalism* and *emergentism*.

Problem of other minds   A problem posed by the following claims: (1) we often know what other people think and how they feel; (2) what other people think and how they feel belong to a private, subjective domain; (3) if what other people think and how they feel belong to a private, subjective domain, then we cannot know what other people think and how they feel as often as we suppose. *Eliminative physicalists*, some *substance dualists*, and some *dual-attribute theorists* reject Claim (1). *Hylomorphists* and *behaviorists* reject Claim (2) in favor of a *direct access thesis*, and many philosophers reject Claim (3) in favor some *inferential access thesis*.

Problem of psychophysical emergence   A philosophical problem posed by the following claims: (1) we are conscious beings; (2) we are composed entirely of nonconscious parts; (3) no number of nonconscious parts could combine to produce a conscious whole; (4) the properties of a whole are determined by the properties of its parts. *Eliminative physicalists* reject Claim (1). *Panpsychists* and *panprotopsychists* reject Claim (2), as do *substance dualists*, *idealists*, and *nonorganismic dual-attribute theorists* albeit for different reasons. Many *emergentists*, *epiphenomenalists*, *physicalists*, and *neutral monists* reject Claim (3), *hylomorphists* reject Claim (4), and some *mind–body pessimists* claim that the problem is entirely insoluble.

Properties   The ontological correlates of predicates. Properties are expressed by predicates. The property of being red, for instance, is expressed by the predicate 'is red'. Likewise, the property of believing that $2 + 2 = 4$ is expressed by the predicate 'believes that $2 + 2 = 4$'. Mental properties are expressed by mental predicates such as 'is in pain', 'hopes that it will not rain', 'believes that there are eight planets in our solar system'. Physical properties are expressed by physical predicates such as 'has a mass of 3 kg'.

Property dualism   The claim that there are mental properties, that there are physical properties, and that mental and physical properties are distinct. Property dualism is the defining characteristic of all dualistic theories, both *dual-attribute theories* and forms of *substance dualism*. *Nonreductive physicalism* is sometimes characterized as a property dualistic theory because some forms of it such as *realization physicalism* distinguish between *higher-* and *lower-order properties*. But this is a misleading characterization since it suggests that *physicalism* is not committed to the claim that everything is physical including all properties. Property dualism is a commitment to the existence of two different kinds of first-order properties. Properties of neither sort, in other words, are mere logical constructions.

Propositional attitudes   *See* Intentionality.

Protoconscious states   *See* Panprotopsychism.

Protomental states   *See* Panprotopsychism.

Psychological-continuity theory of personal identity   The view that being the same person over time consists in maintaining psychological continuity over time. Four-year-old Eleanor is the same person as 40-year-old Eleanor on this account because there is a continuity between 4-year-old Eleanor's mental states and 40-year-old Eleanor's mental states. Psychological-continuity accounts of personal identity encounter problems with *fission*. Some philosophers handle these problems by endorsing *temporal parts theory*. Others reject the psychological-continuity theory in favor of *animalism* which implies that our identity over time consists in being the same animal over time.

Psychophysical coincidence   The claim that the same individual can have both mental and physical properties. Psychophysical coincidence is rejected by *substance dualists* and *eliminativists*, but endorsed by *dual-attribute theorists*, *reductive physicalists*, and *nonreductive physicalists*, among others.

Psychophysical identity theory   A *reductive physicalist* theory that claims that mental states will be identified with states of the nervous system through empirical investigation – a process of *theoretical identification*.

Public conception of mental phenomena   *See* Private versus public conception of mental phenomena.

Putnam, Hilary (1926–)   American philosopher and prolific contributor to philosophy of mind. Putnam was an early supporter of the *theory model of psychological discourse*, a critic of *logical behaviorism*, and a defender of *empirical essentialism*. He is perhaps best known, however, as the originator and later critic of *functionalism*, and as the originator of *Twin Earth thought experiments* in favor of *externalism*. His students include *Ned Block*, *Jerry Fodor*, and *Jaegwon Kim*. Few if any philosophers have had an influence on philosophy of mind in the twentieth century as profound as Putnam's.

Qualia   A Latin word that means qualities. The corresponding singular term is 'quale'. Qualia are supposed to be the qualitative or phenomenal features of *conscious* experiences. Paradigmatic examples include sensations and pains. The philosopher *Thomas Nagel* introduced the expression 'what it's like' to refer to qualia. There is something it's like to experience a pain, or a flavor, or an odor. What it's like cannot be expressed verbally, say many exponents of qualia; to know what something is like someone must experience it him or herself. Critics of *physicalism* and similar theories often appeal to qualia. Examples of their arguments include the *knowledge argument*, and other *qualia-based arguments*, as well as the argument for *epiphenomenalism*. There are several arguments against the existence of qualia including the argument for *eliminative physicalism*, the appeal to *ontological naturalism*, *Dennett's* argument against qualia, and Wittgenstein's *private language argument*.

Qualia-based arguments   Arguments that appeal to the existence of qualia in an effort to show that physicalism and similar theories are false. According to the arguments, it is possible for two systems, A and B, to be physically indistinguishable and yet differ in their phenomenal states or *qualia*: Perhaps A and B experience different qualia (the possibility of inverted qualia) or perhaps A has qualia while B altogether lacks them (the possibility of absent qualia: B would be a qualia zombie). Either way, if physicalism is true, then absent and inverted qualia should be impossible. If they are possible, therefore, physicalism must be false.

Qualia zombies   *See* Qualia-based arguments.

Quine, Willard van Orman (1908–2000)   Prominent American philosopher. Quine contributed to the demise of *logical positivism* and was also the teacher of the philosophers *Donald Davidson*, *David Lewis*, and *Daniel Dennett*, all of whom have made important contributions to the philosophy of mind. Quine seems to have favored some type of *behaviorism* early in his career, but he also expressed sympathy at times for *eliminativism*, and later endorsed *Davidson's anomalous monism*.

Radical behaviorism   *See* Behaviorism (in psychology).

Rationality   To describe people's behavior in terms of their beliefs, desires, and other intentional mental states is to classify that behavior as something that is explainable by appeal to reasons. It is important to distinguish nonrational behavior from irrational behavior. Nonrational behavior is behavior that is not explainable by appeal to reasons. The behavior of a rock, for instance, is nonrational. Irrational behavior, on the other hand, is behavior that is explainable by appeal to reasons, but that fails to satisfy certain criteria for rational evaluation. If I act contrary to what I believe is in my best interests, then I act irrationally but not nonrationally.

Reactive attitude theories of free will and moral responsibility   Compatibilist theories that ground moral responsibility in ordinary social practices involving reactive attitudes such as gratitude and resentment. The term 'reactive attitudes' is due to the philosopher *P. F. Strawson*. Critics argue that reactive attitude theories fail to capture our intuitions about what constitutes moral responsibility.

Realism versus Instrumentalism   *See* Instrumentalism.

Realization   A relation between abstract and concrete descriptions or things. An abstract object such as a rectangle is said to be realized in a piece of wood or metal. Likewise, an abstract procedure such as an algorithm is said to be realized in the gears or circuits of a calculator. According to *functionalism*, mental properties are abstract properties; they are *higher-order properties* that are realized by lower-order properties. My beliefs, desires, pains, and other mental states are realized by states of the brain, for instance. If mental states can also be realized in other kinds of things, then they are *multiply realizable*.

Realization physicalism   A form of *nonreductive physicalism* that combines *physicalism* with *functionalism*. Realization physicalism claims mental properties, and *special scientific* properties generally, are realized by lower-level properties. *Higher-level properties*, it says, are *higher-order properties*, logical constructions that quantify over other properties. Arguments against realization physicalism include *Kim's trilemma* and the *exclusion argument*, as well as arguments that target *functionalism* and *physicalism*.

Reduction   The ability of one theory or conceptual framework to take over the descriptive and explanatory roles of another. The most influential account of reduction was articulated by the philosopher of science Ernest Nagel (1901–1985). On Nagel's view, Theory B can take over the descriptive and explanatory roles of Theory A if Theory A's laws can be explained by Theory B's laws. Nagel took theories to be sets of law statements, and he followed *Carl Hempel* in taking explanation to be deduction from law statements. On Nagel's view, therefore, reduction consists of the law statements of one theory being deducible from the law statements of another. That deduction may require *bridge principles* if the vocabulary of the reduced theory has predicates or terms not included in the vocabulary of the reducing theory. Biologists and scientists working in biological subdisciplines such as neuroscience often use the word 'reduction' to refer not to the ability of one theory to take over the descriptive and explanatory roles of another, but to refer to the method of *functional analysis*.

Reductionism   *See* Reductive physicalism.

Reductive physicalism   A form of physicalism that claims that psychological categories correspond to physical categories in some straightforward way. Examples include the *psychophysical identity theory* and *logical behaviorism*. According to reductivists, for instance, what we call 'pain' is really just a physical state such as a state of the brain. The mental and physical conceptual frameworks are just two different frameworks for describing the very same things. By contrast, *eliminative physicalists* deny that terms such as 'pain' refer to anything in reality, and *nonreductive physicalists* deny that psychological categories correspond to physical categories in a straightforward way. Reductive physicalism gets its name because it implies psychophysical *reduction*; it implies that physical discourse can take over the descriptive and explanatory roles of psychological discourse.

Reductivism *See* Reductive physicalism.

Representational theories of consciousness Representational theories claim that phenomenal *consciousness* can be understood in terms of *mental representation*. They deny that qualia are private nonrelational phenomena, and claim instead that the qualitative features we experience are features of objects we experience themselves – features that we represent internally with our sensory organs. Redness we experience when looking at a tomato, for instance, is a property of the tomato itself which is represented with an internal state of the nervous system that registers the presence of that property in the environment. Physicalists have appealed to representational theories of consciousness in an effort to respond to *qualia-based arguments* against their view.

Rule Alpha A premise in the *consequence argument*. It says that what is necessarily the case is not in our control.

Rule Beta A premise in the *consequence argument*. It says that if X is not in our control, and Y is a necessary consequence of X, and it is not in our control that Y is a necessary consequence of X, then Y is not in our control either.

Russell, Bertrand (1872–1970) A British philosopher and prolific writer best known in philosophy of mind for defending *neutral monism* and inspiring *logical positivism*.

Ryle, Gilbert (1900–1976) British philosopher who taught ancient philosophy at Oxford. He is best known for his book *The Concept of Mind*. Ryle and his contemporary at Cambridge, *Ludwig Wittgenstein*, are often classified as *logical behaviorists*. There are nevertheless good reasons to think they were merely opponents of a *private conception of mental phenomena* who wanted to reject the *inferential access thesis*.

Scientific Revolution A label attached to a series of monumental changes in the way people approached the study of the natural world during the sixteenth and seventeenth centuries. The scientific ideas of *Aristotle* had dominated Western thought for over a thousand years when the sixteenth-century astronomer Nicolaus Copernicus proposed a new model of the universe. Contrary to Aristotle, Copernicus claimed that the Earth orbited the Sun not vice versa. In order to prove the Copernican model of the universe true, Galileo Galilei and other leaders of the Scientific Revolution developed new tools and techniques for studying the natural world. Those techniques ultimately showed that it was not just Aristotle's cosmology that was wrong, but almost every aspect of his science. The Scientific Revolution involved more than a rejection of Aristotelian science, however; it involved a rejection of Aristotelian philosophy as well. In its place people erected a new philosophy based on dichotomies: freedom versus determinism, fact versus value, mind versus body. These dichotomies are responsible for many of the problems of modern philosophy. The task of philosophy since the Scientific Revolution has been to resolve the tensions they generate – to explain how we can be free, mental, moral beings if we inhabit a universe that at a fundamental physical level has none of these features. An example is the *problem of free will and determinism*. Philosophy of mind tries to resolve the problems generated by the mind–body or mental–physical dichotomy. These are called *mind–body problems*.

Searle, John (1932–) American philosopher best known in philosophy of mind for his work clarifying the nature of *intentionality* and for advancing the *Chinese room argument* against *functionalism* and *strong AI*. Searle endorses an *emergentist* theory of dubious coherence. He claims that mental properties are both realized in and caused by states of the brain, yet on standard accounts *realization* is incompatible with causation, and Searle does not offer a clear competing account. Nor is it clear how his account manages to avoid the problems besetting emergentism and realization physicalism such as the *problem of mental causation*.

Sellars, Wilfrid (1912–1989) American philosopher best known for his essay 'Empiricism and the Philosophy of Mind' in which he anticipated many of the problems and ideas that would take center stage in later mind–body debates. Examples include the *theory model of psychological discourse*, the *psychophysical identity theory*, and problems concerning phenomenal *consciousness* and *qualia*.

Semicompatibilism A *compatibilist* theory that grounds moral responsibility in exercising the right kind of control over actions. Unlike other compatibilist theories, however, semicompatibilism denies that free will is compatible with *determinism*. Semicompatibilists thus deny that moral responsibility requires free will. Critics argue that semicompatibilism fails to capture our intuitions about what constitutes moral responsibility.

Sensorimotor contingencies Also called 'sensorimotor expectations': lawlike relations among sensation, movement, and the environment. I know implicitly, for instance, that if I were to move my head around the object in front of me it would present me with a different visual profile. Exponents of *sensorimotor theories of consciousness* claim that the qualitative aspects of our experience are constituted in part by our implicit knowledge of sensorimotor contingencies.

Sensorimotor theories of consciousness Sensorimotor theories claim that the qualitative features of experience can be given an account in terms of patterns of sensorimotor interaction with the environment. What it's like to see red, for instance, is constituted by the range of ways we respond to and interact with red objects using our senses and motor abilities. These forms of interaction involve implicit knowledge of *sensorimotor contingencies*. Because sensorimotor theories of consciousness take conscious experiences to be patterns of environmental interaction, they mesh neatly with a *hylomorphic theory of mind*. Physicalists, however, can also appeal to them in an effort to respond to *qualia-based arguments* against their view.

Simple indeterminism A form of *libertarianism* that claims that actions are completely uncaused. Critics allege that simple indeterminist theories face a problem with control: if an agent's actions are completely uncaused, then the agent is not in control of their occurrence and, in that case, the agent cannot be held morally accountable for them.

Smart, J. J. C. (1920–)   Australian philosopher best known in philosophy of mind for defending the *psychophysical identity theory* by appeal to *Ockham's razor*.

Soft determinism   A *compatibilist* theory that also endorses *determinism*. Soft determinism is contrasted with *hard determinism*.

Soul (Greek *psyche*, Latin *anima*)   An ambiguous term often used in philosophy of mind to describe a version of *substance dualism*. A soul is supposed to be a nonphysical entity attached to a body. According to an older definition, however, soul is the principle of life, the whatever-it-is that distinguishes a living thing from a nonliving one. Greek natural philosophers such as *Democritus* claimed that this was something that could be described at a fundamental physical level such as a large proportion of round atoms. Philosophers influenced by *Plato*, on the other hand, claimed that soul was a nonphysical entity present in a living thing. Finally, philosophers influenced by *Aristotle* claimed that soul was the structure or organization of fundamental physical materials in a living thing. The distinctions among Greek naturalist, Platonist, and Aristotelian *hylomorphic* views of soul were later reflected in the distinctions among mechanists, vitalists, and organicists in modern biology.

Soul view of persons   A term used in this text to refer to the view that we are animals that have nonphysical components – *souls*.

Special sciences   Sciences other than fundamental physics such as chemistry, biology, psychology, and social sciences such as economics. Fundamental physics is supposed to be the one general science whose laws apply everywhere without exception. By contrast, the laws of the special sciences are limited to specific domains – living things in the case of biology, for instance, or mental things in the case of psychology. The term 'special science' is also used to refer to conceptual frameworks that are not strictly speaking scientific such as ordinary psychological discourse.

Strawson, P. F. (1919–2006)   British philosopher best known in philosophy of mind for defending a *dual-attribute theory* and a *reactive attitude* approach to free will. P. F. Strawson is the father of philosopher Galen Strawson (1952–) who is known in philosophy of mind as an exponent of *qualia* and for advancing arguments against the existence of free will and moral responsibility.

Strong AI   *See* Artificial Intelligence.

Strong supervenience   *See* Supervenience.

Subjectivity versus objectivity   The idea that mental states are subjective is the idea that they are accessible in principle to only one person – the person whose mental states or experiences they are. Objective phenomena, by contrast, are accessible in principle to more than one person. Bodily behavior, for instance, is supposed to be objective. In philosophy of mind, the subjective–objective distinction is closely related to the internal–external or inner–outer distinction. Some views claim that our mental states comprise inner, subjective domains that are accessible only to the people whose experiences they are while our bodily behavior belongs to an outer, objective domain that is accessible to other people. This picture gives rise to the *inferential access thesis*. The notion of subjectivity is also related to the idea that each of us occupies a unique point of view. *Thomas Nagel* claims that science is an effort to achieve an objective outlook – a view from nowhere – that is free from the particularities of any one subjective point of view.

Substance dualism   A mind–body theory that endorses *property dualism* but denies *psychophysical coincidence*. According to substance dualists there are not only two different kinds of properties; there are two different kinds of individuals or substances having those properties: individuals having only mental properties (persons), and individuals having only physical properties (bodies). By itself substance dualism does not specify how persons and bodies are related, so there are *interactionist* and noninteractionist forms of it. Substance dualists defend their theory by appeal to a *modal argument*.

Supervenience   The idea that entities (properties, events, descriptions) cannot differ in one respect without differing in another. To say that A-properties supervene on B-properties, for instance, is to say that two things, x and y, cannot differ from each other in A-respects without differing from each other in B-respects. If x and y have all the same B-properties, then they must have all the same A-properties; B-twins, in other words, must be A-twins. There are different kinds of supervenience relations: weak, global, and strong, for instance. A-properties weakly supervene on B-properties exactly if for any individuals x and y in world w, if x and y are physical twins in w, they must also be mental twins in w. A-properties globally supervene on B-properties, on the other hand, exactly if worlds with indistinguishable distributions of B-properties over individuals would also have indistinguishable distributions of A-properties over individuals. And A-properties strongly supervene on B-properties exactly if it is impossible for x in world w_1 and y in world w_2 to differ from each other in respect of their A-properties without differing from each other in respect of their B-properties. During the 1980s and 1990s many philosophers believed that some type of supervenience relation would provide the basis for a workable form of *nonreductive physicalism*. Their optimism has since cooled in light of criticisms advanced by philosophers like *Jaegwon Kim*.

Supervenience argument   *See* Exclusion argument.

Supervenience physicalism   A form of *nonreductive physicalism* that claims that *special scientific* phenomena *supervene* on physical phenomena. Supervenience physicalism faces several serious problems and has been forcefully criticized by *Jaegwon Kim*.

Teleological functionalism   A type of *functionalist* theory that places restrictions on the kinds of systems that can realize mental states. To realize mental states, teleological functionalists say, a system must have parts that serve a purpose in the system; they must have a *function* in a teleological sense, a sense that differs from the notion of function employed by classic functionalist theories. By placing restrictions on *realization*, teleological functionalists look to respond to the *liberalism objection to functionalism*.

Temporal parts theory   The claim that objects consist not just of spatial parts but of temporal parts as well. Objects are not just spread out in space, in other words; they are spread out in time as well. Exponents of *psychological-continuity* accounts of personal identity sometimes appeal to temporal parts theory to solve problems with *fission*.

Theoretical identification   The process of identifying entities postulated by one theory with entities postulated by another theory through scientific investigation. The notion of theoretical identification factors centrally in the *psychophysical identity theory*. There are at least two models of theoretical identification. *J. J. C. Smart* proposed that theoretical identification was a result of *Ockham's razor*. *David Lewis* and *David Armstrong* argued that it was instead an implication of the *transitivity of identity*: if pain, say, is by definition the state caused by burns, and we discover empirically that brain state B is the state caused by burns, then pain must be identical to brain state B.

Theory model of psychological discourse   A popular account of psychological language suggested by *Wilfrid Sellars* and *Hilary Putnam* among others, but defended principally by *Paul and Patricia Churchland*. According to the theory model, psychological discourse is or is like a scientific theory that postulates hypothetical entities (mental states) whose relations to one another are supposed to explain observable human behavior. Critics of the theory model include exponents of the *pattern expression theory* of psychological language such as *hylomorphists*.

Token physicalism   *See* Type versus token physicalism.

Transitivity of identity   The principle that if $x = y$, and $y = z$, then $x = z$. The transitivity of identity is central to the model of *theoretical identification* endorsed by *David Lewis* and *David Armstrong*.

Turing, Alan (1912–1954)   British mathematician considered to be the father of computer science. He is best known in philosophy of mind for the *Turing test*.

Turing machine   A Turing machine is an abstract description of an input–output system. It is named after *Alan Turing*, and is the basis of *functionalist* thinking about the mind.

Turing test   A thought experiment proposed by the British mathematician *Alan Turing*. A human judge interacts using a text-only apparatus with a human, on the one hand, and with a machine on the other. If the judge cannot tell which interlocutor is the human and which the machine, the machine is said to pass the Turing test. Turing suggested that intelligence consists in nothing but correlating inputs with outputs in the right kinds of ways, and hence a machine that passes the Turing test should count as an intelligent being. This idea inspired *functionalism*.

Twin Earth thought experiments   Cases described by *Hilary Putnam* in which two individuals (or a single individual considered in two different circumstances) inhabit environments that differ in some respect, and that environmental difference is responsible for a difference in their beliefs, desires, and other propositional attitudes. In Gabriel's environment people drink H_2O. In Xavier's environment, there is no H_2O, but another substance, XYZ, not found in Gabriel's environment. XYZ is indistinguishable from H_2O in all of its macroscopic features, so in Xavier's environment it is XYZ that people drink. Xavier has never encountered H_2O, and Gabriel has never encountered XYZ, but ordinary speakers of English in both environments make the same utterances concerning the stuff they call 'water'. What they refer to when they make those utterances, however, is different. When Gabriel says, "I want some water," he is talking about H_2O, the stuff he has always drunk in the past. When Xavier says, "I want some water," he is talking about XYZ, the stuff he has always drunk in the past. The same is true of Gabriel's and Xavier's mental states: Gabriel wants H_2O, Xavier wants XYZ. Gabriel and Xavier have different thoughts, then. Gabriel's thoughts concern H_2O, while Xavier's concern XYZ, and the reason is that they have been interacting in their respective environments with different kinds of stuff. People's beliefs, desires, and other propositional attitudes thus depend on environmental conditions such as the kinds of stuff they typically interact with.

Type–token distinction   A distinction originally drawn by the American philosopher Charles Sanders Peirce (1839–1914). A type is a general category and individual tokens are its members. The five quarters in my pocket are five tokens of a single type. In philosophy of mind the type–token distinction is often used as a way of describing the difference between *reductive physicalism* and *nonreductive physicalism*. *See* type versus token physicalism.

Type versus token physicalism   A way of drawing the distinction between reductive and nonreductive physicalism based on the type–token distinction. *Nonreductive physicalism* is called 'token physicalism' because it claims that every token, that is every particular individual or event, is a physical token even though not every type is a physical type. The types of individuals, properties, or events postulated by the *special sciences*, for instance, are not physical types. *Reductive physicalism*, on the other hand, is often called 'type physicalism' because it claims that the categories or types postulated by the special sciences correspond directly to the categories or types postulated by physics. Every token is thus a physical token, but in addition every type is a physical type. Because the type–token distinction can be applied to a broad range of ontological categories, the distinction between type and token physicalism is not fully informative unless we know what the types and tokens in question are, and for that reason other formulations of physicalist theories are preferable.

Verifiability theory of meaning   A doctrine of *logical positivism*. It claims that the meaning of a statement consists in its verification conditions, the conditions sufficient for knowing that the statement is true. According to logical positivists, statements could be verified in only two ways: empirically through scientific investigation, or analytically by analyzing the meaning of the statement's predicates and terms. Utterances that could not be verified in either way were meaningless, according to positivists. The verifiability theory of meaning was discredited for several reasons, not the least of which was that it was self-referentially incoherent: it did not satisfy its own criterion of meaningfulness since the claim that the meaning of a statement consists in its verification conditions can be verified neither empirically nor analytically.

Weak AI   *See* Artificial Intelligence.

Weak supervenience   *See* Supervenience.

What it's like   *See* Qualia.

Wittgenstein, Ludwig (1889–1951)   Influential Austrian philosopher who taught at Cambridge University. His best known works are the *Tractatus Logico-Philosophicus* and the posthumously published *Philosophical Investigations*. The former was an inspiration to *logical positivists* despite Wittgenstein's antipathy toward the positivist movement. After writing it Wittgenstein left professional philosophy to teach elementary-school children in a remote Austrian village. He subsequently developed or perhaps abandoned (which is a contested matter) the views he articulated in the *Tractatus*. The results eventually led to the *Philosophical Investigations*. The latter work has been very influential in the philosophy of mind largely on account of the *private language argument*, a collection of considerations that challenge the coherence of a *private conception of mental phenomena*. Wittgenstein, like his contemporary *Gilbert Ryle*, has often been described inaccurately as a *logical behaviorist* perhaps because he suggested a *pattern expression theory of psychological language* of the sort endorsed by *hylomorphists*.

References

ALEXANDER, SAMUEL. 1966. *Space, Time, and Deity*, Gifford Lectures. New York: Dover Publications.

AQUINAS, THOMAS. 1964. *Summa Theologiae*. Edited by Thomas Gilby. Cambridge: Blackfriars.

AQUINAS, THOMAS. 1995. "Commentary on Paul's First Epistle to the Corinthians." In *The Gifts of the Spirit: Selected Spiritual Writings*, edited by Benedict M. Ashley, 21–78. Hyde Park: New City Press.

AQUINAS, THOMAS. 1999. *A Commentary on Aristotle's De Anima*. Translated by Robert Pasnau. New Haven: Yale University Press.

ARISTOTLE. 1984. *The Complete Works of Aristotle*. Edited by Jonathan Barnes. 2 vols. Princeton: Princeton University Press.

ARMSTRONG, D. M. 1981. *The Nature of Mind and Other Essays*. Ithaca: Cornell University Press.

ARMSTRONG, D. M. 1993. *A Materialist Theory of the Mind*. 2nd edn. New York: Routledge.

AYALA, F. A. 1968. "Biology as an Autonomous Science." *American Scientist* 56: 207–21.

AYER, A. J. 1952. *Language, Truth, and Logic*. New York: Dover Publications.

BAKER, LYNNE RUDDER. 2000. *Persons and Bodies: A Constitution View*. New York: Cambridge University Press.

BALLARD, DANA. 1996. "On the Function of Visual Representation." In *Perception*, edited by Kathleen Akins, 111–31. New York: Oxford University Press. Reprinted in *Vision and Mind: Selected Readings in the Philosophy of Perception*, edited by Alva Noë and Evan Thompson.

BARNES, JONATHAN. 1971–2. "Aristotle's Concept of Mind." *Proceedings of the Aristotelian Society* 72: 101–14.

BARNES, JONATHAN. 1979. *The Presocratic Philosophers*. 2 vols. Boston: Routledge.

BARNES, JONATHAN. 2001. *Early Greek Philosophy*. 2nd edn. New York: Penguin Books.

BECHTEL, WILLIAM. 2007. "Reducing Psychology While Maintaining Its Autonomy Via Mechanistic Explanation." In *The Matter of the Mind: Philosophical Essays on Psychology, Neuroscience, and Reduction*, edited by Maurice Kenneth Davy Schouten and Huibert Looren de Jong, 172–98. Malden: Blackwell Publishers.

BENNETT, JONATHAN FRANCIS. 1988. *Events and Their Names*. Indianapolis: Hackett Publishing Co.

BENNETT, M. R., and P. M. S. HACKER. 2003. *Philosophical Foundations of Neuroscience*. Malden: Blackwell Publishers.

BERKELEY, GEORGE. 1998a [1710]. *A Treatise Concerning the Principles of Human Knowledge*. Edited by Jonathan Dancy. New York: Oxford University Press.

BERKELEY, GEORGE. 1998b [1713]. *Three Dialogues between Hylas and Philonous*. Edited by Jonathan Dancy. New York: Oxford University Press.

BICKLE, JOHN. 1998. *Psychoneural Reduction: The New Wave*. Cambridge, MA: MIT Press/A Bradford Book.

BICKLE, JOHN. 2003. *Philosophy and Neuroscience: A Ruthlessly Reductive Account*. Dordrecht: Kluwer Academic.

BIGELOW, JOHN C., and ROBERT PARGETTER. 1990. "Acquaintance with Qualia." *Theoria* 61/3: 129–47.

BLOCK, NED. 1980. "Troubles with Functionalism." In *Readings in Philosophy of Psychology*, edited by Ned Joel Block, 268–305. Cambridge, MA: Harvard University Press.

BLOCK, NED, and JERRY A. FODOR. 1972. "What Psychological States Are Not." *Philosophical Review* 81/2: 159–81.

BRENTANO, FRANZ CLEMENS. 1973. *Psychology from an Empirical Standpoint*. Translated by Margaret Schättle and Linda L. McAlister. Edited by Oskar Kraus and Linda L. McAlister. New York: Humanities Press.

BROAD, C. D. 1925. *The Mind and Its Place in Nature*. London: Paul, Trench, Trubner.

BURGE, TYLER. 1979. "Individualism and the Mental." *Midwest Studies in Philosophy* 4: 73–121.

BURGE, TYLER. 1982. "Other Bodies." In *Thought and Object*, edited by Andrew Woodfield, 97–120. New York: Oxford University Press.

BURGE, TYLER. 1989. "Individuation and Causation in Psychology." *Pacific Philosophical Quarterly* 70: 303–22.

BURGE, TYLER. 2007. *Foundations of Mind*. New York: Oxford University Press.

BURNYEAT, M. F. 1992. "Is an Aristotelian Theory of Mind Still Credible? (A Draft)." In *Essays on Aristotle's De Anima*, edited by Martha Craven Nussbaum and Amélie Rorty, 15–26. New York: Oxford University Press.

BUTTERFIELD, HERBERT. 1997. *The Origins of Modern Science: 1300–1800*. Rev. edn. New York, NY: The Free Press.

BYRNE, ALEX, and HEATHER LOGUE. 2009. *Disjunctivism: Contemporary Readings*. Cambridge: MIT Press.

BYRNE, RICHARD W., and ANDREW WHITEN. 1988. *Machiavellian Intelligence: Social Expertise and the Evolution of Intellect in Monkeys, Apes, and Humans*. New York: Oxford University Press.

CAMPBELL, NEIL A. 1996. *Biology*. 4th edn. Benjamin/Cummings Publishing Company, Inc.

CAMPBELL, NEIL A., and JANE B. REECE. 2009. *Biology*. 8th edn. San Francisco: Pearson Benjamin Cummings.

CARNAP, RUDOLPH. 1959. "Psychology in Physical Language." In *Logical Positivism*, edited by A. J. Ayer, 165–98. Glencoe: Free Press.

CARRUTHERS, PETER. 2003. *Phenomenal Consciousness: A Naturalistic Theory*. Cambridge: Cambridge University Press.

CARTWRIGHT, NANCY. 1999. *The Dappled World: A Study of the Boundaries of Science*. New York: Cambridge University Press.

CAUSEY, ROBERT L. 1977. *Unity of Science*. Boston: D. Reidel Publishing Co.

CHALMERS, DAVID JOHN. 1996. *The Conscious Mind*, Philosophy of Mind Series. New York: Oxford University Press.

CHALMERS, DAVID JOHN. 2002. "Consciousness and Its Place in Nature." In *Philosophy of Mind: Classical and Contemporary Readings*, edited by David John Chalmers, 247–72. New York: Oxford University Press.

CHISHOLM, RODERICK M. 1948. "The Problem of Empiricism." *Journal of Philosophy* 45 / 19: 512–17.

CHISHOLM, RODERICK M. 1957. *Perceiving: A Philosophical Study*. Ithaca: Cornell University Press.

CHISHOLM, RODERICK M. 1989. "Is There a Mind–Body Problem?" In *On Metaphysics*, 119–28. Minneapolis: University of Minnesota Press.

CHISHOLM, RODERICK M. 2002. "Human Freedom and the Self." In *Free Will*, edited by Robert Kane, 47–58. Malden: Blackwell Publishers.

CHRISTENSEN, SCOTT M., and DALE R. TURNER. 1993. *Folk Psychology and the Philosophy of Mind*. Hillsdale: Lawrence Erlbaum.

CHURCHLAND, PATRICIA SMITH. 1986. *Neurophilosophy*. Cambridge, MA: MIT Press.

CHURCHLAND, PAUL M. 1981. "Eliminative Materialism and the Propositional Attitudes." *Journal of Philosophy* 78: 67–90.

CHURCHLAND, PAUL M. 1984. *Matter and Consciousness*. Cambridge, MA: MIT Press.

CHURCHLAND, PAUL M. 1989. *A Neurocomputational Perspective: The Nature of Mind and the Structure of Science*. Cambridge, MA: MIT Press.

CLARKE, RANDOLPH. 1993. "Toward a Credible Agent-Causal Account of Free Will." *Nous* 27/2: 191–203.

CLARKE, RANDOLPH. 1996. "Agent Causation and Event Causation in the Production of Free Action." *Philosophical Topics* 24/2: 19–48.

COHEN, MARC. 1992. "The Credibility of Aristotle's Philosophy of Mind." In *Essays on Aristotle's De Anima*, edited by Martha Craven Nussbaum and Amélie Rorty, 57–73. New York: Oxford University Press.

CONEE, EARL. 1994. "Phenomenal Knowledge." *Australasian Journal of Philosophy* 72/2: 136–50.

CRANE, TIM, and D. H. MELLOR. 1990. "There Is No Question of Physicalism." *Mind* 99: 185–206.

CRAVER, CARL F. 2007. *Explaining the Brain: Mechanisms and the Mosaic Unity of Neuroscience*. New York: Oxford University Press.

CUMMINS, ROBERT E. 1975. "Functional Analysis." *Journal of Philosophy* 72: 741–64.

DAVIDSON, DONALD. 1993. "Thinking Causes." In *Mental Causation*, edited by John Heil and Alfred R. Mele, 3–18. New York: Oxford University Press.

DAVIDSON, DONALD. 2001a. "Actions, Reasons, and Causes." In *Essays on Actions and Events*, 3–20. New York: Oxford University Press.

DAVIDSON, DONALD. 2001b. "Events as Particulars." In *Essays on Actions and Events*, 181–88. New York: Oxford University Press.

DAVIDSON, DONALD. 2001c. "Mental Events." In *Essays on Actions and Events*, 207–24. New York: Oxford University Press.

DAVIDSON, DONALD. 2001d. "Psychology as Philosophy." In *Essays on Actions and Events*, 229–38. New York: Oxford University Press.

DAVIDSON, DONALD. 2001e. "Rational Animals." In *Subjective, Intersubjective, Objective*, 95–106. New York: Oxford University Press.

DAVIDSON, DONALD. 2001f. "The Individuation of Events." In *Essays on Actions and Events*, 163–80. New York: Oxford University Press.

DAVIDSON, DONALD. 2001g. "Thought and Talk." In *Inquiries into Truth and Interpretation*, 155–70. New York: Oxford University Press.

DECETY, J., and J. GREZES. 1999. "Neural Mechanisms Subserving the Perception of Human Action." *Trends in Cognitive Science* 3: 172–78.

DENNETT, DANIEL CLEMENT. 1978. "On Giving Libertarians What They Say They Want." In *Brainstorms*, 286–99. Montgomery: Bradford Books.

DENNETT, DANIEL CLEMENT. 1984. *Elbow Room: The Varieties of Free Will Worth Wanting*. Cambridge: MIT Press.

DENNETT, DANIEL CLEMENT. 1987. *The Intentional Stance*. Cambridge, MA: MIT Press.

DENNETT, DANIEL CLEMENT. 1991a. *Consciousness Explained*. Boston: Little, Brown, and Co.

DENNETT, DANIEL CLEMENT. 1991b. "Real Patterns." *Journal of Philosophy* 88/1: 27–51.

DENNETT, DANIEL CLEMENT. 1993. "Quining Qualia." In *Readings in Philosophy and Cognitive Science*, edited by Alvin I. Goldman, 381–414. Cambridge, MA: MIT Press.

DESCARTES, RENÉ. 1984. *The Philosophical Writings of Descartes*. Translated by John Cottingham, Robert Stoothoff, and Dugald Murdoch. 3 vols. New York: Cambridge University Press.

DEVITT, MICHAEL, and KIM STERELNY. 1999. *Language and Reality: An Introduction to the Philosophy of Language*. 2nd edn. Cambridge, MA: MIT Press.

DEWEY, JOHN. 1958. *Experience and Nature*. New York: Dover Publications.

D'HOLBACH, BARON. 1999 [1770]. *System of Nature*. Translated by H. D. Robinson and Alastair Jackson. Manchester: Clinamen Press.

DRETSKE, FRED I. 1988. *Explaining Behavior: Reasons in a World of Causes*. Cambridge, MA: MIT Press/A Bradford Book.

DRETSKE, FRED I. 1995. *Naturalizing the Mind*. Cambridge, MA: MIT Press.

DUNBAR, ROBIN. 1996. *Grooming, Gossip, and the Evolution of Language*. Cambridge, MA: Harvard University Press.

DWORKIN, GERALD. 1988. *The Theory and Practice of Autonomy*. New York: Cambridge University Press.

EDDINGTON, ARTHUR STANLEY. 1928. *The Nature of the Physical World*. New York: Macmillan Company.

EDWARDS, PAUL. 2002. "Hard and Soft Determinism." In *Free Will*, edited by Robert Kane, 59–69. Malden: Blackwell Publishers.

EKMAN, PAUL. 2007. *Emotions Revealed: Recognizing Faces and Feelings to Improve Communication and Emotional Life*. 2nd edn. New York: Owl Books.

EKSTROM, LAURA WADDELL. 2001. *Agency and Responsibility: Essays on the Metaphysics of Freedom*. Boulder: Westview Press.

FEIGL, HERBERT. 1958. "The 'Mental' and the 'Physical'." In *Minnesota Studies in the Philosophy of Science*, edited by Herbert Feigl, Michael Scriven, and Grover Maxwell, 370–497. Minneapolis: University of Minnesota Press.

FEYERABEND, PAUL. 1963. "Materialism and the Mind–Body Problem." *Review of Metaphysics* 17/1: 49–66.

FISCHER, JOHN MARTIN, and MARK RAVIZZA. 1998. *Responsibility and Control: A Theory of Moral Responsibility*. New York: Cambridge University Press.

FLANAGAN, OWEN J. 1991. *The Science of the Mind*. 2nd edn. Cambridge, MA: MIT Press.

FODOR, JERRY A. 1968. *Psychological Explanation*. New York: Random House.

FODOR, JERRY A. 1974. "Special Sciences, or, The Disunity of Science as a Working Hypothesis." *Synthese* 28: 97–115.

FODOR, JERRY A. 1975. *The Language of Thought*. Cambridge, MA: Harvard University Press.

FODOR, JERRY A. 1987. *Psychosemantics: The Problem of Meaning in the Philosophy of Mind*. Cambridge, MA: MIT Press.

FOSTER, JOHN. 1982. *The Case for Idealism*. Boston: Routledge.

FOSTER, JOHN. 1991. *The Immaterial Self: A Defence of the Cartesian Dualist Conception of the Mind*. New York: Routledge.

FOSTER, JOHN. 1993. "The Succinct Case for Idealism." In *Objections to Physicalism*, edited by Howard Robinson, 293–313. New York: Oxford University Press.

FRANKFURT, HARRY. 1969. "Alternative Possibilities and Moral Responsibility." *Journal of Philosophy* 66: 829–39.

FRANKFURT, HARRY. 1988. *The Importance of What We Care About*. New York: Cambridge University Press.

GARBER, DANIEL. 1982. "Understanding Interaction: What Descartes Should Have Told Elisabeth." *Southern Journal of Philosophy* 21, Supplement: 15–32.

GARDNER, HOWARD. 1985. *The Mind's New Science*. New York: Basic Books.

GEACH, PETER. 1967. *Mental Acts*. New York: Humanities Press.

GENDLER, TAMAR, and JOHN HAWTHORNE. 2002. *Conceivability and Possibility*. New York: Oxford University Press.

GIBBS, RAYMOND W. 2006. *Embodiment and Cognitive Science*. New York: Cambridge University Press.

GIBSON, JAMES JEROME. 1986. *The Ecological Approach to Visual Perception*. Hillsdale: Lawrence Erlbaum.

GINET, CARL. 1990. *On Action*. New York: Cambridge University Press.

GINET, CARL. 1996. "In Defense of the Principle of Alternative Possibilities: Why I Don't Find Frankfurt's Argument Convincing." *Philosophical Perspectives* 10: 403–17.

GOLDMAN, ALVIN I. 1970. *A Theory of Human Action*. Englewood Cliffs: Prentice-Hall.

GOLDMAN, ALVIN I. 1993. "Consciousness, Folk Psychology, and Cognitive Science." *Consciousness and Cognition* 2: 364–82.

GRANGER, HERBERT. 1996. *Aristotle's Idea of the Soul*. Dordrecht: Kluwer Academic.

HALDANE, JOHN. 1988. "Understanding Folk." *Proceedings of the Aristotelian Society* Supplementary Volume 62: 223–54.

HALDANE, JOHN. 1998. "A Return to Form in the Philosophy of Mind." *Ratio* 11/3: 253–77.

HALL, A. RUPERT. 1981. *From Galileo to Newton*. New York: Dover Publications.

HANKINS, THOMAS L. 1985. *Science and the Enlightenment.* New York: Cambridge University Press.

HARMAN, P. M. 1982. *Energy, Force, and Matter: The Conceptual Development of Nineteenth-Century Physics.* New York: Cambridge University Press.

HART, W. D. 1988. *The Engines of the Soul.* New York: Cambridge University Press.

HARTMAN, EDWIN. 1977. *Substance, Body, and Soul: Aristotelian Investigations.* Princeton: Princeton University Press.

HASLANGER, SALLY. 1989. "Endurance and Temporary Intrinsics." *Analysis* 49/3: 119–25.

HEIL, JOHN, and ALFRED R. MELE, eds. 1993. *Mental Causation.* New York: Oxford University Press.

HEMPEL, CARL. 1950. "Problems and Changes in the Empiricist Criterion of Meaning." *Revue Internationale de Philosophie* 41: 41–63.

HEMPEL, CARL. 1965. *Aspects of Scientific Explanation.* New York: Free Press.

HEMPEL, CARL. 1969. "Reduction: Ontological and Linguistic Facets." In *Philosophy, Science, and Method: Essays in Honor of Ernest Nagel,* edited by Sidney Morgenbesser, Patrick Suppes, and Morton Gabriel White, 179–99. New York: St Martin's Press.

HEMPEL, CARL. 1980. "The Logical Analysis of Psychology." In *Readings in Philosophy of Psychology,* edited by Ned Joel Block, 14–23. Cambridge, MA: Harvard University Press.

HOBBES, THOMAS. 1991 [1642]. *Man and Citizen: De Homine and De Cive.* Edited by Charles T. Wood, T. S. K. Scott-Craig and Bernard Gert. Indianapolis: Hackett Publishing Co.

HOBBES, THOMAS. 1996 [1651]. *Leviathan.* Edited by Richard Tuck. New York: Cambridge University Press.

HOLT, EDWIN B. 1973. *The Concept of Consciousness.* New York: Arno Press.

HONDERICH, TED. 1982. "The Argument for Anomalous Monism." *Analysis* 42: 59–64.

HONDERICH, TED. 2002. *How Free Are You?* 2nd edn. New York: Oxford University Press.

HOOKER, CLIFFORD. 1981. "Towards a General Theory of Reduction." *Dialogue* 20/1: 38–59.

HORGAN, JOHN. 2005. "The Forgotten Era of Brain Chips." *Scientific American* 293: 66–73.

HORGAN, TERENCE. 1984. "Jackson on Physical Information and Qualia." *Philosophical Quarterly* 34/135: 147–52.

HORGAN, TERENCE. 1994. "Physicalism(1)." In *A Companion to the Philosophy of Mind,* edited by Samuel D. Guttenplan, 471–79. Cambridge: Blackwell Publishers.

HUDSON, HUD. 2001. *A Materialist Metaphysics of the Human Person.* Ithaca: Cornell University Press.

HUME, DAVID. 2007 [1748]. *An Enquiry Concerning Human Understanding and Other Writings.* Edited by Stephen Buckle. New York: Cambridge University Press.

HUSSERL, EDMUND. 1970 [1900–1]. *Logical Investigations.* Translated by J. N. Findlay. 2 vols. New York: Humanities Press.

HUXLEY, T. H. 1874. "On the Hypothesis That Animals Are Automata, and Its History." *Nature* 10: 362–66.

JACKSON, FRANK. 1982. "Epiphenomenal Qualia." *Philosophical Quarterly* 32: 127–36.

JACKSON, FRANK. 1986. "What Mary Didn't Know." *Journal of Philosophy* 83: 291–95.

JACKSON, FRANK. 1998. "Postscript on Qualia." In *Mind, Methods and Conditionals: Selected Essays,* 76–9. London: Routledge.

JACKSON, FRANK. 2003. "Mind and Illusion." In *Minds and Persons*, edited by Anthony O'Hear, 251–72. New York: Cambridge University Press.

JAMES, WILLIAM. 1984a [1904]. "A World of Pure Experience." In *William James: The Essential Writings*, edited by Bruce W. Wilshire, 178–97. Albany: State University of New York Press.

JAMES, WILLIAM. 1984b [1904]. "Does 'Consciousness' Exist?'" In *William James: The Essential Writings*, edited by Bruce W. Wilshire, 162–77. Albany: State University of New York Press.

JAWORSKI, WILLIAM. 2009. "The Logic of How-Questions." *Synthese* 166: 133–55.

JAWORSKI, WILLIAM. "Mind and Multiple Realizability." Internet Encyclopedia of Philosophy, http://www.iep.utm.edu/mult-rea/

KANE, ROBERT. 1985. *Free Will and Values*. Albany: State University of New York Press.

KANE, ROBERT. 1996. *The Significance of Free Will*. New York: Oxford University Press.

KANE, ROBERT. 1999. "Responsibility, Luck, and Chance: Reflections on Free Will and Indeterminism." *Journal of Philosophy* 96/5: 217–40.

KANE, ROBERT. 2001. *The Oxford Handbook of Free Will*. New York: Oxford University Press.

KANE, ROBERT. 2002. *Free Will*. Malden: Blackwell Publishers.

KANE, ROBERT. 2005. *A Contemporary Introduction to Free Will*. New York: Oxford University Press.

KANT, IMMANUEL. 1993 [1785]. *Grounding for the Metaphysics of Morals*. Translated by James W. Ellington. 3rd edn. Indianapolis: Hackett Publishing Co.

KANT, IMMANUEL. 1998 [1781]. *Critique of Pure Reason*. Translated by Paul Guyer and Allen W. Wood. New York: Cambridge University Press.

KENNY, ANTHONY. 1968. "Cartesian Privacy." In *Wittgenstein: The Philosophical Investigations*, edited by George Pitcher, 352–70. Notre Dame: University of Notre Dame Press.

KENNY, ANTHONY. 1973. *Wittgenstein*. Cambridge, MA: Harvard University Press.

KENNY, ANTHONY. 1989. *The Metaphysics of Mind*. New York: Oxford University Press.

KIM, JAEGWON. 1972. "Phenomenal Properties, Psychophysical Laws and the Identity Theory." *The Monist* 56: 178–92. Selections reprinted in *Readings in Philosophy of Psychology*, 2 vols, edited by Ned Block, 234–6. Cambridge, MA: Harvard University Press.

KIM, JAEGWON. 1989. "The Myth of Nonreductive Physicalism." *Proceedings of the American Philosophical Association* 63: 31–47. Reprinted in *Supervenience and Mind*.

KIM, JAEGWON. 1992a. "'Downward Causation' in Emergentism and Nonreductive Physicalism." In *Emergence or Reduction?: Essays on the Prospects of Nonreductive Physicalism*, edited by Ansgar Beckermann, H. Flohr, and Jaegwon Kim, 119–38. Berlin: W. de Gruyter.

KIM, JAEGWON. 1992b. "Multiple Realizability and the Metaphysics of Reduction." *Philosophy and Phenomenological Research* 52/1: 1–26. Reprinted in *Supervenience and Mind*.

KIM, JAEGWON. 1993a. "Events as Property Exemplifications." In *Supervenience and Mind*, 33–52. New York: Cambridge University Press.

KIM, JAEGWON. 1993b. *Supervenience and Mind*. New York: Cambridge University Press.

KIM, JAEGWON. 1993c. "The Non-Reductivist's Troubles with Mental Causation." In *Mental Causation*, edited by John Heil and Alfred R. Mele, 189–210. Oxford: Clarendon Press. Reprinted in *Supervenience and Mind*.

KIM, JAEGWON. 1998. *Mind in a Physical World: An Essay on the Mind–Body Problem and Mental Causation.* Cambridge, MA: MIT Press.

KIM, JAEGWON. 1999. "Making Sense of Emergence." *Philosophical Studies* 95/1: 3–36.

KIM, JAEGWON. 2005. *Physicalism, or Something near Enough.* Princeton: Princeton University Press.

KIM, JAEGWON. 2006. "Emergence: Core Ideas and Issues." *Synthese* 151/3: 547–59.

KOLB, BRYAN, and IAN Q. WHISHAW. 2003. *Fundamentals of Human Neuropsychology.* 5th edn. New York: Worth Publishers.

KOSSLYN, STEPHEN MICHAEL. 1994. *Image and Brain: The Resolution of the Imagery Debate.* Cambridge, MA: MIT Press.

KOSSLYN, STEPHEN MICHAEL. 2006. "Mental Imagery and the Brain." In *Progress in Psychological Science around the World: Proceedings of the 28th International Congress of Psychology,* edited by Qicheng Jing, 195–209. New York: Psychology Press.

KRIPKE, SAUL A. 1980. *Naming and Necessity.* Cambridge, MA: Harvard University Press.

KUHN, THOMAS S. 1996. *The Structure of Scientific Revolutions.* 3rd edn. Chicago: University of Chicago Press.

LA METTRIE, JULIEN OFFRAY DE. 1996 [1747]. *Machine Man and Other Writings.* Edited by Ann Thomson. New York: Cambridge University Press.

LAPLACE, PIERRE SIMON. 1951. *A Philosophical Essay on Probabilities.* Edited by Frederick Wilson Truscott. New York: Dover Publications.

LEDOUX, JOSEPH. 1996. *The Emotional Brain.* New York: Simon and Schuster.

LEIBNIZ, GOTTFRIED WILHELM. 1989. *Philosophical Essays.* Edited by Roger Ariew and Daniel Garber. Indianapolis: Hackett Publishing Co.

LEVINE, JOSEPH. 1983. "Materialism and Qualia: The Explanatory Gap." *Pacific Philosophical Quarterly* 64: 354–61.

LEWIS, DAVID. 1966. "An Argument for the Identity Theory." *Journal of Philosophy* 63: 17–25.

LEWIS, DAVID. 1972. "Psychophysical and Theoretical Identifications." *Australasian Journal of Philosophy* 50/3: 249–58.

LEWIS, DAVID. 1980. "Mad Pain and Martian Pain." In *Readings in Philosophy of Psychology,* edited by Ned Block, 216–22. Cambridge, MA: Harvard University Press.

LEWIS, DAVID. 1983. "Postscript to 'Mad Pain and Martian Pain'." In *Philosophical Papers, Vol.1,* 130–32. New York: Oxford University Press.

LEWIS, DAVID. 1986. *On the Plurality of Worlds.* Malden: Blackwell Publishers.

LEWIS, DAVID. 1988. "Rearrangement of Particles: Reply to Lowe." *Analysis* 48/2: 65–72.

LEWIS, DAVID. 2003. "Survival and Identity." In *Personal Identity,* edited by Raymond Martin and John Barresi, 144–67. Malden: Blackwell Publishers.

LOAR, BRIAN. 1990. "Phenomenal States." *Philosophical Perspectives* 4: 81–108.

LOCKE, JOHN. 1959 [1690]. *An Essay Concerning Human Understanding.* 2 vols. New York: Dover Publications, Inc.

LOUX, MICHAEL J. 2002. *Metaphysics: A Contemporary Introduction.* 2nd edn. New York: Routledge.

LOWE, ERNEST J. 1987. "Lewis on Perdurance Versus Endurance." *Analysis* 47/3: 152–54.

LOWE, ERNEST J. 1988. "The Problems of Intrinsic Change: Rejoinder to Lewis." *Analysis* 48/2: 72–77.

LOWE, ERNEST J. 1996. *Subjects of Experience.* New York: Cambridge University Press.

LYCAN, WILLIAM G. 1987. *Consciousness.* Cambridge, MA: MIT Press.

LYCAN, WILLIAM G. 1990. *Mind and Cognition: A Reader*. Cambridge: Blackwell Publishers.

LYCAN, WILLIAM G. 1996. *Consciousness and Experience*. Cambridge, MA: MIT Press.

MACH, ERNST. 1959. *The Analysis of Sensations, and the Relation of the Physical to the Psychical*. New York: Dover Publications.

MacINTYRE, ALASDAIR C. 1999. *Dependent Rational Animals: Why Human Beings Need the Virtues*. Chicago: Open Court.

MALCOLM, NORMAN. 1956. "Dreaming and Skepticism." *Philosophical Review* 65: 14–37.

MALEBRANCHE, NICOLAS. 1997a [1688]. *Dialogues on Metaphysics and on Religion*. Edited by Nicholas Jolley and David Scott. New York: Cambridge University Press.

MALEBRANCHE, NICOLAS. 1997b [1674–5]. *The Search after Truth*. Edited by Thomas M. Lennon and Paul J. Olscamp. New York: Cambridge University Press.

MARTIN, RAYMOND, and JOHN BARRESI. 2003. *Personal Identity*. Malden: Blackwell Publishers.

MAYR, ERNST. 1982. *The Growth of Biological Thought: Diversity, Evolution, and Inheritance*. Cambridge: Belknap Press.

MAYR, ERNST. 1988. *Toward a New Philosophy of Biology: Observations of an Evolutionist*. Cambridge: Belknap Press.

McCANN, HUGH. 1998. *The Works of Agency: On Human Action, Will, and Freedom*. Ithaca: Cornell University Press.

McCLOSKEY, MICHAEL. 1983. "Intuitive Physics." *Scientific American* 248/4: 122–30.

McDOWELL, JOHN HENRY. 1994. *Mind and World*. Cambridge, MA: Harvard University Press.

McGINN, COLIN. 1989. "Can We Solve the Mind–Body Problem?" *Mind* 98: 349–66.

McGINN, MARIE. 1997. *Wittgenstein and the Philosophical Investigations*, Routledge Philosophy Guidebooks. New York: Routledge.

McLAUGHLIN, BRIAN. 1992. "The Rise and Fall of British Emergentism." In *Emergence or Reduction?: Essays on the Prospects of Nonreductive Physicalism*, edited by Ansgar Beckermann, H. Flohr, and Jaegwon Kim, 49–93. Berlin: W. de Gruyter.

MEEHL, PAUL E., and WILFRID S. SELLARS. 1956. "The Concept of Emergence." In *Minnesota Studies in the Philosophy of Science*, edited by Herbert Feigl and Michael Scriven, 239–52. Minneapolis: University of Minnesota Press.

MELE, ALFRED R. 1995. *Autonomous Agents: From Self-Control to Autonomy*. New York: Oxford University Press.

MELNYK, ANDREW. 2003. *A Physicalist Manifesto*. New York: Cambridge University Press.

MELTZOFF, A. 1995. "Understanding the Intentions of Others: Re-Enactment of Intended Acts by 18-Month-Old Children." *Developmental Psychology* 31: 838–50.

MERLEAU-PONTY, MAURICE. 1962. *Phenomenology of Perception*. Translated by Colin Smith. New York: Routledge.

MILL, JOHN STUART. 1965 [1843]. *A System of Logic*. 8th edn. New York: Longmans.

MILLER, JONATHAN. 1982. *The Body in Question*. New York: Vintage Books.

MORGAN, C. LLOYD. 1923. *Emergent Evolution*, Gifford Lectures. London: Williams and Norgate.

MYIN, ERIK, and J. KEVIN O'REGAN. 2009. "Situated Perception and Sensation in Vision and Other Modalities: A Sensorimotor Approach." In *The Cambridge Handbook of Situated Cognition*, edited by Philip Robbins and Murat Aydede, 185–200. New York: Cambridge University Press.

NAGEL, ERNEST. 1979. *The Structure of Science*. 2nd edn. Indianapolis: Hackett Publishing Co.

NAGEL, THOMAS. 1974. "What Is It Like to Be a Bat?" *Philosophical Review* 84: 435–50.

NAGEL, THOMAS. 1989. *The View from Nowhere*. New York: Oxford University Press.

NEMIROW, LAURENCE. 1990. "Physicalism and the Cognitive Role of Acquaintance." In *Mind and Cognition: A Reader*, edited by William G. Lycan, 490–99. Oxford: Blackwell Publishers.

NIELSEN, KAI. 2002. "The Compatibility of Freedom and Determinism." In *Free Will*, edited by Robert Kane, 39–46. Malden: Blackwell Publishers.

NOË, ALVA. 2004. *Action in Perception*. Cambridge, MA: MIT Press.

NOË, ALVA. 2009. *Out of Our Heads: Why You Are Not Your Brain, and Other Lessons from the Biology of Consciousness*. New York: Hill & Wang.

NOË, ALVA, and J. KEVIN O'REGAN. 2002. "On the Brain-Basis of Visual Consciousness: A Sensorimotor Account." In *Vision and Mind: Selected Readings in the Philosophy of Perception*, edited by Alva Noë and Evan Thompson, 567–98. Cambridge, MA: MIT Press.

NOË, ALVA, and EVAN THOMPSON. 2002. *Vision and Mind : Selected Readings in the Philosophy of Perception*. Cambridge, MA: MIT Press.

NUSSBAUM, MARTHA C., and HILARY PUTNAM. 1992. "Changing Aristotle's Mind." In *Essays on Aristotle's De Anima*, edited by Martha Craven Nussbaum and Amélie Rorty, 27–56. New York: Oxford University Press.

O'CONNOR, TIMOTHY. 2000. *Persons and Causes: The Metaphysics of Free Will*. New York: Oxford University Press.

OLSON, ERIC T. 1997. *The Human Animal: Personal Identity without Psychology*. New York: Oxford University Press.

OLSON, ERIC T. 2007. *What Are We?: A Study in Personal Ontology*. New York: Oxford University Press.

OPPENHEIM, PAUL, and HILARY PUTNAM. 1958. "The Unity of Science as a Working Hypothesis." In *Minnesota Studies in the Philosophy of Science*, edited by Herbert Feigl, Michael Scriven, and Grover Maxwell, 3–36. Minneapolis: University of Minnesota Press.

O'REGAN, J. K. 2009. "Sensorimotor Approach to (Phenomenal) Consciousness." In *The Oxford Companion to Consciousness*, edited by T. Baynes, A. Cleeremans, and P. Wilken, 588–93. Oxford: Oxford University Press.

OSMUNDSEN, JOHN A. 1965. "'Matador' with a Radio Stops Wired Bull." *New York Times*, May 17.

PENFIELD, WILDER. 1975. *The Mystery of the Mind: A Critical Study of Consciousness and the Human Brain*. Princeton: Princeton University Press.

PENFIELD, WILDER, and PHANOR PEROT. 1963. "The Brain's Record of Auditory and Visual Experience: A Final Summary and Discussion." *Brain* 86: 595–696.

PENROSE, ROGER. 1990. *The Emperor's New Mind: Concerning Computers, Minds, and the Laws of Physics*. New York: Oxford University Press.

PENROSE, ROGER. 1994. *Shadows of the Mind: A Search for the Missing Science of Consciousness*. New York: Oxford University Press.

PENROSE, ROGER, and M. S. LONGAIR. 1997. *The Large, the Small and the Human Mind*. New York: Cambridge University Press.

PEREBOOM, DERK. 2001. *Living without Free Will*. New York: Cambridge University Press.

PERRY, JOHN. 1975. *Personal Identity*. Berkeley: University of California Press.

PERRY, RALPH BARTON. 1968. *Present Philosophical Tendencies*. New York: Greenwood Press.

PLACE, U.T. 1956. "Is Consciousness a Brain Process?" *British Journal of Psychology* 47: 44–50.

PLANTINGA, ALVIN. 1974. *The Nature of Necessity*. New York: Oxford University Press.

PLATO. *Complete Works*. 1997. Edited by John M. Cooper and D. S. Hutchinson. Indianapolis: Hackett Publishing Co.

POLAND, JEFFREY STEPHEN. 1994. *Physicalism*. New York: Oxford University Press.

PUCCETTI, ROLAND. 1973. "Brain Bisection and Personal Identity." *British Journal for the Philosophy of Science* 24: 339–55.

PUTNAM, HILARY. 1970. "On Properties." In *Essays in Honor of Carl G. Hempel*, edited by N. Rescher. Dordrecht: D. Reidel. Reprinted in HILARY PUTNAM, 1975, *Mathematics, Matter and Method: Philosophical Papers*, Vol. 1, 305–22. New York: Cambridge University Press.

PUTNAM, HILARY. 1975a. "Brains and Behavior." In *Mind, Language, and Reality: Philosophical Papers*, Vol. 2, 325–41. New York: Cambridge University Press.

PUTNAM, HILARY. 1975b. "Robots: Machines or Artificially Created Life?" In *Mind, Language, and Reality: Philosophical Papers*, Vol. 2, 386–407. New York: Cambridge University Press.

PUTNAM, HILARY. 1975c. "The Meaning of 'Meaning'." In *Mind, Language, and Reality: Philosophical Papers*, Vol. 2. New York: Cambridge University Press.

PUTNAM, HILARY. 1975d. "The Meaning of 'Meaning'." *Minnesota Studies in the Philosophy of Science* 7: 131–93.

PUTNAM, HILARY. 1975e. "The Mental Life of Some Machines." In *Mind, Language, and Reality: Philosophical Papers*, Vol. 2, 408–28. New York: Cambridge University Press.

PUTNAM, HILARY. 1975f. "The Nature of Mental States." In *Mind, Language, and Reality: Philosophical Papers*, Vol. 2, 429–40. New York: Cambridge University Press.

PUTNAM, HILARY. 1980. "Philosophy and Our Mental Life." In *Readings in Philosophy of Psychology*, edited by Ned Joel Block, 134–43. Cambridge, MA: Harvard University Press.

PUTNAM, HILARY. 1988. *Representation and Reality*. Cambridge, MA: MIT Press.

PUTNAM, HILARY. 1999. *The Threefold Cord: Mind, Body, and World*. New York: Columbia University Press.

QUINE, W. V. O. 1964. "Two Dogmas of Empiricism." In *From a Logical Point of View*. Cambridge: Harvard University Press.

QUINE, W. V. O. 1966. "On Mental Entities." In *The Ways of Paradox and Other Essays*. Cambridge, MA: Harvard University Press.

QUINE, W. V. O. 1985. "States of Mind." *Journal of Philosophy* 82: 5–8.

REA, MICHAEL C. 1997. *Material Constitution: A Reader*. Lanham: Rowman & Littlefield.

REID, THOMAS. 2002 [1785]. *Essays on the Intellectual Powers of Man*. Edited by Derek Brookes and Knud Haakonssen. University Park: Pennsylvania State University Press.

REID, THOMAS, WILLIAM HAMILTON, and DUGALD STEWART. 1872. *The Works of Thomas Reid*, Vol. 1. 6th edn. Edinburgh: Maclachlan and Stewart.

RESCHER, NICHOLAS. 1998. "Idealism." Reprinted in *Reason, Method, and Value: A Reader on the Philosophy of Nicholas Rescher*, edited by Dale Jacquette, 389–404. Frankfurt: Ontos-Verlag, 2009.

ROBINSON, HOWARD. 1983. "Aristotelian Dualism." *Oxford Studies in Ancient Philosophy* 1: 123–44.

RORTY, AMÉLIE OKSENBERG. 1976. *The Identities of Persons*. Berkeley: University of California Press.

RORTY, RICHARD. 1965. "Mind–Body Identity, Privacy, and Categories." *Review of Metaphysics* 19/1: 24–54.

ROSEN, GIDEON. 2002. "The Case for Incompatibilism." *Philosophy and Phenomenological Research* 64/3: 699–706.

ROSENTHAL, DAVID M. 2005. *Consciousness and Mind*. New York: Oxford University Press.

ROSS, G. R. T. 1973. *De Sensu and De Memoria*. New York: Arno Press.

ROSSI, T., F. TECCHIO, P. PASQUALETTI, et al. 2002. "Somatosensory Processing During Movement Observation in Humans." *Clinical Neurophysiology* 113/1: 16–24.

RUSSELL, BERTRAND. 1956. "Mind and Matter." In *Portraits from Memory and Other Essays*, 145–65. New York: Simon and Schuster.

RUSSELL, BERTRAND. 2005 [1921]. *The Analysis of Mind*. Mineola: Dover Publications.

RYLE, GILBERT. 1949. *The Concept of Mind*. New York: Barnes & Noble.

SAYRE, KENNETH M. 1976. *Cybernetics and the Philosophy of Mind*. Atlantic Highlands: Humanities Press.

SCHAFFNER, KENNETH F. 1967. "Approaches to Reduction" *Philosophy of Science* 34/2: 137–47.

SEARLE, JOHN R. 1980. "Minds, Brains, and Programs." *Behavioral and Brain Sciences* 3/3: 417–57.

SEARLE, JOHN R. 1983. *Intentionality*. New York: Cambridge University Press.

SEARLE, JOHN R. 1992. *The Rediscovery of the Mind*. Cambridge, MA: MIT Press.

SEARLE, JOHN R. 2004. *Mind : A Brief Introduction*. New York: Oxford University Press.

SELLARS, WILFRID. 1956. "Empiricism and the Philosophy of Mind." In *Minnesota Studies in the Philosophy of Science*, edited by Herbert Feigl and Michael Scriven, 127–96. Minneapolis: University of Minnesota Press.

SELLARS, WILFRID. 1963. "Philosophy and the Scientific Image of Man." In *Science, Perception and Reality*, 1–40. New York: Humanities Press.

SELLARS, WILFRID. 1965. "The Identity Approach to the Mind–Body Problem." *Review of Metaphysics* 18/3: 430–51.

SHAPIN, STEVEN. 1998. *The Scientific Revolution*. Chicago: University of Chicago Press.

SHAPIRO, LAWRENCE A. 2004. *The Mind Incarnate*. Cambridge, MA: MIT Press/A Bradford Book.

SHARPE, ROBERT A. 1987. "The Very Idea of a Folk Psychology." *Inquiry* 30: 381–93.

SHEPARD, ROGER N., and JACQUELINE METZLER. 1971. "Mental Rotation of Three-Dimensional Objects." *Science* 171: 701–03.

SHOEMAKER, SYDNEY. 1984. "Personal Identity: A Materialist's Account." In *Personal Identity*, edited by Sydney Shoemaker and Richard Swinburne, 67–132. Oxford: Blackwell Publishers.

SIDER, THEODORE. 2001. *Four-Dimensionalism: An Ontology of Persistence and Time*. New York: Oxford University Press.

SIMPSON, GEORGE GAYLORD. 1964. *This View of Life: The World of an Evolutionist*. New York: Harcourt.

SKLAR, LAWRENCE. 1967. "Types of Inter-Theoretic Reduction." *British Journal for the Philosophy of Science* 18/2: 109–24.

SLAKEY, THOMAS J. 1961. "Aristotle on Sense Perception." *Philosophical Review* 70/4: 470–84.

SMART, J. J. C. 1959. "Sensations and Brain Processes." *Philosophical Review* 68: 141–56.

SMART, J. J. C. 1961. "Free-Will, Praise and Blame." *Mind* 70/279: 291–306.

SMILANSKY, SAUL. 2000. *Free Will and Illusion*. New York: Oxford University Press.

SOKOLOWSKI, ROBERT. 2000. *Introduction to Phenomenology*. New York: Cambridge University Press.

SOMMERHOFF, GERD. 1969. "The Abstract Characteristics of Living Systems." In *Systems Thinking: Selected Readings*, edited by F. E. Emery, 147–202. Harmondsworth: Penguin.

SOSA, ERNEST. 1984. "Mind–Body Interaction and Supervenient Causation." *Midwest Studies in Philosophy* 9: 271–81.

SPERRY, ROGER. 1975. "Mental Phenomena as Causal Determinants in Brain Function." *Process Studies* 5: 247–56.

STERELNY, KIM. 1990. *The Representational Theory of Mind: An Introduction*. Oxford: Blackwell Publishers.

STICH, STEPHEN P. 1983. *From Folk Psychology to Cognitive Science: The Case against Belief*. Cambridge, MA: MIT Press.

STRAWSON, GALEN. 1986. *Freedom and Belief*. New York: Oxford University Press.

STRAWSON, GALEN. 1994. "The Impossibility of Moral Responsibility." *Philosophical Studies* 75: 5–24.

STRAWSON, P. F. 1959. *Individuals: An Essay in Descriptive Metaphysics*. London: Methuen.

STRAWSON, P. F. 1974. "Freedom and Resentment." In *Freedom and Resentment and Other Essays*, 1–28. New York: Routledge.

SWINBURNE, RICHARD. 1997. *The Evolution of the Soul*. New York: Oxford University Press.

TANNER, NORMAN P., ed. 1990. *Decrees of the Ecumenical Councils*. 2 vols. Washington, DC: Georgetown University Press.

TAYLOR, RICHARD. 1992. *Metaphysics*. 4th edn. Englewood Cliffs: Prentice-Hall.

TOMASELLO, MICHAEL. 2003. *Constructing a Language: A Usage-Based Theory of Language Acquisition*. Cambridge, MA: Harvard University Press.

TOMASELLO, MICHAEL. 2008. *Origins of Human Communication*. Cambridge, MA: MIT Press.

TURING, ALAN. 1950. "Computing Machinery and Intelligence." *Mind* 49: 433–60.

TYE, MICHAEL. 1995. *Ten Problems of Consciousness*. Cambridge, MA: MIT Press.

TYE, MICHAEL. 2000. *Consciousness, Color, and Content*. Cambridge, MA: MIT Press.

UNGER, PETER K. 2006a. "I Do Not Exist." In *Philosophical Papers*, 36–52. New York: Oxford University Press.

UNGER, PETER K. 2006b. "The Problem of the Many." In *Philosophical Papers*, 113–82. New York: Oxford University Press.

UNGER, PETER K. 2006c. "Why There Are No People." In *Philosophical Papers*, 53–109. New York: Oxford University Press.

VAN FRAASSEN, BAS C. 1980. *The Scientific Image*. New York: Oxford University Press.

VAN INWAGEN, PETER. 1983. *An Essay on Free Will*. New York: Oxford University Press.

VAN INWAGEN, PETER. 1990. *Material Beings*. Ithaca: Cornell University Press.

WALLACE, R. JAY. 1994. *Responsibility and the Moral Sentiments*. Cambridge, MA: Harvard University Press.

WATSON, GARY. 1975. "Free Agency." *Journal of Philosophy* 24: 205–20.

WATSON, GARY. 2003. *Free Will.* 2nd edn. New York: Oxford University Press.

WESTFALL, RICHARD S. 1977. *The Construction of Modern Science.* New York: Cambridge University Press.

WHITEN, ANDREW, and RICHARD W. BYRNE. 1997. *Machiavellian Intelligence II: Extensions and Evaluations.* New York: Cambridge University Press.

WEINTRAUB, PAMELA. 1984. *The Omni Interviews.* New York: Tickner and Fields.

WIDERKER, DAVID. 1995. "Libertarianism and Frankfurt's Attack on the Principle of Alternative Possibilities." *Philosophical Review* 104/2: 247–61.

WIDERKER, DAVID, and MICHAEL MCKENNA. 2003. *Moral Responsibility and Alternative Possibilities: Essays on the Importance of Alternative Possibilities.* Burlington: Ashgate.

WIGGINS, DAVID. 1980. *Sameness and Substance.* Cambridge, MA: Harvard University Press.

WILKES, KATHLEEN V. 1978. *Physicalism.* Atlantic Highlands: Humanities Press.

WILKES, KATHLEEN V. 1991. "Relationship between Scientific Psychology and Common Sense Psychology." *Synthese* 89: 15–39.

WILLIAMS, BERNARD. 1986. "Hylomorphism." *Oxford Studies in Ancient Philosophy* 4: 189–99.

WIMSATT, WILLIAM C. 1985. "Forms of Aggregativity." In *Human Nature and Natural Knowledge*, edited by Marjorie Grene, Alan Donagan, Anthony N. Perovich, and Michael V. Wedin. Dordrecht: Reidel.

WITTGENSTEIN, LUDWIG. 2001 [1953]. *Philosophical Investigations.* Translated by G. E. M. Anscombe. 3rd edn. Malden: Blackwell Publishers.

WOLF, SUSAN R. 1990. *Freedom within Reason.* New York: Oxford University Press.

WYMA, KEITH. 1997. "Moral Responsibility and the Leeway for Action." *American Philosophical Quarterly* 34: 57–70.

YOUNG, J. Z. 1971. *An Introduction to the Study of Man.* Oxford: Clarendon Press.

Acknowledgments

I am grateful to many people for helping to bring this book to completion. They include many students, among whom Charlie Lassiter, Vince Evans, Carlo DaVia, and Shane Wilkins deserve special mention. Other people whose feedback has improved the final draft include Joe Corabi, Bryan Frances, and two anonymous reviewers for Wiley-Blackwell. I am grateful to Jeff Dean for his constant support throughout the project, and to Tiffany Mok, Sarah Dancy, and Claire Creffield for their unflagging effort in the final stages of production. Above all, I am grateful to Cecilia Jaworski, and to Alexander, Madeleine, Eleanor, Gabriel, and Xavier Jaworski for bearing patiently with me and with all the thought experiments I've subjected them to.

Index

Philosophy of Mind: A Comprehensive Introduction, First Edition. William Jaworski.
© 2011 William Jaworski. Published 2011 by Blackwell Publishing Ltd.